FOURTH EDITION

GUIDING CHILDREN'S LEARNING OF MATHEMATICS

LEONARD M. KENNEDY
California State University, Sacramento

Wadsworth Publishing Company
A Division of Wadsworth, Inc.
Belmont, California

Education Editor: Bob Podstepny
Production Editor: Leland Moss
Managing Designer: Detta Penna
Text Designer: Sharon Smith
Copy Editor: Yvonne Howell
Technical Illustrator: J & R Technical Services
Cover Designer: Sharon Smith

Printed in the United States of America

1 2 3 4 5 6 7 8 9 10—88 87 86 85 84

ISBN 0-534-02989-2

Library of Congress Cataloging in Publication Data
Kennedy, Leonard M.
  Guiding children's learning of mathematics.

  First–3rd editions published under title: Guiding
children to mathematical discovery.
  Includes bibliographies and index.
  1. Mathematics—Study and teaching (Elementary)
I. Kennedy, Leonard M. Guiding children to mathematical
discovery. II. Title.
QA135.5.K43 1983   372.7   83-14507
ISBN 0-534-02989-2

Table of Contents

Preface

This book is for preservice and inservice teachers of mathematics in the elementary school. It presents a program based on the research of learning theorists, such as Piaget, Skemp, and Gagne, and on successful classroom practices. The book emphasizes the need for presenting mathematics through carefully sequenced activities in which the structure of mathematics is highlighted. Through such a program, children first develop an understanding of basic concepts and principles by engaging in activities with appropriate models of the mathematics they are learning. Upon achieving this understanding, children formulate the generalizations that make for more permanent learning and learn the computational and other skills they need to use mathematics effectively now and in the future.

The material in this text will help you present mathematics concepts in ways that lead children to see their relevance in a wide variety of situations. Numerous examples show you how a classroom can be organized to meet the varying needs of children; the roles of teacher-directed lessons, learning centers, and mathematics laboratories are clearly explained. The topics recommended by the National Council of Supervisors of Mathematics as the basic content for today's elementary school mathematics program are discussed in this text. Activities and materials for introducing each topic to children and developing their understanding of it are presented. A wide variety of materials and procedures for dealing with each topic is featured.

The fourth edition of this book bears a new title: *Guiding Children's Learning of Mathematics*. The title was changed from *Guiding Children to Mathematical Discovery* to reflect current thinking about the content of elementary school mathematics and the ways it should be presented to children. The book now emphasizes the importance of a teacher-guided approach with careful attention for sequencing subtasks for each topic until children attain an understanding of the topic. It retains the easy-to-read style of writing and plentiful illustrations that made earlier editions so popular.

CHANGES IN THIS EDITION

The text has been thoroughly revised to reflect current thinking about content and procedures in today's school mathematics program.

1. Chapter 1 discusses the basic topics included in a comprehensive program.

2. Chapter 2 emphasizes theories of learning that play a role in determining effective modes of instruction. Theories of Piaget, Skemp, and Gagne are brought together to formulate a theory of instruction that integrates goals, procedures, and subtasks of a topic.

3. Chapter 3 discusses five factors of readiness and ways to diagnose children's standing in relation to each factor. The need for a diagnostic-prescriptive approach to teaching is presented through discussion of how it meets the needs of special students.

4. Chapter 4 is new. It discusses mathematics anxiety and its impact on students, particularly females and minorities. Causes of and ways to lessen the intensity of anxiety are presented.

5. Chapter 5 stresses problem solving. Eleven strategies and Polya's four-step problem-solving process, adapted for elementary school children, are discussed. Ways to improve children's treatment of word problems and estimation are also included.

6. A new feature is the inclusion of many problems and activities to demonstrate how teachers can present material to children. These begin in Chapter 5, where many problems are presented, and continue in Chapters 7 through 16, where activities for presenting topics are displayed.

7. Chapter 6 presents a revised section on calculators and a new one in which computers are discussed.

8. Beginning with Chapter 7 and continuing through the next nine chapters, there is a section devoted to special students—both learning handicapped and the gifted and talented. Suggestions of materials and procedures for helping these students deal with the chapter's subject are presented. These discussions suggest ways to strengthen special students' understanding of a topic by supplementing regular instruction with special materials and/or procedures.

9. Chapters 7 through 11 deal with whole numbers and operations with them. Each chapter stresses the need for manipulative experiences before pictorial and abstract work with numbers and operations. Fractional numbers expressed as common and decimal fractions and percent are the subject of Chapters 12 and 13. A rationale for teaching common fractions is included along with materials and procedures for teaching the four operations with both common and decimal fractions.

10. Chapter 14 contains information about measurement, with an emphasis on the metric system. The scope-and-sequence chart presents an order of presentation that begins with young children's experimentation in nonstructured situations, and then with both nonstandard and standard units of measure. New sections deal with instruction about money and telling time.

11. Chapters 15 and 16 contain information about geometry (15) and number theory, probability, and statistics (16). Each chapter contains many activities that can be used as the basis for lessons about these topics.

12. Chapter 17 is new. It discusses teacher-directed lessons, learning centers, and mathematics laboratories. A seven-step teacher-directed lesson plan is featured.

13. More than twenty activities using a calculator are interspersed throughout Chapters 8, 10, 11, 13, and 16. Many of these pertain to work in basic areas, while others are for enriching children's experiences in mathematics.

The author is indebted to Professors Joan C. Carson, University of Mississippi; Marilyn Sue Ford, Arizona State University; Loye Y. Hollis, University of Houston; K. Allen Neufeld, University of Alberta; Carole J. Reesink, Bemidji State University; and Edward A. Silver, San Diego State University for their many suggestions for improving the book. I especially thank Professor Steve Tipps of the University of Virginia whose many thoughtful comments contributed much to the quality of this book. I hope all the reviewers find some way in which their views have been reflected in the fourth edition. Naturally, I accept full responsibility for any shortcomings they or anyone else may find in the book. The continuing support of my wife, Mary, has made this book a reality.

How to Use This Book

Each chapter of this book begins with a list of performance objectives that explain what you may expect to gain from the chapter. The objectives for each chapter should be read before reading the chapter itself. Within every chapter is a *self-check* for each objective. Each self-check should be answered to determine how successfully you understand the mathematical concepts and the procedures for using teaching materials and learning aids.

If you perform the self-checks successfully, you will acquire the understanding and skills required to become a successful teacher of elementary school mathematics. Each time that you feel unsatisfied with a self-check, you should review the materials upon which it is based, or read other material dealing with the objective. Then repeat the self-check.

At the end of each chapter are Study Questions and Activities. These will add depth and breadth to the understanding of the concepts and procedures included in the chapter. Complete as many of these as time, energy, and inclination dictate. A list of key terms also appears at the end of each chapter. You should read these lists to review the important terms and restudy sections of a chapter that contain a discussion of any term about which you are uncertain. There are annotated reading lists at the end of each chapter that offer a selection of additional material.

There are three appendices. Appendix A contains lists of common prefixes and suffixes of mathematical terms, their derivations, and their meanings. Appendix B contains addresses of companies that produce computer software for mathematics and Appendix C lists addresses of companies that produce and distribute mathematics learning aids. You can write to these places for information about current programs and learning aids.

I hope you will find this book interesting and helpful.

Leonard M. Kennedy

1

Mathematics in the Elementary School

Upon completion of Chapter 1 you will be able to:

1. Name orally or in writing ten basic skills commonly included in today's mathematics programs.

2. Explain why the mathematics curriculum should be organized around problem solving.

3. Explain why elementary school children should be introduced to calculators and computers.

4. Identify three types of numbers to which children are introduced.

5. Name the two basic number operations and their inverses.

6. Name four basic properties included in elementary programs, and give an example of how each one is used for the operation(s) to which it applies.

7. Distinguish between discrete and continuous objects, and give examples of continuous objects.

8. Name at least two reasons for including geometry in a mathematics program, and cite examples that illustrate the validity of the reasons.

9. Name at least three reasons for including number theory activities in a program.

10. Name at least four reasons for including the study of probability in the elementary school program.

11. Name four types of graphs used by elementary school children.

Every teacher faces the challenge of preparing children to live in an ever-changing world. Today's elementary school children will reach adulthood near the beginning of the twenty-first century. No one can predict what life will be like then. Therefore teachers must help children prepare for a life of continuing education so they can cope with the unknown changes to come.

For the teacher of mathematics in the elementary school, the challenge means that they will need to help children acquire a background of understandings and skills in mathematics that will allow them to face the next century with confidence. A list of the basic skills each student should acquire was developed in 1977 by the **National Council of Supervisors of Mathematics** (NCSM). Their position paper identifies ten basic skills that students should develop before they complete high school:

- Problem solving

- Applying mathematics in everyday situations

- Alertness to the reasonableness of results

- Estimation and approximation

- Appropriate computation skills

- Geometry

- Measurement

- Reading, interpreting, and constructing tables, charts, and graphs

- Using mathematics to predict

- Computer literacy[1]

In 1980 **The National Council of Teachers of Mathematics** issued *An Agenda for Action: Recommendations for School Mathematics in the 1980s.* In this agenda the group recommends that:

- Problem solving be the focus of school mathematics in the 1980s.

- Basic skills in mathematics be defined to encompass more than computational facility.

- Mathematics programs take full advantage of the power of calculators and computers at all levels.[2]

The recommendations of both organizations acknowledge the fact that in a rapidly changing technological society a limited number of facts about measurement, geometry, and other areas of mathematics and a narrow range of computational and problem-solving skills will not prepare children for the future. Rather, as the NCSM says:

---

[1] National Council of Supervisors of Mathematics, "Position Paper on Basic Skills," *Arithmetic Teacher*, XXV, No. 1 (October 1977), pp. 19–22.

[2] The National Council of Teachers of Mathematics, *An Agenda for Action: Recommendations for School Mathematics in the 1980s* (Reston, Virginia: The Council, 1980), p. 1.

There are many reasons why basic skills must include more than computation. The present technological society requires daily use of such skills as estimating, problem solving, interpreting data, measuring, predicting, and applying mathematics to everyday situations. The changing needs of society, the explosion of the amount of quantitative data, and the availability of computers and calculators demand a redefining of priorities for basic mathematical skills.[3]

Authors and publishers of elementary school textbook series also recognize that children need a comprehensive mathematics program. An examination of four series published in 1980 and 1981 revealed that with the exception of computer literacy, all of the basic skills in the NCSM position paper are included. However, the major emphasis in each series is on computational skills using whole and fractional numbers. In order to strengthen children's understanding and knowledge of all skills, teachers need to supplement textbooks with other materials. This book and the references it contains discuss materials and procedures for teaching mathematics in ways that will expand children's knowledge and understandings beyond that which they can obtain from textbooks alone.

***Self-check
of Objective 1***

Ten basic mathematical skills have been identified by the National Council of Supervisors of Mathematics. Name them before continuing your reading.

SKILL AREAS INCLUDED IN THIS BOOK

This book is organized around eight **skill areas** which encompass the ten basic skills listed by the NCSM. Each of the eight skill areas is discussed in one or more of the book's chapters:

- Problem solving, applications, and estimation
- Calculators and computers
- Numbers and operations
- Measurement
- Geometry
- Number theory
- Probability and statistics
- Tables and graphs

---

[3] National Council of Supervisors of Mathematics, p. 21.

An overview of each skill area is presented here to heighten your awareness of its importance and role in a comprehensive elementary school mathematics program.

1. Problem Solving, Applications, and Estimation

Providing individuals with skills and understandings to efficiently solve a wide range of personal, professional, and social problems is the primary reason for mathematics instruction in schools. As indicated in *An Agenda for Action,* the National Council of Teachers of Mathematics believes that the mathematics curriculum should be organized around problem solving. **Problem solving** is done when an individual uses strategies and skills to determine the answer to a new, unfamiliar problem. Children need opportunities to learn how to analyze problems, devise and carry out plans for their solutions, and look back to judge the reasonableness of the results. There are strategies that children must learn if they are to become skillful problem solvers. A list of the strategies discussed in this book is on page 82. Before students can apply strategies effectively, they must have a good understanding of the mathematics upon which the strategies are based, such as numbers, computation, measurement, geometry, statistics, probability, and number theory.

As children learn each of the basic skills, they need opportunities to see how their new knowledge is used to solve problems. Teachers should take advantage of in- and out-of-school situations to present settings that show how computing, measuring, graphing, and other skills are used in everyday situations and in solving unfamiliar problems. Chapter 5 contains examples of problems that are appropriate for elementary school children and discusses strategies for solving them. Examples of everyday situations that can be used to introduce new topics are included in chapters that deal with computation and the other skill areas.

Children learn to round off numbers and to judge quantities, distances, lengths, capacities, and weights in order to make reasonable estimates and determine approximate answers. **Approximate answers** are used in situations in which exact answers are not required and in judging the reasonableness of results when exact answers are necessary. These topics are also discussed in Chapter 5.

Explain orally or in writing why the mathematics curriculum should be organized around problem solving.

Self-check of Objective 2

2. Calculators and Computers

Calculators have become commonplace in everyday life. Surveys completed by the Calculator Information Center show that a majority of children has access to a calculator.[4] Kindergarten and first-grade children can learn to use calculators as aids for counting by ones, twos, fives, and tens; older children can use them for computing with whole numbers and fractional numbers expressed as decimal fractions. Once they have learned to use calculators for counting and computing, students can use the machines as tools for solving problems. Calculators are particularly useful when children are confronted by a problem for which they know the operation but cannot perform the computation because large numbers are involved. Calculators also can be a valuable mathematics learning aid for many learning-handicapped children. According to the Calculator Information Center, ". . . achievement [for all students] will not be harmed and may be enhanced when calculators are used. Furthermore the evidence indicates content is taught better when calculators are used than when they are ignored."[5]

An examination of publications devoted to **computers** reveals that these machines now have applications that were unheard of just a few years ago. A recent issue of *Apple, the Personal Computer Magazine*[6] discusses how people use one type of personal computer to design furniture and boots; create pictures and weave fabrics of unique design; make special animated effects for movies; compose, perform, record, and teach music; and write and edit manuscripts (this revision of *Guiding Children's Learning of Mathematics* is being done on a computer with a commercially developed word-processing system).

Such applications represent only a portion of the ways small computers are used, and we have not even considered the capabilities of the larger, more sophisticated systems available to business, industry, and government. Nevertheless these examples illustrate the point that school children need to learn about computers. There are few children in today's schools who will not work directly with computers in the future, and even those few will come in contact with computers in many ways. In schools where computers are available, children should learn to use them for solving problems and dealing with numerical, written, and graphic information and as one way of getting drill and practice in mathematics. Children in schools where the machines are not available should be given a unit that contains information that acquaints them with computers and their uses. Some elementary school teachers believe students should be

---

[4] Marilyn M. Suydam, *The Use of Calculators in Precollege Education* (Columbus, Ohio: Calculator Information Center, August 1982), p. 3.

[5] Suydam, p. 10.

[6] Published by Apple Computer, Inc., 10260 Bandley Drive, Cupertino, CA 95014.

introduced to programming skills and include instruction about this in their programs.

There are computer-managed instruction systems to help teachers evaluate children's knowledge and understanding of mathematics, place children in a learning sequence, maintain records, and do other routine tasks. Once a child's place in a learning sequence is determined, the computer program provides some of the instruction and practice the child needs. Management programs will not replace teachers but will simplify some tasks and give teachers more time for working directly with children.

Explain orally or in writing why calculators should be a part of the mathematics curriculum. Do the same for computers.

Self-check of Objective 3

3. Numbers and Operations

Most of the time spent on mathematics in the elementary school is devoted to **numbers** and **operations.** By the time children complete the sixth grade, most of them will have had experiences with whole numbers and rational numbers expressed as decimal and common fractions and as percents. Some children will also have had experiences with integers expressed as negatives of the nonzero whole numbers. Children learn that **whole numbers** are used to count objects in collections, or sets. **Fractional numbers** are used when part of a unit or part of a set is considered. **Integers** are used for expressing temperature, time, distance, and altitude and for other situations in which both direction and magnitude must be indicated. Children must have a clear understanding of each of these types of numbers and of the Hindu–Arabic numeration system, which provides the words and symbols for expressing numbers in each system. Otherwise their abilities to count, compute, and measure and to use mathematics to solve problems will be severely limited.

The basic number operations are **addition** and **multiplication** and their inverses, **subtraction** and **division.** In order to perform each operation, a child learns an **algorithm,** which is a set of rules or procedures for processing numbers for operations. For example, a common procedure for completing the subtraction in the margin is the *decomposition* algorithm. When this algorithm is used, it is necessary to "borrow" a ten and rename it 10 ones, giving a total of 13 ones and leaving 7 tens. Now the subtraction can be completed by subtracting 6 from 13, 2 from 7, and 4 from 5 and recording the difference, 157. (There are other al-

$$
\begin{array}{r}
583 \\
-426 \\
\hline
\end{array}
$$

$$
\begin{array}{r}
5\overset{7}{8}3 \\
-426 \\
\hline
\end{array}
$$

$$
\begin{array}{r}
5\overset{7}{8}3 \\
-426 \\
\hline
157
\end{array}
$$

gorithms for completing this subtraction; some of them are discussed in Chapter 10.)

There are properties that apply to certain of the basic operations which children can learn to use in meaningful ways. For example, they can change the order of addends when they add without affecting the sum: $3 + 4$ yields the same answer as $4 + 3$. This demonstrates the **commutative property** for addition. The commutative property also applies to multiplication but not to subtraction and division.

The **associative property** also applies to both addition and multiplication but not to subtraction and division. In the set of whole numbers, $(3 + 4) + 6 = 3 + (4 + 6)$. In the first part of the equation the parentheses indicate that 3 and 4 are to be added first, and then 7 and 6 are to be added to make 13. In the second part the parentheses indicate that 4 and 6 should be added first, and then 3 and 10 are added to make 13. In either half of the equation, the sum is 13. An example for multiplication is $(2 \times 5) \times 6 = 2 \times (5 \times 6)$.

$$\begin{array}{r} 36 \\ \times 4 \\ \hline \end{array}$$

The **distributive property** applies to multiplication over addition. It makes it possible to complete a multiplication algorithm in stages when numbers like 4 and 36 are multiplied. To complete the algorithm in the margin, 36 is thought of as 3 tens and 6 ones. The product of 4 and 6 is recorded first; then the product of 4 and 30 is recorded. The sum of these partial products is then recorded. The distributive property is also used when performing division. The division of 36 by 3 can be explained as $36 \div 3 = (30 + 6) \div 3 = (30 \div 3) + (6 \div 3) = 10 + 2 = 12$.

$$\begin{array}{r} 36 \\ \times 4 \\ \hline 24 \\ 120 \\ \hline 144 \end{array}$$

Children also learn that there are identity elements for operations performed on numbers. An **identity element** is a number that when operated on with another number results in the other number. Zero is the identity for addition. In the set of whole numbers, $3 + 0 = 3$. In multiplication the identity is one, that is, $1 \times 3 = 3$.

Number sentences are used to record and communicate mathematical ideas. As children study mathematics, they learn that number sentences are a form of shorthand used to make statements about number situations. One important problem-solving skill is to analyze a problem situation and write a number sentence for it. Once a number sentence is determined, it can be rewritten in algorithm form so the necessary computation can be performed.

It is important that children develop systematically and meaningfully their knowledge of numbers, the Hindu–Arabic numeration system, and operations and algorithms. As a teacher you must plan activities that take into account each child's level of maturity and understanding of mathematical concepts and that clearly show relationships among and between numbers and operations. Also, use common situations as settings in which you introduce operations and their algorithms to acquaint children with ways the operations are used to solve problems. Chapters 9 through 13 present materials and procedures for introducing operations for whole and fractional numbers and algorithms for computing with each operation.

Name orally or in writing three types of numbers to which elementary school children are introduced.

Two basic operations and their inverses are introduced in the elementary school. Name them.

Four number properties that apply to one or more of the operations are discussed. Name each property and write examples that illustrate how each one is used for the operation(s) to which it applies.

Self-check of Objectives 4, 5, and 6

4. Measurement

Children's in- and out-of-school activities bring them into frequent contact with both discrete and continuous materials. **Discrete materials** are things that are counted, such as marbles and oranges. **Continuous materials** are things that cannot be counted, such as the weight of a package of meat and the length of a piece of ribbon. Continuous materials are measured rather than counted. The types of measures treated in this book are linear, perimeter, area, volume (both capacity and cubic units), weight, time, and temperature.

When the Metric Conversion Act was signed into law by President Gerald Ford in 1975 it was believed that the United States would make a transition from the **English (customary) system** of measures to the **metric system.** It was anticipated that the changeover would be completed in a relatively few years. Such has not been the case, however, and both systems are used today. As long as children live in a society where both systems are used, they will need to learn about and use units for the two systems. Units from the metric system are used as examples for activities in this book. Teachers can easily substitute customary units for metric units in each of the activities to give children experiences with them.

Give an example of both a discrete and a continuous object. Give examples of continuous objects you believe should be available for children to measure.

Self-check of Objective 7

5. Geometry

Until recently elementary school children studied **geometry** only briefly. They learned to recognize some geometric shapes and became acquainted with formulas for determining areas and perimeters of simple plane figures. Today geometry has a much more prominent role in the program. Through activities both inside and outside of the classroom children develop an intuitive understanding of basic geometric concepts.

A greater amount of geometry is included because we recognize that children can learn and use many geometric concepts, that its study encourages creativity and inquiry, and that it provides children with a break from the study of numbers and computation.

We regularly see geometric shapes and forms in both human-made and natural objects. In human-made objects they are often a necessary part of the object's structure. Geometric shapes are used in many ways for aesthetic reasons; their use in art from all periods of history is widely recognized. In school the study of geometry begins with an examination of objects so that children can develop an understanding of two- and three-dimensional figures. Later, carefully selected models are used to introduce certain specific geometric concepts. For example, models of cubes, prisms, and pyramids give opportunities for classifying figures according to the shapes of their faces and/or the number of edges and vertices. As children mature, they refine the language they use to describe each figure.

Coordinate graphing is a topic included in most mathematics programs, as are the concepts of similarity, congruence, and symmetry. The study of geometric transformations is appropriate for some elementary school children.

Self-check of Objective 8

Several reasons for including geometry in the elementary school program are given. Can you cite at least two? Can you also give examples that illustrate the validity of each of these reasons?

6. Number Theory

The study of **number theory** introduces children to odd and even numbers, **prime** and **composite numbers,** and concepts such as **least common multiple** (LCM) and **greatest common factor** (GCF). There are several reasons for including number theory in a program. Children who are familiar with the concept of least common multiple can use LCMs to determine the lowest common denominators when adding and subtracting unlike common fractions. Knowledge of greatest common factor is helpful when simplifying common fractions (reducing to lowest terms).

Another reason for including number theory is that it is interesting to many children. A properly taught unit gives a program a motivating factor that might otherwise be missing. The study of number theory also provides many opportunities for children to practice mathematical skills, such as addition or multiplication involving the basic facts for these operations.

7. Probability and Statistics

The preface of the 1981 yearbook of the National Council of Teachers of Mathematics, *Teaching Statistics and Probability*, contains five reasons why **statistics** and **probability** are appropriate topics for school mathematics:

- They provide meaningful applications of mathematics at all levels.

- They provide methods for dealing with uncertainty.

- They give us some understanding of the statistical arguments, good and bad, with which we are continually bombarded.

- They help consumers distinguish sound use of statistical procedures from unsound or deceptive uses; and

- They are inherently interesting, exciting, and motivating topics for most students.[7]

Elementary school children are not likely to face situations in which an understanding of probability and statistics is crucial, but situations requiring some use of these topics do arise frequently and are of importance and interest to them. Work with statistics can begin as early as kindergarten, where children can make surveys to determine their favorite television shows or video games or the kinds of pets each one has. As the years pass, children's skills in handling data meaningfully should be nurtured as they collect, organize, display, and interpret information from a variety of sources. Simple experiments give children opportunities to develop an intuitive understanding of certain probability concepts and procedures. A strong emphasis should always be placed on the application of knowledge about statistics and probability in problem-solving situations.

An additional benefit of activities with statistics and probability is that they frequently provide opportunities to work with arithmetic skills such as addition, subtraction, multiplication, and division. Much of the work with these topics can be done through independent individual or small-group investigations.

---

[7]Albert P. Schulte, ed., *Teaching Statistics and Probability, 1981 Yearbook* (Reston, Virginia: The National Council of Teachers of Mathematics, 1981), p. ix.

Three reasons for including number-theory activities in a program are cited. Name the three reasons.

Five reasons that support inclusion of probability and statistics in the mathematics curriculum are presented. Name at least four of the reasons.

8. Tables and Graphs

Tables and **graphs** are used to organize data so that trends and patterns can be determined and problems involving the data can be solved. Among the graphs children learn to make and interpret are object, picture, bar, and line graphs. Object and picture graphs can be used by kindergarten and first-grade children to organize information about themselves, such as their favorite ice-cream flavors and birth months. Older children use bar and line graphs to organize and display data they gather and make more sophisticated interpretations of data in tables and graphs. Children should learn to determine trends and make predictions from tables and graphs they and others have made. Examples of how graphs are used to solve problems are given in Chapter 5; examples of the four graphs named above are in Chapter 16.

Name four types of graphs appropriate for elementary school children.

SUMMARY

In 1977 the National Council of Supervisors of Mathematics identified ten mathematics skills that children should develop by the time they complete high school. With the exception of computer literacy, elementary school mathematics textbook series include information about each of the skills. The emphasis in the series is on computation, however, so teachers must supplement textbooks with outside activities dealing with the other skills so that children will have a comprehensive program. Problem solving, application, and estimation skills are important and are included in all programs. The ever-expanding use of computers demands that students become familiar with the operation of these machines and learn about their uses. Number systems, the Hindu–Arabic numeration system, and operations on numbers receive much attention in schools.

The whole numbers, positive fractional numbers, and integers—and operations on them—are studied from kindergarten on. Addition and multiplication and their inverses, subtraction and division, are operations that are studied in elementary school. Knowledge of the commutative, associative, and distributive properties and the role of identity elements contributes to children's understanding of numbers and operations.

Measurement of continuous objects is emphasized through study of both the metric and customary systems of measure. The study of geometry encourages creativity and inquiry in children. Number theory, statistics, and probability help develop skills that are useful in other areas of the curriculum as well as in mathematics, serve to motivate many children, and provide opportunities for children to practice the basic operations. Tables and graphs help children develop thinking skills and improve their ability to understand and solve problems of daily living.

STUDY QUESTIONS AND ACTIVITIES

1. Examine a book for each of three different grades in an elementary mathematics series to determine which of the ten basic skills identified by the National Council of Supervisors of Mathematics are included in each book. Estimate the approximate amount of coverage devoted to each skill.

2. The National Council of Teachers of Mathematics believes that the basic skills in mathematics must be defined to encompass more than computational facility. Several authors listed in this chapter's reading list have written about the "back-to-basics" movement. Read one of the articles; summarize the author's concerns. Talk to teachers, administrators, parents, and school-board members in a district with which you are acquainted to find out what they consider to be "basic" in a mathematics program. Do their comments indicate a narrow or broad view of what is basic?

KEY TERMS

National Council of Supervisors of
    Mathematics
National Council of Teachers of
    Mathematics
skill areas
problem solving
approximate answers

calculators
computers
numbers
operations
whole numbers
fractional numbers
integers

addition   metric system
subtraction   geometry
multiplication   coordinate graphing
division   number theory
algorithm   prime numbers
commutative property   composite numbers
associative property   least common multiple
distributive property   greatest common factor
identity element   statistics
discrete materials   probability
continuous materials   tables
English (customary) system   graphs

FOR FURTHER READING

Arithmetic Teacher, February 1979, has the theme "The Case for the Comprehensive Mathematics Curriculum" and identifies topics other than "basics" that are important. Articles deal with probability, statistics, geometry, estimation, computers, and other topics.

Bell, Max S. "Early Teaching for Effective Numeracy," *Arithmetic Teacher*, XXVII, No. 4 (December 1980), p. 2. Bell argues that there are many numerical concepts that kindergarten and primary-grade children should learn besides computation. These noncalculation aspects of numbers will enrich and improve the primary program.

Brodinsky, Ben. "Back to the Basics: The Movement and Its Meaning," *Phi Delta Kappan*, LVVIII, No. 7 (March 1977), pp. 522–527. Discusses the forces behind "back to basics," its strengths and weaknesses, its supporters, educators' responses, and other points associated with the movement. While not devoted strictly to mathematics, the article clearly identifies the problems teachers face as a result of one of today's major influences on what is taking place in classrooms across the country.

Fey, James T. "Mathematics Teaching Today: Perspectives from Three National Surveys," *Arithmetic Teacher*, XXVII, No. 2 (October 1979), pp. 10–14. The information contained in this article summarizes surveys dealing with the content of elementary mathematics textbook series, patterns of instructional organization and style, and the perceptions of the abilities, problems, and needs of teachers.

Glennon, Vincent J. "Mathematics: How Firm the Foundation?" *Phi Delta Kappan*, LVII, No. 5 (January 1976), pp. 302–305. Glennon reviews a number of influences on mathematics—the "new math," "back-to-basics" movements, Piaget and other theorists, and individualization and grouping trends. Then he pleads for a continued emphasis on sequential, systematic, and structured teaching using appropriate techniques for individualizing and teaching.

Kilpatrick, Jeremy. "Stop the Bandwagon, I Want Off," *Arithmetic Teacher*, XXVIII, No. 8 (April 1981), p. 2. Kilpatrick argues against taking a bandwagon approach to the teaching of problem solving. He believes that although problem solving is important, it should be viewed in perspective and not reduced to a slogan.

National Council of Supervisors of Mathematics. "Position Paper on Basic Goals," *Arithmetic Teacher*, XXV, No. 1 (October 1977), pp. 19–21. There is a need for a clear definition of the goals of school mathematics. The goals must be broader than computational skills alone. The Council's position paper identifies ten basic skills to be developed by completion of high school and gives a rationale for a broad definition of basic skills.

National Council of Teachers of Mathematics. *An Agenda for Action, Recommendations for School Mathematics of the 1980s* (Reston, Va.: The Council, 1980). The Council makes eight recommendations that deal with content, instruction, evaluation of programs, amount of mathematics for students, teachers, and support for programs.

Shulte, Albert P. "Four Essential Forward Steps," *Arithmetic Teacher*, XXVIII, No. 3 (November 1980), p. 2. Shulte contends that children need to be given a broader view of computation, see an increased emphasis on mathematical modeling, deal with more nontextbook problems to solve, and have more measurement activities.

2

Foundations for Effective Teaching

Upon completion of Chapter 2 you will be able to:

1. Name four stages of mental growth through which Piaget said each person progresses, and give examples of how this theory influences the way mathematics is taught.

2. Describe the nature of the activity at each level of Skemp's two-level director system for learning.

3. Describe what Gagne means when he refers to the hierarchy of steps for a topic, and state a reason why it is important to keep the hierarchy for a topic in mind when learning activities are planned.

4. Explain the three elements of a model designed to help teachers make decisions about teaching mathematics.

5. Describe the information contained in a textbook series scope-and-sequence chart.

6. Explain how performance objectives can be used when a sequence of activities for children is planned.

A mathematics curriculum as comprehensive as the one described in Chapter 1 presents a great challenge to every teacher who wishes to develop and offer a program of instruction that helps every child acquire a broad background of mathematical knowledge, understandings, and skills. What background do you, who ultimately will be responsible for the mathematics instruction of a group of children, need in order to meet this challenge? For one thing you must know the mathematics you will teach. If you do not know all the mathematics involved in the basic skills needed for a broad curriculum, you should plan now to overcome your weaknesses before you begin working with children. You may do this by studying mathematics-content books for teachers or by enrolling in an appropriate course in a junior college or four-year institution.

You need to know some of the research into learning that provides a theoretical basis for the way you plan and organize children's experiences. Since all children are not alike, you need knowledge about ways to assess children's levels of mental maturity, knowledge of mathematics, and attitudes toward the subject. Mathematics anxiety inhibits the learning of many persons; you need to know some of its causes and ways to lessen its incidence. You need knowledge of how calculators and computers are used in elementary school programs. Naturally you need to know materials and procedures for teaching specific topics. And finally you must be able to organize your classroom for effective instruction. A careful reading of this book and thoughtful responses to the self-checks and end-of-chapter study questions will provide much of the understanding, knowledge, and skills you need to be an effective mathematics teacher.

This chapter focuses on research into learning and some implications of this research for teaching mathematics. First, theories developed by Jean Piaget, Richard Skemp, and Robert Gagne are discussed. Next, a model is used to show how to take these theories into account as lessons are planned. The chapter concludes with a discussion of scope-and-sequence charts and lists of performance objectives and of ways they can be used for determining a sequence of learning activities.

RECENT STUDIES OF LEARNING

Research into learning provides information that teachers, textbook writers, and other curriculum planners use to develop mathematics programs. During the nineteenth century the **mental-discipline theory** had the greatest influence on mathematics teaching. According to this theory the mind is like a muscle and benefits from exercise as muscles do. Mathematics was used to give the mind much of its exercise, and lengthy computations that were largely devoid of meaning were contained in textbooks of the period. Instruction emphasized ways to copy and compute examples carefully.

Early in the present century Edward Thorndike's **stimulus–response theory** replaced the mental-discipline theory. This theory was based on the belief that learning occurs when a bond, or connection, has been established between a stimulus and a response. To learn mathematics, children were given practice (drill) exercises consisting of many number combinations so they could establish the bond between each combination and its correct response. Little, if any, time was spent helping children understand what they were doing.

In the 1930s William Brownell introduced his **meaning theory,** which is based on the belief that children must understand what they are learning if learning is to be permanent. One way children develop an understanding of mathematics is to use objects as they learn concepts such as counting and place value. This theory supports children's working with many manipulative materials, such as those described in this book, and is valid as the basis for many classroom practices.

1. Jean Piaget

The most influential of recent learning theorists is Jean Piaget. Some programs present mathematics in ways based entirely on his theories; examples are *Mathematics the Piaget Way,*[1] developed for the primary grades in the Tower-Soudan Schools in Minnesota, and Baratta-Lorton's *Mathematics Their Way.*[2] Piaget's ideas are incorporated in other programs through the use of **concrete–manipulative materials** to lay foundations and develop children's understanding of mathematics.

Piaget's research led him to conclude that ideally each individual passes through four stages as thought processes develop and mature, gradually progressing from one stage to the next over the years. Teachers who are aware of the characteristics of children's thought processes at each stage can judge where each child is in terms of mental development. Piaget's four stages are:

- The sensorimotor stage (zero to two years)

- The preoperational stage (two to seven years)

- The concrete operations stage (seven to twelve years)

- The formal operations stage (twelve years and older)

a. Sensorimotor Stage The **sensorimotor stage** occupies the period of an infant's life prior to the onset of verbal communication. Teachers are not directly concerned with children this young, but they should know that even at this early age the foundations for later mental growth and mathematical learning are developed. Initially an infant's actions are random and uncoordinated, and events are disconnected. For a baby, persons and objects cease to exist when they are out of sight. Later the children are able to coordinate their actions, and they begin to connect present events with past experiences. By the end of the sensorimotor stage they are able to recognize familiar individuals and objects and to hold mental images of them after they are out of sight.

---

[1] A. Dean Hendrickson, *Mathematics the Piaget Way* (St. Paul: Minnesota Council on Quality Education, State Department of Education, 1981).

[2] Mary Baratta-Lorton, *Mathematics Their Way* (Barrington, Illinois: Addison-Wesley Publishing Company, Inc., 1976).

b. Preoperational Stage   The **preoperational stage** occurs between the ages of two years and about seven years. Its onset is marked by the child's first use of words and of objects and symbols to stand for other objects. A. Dean Hendrickson describes preoperational children:

> Children who are not yet concrete operational are most likely to make judgments about situations based on immediate appearances of things.
> . . . Preoperational thinkers tend to center on single features rather than to coordinate features, often making decisions based on one attribute and then switching to a different attribute. . . .
> (They) tend to focus on states and to ignore the transformations made in going from one state to another. In a similar fashion, the child's thinking is irreversible in that an opposite set of transformations needed to reverse a change, or a compensatory plan to undo something, cannot be conceptualized.
> In forming classes, or part whole relations, the preoperational or transitional child finds it difficult to see that one class can be a subclass of a larger one. . . .[3]

Piaget described three levels of understanding of quantity and number within this period.[4] Children first make what Piaget called a "global comparison of quantities or amounts." For example, when shown two containers that are the same size, each holding the same number of beads, preoperational thinkers believe that the number of beads in one container changes when the beads are poured into another container of different size or shape; the quantity seems to increase or decrease depending on how the beads appear in the new container.

Later, children establish what Piaget called "intuitive correspondence without lasting equivalence." Children believe that the number of beads should remain the same when poured from one container to another. Yet, when the second container is substantially different, they believe the number of beads changes. They are unable to maintain the conservation of quantity.

Finally, children reach a mature level of understanding about quantity and number when they establish and maintain a lasting correspondence between the elements in two sets, even though the configurations of the sets are changed. Now they know that the number of beads remains unchanged regardless of differences in the containers holding them.

Piaget did not associate these stages of understanding with school grades. It is accurate to say, however, that children in Piaget's experiments were of the ages of children in preschool and kindergarten classes and grades one and two. It is also accurate to say that some children did not reach the level of lasting correspondence until the age of seven. Teachers who are aware of this research and who know each of their

---

[3] A. Dean Hendrickson, pp. 2–3. (Used by permission.)

[4] Jean Piaget, *The Child's Concept of Number* (New York: The Humanities Press, 1952). See Part I, Sec. II and Part III, Sec. IX.

children's level of understanding will not prematurely introduce operations that depend upon lasting correspondence, such as addition and subtraction. Rather they will wait until each child has achieved this level of development.

c. Concrete-Operations Stage

Children enter the **concrete-operations stage** at about age seven. Now they begin to form mental images of objects and to think in terms of the whole rather than the parts. They can mentally integrate parts to make a whole and can separate a whole into its parts. Students who are able to do these sorts of mental activities, called **operations** by Piaget, have achieved what he called **reversibility.** He believed children must internalize these mental operations before they can think logically.

This belief supports children's use of a wide variety of concrete–manipulative and other materials as they learn mathematics. Because the mental images children create and move about in their minds are a product of their experiences, those who see and manipulate an abundance of objects, shapes, and symbols have clearer mental images than those whose experiences are meager. By the time this period comes to a close, children who have had a variety of meaningful experiences will have mastered many operations. Toward the end, children will think effectively without concrete materials.

d. Formal-Operations Stage

The **formal-operations stage** is reached by individuals who are able to form hypotheses, analyze situations to consider all factors that bear on them, draw conclusions, and test them against reality. Transition to this stage occurs at about age twelve, when children generally move into the adult stage of thinking.

Piaget contended that as children move from one stage to the next no stage is ever skipped. To the question of whether it is possible to accelerate children through the stages, he replied: "It's probably possible to accelerate, but maximal acceleration is not desirable. There seems to be an optimal time. What this optimal time is will surely depend upon each individual and on the subject matter. We still need a great deal of research to know what the optimal time will be." [5]

---

[5] Jean Piaget, quoted in Frank G. Jennings, "Jean Piaget: Notes on Learning," *Saturday Review* (May 20, 1967), p. 82.

Self-check of Objective 1

Piaget's research has influenced the way children are taught. Identify Piaget's four stages of mental growth; then describe orally or in writing ways this theory of mental development influences instruction in mathematics.

2. Richard Skemp

Skemp is an English mathematician–psychologist who believes that much human activity is goal directed and that in order to understand people's actions it is necessary to know their goals. He says that intelligence is a kind of learning which leads to the achievement of goal states by a variety of means.[6] A **two-level director system** guides learning. At the first level the manipulation of objects in in- and out-of-school environments provides the learner with physical activities that form the basis for further learning and the internalization of ideas. Second-level actions are built on those of the first level and are mental rather than physical.[7]

Skemp also believes that in order for learning to be useful to an individual the common properties of experiences must be brought together to form a conceptual structure, or schema.[8] For the teacher this means that the structure of mathematics must be made clear to children before they can use prior knowledge as a basis for further learning or effectively apply their knowledge to the solution of problems. Skemp says this about the importance of structure: "The study of the structures themselves is an important part of mathematics; and the study of the ways in which they are built up, and function, is at the very core of the psychology of learning mathematics."[9] He advocates a physical environment that gives children opportunities to interact with objects during the early stages of learning a concept. They also need time to reflect and a chance to act on knowledge so they can organize their thoughts and internalize their learning.[10]

3. Robert Gagne

Most of Gagne's studies have dealt with investigations of what he calls the **hierarchy of steps** through which a learner must pass in order to complete a task.[11] He has concluded that learning is improved when the subtasks needed to arrive at a specific task are first established and or-

---

[6] Richard S. Skemp, "Mathematics as an Activity of Our Intelligence: A Model for Diagnosis and Remediation of Learning Difficulties in Mathematics," in Ian D. Beattie, ed., 1981 *Research Monograph. Research Reports from the Seventh Annual National Conference on Diagnostic and Prescriptive Mathematics* (Bowling Green, Ohio: The Research Council for Diagnostic and Prescriptive Mathematics, 1982), pp. 2–4.

[7] Skemp, pp. 4–5.

[8] Skemp, p. 7.

[9] Richard S. Skemp, *The Psychology of Learning Mathematics* (Hammondsworth, England: Penguin Books, Ltd. A Pelican Original. Copyright © Richard S. Skemp, 1971), p. 39.

[10] Skemp, "Mathematics as an Activity of Our Intelligence: A Model for Diagnosis and Remediation of Learning Difficulties in Mathematics," p. 9.

[11] See Robert M. Gagne, *The Conditions of Learning*, 3rd ed. (New York: Holt, Rinehart and Winston, Inc. 1977).

dered and then are taught in sequence until the target task has been accomplished. Figure 2-1 shows one sequence that might be used to teach children to subtract whole numbers. The target task, or goal, is the ability to subtract a pair of whole numbers of any size. The subordinate tasks leading to the target task are listed in sequence, beginning with the simplest one at the bottom of the flow chart. According to Gagne, learning is facilitated by assuring that each student learns and understands each of the subordinate tasks in sequence until the target task is accomplished. The accomplishment of most target tasks in elementary school mathematics requires several years of study. Work with subtraction of whole numbers begins in kindergarten and is usually not concluded until grade five or six.

**Self-check
of Objectives 2 and 3**

The nature of the activity differs for each level of Skemp's two-level director system for learning. What is the nature of activity at the first level? At the second level?

Explain what Gagne means when he refers to a hierarchy of steps for a topic. Identify a target task other than subtraction that will trouble a child who has not accomplished the prerequisite subtasks.

APPLYING THEORY TO PRACTICE

One way to learn how to apply different theories of learning to your teaching is to study a **model.** In the model used here, subtraction of whole numbers is the topic discussed. The model is a cubelike structure composed of smaller cubes, or cells (Figure 2-2). Each dimension of the model deals with one of three equally important factors to consider as you plan experiences for children:

- A set of broad goals, or objectives, for children

- A teaching–learning sequence

- A sequence of subtasks for a topic

1. Goals, or Objectives

First consider goals for the children you teach. The goals presented here refer to four types of mathematical behavior:

- Knowledge of facts and skills

- Demonstration of understanding and comprehension

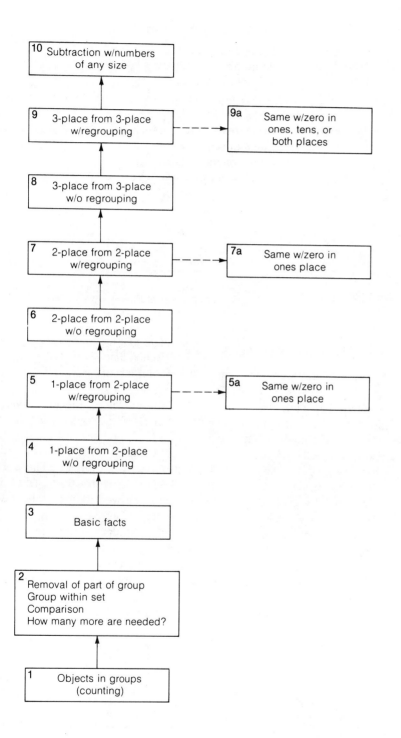

FIGURE 2-1

A sequence of steps for learning to subtract whole numbers

FIGURE 2-2
A model for decision making
in mathematics teaching.
Source: Based on material in
Edward G. Begle and James
W. Wilson, "Evaluation of
Mathematics Programs,"
Mathematics Education (Chi-
cago: National Society for the
Study of Education, 1970).

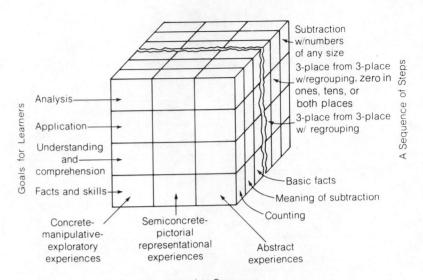

A Teaching–Learning Sequence

- Application of mathematics in a variety of situations

- Analysis of relationships and patterns in nonroutine ways[12]

These four behaviors are represented in the model by the four layers,
beginning at the bottom with knowledge of facts and skills. Each layer
is labeled at the model's left.

Facts and skills are the least cognitively complex types of mathematical behavior and are the easiest to select, teach, and evaluate. There are
100 basic subtraction facts, such as $8 - 3 = 5$ and $6 - 6 = 0$. Skill is
demonstrated by a child who computes the answer for examples like
$63 - 14 = \square$ and $92 - 48 = \square$ using the decomposition algorithm.

The second level of mathematical behavior—**understanding and comprehension**—is more complex than knowledge of facts and skills. It requires that a child be able to use principles and concepts to explain the
meaning of a fact or operation. Students who have a good understanding
of subtraction not only can determine the answer for an example like
$63 - 14 = \square$ but also can explain the meaning of each step in the algorithm they use.

The third level of mathematical behavior is **application.** Students

---

[12]These categories are adapted from Edward G. Begle and James W. Wilson, "Evaluation
of Mathematics Programs," *Mathematics Education* (Chicago: National Society for the Study
of Education, 1970), pp. 367–404. Other categories are found in Benjamin S. Bloom, ed.,
*Taxonomy of Educational Objectives, The Classification of Educational Goals, Handbook I;
Cognitive Domain* (New York: Longmans, Green and Co., 1956); and Len Pikaart and
Kenneth J. Travers, "Teaching Elementary School Mathematics: A Simplified Model,"
Arithmetic Teacher, XX, No. 5 (May 1973), pp. 332–342.

achieve this goal when they are able to apply the facts and skills, concepts, and principles they have learned to everyday situations and to the solution of nonroutine problems. They know that subtraction is frequently applied in routine ways, such as when it is used to determine the difference in the capacities of two auditoriums. At other times the problem is such that the means of solution is not immediately obvious. Now students must analyze a situation to determine possible strategies and select the appropriate one(s). Students with a good understanding of subtraction will recognize when to use it to help solve nonroutine problems.

Analysis is the highest mathematical behavior represented in the model. It requires that students engage in the type of abstract thinking associated with Piaget's fourth stage of mental development. It requires the detection of patterns and relationships and the organization of ideas into well-ordered, and sometimes complex, structures. Analysis is demonstrated by a student who explains why the difference between an odd and an even number is always an odd number and the difference between two even or two odd numbers is always an even number. This level of mathematical behavior is not usually achieved by children until they are in the upper grades of elementary school. There are many who do not achieve it at all while in elementary school.

The National Council of Supervisors of Mathematics developed their list of basic mathematical skills in 1977 because they viewed with alarm the emphasis that was being placed on a narrow view of "basics." They saw that instruction was being concentrated on facts and skills, while other types of mathematical behavior were being deemphasized. Children whose work is confined largely to the lowest level of behavior can learn to compute accurately and rapidly, but they will possess few other mathematical behaviors or skills. All children should be moved to the highest level of mathematical behavior they are capable of performing. The second dimension of the model, which deals with a three-tier teaching–learning sequence built on the theories of Brownell, Piaget, and Skemp, will help you see how to develop the higher levels of mathematical behavior.

2. A Teaching–Learning Sequence

Brownell's meaning theory stresses that children must understand what they are learning if learning is to be permanent, whereas Piaget and Skemp contend that children acquire understanding through the manipulation of objects and the internalization and structuring of concepts. These beliefs support the practice of beginning new work at a concrete–manipulative level of activity, where children use materials that are designed and/or organized in ways that foster thinking about mathematical concepts. This work, the first stage in the **teaching–learning sequence**, provides the mental images children need in order to perform the mental operations that lead to the internalization of concepts. The second stage in the sequence is the pictorial representation of materials, where pictures or models are used in place of the actual materials. Children are ready for the abstract stage of the teaching–learning sequence when they are capable of using numerals and other mathematical symbols as they work and do not require real or pictured objects.

This teaching–learning sequence is represented in Figure 2-2 by columns of cells that extend left to right across the model. **Concrete-manipulative experiences** are at the left, **semiconcrete-pictorial experiences** are in the middle, and **abstract experiences** are at the right.

The following illustration of this part of the model shows a sequence of teaching–learning activities used to develop first graders' understanding of how subtraction is used to compare the sizes of two collections of objects. It begins at the concrete–manipulative level as children work with small colored plastic airplanes. Each child is directed to count out a group of eight blue airplanes and a group of three red airplanes, for example. To determine how many more blue than red planes have been counted, a child matches each red plane with a blue plane until all of the red planes have been matched. The number of unmatched blue planes is the difference in the sizes of the two groups. Many activities with these and similar objects are used to provide the concrete experiences children need to understand how to use subtraction to compare sets of objects.

Later the children are given activity pages, perhaps from their workbooks, that contain pictures of real objects and representations of objects, such as colored squares, circles, and other shapes grouped to show pairs of sets. Rather than making the matchings directly, a child draws lines between the pictured objects in two sets to match them. The number of unmatched pictures in the larger set is the difference in the sizes of the two sets.

Eventually, subtraction sentences like $8 - 3 = 5$ will be introduced to represent earlier actions with objects (concrete mode) and pictures (semiconcrete mode). The children's activities will also involve them in writing sentences and answers for situations such as these: "Joanie has 17 baseball cards, while Johnny has 8. Joanie has how many more cards than Johnny?" "Juan made 8 wreaths for the classroom; Tricia made 6. How many fewer wreaths did Tricia make than Juan?"

3. A Sequence of Steps

Gagne's research indicates that one way to improve learning is to determine the sequence of steps or subtasks that lead to accomplishment of the target task and teach the steps in order. Figure 2-1 shows one sequence of steps for teaching children to subtract whole numbers; these steps are represented in the model (Figure 2-2) by rows of cells that extend from front to back. Counting, which is a prerequisite skill for each of the operations, is shown at the front; the target task is at the back. (The intermediate steps that cannot be shown in the model are in the flow chart.) As you plan activities, subtraction in our example, you need to be aware of the sequence of steps and where each of your children is in relation to the steps to avoid having children spend time with concepts and skills they already understand or having them try to cope with those for which they lack the necessary background. (A sequence of steps for each of the operations addition, multiplication, and division with whole numbers is contained in chapters dealing with those topics.)

4. Integrating the Three Dimensions

We will now consider how the three dimensions of the model are brought together to plan effective lessons. The following situations illustrate how three teachers brought goals for learners, the teaching–learning sequence, and the sequence of steps for subtraction together as they planned their lessons.

A first-grade teacher plans to present a lesson that will help children understand how to use subtraction in take-away situations. The teacher is aware of Brownell's meaning theory and of the research by Piaget and Skemp indicating that in order for children to understand a concept, they need opportunities to use objects at the early stages of learning. Because this is a new concept, the teacher will have children work with plastic disks as he teaches the lesson.

Now visualize the place of this work in the model. It is represented by a cell located in the model's second layer (comprehension–understanding), at the left (concrete–manipulative), and in the second row from the front (meaning of subtraction).

A third-grade teacher wants to introduce subtraction of three-place numbers from three-place numbers with regrouping (borrowing). She is aware of research about learning, so she will use concrete materials to help children understand why regrouping is necessary. She is also aware that she will help children realize why it is important to learn this type of subtraction if she presents real-world situations that use it. She begins with a story problem, such as: "There are 362 greeting cards in a rack. During the next week 295 are sold. How many cards remain to be sold?" The children use beansticks (place-value materials they can make) to represent the greeting cards as they deal with this new type of subtraction.

This work is represented in the model by a pair of cells, because it deals with both understanding–comprehension and application. The cells are in the two middle layers, at the left, and toward the back in the eighth row (three-place from three-place with regrouping).

As children's background of concepts and skills matures, it is possible to deal with new concepts at the abstract level of the teaching–learning sequence.

A fifth-grade teacher wants children to learn a quick way to subtract 298 from 602. She knows that the children have a good understanding of place value, different ways to express numbers, and the decomposition algorithm. She uses this sequence of questions:

Teacher: How many tens are there in 602?

Children: There are 60.

T: If we regroup (borrow) one ten to make twelve ones, how many tens are left?

C: There are 59 tens.

T: Let's see how we can use what we have just done to complete the subtraction of 298 from 602 with just one regrouping instead of two. Who can tell me what to do?

C: We can rename 602 as 59 tens and 12 ones. Then we can complete the subtraction by subtracting 8 from 12, 9 from 9, and 2 from 5. The answer is 304.

This lesson develops understanding of a new way to deal with a particular type of subtraction but uses neither concrete nor pictorial materials. It is represented by a cell in the second layer (understanding), at the right (abstract), and in row 9a (three-place from three-place with zero in the tens place of the minuend).

Self-check of Objective 4   Identify the three dimensions of the decision-making model. Explain orally or in writing the significance of each dimension to the planning of mathematics units and daily lessons.

INFORMATION ABOUT SEQUENCES OF TASKS

Fortunately it is not necessary for teachers to devise their own list of subtasks for teaching a topic. The authors of textbook series and other curriculum planners have done this, and their lists are ready to use. **Scope-and-sequence charts** provided with children's textbook series are one source of the sequence for different topics. Another source is a list of **performance objectives**. These lists accompany some commercially produced materials and have been prepared by some districts for their teachers.

1. Scope-and-Sequence Charts

Textbook series provide the basis for many school districts' mathematics programs. The content of a textbook series is easily determined by ex-

amining a scope-and-sequence chart, which is contained in the teacher's manual. A scope-and-sequence chart gives a listing of all of the mathematics topics that are contained in the series. Each major topic is usually listed separately at the top of the chart. A grade-by-grade list identifies the subtasks for each topic and the order in which they are presented.

A part of the scope-and-sequence chart for the Scott, Foresman and Company's *Mathematics Around Us* series is shown in Table 2-1. The chart

TABLE 2-1   Scope and sequence chart*

	1	2	3
Whole Numbers: Subtraction	Meaning of subtraction, 52–54, 89–90 Basic facts: minuends • Through six, 55–62, 91–92, 96–100 • Through nine, 126–140, 144 • Through twelve, 163–179, 242 • Through eighteen, 285–296, 298 Zero in, 93–94 Families of facts, 126, 129–130, 135–136, 140, 162–164, 167–168, 171–172, 175, 198, 285, 287, 289–291 Names for numbers, 52–54, 173–174, 288 Computation with no renaming, 303–306	Meaning of subtraction, 58–59 Basic facts: minuends • Through nine, 60–70 • Through twelve, 107–110, 113–116 • Through eighteen, 123, 125–131, 133–134 Zero in, 61 Families of facts, 63–64, 67–68, 70, 104–110, 113–114, 129–130 Names for numbers, 111–112, 124 Computation with no renaming 229–230 Renaming, 231–234 Computation with one renaming • Two digit, 235–240, 243–248, 255–258, 287–288, 291 • Three digit, 285–286, 289–290	Basic facts, 28–33 Families of facts, 36–37 Names for numbers, 38 Computation with no renaming, 104–105 Renaming, 106–107 Computation with one renaming • Renaming tens, 106–111, 114–117, 120 • Renaming hundreds, 106–107, 112–117, 120 • Money, 118–119 • Four-digit numbers, 218–221 • Checking, 216–217 Computation with two renamings, 222–223, 226–230 Computation with zero, 224–230 Computation with large numbers (Side Trip), 231

	4	5	6
	Basic facts, 42–45 Renaming, 48–49 Computation • One renaming, 50–51 • More than one renaming, 52–55, 58–59 • With zeros, 56–59 • Mental computation (Side Trip), 60–61 • Checking, 68–69 • Money, 72–73 • Large numbers (Side Trip), 80–81 Estimating differences, 46–47 Missing addends, 76–77	Basic facts, 10–11 Computation • One renaming, 20–21 • More than one renaming, 22–25 • With zero, 24–25 • Money, 32–33 • Checking, 20–21 Estimating differences, 26–27 Missing addends, 34–35	Computation • One renaming, 12–13 • More than one renaming, 14–15 • With zero, 14–15 • Checking, 12–13 Estimating differences, 18–19 Missing addends, 22–23

*From *Scott, Foresman Mathematics K–8*, Teacher's Edition, by L. Carey Bolster, et al. Copyright © 1980 by Scott, Foresman and Company. Used by permission.

shows which subtraction subtasks are presented in each of the grades and the sequence in which they are presented.

2. Performance Objectives

Some commercial programs and most district-produced programs do not have scope-and-sequence charts. Many of these programs do have lists of performance objectives, which frequently list the order in which a sequence of activities should be presented. In addition to showing a sequence for the objectives, the list contains descriptions of how children will demonstrate that they have accomplished the objectives.

Here are performance objectives for work with mass (weight) measurement from one district's program:

1. Given two objects of different weights, each of which can be lifted by a child with one hand, the student will identify the heavier or lighter object.

2. Given a balance with a pan or platform at the end of each arm and a collection of objects having slightly different weights, the student will use the balance to compare the weights of any two objects.

3. Given a balance with a pan or platform at the end of each arm and a collection of objects, such as different-sized wooden blocks, the student will use nonstandard units, such as dried beans or marbles, to weigh each object.

4. Given a balance scale and a set of gram weights to 1000 grams, the student will weigh objects weighing less than 1 kilogram to the nearest gram.

5. Given a metric bathroom scale, the student will weigh himself or herself to the nearest kilogram.

6. Given a balance scale, the student will weigh objects weighing less than two kilograms, recording the weight as grams and kilograms, for example, 1364 grams and 1.364 kilograms.

7. Given an incomplete table of metric units of weight, the student will complete the table to show the number of milligrams, centigrams, and decigrams in a gram, and the number of grams in a dekagram, hectogram, and kilogram.

8. Given a metric balance scale, pound and ounce weights, and a kilogram weight, the student will show that there are a little more than two pounds in a kilogram.

These performance objectives show the concepts and skills involved in learning the metric system of weight. They tell what children should know and be able to do by the time they complete the sixth grade. They also give a suggested sequence for presenting the concepts and skills.

The scope-and-sequence charts and lists of performance objectives contained in published materials or district program guides are valuable sources of information. You should become acquainted with these materials and use them when you plan activities for your children.

Scope-and-sequence charts are discussed, and an example is given. Describe orally or in writing the information contained in a typical scope-and-sequence chart.

    Explain what a performance objective is and tell how lists of objectives can be helpful in determining a sequence of activities for children.

Self-check
of Objectives 5
and 6

SUMMARY

Procedures for presenting mathematics to children have changed as new theories of learning and instruction have been introduced. The mental-discipline and stimulus–response theories governed instructional practices in the last century and early part of the present century. Brownell introduced the meaning theory in 1935. Recently the theories of Piaget, Skemp, and Gagne have influenced instruction. Piaget emphasized the importance of considering children's levels of cognitive development, and Skemp and Gagne have stressed the need for considering structure and sequence in presenting topics to children. A model illustrates how mathematical behaviors, or goals for children, a teaching–learning sequence, and the sequence of subtasks for a topic can be brought together when lessons are planned. Scope-and-sequence charts and lists of performance objectives are sources of information about a topic's subtasks and the order in which they should be presented to children.

STUDY QUESTIONS AND ACTIVITIES

1. Read from books and articles that interpret Piaget's theories of mental development to learn more about the four stages of cognitive growth and the characteristics of children in each stage. The articles and books on this subject in this chapter's reading list will be useful.

2. Select a teacher's manual for the mathematics textbook for one elementary school grade. Examine the scope-and-sequence chart

and list the skill areas from the NCSM list in Chapter 1 that are contained in that book. Then select one skill area and list the subtasks for it that are presented in the grade you select.

3. Look at a textbook's teacher's manual, a filmstrip or cassette program's manual, the manual for a computer-assisted instructional program, and a mathematics laboratory kit to see which, if any, have performance objectives. When you find one that has performance objectives, examine and critique the material to see how well it helps children meet the objectives.

4. Read Skemp's article on instrumental and relational understanding (see the reading list). Distinguish between the two types of understanding. Based on your experiences with mathematics, which of these understandings have you developed? Give examples of either or both types of understanding you presently possess. Can you think of any situations in which instrumental understanding might be preferred over relational understanding?

KEY TERMS

mental-discipline theory	model
stimulus–response theory	facts and skills
meaning theory	understanding and comprehension
concrete–manipulative materials	application
sensorimotor stage	analysis
preoperational stage	teaching–learning sequence
concrete-operations stage	concrete-manipulative experiences
operations	semiconcrete–pictorial experiences
reversibility	abstract experiences
formal-operations stage	scope-and-sequence charts
two-level director system	performance objectives
hierarchy of steps	

FOR FURTHER READING

Adler, Irving. "Mental Growth and the Art of Teaching," *Arithmetic Teacher*, XIII, No. 7 (November 1966), pp. 576–584. A discussion of a dozen facets of Piaget's theory of mental growth and thirteen implications of the theory for teaching mathematics.

Brown, Sue D., and Donald E. Brown. "A Look at the Past," *Arithmetic Teacher*, XXVII, No. 5 (January 1980), pp. 34–37. Teaching methods of the past century, as reflected in mathematics books, are briefly described. Excerpts from many books are presented.

Duckworth, Eleanor. "Piaget Rediscovered," *Arithmetic Teacher*, XI, No. 7 (November 1964), pp. 496–499. A discussion of Piaget's theories on intellectual development, teaching, and teacher training.

Dyrli, Odvard E. "Programmed Piaget," *Learning*, V, No. 2 (October 1976), pp. 78–80, 82, 84, 86. A 22-unit "program" helps the reader understand Piaget's four levels of cognitive development and their implications for the teacher. This article is recommended as good for the novice with regard to Piaget's theories.

Elkind, David. "What Does Piaget Say to the Teacher?" *Today's Education*, LXI, No. 8 (November 1972), pp. 46–48. Piaget's interview technique is used to identify some of the implications of his research for teachers. Three aspects of the technique and how they might affect teaching are reviewed.

Fennema, Elizabeth. "Manipulatives in the Classroom," *Arithmetic Teacher*, XX, No. 5 (May 1973), pp. 350–352. Seven reasons for using manipulatives, or learning aids, while teaching mathematics are discussed. The author also cautions against the use of manipulatives in a random way.

Gagne, Robert M. *The Conditions of Learning*, 3rd ed. (New York: Holt, Rinehart and Winston, 1977). A presentation of Gagne's latest views on how learning takes place. While this book deals with learning in general, many of the examples pertain to mathematics.

Gibb, E. Glenadine. "Teaching Effectively and Efficiently," *Arithmetic Teacher*, XXIX, No. 7 (March 1982), p. 2. Gibb discusses different interpretations of what efficiency and effectiveness in mathematics are. She concludes by saying that if changes in curriculum are to take place, the expected learning outcomes and expected content cannot be overlooked.

Hamrick, Kathy B. "Are We Introducing Mathematics Symbols Too Soon?" *Arithmetic Teacher*, XXVIII, No. 3 (November 1980), pp. 14–15. Hamrick believes that children must first learn to talk about mathematics before they use symbols. Their ability to discuss mathematics meaningfully arises from work with both manipulative and pictorial materials.

Lovell, Kenneth R. "Intellectual Growth and Understanding Mathematics: Implications for Teaching," *Arithmetic Teacher*, XIX, No. 4 (April 1972), pp. 277–282. Lovell discusses the implications of Piaget's research for the mathematics educator.

Masalski, William J. "Mathematics and the Active Learning Approach," *Arithmetic Teacher*, XXVI, No. 1 (September 1978), pp. 10–12. Active learning, which involves students in physical interaction with materials and/or the environment, can be promoted through use of organizing centers, open-ended tasks, and the solution of good problems. Defines each means of active learning and gives examples.

Nasca, Donald. "Math Concepts in the Learner Centered Room," *Arithmetic Teacher*, XXVI, No. 4 (December 1978), pp. 48–52. Nasca identifies three stages in the acquisition of mathematical concepts. Premature emphasis on symbolism interferes with concept learning. Examples of topics presented in ways that stress understanding are illustrated.

O'Hara, Ethel. "Piaget, the Six-Year-Old, and Modern Math," *Today's Education*, LXIV, No. 3 (September/October 1975), pp. 32–36. Piaget's four stages of cognitive growth are briefly reviewed. The focus is on preoperative first graders and what their level of cognitive development means for the mathematics program.

Piaget, Jean. *The Child's Conception of Number* (New York: The Humanities Press, 1952). Piaget describes, with many anecdotes regarding children's reactions, his research into how children think about numbers.

Skemp, Richard R. *The Psychology of Learning Mathematics* (Hammondsworth, England: Penguin Books, Ltd., 1971). This book deals with how mathematics is learned rather than how it is taught. The first half looks at the thought patterns people adopt when they do mathematics, and analyzes them psychologically. The second half applies the psychology of the first half to the learning of mathematics, beginning with the child's first concepts of number.

———. "Relational Understanding and Instrumental Understanding," *Arithmetic Teacher*, XXVI, No. 3 (November 1978), pp. 9–15. Relational understanding indicates that the learner knows the relationships among parts—knows the schema—of a topic or concept, while instrumental understanding relies on rules only. The advantages of relational understanding outweigh those of instrumental understanding, according to Skemp, even though it is a harder type of understanding to develop.

Weaver, J. F. "A Play in Search of an Enlightened Ending," *Arithmetic Teacher*, XXVII, No. 2 (October 1979), pp. 2–3. Six misuses of mathematics, culled from a variety of sources, form the first act of the "play." The second act features the 1979 president of the National Council of Teachers of Mathematics. The unfinished portion points out that children must have a wealth of relevant experiences within a variety of contexts if they are to become quantitatively literate.

———. "Some Concerns about the Application of Piaget's Theory and Research in Mathematics Learning and Instruction," *Arithmetic Teacher*, XIX, No. 4 (April 1972), pp. 263–270. Discusses cases where Piaget's evidence has been disregarded in teaching and also where his research has been unnecessarily invoked.

3

Assessment Procedures for Mathematics

Upon completion of Chapter 3 you will be able to:

1. Name five components of readiness for mathematics and explain the significance of each one to mathematics teaching–learning.

2. Describe the kinds of information revealed by Piagetian-type tests, and discuss the importance of such information.

3. Distinguish between achievement and diagnostic tests, and describe the values of analytical diagnostic tests for program planning.

4. List steps in preparing a criterion-referenced diagnostic test.

5. Name three types of attitude tests, and give examples of items for each type.

6. Identify at least five sources of information about children's mathematical backgrounds besides tests.

7. Identify four general groups of exceptional children whose handicaps may affect their learning in mathematics.

8. Describe three learning disabilities which affect performance in mathematics.

9. Describe the type of information about mathematics that is needed for the individualized educational plan of a learning-handicapped child.

10. Identify three clusters of traits possessed by gifted and talented individuals, and name some of the characteristics of each cluster.

11. Describe two ways of providing for the mathematical needs of gifted and talented children.

The success of a mathematics program depends on how well it relates to children's levels of cognitive growth, skills and understandings, and attitudes toward the subject. Current and accurate information about each child is essential before good planning can be done. This chapter provides information about five components of readiness you need to consider as you plan activities, techniques for gathering information about each child's current status in each of the components, and special students and mathematics.

COMPONENTS OF READINESS

In a paper delivered at the first National Conference on Remedial Mathematics held at Kent State University in 1974, Robert Underhill named five components, or areas, of readiness that teachers need to consider as they plan and teach mathematics:

- Content readiness
- Pedagogical readiness
- Maturational readiness
- Affective readiness
- Contextual readiness [1]

1. Content Readiness

Gagne and Skemp stress the importance to a learner of knowing and understanding prerequisite tasks and structure before embarking on further work with a topic. **Content readiness** refers to the mathematical skills and knowledge possessed by a child. It is concerned with how well a child knows and understands a topic's subtasks. For example, children have content readiness for learning to subtract two three-place numbers with regrouping (subtask 9 in the flowchart in Figure 2-1) if they know and understand the sequence of subtasks that precede this new type of subtraction. Diagnostic tests, evaluation of work products, interviews, and observations of children at work are some sources of information about content readiness.

---

[1] Robert B. Underhill, "Classroom Diagnosis," in Jon L. Higgins and James W. Heddens, eds., *Remedial Mathematics: Diagnostic and Prescriptive Approaches* (Columbus, Ohio: ERIC Center for Science, Mathematics, and Environmental Education, College of Education, The Ohio State University, 1976), pp. 33–35. Used by permission.

2. Pedagogical Readiness

Work with a variety of materials—concrete, pictorial, graphic, and symbolic—is advocated as the means by which children gain the experiences they need for understanding mathematics, and many materials are illustrated and discussed in this book. **Pedagogical readiness** is concerned with the learner's understanding of learning aids and how the aids illustrate processes and concepts. An example of a mathematics learning aid is a set of beansticks. (These materials, which children can make themselves, are discussed in Chapters 8, 10, and 11.) Beansticks can be used to illustrate the meaning of the decomposition algorithm for whole-number subtraction. Children have pedagogical readiness for using beansticks to understand this algorithm if they know how beansticks represent place-value positions in numbers and how exchanges between beans in adjacent positions (regroupings) are made. Observations of a child at work with learning aids, listening to the verbal contributions a child makes during lessons in which aids are used, and interviews are some of the ways you can determine a child's pedagogical readiness.

3. Maturational Readiness

Maturational readiness in the Piagetian sense is considered here. Underhill states that a child's level of maturation places constraints on the level of knowing a child may achieve with reference to a concept but does not preclude the child from learning some things. "Learner progress is limited but not halted by his capabilities of conservation, reversibility, attending to sequencing, and attending to two or more variables at a time."[2] Piagetian-type tests, observations of children at work, and their verbal contributions during discussions and activities are sources of information about maturational readiness.

4. Affective Readiness

Children's attitudes toward mathematics have a large bearing on how they approach the subject. A child who possesses a good attitude toward mathematics, realizes that knowledge of mathematics broadens occupational choices and enriches personal life, and has few anxieties about the subject has high **affective readiness** and is more likely to approach the subject positively and experience success than one whose affective readiness is low. Attitude tests, observations of a child at work, evaluation of work products, and interviews with both the child and the parents or guardians are sources of information about affective readiness.

Mathematics anxiety, or fear of mathematics, has a profound effect on

---

[2]Underhill, p. 34.

a learner's attitude toward the subject. Historically, females and minorities have been under-represented in mathematics courses in high schools and universities. One reason is that they have been particularly vulnerable to mathematics anxiety. Chapter 4 presents specific information about mathematics anxiety, its special impact on females and minorities, and classroom practices that lessen its incidence and severity.

5. Contextual Readiness

Contextual readiness refers to a child's level of awareness of the uses of mathematics. A child who is aware of real-world uses of mathematics is more likely to become involved in activities dealing with a topic, such as subtraction of three-place numbers with regrouping, than one who is unaware of its applications. Underhill says this about contextual readiness: "Extra-school experiences or experiences of the child's not-at-school world should be related whenever possible to school learning. Whenever a concept of a discipline can be placed into a context (preferably extra-school) familiar to the learner, he will be more ready for it than when it is not."[3]

Underhill names five components of readiness to consider when planning activities. List each component and discuss its implications for teaching mathematics.

Self-check of Objective 1

ASSESSMENT PROCEDURES

Current information about each child's status with regard to the five areas of readiness can be obtained in a variety of ways. Written tests are commonly used and come to mind immediately when assessment procedures are considered. Tests are important but cannot provide the comprehensive information that is needed to make a good match between a child and program. Systematic use of the following procedures will provide the information you need about each child:

- Tests

- Evaluation of daily work

- Observations of children

- Interviews with children

[3] Underhill, pp. 34–35.

- Evaluations of children's uses of mathematics
- Parent–teacher conferences

1. Tests

Several types of tests are available. This section acquaints you with Piagetian-type, commercial achievement and diagnostic, teacher-made diagnostic, and attitude tests.

a. Piagetian-type Tests Based on Piaget's theory of cognitive development, **Piagetian-type tests** are designed to provide information about a child's mental maturity. Each test deals with a specific topic, such as logical classification, ordering and seriation, time, and logical thought, and is patterned after the manner in which Piaget conducted his original research.

Piagetian-type tests are especially helpful for kindergarten and primary-grade teachers who want to establish where a child is in regard to the transition from the preoperational stage to the concrete-operational stage of development.

Three books written for the Nuffield project in Great Britain by a team from Piaget's Geneva Institute are sources of Piagetian-type tests. The Nuffield project relied heavily on Piaget's theories to develop a mathematics program for British children. The project published a series of guides for teachers in infant and junior schools. (These schools correspond to our elementary schools.) Three of the guides, *Checking Up I*, *Checking Up II*, and *Checking Up III*, contain tests for determining children's levels of cognitive development.[4] A part of the checkup for one-to-one correspondence is reproduced in Table 3-1. The materials and procedures for administering the test, along with typical children's replies, are given. Note that replies are organized in groups that correspond to the three levels of thinking Piaget found within the preoperational stage. Responses like those in *c* indicate that children have reached the level of lasting correspondence. The tests are administered on a one-to-one basis.

---

[4] These three and other Nuffield books are available in the United States from John Wiley and Sons, Inc.

Self-check of Objective 2

The sample page from *Checking Up I* shows a Piagetian-type test. Describe the kind of information about children revealed by such tests. Why is the information important to teachers of young children?

Summary Checkup OC†	Typical Replies
One-to-one correspondence and transitivity	*a* [Children with an immature understanding of OC]
Objective	*The child may argue that because the line now looks different there are not as many bricks as counters. He may say:*
Transitivity: if A = B and B = C, then A = C.	*"There are fewer counters because the line is shorter,"*
Material	*or*
A collection of counters, say twelve (A)	*"There are more because the line is longer."*
A collection of small bricks (B)	*Children may also say:*
A collection of small miscellaneous objects (C)	*"There are more counters because they are close together."*
Part 1	*b* [Children with a developing understanding of OC]
Procedure	*The children will say that there are as many bricks as counters but will not be able to justify their reply.*
The teacher should spread out nine counters on the table and ask the child: "Can you put on the table as many bricks as there are counters?"	*c* [Children with a mature understanding of OC]
	Children will say that there are as many bricks as counters. They will be able to justify their reply in the following manner:
Note	*i*
Should the child not be able to establish this initial correspondence, then the teacher should let him have further practice.	*"It doesn't matter if they are in a long line because they are exactly the same bricks as before when they were in front of the counters,"*
	or
Once the child has established a one-to-one correspondence between the two collections the teacher should ask the child if he needs the remaining bricks.	*"You haven't put any more, and you haven't taken any away."*
	ii
	"You can put them back as they were before, and you'll see that they are the same."
Note	*iii*
Should the child, with the remaining bricks, fill in a space in the line of bricks already arranged, the teacher should remove the remaining bricks and ask the child:	*"The line is longer but there's more space between the bricks,"*
	or
"Are there as many bricks as counters?"	*"The line is shorter and there's less space between the counters."*
"Why?"	*Only those children giving replies b or c should go on to Part 2.*
Once the child's reply has been given, the teacher should then tell the child: "We are now going to spread out the bricks."	
The teacher should do this in such a way that the line of bricks is longer than the line of counters, and then ask: "Are there as many bricks as counters?" "Why?"	

*The Nuffield Foundation, *Checking Up I* [London: John Murray (Publishers), Ltd., 1970], p. 34. (Used by permission.)

†OC = one-to-one correspondence

In addition to the Nuffield books, Richard Copeland's books *How Children Learn Mathematics* and *Diagnostic and Learning Activities in Mathematics for Children*[5] are useful sources of information about how to develop Piagetian-type tests.

b. Commercial Tests Commercial companies publish both achievement and diagnostic tests. **Achievement tests** are designed to assess what a child knows about a particular subject or group of subjects. For example, the *SRA Achievement Test*[6] provides information about reading, mathematics, and language arts in the primary grades and about these three plus social studies, science, and reference skills in the intermediate grades. Within an area, there are subtests dealing with different aspects of the subject, such as computation, problem solving, and concepts in mathematics. An example of a single-subject achievement test is the *Tests of Achievement in Basic Skills—Mathematics Skills*[7] which contains subtests titled "Arithmetic Skills," "Geometry–Measurement–Application," and "Modern Concepts" and has forms for grades K–1–2, 3–4, and 4–6 in the elementary school.

Commercially published achievement tests have standardized procedures for administering them, analyzing results, and determining a child's grade level or percentile score. Norms that indicate typical performance for children at each grade level are used to determine a particular child's achievement in relation to other children. Standardized achievement tests are frequently used in state- or district-wide testing programs, where they are administered to all children or to those in selected grades according to a prescribed schedule. These tests are useful for determining a child's grade placement and as screening devices for indicating which children have weaknesses that need further diagnosis.

Textbook series usually have sets of achievement tests that cover the mathematics content. These tests serve some of the same purposes as standardized tests but deal with the content of a single series only. Examples of a set of program tests are the beginning-of-the-year inventory and end-of-year mastery tests that accompany the *HBJ Mathematics*[8] series.

Achievement tests serve useful purposes, but they do not always yield sufficient information to determine a child's specific spot in a program. A more comprehensive, analytical diagnosis is sometimes needed before

---

[5] Richard W. Copeland, *How Children Learn Mathematics*, 3rd. ed. (New York: Macmillan Publishing Company, Inc., 1979) and *Diagnostic and Learning Activities in Mathematics for Children* (New York: Macmillan Publishing Company, 1974).

[6] *SRA Achievement Series* (Chicago: Science Research Associates, 1978).

[7] *Tests of Achievement in Basic Skills—Mathematics Skills* (San Diego: Educational and Industrial Testing Service).

[8] Lola J. May, Shirley M. Frye, and Donna Cyrier Jacobs, *HBJ Mathematics* (New York: Harcourt Brace Jovanovich, Publishers, 1981).

the right placement can be made. An analytical diagnosis frequently includes a criterion-referenced diagnostic test as one source of information. Such tests are frequently based on performance objectives and contain items that test a child's comprehension of mathematics and skill in computing.

Commercial **diagnostic tests** are useful as long as their items match the objectives of a school's program. The *Keymath Diagnostic Arithmetic Test* [9] is a test that is administered to one child at a time. The test administrator shows the student a page from the test book, gives oral instructions, and receives the student's oral response. A record of responses is made on a record sheet provided with the test. In addition to oral responses, children write answers on a separate test paper to demonstrate skill in addition, subtraction, multiplication, and division computation.

The *Stanford Diagnostic Achievement Test* [10] is an example of a group test. There is a test for each of four grade ranges: 1.6–4.5, 3.6–6.5, 5.6–8.5, and 7.6–13. Subtests deal with number systems and numeration, computation, and application.

Chapter pretests and posttests in textbooks are often criterion-referenced tests that are useful for diagnosing children's understandings and skills for each chapter's content.

c. Teacher-made Tests   It is often the case that commercial and textbook tests are unavailable or are unsuitable for a given teacher's purpose. When this is true, **teacher-made tests** must be prepared. These four steps will help you to prepare and use your own diagnostic tests:

- Choose the test's topic(s).

- Choose the objectives.

- Select procedures and design the test.

- Analyze the results.

Choose the test's topic(s). If you are a kindergarten or first-grade teacher, you will select topics such as one-to-one correspondence; rote and rational counting to 20 (or 50, or 100); numeral recognition; matching numerals with sets; classifying objects by size, shape, and color; and comparing objects by length, volume, and size. The number of topics you select will be limited to those you can test on a one-to-one basis in about ten minutes. For one test session you might choose the first four from the ones just listed.

A diagnostic test for older children will usually be restricted to one topic, such as subtraction with whole numbers, the meaning of rational

---

[9] *Keymath Diagnostic Arithmetic Test* (Circle Pines, Minnesota: American Guidance Services, Inc., 1976).

[10] *Stanford Diagnostic Achievement Test* (New York: Harcourt Brace Jovanovich, Inc., 1976).

numbers expressed as common fractions, or linear measurement. A test will often cover only a few subtasks rather than all of them. For example, a subtraction test for grade three might begin with subtask 5 and continue through subtask 7a from the sequence in Figure 2-1.

Choose the objectives. Once you have chosen your topic(s), select performance objectives that are appropriate for your children. These may come from an already prepared list, or you may need to write your own. Topics from a text's scope-and-sequence chart for your grade or flow charts of subtasks for a topic will guide you when you prepare your own.

You also need to determine the mathematical behaviors you want your children to demonstrate on the test. The five objectives that follow are based on the first four kindergarten–primary grade topics listed previously and deal with facts and skills (numbers 2, 3, and 4 in the following list) and understanding and comprehension (1 and 5) from the model in Figure 2-2.

1. Given a collection of up to 10 objects arranged in a straight line, the learner will make a one-to-one matching using similar objects.

2. The learner will count orally to 20.

3. Given a collection of 20 objects, the learner will count them.

4. When shown cards containing the numerals 0 through 9, the learner will say the number named on each one.

5. Given pictures of 1 to 9 objects and numeral cards for the numbers 1 to 9, the learner will match each picture with the numeral card that tells how many objects are in it.

The following objectives are for subtask 5 in the subtraction sequence and deal with (1) facts and skills, (2) understanding and comprehension, and (3) application.

1. Given a subtraction combination like $43 - 9 = \square$, the learner will determine the answer using paper and pencil.

2. Given a subtraction combination like $43 - 9 = \square$, the learner will give an oral explanation of the steps involved in using the decomposition algorithm to determine the answer.

3. Given a subtraction combination like $43 - 9 = \square$, the learner will write an appropriate word problem.

A similar objective should be written for each of the other subtasks and types of mathematical behaviors that are to be tested.

Select procedures and design the test. Once topics and objectives are selected, the next step is to determine how children will be tested. Some tests must be administered to one child at a time, whereas others are given to a group or entire class. To test performance on the five kindergarten–first grade objectives, these procedures can be used:

1. Arrange 6 red poker chips in a straight line with a 1-inch space between each chip. Give the child 6 blue chips with instructions to match the blue chips with the red chips. Demonstrate what a match is, if necessary. Repeat with both larger and smaller sets of chips.

2. Tell the child to count to 20.

3. Arrange 20 red chips on one side of a desk or large sheet of paper (Figure 3-1), and tell the child to count while moving them one at a time to the other side.

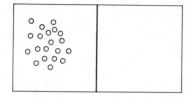

FIGURE 3-1
Set-up for testing a child's ability to count

4. Show one at a time and in mixed order a set of cards, each containing one of the numerals 0–9. Ask the child to tell you the number named on each card.

5. Use dot cards, like those in Figure 3-2, and numeral cards. Arrange the dot cards in random order in a line. Tell the child to match each numeral card with the correct dot card.

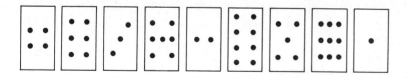

FIGURE 3-2
Cards for testing a child's ability to match quantity and numeral

You can record each child's response on a prepared record card. A 4-by-6 card like the one in Figure 3-3 is useful for this test. Circle numerals that indicate responses for numbers 1, 4, and 5. Write in numerals that tell how high each child counts in procedures 2 and 3.

Paper and pencil tests are commonly used to test children's knowledge of facts and skills. The test in Figure 3-4 contains fifteen items, three for each of the subtasks 5 through 7a in the subtraction sequence in Figure 2-1. No more than 15 items are necessary. It is assumed that a child who gets two or all three of the items for a particular subtask correct has developed computational skill with that type of subtraction. On the other hand, a child who misses two or all three of a particular type probably needs further work with that type of subtraction. Note that the items are

```
┌─────────────────────────────────────────────────────────┐
│                                                           │
│   Name ____ Grade ____ Teacher ____ Date _____           │
│                                                           │
│   1. One-to-one matching: Sets of 6  3  9  5              │
│                                                           │
│   2. Oral rote counting to _____                         │
│                                                           │
│   3. Rational counting to _____                          │
│                                                           │
│   4. Identification of numerals: 0, 1, 2, 3, 4, 5, 6, 7, 8, 9  │
│                                                           │
│   5. Matching sets and numerals: 1, 2, 3, 4, 5, 6, 7, 8, 9    │
│                                                           │
└─────────────────────────────────────────────────────────┘
```

$$\begin{array}{r} 42 \\ -29 \\ \hline \end{array}$$

mixed on the page rather than grouped by type. This forces a child to think about each separate item rather than relying on a pattern to complete the second and third of a type after one example is completed. A wide variety of basic facts is included in the 15 examples. Do not set a time limit for completing a diagnostic test; give each child all the time needed to complete the test.

To test understanding and comprehension of a particular type of subtraction, give an example like the one in the margin and ask the child to "think aloud" as the work is completed: "Tell me what you do when you complete this subtraction example." Do not interrupt or attempt to correct any faulty steps as the child works. Do note errors and possible reasons for them so you can help the child later. By requesting a written word problem for each of two or three subtasks from the sequence, you can test a child's recognition of how subtraction is applied in routine situations.

Analyze the results. The purpose of a diagnostic test is to help you determine a child's strengths and weaknesses in mathematics. Therefore it is necessary that you carefully analyze responses for each test you administer. The analysis requires attention to more than the number of items missed. You must note such things as the types of examples that are done correctly or incorrectly and patterned errors that indicate faulty thinking and misunderstandings. Patterned errors are errors a child repeats as work of a given type is completed. For example, a child might complete subtraction by using the process demonstrated by these examples:

$$\begin{array}{r} 42 \\ -19 \\ \hline 37 \end{array} \qquad \begin{array}{r} 67 \\ -49 \\ \hline 22 \end{array} \qquad \begin{array}{r} 85 \\ -37 \\ \hline 53 \end{array}$$

Name _____

Date _____

Subtraction with Whole Numbers

A 36
  − 7

B 43
  − 21

C 40
  − 8

D 36
  − 19

E 43
  − 9

F 50
  − 27

G 70
  − 2

H 45
  − 22

I 60
  − 25

J 38
  − 19

K 80
  − 29

L 78
  − 42

M 90
  − 3

N 86
  − 18

O 31
  − 4

FIGURE 3-4
Sample subtraction diagnostic test

This error, in which the child subtracts the smaller from the larger number regardless of where they appear in the algorithm, is common among schoolchildren. It results from an unclear understanding of subtraction and failure to grasp the regrouping, or borrowing, process. Basic-fact errors should be detected if they occur. Patterned and basic-fact errors are usually easy to overcome if they are detected early and corrected before they are practiced and become habitual. The reasons for errors cannot always be determined by examination of a child's written work. Interviews during which you have a child explain an algorithm's steps or other work will often reveal the reason. Interviews are discussed later.

***Self-check
of Objectives 3 and 4***

Criterion-referenced tests are used to diagnose children's knowledge and understanding of mathematics. Distinguish between a criterion-referenced diagnostic test and an achievement test. Tell why diagnostic tests are important in program planning.

You may have to prepare a diagnostic test one day. List the steps to follow when you do.

d. Attitude Tests   Success in mathematics is usually positively correlated with positive attitudes toward the subject. **Attitude tests** are one way to determine children's feelings about mathematics. A variety of tests are available, including semantic-differential forms, attitude scales, and sentence completion forms.

A **semantic-differential test** contains a set of antonyms. Between each pair of antonyms is a seven-point scale on which an individual marks a point to indicate which word more closely represents that person's feeling about a subject. To prepare such a scale for mathematics, you would use a series of word pairs like these:

worthwhile . . . . . . worthless

easy . . . . . . difficult

boring . . . . . . challenging

Children mark the point that best expresses their individual feelings. A mark in the center can be scored 0. A plus 1, 2, or 3 is given to a mark in the direction of a positive expression, and a negative 1, 2, or 3 is given to a mark in the direction of a negative expression. The greater the positive score, the more positive is a student's attitude toward mathematics; a score near zero indicates a neutral attitude, and a negative score shows a dislike for mathematics.

Mathematics Attitude Scale

Directions: Please write your name in the upper right-hand corner. Each of the statements on this opinionnaire expresses a feeling or attitude toward mathematics. You are to indicate, on a five-point scale, the extent of agreement between the attitude expressed in each statement and your own personal feeling. The five points are: Strongly Disagree (SD), Disagree (D), Undecided (U), Agree (A), Strongly Agree (SA). Draw a circle around the letter or letters giving the best indication of how closely you agree or disagree with the attitude expressed in each statement.

1. I am always under a terrible strain in a mathematics class.   SD D U A SA
2. I do not like mathematics, and it scares me to have to take it.   SD D U A SA
3. Mathematics is very interesting to me, and I enjoy arithmetic and mathematics courses.   SD D U A SA
4. Mathematics is fascinating and fun.   SD D U A SA
5. Mathematics makes me feel secure, and at the same time it is stimulating.   SD D U A SA
6. My mind goes blank and I am unable to think clearly when working mathematics.   SD D U A SA
7. I feel a sense of insecurity when attempting mathematics.   SD D U A SA
8. Mathematics makes me feel uncomfortable, restless, irritable, and impatient.   SD D U A SA
9. The feeling that I have toward mathematics is a good feeling.   SD D U A SA
10. Mathematics makes me feel as though I'm lost in a jungle of numbers and can't find my way out.   SD D U A SA
11. Mathematics is something that I enjoy a great deal.   SD D U A SA
12. When I hear the word mathematics, I have a feeling of dislike.   SD D U A SA
13. I approach mathematics with a feeling of hesitation, resulting from a fear of not being able to do mathematics.   SD D U A SA
14. I really like mathematics.   SD D U A SA
15. Mathematics is a course in school that I have always enjoyed studying.   SD D U A SA
16. It makes me nervous to even think about having to do a mathematics problem.   SD D U A SA
17. I have never liked mathematics, and it is my most dreaded subject.   SD D U A SA
18. I am happier in a mathematics class than in any other class.   SD D U A SA
19. I feel at ease in mathematics, and I like it very much.   SD D U A SA
20. I feel a definite positive reaction toward mathematics; it's enjoyable.   SD D U A SA

FIGURE 3-5
Mathematics attitude scale.

Source: Lewis R. Aiken, Jr., "Research on Attitudes Toward Mathematics," *Arithmetic Teacher*, March 1972, copyright © 1972 by the National Council of Teachers of Mathematics. Used by permission.

An **attitude scale** is the most popular device for obtaining children's feelings about school subjects. The type of attitude scale shown in Figure 3-5 is commonly used in the intermediate grades and beyond. An attitude scale yields a positive–neutral–negative score.

This scale can be simplified for younger children. Some primary teachers give children a response sheet that omits the statements and replaces the letters with three "faces" for each item. Children indicate their feelings by marking a "happy," "neutral," or "sad" face as their teacher reads each item.

A **sentence-completion form** is sometimes used to obtain information about a child's feelings. Rather than responding to prescribed items, the children are free to say whatever they want about a single topic or several topics. Items like these are used:

1. I think mathematics . . .

2. My mathematics class . . .

3. I like (or do not like) mathematics . . .

Items on a sentence-completion form do not yield positive–neutral–negative scores. However, they may give a better reflection of a child's feelings than either the semantic-differential form or an attitude scale because of the freedom of expression they allow.

Scores on attitude scales are less valid in elementary school than in higher grades. (Validity refers to the degree to which a score reflects a child's true feelings about a subject.) This is so because younger children have less stable attitudes and less insight into their feelings than older students.[11]

A further discussion of attitudes, particularly negative attitudes that lead to mathematics anxiety, is contained in Chapter 4.

Self-check of Objective 5	Three types of attitude tests are described. Name each type, and give your own example of an item for each one.

2. Evaluation of Work Products

During the course of a school year, children make and use models and complete many worksheets, tables, graphs, charts, and other work products. Some are the result of an activity related to the introduction of a new topic, others come from practice exercises dealing with algorithms or other skills, and some come from enrichment activities. **Evaluation** of children's work products will provide you with much information about how well they understand what they are doing and their skill in perform-

---

[11]Lewis R. Aiken, Jr., "Research on Attitudes Toward Mathematics," *Arithmetic Teacher*, XIX, No. 3 (March 1972), p. 230.

ing routine tasks. Their written responses on practice pages should receive special attention. Incorrect responses should be analyzed carefully to determine if patterned and basic-fact errors occur.

When analysis of a child's written work reveals many errors, the topic may be too difficult for that child. If this is so, an adjustment should be made in the child's work. To constantly ask children to perform tasks for which they are not ready will lead to discouragement, possibly so much that they will quit trying to learn.

3. Observation of Children

You will find that **observation** of each child during class discussions, tests, and work periods pays big dividends: information is revealed about a child's interests in and attitudes toward mathematics, knowledge and understanding of the subject, and applications of mathematics in problem-solving situations. As children discuss a topic, note each child's contributions. Do some children tend to dominate the discussion? Are there some who never or infrequently contribute? What is the quality of each child's contribution? Does a child reveal the development of insights into the topic as it is discussed?

While children use learning aids, you should observe them carefully for clues that indicate how well they are developing an understanding of the aids and their uses. Are there children who use a device in a mechanical manner, applying it in an imitative way? Do others reveal that they understand the meaning of the device by applying it to new situations or in original ways? Do some children use several different devices to represent or illustrate a given process? Do some rely on learning aids more than their levels of maturity suggest they should?

You should observe children during tests and study periods to note work habits, use of materials, and ability to perform operations on numbers. When children begin work immediately and apply themselves consistently, you can usually conclude that they understand what they are doing. On the other hand, children who are slow getting to work or cannot keep their minds on it show that they may not understand the work. By circulating among the children as they work, you can observe those who are having difficulty and give them immediate assistance in nontest situations. Often a child can overcome difficulty in a short time with immediate help. If several children have a common problem, they should be formed into a small group for special assistance.

You should observe children from time to time as they use measuring instruments such as rulers, scales, and thermometers. If they use them incorrectly, they should get immediate help from you or another child.

Children should receive encouragement as they work. A soft-spoken "That's the way" or "You're on the right track" is often the only praise needed by children who are uncertain about whether they are working correctly.

4. Interviews with Children

Interviews are used in both planned and spontaneous situations. A planned interview occurs as a part of a diagnostic program when you schedule a time for a child to explain how the subtraction algorithm is completed. A spontaneous interview might occur when you observe a child who is unable to complete a task for a daily assignment and you have an on-the-spot discussion about the student's problem. In either event, you ask questions that help the child reveal misconceptions and faulty thinking.

A teacher who has good rapport with students can also use interviews to discuss a child's feelings about mathematics. Interviews need not be lengthy; 2 or 3 minutes are usually sufficient.

5. Evaluation of Children's Uses of Mathematics

How children use mathematics during the school day outside of the mathematics class and in extra-school situations reveals much about their skills, understandings, and attitudes. When children use charts and graphs to organize and report data during a science or social-studies project, make accurate measurements in art, and record times accurately during a sporting event, it indicates that they are comfortable with mathematics and recognize its value. You must be alert to the ways children use mathematics and give guidance and assistance so they will broaden their in- and extra-school uses. You should also help children evaluate each finished project to determine if it serves its intended purpose.

6. Parent–Teacher Conferences

Parents or guardians of a child can provide valuable information often unavailable from any other source. The parents of a young child can tell about the extent to which the child has been exposed to activities that provide experiences with numbers. Parents of an older child can tell you if the child reads books about mathematics, works number puzzles, and pursues other mathematical interests or whether mathematics is shunned at home. A parent's personal anxiety about mathematics is frequently revealed during a conference. A parent may also talk about how important it is that the child excel in mathematics. Children respond to parents' attitudes and pressures to succeed in different ways. Some become anxious themselves or blame their failure on an "inherited" inability to learn mathematics. One child may respond to pressure with no problems, whereas another buckles under the pressure, fails, and dislikes mathematics. Children sometimes experience problems because of a conflict between the way a topic is taught in school and the way parents think it should be learned. Problems that arise because of parental attitudes, pressures, and ways of doing mathematics should be discussed openly and frankly during conferences. At the same time parental help and support to work at home should be sought and planned.

There are sources of information about children's mathematical backgrounds besides tests. Name five of them, and tell why each one is an important part of an assessment program.

Self-check of Objective 6

DIAGNOSTIC–PRESCRIPTIVE TEACHING

Information about children's levels of mental maturity; strengths and weaknesses in facts and skills, understandings and comprehension, and applications; and attitudes toward mathematics provides the basis for planning and prescribing appropriate activities for each child. The majority of children in a class experience no special problems in learning mathematics when the elements of the model in Chapter 2—goals for children, teaching–learning sequence, and sequence of steps for a topic— are properly accounted for in their units and daily work. There are two groups of children for whom different provisions need to be made so that their activities meet their special needs. These are students with learning handicaps and gifted–talented students.

1. Learning-Handicapped Children

The Education for All Handicapped Children Act (PL 94-142) requires that all handicapped children between the ages of three and eleven have the opportunity for free public education in what is called "the least restrictive environment." This means that children who formerly may have been taught in special schools or classes are now in regular classrooms for all or part of their education.

Learning-handicapped children are a heterogeneous lot, just as are children in any large group. Even so, there are categories of exceptionality that help differentiate children with one sort of handicap from those with another type. Four categories of handicaps are discussed here:

- Learning disabilities

- Sensory handicaps

- Physical impairments

- Social–emotional impairments

(Children handicapped because of mental retardation are not discussed in this book.)

a. Learning Disabilities   Some children have **learning disabilities** that prevent them from learning in the same ways as most children. For example, there may be a visual discrimination deficit that causes a child to confuse similar numerals, such as "*3*" and "*5*," and signs of operation, such as "+" and "×." Nancy Bley and Carol Thornton developed a table (Table 3-2) to use as an aid in identifying learning-disabled children.

TABLE 3-2   Examples of learning disabilities affecting performance in mathematics*

	Visual Deficit	Auditory Deficit
Perceptual Figure-ground	May not finish all problems on page	Trouble hearing pattern in counting
	Frequently loses place	Difficulty attending in the classroom
	Difficulty seeing subtraction within a division problem	
	Difficulty reading multidigit number (see closure)	
Discrimination	Difficulty differentiating coins	Cannot distinguish between 30 and 13 (see receptive language)
	Difficulty differentiating between or writing numbers (3 for 8; 2 for 5)	Difficulty with decimal numbers
	Cannot discriminate between operation symbols	
	Cannot discriminate between size of hands on clock	
	Difficulty associating operation sign with problem (see abstract reasoning)	
Reversal	Reverses digits in a number (may also be a sequential memory problem)	
	Difficulty with regrouping	
Spatial	Trouble writing on lined paper	Difficulty following directions using ordinal numbers
	Difficulty with concept of before/after, so trouble telling time	
	Trouble noticing size differences in shapes	
	Trouble with fraction concept due to inability to note equal-sized parts	
	Difficulty writing decimals	
	Difficulty aligning numbers	
	Difficulty with ordinal numbers	
	Difficulty writing fractional numbers (may also be reversed)	

	Visual Deficit	Auditory Deficit
Memory Short-term	Trouble retaining newly presented material Difficulty copying problems from the board (may be spatial)	Difficulty with oral drills Difficulty with dictated assignments
Long-term	Inability to retain basic facts or processes over a long period Difficulty solving multioperation computation	
Sequential	Difficulty telling time Difficulty following through a multiplication problem Difficulty following through long division problems Difficulty solving column addition problems Difficulty solving multistep word problems	Cannot retain story problem that is dictated
Integrative Closure	Difficulty visualizing groups Difficulty reading multidigit number (see figure-ground) Difficulty with missing addends and missing factors Inability to draw conclusions, therefore trouble noticing and continuing patterns Difficulty with word problems Trouble continuing counting pattern from within a sequence	Difficulty counting on from within a sequence
Expressive language	Rapid oral drills very difficult	Difficulty counting on Difficulty explaining why a problem is solved as it is
Receptive language	Difficulty relating word to meaning (may be spatial) Difficulty with words that have multiple meanings	Difficulty relating word to meaning Difficulty writing numbers from dictation
Abstract reasoning	Inability to solve word problems Inability to compare size of numbers, using symbols Cannot understand patterning in counting Difficulty with decimal concept	

*Reprinted from *Teaching Mathematics to the Learning Disabled* by Nancy S. Bley and Carol A. Thornton by permission of Aspen Systems Corporation, © 1981.

The table names three types of learning disabilities: perceptual, memory, and integrative. Several subcategories for each disability are listed. Examples of some of the behaviors manifested by children who possess a given disability are also listed. Many of the behaviors are characteristic of children commonly considered to be lazy, inattentive, daydreamers, or disinterested. Rather than recognizing that a learning disability may exist, teachers frequently reprimand children who exhibit these behaviors and admonish them to pay attention, try harder, or otherwise shape up. Rather than reprimanding a child who is not learning at the same rate as the other students, you should consider the possibility that one or more learning disabilities exist. At the present time there are no tests or other devices for pinpointing disabilities. However, being aware that disabilities do exist and knowing ways they are manifested in a child's behavior increases the likelihood that you will recognize any learning-disabled children in your classroom. Observations of children during discussions and as they work individually or in small groups, and careful examinations of their written work, will provide clues.

Self-check of Objectives 7 and 8

Four categories of learning handicaps are discussed. Name them before you continue your reading.

Describe briefly each of the learning disabilities listed in Table 3-2.

b. Sensory Handicaps   Two **sensory handicaps** that affect children's ability to learn mathematics are visual and auditory (hearing). Naturally there are variations in the severity of sensory losses among children. Children with minor visual deficiencies can usually have prescription glasses, and as long as the glasses are properly fitted and are worn as prescribed, visual losses are no problem. Visually impaired children require large-print materials or special devices in order to read mathematics books and other printed material. Educationally blind children must use Braille material.

Visually impaired and blind children usually adapt easily to the classroom. Their capabilities for learning mathematics are equal to those of their normally sighted peers.[12] Because they often have difficulty in putting ideas together to form concepts, you must present well-sequenced concrete learning experiences during which you help these children organize their thoughts about what they feel and hear, so they can form generalizations about the topics they are studying.

[12]Howard H. Spicker and James McLeskey, "Exceptional Children in Changing Times," in Vincent J. Glennon, ed., *The Mathematical Education of Exceptional Children and Youth, An Interdisciplinary Approach* (Reston, Virginia: National Council of Teachers of Mathematics, 1981), p. 15.

Three factors determine the severity of a child's hearing loss: the age at which the loss occurred, the severity of pitch and frequency losses, and the degree to which the loss has affected language development.[13] A child born with a total hearing loss will have much more difficulty developing and using language than one whose loss is less severe or whose date of onset was after language development had begun. The degree of loss affects the manner in which the child is able to adjust to the classroom. For some children you will need to make only minor or no adjustments in the ways you teach, but a special mathematics program will be needed for others.

c. Physical Impairments   There are great variations in the **physical impairments** that affect children's ability to function in the classroom. They range from health problems such as asthma and diabetes to nervous system disorders like cerebral palsy and epilepsy. Among children with the same impairment, the degree of severity also varies. Since each case is unique, each child's mathematics program must be unique, too. Many children require only minor adjustments, whereas those whose conditions prevent them from writing and/or manipulating teaching–learning materials require special learning aids and ways of responding to assignments. Specially adapted computer setups have touch and/or light panels that allow students to respond to the computer's program. Most of the teaching–learning materials used with nonhandicapped children are suitable for many physically impaired children. When the severity of the handicap is great enough to affect future vocational plans and social competency, major adjustments under the direction of specialists are needed.

d. Emotional Handicaps   Children with **emotional handicaps** are defined in Public Law 94-142 as being those with a history of having their school performance affected by one or more of these conditions: (1) inability to build and maintain satisfactory interpersonal relations with fellow students or teacher, (2) inappropriate behavior or feelings under normal classroom conditions, (3) deep moods of unhappiness or depression, and (4) a tendency to develop physical symptoms to fears. The definition also includes schizophrenic and autistic children.[14] J. F. Weaver and William Morse broaden the definition to include socially maladjusted children, who make up a large part of the segment of children who have problems in school. They use the expression "socially–emotionally impaired" (SEI) when discussing these children.[15]

---

[13] Spicker and McLeskey, p. 16.

[14] J. F. Weaver and William C. Morse, "Teaching Mathematics to Socially and Emotionally Impaired Pupils," in Vincent J. Glennon, ed., *The Mathematical Education of Exceptional Children and Youth, an Interdisciplinary Approach* (Reston, Virginia: National Council of Teachers of Mathematics, 1981), p. 96.

[15] Weaver and Morse, pp. 96–97.

According to Weaver and Morse, teachers need to have empathy for socially–emotionally impaired children and be able to accept them, be able to structure the classroom social climate so that SEI children are supported by their classmates, and plan mathematics activities to fit each child.

e. Planning for Handicapped Children   A teacher does not work alone when plans for handicapped children are developed. PL 94-142 prescribes that an **individualized educational plan** (IEP) be developed for each child. The plan is prepared by a team composed of the child's parent(s), teacher, a person other than the teacher who is qualified to provide or supervise the program, and the child when appropriate. Possibly other persons—school psychologist, special education teacher, or mathematics specialist—may be on the team. Each person provides input for the plan's development, with the overall plan reflecting the group's considered judgment about what is best for the student.

These generalizations should be considered as a plan is developed:

- All handicapped children progress through Piaget's stages of mental development. The rate at which they progress and the level of attainment varies according to the type and degree of handicap. Piagetian-type tests and diagnostic tests are useful for determining the level of mental development and the mathematical skills and understandings of handicapped children.

- The sequence of subtasks for a topic must be considered when selecting content. Gaps in a child's knowledge and understanding are often more critical when handicaps are present because the handicaps make catching up and bridging gaps difficult and time-consuming.

- Appropriate learning objectives based on criterion-referenced diagnostic tests should be established for each child.

- The teaching–learning sequence—concrete–manipulative, pictorial–representational, and abstract—should be followed with most handicapped children. These children are capable of learning concepts and solving problems, so rote learning and memorization are not appropriate modes of learning for them.

Self-check of Objective 9   Describe briefly the kind of information about mathematics that is needed for the individualized educational plan for a learning handicapped child.

2. Gifted and Talented Children

No single criterion can be used to identify a **gifted** student. Formerly a score in the top 1 percent on a standardized intelligence test was a commonly used criterion. Now it is recognized that giftedness manifests itself in many ways. H. Laurence Ridge and Joseph Renzulli identify three clusters of traits that are possessed by individuals at the upper end of the creativity–productivity scale:

- Above-average general ability
- Task commitment
- Creativity [16]

Scores on general intelligence tests are one source of information to use when identifying gifted and talented children. However, when scores alone are used, children with potential for high levels of achievement are omitted. Students who immerse themselves in a particular area of interest (task commitment) and who show originality of thinking and diversity in approaches and inventive solutions to problems (originality) possess qualities of giftedness that warrant consideration when the gifted are identified. Your awareness of traits for each cluster will help you identify potentially gifted and talented children. The following are some common traits:

Above-average general ability
- accelerated pace of learning—earlier and faster
- sees relationships—readily grasps "big ideas"
- higher levels of thinking—applications and analysis easily accomplished
- verbal fluency—large vocabulary, expresses self well verbally and in writing
- extraordinary amount of information
- intuition—easily leaps from problem to solution
- tolerates ambiguity
- achievement and potential have close fit
- masters advanced concepts in field of interest

Task commitment
- highly motivated
- self-directed
- accepts challenges, may be highly competitive
- extended attention to one area of interest

---

[16] H. Laurence Ridge and Joseph S. Renzulli, "Teaching Mathematics to the Talented and Gifted," in Vincent J. Glennon, ed., *The Mathematical Education of Exceptional Children and Youth, an Interdisciplinary Approach* (Reston, Virginia: National Council of Teachers of Mathematics, 1981), pp. 196–201.

- reads avidly in area of interest
- relates every topic to own area of interest
- industrious and persevering
- high energy and enthusiasm

Creativity
- curious
- imaginative and perceptive
- questions standard procedures
- original approaches and solutions
- flexible
- risk taker and independent

Gifted and talented children are sometimes placed in a special program in their own or another school. If a special program is not available, you will have to provide for their needs in your class. Although no area of the curriculum should be neglected, gifted and talented children do need frequent opportunities to work in self-selected areas of special interest.

Not all gifted and talented children are equally interested in mathematics, so you cannot expect the same level of accomplishment from each one. However, you should expect that all gifted and talented children will learn basic concepts, skillfully compute with both whole and fractional numbers, use common instruments of measure, and apply mathematics in both in- and out-of-school situations. They will not learn basic concepts and skills by chance; they must participate in a planned, systematic program to develop them. Experiences at the concrete–manipulative and pictorial levels of learning are important for these children, but will often be briefer than for others, as will the time they need to practice facts and algorithms.

In addition to learning basic concepts and skills, gifted and talented children need other mathematical experiences. Two ways of providing additional mathematical experiences are commonly used. **Horizontal enrichment** provides opportunities for children to explore a variety of topics not a part of the usual program. Historical numeration systems and computational processes, nondecimal numeration systems, puzzles, and unusual problems are examples of topics that are commonly used for horizontal enrichment. Examples of topics that are suitable for this type of enrichment are presented in several of the chapters that follow. When **vertical enrichment** is used, gifted and talented children speed up their study of the regular topics and move on to work that commonly appears in later grades.

Ridge and Renzulli recommend a program that provides three types of activities. First there are general exploratory activities to stimulate interest in specific subject areas. Classroom centers; visits to museums, computer centers, and science laboratories; and talks by pilots, computer programmers, and scientists are examples of first-level activities. Second-level activities build on the first. After choosing an area of interest through first-level activities, a child receives individual or group training to develop processes that are needed to pursue the topic. Library-research skills, facility with special instruments of measure, and knowledge of ways to record special data are developed in phase two. At the third level the student undertakes an individual or small-group study of a topic. When the study is completed, the student(s) shares the results with classmates through an oral or written report, a classroom or school display, a school assembly, or other form of presentation.[17] An example of how this plan can be used in the area of measurement is described in Chapter 14.

Ridge and Renzulli say that three clusters of traits should be used to identify gifted and talented children. Identify each cluster, and name at least three traits for each one.

Give a brief description of two plans for providing for the special needs of gifted and talented children.

Self-check of Objectives 10 and 11

SUMMARY

Five types of readiness should be considered as mathematics programs are planned and developed: content, pedagogical, maturational, affective, and contextual. Children's levels of knowledge of facts and skills, understanding and comprehension, and abilities to apply mathematics must be assessed periodically. Piagetian-type tests provide information about children's levels of cognitive development. Achievement tests give useful information about children's general levels of accomplishment, and criterion-referenced diagnostic tests give specific information that is helpful in placing children in a program. Attitudes toward mathematics can be determined by semantic-differential tests, sentence-completion forms, and attitude scales. Other assessment techniques can be used to obtain information that tests cannot supply. These include analysis of daily work, observation of children at work, interviews with children, observation of their uses of mathematics, and parent–teacher conferences.

Assessment procedures provide information for developing programs for all students. A learning-handicapped child must have a special individualized education plan developed by a team of people acquainted with the child. Learning handicaps include learning disabilities, sensory impairments, physical impairments, and emotional maladjustments. Many materials and procedures used with nonhandicapped children can be used with handicapped children. The nature of some handicaps require that

[17] Ridge and Renzulli, pp. 218–222.

major adjustments be made for children who possess them. Materials and procedures must be adapted to meet their very special needs. Gifted and talented children have above-average general ability, task commitment, and creativity. They need programs that provide for their special abilities and needs.

STUDY QUESTIONS AND ACTIVITIES

1. Use the materials from *Checking Up I* quoted in this chapter, from one of the *Checking Up* books, or from another source to conduct a brief study of some aspect of kindergarten or first-grade children's concepts of mathematics. Which level of understanding has each child attained? How can teachers at the primary level use Piaget's ideas and investigative techniques to improve their teaching?

2. Examine a newly published commercial diagnostic test and its manual. What specific mathematical skills and understandings does it diagnose? Critique the test in terms of the attention it gives to facts and skills, comprehension and understandings, and applications of mathematics. Do you believe there is a good balance?

3. Compare the test you examined for study question 2 with a contemporary textbook series. Are the same skills and understandings in both the test and text? How closely do vocabulary and mathematical notation of the two agree? What difficulties might arise for children when a test and a book do not use the same vocabulary and notation?

4. Use this chapter's suggestions for preparing a teacher-made diagnostic test to make a test. Select a topic, select a sequence of five subtasks from a hierarchy for it, write appropriate objectives, and then prepare items and design your test.

5. Administer your diagnostic test to a group of children. Analyze each paper carefully to determine if there are patterned errors. Describe any patterned errors you find.

6. Chapter 2 of Ashlock's book (see reading list) contains many examples of error patterns. Analyze the errors on several pages and identify the pattern for each page.

7. Interview a teacher who has one or more handicapped students mainstreamed for mathematics. What provisions are included in each child's individualized education plan to account for special needs in mathematics? How are these needs met in the classroom?

KEY TERMS

content readiness
pedagogical readiness
maturational readiness
affective readiness
contextual readiness
Piagetian-type tests
achievement tests
diagnostic tests
teacher-made tests
attitude tests
semantic-differential test
attitude scale
sentence-completion form

evaluation
observation
interviews
learning-handicapped children
learning disabilities
sensory handicaps
physical impairments
emotional handicaps
individualized educational plan
gifted
horizontal enrichment
vertical enrichment

FOR FURTHER READING

Arithmetic Teacher, XXVII, No. 3 (November 1979). This issue contains eight articles that focus on assessment.

————, XXVIII, No. 6 (February 1981). Eleven articles in this issue deal with mathematics for gifted students.

Ashlock, Robert B. *Error Patterns in Computation*, 3rd ed. (Columbus, Ohio: Charles E. Merrill Publishing Company, 1982). Children's computational work was studied to determine patterns of errors. This semiprogrammed book gives the reader the opportunity to study error patterns and establish procedures for helping children overcome them.

Bley, Nancy S., and Carol A. Thornton. *Teaching Mathematics to the Learning Disabled* (Rockville, Maryland: Aspen Systems Corporation, 1981). Chapter 1 discusses learning disabilities and general procedures for dealing with them in the classroom. Each of the other chapters presents information about teaching specific topics.

Carpenter, Thomas P., and others. "Student's Affective Responses to Mathematics: Results and Implications from National Assessment," *Arithmetic Teacher*, XXVIII, No. 2 (October 1980), pp. 34–37, 52–53. The results of the second National Assessment of Educational Progress section on attitudes indicated that a majority of the 9-year-old children liked mathematics. The article discusses children's responses and presents major findings from the survey.

Engelhardt, Jon M. "Using Computational Errors in Diagnostic Teaching," *Arithmetic Teacher*, XXIX, No. 8 (April 1982), pp. 16–19. Engelhardt discusses four types of errors: mechanical, careless, conceptual, and procedural. Teachers must attend to each type of error and not concentrate on procedural errors, which they commonly do according to the author.

Fowler, Mary Anne. "Diagnostic Teaching for Elementary School Mathematics," *Arithmetic Teacher*, XXVII, No. 7 (March 1980), pp. 34–37. Diagnostic teaching requires three things: determination of types of errors, rationale for each type of error, and establishment of what needs to be learned in order to overcome each type of error. The article discusses diagnostic teaching in the elementary school.

Freeman, Donald J. and others. "A Closer Look at Standardized Tests," *Arithmetic Teacher*, XXIX, No. 7 (March 1982), pp. 50–54. Four standardized tests are discussed. The authors found considerable variation in their contents. A test should be selected carefully to provide the closest possible match between its content and a program's content.

Glennon, Vincent J., ed. *The Mathematical Education of Exceptional Children and Youth, an Interdisciplinary Approach* (Reston, Virginia: National Council of Teachers of Mathematics, 1981). The book presents information about teaching mathematics to different types of exceptional children.

Michaels, Linda A., and Robert A. Forsyth. "Measuring Attitudes Toward Mathematics? Some Questions to Consider," *Arithmetic Teacher*, XXVI, No. 4 (December 1978), pp. 22–25. The authors identify a number of factors to consider when preparing to test children's attitudes toward mathematics. They discuss points related to how to collect data, the attitudes to assess, types of items and their uses, length of scale, and validity.

Norton, Mary Ann. "Improve Your Evaluation Techniques," *Arithmetic Teacher*, XXX, No. 9 (May 1983), pp. 6–7. Discusses ways to evaluate students' understandings and skills by means other than tests. Observation and student-response techniques are stressed.

Rudnitsky, Allan N., Priscilla Drickamer, and Roberta Handy. "Talking Mathematics with Children," *Arithmetic Teacher*, XXVIII, No. 8 (April 1981), pp. 14–16. Presents guidelines and strategies for conducting interviews about mathematics.

Shaw, Robert A. and Philip A. Pelosi. "In Search of Computational Errors," *Arithmetic Teacher*, XXX, No. 7 (March 1983), pp. 50–51. Observations and student interviews reveal the nature of students' computational errors. Four situations are discussed.

Scheer, Janet K. "The Etiquette of Diagnosis," *Arithmetic Teacher*, XXVII, No. 9 (May 1980), pp. 18–19. Presents 12 guidelines to proper etiquette in diagnosis.

4

Mathematics Anxiety

Upon completion of Chapter 4 you will be able to:

1. Describe mathematics anxiety, or mathophobia.

2. Explain why mathematics anxiety is a critical problem for many students, particularly females and ethnic minorities.

3. Give examples of how teachers' beliefs and practices can cause mathematics anxiety.

4. Describe ways teachers can lessen mathematics anxiety.

"My first awareness that I couldn't do mathematics came in the sixth grade when I found that I could never figure out how to do word problems. Later, I had difficulty doing division with fractions and working percent problems. By the time I was in the seventh grade I dreaded going to math classes."

"The problem got so bad in the ninth grade that it seemed like a wall arose between my eyes and my mind every time I faced anything to do with math. Nothing in class or the book made any sense at all. Today I avoid situations that involve numbers. Why, I even walk rather than take a cab because I don't have to figure a tip if I walk."

These statements are typical of those made by adults who are victims of mathematics anxiety. **Mathematics anxiety,** or **mathophobia,** is a serious problem for many people. Some researchers who have studied the problem contend that a majority of adults suffer from mathematics anxiety to some degree.[1] Even though the problem does not usually manifest

[1] See Mitchell Lazarus, "Mathophobia: Some Personal Speculations," *The National Elementary Principal*, LIII, No. 2 (January/February 1974), pp. 16–22, and Sheila Tobias, *Overcoming Math Anxiety* (New York: W. W. Norton and Company, Inc., 1978).

itself until after elementary school, evidence shows that it frequently gets its start there. Mathematics anxiety is discussed in this chapter, with special attention given to its effects on females and minorities.

MATHEMATICS ANXIETY

Mathematics anxiety is a fear of mathematics or an intense, negative emotional reaction to the subject. For students it may evoke such strong feelings that they go to great extremes to avoid taking mathematics courses or courses that require a mathematics background. Mathophobes often choose not to go to college, or they take majors that require little or no mathematics.

Mathematics anxiety is a particularly acute problem for females and minorities. When anxiety causes them to limit their high school or university mathematics courses, they are blocked from earning degrees in majors that can help them achieve equity in the professions and other areas of employment. A 1972 survey by sociologist Lucy Sells shows that though 57 percent of the male students who entered the Berkeley campus of the University of California had four years of high-school mathematics, only 8 percent of the female students had the same background.[2] Sells also reports a 1978 survey of California high-school students that showed that 79 percent of Asian students and 72 percent of white students were in a sequence of courses leading to calculus. On the other hand, only 25 percent of Hispanic students and 20 percent of black students were in such a sequence of courses. While 40 percent of all students taking mathematics courses were black, they comprised 79 percent of the students in remedial courses without access to even high-school algebra and geometry. Only 5 percent of black students were enrolled in trigonometry, elementary functions, and calculus.[3]

The lack of high-school mathematics blocks access for many students, particularly females and minorities, to majors in science, medicine, engineering, business, and other fields in which mathematics is important. Although more recent surveys show that the number of females with sufficient mathematics to choose any major they wish is increasing,[4] there

---

[2] Lucy W. Sells, "Mathematics—A Critical Filter," *The Science Teacher*, XXXXV, No. 2 (February 1978), p. 28.

[3] Lucy W. Sells, "The Mathematics Filter and the Education of Women and Minorities," in *Women and the Mathematical Mystique*, Lynn H. Fox, Linda Brody, and Dianne Tobin, eds. (Baltimore: The Johns Hopkins University Press, 1980), p. 68.

[4] See June M. Armstrong, "Achievement and Participation of Women in Mathematics: Results of Two National Surveys," *Journal of Research in Mathematics Education*, XII, No. 5 (November 1981), pp. 365–366; John Ernest, "Mathematics and Sex," *American Mathematical Monthly*, LXXXIV, No. 8, (October 1976), pp. 601–602; Sheila Tobias, "Managing Math Anxiety: A New Look at an Old Problem," *Children Today*, VII, No. 5 (September/October 1978), p. 8.

are still too many females and minorities who are blocked from some majors because of too little mathematics.

The inability to enter college and university major programs is not the only limitation placed on future occupations by a lack of mathematics. It is estimated that background in high-school algebra and geometry alone may make a difference of 25 percent in scores for examinations required to enter many civil-service positions and industrial jobs.[5] In a rapidly changing society it is unlikely that an individual will remain in the same occupational field for a lifetime. Old jobs are eliminated, and new ones, which often require a knowledge of mathematics, replace them. A good mathematical background is a requirement for persons in most managerial positions. Persons who must make occupational shifts or who aspire to move up in their chosen fields are denied opportunities to do so if they have an insufficient knowledge of mathematics.

Persons who are mathematically anxious experience limitations in their personal lives, also. The individual who is fearful of having to figure the amount of tip for a taxi ride or a restaurant meal, who cannot balance a checkbook or read newspaper charts and graphs, or who cannot estimate the cost of a vacation is unable to cope with many of the problems of daily living.

The extent to which a person is affected by mathematics anxiety varies in two ways: the level of mathematics at which a person can function and the intensity of the anxiety.[6] Some persons can do little more than add a column of three numbers without panicking. Others manage well with the simpler aspects of arithmetic but falter when faced with work at a higher level, such as common and decimal fractions and percent. Any form of higher mathematics is the downfall of many.

Some persons are bothered only slightly by mathematics anxiety and are not seriously affected. Some have more intense anxiety but realize that mathematics is a necessary part of their education; they take courses with some degree of success but stop as soon as they meet the requirements for a job or higher education. Others take the minimum course(s) needed to get a high-school diploma and endure classes as best they can. Persons with a strong aversion toward mathematics experience much stress, and their lives are handicapped in many ways.

[5] Sheila Tobias, "Managing Math Anxiety: A New Look at an Old Problem," p. 7.

[6] Mitchell Lazarus, p. 17.

Self-check of Objectives 1 and 2

Describe what mathematics anxiety is.

Discuss reasons why mathematics anxiety is a critical problem for many people. Describe its special impact on females and minority students.

CAUSES OF MATHEMATICS ANXIETY

Even though mathematics anxiety does not usually manifest itself until after elementary school, teachers at all levels need to be aware of it and some of its causes.

1. Teachers' Attitudes and Beliefs

Teachers' own attitudes toward mathematics and their beliefs about students' capabilities for learning it have a great bearing on how they treat students and conduct their classes. Teachers themselves, particularly those in elementary school, are often victims of mathematics anxiety. John Ernest reported that a survey of 75 future teachers at the Santa Barbara campus of the University of California showed that 14 percent actually disliked or hated mathematics, and another 26 percent showed an indifference toward it.[7] Ernest concluded that 40 percent of the prospective teachers are likely to transmit their less-than-positive attitudes toward mathematics to students. Although Ernest and others who report similar findings do not attribute such attitudes to mathematics anxiety, there is no reason to believe that it is not a contributing factor.

In addition to their personal feelings toward mathematics, teachers often hold erroneous beliefs about students' capabilities for learning mathematics. There has been a common belief that males have an aptitude for learning mathematics that females do not possess.[8] Support for this has come from the fact that males outnumber females in mathematics-oriented careers by large numbers and that males as a group have higher scores than females as a group on tests such as the mathematics portion of the Scholastic Aptitude Test and the high-school portion of the National Assessment of Educational Progress mathematics tests. Research recently completed by Elizabeth Fennema and Julia Sherman shows that conclusions drawn from comparisons of scores on such tests are erroneous, because they do not take into account the amount of mathematics that students have had before they take the tests. Fennema reports:

> In summary, the following can be concluded about sex-related differences in mathematics learning in the United States in 1978: (1) No sex-related differences are evident—at any cognitive level, from computation to problem solving—at the elementary level (this conclusion has been accepted for a number of years); (2) after elementary school, differences do not always appear; (3) starting at about the seventh grade, if differences appear, they tend to be in the males' favor, particularly on tasks involving mathematical reasoning; (4) there is some evidence that sex-related differ-

---

[7] John Ernest, p. 600.

[8] Elizabeth Fennema, "Women and Girls in Mathematics Equity in Mathematics Education," *Educational Studies in Mathematics*, X, No. 4, (November 1979), p. 389.

ences in mathematics learning in high school may not be as great in 1978 as they were in previous years; and (5) conclusions reached about male superiority have often been gathered from old studies in which the number of mathematics courses taken was not controlled. Therefore, males with more mathematics background were being compared with females with less mathematics background. In reality, then, the comparison was not between females and males but between students who had studied mathematics from one to three years in high school and students who had studied mathematics for two to four years of high school.[9]

The conclusion that males are superior to females in mathematics, even though erroneous, has led many persons to think of mathematics as a male domain, especially a white-male domain. Teachers who think that this is true often treat females differently. There is little, if any, difference in treatment in the primary grades. As children advance, however, teachers frequently interact more with males, paying more attention to their problems, giving them more help and praise, and expecting a higher level of achievement. Males are encouraged to be more independent as they work, while females are encouraged to be more dependent.[10] Fennema believes that this **stereotype** is a partial reason for the less-positive attitudes of females toward mathematics. The stereotype is transmitted to girls in both subtle and nonsubtle ways until many of them believe that mathematics is inappropriate for them. They become anxious about succeeding in mathematics because they must, in part at least, deny their femininity.[11]

Minorities also are often treated as though they lack ability in mathematics. In addition some minorities face another problem. Rodney Brod of the University of Montana found that teachers tended to give white students the benefit of the doubt when grading but seldom extended the practice to native American Indian students.[12]

Research into the causes of anxiety and mathematics avoidance indicates that one of the strongest influences on attitude is students' confidence in their own ability to learn mathematics. Students who are confident become increasingly autonomous and self-reliant in mathematics. They attribute success to their own ability and commitment to learning. Students who are less confident depend on others for help and work at

---

[9] Elizabeth Fennema, "Sex-Related Differences in Mathematics: Where and Why," in *Women and the Mathematical Mystique*, Lynn H. Fox, Linda Brody, and Dianne Tobin, eds. (Baltimore: The Johns Hopkins University Press, 1980), p. 81. Used by permission.

[10] Elizabeth Fennema, "Teachers and Sex Bias in Mathematics," *Mathematics Teacher*, LXXIII, No. 3 (March 1980), pp. 169–170.

[11] Elizabeth Fennema, *Women and Mathematics: State of the Art Review*, Paper presented at the Equity in Mathematics Core Conference sponsored by the National Council of Teachers of Mathematics, Reston, Virginia, February 19–21, 1982, p. 7.

[12] Claudette Bradley, *The State of the Art of Native American Mathematics Education*, Paper prepared for Equity in Mathematics Core Conference sponsored by National Council of Teachers of Mathematics, Reston, Virginia, February 19–21, 1982, p. 3.

lower cognitive tasks. They are more likely to attribute whatever success they have to luck rather than to ability or effort. Females have a greater tendency to attribute success to luck, whereas males tend to credit ability and effort.[13]

Although specific reasons for a given student's lack of confidence cannot be identified, it is correct to say that actions that might undermine a student's confidence should be avoided. Therefore teachers must recognize the damage that can be done to females and minorities by **differential treatment** that is based on a mistaken belief about their capabilities to learn mathematics.

2. Teaching Practices That Foster Anxiety

Adults often engage in group discussions as part of their therapy at workshops designed to lessen mathematics anxiety. Almost without exception they report that certain teacher practices and expectations contributed to their anxieties. Five practices are discussed here:

- Emphasis on memorization
- Emphasis on speed
- Authoritarian teaching
- Emphasis on doing one's own work
- Lack of variety in teaching–learning processes

a. Emphasis on Memorization   Most children can and should be expected to memorize the basic facts for the four operations with whole numbers and learn an algorithm for each operation. However, when they are expected to learn these facts and processes by **memorization** alone and in a manner devoid of meaning, many children experience learning problems. Rather than seeing mathematics as a structured body of knowledge, they learn a disconnected collection of facts and rules. Children usually keep up in the early grades where there are few facts and rules, although even then there are some who lag behind. By the time they reach the fifth and sixth grades many children are overwhelmed by all they are expected to memorize. Assignments are a chore to finish. They dread having to take tests. They cannot apply what they have learned, because they see little or no connection between mathematics and the real world. Many of these children are filled with anxiety by the time they reach junior high school and vow to quit mathematics as soon as possible.

---

[13] Elizabeth Fennema, pp. 6, 9.

b. Emphasis on Speed Memorization and **speed** usually go hand in hand. Teachers use drills, timed tests, and relays and games that put a premium on speed to foster memorization. Some children can quickly recall memorized facts and processes and are not affected by these tactics. Others, however, work more deliberately. When these children are forced to work at uncomfortable speeds, they often become apprehensive about their ability to cope with mathematics. Deliberate and persistent workers should be given time to complete their assignments without pressure. They also need praise and credit equal to that given to students who finish more quickly.

c. Authoritarian Teaching Persons in mathematics anxiety workshops frequently recall how their teachers gave them a step-by-step procedure, along with a list of rules, for doing long division or other procedures. Teachers often stated that theirs was the only acceptable way to do the work and that other methods would be viewed with disfavor. This is **authoritarian teaching** of mathematics. Authoritarian teachers also emphasize correct answers and give no credit for children's processes. When emphasis is placed on a "right way" of working along with right answers, children often think of mathematics as being inflexible and lacking in creativity.[14]

d. Emphasis on Doing One's Own Work Teachers commonly expect children to work alone in mathematics. From the primary grades on, children are admonished to "Do your own work." Children are often forbidden to seek help from a classmate. Sheila Tobias says that teachers should provide opportunities for children to do mathematics in small groups, so they can work together on problem-solving strategies and processes and compare answers.[15] There are many times, particularly during the concrete–manipulative stage of the teaching–learning process, when children can be formed in small groups to work on a new topic.

e. Lack of Variety in the Teaching–Learning Process Lorelei Brush reported in her study of New England students in grades six to twelve that one of the major reasons given for disliking mathematics was **lack of variety** and boredom.[16]

. . . These students enjoy being presented with problems which make them think, they derive satisfaction from satisfactorily answering a tough

---

[14] Wade H. Sherard, "Math Anxiety in the Classroom," *The Clearing House*, LV, No. 3 (November 1981), p. 104.

[15] Sheila Tobias, "Stress in the Math Classroom," *Learning*, IX, No. 6 (January 1981), p. 38.

[16] Lorelei Brush, *Encouraging Girls in Mathematics* (Cambridge, Mass.: Abt Books, 1980), p. 49.

question, and they do not enjoy repetitive assignments which require them to solve a series of very similar problems.[17]

The common practice of centering mathematics instruction around a textbook, **speed drills,** and **timed tests** is uninspiring and repetitive, and contributes to many children's dislike of mathematics. The type of teaching advocated in this book provides you with a repertoire of skills and procedures that will provide the variety you need to help children maintain their interest as they learn mathematics.

You have read how teachers' beliefs and practices can cause mathematics anxiety. Describe at least two each of the anxiety-causing beliefs and practices.

Self-check of Objective 3

LESSENING MATHEMATICS ANXIETY

Mathematics is so important for today's students that anxiety must not be allowed to cause any student to discontinue study of the subject. Teachers cannot let their attitudes and practices contribute to mathematics anxiety. The practices that follow are ones that are helpful for reducing **stress** in the classroom, improving students' attitudes, and encouraging them to continue their study of mathematics.

- Provide a **relaxed, unhurried atmosphere** within which children work without pressure. Assignments should not be excessive for the in- and out-of-school time children have to devote to mathematics. Children should know that they will complete each assignment in a reasonable time if they stay on task.

- Treat male and female students alike; avoid differential treatment based on the belief that mathematics is a male domain.

- Help children be aware of the usefulness of the mathematics they are learning. Help them see ways mathematics is applied to the solution of both everyday and nonroutine problems. Provide information about occupations that require a mathematics background. Careers as diverse as agriculture, business, elementary education, food science, geography, and pre-medicine require at least two years of high-school mathematics. Students must keep their options open, because many careers are requiring an increasing amount of mathematics. A list of addresses at the end of this chapter identifies sources of information about careers that

---

[17]Lorelei Brush, p. 50.

require advanced mathematics and about other topics related to anxiety and equity in mathematics.

- Use **diagnostic teaching techniques** based on the teaching–learning model presented in Chapter 2.

- Give credit for processes as well as correct answers. Do not insist that work be done "the teacher's" way. Lorelei Brush reports that one of the primary reasons for students' dislike of mathematics is that as the years pass they spend an increasing amount of time learning what is already known and less time contributing their own ideas. She recommends that children be given opportunities to figure out for themselves, alone or in small groups, more of what they learn. Open discussions give students opportunities to express their ideas about and to internalize what they are learning.[18]

- Avoid **insensitive teaching behaviors,** such as humiliation and ridicule. Children's incorrect responses are usually the result of an incomplete understanding of a concept or procedure. Children who are "put down" for incorrect responses become reluctant to speak out, and teachers lose opportunities to analyze and correct faulty thinking.

- Do not let yourself get in a rut. Use the materials and teaching–learning processes described in this book. Become acquainted with other mathematics resource books and journals. The *Arithmetic Teacher* contains descriptions of many worthwhile materials and procedures. It is a must for every conscientious teacher of elementary-school mathematics.

- Do not overemphasize one aspect of mathematics, such as computation, at the expense of other areas.

- Do not use mathematics as punishment. Children view with distaste work that is assigned as a penalty for misbehavior or other classroom infractions.

- Maintain a positive attitude toward mathematics. If you are a mathematically anxious person, do not be afraid to admit it. You are not alone! Also, *do something about it!* Books and articles contained in this chapter's bibliography will help.

[18] Lorelei R. Brush, "Some Thoughts for Teachers on Mathematics Anxiety," *Arithmetic Teacher*, XXIX, No. 4 (December 1981), pp. 38–39.

Self-check of Objective 4

You have just read ten ways to lessen mathematics anxiety in your classroom. Can you recall and list them?

SUMMARY

Mathematics anxiety is a fear of mathematics created by conditions inside and outside of school that cause a person to avoid mathematics to some degree. Mild anxiety causes people to feel uncomfortable when they take a mathematics test or when other people observe them compute the cost of a tip. Anxiety causes many students to discontinue taking mathematics courses as soon as they can. Students who avoid mathematics courses in high school are effectively blocked from university majors that require a good mathematics background. These people are shut out of many careers. Some writers contend that a majority of adults suffer from mathophobia; all agree that it is more prevalent among females and ethnic minority persons. The problem is particularly acute for females and minorities, because they cannot enter many careers that will give them equity in employment and society.

Teachers frequently have beliefs and behaviors that contribute to mathematics anxiety. One prevalent belief is that mathematics is a white-male domain. Teachers, parents, and counselors transmit this erroneous belief to girls and minorities in many direct and indirect ways. Differential treatment causes many females and minorities to lack confidence in their capabilities in mathematics. Lack of confidence in one's own ability is a major cause of anxiety. Not all teachers possess positive attitudes toward mathematics; their own negative attitudes are often transmitted to students. Classroom practices that emphasize memorization and speed, authoritarian teaching, and a lack of variety in mathematics activities contribute to mathematics anxiety.

Teachers should provide a relaxed atmosphere, help children understand what they learn, use a variety of procedures and materials, accept alternate solutions, help children to understand the usefulness of mathematics, and use other practices that lessen anxiety.

SOURCES OF MATERIAL ABOUT ANXIETY AND EQUITY

Board of Education for the City of Toronto
155 College Street
Toronto, M5T 1P6 Canada
  Produced *The Invisible Filter,* a report of the effects of discontinuing the study of mathematics.

Clark Irwin and Co., Ltd.
791 St. Clair Avenue, W.
Toronto, M6C 1B8 Canada
  Publishes two posters: "Dropping Math? Say Good-bye to 82 Jobs" and "Mathophobia."

Chicago Associates for Social Research
410 S. Michigan Avenue, Suite 525
Chicago, IL 60605

Headquarters for "Minorities in Mathematics," an organization that collects and disseminates information about mathematics and minorities.

Department of Curriculum and Instruction
School of Education
The University of Kansas
Lawrence, KA 66045

COMETS Profiles (Career Oriented Modules to Explore Topics in Science) are 24 biographical sketches of women in science, plus accompanying language-arts activities.

Math/Science Network
Lawrence Hall of Science
University of California
Berkeley, CA 94720

An association of 500 scientists, educators, engineers, community leaders, and parents who work cooperatively to increase the participation of females in scientific and technical careers. Network activities and materials are designed for students of all ages. Network publications that contain useful material for elementary school teachers are *Math for Girls and Other Problem Solvers* by Diane Downie, Twila Slesnick, and Jean Kerr Stenmark and *Use Equals to Promote the Participation of Women in Mathematics* by Alice Kaseberg, Nancy Kreinberg, and Diane Downie.

Women's Educational Equity Act Publishing Center
Educational Development Center
55 Chapel Street
Newton, MA 02160

The Women's Educational Equity Act was passed by Congress in 1974 with the goal of promoting educational equity for girls and women in the United States. The U.S. Department of Education provided grants for the development of materials and programs. The catalog *Resources for Educational Equity* contains descriptions of materials and programs for elementary, secondary, and postsecondary levels of education. The WEEA Publishing Center maintains a toll-free line (800-225-3088) for persons outside Massachusetts who seek assistance in choosing and implementing programs. The phone number for Massachusetts residents is 1-617-969-7100.

Women and Mathematics Education
Education Department
George Mason University
Fairfax, VA 22030

Women and Mathematics Education (WME) is an organization of concerned teachers, counselors, and other individuals who have organized to promote the study of mathematics by girls and women. It serves as a network to put teachers in touch with others who have similar interests, publishes a newsletter, and distributes materials concerning women and mathematics.

STUDY QUESTIONS AND ACTIVITIES

1. According to Kogelman and Warren, each of the following statements is a myth about mathematics that contributes to mathematics anxiety. Read each myth, and write a short statement in which you give your reaction to it.

ONE: Men are better in math than women.
TWO: Math requires logic, not intuition.
THREE: You must always know how you got your answer.
FOUR: Math is not creative.
FIVE: There is a best way to do a math problem.
SIX: It's always important to get the answer exactly right.
SEVEN: It's bad to count on your fingers.
EIGHT: Mathematicians do problems quickly, in their heads.
NINE: Math requires a good memory.
TEN: Math is done by working intensely until the problem is solved.
ELEVEN: Some people have a "math mind" and some don't.
TWELVE: There is a magic key to doing math.[19]

2. A series of Mathematics Equity Conferences was conducted by the National Council of Teachers of Mathematics in 1982–1983. Participants were encouraged to survey children in local schools to determine prevailing conditions pertaining to equity for females and minorities in their communities. This Sentence Completion Task was one source of data from children.

SENTENCE COMPLETION TASK

Name   Age Sex Date
1. On weekends I spend my time . . .
2. When I grow up I hope to work in . . .
3. I do not like people who . . .
4. My parents want me to study more . . .
5. I look forward to . . .
6. The subject in school that will help me most when I get a job is . . .
7. When I grow up my parents want me to work as . . .
8. When I was younger . . .

Duplicate the Sentence Completion Task and administer it to at least 20 students in grades 3–6. This can be done in a group situation in most cases, although you may secure oral answers

---

[19] Stanley Kogelman and Joseph Warren, *Mind over Math* (New York: The Dial Press, 1978), pp. 30–43.

on a one-to-one basis if you wish. Identify each answer sheet by sex, race, or ethnic group. Divide the sheets into groups by male–female or minority–nonminority. Look for patterns to the answers for numbers 2, 4, 6, and 7. If possible, summarize your data in a table and graph. Write one paragraph summarizing your data and identifying the problem you feel needs to be addressed in your school.

3. Another source of information for the conferences was a picture task. Kindergarten through third graders were asked to "Draw a picture of yourself when you are grown up and at work." Have children in your class do this. Then have each one write or dictate some statements for you to record with the picture. Indicate sex, race, or ethnic group for each picture. Separate the pictures according to the occupations they indicate, for example, scientist, professional athlete, truck driver, doctor, teacher, nurse, homemaker, and so forth. Write one paragraph summarizing your data and identifying the problem you feel needs to be addressed in your school.

4. Read Brush's article in the December 1981 *Arithmetic Teacher* (see reading list). Write a statement explaining how you can prevent your students from developing the four attitudes reported to Brush by students in her study.

5. Contact one of the sources listed above for information about their services and materials. Write a brief description of how the source can help you reduce anxiety and promote equity in your classroom.

KEY TERMS

mathematics anxiety	lack of variety
mathophobia	speed drills
stereotype	timed tests
differential treatment	stress
memorization	relaxed, unhurried atmosphere
speed	diagnostic teaching techniques
authoritarian teaching	insensitive teaching behaviors

FOR FURTHER READING

Armstrong, Jane M. "Achievement and Participation of Women in Mathematics: Results of Two National Surveys," *Journal of Research in Mathematics Education*, XII, No. 5 (November 1981), pp. 356–372.

The results of national surveys by the Women in Mathematics Project group in 1978 and the National Assessment of Educational Progress group in 1977–78 are reported to provide information on mathematics achievement and participation by both males and females. Data from both surveys and generalizations about the findings are reported.

Brush, Lorelei. *Encouraging Girls in Mathematics* (Cambridge, Mass.: Abt Books, 1980).
Brush summarizes the findings from her study of students' attitudes toward mathematics and provides information about ways to help girls overcome anxiety and choose mathematics careers.

————. "Some Thoughts for Teachers on Mathematics Anxiety," *Arithmetic Teacher*, XXIX, No. 4 (December 1981), pp. 37–39. Some reasons for not liking mathematics reported by students are summarized. Brush discusses actions teachers can take to prevent mathematics anxiety.

Donady, Bonnie, and Sheila Tobias. "Math Anxiety," *Teacher*, LXXXXV, No. 3 (November 1977), pp. 71–74.
Donady and Tobias, who were then associated with the Math Clinic at Wesleyan University in Middletown, Connecticut, discuss causes and results of mathematics anxiety, with particular emphasis on females. The article contains a list of then-existing mathematics reinforcement programs and materials.

Ernest, John. "Mathematics and Sex," *American Mathematical Monthly*. LXXXIII, No. 8 (October 1976), pp. 595–614.
The article concentrates on sex differences in mathematical education, beginning with grade two and following through to the research mathematician. It is a comprehensive report of the status of women in mathematics education during the early 1970s.

Fennema, Elizabeth. "Women and Mathematics: Does Research Matter?" *Journal for Research in Mathematics Education*, XII, No. 5 (November 1981), pp. 380–385.
Fennema cites a number of myths about abilities and interests in mathematics. These myths have been damaging but are amenable to change. Causes that are due to social factors can be modified, and educators have a responsibility to know the truth about females' abilities and interests in mathematics.

————. "Teachers and Sex Bias in Mathematics," *Mathematics Teacher*, XXXIII, No. 3 (March 1980), pp. 169–173.
Research evidence supporting the belief that teachers treat female students differently from male students is cited. Five practices that result in greater equity are listed.

————. "Women and Girls in Mathematics Equity in Mathematics Education," *Educational Studies in Education*, X, No. 4 (November 1979), pp. 389–401. This article discusses beliefs about cognitive, affective, and educational variables in the mathematics education of females. The author concludes that there is nothing inherent that keeps females from learning mathematics. The article contains an extensive bibliography.

————, and Julia Sherman. "Sex Related Differences in Mathematics Achievement, Spatial Visualization, and Affective Factors," *American Education Research Journal*, XIV, No. 1 (Winter 1977), pp. 51–71.

A comprehensive study of 589 female and 644 male, predominantly white, students in grades 9–12 revealed few sex-related cognitive differences but many attitudinal differences. The study strongly supports the contention that sex differences are the result of socio-cultural rather than cognitive forces.

Fox, Lynn H. "Mathematically Able Girls: A Special Challenge," *Arithmetic Teacher*, XXVIII, No. 6 (February 1981), pp. 22–23.
Recent research indicates that many able girls elect not to continue their study of mathematics beyond minimum required courses. Fox discusses six practices that will encourage mathematically able girls to continue their studies.

————, Linda Brody, and Diane Tobin. *Women and the Mathematical Mystique* (Baltimore, Maryland: The Johns Hopkins University Press, 1980).
This book contains a collection of articles that deal with women and mathematics.

Hannafin, Michael J. "Effects of Teacher and Student Goal Setting and Evaluations on Mathematics Achievement and Student Attitudes," *The Journal of Educational Research*, LXXIV, No. 5 (May/June 1981), pp. 323–326.
The author cites a study that shows that children who are given the opportunity to participate in establishing goals in mathematics have a better sense of what they can accomplish than their teachers. Students given opportunities for self-regulation of instruction had greater confidence in their ability to manage portions of their instruction than those who did not.

Hill, Jan. "The Nonsexist Classroom," *Instructor*, LXXXIX, No. 7 (February 1980), pp. 78–80.
Discusses ways to lessen sex stereotypes about female and male roles in an elementary classroom. Includes a consciousness-raising attitude scale for teachers prepared by Barbara Samuels.

Hodges, Helene L. B. "Learning Styles: Rx for Mathophobes," *Arithmetic Teacher*, XXX, No. 7 (March 1983), pp. 17–20.
Describes three mathophobic children, and discusses four aspects of learning styles teachers should consider to lessen mathematics anxiety in students.

Kogelman, Stanley, and Joseph Warren. *Mind Over Math* (New York: The Dial Press, 1978).
Discusses causes of mathematics anxiety and describes processes for lessening it.

Lazarus, Mitchell. "Mathophobia: Some Personal Speculations," *The National Elementary Principal*, LIII, No. 2 (January/February 1974), pp. 16–22.
Gives a good explanation of mathophobia (mathematics anxiety), some causes, and some effects on ordinary adult life.

Sells, Lucy. "Mathematics: A Critical Filter," *The Science Teacher*, XXXXV, No. 2 (February 1978), pp. 28–29.
This was one of the first articles to call attention to the fact that females are blocked from taking many courses of advanced study by a lack of mathematics courses in high school.

Sherard, Wade H. "Math Anxiety in the Classroom," *The Clearing House*, LV, No. 3 (November 1981), pp. 106–110.

The author cites some causes of anxiety and discusses eight practices that help reduce it.

Tobias, Sheila. "Managing Math Anxiety: A New Look at an Old Problem," *Children Today*, VII, No. 5 (September/October 1978), pp. 7–9, 36.
Discusses mathematics anxiety and describes how clinical intervention can help students and adults overcome it.

————. "Math Anxiety: What You Can Do About It," *Today's Education*, LXIX, No. 3 (September/October 1980), pp. 26GS–29GS.
Tobias states that elementary school teachers who feel uncomfortable about teaching mathematics owe it to their students to overcome their feelings of anxiety. She discusses some ways teachers can overcome anxieties.

————. *Overcoming Math Anxiety* (New York: W. W. Norton and Company, Inc., 1978).
Gives reasons cited by clinic participants for their anxieties and contains chapters that discuss ways individuals can lessen mathematics anxiety.

————. "Stress in the Math Classroom," *Learning*, IX, No. 6 (January 1981), pp. 34, 37–38.
Tobias discusses four causes of anxiety and presents alternative practices for lessening its incidence.

————, and Carol Weissbrod. "Anxiety and Mathematics: An Update," *Harvard Educational Review*, L, No. 1 (February 1980), pp. 63–70.
Updates research on sex-related differences in mathematics and anxiety to point up the link between the two and their impacts on females and minorities. Contains an extensive bibliography.

5

Problem Solving

Upon completion of Chapter 5 you will be able to:

1. Describe in general terms the meaning of problem solving.

2. Identify 11 problem-solving strategies for elementary school children, and apply each strategy to the solution of one or more problems.

3. Identify the four stages of a sound problem-solving process.

4. Describe ways teachers can help children develop competence in solving textbook and test story problems.

5. Identify three types of estimation skills children should learn, and give an example of each type.

In early schools the task of preparing students for roles in society was much simpler than in schools today. In a slow-changing society mathematical skills necessary for business, industry, and home were easily determined and taught. But over the years occupational skills and mathematical requirements have expanded and become less definite. A fast-changing technological world offers few occupations for which mathematical requirements can be explicitly defined and developed during one's school years. Rather, today's students must understand a wide range of concepts and skills and must learn problem-solving strategies that have broad applications.

One of the primary goals of school mathematics is to help children develop problem-solving skills. Both the National Council of Supervisors of Mathematics and the National Council of Teachers of Mathematics stress the importance of problem solving. It heads the list of basic skills identified in the NCSM's 1977 statement[1] and is the focus of school mathematics in the NCTM's *Agenda for Action.*[2]

The term **problem solving** is used in this book to describe the actions an individual takes in any problem situation for which steps to its immediate solution are not apparent but for which a solution exists. Before a problem can be said to exist, the individual must be committed to finding a solution.

When this definition is used, story problems in textbooks need to be recognized for what they are: exercises in vicarious problem solving. They supplement the real problems children encounter during their in-school and extra-school activities. As far as possible, problem-solving experiences should result from real problems encountered in science, social studies, art, and other in-school activities. (Children solve problems in extra-school situations, but teachers have little control over these.) Alert teachers see to it that children have many problem-solving experiences by planning lessons for all subjects so that problems that require mathematical solutions are included.

Children's experiences in other curricular areas do not provide enough problem-solving experiences to establish proficiency, so textbook word problems and problems from other sources are a valuable part of a mathematics program.

A problem for one person is not necessarily a problem for another. School children face many situations which, on first encounter, are problems but which become routine over time. Primary-grade children who gather data about their favorite video games need help in organizing and presenting their information to share with others. Upper-grade children who have had many table- and graph-making experiences will routinely prepare a table or graph to present data for such a situation. One important reason for stressing problem solving is to help children master skills and strategies so they can attack situations in routine ways rather than facing each one as a new problem to be solved.

Elementary-school children can learn the 11 strategies presented in this chapter. Each strategy is accompanied by one or more problems. You should try to solve each problem before you read its solution. The chapter also contains information about a four-step problem-solving process,

[1] National Council of Supervisors of Mathematics, "Position Paper on Basic Skills," *Arithmetic Teacher*, XXV, No. 1 (October 1977), p. 20.

[2] National Council of Teachers of Mathematics, *An Agenda for Action: Recommendations for School Mathematics in the 1980s*, (Reston, Virginia: The Council, 1980), p. 1.

Explain orally or in writing what is meant by the term *problem solving*.

**Self-check
of Objective 1**

suggestions for improving children's work with textbook and test story problems, and ways to help children learn to make accurate estimates.

PROBLEM-SOLVING STRATEGIES

When faced with a problem, a person must explore the situation and select one or more **strategies** that can be used to solve it. A good problem solver has a repertoire of strategies from which to choose. These strategies are applicable to a wide variety of problems:

- Look for patterns.
- Draw a diagram or picture.
- Make a model.
- Construct a table or graph.
- Guess and check.
- Account for all possibilities.
- Act it out.
- Write a mathematical sentence.
- Restate the problem.
- Identify wanted–given information.
- Break set, or change your point of view.

Keep the following points in mind when you are presenting strategies to children:

- Most strategies are applicable to a variety of problems. None has a "best" problem to which it applies.
- A strategy may be applied in different ways to different types of problems.
- A problem may be solved in several ways. It is not always necessary to use a particular strategy for a given problem.
- Children will not all reach the same level of sophistication in using each strategy.
- Processes of selecting and using strategies are as important as correctly solving a problem. Children should receive credit for choosing and using an appropriate strategy, even when their solutions are not entirely correct.

- All children need opportunities to learn and use problem-solving strategies.

1. Look for Patterns

Patterns appear in many natural and person-made objects and situations. They are prominent in mathematics, so finding and using patterns have wide applicability in mathematical problem solving. Kindergarten and primary-grade children can find patterns in strings of colored beads, arrangements of blocks, and beats of a drum. Later, primary children should investigate number patterns such as odd–even and skip-counting. They can complete patterns begun by others and create their own.

Older children can work with patterns that are more abstract and less obvious. In each of the two problems that follow, which are suitable for fifth or sixth graders, you are to determine a pattern. Once you have determined the pattern, use it to formulate a general rule for solving the problem.

PROBLEM 5-1 Triangular Numbers

Triangular numbers were first studied by the Greeks, who were interested in relationships between numbers and geometry. The dot triangles illustrate the first four triangular numbers.

- Write the first four triangular numbers.
- Draw a picture of the next triangular number. Add this number to your list.
- Study your list to see if you can determine a pattern in it. Write any pattern you find.
- List the next three triangular numbers.
- Determine, if you can, a general rule for finding the total number of dots in a triangle with any number of dots along one side. Write your rule as a formula. Use your rule to determine the number of dots in a triangle with 15 dots along one side.

This sequence lists the set of triangular numbers:

1, 3, 6, 10, 15, . . .

Each triangular number greater than 1 is the sum of two or more consecutive whole numbers, beginning with 1:

$$1 = 1$$
$$1 + 2 = 3$$
$$1 + 2 + 3 = 6$$
$$1 + 2 + 3 + 4 = 10$$
$$1 + 2 + 3 + 4 + 5 = 15$$

and so on.

The number of dots in a triangle is the sum of the number of consecutive whole numbers, beginning with 1, named by the number of dots along one side. The number of dots in a triangle with eight dots along one side is the sum of $1 + 2 + 3 + 4 + 5 + 6 + 7 + 8$, or 36.

A rule for finding the number of dots in an n-dots-to-a-side triangle is $n(n + 1) \div 2$.

When Carl Gauss, the famous mathematician, was a child, a teacher who wanted to keep him busy told him to add the first hundred whole numbers. Gauss used the rule given above and was finished almost as soon as his teacher turned his back.

PROBLEM 5-2   Towers of Hanoi

Towers of Hanoi is an ancient puzzle in which rings are moved from one post to another. In the picture, five rings are on one of the three posts. The problem is to determine the least number of moves required to move the five to either of the other posts.

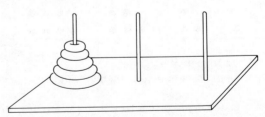

Rules prescribe how moves are made. A larger ring can never be placed on top of a smaller one, and at the end the rings must appear as they did at the beginning. (Use the third post to store in-transfer rings as the moves are made.) Problem: What is the minimum number of moves required to transfer the five rings?

- How many moves are required to move one ring? Two rings? Three rings? Four rings?
- Do you see a pattern you can use to determine the number of moves for five? List any patterns you have found.
- How many moves do you think are required to move six rings? Seven rings?
- Determine, if you can, a general rule you can use to find the minimum

number of moves required to transfer n rings. Use your rule to determine the number of moves required for a dozen rings.

- Compare your rule and answers with those of a classmate.

This table shows the moves for 1, 2, 3, 4, and 5 rings:

Number of rings	Number of moves	Differences between number of moves
1	1	0
2	3	2
3	7	4
4	15	8
5	31	16

The numbers in the third column increase as successive powers of 2: $2^1 = 2$, $2^2 = 4$, $2^3 = 8$, $2^4 = 16$, ... A comparison of the numbers in columns 2 and 3 shows that each number in column 2 is one less than twice the number to its right in column 3.

A rule for determining the moves required to transfer n rings is $2^n - 1$, where n indicates the number of rings.

2. Draw a Diagram

Diagrams range from a simple number line illustrating the whole numbers 0 through 10 to blueprints for an interplanetary rocket. Children should be introduced to diagrams early and should use them throughout their school years. Diagrams serve as one means of making the transition from manipulative experiences to abstract operations. A child who is able to translate a problem situation into a clear diagram demonstrates an accurate perception of the problem. Simple picture diagrams can be used for the first two problems that follow. Venn diagrams are useful for the third and fourth problems.

PROBLEM 5-3   Leaving Adamsville

Leaving Adamsville
Barlow—82 kilometers
New Hampton—
  230 kilometers

How many miles must you travel until you are half way between Barlow and New Hampton?[3]

The road sign gives the information needed to fill in a diagram. The diagram shows that it is 148 kilometers from Barlow to New Hampton. Half that distance is 74 kilometers. Add 74 to 82 to determine the distance to go from Adamsville to be half way between the two towns.

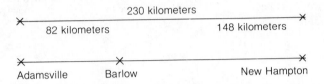

230 kilometers

82 kilometers   148 kilometers

Adamsville   Barlow   New Hampton

PROBLEM 5-4   Standing Atop an Object

When you stand atop a 10- to 20-foot tall object and look down, the object appears much higher than when you are below the object and look up. Is there a physical explanation for this, or is it just psychological?[4]

The diagram shows that the length of your line of vision is greater when you are on top looking down (A) than when you are at the bottom looking up (B). The distance for A is the distance of B plus twice your eye height (the distance from your feet to your eyes).

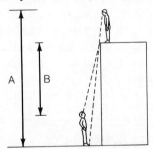

A B

A **Venn diagram** is a special kind of diagram that is used to show relationships between and among members of two or more sets. Children can use simple Venn diagrams as they work with attribute materi-

---

[3] Adapted from Carole Greenes and others, *Techniques of Problem Solving: Problem Card Decks* (Palo Alto: Dale Seymour Publications, 1980), Card 48-C.

[4] Ohio Department of Education, *Problem Solving—A Basic Mathematics Goal, Book 1, Becoming a Better Problem Solver* (Columbus: The Department), p. 24. (Used by permission.)

als as discussed on pages 150–153. These diagrams can also be used to determine greatest common factors of common fractions and to determine least common multiples. Use Venn diagrams to solve the next two problems.

PROBLEM 5-5 The Dog Kennel

John and Joe owned four dogs jointly. John owned three himself. Altogether they had twelve dogs in a kennel. How many did each have?[5]

Use two circles in your Venn diagram, because there are two boys. The *3* in John's circle represents the three dogs he owns alone, and the *4* represents the dogs they own jointly. The *5* in Joe's circle is the difference between 12 and (3 + 4) and represents the dogs Joe owns alone.

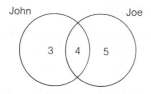

PROBLEM 5-6 The Math Teacher

A math teacher conducted a survey in her classes. 42 students chewed gum in class; 55 talked incessantly; and 25 fell asleep during class. Four people both talked and fell asleep but didn't chew gum. Six students fell asleep and chewed gum, but at least didn't talk. Forty students only talked. Ten students talked and chewed gum, but didn't fall asleep. How many students were there in all? How many students talked and chewed gum and fell asleep (UGH)?[6]

Use a three-circle diagram. First fill in the information you know for certain (underlined in the diagram). Once this information is in place, use it to determine the unknown information. The known information accounts for 54 of the 55 talkers (40 + 10 + 4 = 54). This tells you that

[5] Adapted from Maria Marolda, *Attribute Games and Activities* (Palo Alto: Creative Publications, 1976), p. 141. (Used by permission.)

[6] Maria Marolda, p. 141. (Used by permission.)

there can be but one student who talked, chewed gum, and slept. Once you know this, you can determine the number of students who only sleep or only chew gum.

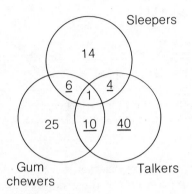

The total number of students is 100 (40 talkers only, 14 sleepers only, 25 chewers only, 10 talkers–chewers, 6 sleepers–chewers, 4 talkers–sleepers, and 1 sleeper–talker–chewer.

3. Make a Model

A **model** is similar to a diagram, but objects rather than drawings are used. Play money is frequently used in primary grades to give children practice with buying and selling, and model clocks are used in time-telling lessons. Three-dimensional models of cubes, pyramids, and other geometric solids are used as children learn about these figures. An advantage of models over diagrams is that they can be moved about as the learner deals with a problem. Use disks for the first problem and squares of paper for the second problem that follows.

PROBLEM 5-7   Cycle Riders

I counted 7 cycle riders and 19 cycle wheels go past my house Saturday morning. How many bicycles and how many tricycles passed my house?[7]

Use different arrangements of two and three disks as wheels until you have the answer. These "wheels" show that 2 bicycles and 5 tricycles are ridden by the 7 riders.

---

[7] Ohio Department of Education, p. 16. (Used by permission.)

Bicycles   Tricycles

PROBLEM 5-8   Stamp Collectors

Marcia has three times as many stamps as her brother. If her brother had eight more stamps, they would have the same number of stamps. How many stamps does Marcia have?[8]

The problem tells you that Marcia has three times as many stamps as her brother. Use squares of paper to show this ratio. The model shows that if Marcia has 12 stamps, her brother has 4 stamps. When each child has this many stamps, the brother can match Marcia by getting 8 more stamps.

Marcia's stamps

Brother's stamps

4. Construct Tables or Graphs

Statistics are used by planners in many fields. An architect uses information about a new building's occupants to plan rooms, furnishings, and safety features; an insurance actuary uses data about births, deaths, and ages to establish insurance rates; and a shipping agent uses data about production schedules and product destinations to plan shipping schedules.

The statistical **data** collected and used by children are simpler but just as real as in these examples. Some of the sources recommended by the National Council of Teachers of Mathematics are listed here: [9]

---

[8] Carole Greenes, Card 44-C.

[9] National Council of Teachers of Mathematics, "Collecting, Organizing, and Interpreting Data," in *More Topics in Mathematics* (Washington, D.C.: The Council, 1969), pp. 450–451. (Used by permission.)

- Shoe sizes of the pupils in the classroom
- Heights of the children
- Weights of the children
- Color of eyes or hair of the children
- Enrollment in classes, clubs, or events
- The favorite colors of the children
- TV programs seen the night before class
- Record of the temperatures for a week in a particular place in the room at three different times each day
- Birthdays of the children
- Weekly growth of a plant from seed to maturity
- Number of blocks each child lives from school
- The time taken for each classroom activity during the day
- Each pupil's favorite kind of meat
- Where each child went on vacation
- Kinds of books read by the children

Each of these gives children the opportunity to collect data from firsthand sources—themselves, their classmates, children in other classes, and adults in their school. Firsthand data are preferred over information from almanacs, encyclopedias, or textbooks, because they have greater meaning to children. Also, children get valuable experience in collecting, organizing, and interpreting their own data. Later they can read and interpret ready-made tables and graphs.

Once children have gathered data, they need to use **tables and graphs** to organize and interpret their information. The table and graph in Figure 5-1 show how one group of children organized data about the colors of the shoes they wore over a period of days. They used the table (a) to record the daily shoe count. Then they put the information on the bar graph (b). They could then compare the number of shoes for each day and from day to day.

Children should learn to use and interpret circle graphs. These graphs are based on fractional parts of a whole and often show percents, so children should not use them before they have an understanding of percent. The following topics from the NCTM list are sources of data for circle graphs:

- The favorite colors of the children
- TV programs seen the night before

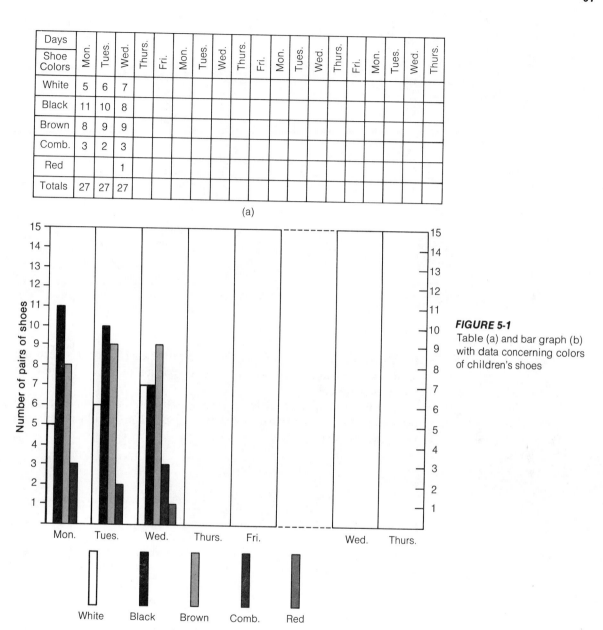

Days Shoe Colors	Mon.	Tues.	Wed.	Thurs.	Fri.	Mon.	Tues.	Wed.	Thurs.	Fri.	Mon.	Tues.	Wed.	Thurs.	Fri.	Mon.	Tues.	Wed.	Thurs.
White	5	6	7																
Black	11	10	8																
Brown	8	9	9																
Comb.	3	2	3																
Red			1																
Totals	27	27	27																

(a)

(b)

FIGURE 5-1
Table (a) and bar graph (b) with data concerning colors of children's shoes

- Each child's favorite kind of meat
- Kinds of books read by the children

The graph in Figure 5-2 shows the color choices of a group of children. The children who are sampled comprise the total population (100 percent) for the graph. The number of children liking a certain color are

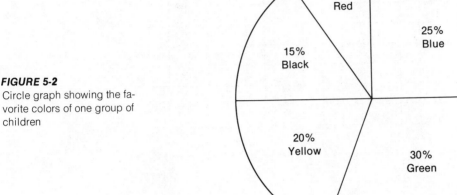

FIGURE 5-2
Circle graph showing the favorite colors of one group of
children

some percent of the total. Once the percent for each color has been determined, the children must determine the portion of the circle's interior
that will represent it.

In addition to systematically presenting statistical data, a table or graph
can be used to organize data for solving a problem, as illustrated with
these two problems.

PROBLEM 5-9   Two Unique Rectangles

There are only two rectangles whose sides are whole numbers and whose
area and perimeter are the same number. What are they?[10]

The strategy here is to use a series of tables showing length, width, perimeter, and area for rectangles.

- Start with a table that shows a 1-by-1 rectangle and increases a
  pair of sides by units of 1:

---

[10] Ohio Department of Education, p. 10. (Used by permission.)

Length	Width	Perimeter	Area
1	1	4	1
2	1	6	2
3	1	8	3

Will this table produce a solution? Why?

- Make another table.

Length	Width	Perimeter	Area
2	2	8	4
3	2	10	6
4	2	12	8

Will this table produce a solution? Why?

- Your next table begins with a 3-by-3 rectangle. Does it yield a solution?

Length	Width	Perimeter	Area
3	3	12	9
4	3	14	12
5	3	16	15
6	3	→ 18	→ 18
7	3	20	21
8	3	22	24

We have one answer. The numbers beyond the matched pair will not yield another answer. Why?

- The next table looks like this:

Length	Width	Perimeter	Area
4	4	→ 16	→ 16
5	4	18	20

This table yields the second answer.

PROBLEM 5-10   Knitting a Sweater

Jack is knitting a sweater. The directions say that every 7 rows of stitches will make 1 inch of sleeve. If a sleeve is 16 inches long, how many rows of stitches will it have?

Both a table and graph are useful here. How do they help you find the answer?

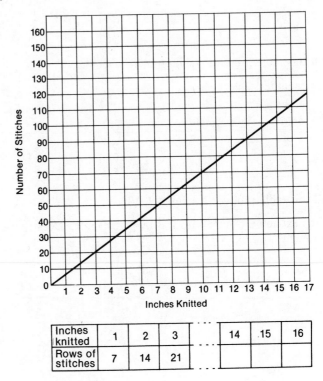

Inches knitted	1	2	3	···	14	15	16
Rows of stitches	7	14	21	···			

5. Guess and Check

One of the least appreciated strategies is *Guess and check*. Guessing for the solution of a problem is frequently associated with aimless casting about for an answer. We do not advocate blind guessing, but we whole-heartedly do encourage educated guesses.

What is the difference?

An educated guess is based on the problem solver's careful attention to pertinent aspects of the problem, though not necessarily in a formal man-ner. This information is assimilated with his previous experiences to pro-duce a hypothesized answer which the guesser has some reason to expect to be "in the right ball park."

As a strategy, the key element is *and check*. In other words, the prob-lem solver makes an educated guess *and then checks* it against the problem conditions to determine how to improve his guess. He repeats this pro-cess until he has an acceptable answer.[11]

This problem is a good one for children to solve with the **guess-and-check** strategy.

---

[11] Ohio Department of Education, p. 17. Emphasis in original. (Used by permission.)

PROBLEM 5-11 Buying Stamps

It costs 20 cents to mail a letter and 13 cents to mail a postcard. Reggie spent $3.23 for postage to mail messages to 20 friends. How many letters and how many postcards did he mail?

It may be helpful to construct a table to keep track of your guesses. For example, let the first guess be 10 letters and 10 postcards and calculate the cost.

Letters (20¢ each)		Postcards (13¢ each)		Totals	
Number	Cost ($)	Number	Cost ($)	Number	Cost ($)
10	2.00	10	1.30	20	3.30
9	1.80	11	1.43	20	3.23

The first guess gave an incorrect answer but did yield good information. Because $3.30 is greater than the amount of money Reggie spent, we know we need to reduce the number of letters and increase the number of postcards. When we do this, we get the correct answer on our next guess.

6. Account for All Possibilities

This strategy works well when there is a limited number of possibilities to be considered. Tables are frequently used to organize information when this strategy is used. In the first of the two problems that follow, this strategy uses the Cartesian-product, or cross-product, concept of multiplication in a realistic situation. All possible combinations of ice creams and toppings are made to show the different sundaes an ice-cream parlor can make.

PROBLEM 5-12 The Ice Cream Parlor

An ice-cream parlor has four flavors of ice creams and six flavors of toppings. Are there enough combinations of ice creams and toppings so that 19 children can each have a different sundae?

Make a table in which the topping flavors are listed down the side and ice cream flavors across the top. Show each ice cream–topping combination as ordered pairs in the table.

Topping	Ice cream			
	Vanilla	Coffee	Banana	Walnut
Marshmallow	M–V	M–C	M–B	M–W
Cherry	Ch–V	Ch–C	Ch–B	Ch–W
Chocolate	Choc–V	Choc–C	Choc–B	Choc–W
Strawberry	S–V	S–C	S–B	S–W
Caramel	Car–V	Car–C	Car–B	Car–W
Raspberry	R–V	R–C	R–B	R–W

PROBLEM 5-13   Buying Fertilizer

You need 17 pounds of fertilizer, which comes in 3-lb or 5-lb bags. How many bags of each size do you buy to obtain at least that amount at the lowest cost?[12]

You can systematically account for the weight and cost of each combination of bags that will yield at least 17 pounds of fertilizer. (It is not necessary to record all possibilities; you need list only the combinations that give at least 17 pounds of fertilizer.) This table shows that the best price actually gives the customer more fertilizer than the second-best price.

---

[12]Ohio Department of Education, p. 11. (Used by permission.)

Number of 5-lb bags	Cost ($)	Number of 3-lb bags	Cost ($)	Total weight (lb)	Total cost ($)
4	13.00			20	13.00
3	9.75	1	2.29	18	12.04
2	6.50	3	6.87	19	13.37
1	3.25	4	9.16	17	12.41
		6	13.74	18	13.74

7. Act it Out

The **acting-out** strategy is different from **dramatization.** Children who dramatize replicate a real-world situation without solving a problem. In the primary grades a classroom store stocked with empty food and household-product containers can be used to give children experiences buying and selling their store's products. Older students may earn credits for accurate and on-time work, good behavior, courtesy, and so on, which are placed in a classroom bank. Checks are drawn against these credits to buy free time, opportunities to play games, and other rewards. In both situations children learn worthwhile consumer skills but solve no problems.

The acting-out strategy is often spontaneous and is usually not very elaborate. Consider the two situations that follow. What characters or props are needed for each one?

PROBLEM 5-14 Fox, Goose, and Grain

You are transporting a fox, a goose, and a bucket of grain to market, and you come to a river. There is a rowboat large enough for you and only one commodity. You must keep these factors in mind as you plan your crossings: If you leave the fox with the goose, the goose will be eaten; and if you leave the goose with the grain, the grain will be eaten. How will you get the grain and the animals across the river?

Use three objects to represent the commodities, and carry them across a "river" to determine if your plan is a good one. One scheme for crossing the river is as follows: (1) Leave fox and grain, take goose across and return. (2) Leave fox, take grain across and return with goose. (3) Take fox across, leave goose and return. (4) Take goose across and continue your journey.

PROBLEM 5-15   Horse Trading

A woman buys a horse for $60, sells it for $70, buys it back for $80, and sells it for $90. How much does the woman make or lose in the horse-trading business? [13]

Get two friends, one to act as the horse and the other the buyer. Use play money, and carry out the transactions.

8. Write a Mathematical Sentence

Children at all grade levels should be encouraged to write **mathematical sentences** to express problem situations. A mathematical sentence serves two purposes: It shows that a student understands a problem situation, and it shows what computation is needed to solve a problem. A child who can write a correct sentence for the following problem demonstrates understanding of the situation and can proceed to determine the answer.

PROBLEM 5-16   Airplane Trip

An airplane flew from San Francisco to Los Angeles (347 miles), from Los Angeles to El Paso (701 miles), from El Paso to Houston (676 miles), and from Houston to New Orleans (318 miles). How far did the airplane fly? Write a mathematical sentence to show that you understand this problem.

A sentence for this problem is $347 + 701 + 676 + 318 = \square$.

9. Restate the Problem

Sometimes a problem is not understood at the time it is first read. A careful second reading followed by a restatement of the problem often makes it clear. At other times the substitution of smaller or more familiar numbers may be helpful when large or unfamiliar numbers appear in a problem. Children who are able to restate even the simplest problems in their own words demonstrate understanding. There are times when restatement leads directly to a solution.

---

[13] Ohio Department of Education, p. 15. (Used by permission.)

PROBLEM 5-17   At the Five and Dime

I bought some items at the Five and Ten store. All the items were the same price and I bought as many items as the number of total cents in the cost of each item. My bill was $2.25. How many items did I buy?[14]

The problem says I bought as many items as the number of cents each item cost. The number of items equals the number of cents, so $n \times n =$ total cost. I must determine the number that when multiplied by itself equals 225. This is the square root of 225, or 15. A calculator with a square-root key is helpful here.

PROBLEM 5-18   Wine and Cork

A bottle of corked wine cost $10.00. The wine is valued at $9.00 more than the cork and bottle.
   What is the value of the wine?

Be careful with this one. At first glance it appears that the wine cost $9.00 and the bottle and cork cost $1.00. But $9.00 is not $9.00 more than $1.00. A guess-and-check strategy can now be used, if necessary, to check other combinations. The wine's value is $9.50, and the cork and bottle are worth 50 cents.

10. Identify Wanted–Given Information

The **wanted-given** strategy is used when a person examines the problem to find out what is wanted and what is given. What is wanted may be a sum, difference (unknown addend), a product, a quotient (unknown factor), or some other answer. What is given is often a pair (or more) of addends, a sum and a known addend, a pair of factors, a product and a known factor, or a combination of these. Activities for this strategy are discussed later in this chapter.

11. Breaking Set, or Change Your Point of View

Various factors can make a problem difficult. Most we have no control over, but one that is within our discretionary power is the perspective we

---

[14]Ohio Department of Education, p. 29. (Used by permission.)

take of the problem. Upon meeting most problems, we tend to quickly adopt a particular point of view. We speedily formulate a plan of attack and then implement it to determine whether it produces a solution. If our plan is not successful, the tendency is to return to the same point of view and adopt a new plan. This may be successful. But it may also involve a circle of faulty logic based upon an incorrect or nonproductive initial perspective.

The real culprit in this process is failure to examine adequately the problem initially. The better we understand the full nature of a problem, the more likely we are to choose a successful line of attack. However, it is human nature to progress rapidly through the problem-identification stage. We should therefore acknowledge this human frailty and provide a means to escape from a failure cycle created by an unsuccessful initial view of a problem.

We recommend the strategy CHANGE YOUR POINT OF VIEW. That is, cease current problem efforts, discard any previous notions about the problem, and try to redefine the problem in a completely different way. Unlike RESTATING THE PROBLEM, changing your point of view requires a major shifting of focus upon the problem components. Elements which were emphasized are now downplayed or perceived in a different manner. Other problem features are highlighted that previously may have been given very little consideration. We try to imagine how the problem state could be achieved in ways other than initially conceived.[15]

Apply the **breaking-set** strategy to each of the following problems.

PROBLEM 5-19   The Farmer's Trees

A farmer planted 10 trees in 5 rows of 4 trees each. How did she do this?

PROBLEM 5-20   Checkers

How could a man and a woman play five games of checkers and each win the same number of games without any ties?[16]

PROBLEM 5-21   Triangles

How can you arrange six new lead pencils to form four congruent equilateral triangles?

---

[15] Ohio Department of Education, p. 16. (Used by permission.)

[16] This and the tree problem are adapted from Robert J. Sternberg and Janet E. Davidson, "The Mind of the Puzzler," *Psychology Today*, XVI, No. 6 (June 1982), p. 37.

Solutions to these three problems are not given here. You are on your own. Compare your answers with those of your co-workers.

You have read 11 problem-solving strategies. Can you name eight of them and give an example of a problem for which each one is applicable?

Self-check of Objective 2

A FOUR-STEP PROBLEM-SOLVING PROCESS

A repertoire of problem-solving strategies helps a person be an effective problem solver. However, strategies alone are not sufficient. One must also possess knowledge of the **problem-solving process** itself. George Polya is a mathematician who studied problem solving during his career at Stanford University. His book *How to Solve It* [17] was first published in 1945 as a guide for university students. His four-step process is also useful for precollege students; a simplified version is advocated for elementary school children. Polya's four steps are

- Understanding the problem
- Devising a plan
- Carrying out the plan
- Looking back

1. Understanding the Problem

The first step is to understand the problem. Study the situation to determine what is given, what is to be found, and what is needed. Is the information that is given sufficient? If not, what more is needed? Perhaps a model or diagram will help. Do not forget about breaking set, or taking a different point of view.

PROBLEM 5-22 $63.00

How is it possible to have $63.00 in bills without having any one-dollar bills?

[17] George Polya, *How to Solve It* (Garden City, New York: Doubleday Anchor Books, Doubleday and Company, Inc., 1957).

PROBLEM 5-23 Candlestick Park

Could all of the students in our school be seated in Candlestick Park in San Francisco? Could all of the people living in Elk Grove, California be seated in Candlestick Park? All of the people living in Sacramento, California?

- Analyze each of the preceding problems; then write statements that show you understand each one.

2. Devising a Plan

Once a problem is understood, a plan for solving it must be devised. Consider previously solved problems to determine if strategies used earlier can be used now. Is there a general rule that applies? Which strategies are appropriate for the problem? Simplify or restate the problem if necessary. Is the plan complete? Does it take into account all aspects of the problem? Will it yield a complete answer?

- Write a description of each of your plans for solving the preceding problems.

3. Carrying Out the Plan

As a plan is carried out, each step should be checked. Is all computation reasonable? Do charts and graphs contain all pertinent information? Are the data leading to useful answers? Are guesses reasonable ones? (Do not waste time on wild guesses.)

- If possible, complete the preceding problems.

4. Looking Back

According to Polya, this is a very important step. Teachers and children both need to go beyond the solution. Now is the time to discuss whether the result could have been derived differently. Was the chosen strategy the best or most efficient? Was it applied correctly? Also consider other past and potential problems to help children learn that there are classes of problems for which certain strategies and general rules are applicable.

- Think about the approach and process you used with each of the two problems. Tell whether you could have done anything differently to make your work more efficient.

List the steps in Polya's problem-solving process, and indicate the significance of each one.

*Self-check
of Objective 3*

WORD PROBLEMS

You are encouraged to present many in-school activities that expose children to realistic problems. Teachers who do this know that many problem-solving strategies can be learned this way. There are times, however, when **word problems** must be used to broaden children's exposure to strategies. Word problems also provide realistic settings in which to introduce new topics.

Results of the second National Assessment of Educational Progress mathematics test indicate that 9- and 13-year-old children could solve word problems involving a single operation nearly as well as they could compute answers to algorithms for the same operation. They were more skillful in computing answers and solving problems involving addition and subtraction with whole numbers than they were with multiplication and division.[18] The downfall of most students was work with less-familiar problems, such as multistep problems, and those with too much or too little information. This led Carpenter and his associates to recommend that more attention be given to such problems.[19]

In addition to the strategies and four-step process already discussed, attention should be directed to activities that deal with

- Reading in mathematics
- Children's own problems
- Extraneous and too-little information

1. Reading in Mathematics

Children's achievement in mathematics is affected by their language development. Generally children who lack adequate language mastery have more difficulty in achieving success in mathematics than those whose

---

[18]Thomas P. Carpenter and others, "Solving Verbal Problems: Results and Implications from National Assessment," *Arithmetic Teacher*, XXVIII, No. 1 (September 1980), pp. 9–10.

[19]Carpenter, pp. 10–11.

mastery is good. Even children whose language development is normal may experience problems with reading in mathematics.

One aspect of the problem is the vocabulary of mathematics. Many words used in mathematics are already familiar in other contexts, so their mathematical meanings need special attention. For example, *base, difference,* and *product* have meanings apart from those used in mathematics. Other words, such as *array, quotient,* and *commutative,* may be new when children first encounter them in mathematics. Earp and Tanner suggest that both types of words should be developed through an oral-language process. They offer these suggestions:

- Much oral language should be used in mathematics classrooms. More time should be spent discussing mathematical ideas than is commonly used.

- Mathematics vocabulary should be taught in ways similar to those for teaching vocabulary in a reading lesson. Children should hear, see, and say mathematical words, pronounce them by syllables, and use them in written and oral sentences.

- Mathematical statements in textbooks should be rewritten or paraphrased by both children and teachers.

- The cloze procedure should be used. With this procedure a blank replaces every nth word in a sentence or statement. Children complete each one by filling in the blanks with suitable words.[20]

The symbols of mathematics, that is, signs of operation ($+$, $-$, $\times$, $\div$), of relation ($=$, $<$, $>$, $\neq$), and others, must be clearly understood. Abbreviations, such as cm, L, lb, and #, and commonly used Greek and Latin prefixes and suffixes, such as bi-, centi-, geo-, para-, -hedron, and -gon, should receive special attention. (Appendix A gives the meanings of commonly used Greek and Latin prefixes and suffixes.) A classroom chart to which each new symbol, abbreviation, prefix, and suffix is added when introduced will remind children of the meanings.

Children must learn to read mathematics slowly and carefully. Greater attention must be given to detail when reading in mathematics than when reading a story. (The first two steps of the four-step problem-solving process deal with this.)

Looking for clues in word problems is often taught as a strategy for determining which procedures to use. Examples of clue words within sentences are: "How many are there in all (or altogether)?" (Addition). "What is the difference?" and "How many are left?" (Subtraction). However, such clues are so limited in value as to be almost useless; many

---

[20]N. Wesley Earp and Fred W. Tanner, "Mathematics and Language," *Arithmetic Teacher,* XXVIII, No. 4 (December 1980), p. 34.

children use them improperly, thinking they suggest one operation when another is appropriate.

PROBLEM 5-24   Bob's Marbles

Bob had thirty-six marbles. When his father gave him a new bag of marbles, Bob counted all of them and found he had fifty-one altogether. How many marbles did his father give him?

The word *altogether* in this problem incorrectly suggests addition. Another weakness of the clue-word strategy is that many problems do not include useful clues. If the clue-word approach is the only, or primary, strategy a child has, there will be many times the child will give up or resort to guessing.

2. Children's Own Problems

Personalized word problems have the advantage of matching children's interests and using settings and vocabulary with which they are familiar. They are also valuable for checking children's understanding of mathematics.

The **language–experience approach** can be used to introduce primary-grade children to word problems. With this approach, you set up situations that children act out.

ACTIVITY 5-1   The Books

- Begin with a stack of 13 books. Give eight of them to a child and keep five. Discuss your actions. How many books at first? How many were given to Bobbie? How many did I keep?
- Have a child tell a story about the books; write it on the chalkboard or a chart.

Repeat activities of this sort over time until children are fluent in interpreting actions and telling stories about them.

Another activity is to have children make up problems for sentences that you specify.

ACTIVITY 5-2 Making up Word Problems

- Write these sentences on the chalkboard: $12 - 8 = 4$ and $3 + 7 = 10$.
- Instruct the children to make up a word problem for the subtraction sentence and one for the addition sentence.
- Have volunteers tell their stories. Discuss each one to see how it fits its sentence.

Children's stories may be written or oral, depending upon their writing skills.

The language–experience approach can be modified for older children. Instead of acting out a problem (the sizes of numbers used make this cumbersome), present a number sentence like $436 + 389 = 825$. Discuss situations that could give rise to the sentence. At first, children's contributions may be limited, but with experience they will generate many situations. Practice should follow discussion. At first, present them with clearly specified conditions.

ACTIVITY 5-3 Subtraction Word Problem

Make up a word problem involving subtraction in which a two-digit number is subtracted from a two-digit number and for which regrouping (borrowing) is necessary. Example: $53 - 19 = 34$.

As children gain experience in writing word problems, your directions can become less specific. Now you might direct them to make up a word problem dealing with an extra-school experience such as measuring a garden plot, doubling ingredients for a recipe, or ordering Girl Scout cookies. Encourage them to discuss this assignment with and solicit suggestions for problems from adults at home.

Children's problems should be shared. One way to share is to exchange problems during a work period. Discuss solutions before the period's close. Another way is to have children put each problem on a 4×6 card for a classroom file. Children can work with these cards during problem-solving practice periods, as part of a planned mathematics contract, or as self-selected free-time activities. Over time, you will accumulate a collection of personalized problems to supplement or replace textbook problems.

3. Extraneous or Too-Little Information

Word problems with too much or too little information should be assigned and discussed from time to time. Each problem should be studied carefully to determine what information is given. Statements that do not contain questions or numbers provide practice in determining what is lacking. Here are examples of problems for these types of exercises:

- A car can go 17 miles on 1 gallon of gas. How far can it travel on one tank of gas?

- Jack had $5.00 in his bank. He then worked for 6 hours and earned $3.25 an hour. How much money did he earn for his work?

- An airplane has a top speed of 1100 miles an hour. It flew at this speed for 3 hours.

- Jack bought a new baseball glove. How much change did he receive?

Read each problem. Does it provide too much or too little information? Change each one in a way that you think makes it a good story problem.

You have read about three types of activities that help children learn to solve word problems. Name each activity, and describe its contribution toward improving a child's skill in dealing with word problems.

Self-check of Objective 4

ESTIMATION

Estimation skills have wide application in mathematics. Children need to learn how to make reasonable estimates when giving answers to problems and when computing, measuring, and determining quantities of objects.

1. Estimating Answers

Skill in estimating answers has gained importance as people have become aware of its use in problem solving. One part of the carry-out-the-plan phase of the problem-solving process is to check the accuracy of each step. Estimation is often used to do this. Whether a calculator or a paper

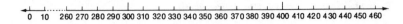

FIGURE 5-3
Number line used to help
children round off numbers to
the nearest hundred

and pencil are used, estimation is useful for judging the reasonableness of one's work.

Before children can estimate answers, they must know how to **round off** numbers to the nearest ten, hundred, or thousand. To estimate the answer for the addition shown in the margin, a person must first round each addend to the nearest hundred. A number line such as the one in Figure 5-3 is useful for helping children see that 290 is nearer to 300 than to 200. When 290 is located on the line and the steps are counted between 290 and 200 and between 290 and 300, the reason for rounding off 290 as 300 becomes clear. After all four numbers have been rounded off, the answer can be estimated by adding only the hundreds.

When children in elementary school are taught to round off numbers to the nearest ten, they learn that the numbers 31, 32, 33, and 34 are rounded to 30 and that the numbers 36, 37, 38, and 39 are rounded to 40. Children can use a number line to see that 31, 32, 33, and 34 are closer to 30 than to 40 and that 36, 37, 38, and 39 are closer to 40 than to 30. When 35 is considered, however, the number line shows that it is as close to 30 as to 40. Children will need to be given a rule for rounding off numbers that end in five. A commonly used rule is to round off the numbers to the next higher ten. By applying this rule to the number 35, the children learn to round it off to 40.

```
290
320
380
+430
```

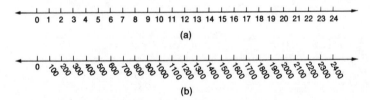

FIGURE 5-4
Number lines used to help
children learn to round off
numbers to (a) the nearest ten
and (b) the nearest thousand

A number line similar to the one in Figure 5-4(a) is useful for rounding numbers to ten, and the one in Figure 5-4(b) can be used to round numbers to the nearest thousand. These lines can be made on adding machine tape and fastened to the classroom walls. (A way to use a calculator for learning to round off numbers is explained in the next chapter.) After the children have learned to round off numbers to the nearest ten, hundred, and thousand, help them work with numbers that are to be rounded off first to the nearest ten, then to the nearest hundred, and then to the nearest thousand. Activities like the following are useful:

ACTIVITY 5-4   Rounding Off

- Round off each of these numbers to the nearest ten:

  3291   4648   13,689

- Round off each number to the nearest hundred.
- Round off each number to the nearest thousand.

Skill in estimating answers can be developed through exercises like the following:

PROBLEM 5-25   Estimation

Estimate an answer for each of these examples:

$$
\begin{array}{cccccc}
23 & 18 & 67 & 63 & 48 & 61 \\
+49 & +21 & +42 & -21 & -19 & -18
\end{array}
$$

Estimate an answer for each of these examples:

$$
\begin{array}{cccc}
62 & 73 & 978 & 439 \div 11 = \square \\
\times\ 3 & \times 21 & \times\ 48 & 698 \div 35 = \square
\end{array}
$$

Give an estimated answer for each of these word problems.
- What is the cost of a 39-cent can of fruit and a 48-cent quart of milk?
- Each bus carries 28 passengers. How many passengers can six buses carry?
- There are how many 29s in 612?

Children may compute the problems or use calculators to determine exact answers against which to judge their estimates.

Sometimes an estimated rather than an exact answer will solve a problem. This is true of the following situations:

PROBLEM 5-26   More Estimation

Use estimation to solve these problems:
- Sally wants to buy a baseball glove that costs $12.95 and a baseball that costs $3.25. She has $18.00. Is this enough money to purchase the ball and glove?
- A jet plane can carry enough fuel to remain airborne for 5 hours of flight at top speed. If it flies at a top speed of 890 miles per hour, can it make a round trip of 5000 miles without having to refuel?

Estimation is used to help children learn to place the decimal point properly when multiplying and dividing with decimal fractions. Activities dealing with these applications are given in Chapter 13.

2. Estimating Measurements

Skills in estimating with measures have wide application. Instruction in this aspect of estimation must be planned as an integral part of children's measurement experiences. Estimation activities are presented in Chapter 14, which deals with measurement.

3. Estimating Quantities

A popular means of attracting customers to a business is to place a jar of gum balls (or similar objects) in a store's window along with an invitation to make a guess about the number of gum balls. The prize-winning guess is sometimes exact; more often it is just close. Other answers range from ridiculously low to outrageously high. The grossly wrong answers occur because many persons lack an understanding of what numbers mean. Even though they can say a number like 3698, they have no notion of what that many gum balls looks like. An answer of 392 or 10,348 is perfectly all right with them.

First graders use beansticks, bundles of tongue depressors, and commercial materials like Cuisenaire Rods and Blocks to conceptualize the meanings of relatively small numbers. A computer printout showing several hundred, several thousand, or even a million dollar signs is an impressive way to show a large quantity of something. Once primary-grade children understand the meanings of numbers, they should have periodic experiences in estimating quantities.

Activities such as the following give children practice in estimating quantities:

ACTIVITY 5-5   Guessing Dots

- Show children a card and ask them to guess how many dots are on it. Allow time for them to make their guesses. Accept all responses.

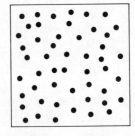

- Discuss strategies used by those whose guesses were close. Include the following strategies if they are not given by the children:
  - Count the dots across the top (or bottom) and down one side. There are about seven each way. There are about 49 (or 50) dots on the card.
  - Fold the card so only one-fourth shows. Count the dots on one-fourth of the card. Multiply this answer by four.
- Repeat with larger cards containing more dots.

This activity is a good one for older children:

ACTIVITY 5-6   Beans in the Jar

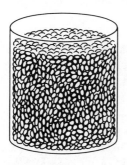

- Display a jarful of lima beans on a table. Leave a ruler, a small paper cup, a tablespoon, and the bottom part of an egg carton next to the jar. Give children time during the next day or two to guess how many beans are in the jar. Tell them they may use any strategy they wish short of removing and counting the beans.
- Accept and list guesses; then discuss strategies, including the following:
  - Measure the depth of the beans in the jar. One layer is about one centimeter deep and contains — beans. The beans are — centimeters deep, so there are about — beans in the jar.
  - There are an average of — beans in one paper cup. (Count beans in three or four cups and determine their average.) There appear to be about — cups of beans in the jar, so there are about — beans.
  - There are about — beans in one tablespoon. Pour twelve tablespoonsful into the egg carton, one spoon per section. There are about — beans in one carton and about — cartons of beans in the jar. So there are about — beans in the jar.
- Count the beans. (Can you devise a way to do this so that you reinforce children's understanding of place value and large numbers?)
- Discuss the strategies in terms of whether one is more useful than another or whether they are equally useful. Under what circumstances

might one strategy be better than another? (Consider the different sizes of objects that might be put in the jar.)

**Self-check
of Objective 5**

Name three types of estimation skills children should develop.

SUMMARY

Problem solving is described in this book as the set of actions a person takes when faced with a problem for which an immediate solution is not apparent. There must be both a solution and desire by an individual to find it in order for a problem to exist. A person must have a repertoire of mathematical problem-solving strategies and skills. The following strategies are among those that elementary school children can learn: look for a pattern, draw a picture or diagram, use a model, construct a table and/or graph, guess and check, account for all possibilities, act it out, write a mathematical sentence, restate the problem, identify wanted–given information, and break set, or change point of view.

George Polya explained a four-step problem-solving process that has been adapted for elementary school children. The four steps are understand the problem, devise a plan, carry out the plan, and look back to evaluate the plan and solution.

Children learn strategies and the problem-solving process through both in-school real-world word problems and textbook, problem-card, and personal word problems. Word problems need special attention. Procedures used to teach vocabulary in a reading lesson should be used to teach vocabulary in mathematics. The clue-word strategy for solving word problems is of little worth and should not be used. Children's own word problems have an advantage over published problems because their settings and vocabulary are familiar. Problems with too much or too little information and without questions should be analyzed and revised so they are meaningful.

Skills in estimating answers, measures, and quantities need to be systematically developed. The ability to round off numbers is a prerequisite for estimating answers.

STUDY QUESTIONS AND ACTIVITIES

1. Examine a primary-grade and an intermediate-grade book from a contemporary elementary-school mathematics series to deter-

mine which of the 11 problem-solving strategies are included. Does the teacher's manual or textbook contain activities for developing specific strategies? Are word problems and other problem-related materials organized to introduce and develop understanding of the strategies in a systematic way? Based on your examination, what (if anything) would a teacher need to do in order to supplement the textbook material to give children a comprehensive problem-solving program?

2. Make up, recall from previous experiences, or locate in published sources one problem for each of the 11 strategies. Indicate the grade range for which you think each one is appropriate. Name the source of any published problems.

3. Read Kilpatrick's article (see reading list). How can you prevent problem solving from becoming a mere slogan, which you will push for awhile and then drop, as Kilpatrick fears will happen?

KEY TERMS

problem solving
strategies
patterns
diagrams
Venn diagram
model
statistics
data
tables and graphs
guess-and-check

acting out
dramatization
mathematical sentences
wanted-given
breaking-set
problem-solving process
word problems
language-experience approach
estimation
round off

FOR FURTHER READING

Arithmetic Teacher, XXIX, No. 6 (February 1982). This issue contains ten articles about problem solving. There are both how-to and opinion articles.

Carpenter, Thomas P., and others. "Solving Verbal Problems: Results and Implications from National Assessment," *Arithmetic Teacher*, XXVIII, No. 1 (September 1980), pp. 8–12. In the second National Assessment of Educational Progress mathematics test, children performed well with one-step problems but did less well with other problem types. Teaching processes that move beyond one-step problems are needed so that children will develop skill with complex and nonroutine problems.

Charles, Randall I. "Evaluation and Problem Solving," *Arithmetic Teacher*, XXX, No. 5 (January 1983), pp. 6–7. Processes for evaluating achievement in problem solving are discussed. Five schemes for recording information are described.

―――. "Get the Most Out of 'Word Problems'," *Arithmetic Teacher*, XXIX, No. 3 (November 1981), pp. 39–40.

Most textbook word problems illustrate applications of mathematics topics. Charles describes ways to make these same problems fulfill the roll of developing mathematical concepts and improving problem-solving skills.

Davidson, James E. "The Language Experience Approach to Story Problems," *Arithmetic Teacher*, XXV, No. 1 (October 1977), p. 28. Having children write and solve their own story problems based on personal experience helps avoid some of the pitfalls of textbook problems—low reading comprehension, lack of experience with the problem situations, unfamiliarity with the language of the situations, and irrelevancy of the problems.

DeVault, M. Vere. "Doing Mathematics is Problem Solving," *Arithmetic Teacher*, XXVIII, No. 8 (April 1981), pp. 40–43. There are four types of problem-solving experiences in a good mathematics curriculum. Each type has a definite contribution to make to children's problem-solving abilities.

Greenes, Carole E., and Linda Schulman. "Developing Problem-Solving Ability with Multiple-Condition Problems," *Arithmetic Teacher*, XXX, No. 2 (October 1982), pp. 18–21. Polya's four-step problem-solving model is applied to problems having more than one condition. Guess-the-number problems are used as examples for discussing procedures for all grades.

Johnson, David C. "Teaching Estimation and Reasonableness of Results," *Arithmetic Teacher*, XXVII, No. 1 (September 1979), pp. 34–35.

Johnson makes an appeal for more formal treatment of estimation and checking for "reasonableness of results." He discusses ways to do this.

Jones, Billie M. "Put Your Children in the Picture for Better Problem Solving," *Arithmetic Teacher*, XXX, No. 8 (April 1983), pp. 30–33.

Problems based on information contained in the *Guinness Book of World Records* and the mathematical and reading skills required to solve them are presented. Five different problems are discussed.

Kilpatrick, Jeremy. "Stop the Bandwagon, I Want Off." *Arithmetic Teacher*, XXVIII, No. 8 (April 1981), p. 2.

Kilpatrick pleads for substance to the slogan "Problem solving should be the focus of the curriculum." Otherwise, it will be something a "teacher tried, but didn't like" as with so many other educational fads.

Krulik, Stephen. "Problem Solving: Some Considerations," *Arithmetic Teacher*, XXV, No. 3 (December 1977), pp. 51–52. Presents and elaborates on three criteria for identifying a "problem." Describes seven ways to help children become better problem solvers; some are accompanied by examples.

Lee, Kil S. "Guiding Young Children in Successful Problem Solving," *Arithmetic Teacher*," XXIX, No. 5 (January 1982), pp. 15–17.

Three problem situations and ways children can tackle each one are discussed. Polya's model is the basis for children's processes.

Moses, Barbara. "Individual Differences in Problem Solving," *Arithmetic Teacher*, XXX, No. 4 (December 1982), pp. 10–14.

Children's varying levels of understanding and skills need to be considered during problem-solving activities. Examples of materials and procedures for developing understanding and skills are illustrated and discussed.

Muller, Adelyn C., and Ray Kurtz. "Students Like Personalized Word Problems," *Arithmetic Teacher*, XXVIII, No. 9 (May 1981), pp. 13–14. Word problems that relate to each child are more motivating than the general word problems in textbooks. Ways to teach children to write their own problems are presented.

Polya, George. *How to Solve It* (Garden City, NY: Doubleday Anchor Books, 1957).
Problems are solved by a process called *heuristic reasoning,* in which a systematic investigation of a problem is made to determine a solution. A four-step process is recommended by Polya.

Trafton, Paul R. "Estimation and Mental Arithmetic: Important Components of Computation," *Developing Computational Skills*, 1978 Yearbook of the National Council of Teachers of Mathematics. (Reston, Va.: The Council, 1978), pp. 196–213.
Explains and illustrates the uses of estimation in problem solving and computation, processes for developing estimation skills, and ways to develop mental arithmetic skills.

Walter, Marion. "Frame Geometry: An Example in Posing and Solving Problems," *Arithmetic Teacher*, XXVIII, No. 2 (October 1980), pp. 16–18.
A picture-frame-making problem is posed. How many different frames can be made? Strategies for this and similar problems are considered.

Wirtz, Robert W., and Emily Kahn. "Another Look at Applications in Elementary School Mathematics," *Arithmetic Teacher*, XXX, No. 1 (September 1982), pp. 21–25.
A distinction is made between application and problem solving. Children's personalized problems are the focus of this article.

6

Calculators and Computers

Upon completion of Chapter 6 you will be able to:

1. Explain the role of calculators in the elementary school mathematics program.

2. Outline briefly the historical development of computers.

3. Describe a microcomputer and identify its main components.

4. Distinguish between computer hardware and software.

5. Describe three uses of computers by elementary school children.

6. Explain the meaning of computer awareness for elementary school students.

7. Identify six factors to consider when planning children's programming experiences.

Electronic technology has come to the elementary classroom. One need only look at titles of new journals to grasp the impact that the calculator, computer, and preprogrammed devices are making on instruction and classroom activities; examples are *The Computing Teacher, Educational Computer, Electronic Learning,* and *Technological Horizons in Education Journal.* Increasingly, mathematics journals and those for other subjects contain articles about calculator and computer applications. It is a rare teachers' conference that does not have workshops and other sessions about calculators and computers, as well as computer equipment and software displays.

CALCULATORS IN THE ELEMENTARY SCHOOL

The National Council of Teachers of Mathematics recommended in *An Agenda for Action* that schools make problem solving the focus of school mathematics. The Council also recommended that schools take advantage of the **calculator** at all levels. Schools that put the second recommendation into practice will be well on the road to implementing the first, because the calculator fits nicely into problem-solving activities. A calculator frees children from routine computation, which is sometimes tedious and time-consuming, and gives them time to consider problems and what to do to solve them. Articles in *Arithmetic Teacher* and other journals confirm that children who use calculators generally become better problem solvers than those who do not use them.

In addition to serving as a problem-solving tool, calculators have other uses in the classroom:

- Developing understanding of numbers. A calculator enables children to count by ones, twos, fives, or any other number very quickly. By pressing the ☐ key, the ⊞ key, the ☐ key again, and the ⊟ key a child can count by ones to any number. A child who counts to 1000 this way gains insight into both the sequence of numbers and large numbers. Children can also learn about place value with a calculator; they learn the meaning of 6 in the number 468 when they see that to replace the 6 with a 0, they have to subtract 60.

- Gain insight into operations. Calculators can be used to develop understanding of operations and show the rationale for their algorithms. Children who begin with 384 and repeatedly subtract 64 to divide 384 by 64 will have a better understanding of the repeated subtraction algorithm for dividing whole numbers. The multiplication algorithm in the margin can be completed in stages on a calculator. By finding 9×362, 80×362, and 400×362, recording the separate products, and then determining their sum, a child gains insight into how the commonly used algorithm works.

- Extend children's mathematical experiences. The calculator opens the door to many experiences that children might otherwise bypass, because the necessary computations are tedious and time-consuming. For example, children can study the pattern that develops as these multiplications are completed:

$$1 \times 1$$
$$11 \times 11$$
$$111 \times 111$$
$$1111 \times 1111$$

Once these are completed, children can predict the product of $11,111 \times 11,111$. Does the calculator show that the prediction is accurate? (Most calculators will not have a display large enough to show the complete product but will show enough to check the prediction's accuracy.) There are many similar patterns children can study.

- Rounding off and estimating. A calculator user should first estimate an answer and then determine if the machine's answer is in the "ball park." An answer that does not reasonably match an estimate should be redone to confirm that it is either accurate or incorrect. Estimated answers are frequently used in problem-solving situations. Rounded numbers are used in most estimations that involve computed answers. Children can use a calculator to learn how to round off numbers. To round off a number, say 74, to the nearest ten, first display the number; then count backward by 1s from 74 to 70. Reset the number 74 and count by 1s to 80. Because the count to 70 is completed in four steps, and the count to 80 requires six steps, 74 is rounded off to 70. A similar process is used for rounding off to the nearest hundred or thousand.

Work with calculators should not replace knowledge of basic facts and paper-and-pencil computation skills. Even though calculators will produce correct answers for all computations, a child must know which keys to press and the order in which to press them. This knowledge comes from a good understanding of each operation and the algorithms by which it can be processed. Children should not become so reliant on calculators that they use them when simple mental or paper-and-pencil processes are more efficient. A minority of children have difficulty learning facts and computation skills. A calculator may make it possible for these children to learn to compute and to gain a more positive attitude toward the subject.

Studies of calculators in the elementary school indicate that they enhance learning of computational skills and problem-solving processes or at least are not detrimental. Robert Reys and his associates report that many teachers who have used calculators say that the machines enable children to work more problems and to cover more topics. More than 80 percent of the teachers in Reys' study reported that students were more eager to work and had an enhanced confidence in their abilities to solve problems.[1] This last finding suggests that calculators may be helpful in lessening mathematics anxiety, which if true is a further justification for their use.

Calculators have the same form of circuitry as computers. In fact some have memory functions and programmable features that surpass those of some computers; such calculators are not useful for elementary-school mathematics programs. Most persons recommend that elementary-school children use one with algebraic rather than arithmetic logic. The alge-

---

[1] Robert Reys, *et al.*, "Hand Calculators—What's Happening in Schools Today?" *Arithmetic Teacher*, XXVII, No. 6 (February 1980), p. 41.

braic calculator has a separate key for each operation—⊞, ⊟, ⊠, and ⊞—and one for ⊟. The order of pressing each key on an algebraic calculator follows the order of numerals and symbols in a number sentence. To add $7 + 3 =$, the �7 key, the ⊞ key, the ③ key, and the ⊟ key are pressed in that order.

Do not consider a calculator with less than an eight-digit display. The machine should have a floating decimal. Another feature to consider, at least for children in grades four through six, are memory keys. A calculator with four-key memory stores intermediate answers as the multistep computation is completed. Percent and square-root keys are also useful for older children. Size is another factor to consider, especially when machines are selected for very young or physically handicapped children. Many of the very small machines that are now made are unsuitable for these children. An AC adapter makes it possible to plug a calculator into any convenient outlet, although improvements in battery longevity make this less important than formerly.

One special-purpose calculator is particularly useful for teachers. This machine has been modified so that light passes through the display area to project the readout from an overhead projector to a screen (Figure 6-1). It is useful for whole-class instruction about calculators. It costs little more than an ordinary calculator.[2]

In spite of the availability of calculators, their widespread use among adults, and evidence of their usefulness to children, many teachers and lay persons object to having them in the elementary school. Teachers who choose to use them may need to justify their position to other teachers, administrators, and parents. Before you have children use calculators, you should determine if there is a policy governing their use in your school. If there is, make certain your plans are consistent with the policy. If there is none, perhaps you can help establish one. In the absence of a school or district policy, you should discuss your plans with your principal. Be able to explain how you will have children use them, and point out their benefits to children. Have procedures for using them. Decide whether children will use them at their desks or at a calculator center. Also decide whether a child will be permitted to take a machine home. If you do permit this, have reasons and a checkout plan.

The number of calculators you need depends upon how children will use them. In the primary grades, two to four machines are sufficient for a class. Children work in centers where free investigations for exploring and verifying mathematical ideas and problem-card activities are completed. A calculator becomes a teaching and problem-solving tool in the intermediate grades, so more machines are needed. It is recommended that no more than two children work with a single machine, so 15 to 18 are needed for most classes. Once you have introduced calculators into your program, there will probably be children who will want to bring

---

[2] The Educator Overhead Calculator is available from Stokes Publishing Company, P.O. Box 415, Palo Alto, CA 94302.

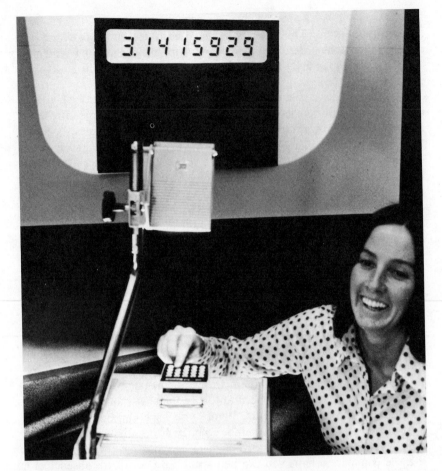

FIGURE 6-1

An overhead calculator.
Photo courtesy of Stokes Publishing Company, Palo Alto, California.

their own. Rules for using personal calculators should be the same as for classroom machines.

**Self-check
of Objective 1**

Describe four of the uses of a calculator in an elementary school program.

COMPUTERS IN THE ELEMENTARY SCHOOL

Each of the earlier editions of this book contains a brief reference to **computers.** However, because uses of computers in elementary schools were very limited, no detailed information about them is included. Since the third edition was published in 1980, the situation has changed. Now microcomputers and instructional programs for them are available. The National Council of Teachers of Mathematics recommends that "Mathematics programs take full advantage of the power of computers at all grade levels."[3] They state that students should have access to computers that are integrated into the core mathematics program, that a computer-literacy course should be a part of every student's general education, and that uses of computers in homes and schools should be coordinated.[4]

1. Historical Overview

The first operational computer, called ENIAC, was developed at the University of Pennsylvania in 1945. It occupied most of the space in a large room and required much electricity to operate and cool it. Nevertheless it proved its worth by demonstrating that a computer could drastically reduce the time required for completing complex computations. By 1951 the UNIVAC I computer was developed as the first commercially produced computer. About 100 units were sold to large universities, businesses, and government agencies. These and other early computers operated with vacuum tubes and were bulky, hot, and unreliable.

In the 1960s, transistors and diodes replaced vacuum tubes and computers became smaller, less expensive to purchase and operate, and more reliable. Still they were too expensive for schools at the precollege level. However, nearly 200 colleges and universities had computers, which first were used for administrative purposes. As computers became more common, some educators recognized their potential as a teaching tool. Patrick Suppes and his associates at Stanford University, and others, did early work with computer-assisted instruction at the precollege level. Students worked in their school at terminals that were connected by telephone lines to a computer they shared with students in other schools. These early studies showed that computers could have a positive impact on children's learning. However, the costs of computers prevented schools from taking advantage of this new aid to learning.

The breakthrough that made it feasible for schools to purchase and use computers occurred in the 1970s. This was the development of the **integrated circuit,** a fingernail-sized silicon chip that contains all of the circuit elements needed to replace wired-together transistors and resistors. Integrated circuits first appeared in **minicomputers,** which were developed in the early seventies. These machines occupied less space and were far less expensive than earlier models. Smaller colleges and some high schools used minicomputers for administrative and instructional purposes. By the end of the 1970s **microcomputers** the size of typewriters were developed. Microcomputers are also called **personal computers**

---

[3]National Council of Teachers of Mathematics, *An Agenda for Action: Recommendations for School Mathematics of the 1980s* (Reston, Virginia: The Council, 1980), p. 8.

[4]National Council of Teachers of Mathematics, pp. 9–10.

because their small size and low cost make it feasible for individuals to own one for personal use at home.

Some microcomputers cost as little as $100; most cost less than $2000. Many do the same work as earlier machines that cost thousands of dollars. Microcomputers are capable of processing data, graphics, and words; storing and retrieving information; synthesizing voices and music; and communicating with like-sized and bigger computers anywhere in the world. Their small cost puts them within the reach of schools at all levels. Their role in society and the role they can play in education make it essential that schools use them.

**Self-check
of Objective 2**

A brief historical overview of computers has been given. Describe the developments that led to affordable computers for elementary schools.

2. What is a Computer?

A computer is a machine designed for the input, storage, manipulation, and output of symbols (digits, letters, punctuation). It can automatically and very rapidly follow a step-by-step set of directions (called a computer program) that has been stored in its memory.[5]

Every computer, regardless of type, has these components:

- Input device(s)
- Central processing unit (CPU)
- Storage units, primary and secondary
- Output device(s)

a. Input Devices   Information is put into a computer by means of various types of **input devices.** A keyboard is most frequently used on a microcomputer. The key arrangement is like that of a typewriter, with additional special keys to control functions peculiar to the computer. Other input devices include touch panels, through which students give input by touching spots on the display screen; graphic input panels, which allow a student to use a stylus to write words or numbers or draw pictures that are transferred to the computer; and voice input devices. The special input devices are of particular interest to educators, because they

---

[5] David Moursund, *Teacher's Guide to Computers in the Elementary School* (Eugene: International Council for Computers in Education, University of Oregon, 1980), p. 7.

make it possible for very young children and those with physical handicaps, such as visual impairments or cerebral palsy, to use computers in ways a keyboard does not permit. Other input devices are magnetic tape, punched cards (commonly called IBM cards), electro-sensitive forms (such as pencil-marked test-answer sheets), and communication hookups connected with other computers. All of these devices are available for one or more of the microcomputers commonly found in schools.

b. Central Processing Units   The **central processing unit** (CPU) is the part of a computer that manipulates information and data. In microcomputers it is a silicon chip called a **microprocessor.** It executes the step-by-step instructions given by the person or program operating the machine. It contains one unit that can read and understand an instruction and another arithmetic–logic unit that performs the actual work. A microcomputer operates with remarkable speed, executing thousands of instructions per second.

c. Storage Units   Primary **storage units** are chips within the computer that temporarily store instructions from the program that is being used and data fed to it by the operator. As the CPU receives data and executes instructions, information is transferred to the primary storage unit. Primary storage is temporary, so information that is to be saved must be transferred to a secondary, or permanent, storage unit. On most microcomputers the secondary storage unit is either a cassette recorder with tape storage or a disk drive with floppy-disk storage. Both units store information on a magnetic-oxide-coated surface. There are two sizes of disk drives, one that holds 5¼-inch disks and one that holds 8-inch disks. A disk drive has several advantages over a cassette recorder. It can quickly locate and retrieve information from any spot on a disk, whereas a recorder must run through a tape to seek a particular piece of information. It is also more reliable and has a greater capacity. A 5¼-inch disk stores 100,000 to 200,000 digits, letters, punctuation marks, and spaces, but a 15-minute tape holds only 32,000 to 65,000.

The power of a microcomputer is determined by the capacity of its primary storage unit, which is measured in kilobytes (K). One K has a value of 2^{10}, or 1024. Thus a 48K machine stores about 50,000 bytes, or individual units of information, and has six times the capacity of an 8K computer.

d. Output Devices   The most common **output device** is a monitor, which is either a television set or a device very much like a television set that is used exclusively with a computer. Some computers are capable of producing output in color, so both color and black-and-white monitors are used. Monitors produce temporary, or softcopy, output. A printing device is one way of producing permanent, or hardcopy, output. Printers can produce typewriter-style copy and graphic displays. Special printers that produce Braille copy are of interest to educators of the blind. Several

FIGURE 6-2
Typical microcomputer setup,
with computer, two disk
drives, a monitor, and a
printer. Photo courtesy of Apple Computer, Inc., Cupertino, California.

microcomputers are capable of outputting voice and music. A typical
microcomputer setup is illustrated in Figure 6-2, which shows a computer, two disk drives, a monitor, and a thermal printer.

***Self-check
of Objective 3***

List the components of a microcomputer, describe the function of each part,
and name at least two examples of the following components: input device,
output device, secondary storage unit.

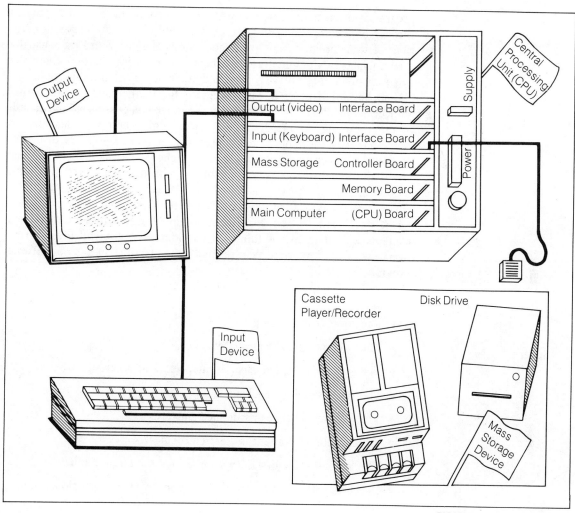

Output Device

Central Processing Unit (CPU)

Supply

Power

Output (video)   Interface Board

Input (Keyboard) Interface Board

Mass Storage   Controller Board

Memory Board

Main Computer   (CPU) Board

Input Device

Cassette Player/Recorder   Disk Drive

Mass Storage Device

FIGURE 6-3

A basic microcomputer system. Diagram from Robert Kansky, "The CPU and You: Mastering the Microcomputer," *Arithmetic Teacher*, XXX, No. 6 (February 1983), p. 53. Used by permission.

3. Computer Software

Hardware devices carry out the various functions of a computer. Equally important are programs, called **software,** which give instructions to a computer. A program is stored on a cassette tape or disk and is placed into the computer's primary storage unit through the cassette recorder or disk drive. From there it gives instructions to the central processing unit, which carries out the program's functions.

Programs are available for every elementary-school subject area. There are two general types of programs: **computer-assisted instruction** (CAI) programs for drills, tutorials, simulations, and educational games and **computer-managed instruction** (CMI) programs. A comprehensive CMI program provides pre- and post-tests, develops independent educational programs for each student, monitors each one's progress, and maintains records of accomplishment for each student. Names and brief descriptions of some programs are given later in this chapter. Software is usually accompanied by **documentation,** which is written information about the program, including purpose, intended audience, cost, and directions.

The development of a good program for mathematics or any other subject is time-consuming and costly. Few persons possess sufficient skill in programming, knowledge of a subject, and expertise in teaching to single-handedly develop a sound program. A team composed of a programmer, subject-matter specialist, and teacher or learning specialist may spend thousands of hours to develop an educationally sound program. Before any program is purchased, it should be evaluated carefully. Guidelines for evaluating software have been developed. One evaluation form, developed by the Northwest Regional Educational Laboratory, contains a 21-item list of things to consider. The list will give you an overview of the important features and characteristics of a good software program.

- The content is accurate.
- The content has educational value.
- The content is free of race, ethnic, sex, and other stereotypes.
- The purpose of the package is well defined.
- The package achieves its defined purpose.
- Presentation of content is clear and logical.
- The level of difficulty is appropriate for the target audience.
- Graphics/color/sound are used for appropriate instructional reasons.
- Use of the package is motivational.
- The package effectively stimulates student creativity.
- Feedback on student responses is effectively employed.
- The learner controls the rate and sequence of presentation and review.
- Instruction is integrated with previous student experience.
- Learning can be generalized to an appropriate range of situations.
- The user support materials are comprehensive.
- The user support materials are effective.

- Information displays are effective.

- Intended users can easily and independently operate the program.

- Teachers can easily employ the package.

- The program appropriately uses relevant computer capabilities.

- The program is reliable in normal use.[6]

Descriptors—strongly agree, agree, disagree, strongly disagree, and not applicable—are used to judge each item. At the conclusion of an evaluation, the evaluator is asked to recommend the program highly, recommend it with few or no changes, recommend it only if certain changes are made, or reject it; to describe its strengths and weaknesses; and to describe potential uses.

Software is available from several sources: commercial software, consortium software, and teacher-developed software. Both computer-assisted instruction and computer-managed instruction programs are available from commercial sources. Programs vary from single-disk drill-and-practice programs dealing with a single topic, such as multiplication, to complex management programs covering a range of grades. An advantage of commercial programs is that they can be readily used by both treachers and children who are not experienced computer users. A disadvantage of commercial programs is that they are static and cannot be changed to add or delete information for a particular group of children.

A computer consortium is a partnership of persons who have joined to promote the use of computers in schools. The Minnesota Educational Computing Consortium [7] assists users and educational member systems in coordinating and using computer resources. The organization develops software programs and provides technical and training services. Many Minnesota school districts are consortium members; districts in other states also participate. Consortium members pay a fee that gives them access to software developed by the consortium. The same advantages and disadvantages of commercial software apply to consortium software.

Teacher-produced programs can be made to fit the needs of a particular group of students. Thus they overcome a major weakness of commercial and consortium programs. However, few teachers possess the programming skills needed for developing their own materials. **Authoring tools** are available for teachers who want to develop their own programs but who lack advanced programming skills. An authoring tool

---

[6] Microsift, Northwest Regional Educational Laboratory, Portland, Oregon. (Used by permission.)

[7] Minnesota Educational Computing Consortium, 2520 Broadway Drive, St. Paul, MN 55113.

provides the framework around which a program is built and gives step-by-step instructions to guide a teacher in filling in details for a computer lesson. Once a program has been developed, it can be saved on tape or disk and placed in a school's software library.

There are two types of authoring tools. One is an authoring system, which provides a framework around which a lesson is developed; it can be used for lessons in most elementary-school subject areas. In this example for mathematics, the system's directions are in capital letters, and the teacher's responses follow.

```
WHAT IS THE NAME OF THIS LESSON?
Quadrilaterals
TYPE THE TEXT THAT IS TO BE DISPLAYED.
This lesson is about quadrilaterals.
QUESTION # 1:
Do you know the name of at least one
quadrilateral?
CORRECT ANSWERS:
Square
Rectangle
Parallelogram
Rhombus
Trapezoid
Kite
FEEDBACK FOR CORRECT RESPONSES:
Great! Excellent!
NUMBER OF TRIES:
2
HINT AFTER FIRST WRONG ANSWER:
The shape of the classroom door is a
quadrilateral.
EXPECTED WRONG ANSWER:
Triangle
FEEDBACK FOR EXPECTED WRONG ANSWER:
Sorry, a triangle has only three sides.
FEEDBACK FOR UNEXPECTED ANSWERS:
Sorry, that is not a quadrilateral. A
quadrilateral is a plane figure with four sides.
DO YOU HAVE ANOTHER QUESTION?
(Y/N).
```

PILOT (Programmed Instruction Learning Or Teaching) is a simple programming language developed for preparing computerized lessons. It has greater flexibility than the system already described but requires more time to learn and use. It has special commands that allow a teacher to create her own lesson format, rather than following a prescribed framework. There are PILOT programs for most microcomputers.

COMPUTERS IN THE CLASSROOM

1. Learning by Computer

Computer programs provide children with opportunities for drill and practice and for engaging in interactive learning through tutorial and simulation programs. **Logo** is a computing language simple enough that children can use it to write their own programs, freeing them from simply reacting to information provided by a program. It can be used to illustrate many mathematical ideas.

a. Drill and Practice Elementary-school children are expected to learn many facts and skills for recall from memory. The capabilities of a computer make it well-suited for providing drill and practice in mathematics. It can be programmed to provide straightforward practice on the basic facts, or it can provide a complete management system for a range of mathematics skills for several grades. An example of a simple basic-facts-drill program is *Prescriptive Math Drill,*[8] which presents sets of facts grouped by operation and according to difficulty. *Meteor Multiplication* is an arcadelike program that features a space motif. Children try to knock flaming meteors containing multiplication combinations from the sky before their space station is consumed by one of the meteors.[9] An example of a comprehensive drill-and-practice program is *Milliken Math Sequences.*[10] This is a 12-disk objective-based program that provides drill-and-practice in computation, numeration, measurement, and the laws of arithmetic for students from first through eighth grades. The contents of this program parallel most textbook programs and can be used in a classroom or mathematics laboratory to provide practice to supplement textbook materials or for either remediation and enrichment. This program has pre- and post-tests for placing children in the program and testing progress and provides both individual and class records.

David Moursund reports that drill-and-practice is the most common use of computer-assisted instruction. He also states that extensive research over the years has proven computerized drill and practice to be an effective aid to learning but that using a computer for drill alone cannot justify its cost.[11]

---

[8]*Prescriptive Math Drill* (Hartley Courseware, Inc., P.O. Box 431, Dimondale, MI 48821).

[9]Developmental Learning Materials, One DLM Park, Allen, TX 75002.

[10]*Milliken Math Sequences* (Milliken Publishing Company, 1100 Research Blvd., St. Louis, MO 63132).

[11]David Moursund, *Introduction to Computers in Education for Elementary and Middle School Teachers* (Eugene, Oregon: International Council for Computers in Education, University of Oregon, 1981), p. 24.

b. Tutorials and Simulation   A **tutorial** differs from a drill-and-practice program by providing primary instruction as well as practice. A tutorial program that provides branching to account for different levels of student comprehension is preferred over a program that cannot individualize instruction. A typical program instructs children about the meaning of common fractions, operations with common fractions, cancellation, reduction, and other fraction concepts.

A map is a model of all or part of the world, whereas a terrarium is a model of a biological environment. In the domain of computers, simulation programs model a situation in science, economics, art, or some other field to provide a realistic setting in which students study alternative futures. For example, *Sell Bicycles* [12] sets up an environment in which a student plays the role of manager of a bicycle-manufacturing company who must determine production figures, an advertising budget, and selling prices. Three similar programs from the MECC are *Sell Apples* (grades 3–6), *Sell Lemonade* (grade 6), and *Sell Plants* (grade 4–6). Their *Solar Distance* is a science program that involves students in comparing time and speed for various vehicles in simulated trips to the planets, and *Oregon* simulates a wagon train trip to Oregon in 1847, during which participants must handle finances for the trip. Each of these and similar simulation programs involves students in problem-solving situations for which a variety of strategies are required.

c. Collaboration Between Children and Computers   In most situations in which computers are used, children react to the computer rather than act upon it themselves. Drill-and-practice programs offer little or no opportunities for children to be creative. Tutorial and simulation programs do require some reasoned input as strategies are selected and applied, but they must be acted upon within a set of prescribed limits.

Logo, a simple computer program language, gives children the means to develop their own programs. It was developed in the Artificial Intelligence Laboratory at the Massachusetts Institute of Technology by Seymour Papert and his associates.

> Logo is the name for a philosophy of education and for a continually evolving family of computer languages that aid its realization. Its learning environments articulate the principle that giving people personal control over powerful computational resources can enable them to establish intimate contact with profound ideas from science, from mathematics, and from the art of intellectual model building. Its computer languages are designed to transform computers into flexible tools to aid in learning, in playing, and in exploring.
> . . . We try to make it possible for even young children to control the computer in self-directed ways, even at their very first exposure to Logo. At the same time, we believe Logo should be a general purpose programming system of considerable power and wealth of expression. . . . More

---

[12]*Sell Bicycles* was developed by the Minnesota Educational Computer Consortium.

than 10 years of experience at MIT and elsewhere have demonstrated that people across the whole range of "mathematical aptitude" enjoy using Logo to create original and sophisticated programs. Logo has been successfully and productively used by preschool, elementary, junior high, senior high, and college students, and by their instructors.[13]

Logo simplifies programming by combining commands into groups called procedures, with these procedures serving as steps to other procedures, and so on. There is a simplified process for executing commands and for defining, executing, and modifying procedures. Another feature of Logo is the incorporation of a programming area called turtle geometry. A turtle is a computer-controlled "cybernetic animal" that lives on the display screen and responds to Logo commands that make it move forward, backward, and to the left or right. Backward and forward movements are controlled by units of distance, and turns are controlled by degrees. The turtle can be instructed to leave a line that indicates direction and distance. The following command produces a square (FD 70 means forward 70 units, and RT 90 means right 90 degrees):

```
TO SQUARE SIDE

    FD 70
    RT 90
    FD 70
    RT 90
    FD 70
    RT 90
    FD 70
```

Turtle geometry allows students to investigate a wide range of mathematical concepts. (There is even a mechanical robotic turtle that can be directed to execute the above commands and draw a square on a sheet of paper placed on the floor.)

Children can also use the Logo language to develop their own drill-and-practice programs, randomly generate sentences (which helps them learn nouns and verbs), and create games. There are Logo software programs for most computers used in elementary schools.

[13] Harold Abelson, *Logo for the Apple II* (Peterborough, New Hampshire: BYTE/McGraw-Hill, 1982), p. ix.

Prepare an oral or written statement that distinguishes between computer hardware and software.

Three different uses of computers by children have been described. Identify each one and explain how each use differs from the others.

Self-checks of Objectives 4 and 5

2. Computer Awareness

New technologies are often the source of fear and apprehension. Many people believe that soon their lives will be controlled by intimidating machines and that there will be widespread job displacement of humans by computers and robots. The more students (and adults) know about computers, the less likely they are to harbor unfounded fears of them. **Computer-awareness** courses are designed to acquaint students with computers and their uses and to provide information about career opportunities with computers.

A teaching unit about computers and career opportunities is frequently the means for presenting information to children in grades 4 through 6. A comprehensive unit will include these topics: the history of computing and computers, hardware and software, computer applications, and career opportunities. Information should not be presented through lectures. Instead, children should become involved in library research, field trips, hands-on experiences with microcomputers, and other investigation-oriented activities.

a. History of Computing and Computers

1. Make a collection of historical algorithms: the lattice method of multiplying, Russian Peasant and finger multiplication, Babylonian multiplication and division, Egyptian algorithms for whole numbers and common fractions.[14]

2. Make a collection of computing devices, including Napier's rods, Genaille's rods, abacuses (many versions have been used throughout the world), early mechanical digital calculators (some were developed in the 1600s), electric calculators, and contemporary calculators. Replicas, models, pictures, and actual devices can be made or obtained by children. Used mechanical calculators are sometimes available at little or no cost from business machine companies.

3. Have children prepare reports on persons who developed computing devices, such as Blaise Pascal (1623–1662) who was in his teens when he developed a mechanical digital calculator for adding, Gottfried Leibniz (1646–1716) who invented a four-function calculator about 1671, and Charles Babbage (1792–1871) who designed the first modern calculating machine in the 1800s.[15]

---

[14] See National Council of Teachers of Mathematics, *Historical Topics for the Mathematics Classroom* (Washington, D.C.: The Council, 1969), Chapter 3.

[15] See James R. Newman, *The World of Mathematics*, Vol. 1 (New York: Simon and Schuster, 1956), pp. 515–518 for a brief history of calculating machines. *Men of Mathematics* by E. T. Bell (New York: Simon and Schuster, 1937) contains biographies of Pascal and Leibniz which may be of interest to more able fifth- and sixth-grade children.

Ada Lovelace developed ideas for a programming language for Babbage's machine. A programming language developed by the U.S. military services is called ADA in her honor.[16]

4. Collect pictures and information about computers. Include EN-IAC, UNIVAC, and other early computers. Compare a microcomputer with the early machines. What are their similarities and differences?

b. Computer Hardware and Software

1. Collect information about input devices. Include pictures of keypunch, phone modem, keyboard, and other devices. Prepare a display of disks and tapes, keypunch cards, test-answer sheets, and other input paraphernalia.

2. Collect information about storage devices. How does a primary storage unit work? How is the capacity of a computer determined? Collect examples of secondary storage paraphernalia, such as keypunch cards, magnetic tape, disks, and Braille and other printouts.

3. How do central processing units work? Learn about the CPU's arithmetic–logic control and its memory units.

4. Investigate different programming languages. Why have different languages been developed? Which languages are most suitable for children? For teachers?

c. Computer Applications

1. Collect examples of how personal computers are used by individuals. Many children come from homes where there are computers. A parent, or the child, can demonstrate ways their computer is used. Game-playing is the most common in-home use, but personal finances, recipe storage, address lists, and other applications are widespread. Do people produce their own programs, or do they use ready-made programs? What determines their choice?

2. Investigate ways computers are used in business, commerce, industry, sports, and government. How are computers used in banking and insurance? in supermarkets? in auto manufacturing? in college or professional football? in the post office? Visit places where computers are used to observe their operation and interview their operators.

---

[16]David Moursund, *Introduction to Computers in Education for Elementary and Middle School Teachers*, p. 45.

3. Investigate and summarize student–school uses. Children who do not have access to computers can view a demonstration and experiment with computer-assisted instruction, word processing, and Logo or BASIC programming languages. Discuss how a computer helps administrators and teachers maintain school records.

4. Investigate the social impact of computers. Recognize that only people can program a computer. What potential problems exist in relation to the computer's impact on human rights and the way we live?

d. Career Opportunities

1. Make a list of computer-related occupations such as systems analysts, system designers, keypunch operators, programmers, and sales representatives. Emphasize that careers are open to all persons. Many video-game programmers are young people; some are still in high school. Invite a local programmer to tell about programming and to demonstrate games or other programs. Secure names of companies to contact from computer magazines and telephone-book yellow pages.

2. Visit and hear speakers from places where computers are used. Children can generate a list of such places with input from parents and acquaintances.

3. Investigate requirements for entry into various computer-training programs. Contact local vocational schools, community colleges, and four-year and graduate schools to learn about training and educational opportunities. Determine the minimum requirements for each program.

Self-check of Objective 6	Computer-awareness activities are designed to acquaint children with computers and their uses. Describe briefly four topics for an elementary-school awareness unit, and list two or three activities for each topic.

3. Programming

Some people believe that programming activities should begin in the elementary school. Gary Bitter, a professor of computer education at the University of Arizona believes that children in grades 4, 5, and 6 should learn BASIC. His reason for choosing BASIC is that it is the most widely used computer language in elementary and secondary schools and it is available for all microcomputers.[17] **BASIC** stands for Beginner's All-Purpose Symbolic Instruction Code and was developed to provide a programming language that is applicable to many situations. There is also a pupil's version of PILOT, which is easier to learn and use than BASIC.[18]

There are other persons,[19] including this author, who believe that most programming activities should be delayed until junior high school. There is no demonstrated need for having instruction in BASIC as part of the elementary-school program for all children. Programming in Logo and simplified PILOT can be learned and used when these programs are available, and BASIC can be an activity for some gifted and talented children.

Before you consider teaching programming to any children, there are several factors to consider:

- The language you will teach. Logo and PILOT can be learned more easily than BASIC.

- The number of computers that are available. Learning a programming language requires time, just as learning to speak, read, and write English does. Each child should have access to a computer for 20 to 30 minutes several times a week.

- Your children's interest in programming. Some children will have a profound and continuing interest, whereas others do not sustain their interest.

- Students from homes with computers may have programming skills and may be able to help their peers learn programming.

- Your understanding and skill. Though it is not necessary that you be an advanced programmer to teach elementary-school children, you need a working knowledge of the language you plan to use.

- The goals you set for your children. Establish objectives and standards of accomplishment to guide their work. These need not be the same for every child.

[17] Gary Bitter, "The Road to Computer Literacy, Part III: Objectives and Activities for Grades 4–6," *Electronic Learning*, II, No. 3 (November/December 1982), p. 44.

[18] David D. Thornburg, "Picture This! Pilot Turtle Geometry," *Classroom Computer News*, II, No. 4 (March/April 1982), pp. 38–39 and 42–43.

[19] See Arthur Luehrmann, "Part V: Computer Literacy, What It Is; Why It's Important," *Electronic Learning*, I, No. 5 (May/June 1982), pp. 20 and 22.

Identify four factors to consider before teaching programming to children.

Self-check
of Objective 7

POSTSCRIPT ON COMPUTERS

New hardware, new software programs, and new programming languages for children and teachers are being developed at a rapid pace. It is not practical to list names and addresses of hardware manufacturers in this book. Persons interested in information about hardware should contact local computer stores for current information and to arrange demonstrations of equipment. Displays at professional conferences and workshops are also sources of current information.

Software has been developed by individuals who have small production companies as well as well-established publishers. Some of the small companies have prospered and continue to operate, whereas others have failed and are no longer in business. Because any listing of software companies may contain names of defunct organizations, correspondence to producers of software may be returned or go unanswered. Appendix B contains the names of companies that were selected with the expectation that they will continue to produce mathematics software and will respond to inquiries about their products.

Many computer-using educators have organized user-groups to share information and teacher-developed software, assist newcomers, and join with others to present a unified voice in establishing goals and standards for computers in education. An umbrella organization for many user groups is the International Council for Computers in Education (ICCE), Department of Computer and Information Science, University of Oregon, Eugene, OR 97403. ICCE publishes *The Computing Teacher*, a journal that includes a wide range of information about computers in education. Some ICCE publications and other journals dealing with computers are included in the further-reading section of this chapter.

PREPROGRAMMED DEVICES

There are microprocessor-based devices other than calculators and computers that are used in the classroom. These are **preprogrammed devices** such as Rainbow,[20] on which a child presses keys to match answers in a drill-and-practice situation in mathematics (and other subjects). Cards present different operations; response time and scores are automatically recorded (Figure 6-4.) These devices do one job only and range in size from small hand-held devices to microcomputer-size units. Preprogramming limits the uses of these machines, which are not substitutes for calculators and computers. They do provide an alternate means of presenting drill-and-practice activities in mathematics that will appeal to some children. Suppliers of these devices include:

---

[20] Available from Educational Insights, 150 W. Carob Street, Compton, CA 90220.

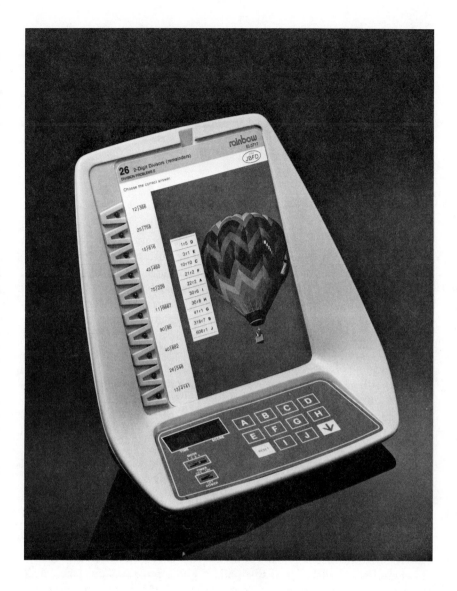

FIGURE 6-4
Preprogrammed learning aid.
Photo courtesy of Educational
Insights, Compton, California.

Centurion Industries, Inc.
167 Constitution Drive
Menlo Park, CA 94025

Hirschco, Inc.
2633 Greenleaf Avenue
Oak Grove Village, IL 60007

Texas Instruments, Inc.
2301 N. University
Lubbock, TX 78408-3508

Educational Insights
150 Carob Street
Compton, CA 90220

Mattel Toys
5150 Rosecrans Avenue
Hawthorne, CA 90250

SUMMARY

The National Council of Teachers of Mathematics has recommended that schools take full advantage of calculators and computers. Calculators can be used by children to solve problems that require complex or tiresome computation, to gain insight into numbers and operations, to investigate areas of mathematics they might otherwise avoid because of the amount of paper-and-pencil computation they would need to perform, and to learn to round numbers. Studies show that calculator use is not detrimental to children's computational skills and that calculators inspire them to do more problem-solving activities. Many children gain confidence in their problem-solving skills when they use calculators. A four-function machine with an eight-digit readout is recommended for elementary-school children; memory, square-root, and percent keys are recommended for older children. Teachers need to develop a plan for using calculators before introducing them to children.

The first computer was placed in operation in 1945. Since then the cost and size of computers have been reduced and their power and reliability increased manyfold. Today it is feasible for schools at all levels to have one or more computers for administrative and instructional purposes. A microcomputer system consists of a computer, input and output devices, and a monitor. A printer may or may not be used. There are computer-assisted instruction (CAI) and computer-managed instruction (CMI) programs in many subject areas. Drill-and-practice, tutorial, and simulation are available in mathematics. These programs must be acted upon within prescribed limits. Programs can be obtained from commercial producers and computer consortiums. Teachers can write their own program with authoring systems, which are programming tools that guide the teacher through the writing process.

A computer-awareness unit will help fourth-, fifth-, and sixth-grade children learn about computers and some of the ways they are used. A unit should include information about job opportunities in computer-related occupations. Some persons recommend that instruction in the BASIC computer language begin in the upper elementary grades. Others, including this author, recommend that instruction for most children be delayed until junior high school. Logo and a simplified version of

PILOT are programming languages most elementary-school children can use.

Preprogrammed devices provide an alternative method of giving children drill-and-practice activities.

STUDY QUESTIONS AND ACTIVITIES

1. Calculators are widely accepted and used by adults. Support for their use by elementary-school children is much less widespread. How do you account for such low acceptance by parents, administrators, and teachers? What is your position on their use in the elementary school?

2. Grayson Wheatley (see reading list) believes much time-consuming computation should be completed with a calculator. Recall your own experiences with such computation in grades 4, 5, and 6. Do you believe the time required for such work was justified? Do you feel the same way about similar work for children today? If children use calculators, what should be done with the time formerly spent on paper-and-pencil computation?

3. Investigate a selected school district to determine the extent to which computers and calculators are used in its elementary schools. Is there a written policy governing their uses? What computer programs are available to children? In your judgment, does the district make full use of the computer and calculator, as recommended by the National Council of Teachers of Mathematics?

4. Conduct a survey of a group of children to determine how many have computers or calculators at home. To what uses are the machines put? If possible, determine parents' attitudes toward computers and calculators in the elementary school. For what purposes do parents believe they should be used in schools?

5. Make a list of things children are expected to memorize for immediate recall by the time they complete grade 6. Include all areas of the mathematics curriculum. Most of the items on your list can be included in drill-and-practice programs. Do you agree with David Moursund that if programs of this sort are the sole use to which a computer is put, the cost of a computer system and software cannot be justified? Give arguments to support your answer.

6. What do you predict will be the status of calculators and computers in elementary schools in ten years? Give evidence to support your prediction.

KEY TERMS

calculator	software
computers	computer-assisted instruction
integrated circuit	computer-managed instruction
minicomputers	documentation
microcomputers	authoring tools
personal computers	PILOT
input devices	Logo
central processing unit	tutorial
microprocessor	computer awareness
storage units	BASIC
output device	preprogrammed devices

FOR FURTHER READING

Arithmetic Teacher, XXIII, No. 7 (April 1976).
>This issue includes one editorial and eleven articles dealing with calculators. Information ranges from opinions, to how to use calculators, and classroom games and activities.

————. XXX, No. 6 (February 1983). This issue focuses on microcomputers in schools. The editorial argues for having children write programs in BASIC and Logo. Ten articles deal with general aspects of computers in schools and three deal specifically with mathematics and computers.

Bartalo, Donald B. "Calculators and Problem-Solving Instruction: They Were Made for Each Other," *Arithmetic Teacher*, XXX, No. 5 (January 1983), pp. 18–21.
>A ten-day sequence of activities involving children with calculators and problem solving is reported along with seven teaching suggestions. The lessons were designed to focus children's attention on problem-solving skills.

Beechhold, Henry F. "Computers in Education: Is 'Educational' Software the Answer?" *Electronic Education*, II, No. 1 (September 1982), pp. 30–31.
>The author contends that rather than using programs designed especially for the classroom, children should use "real-world" programs, such as accounting and word-processing programs, to solve problems. For example, an accounting program might be used to manage a class business.

Bitter, Gary G. "The Road To Computer Literacy, Part III: Objectives and Activities for Grades 4–6," *Electronic Learning*, II, No. 3 (November/ December 1982), pp. 44–48 and 90–91. Bitter discusses computer awareness and programming and presents activities in both areas. Samples of programs in BASIC are given.

Bracey, Gerald W. "Computers in Education, What the Research Shows," *Electronic Learning*, II, No. 3 (November/December 1982), pp. 51–52, 54.
>Bracey reviews research about computers in education and discusses

achievement, affective-motivational, and social outcomes. He also suggests some research that is needed.

Carpenter, Thomas P., and others. "Calculators in Testing Situations: Results and Implications from National Assessment," *Arithmetic Teacher*, XXVIII, No. 5 (January 1981), pp. 34–37.
Some students who completed the mathematics test of the National Assessment of Educational Progress in 1977–78 were given calculators and instructed to use them as they did the test. The results showed that the calculators helped students at all age levels (9, 13, and 17) attain higher scores than peers who had no machines. The authors discuss recommendations concerning calculator use in classrooms.

Computing Teacher. Each edition includes articles dealing with computers in education. Many deal with elementary-school applications.

Duea, Joan, and Earl Ockenga. "Classroom Problem Solving with Calculators," *Arithmetic Teacher*, XXIX, No. 6 (February 1982), pp. 50–51.
Examples of student-created problems and their uses in a classroom are presented. Calculators improve the quality and number of student-produced problems.

Electronic Education. This publication presents articles on a wide range of topics dealing with home and school learning by computers. Its buyer's guide and reviews of books, programs, and new products are sources of current information about microcomputers and learning programs.

Electronic Learning. This journal is published by Scholastic, Inc., which has published weekly newsmagazines for schools for many years. The news section provides up-to-date information about a variety of topics related to computers and schools. It includes reviews of equipment, programs, and other computer-related materials.

Hopping, Lorraine. "Guidelines for Finding and Using Diagnostic/Prescriptive Software," *Electronic Learning*, II, No. 4 (January 1983), pp. 76–78.
The author discusses how diagnostic–prescriptive programs work and are used. Five mathematics programs are listed, along with 12 questions to ask before selecting any program.

Lappan, Glenda, Elizabeth Phillips, and M. J. Winter. "Powers and Patterns: Problem Solving with Calculators," *Arithmetic Teacher*, XXX, No. 2 (October 1982), pp. 42–44.
A study of number patterns generated by working with the powers of numbers provides problem-solving experiences, practice with calculators, and application of calculator skills.

Leuhrmann, Arthur. "Part V: Computer Literacy, What It Is; Why It's Important," *Electronic Learning*, I, No. 5 (May/June 1982), pp. 20 and 22.
The author distinguishes between computer awareness and computer literacy. He likens instruction in programming to instruction in writing and concludes that though each child can learn about programming not every child should become an expert programmer any more than every one should become an expert writer.

Meyer, Phyllis I. "When You Use a Calculator You Have to Think!" *Arithmetic Teacher*, XXVII, No. 5 (January 1980), pp. 18–21.

The experiences of a group of sixth graders with calculators are described. The conclusion was that calculators helped the children think logically as they solved problems.

Morris, Janet P. "Problem Solving with Calculators," *Arithmetic Teacher*, XXV, No. 7 (April 1978), pp. 24–25.
Describes several uses of the calculator. Included are exploring number patterns, discovering relationships, practicing mental estimation, reinforcing inverse operations, problem applications, developing problem-solving techniques, and individualized exploration and enrichment.

Moursund, David. *Calculators in the Classroom: With Applications for Elementary and Middle School Teachers* (New York: John Wiley & Sons, 1981).
This semiprogrammed book presents useful information about calculators and how to use them. Examples of activities for elementary school children are given.

———. *Introduction to Computers in Education for Elementary and Middle School Teachers* (Eugene, Oregon: International Council for Computers in Education, 1981).
The book's goals are to help teachers cope with computers in their schools, give ways to help children cope, and provide a foundation for learning more about computers.

———. *Teacher's Guide to Computers in the Elementary School* (Eugene, Oregon: International Council for Computers in Education, 1980).
This small book summarizes information about computers and their uses in elementary schools. It is good for a quick overview.

Reys, Robert E. "Calculators in the Elementary Classroom: How Can We Go Wrong?" *Arithmetic Teacher*, XXVII, No. 3 (November 1980), pp. 38–40.
This author favors the use of calculators. He discusses ten ways we can go wrong if they are used improperly.

Schleicher, Gordon. "Authoring Systems Can Save Time in Development of CAI," *Electronic Education*, II, No. 3 (November 1982), pp. 20 and 27.
Contrasts an authoring system with a programming system and discusses The Author, a specific authoring system.

Technological Horizons in Education Journal. This journal contains articles on computers. It also has information about other electronic devices, such as video recorders and telecommunications equipment.

Today's Education, LXXI, No. 2 (April/May 1982). This issue has five articles about computers in the classroom.

Wheatley, Grayson. "Calculators in the Classroom: A Proposal for Curricular Changes," *Arithmetic Teacher*, XXVIII, No. 4 (December 1980), pp. 37–39.
Wheatley believes calculators should be used more than they are in mathematics classes. He recommends four areas of work that should receive reduced attention and six areas that need greater emphasis.

Wiebe, James H. "Using a Calculator to Develop Mathematical Understanding," *Arithmetic Teacher*, XXIX, No. 3 (November 1981), pp. 36–38.
Understanding of counting, estimating, and computation can all be improved through calculator work. Examples of activities are given.

Winner, Alice-Ann, and Margo D. McClung. "Computer Game Playing—'Turn-On' to Mathematics," *Arithmetic Teacher*, XXIX, No. 2 (October 1981), pp. 38–39.
The authors discuss the value of computer games, such as Blackjack, Guess My Number, and UFO, to fourth and fifth graders. They believe that concepts are learned and positive attitudes developed as games are played.

7

Teaching the Foundations of Numeration

Upon completion of Chapter 7 you will be able to:

1. Describe materials and activities dealing with discrete and continuous materials, classification, patterns, order and sequence, and spatial relationships.

2. Identify five principles that apply to the counting process.

3. Identify four common errors committed by children who are learning to count.

4. Use markers and numeral cards to show how children can learn to count the number of objects in a collection.

5. Demonstrate a procedure that introduces the meaning of zero.

6. Illustrate two types of materials for providing practice with numeral writing, and explain the difference between the two.

7. Distinguish between the cardinal and ordinal uses of numbers, and describe activities that help children understand ordinal uses.

8. Describe how music and finger-play activities, poems, and stories can enhance children's understanding of number concepts.

9. Describe three areas of number work that are particularly troublesome to children with learning handicaps, and describe at least one activity for each area.

Between 1920 and 1950 formal instruction in mathematics was delayed in many schools until at least the third grade. Children in kindergarten and the first and second grades were generally considered too immature to understand number concepts. Teaching of number concepts was often incidental and unplanned. Some teachers made good use of chance happenings to begin teaching mathematics, some did not, and some taught number concepts only if children exhibited an interest in learning about them.

Today few believe that children below the third grade should be denied a planned program of mathematics instruction. Systematic instruction begins at least as early as grade 1, and in many schools it begins in preschool and kindergarten classes.

EARLY MATHEMATICS EXPERIENCES

Most children understand some mathematical concepts at an early age. It is difficult to identify any particular moment in a child's life when the first numerical or quantitative concepts are acquired. Understanding of mathematical concepts begins imperceptibly and grows so gradually it is almost unnoticeable. It has been observed that children under two years of age have acquired some idea of *more*, usually in connection with food, such as taking the larger cookie or piece of candy when given a free choice.[1] Rochel Gelman and C. R. Gallistel report studies that show that two- and three-year-old children understand the process of counting objects. Although the children were not accurate, they showed that they were aware of the principles involved.[2]

The mathematical understandings children develop in preschool years depend upon their experiences. Many pick up simple number skills through both deliberate and incidental activities. For example, many children are taught to say number words in sequence. Usually this is done without regard to the meaning of the numbers. Such counting is referred to as **rote counting.** Though this skill is not particularly valuable in itself, it is a foundation upon which later work can be built. A deliberate effort to teach meaningful counting occurs when an adult encourages children to count tableware pieces as they help set the table. Children who play at game boards on which moves are determined by dice or spinners learn to count spots on dice and read spinner numerals, as well as to count moves around the board.

Many simple skills are acquired incidentally through play. Not only are these experiences fun but also they help children acquire vocabularies and background upon which later learning is based. In the same way that language is learned spontaneously in play, so are mathematics skills learned. Children use counting processes; fit shapes into forms; make symmetric patterns; build block structures; crawl over, under, and around objects; and engage in other activities with a mathematics orientation.

---

[1] George E. Hollister and Agnes G. Gunderson, *Teaching Mathematics in the Primary Grades* (Boston: D. C. Heath and Company, 1964), pp. 12–13.

[2] Rochel Gelman and C. R. Gallistel, *The Child's Understanding of Number* (Cambridge, Mass.: Harvard University Press, 1978), pp. 131–135.

PRENUMBER EXPERIENCES

Play experiences should continue in preschool, kindergarten, and first grade. A well-equipped classroom will contain a variety of commercial and teacher-made learning materials to help children develop a beginning understanding of:

- Discrete and continuous materials
- Classification
- Patterns
- Ordering and sequencing
- Spatial relationships

1. Discrete and Continuous Materials

Discrete materials are items that can be counted such as blocks and plastic disks, and continuous materials are those that are measured, such as pieces of ribbon or cans of water. Offer free-play and teacher-led activities with both types of materials. Activities you direct provide opportunities to emphasize characteristics of materials that will later be used for classification, patterning, and ordering and sequencing, as well as to develop vocabulary.

Children should have opportunities to learn through play during their preschool and kindergarten years. Ample time is needed for explorations with materials such as the following:

- Water or sand table with cans, plastic containers, and wooden boxes. These materials help children to develop an understanding of conservation of liquid and to learn intuitively the concepts of more and less than, equality, and ratio; they also provide opportunities for counting when the contents of one container are emptied into others. Sand is a suitable substitute for water if liquid is a problem.

- Large, natural-colored hollow blocks for constructions that children can climb on, into, under, and around and smaller, colored blocks for tabletop constructions. Among other things, these materials help develop children's understanding of spatial and size relationships and patterns, as well as providing early experiences that lead to counting of discrete objects.

- Structured materials, such as Cuisenaire rods, Dienes multibase blocks, and Unifix cubes (Figure 7-1). During play, children will discover and describe each material's characteristics and learn the

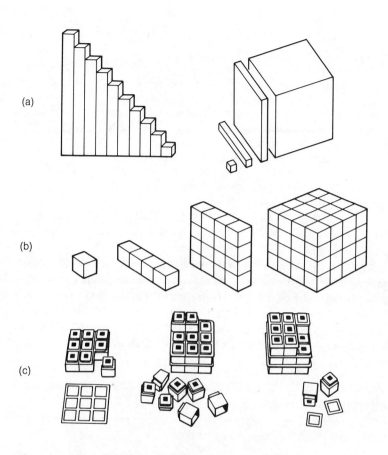

FIGURE 7-1
Structured materials.
(a) Cuisenaire rods, squares,
and blocks. (b) Dienes multibase arithmetic blocks.
(c) Unifix cubes.

foundations upon which understanding of the material's structured properties are built during teacher-directed lessons.

- Books. Children's books with mathematics themes are numerous
  and are fun and colorful. Children should hear them read and
  have time to look at them alone or with a partner. Examples are:
  Harriet Goes to the Circus by Betsy and Girelio Maestro (New
  York: Crown Publishers, Inc., 1977), *Zero Is Not Nothing* by
  Mindel and Harry Sitomer (New York: Thomas Y. Crowell,
  1978), and *Spaces, Shapes, and Sizes* by Jane Srivastava (New
  York: Thomas Y. Crowell, 1980).

- Adult clothes, such as hats, gloves, jackets, boots, and shoes.
  Children delight in "dressing up." At the same time they learn
  about one-to-one matching, pairs, larger and smaller, and other
  mathematics-related ideas.

You should also provide teacher-directed activities with group investigation–discussion and learning-center activities, in which children work
alone or in groups of two or three. The first activity suggests ways to
have children discuss and describe characteristics of familiar objects.

ACTIVITY 7-1 Describing Objects

- Use classroom objects, such as chairs, tables, filing cabinet, chalk, paper towels, and objects you provide, such as swatches of cloth, pieces of sandpaper, lengths of colored dowel rods, geometric shapes, and buttons. Have children describe them by use, color, texture (feel), materials, size, shape, and so on.
- Write experience stories dictated by children:
  "A chair is to sit on."
  "Our chairs are made of metal and plastic."
  "Our chairs are red and green."
  "There are big chairs and small chairs in our classroom."

Activities in which children make one-to-one matchings refine their understanding of the *as many as, more than,* and *fewer than* relations. Magnetic- or flannel-board materials are useful for the first two of the activities that follow. Canoes and paddles can be cut from construction paper and pictures from magazines and catalogs; attach one or more pieces of self-adhesive magnetic tape to the back of each item.[3]

ACTIVITY 7-2 Matching Canoes and Paddles

- Children match canoes and paddles.

- Have the children tell whether there are *as many as, more than,* or *fewer than* when matchings are complete.
- Remove the paddles and hold them in one hand. Ask, "Are there as many paddles as there are canoes?"

---

[3]Adhesive magnetic tape is available from school and business supply establishments.

- Variations: Use airplanes and hangers, cutout dolls and pieces of clothing, and other commonly matched items.

ACTIVITY 7-3 Sorting by Number of Wheels

- Make a pack of cards with pictures of vehicles, toys, and machines that have different numbers of wheels such as cars, bicycles, and one-wheeled cultivators.

Fewer	Same	More

- Place one card in the middle column of the chart. Children sort the cards and place each one in the proper column.

ACTIVITY 7-4 Matching Outlines

- Put outlines of common objects on a large sheet of heavy tagboard.

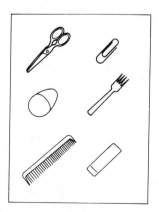

- Children match each real object with its outline.

ACTIVITY 7-5 Comparing Lengths

- Prepare a box of long and short pieces of twine, hair ribbons, shoe-laces, yarn, and so on. Children put them in the proper place on the chart.

Long
Short

---

2. Classification

Knowledge of **classification** schemes and processes is an important characteristic of a good problem solver. Classification skills begin in pre-school, kindergarten, and first grade, where children classify objects according to shape, color, size, thickness, and so on. Older children need opportunities to classify numbers according to odd–even, prime–composite, divisible by, multiple of, and so on. Many different sets of materials have been designed for classification activities. One set of blocks has sixty pieces, with five shapes, three colors, two sizes, and two thicknesses (Figure 7-2). People Pieces and Color Cubes are other commercial attribute materials. A collection of buttons with different colors, shapes,

FIGURE 7-2

Samples of shapes in a set of commercial attribute materials

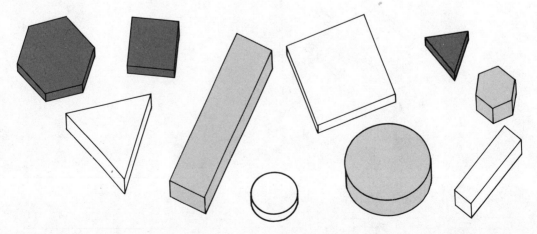

numbers of holes, and sizes, or a set of shapes cut from colored cardboard is easily assembled to substitute for commercial sets.

Children's first experiences with an attribute set should occur in freeplay situations. After a period of unstructured play, many children spontaneously separate a set by one of its attributes: color, shape, or size. Once a child does this, your question: "What did you do with the blocks this time?" may cause the child to reflect upon the scheme used. Do not press those who cannot readily explain a scheme.

When children give evidence that they are ready for structured work, introduce directed activities. Now Venn and tree diagrams can be used to organize the materials.

ACTIVITY 7-6   Classifying by Color

- Put two loops of yarn on a table. Label one *blue* and the other *red*.

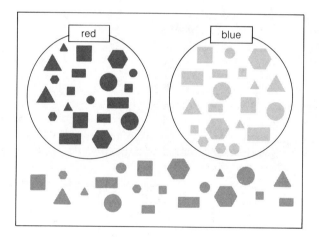

- Direct children to put attribute blocks into each circle according to color.
- Ask questions: "Why is this piece here?" (as you point to a red piece). "Why are these pieces here?" (as you point to the yellow pieces outside of both circles).
- Variations: Change labels so children sort by size, shape, thickness.

ACTIVITY 7-7   Classifying by Color and Shape

- Put down two overlapping circles. Label one *red* and the other one *triangle*.

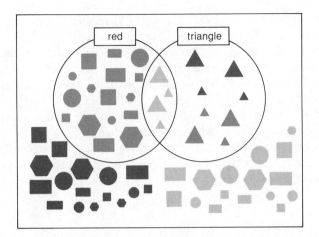

- Direct children to use the labels as guides to put blocks inside the circles.
- Ask questions: "Why are these shapes in this circle?" (as you sweep around the red circle). "Why are these pieces inside both of the circles (as you point to the red triangles). "Why are these pieces inside neither circle?" (as you point to nonred, nontriangular pieces).

___

ACTIVITY 7-8   Matching Colors and Shapes

___

- Draw a tree diagram on a large piece of tagboard. Label each arm. *Red* and *blue* might go on the first branch, with *triangle* and *circle* on the left branch and *square* and *rectangle* on the right branch.

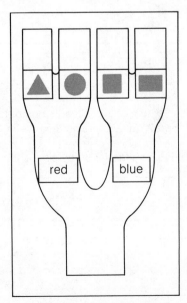

- Have each child select a red or blue attribute piece. Help each one move his or her piece from the bottom to its proper position on a topmost branch.
- Ask questions to direct children's attention to the reasons for the placement of each piece.
- Variations: Different labels can be put on each of the branches, or trees with different arrangements of branches can be used.

3. Patterns

Patterns abound in mathematics. As children work with patterns, they sharpen their perception and develop awareness of order, sequence, shapes, and aesthetics. A pattern center can be established at a table or on the floor in a corner. Pattern materials can be colored beads and lace, pegboards with colored golf tees, pattern blocks, attribute materials, and shapes cut from colored cardboard. Pattern activities are easily directed by problem cards such as those shown in Figure 7-3.

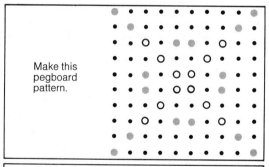

Make this pegboard pattern.

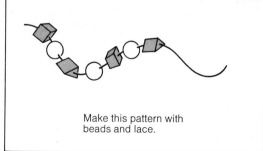

Make this pattern with beads and lace.

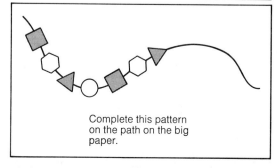

Complete this pattern on the path on the big paper.

FIGURE 7-3
Samples of pattern cards

As children work at pattern centers, check their work from time to time to be certain that they understand what they are doing and to discuss their work.

4. Order and Sequence

Order and sequence apply to both discrete and continuous materials. Through earlier activities with these materials children learned about the materials' characteristics; made one-to-one matchings; compared sets; and made gross comparisons of lengths, masses (weights), and volumes. Now they order sets by quantity and continuous materials by length, mass, and volume.

ACTIVITY 7-9   Ordering by Size

- Use a set of ½-inch dowel rods, each a different length, and a 2 by 4 block with holes of equal depth. Children are to order the dowels according to length, beginning with either the shortest or the longest rod.

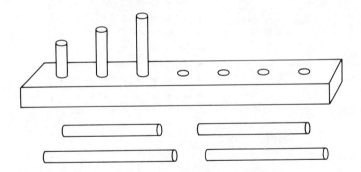

- Variations: Use covered baby-food jars with varying amounts of colored water or rice, paper dolls of various heights to be ordered on a magnetic or flannel board, or metal washers of varying sizes to be fitted over nails in a board.

ACTIVITY 7-10

- Use soup cans with equal-sized ¼-inch dowel rods. Put a can with four rods and one with seven rods before the children.

- Hold up a can with five rods and ask whether it has the same number, more than, or fewer than the four-rod can. Allow children to make a one-to-one matching of the rods, if necessary.
- Compare with the seven-rod can in the same way. Have the children determine where the five-rod can goes in relation to the other two cans.
- Do the same thing with other cans holding fewer than ten rods.
- Variations: Use domino cards, sets of buttons sewn or glued to cards, and sets of small plastic toys glued to cards.

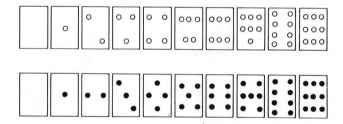

You will help children understand the new concepts if you pay close attention to vocabulary during these activities. For example, when continuous materials are compared, help children use terms such as *shorter than, taller than, longer than, heavier than, lighter than,* and *the same as.* When sets of objects are compared, children should use the terms *fewer than, more than,* and *the same number as.* (Later, when children learn the < and > symbols, the terms *less than* and *greater than* will be learned.)

5. Spatial Relationships

Many play activities lead to preliminary understandings of **spatial relationships.** Children's first work in this area can be through games of follow-the-leader that lead them *around* the blue-flowered bush, *under* the low monkey bar, and *through* the large concrete pipe. Be sure action words are emphasized. In-classroom follow-the-directions games develop spatial understandings and give practice in listening for and following directions: "Go stand *inside* the ring formed by the red hula hoop." "Place the yellow block *on top of* the green block."

Two- and three-step directions should follow the simpler ones: "Go to the *front* of the room, *touch* the chalkboard, and then go stand *beside* the file cabinet."

Later, concepts of *far*, *near*, *left*, *right*, *low*, *high*, and so on can be developed through similar games. Additional activities dealing with spatial relationships are presented in Chapter 15.

These activities for beginners in mathematics do not exhaust the things you can do to lay a firm foundation for later work. If you work with children still in the preoperational stage of mental development, you are encouraged to use some of these books for additional ideas:

Baratta-Lorton, Mary. *Mathematics Their Way* (Menlo Park, Cal.: Addison–Wesley Publishing Company, 1976).

———. *Workjobs* (Menlo Park, Cal.: Addison–Wesley Publishing Company, 1972).

———. *Workjobs II* (Menlo Park, Cal.: Addison–Wesley Publishing Company, 1978).

Copeland, Richard W. *Math Activities for Children* (Columbus, Ohio: Charles E. Merrill Publishing Company, 1979).

Cruikshank, Douglas E., David L. Fitzgerald, and Linda R. Jensen. *Young Children Learning Mathematics* (Boston: Allyn and Bacon, Inc., 1980).

Holt, Michael, and Zoltan Dienes. *Let's Play Math* (New York: Walker and Company, 1973).

Nuffield Mathematics Foundation. *Mathematics, the First Three Years* [London: John Murray (Publishers), Ltd., 1970]. (The Nuffield Foundation books are published in the United States by John Wiley & Sons, Inc., New York.)

Payne, Joseph N., ed. *Mathematics Learning in Early Childhood*, 37th Yearbook (Reston, Va.: National Council of Teachers of Mathematics, 1975).

Self-check of Objective 1

Distinguish between continuous and discrete materials and describe precounting activities children should have with both types of objects. Also describe at least one activity for each of these: classification, pattern, order and sequence, and spatial relationships.

FIRST COUNTING EXPERIENCES

Children enter kindergarten and first grade with varying number experiences and different foundation skills, including counting, so you should use the diagnostic procedures described in Chapter 3 to determine each child's counting skills. The meager backgrounds of some children may indicate that they are not yet ready to begin counting and need more prenumber activities. Other children may have advanced skills and be ready to deal with concepts such as place value as they learn about numbers greater than nine (see Chapter 8). Children who are learning to count need carefully sequenced, teacher-led activities.

Five principles apply to the process of determining the size of a set.

- The **one-to-one principle** involves *ticking off* the items in a collection in such a way that one and only one number is used as each item is counted.

- The **stable-order principle** means that counting numbers are arranged in a sequence that does not change.

- The **cardinal principle** gives special significance to the number named last, because not only is it associated with the last item but it also represents the total number of items in the set. This number, which tells *how many*, is the *cardinal* number of the set.

- The **abstraction principle** states that any collection of real or imagined objects can be counted.

- The **order-irrelevance principle** states that the order in which items are counted is irrelevant.[4]

An understanding of counting is built upon a child's intuitive understanding of the number *one*. There is no way to describe the meaning of *one* other than by holding up one finger, pointing to one marker on a magnetic board, or isolating some other single object in a similar way and then attaching the word *one*, and later, the numeral "1," to it. When an intuitive understanding of *one* is established, *two* can be thought of as *one-more-than one*, *three* as *one-more-than two*, and so on, until a child realizes that each number has a successor.

Gelman and Gallistel identify common errors committed by children who are learning to count:

- A child may make a coordination error. This occurs when the count is not started until after the first item has been touched, which results in an under-count; or when the count continues

---

[4]Rochel Gelman and C. R. Gallistel, *The Child's Understanding of Number* (Cambridge, Mass.: Harvard University Press, 1978).

after the final item has been touched, which results in an over-count.

- A child may make omit errors. This occurs when one or more items are skipped.

- A child may make a double-count error by counting one or more items more than once.

- A child may repeatedly use an idiosyncratic counting sequence such as *one, two, three, five, seven, eight.*[5]

An awareness of these errors will alert you to watch for them as children learn to count.

**Self-check
of Objectives 2 and 3**

Five principles that apply to the counting process are identified. Name and explain each one.

    Identify four errors commonly committed by children who are learning to count.

1. Learning to Count

Children's initial counting experiences should involve only a small number of objects. Activities like the following are recommended:

ACTIVITY 7-11 Counting Small Groups

- Put two markers on a magnetic board. Ask a child to name the number of markers.

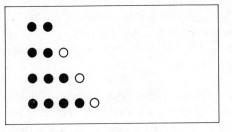

---

[5] Gelman and Gallistel, pp. 106–108.

- When the number *two* has been named, direct the children's attention to other groups of two in the classroom, such as two erasers in the chalkboard rail; have them locate other sets of two.
- Arrange a second set of two on the magnetic board beneath the first set. Put another marker of another color after these two. Ask, "How many markers in this set?"
- When the number *three* has been named, have the children find groups of three in the room. (If your room does not have several natural sets with two or three objects, prearrange some beforehand, such as groups of pictures, books, flowers, and similar objects.)

Sets for the rest of the numbers through nine should gradually be developed and studied in a similar manner. As counting is taught, stress numerical order. Also stress the **cardinal** number by emphasizing it for each set you count: "One, two, *three*." After a child has counted ask, "What is the last number you named? How many shapes (books, disks) in the set?" Figure 7-4 shows how a magnetic board or chart with geometric shapes might appear after all nine numbers have been studied.

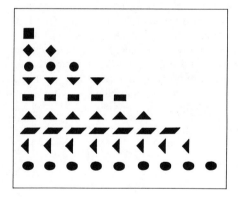

FIGURE 7-4
Geometric shapes used on a sequence-of-sets chart to illustrate the one-more-than, or successor, pattern

There are many counting-center activities you can set up once children learn to count.[6]

Zero requires special attention. It is not a number children are likely to experience before school, and the set with which it is associated, that is, one with no members, is more difficult for children to comprehend than sets that contain objects. Story situations like this one are useful for introducing zero.

[6] For example, see "Sets" and "Number Sequences" in *Workjobs* and "A Photographic Collage of the Developmental Levels" in *Workjobs II*, both by Baratta-Lorton; Chapter 3 in Cruikshank, Fitzgerald, and Jensen; Section One of Leonard M. Kennedy, *Models for Mathematics in the Elementary School* (Belmont, Cal.: Wadsworth Publishing Company, 1967); and Chapter 1 of Mary E. Platts, ed., *Plus*, rev. ed. (Stevensville, Mich.: Educational Services, Inc., 1975).

ACTIVITY 7-12   Learning about Zero

- Put three felt flowers on a flannel board.

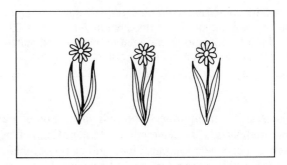

- Say "These are some flowers that were growing in my garden. How many flowers are there?"
- Remove one of the flowers and say "I went to my garden on Saturday and picked one of the flowers. How many were left?"
- Remove the two flowers. "I picked the two flowers on Sunday. How many were left?" Children will respond with: "There aren't any." "They are all gone." "None." Accept all responses.
- Show several empty containers, such as boxes with lids, covered jars, and paper bags, and ask the children to describe their contents. Some will say that they are empty. At this point introduce the word *zero* as the name for the number that tells how many flowers were left in the garden and the number of things in the containers.

Self-check of Objectives 4 and 5

Prepare a set of materials (including objects and numeral cards) that can be used to introduce children to the process of counting.

The flower-garden situation is only one of many that can be used to introduce zero as a number. Children need more than one activity dealing with this concept. Make up a similar story and describe the materials you would use with it.

---

2. Learning to Read and Write Numbers

The initial steps in learning to count take place before children are taught to write numerals. It is not necessary, however, to teach the meaning of all the numbers 0 through 9 before beginning instruction in reading them.

After children have learned the meaning of *two*, *three*, and *four*, the numerals "2," "3," and "4" can be introduced.

Children can match numerals and their sets through exercises with markers. Magnetic or felt numerals are particularly useful because children can put a numeral alongside a set without having to write. Placing a numeral with its set and placing the correct number of markers next to a numeral are the most basic and the simplest exercises.

ACTIVITY 7-13   Matching Numeral and Set Cards

- Put set cards in a pocket chart. Give children numeral cards, beginning with *1*, to put in front of the sets.

1	○
2	○ ○
3	○ ○ ○
4	○ ○ ○ ○
5	○ ○ ○ ○ ○
6	○ ○ ○ ○ ○ ○
7	○ ○ ○ ○ ○ ○ ○
8	○ ○ ○ ○ ○ ○ ○ ○
9	○ ○ ○ ○ ○ ○ ○ ○ ○

- Variations: (1) Begin with *9* and reverse the order of putting the numeral cards in the chart. (2) Put the cards in the chart without regard to order. (3) Put numeral cards in the chart, and have the children put in the set cards.

ACTIVITY 7-14   Matching Domino Cards and Numerals

- Give children domino cards to put in sequence, beginning with *zero*. Have children match each domino card with its numeral card. Later begin with nine and reverse the order.

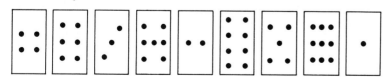

- Variation: Put a card in front of the children. Ask, "Which card goes just before this card?" "Which card goes just after it?" "Who can put the rest of the cards in place?"

Encourage children to identify the number of a set on sight, rather than by counting each time. Most children will learn to recognize sets of four or five. Some will learn common domino patterns for larger sets. Few persons, including adults, will recognize the number of objects in randomly organized sets larger than four or five.

ACTIVITY 7-15   Matching Numeral and Set Circles

- Use magnetized circles of colored cardboard containing a numeral and a set. Cut the circles so that the numeral is on one half and the set on the other half.
- Put the set halves on the board so the children can match each one with the proper numeral half.

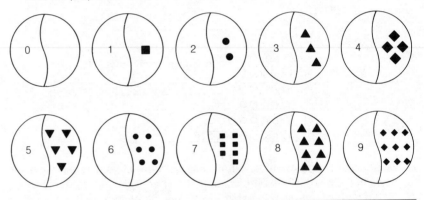

The manuscript form of writing numerals is used almost exclusively, even though most people change to the cursive form for writing words (Figure 7-5).

Write-in textbooks for the first grade include instruction pages on which children can practice writing. A lesson commonly begins with an example of a numeral. Next the numeral is made with broken lines or is rendered in light-colored ink for children to trace. Then only the starting point appears, showing the child where to begin writing the numeral. Last there are spaces in which the child practices writing the numerals with no guidance. Figure 7-6 shows a typical exercise.

FIGURE 7-5

(a) Manuscript form for writing numerals. (b) Cursive form for writing numerals.

1 2 3 4 5 6 7 8 9 0

(a)

1 2 3 4 5 6 7 8 9 0

(b)

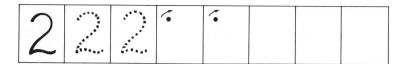

FIGURE 7-6
The sequence of steps for teaching children to write a numeral

The authors of the CDA Math Program[7] advise against requiring children to trace ready-made numerals. They have observed that many children constantly check their progress when they are required to trace models and become upset when they stray too far from the models. The authors recommend that children be given sheets of paper that contain four different numeral models. A sample of one practice page is shown in Figure 7-7. Children practice by writing the numerals in the open spaces in each numeral's box. If they wish, they can trace the models.

As children gain experience in writing numerals, most of them make numerals correctly and neatly during practice sessions. However, some are less careful when some other phase of mathematics is emphasized. Reminding a child of how a particular numeral is formed is usually all that is needed to prevent a bad habit from developing. If a chart showing the correct way to write each numeral is posted in the room, a child who makes an error can look at it to see how a particular numeral should appear. If necessary, the child can go to the chart to trace the numeral a few times with a finger before writing it on paper.

Instruction in reading number words should follow instruction in reading numerals. Even though these words are usually taught during reading lessons, they should also be taught as part of the mathematics program. Many of the exercises used for associating numerals and pattern cards can be used to learn the words and their meanings. The children match cards, numerals, and words by arranging cards in a pocket chart,

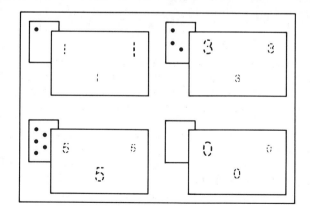

FIGURE 7-7
Sample numeral-writing practice page recommended by *CDA Math* (used by permission)

---

[7] Morton Botel, Robert W. Wirtz, and Max Beberman, *Memo from the Authors of CDA Math—Introducing Children to the Primary CDA Math Program* (Washington, D.C.: Curriculum Development Associates, Inc., 1973), pp. 10–11.

as shown in Activity 7-13, or on flannel or magnetic board. You should also encourage children to use number words in their own stories.

Self-check of Objective 6

Describe the two numeral-writing pages discussed here and tell why the authors of *CDA Math* prefer theirs.

3. Using the Number Line to Relate Sequence and Counting

A **number line** is a useful device for children of all ages. Children in kindergarten and first grade can use a number line marked on the classroom floor as they learn to count. Such a line can be painted or put down with masking tape. The points should be about 14 inches apart, with the numerals that name the points printed on cards rather than on the floor to increase the number line's versatility.

ACTIVITY 7-16   Walking the Number Line I

- Group children so the line runs from their left to their right.

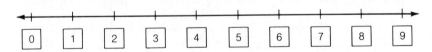

- Have a child stand on *0*. As the child takes a step from *0* to *1*, the children say *one*. Emphasize that it is the step that is counted not the *1* card. The count continues in unison as the child moves to *9*.
- Have each child walk the line while the group counts in unison or the child counts alone.
- Variations: (1) Children begin at *9* and walk from there to *0*. Again, emphasize the number of steps. (2) Remove the cards, mix them, and have one or two children put them in place. (3) Have the children close their eyes while you remove one or two cards, or interchange some. Have the children tell the names of the missing cards or reorder them properly.

Next, children should use a number line placed on the chalkboard. It can be purchased or made from a length of adding machine tape. Place the line within reach of the children, so they can point to numerals *1* through *9* and indicate steps along the line with chalk. Also, a small number line should be attached to each child's desk for individual use.

4. Learning the Ordinal Uses of Numbers

Number is used in the **ordinal** sense when the order of objects in a set is established—first, second, or third.

Textbooks for the primary grades instruct children in the use of *first, second, third, . . . , middle,* and *last.* You should bring up the use of these words and their meanings whenever you can. Times to develop the words' meanings are when children line up, when books are shelved by volume numbers, and when children are learning the order of letters in the alphabet. Children often learn ordinal concepts so well through experiences like these that textbook materials become unnecessary.

What are differences between the cardinal and ordinal uses of numbers? Describe how numbers are used in the ordinal sense.

Self-check of Objective 7

5. Number Rhymes, Songs, and Finger-Play Activities

Number rhymes, songs, and finger-play activities familiarize children with number names and their sequence. Children enjoy poems because of their rhythmic sound and the finger-play activities generated by many of them. Nursery-rhyme books, poetry anthologies, and teacher's manuals for some mathematics series are good sources of songs, rhymes, and poems.

Songs such as "One Little Brown Bird"[8] are enjoyed by young children. The verses of many of these songs give the numbers in sequence. The first three verses of "One Little Brown Bird" are

> One little brown bird, up and up he flew,
> Along came another and that made two.
>
> Two little brown birds, sitting in a tree,
> Along came another one and that made three.
>
> Three little brown birds, then up came one more,
> What's all the noise about? That made four.

Children's records are excellent sources of songs for early number work. Most children listen intently to such songs, eagerly awaiting the chance to join in when the record is repeated.

"Chickadees"[9] is an example of a finger-play.

[8] *Sixty Songs for Little Children* (London: Oxford University Press, 1933). (Used by permission.)

[9] Marion F. Grayson, *Let's Do Fingerplays* (Washington, D.C.: Robert B. Luce, Inc., 1962), p. 60. (Reprinted by permission of Robert B. Luce, Inc.)

Five little chickadees sitting on the floor;
  (Hold up hand, fingers extended.)
One flew away and then there were four.
  (Fold down one finger as each bird flies away.)

Four little chickadees sitting in a tree;
One flew away and then there were three.

Three little chickadees looking at you;
One flew away and then there were two.

Two little chickadees sitting in the sun;
One flew away and then there was one.

One little chickadee sitting alone;
He flew away and then there was none.

Finger-play activities can be found in some teacher's manuals, in Scott and Thompson's *Rhymes for Fingers and Flannelboards*,[10] and in Grayson's *Let's Do Fingerplays*.

**Self-check
of Objective 8**

Explain why teachers of young children should include number songs, finger-play activities, and stories and poems in their mathematics program.

SPECIAL STUDENTS AND COUNTING

Well-equipped settings for free-play activities and well-planned developmental activities are essential for all children. Children with learning handicaps need activities like the ones discussed in this chapter. However, because of their handicaps, many of these children need special attention. For some, the time spent with concrete materials needs to be increased. The reasons for lessons must be made particularly clear, so the children can associate current work with previous activities. This helps them fill in a topic's schema and prevent gaps in their learning. Learning aids must be selected with the children's handicaps in mind. For example, children with visual and certain physical handicaps need large-sized blocks rather than small ones, rigid materials like dowel rods rather than yarn or ribbons for comparing lengths of objects, and textured rather than drawn numerals for numeral recognition.

Certain areas of early number work are troublesome for learning-handicapped children. Some of these areas are discussed, and special activities and materials are recommended.

---

[10] Louise B. Scott and Jesse J. Thompson, *Rhymes for Fingers and Flannelboards* (St. Louis: Webster Publishing Company, 1960).

1. Coordination, Omit, and Double-Counting Errors

Children who commit these errors by making incorrect one-to-one matches between objects and the counting numbers should be encouraged to touch and move objects as they are counted.

ACTIVITY 7-17 Counting by Touch

- Have a child count at a desk top, or on a large sheet of paper, separated into halves by a line down the middle. The child moves each object from the left side to the right side as it is counted.

This activity diminishes the chances that the child will begin or end the count improperly, will fail to count one or more objects, or will double-count some. Once consistent accuracy is achieved when counting this way, have the child count objects aligned in a row, but without moving them.

2. Sequence Errors

Children who have difficulty remembering the sequence of numbers and the numbers that come before and after another number will benefit from *count on* activities. These activities begin at a number other than one; a child begins at a number such as "6" and counts from it.

Before *count on* activities are used, each child must be aware that the last number named is the cardinal number of a set. Be sure that you and the children emphasize the last number: "One, two, *three*." Activities at a walk-on number line can stress sequence and cardinality.

ACTIVITY 7-18 Walking the Number Line II

- Begin by walking the number line yourself and saying, "One, two, three, four. I took four steps."
- Have each child walk on the line and count; then you or the child should state the number of steps the child walked.
- Turn over all cards following a given card, for example, 4. Have a child walk from 0 to 4; then ask, "What will be the number for the next step you take?" Turn over 5; repeat for 6, and so on.

Special practice in *counting on* from small sets should be given these children.

ACTIVITY 7-19 Counting On

---

*Begin with a set of four red poker chips.

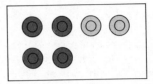

- Have a child count or name the quantity on sight. After the children say "four," put down a blue chip. When the blue chip is in place, have the children say "five." Put down another blue chip and say "six." Continue until nine chips are counted.
- Variations: (1) Begin with sets other than four. (2) Begin with a set of five (or some other number) and count backward as objects are removed one by one.

One teacher observed by the author has children pop an open palm against their forehead as "four" is spoken. This "pops" the number into each child's head. Then as objects are added to the original set, each child holds up a finger for each number as it is counted on. To count backward, the number is again "popped" into the child's head, and a finger is lowered for each number that is counted.

3. Errors in Writing Numerals

Many children commit reversal errors or mistake one numeral for another while learning to write numerals. Most of them outgrow these errors; but the problems persist for some children with learning impairments, particularly those with visual handicaps, visual discrimination and spatial organization problems, and motor coordination weaknesses. Special materials for these children include large numerals cut from felt or sandpaper glued to cards and flat boxes with wet sand in which numerals are drawn. As children use these materials, there is a kinesthetic reaction that helps them remember each numeral's configuration. Numerals written on the chalkboard and traced with chalk or a wet sponge are also helpful. Some children are helped by having someone trace a numeral on their back or on the back of their writing hand just before a numeral is traced or written.

Three areas that are troublesome for children with learning handicaps are discussed. Identify each one, and describe at least one activity for helping these children deal with them.

*Self-check
of Objective 9*

SUMMARY

Mathematics begins for most children before they begin school. Their early play experiences provide a basis for later learning. They should continue to have gamelike activities in preschool, kindergarten, and the first part of grade 1. Many of their activities can concern discrete and continuous materials, classification, patterns, order and sequence, and spatial relationships. Five principles govern the act of counting: the one-to-one, the stable-order, the cardinal, the abstraction, and the order-irrelevant principles. Children frequently miscount because they start or end the count improperly, they skip or double-count items, and they use idiosyncratic counting sequences.

When children are ready for counting, they must have many experiences with a variety of manipulative materials. Carefully planned activities will enable children to understand the meaning of counting and the way numerals are used to record the number of items in a collection, or set. Once children know the meaning of a number, they are ready to read and write its numeral. Reading number words should be a part of the mathematics program. There are two forms of writing numerals, the manuscript and the cursive. Manuscript numerals are used most often. Children learn to write numerals by tracing patterns or making copies alongside already written models. Simple finger-play activities, songs, stories, and poems involving numbers contribute to children's background for learning mathematics.

Children with learning handicaps frequently have difficulty learning to count and to write numerals. Special attention needs to be given to the counting process to avoid coordination, omit, and double-counting errors and to help these children learn the number sequence. Textured numerals, tracing at the chalkboard, and numerals traced on a child's back are necessary for some children as they learn to write numerals.

STUDY QUESTIONS AND ACTIVITIES

1. One way to assure yourself of an adequate assortment of materials and activities when you begin teaching is to make a mathematics-teaching file. Start a file now; then add to it as you read

each chapter of this book. Each of the remaining chapters has one end-of-chapter activity that suggests new activities and materials for each one. Authors of several of the articles in this chapter's reading list suggest counting, sorting and classifying, seriation, and one-to-one matching activities. Use these articles as sources for at least one activity dealing with each of these topics. Do not include activities that are described in this chapter.

2. V. Ray Kurtz (see reading list) reports that 21 percent of the Kansas teachers who responded to a questionnaire about their kindergarten mathematics program indicated that their program was inadequate. Seventy-eight percent said they used an adopted series as the basis for their program, and 67 percent used a consumable workbook. Contact a kindergarten teacher, and discuss the basis for this teacher's program. Are there specific performance objectives? Are any of the competencies that Kurtz considers "clearly not" for kindergarten children in this teacher's program? What teaching–learning materials are used? How does this teacher feel about the adequacy of the program? What changes, if any, would the teacher make?

3. Observe or work with a group of kindergarteners who are counting small collections of objects. Do any of them commit coordination, omit, or double-counting errors? Use procedures from this chapter or elsewhere to help them overcome their errors. Which procedure(s) works best?

4. Nancy Smith and Karla Wendelin (see reading list) name ten strands of concepts commonly taught in kindergarten through grade 3. They identify words associated with each strand and then describe several books that offer opportunities for discussion about the concept and vocabulary. Read one book each for at least four of the strands. List the terms for the strand contained in each of the books. Write a brief description of a lesson that uses one of the books as the basis for a discussion with a group of kindergarten or first-grade children.

KEY TERMS

rote counting	cardinal principle
classification	abstraction principle
patterns	order-irrelevance principle
order and sequence	cardinal
spatial relationships	number line
one-to-one principle	ordinal
stable-order principle	

FOR FURTHER READING

Bruni, James V., and Helene Silverman. "Making and Using Attribute Materials," *Arithmetic Teacher*, XXII, No. 2 (February 1975), pp. 88–95. Describes a 54-piece attribute set made from colored oaktag. Explains activities for children of all elementary grades.

Burton, Grace M. "Helping Parents Help Their Preschool Children," *Arithmetic Teacher*, XXV, No. 8 (May 1978), pp. 12–14. Though intended for preschool teachers, the article suggests many experiences for children that are suitable for kindergarten and some first-grade children. Includes activities dealing with sorting and classifying, counting, geometry, and money.

Ginsburg, Herbert P. "Children's Surprising Knowledge of Arithmetic," *Arithmetic Teacher*, XXVIII, No. 1 (September 1980), pp. 42–44.
Ginsburg cites research that shows that young children exhibit surprising intellectual strengths, ranging from intuitions about *more*, to counting procedures for mental addition, to invented strategies for school arithmetic. Teachers are challenged to tap these hidden resources.

Hamrick, Kathy B. "Are We Introducing Mathematical Symbols Too Soon?" *Arithmetic Teacher*, XXVIII, No. 3 (November 1980), pp. 14–15.
Hamrick believes many children are given symbols too soon. Children are ready for symbols when they can discuss a topic orally, using objects or pictures, if necessary.

Hollis, Loye Y. "Mathematical Concepts of Young Children," *Arithmetic Teacher*, XXIX, No. 2 (October 1981), pp. 24–27.
The author summarizes research about children's knowledge of mathematics and presents a list of competencies for three-, four-, and five-year-old children.

Horak, Virginia M., and Willis J. Horak. "Developing Mathematical Understandings with Bead Strings," *Arithmetic Teacher*, XXX, No. 4 (December 1982), pp. 6–9.
A set of bead strings containing one to ten beads on each string provide opportunities for children to investigate many early number concepts. Activities are described.

Huey, J. Frances. "Learning Potential of the Young Child," *Educational Leadership*, XXIII (November 1965), pp. 117–120. A brief discussion of how preschool children develop concepts and begin to understand symbols; included are ten suggestions to help young children develop concepts and generalizations.

Jensen, Rosalie, and David R. O'Neil. "That's Eggzactly Right!" *Arithmetic Teacher*, XXIX, No. 7 (March 1982), pp. 8–13.
Plastic eggs, egg cartons, and small objects provide counting, ordering, matching, comparing, and other number experiences.

Kurtz, V. Ray. "Kindergarten Mathematics—A Survey," *Arithmetic Teacher*, XXV, No. 8 (May 1978), pp. 51–53. Reporting on a survey made in Kansas, the author gives the competencies that are *clearly*, *questionable*, and *clearly not* for kindergarten children. He also reports that over 75 percent of the teachers use an adopted series as a basis for their program.

Lettieri, Frances M. "Meet the Zorkies: A New Attribute Material," *Arithmetic Teacher*, XXVI, No. 1 (September 1978), pp. 36–39. Zorkies, natives of the planet Zorka, differ in color, and number of eyes, legs, and arms; altogether there are 36. Includes illustrated samples of the 34 activity cards, which deal with attribute discrimination, equivalence and difference relations, ordering relations, and transformations.

Liedtke, W. W. "Rational Counting," *Arithmetic Teacher*, XXVI, No. 2 (October 1978), pp. 20–26. Presents the bases for developing skill in rational counting through classifying, matching, and ordering and patterns. Describes and illustrates materials and procedures for developing children's background in these skills.

———, and L. D. Nelson. "Activities in Mathematics for Preschool Children," *Arithmetic Teacher*, XX, No. 7 (November 1973), pp. 536–541. The authors list a variety of activities with manipulative materials. Three different types of activities are discussed: classification, conservation (one-to-one correspondence), and seriation.

Lindquist, Mary M., and Marcia E. Dana. "Make Counting Really Count—Counting Projects for First and Second Grades," *Arithmetic Teacher*, XXV, No. 8 (May 1978), pp. 4–11. Counting will count for children who engage in the many counting and recording activities described. The headings include: Listing Counts, Drawing Counts, Hunting Counts, Tallying Counts, Collecting Counts, and others.

Smith, Nancy J., and Karla Hawkins Wendelin. "Using Children's Books to Teach Mathematical Concepts," *Arithmetic Teacher*, XXIX, No. 3 (November 1981), pp. 10–15.
The authors identify mathematics concepts for kindergarten and grades 1 through 3 and then name children's books that deal with each one.

Van de Walle, John A. "Track Cards," *Arithmetic Teacher*, XXV, No. 6 (March 1978), pp. 22–26. Teacher-made track cards provide the basis for many kindergarten and primary grade activities enhancing children's thinking, creativity, verbal skills, understanding of certain topological and symmetry concepts, vocabulary, and so on. Includes ten different types of activities, along with directions for preparing track cards.

Yvon, Bernard R., and Eunice B. Spooner. "Variations in Kindergarten Mathematics Programs and What a Teacher Can Do About It," *Arithmetic Teacher*, XXIX, No. 5 (January 1982), pp. 46–52.
The authors surveyed commercial kindergarten mathematics programs and concluded that reliance on a single published program does not give children a well-rounded experience. They describe teacher-made materials for 16 hands-on projects to balance the program.

8

Extending Understanding of Numeration

Upon completion of Chapter 8 you will be able to:

1. Use markers or other objects to demonstrate one-to-many, many-to-one, and many-to-many correspondences, and describe real-life situations that deal with these correspondences.

2. Describe the major characteristics of the Hindu–Arabic numeration system.

3. Illustrate and describe at least three place-value devices, and demonstrate how they are used to help children understand the meaning of numbers greater than 10.

4. Explain why an abacus is a useful device for representing numbers, and demonstrate how to use one to represent a number such as 647,093.

5. Explain skip-counting, and describe activities for helping children learn to skip-count.

6. Distinguish between compact and expanded numerals, and write at least three different expanded forms.

7. Tell a story that can be used to introduce children to integers, and illustrate how number lines can be used to clarify the meaning of these numbers.

8. Describe two calculator activities for helping children understand numbers greater than nine.

9. Identify two problem areas associated with larger numbers that children with learning disabilities often experience, and describe ways of helping children overcome them.

10. Identify two areas of study that can be used to expand gifted and talented students' understanding of numeration.

If children are to work effectively with the **Hindu–Arabic numeration system,** they must understand the system thoroughly and not simply have a rote knowledge of it. Therefore the topics—one-to-many, many-to-one, and many-to-many correspondences; the Hindu–Arabic numeration system; and integers—in this chapter must be presented in a manner that permits children to learn the fundamentals and rationale behind them.

ONE-TO-MANY, MANY-TO-ONE, AND MANY-TO-MANY CORRESPONDENCES

Counting is a process of making a **one-to-one correspondence** between a collection of objects and the natural numbers 1, 2, 3, ... It is important that children understand one-to-one correspondence as the basis for counting. It is important that they recognize that one-to-many, many-to-one, and many-to-many correspondences have useful applications, too.

Examples of **one-to-many correspondences** are place value (1 ten is equal to 10 ones), money (1 nickel is equivalent to 5 pennies), linear measure (1 meter is equivalent to 100 centimeters), and weight measure (1 gram is equivalent to 1000 milligrams). **Many-to-one correspondences** are also illustrated by place value (10 tens equal 1 hundred), money (2 nickels are equivalent to 1 dime), linear measure (12 inches are equivalent to 1 foot), and weight measures (16 ounces are equivalent to 1 pound).

Many rate-type problems are based on these same correspondences. An example is a problem involving distance traveled. "A bicyclist can travel at an average rate of 12 miles in 1 hour. What is the time required to travel 36 miles?" The rate of travel is a many-to-one correspondence, and the answer is a **many-to-many correspondence.** The rate in the problem "If 2 pencils cost 15¢, how many can you buy with 60¢?" is a many-to-many correspondence, as is the answer.

Commercial and teacher-made activities will help children understand these correspondences. *Chip Trading Activities* kits[1] offer a variety of activities.

A kit contains four colors of circular chips, chip boards, chip tills, abacus boards, dice, numeral and operations cards, and manuals (Figure 8-1). The Banker's Game provides opportunities for children to practice many-to-one and one-to-many trades.[2]

[1] Patricia Davidson, Grace Galton, and Arlene Fair, *Chip Trading Activities* (Fort Collins, Colo.: Scott Resources). Used with permission.

[2] This game is adapted from Davidson, Galton, and Fair, *Chip Trading Activities, Book I.* Scott Resources. Used with permission.

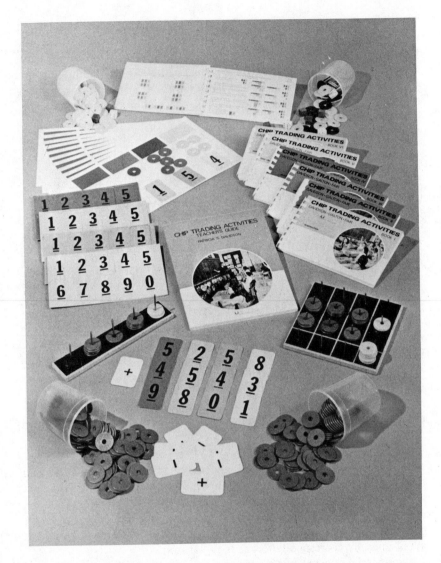

FIGURE 8-1
Chip-trading materials.
Photograph courtesy of Scott
Resources, Fort Collins,
Colorado.

GAME   Banker's Game

- Materials: 1 red, 15 each green, blue, and yellow chips, 1 chip board for banker, 1 chip till for each player, 1 die.
- Players: 3–5 (one acts as banker).
- Order of Play: Roll the die, with highest or lowest roll going first.
- Rules: Banker sets up bank as shown.

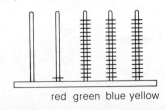

red green blue yellow

Chips are traded this way:

> 1 blue = 3 yellow
> 1 green = 3 blue
> 1 red = 3 green.

The first player rolls the die and asks the banker for the number of chips indicated on it. If the number is 5, the player gets five yellow chips. Three of the yellow chips are exchanged for 1 blue chip; all chips are placed on the chip till. Next players have their turns in order. Play continues until one player gets a red chip.

R	G	B	Y

- Variations: (1) Play can begin with each player having one red chip. Players trade down until one player clears her or his till. (2) The rate of exchange can be different. A 10-for-1 rate gives practice with the base-ten scheme.

Can you use poker chips, or other objects, to demonstrate each of these correspondences: one-to-many, many-to-one, many-to-many? Describe a real-life situation that deals with each correspondence.

*Self-check
of Objective 1*

THE HINDU–ARABIC NUMERATION SYSTEM

In studying our own numeration system, children do not need to be overwhelmed with historical details. Instead they should acquire an understanding of how the system developed.

Early development took place in India. It is likely that our present system evolved from one having twenty symbols: nine for units, nine for tens, one for hundreds, and one for thousands.[3] We know that numerals were used in a place-value scheme by about 600 A.D.[4] Then the forerunners of today's numerals were developed and first appeared in written records in about 700 A.D. These are called Devanagari numerals (Figure 8-2).

---

[3] Florian Cajori, *A History of Mathematics* (New York: The Macmillan Company, 1919), p. 89.

[4] H. A. Freebury, *A History of Mathematics* (New York: The Macmillan Company, 1961), p. 72.

1 2 3 8 4 5 7 < Ɛ O
1   2   3   4   5   6   7   8   9   0

There are conflicting statements about the date of the origin of zero.
Freebury says zero appears in the Devanagari numerals of the eighth century. Smith says, "The earliest undoubted occurrence of a zero in India
is seen in an inscription at Gwalior. In this inscription 50 and 270 are
both written with zeros."[5] He goes on to say that the date of origin will
probably never be known but that it most likely was in India in the ninth
century.[6]

The Arabs' contribution to the advancement of our numeration system
lies more in their transmitting information about it to other parts of the
world than from their refinements of it. The Arabs translated into their
language much of the knowledge of science and mathematics that had
been developed and recorded in Greece, India, and elsewhere. Some of
these Arabic translations are our only sources of knowledge about Greek
and Indian achievements. One translation, called *The Book of al-Khowarazmi on Hindu Number*, explained the use of Hindu numerals. From
the author's name, al-Khowarazmi, came the word *algorithm*,[7] which today means the procedures used to perform number operations. This author also wrote a book called *Al jabr*, which was about reduction and
cancellation. *Al jabr* was much used in Europe where the title was eventually corrupted into *algebra* and came to be used to describe the science
of equations.[8] Today the word names one of the important branches of
mathematics.

The crusades, the increased trade among nations of the Mediterranean
area, and the Moorish conquest of North Africa and Spain resulted in
the spread of the Hindu–Arabic numeration system to many parts of
Europe. Roman numerals and the abacus, which had been spread
throughout Europe during the Roman conquest, were being used there
when the Hindu–Arabic system arrived. Gradually the Hindu–Arabic
system and the use of algorithms were recognized, and for a time the two
systems coexisted. Eventually the *algorists* won out over the *abacists*, and
by the sixteenth century the Hindu–Arabic numeration system was predominant.

The characteristics of the Hindu–Arabic numeration system are summarized and explained in the following paragraphs.

---

[5] David Eugene Smith, *History of Mathematics, Vol. II* (Boston: Ginn & Company, 1953),
p. 69.

[6] Smith, p. 69.

[7] Freebury, *A History of Mathematics*, p. 76.

[8] Freebury, p. 77.

1. There is a base number, which in this system is 10. During their first counting experiences, people undoubtedly used their fingers for keeping track of the count. After all ten fingers had been used, it was necessary to use a supplementary means for keeping track of the count. It was natural that the grouping was based on ten, the number of fingers available.

2. There is a symbol for zero. It is a place holder in a numeral like 302, where it indicates that there are no tens. It is also the number that indicates the size, or numerical value, of a set that has no objects in it.

3. There are as many symbols, including zero, as the number indicating the base. The symbols in the Hindu–Arabic system are 0, 1, 2, 3, 4, 5, 6, 7, 8, and 9.

4. The place-value scheme has a ones place on the right, a base position to the left of the ones place, a base times base (b^2) position next, a base times base times base (b^3) position next, and so on. Beginning at any place in the system, the next position to the left is ten times greater, and the position to the right is one-tenth as large. This characteristic makes it possible to represent fractional numbers as well as whole numbers with the system.

5. The system makes it possible to make computations using only paper and pencil and a standard algorithm. Though the use of the standard algorithms will probably diminish with the advent of the calculator, their place in a mathematics program is assured for the foreseeable future, because of the role they play in helping children understand the four operations. (Each algorithm is explored fully in later chapters.)

State the characteristics of the Hindu–Arabic numeration system.

Self-check
of Objective 2

TEACHING THE HINDU–ARABIC SYSTEM

Classrooms at every level should be well-equipped with place-value materials. Concrete–manipulative materials give young children the means to represent numbers greater than nine in ways that make place-value concepts clearer than when work is begun at the pictorial and abstract levels of the teaching–learning hierarchy. Both commercial and teacher-

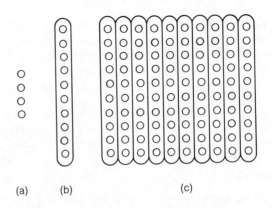

FIGURE 8-3
Set of beansticks showing (a) loose beans, (b) a tens stick, and (c) a hundreds raft

(a)   (b)   (c)

made materials and proportional and nonproportional materials are use-ful. Proportional materials are designed to show that 10 is ten times larger than 1 and that 100 is ten times larger than 10. The Cuisenaire rods, flats, and cubes and Dienes materials shown in Figure 7-1 are commer-cially produced proportional materials. Unifix cubes are proportional when 10 cubes are joined to make a ten-unit piece, and 10 ten-unit pieces are put side-by-side to represent 100. Beansticks are proportional teacher-made materials. Loose beans represent units, 10 beans glued to a coffee-stirrer stick represent ten, and 10 ten-sticks glued together form a raft to represent 100 (Figure 8-3). Tongue depressors and ¼-inch dowel rods are proportional when 10 are bundled together to represent ten, and 10

Tens	Ones

(a)

(b)

FIGURE 8-4
Place-value devices illustrating the meaning of the number 17. (a) Place-value pocket chart. (b) Place-value frames. (c) Place-value box.

Tens	Ones

(c)

tens bundles are bundled to represent 100. Figure 8-4 shows three devices for representing tens and ones with sticks.

Chip trading materials are nonproportional because a single chip of a color different from that of the unit chip represents 10, and a single chip of still another color represents 100. An abacus like the one in Figure 8-6 is also nonproportional because a single bead on a wire represents ten times the value of a bead to its right.

Children's first experiences with **place value** should occur through free play with proportional materials, as suggested in Chapter 7. Before you begin instruction about place value, be certain your children can do rational counting to at least 9 and can read and write the numerals for the numbers 0 through 9. They should also be able to express the numbers 1 through 9 as addition combinations. For example, three can be expressed as "3 + 0," "2 + 1," "1 + 2," and "0 + 3." This ability is not important for the combinations themselves but as a basis for understanding that a number like 15 can be expressed as "1 ten and 5 ones" and as "10 + 5." When children are ready for numbers greater than 9, you can use any of the place-value devices. The following activity is one way to begin:

ACTIVITY 8-1   Place Value with Sticks and Markers

- Use a place-value device with sticks, such as one of those in Figure 8-4, and markers on a magnetic or flannel board. Put 15 markers on the board.
- Select three children: The first to count the objects, the second to represent the count on the device, and the third to record the count with numerals on a chalkboard.
- As the first child counts the markers one by one, the second child puts a stick for each marker in the ones place of the device. At the same time, the third child records the count with numerals written in sequence on the chalkboard.
- Pause at nine and review what has been done so far.
- As the tenth marker is counted and the tenth stick is placed in the ones place, ask, "How many markers has Sue counted?" "How many sticks are in the ones place?" "How can Bob write '10' on the chalkboard?" Demonstrate how to bundle ten sticks to represent 1 ten, and place the bundled sticks in the tens place. "How many tens?" "How many ones?" Explain how "10" is written and its meaning.
- Continue the count by representing "11" with a bundle of ten and a single stick and showing how "11" is written. Do the same with 12, 13, 14, and 15.
- Discuss the meaning of "11" as ten and one, "12" as ten and two, and so on.
- Repeat with different numbers and other children as counters and recorder.

ACTIVITY 8-2   Place Value with Beans and Sticks

- Give each child nineteen loose beans, a tens beanstick, and a place-value mat.

Tens	Ones

- Tell each child to count thirteen loose beans and put them in the ones place on the mat; talk about the number of beans and point out that there are more than nine.
- Tell each child to separate the beans into a group of 10 and a group of 3, and to put the ten beans in the tens place of the mat.
- Have each child exchange the ten loose beans for one tens stick; discuss the fact that there are 1 ten and 3 ones, or 13.
- Write the expanded notations 1 ten and 3 ones = 13 and $10 + 3 = 13$ on the chalkboard and discuss.
- Repeat with other numbers between nine and twenty.

Frequent activities, both teacher-led and with problem cards, games, and individual work sheets are necessary for most children. Children who demonstrate skill and understanding while working under your direction are ready for individual and cooperative work with problem cards and games. Figure 8-5 shows samples of three problem cards, each using a different commercial material. Naturally you will want more than one card for each material. These materials have teacher's guides that contain many activities.[9] Charles Thompson and John Van de Walle describe activities for transition boards, which are teacher-made materials for stressing place value and trading activities in the December 1980 and January 1981 *Arithmetic Teacher*.

After children understand place value through 19, they should continue to work with devices that show place value through 99. Games offer opportunities for children to practice learned skills in group situations. In every grade a good game contributes to learning by giving children additional manipulative experiences with familiar materials. The changed setting in which the materials are used livens the practice session and heightens children's interest in maintaining their skills. An ex-

[9] The Cuisenaire Company of America, 12 Church Street, New Rochelle, NY 10805 has manuals and problem cards for its materials. For Dienes material write McGraw-Hill Company, 1221 Avenue of the Americas, New York, NY 10020; and for Unifix, write Mind/Matter Corporation, P.O. Box 345, Danbury, CT 06810.

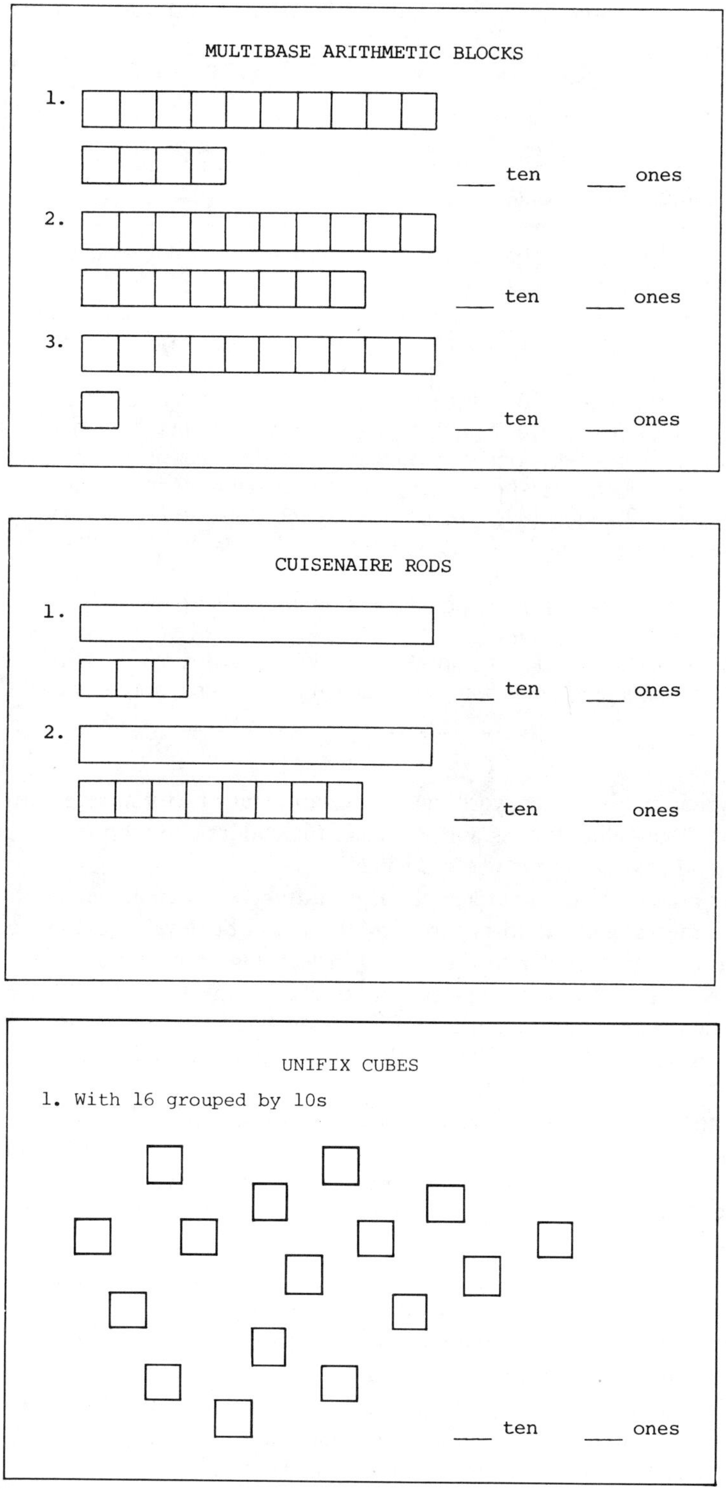

FIGURE 8-5
Problem cards for activities with structured materials

ample of a place-value game for numbers between 9 and 100 is Beans and Sticks.

GAME   Beans and Sticks

- Materials: A set of 18 loose beans, 9 tens sticks, and a place-value mat for each player; one 0–9 spinner.
- Players: 2–4
- Order of Play: Each child spins the spinner; use either high or low to determine first player.
- Rules: The first player spins the pointer and calls out the number at which it stops. The player counts as many beans and puts them in the ones place of the mat. Each player takes a turn. The first player spins again, counts beans, and puts them on the mat. If the count exceeds 9, the player exchanges 10 loose beans for 1 tens stick, and places it on the mat in the tens place. At the end of each play the child tells the number represented on her or his mat. Play continues until one player has a score in the 90s or until an agreed upon number of spins have been made.
- Variation: Use hundreds rafts and two spinners, one designated tens and one designated ones, with mats showing ones, tens, and hundreds.

First-grade mathematics workbooks have abundant pictorial representations of place-value devices and exercises for children's practice at the pictorial and abstract levels of experience.

In later grades children work with larger numbers. Their understanding of the meaning of numbers through 999 should be developed as they engage in activities similar to those used in learning about the numbers through 99. It is not necessary to continue counting objects, but the place-value devices will remain useful in illustrating that 10 tens equal 1 hundred as 10 bundles of 10 markers each are put together to make 1 bundle of 100 in one of the devices.

The flats and rods in Cuisenaire and Dienes sets, and rafts and tens sticks in a set of beansticks, are used to represent numbers between 99 and 999. Cubes are used with flats and rods for numbers between 999 and 9999. Special plastic grids are used to make squares and large cubes of Unifix cubes.

As children work with a device, they also learn how the numeral for 10 tens, or 100, is written. They should note the relationship between the symbol "100" and the markers on the place-value device, a single flat in a set of structured material, or a beanstick raft. As children continue this study, special attention should be given to the tens place when it contains a zero, as in 101. Some of the larger numbers should be practiced until each student understands the place-value concept.

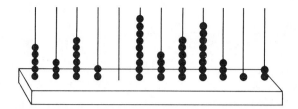

FIGURE 8-6
Abacus representing the
number 536,209,468,312

A classroom **abacus** is an excellent device for extending children's understanding of place value to larger numbers, because it can show numbers that are impractical with other devices. To make one for classroom use, insert pieces of stiff wire into holes drilled in a board; wooden beads can be used for markers. Commercially made abacuses are also available. The abacus in Figure 8-6 has enough rods to represent numbers as large as billions.

A child's first abacus should have only three or four rods. You can use this abacus to demonstrate how it represents numbers. Point out that one bead on the tens rod has the same value (that is, represents the same number) as ten beads on the ones rod (10); one bead on the hundreds rod represents the same number as ten beads on the tens rod (100). Under your guidance children will conclude that each rod represents a place-value position that has a value ten times greater than the position to its immediate right, regardless of where it is on the abacus. By the time they are in the fourth grade most children will, with your help, be able to reverse their thinking to conclude that each place-value position also represents a value that is one-tenth the value of one to its immediate left. As their understanding of place value increases, children will generalize that the Hindu–Arabic numeration system has a place-value scheme based on ten and powers of ten. This same scheme forms the basis of the metric system, a fact that should be capitalized upon as children deal with metric measure.

A place-value chart is a useful means for helping older children understand large numbers (Figure 8-7). Numerals instead of beads are used to represent each place-value position. Children should read the numbers represented on the chart and also put numerals on the chart to represent numbers presented orally.

Hundred billions	Ten billions	Billions	Hundred millions	Ten millions	Millions	Hundred thousands	Ten thousands	Thousands	Hundreds	Tens	Ones
5	3	6	2	0	9	4	6	8	3	1	2

FIGURE 8-7
Place-value chart showing
value of place positions for
the number 536,209,468,312

**Self-check
of Objectives 3 and 4**

Make models or pictures of at least three place-value devices or materials.
Demonstrate with your models or pictures how each device is used to represent the meanings of numbers greater than ten.

Give an explanation of how the abacus can be used to represent large numbers. Represent the number 436,488 on a real or pictured abacus.

SKIP-COUNTING

Skip-counting is used to count objects by a sequence other than ones, such as counting by twos, fives, and tens. It is a useful way to count money, vote tallies, and large collections of objects. Skip-counting is also also used when multiplication is interpreted as repeated addition. Children's first work with skip-counting should build on their knowledge of patterns.

ACTIVITY 8-3   Skip-Counting

- Show children a bead or shape pattern like the ones in Figure 7-1; discuss each pattern.
- Show a pattern that alternates by twos, and have children note the pairs of objects. Count by ones.
- Ask, "Does anyone know another way to count the beads?" If counting by twos is not mentioned, show how it is done.

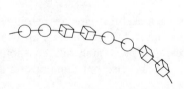

- Count other pairs, such as pennies grouped by twos, pairs of desks placed side by side, and pairs of children in a line.
- Do the same with patterns of five and ten.

ACTIVITY 8-4   Patterns

- Study patterns and skip-counting on a hundreds board.

1	2	3	4	5	6	7	8	9	10
11	12	13	14	15	16	17	18	19	20
21	22	23	24	25	26	27	28	29	30
31	32	33	34	35	36	37	38	39	40
41	42	43	44	45	46	47	48	49	50
51	52	53	54	55	56	57	58	59	60
61	62	63	64	65	66	67	68	69	70
71	72	73	74	75	76	77	78	79	80
81	82	83	84	85	86	87	88	89	90
91	92	93	94	95	96	97	98	99	100

- Examine rows across to observe how counting by twos includes every other space, counting by fives includes every fifth space, and counting by tens includes every tenth space.
- Look at the columns. The number in the ones place is the same in each column, whereas the number in the tens place increases by one.
- A diagonal from top left to bottom right increases by eleven, and one from top right to bottom left increases by nine. Study these diagonals to determine why these patterns occur.

Skip-counting can also be done on a number line. A line on adding-machine tape that extends into the hundreds can be placed above chalkboards and bulletin boards on one or more classroom walls. Mark numbers ending in five with red ink and those ending in zero with blue ink to make it easy to count into the hundreds by fives and tens. Also, have children skip-count by a number beginning at a number that is not a multiple of the counting number. Figure 8-8 shows a part of a count by five beginning at 29.

Patterned skip-counting is beneficial and fun. Rather than using a constant skip count, use one like 1, 5, 7, 11, 13, 17, ...

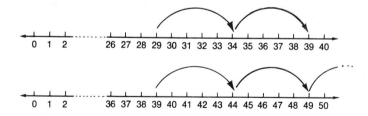

FIGURE 8-8
Number line used to illustrate skip-counting by fives from 29

Give two examples of skip-counting, and describe three activities for helping children skip-count by fives.

***Self-check
of Objective 5***

EXPRESSING NUMBERS WITH EXPANDED NOTATION

Children use both compact and expanded forms of numerals in elementary-school mathematics. In the compact form, the one we normally use, the number 243 is written as "243." There are times, however, when one of the expanded forms is useful. For example, when children are learning about place value, the expanded forms *2 hundreds + 4 tens + 3 ones* and "200 + 40 + 3" emphasize place value in the Hindu–Arabic numeration system. Also, it is best that children know how to express numbers in the simplest expanded form before beginning to add and subtract numbers represented by multidigit numerals, because this form helps children to understand the algorithms better. Another reason to understand **expanded notation** is that, particularly in its exponential form, it serves as a foundation for the study of extremely large and small numbers and their expression in scientific notation.

The simplest form of expanded notation is the expression of a number using a combination of numerals and words; for example, the number 17 is expressed as "1 ten and 7 ones." As children count objects and use place-value devices, you should repeatedly have them interpret the numbers as so many tens and so many ones and write the numerals in both the standard and simple expanded forms. From the use of the form "5 tens and 6 ones" to express the number 56, children move to the shorter "50 + 6" form. A game such as Expanded Notation Concentration provides practice in recognizing and naming expanded forms of numbers.

GAME   Expanded Notation Concentration

Materials: 8 to 12 pairs of cards like those shown.

10 + 2	12
40 + 3	43
30 + 4	34

- Players: 2–3
- Order of Play: Players determine order before the game begins.
- Rules: Shuffle the cards and put them face down on a desk in rows and columns to form a rectangle. The first player turns over a pair of cards and determines if they match. If they do, the player says, "10 plus 2

equals 12," or whatever the numbers are. This pair is kept by the player, who takes another turn. If a pair does not match, they are returned to their places on the desk, and the next player takes a turn. Play continues until all pairs have been matched. The player with the most pairs is the winner.

Other games that provide practice with expanded notation are Place Value Probe, Expando Land, and Spin a Value.[10]

In the second through fourth grades children will apply the expanded form to larger numbers, such as 53,692. As they use an abacus to represent such a number, children should learn to express it in the following ways:

5 ten thousands, 3 thousands, 6 hundreds, 9 tens, and 2 ones

53 thousands, 6 hundreds, 9 tens, and 2 ones

$50,000 + 3,000 + 600 + 90 + 2$, or 50,000
  3,000
  600
  90
  2
  ―――――
  53,692

After children can multiply by ten and powers of ten, they are ready to express numbers in two other forms:

$$(5 \times 10,000) + (3 \times 1000) + (6 \times 100) + (9 \times 10) + (2 \times 1)$$
$$[5 \times (10 \times 10 \times 10 \times 10)] + [3 \times (10 \times 10 \times 10)]$$
$$+ [6 \times (10 \times 10)] + [9 \times 10] + [2 \times 1]$$

When children understand the meanings of these forms, they will have little difficulty learning how to express numbers by exponential notation. It is usually in the sixth grade that children learn to use exponents to indicate powers of ten. In exponential notation, 53,692 is expressed in this way:

$$(5 \times 10^4) + (3 \times 10^3) + (6 \times 10^2) + (9 \times 10^1) + (2 \times 10^0)$$

Any of the place-value devices can be used to regroup numbers to 999, but for numbers larger than 1000, the abacus illustrates the process more conveniently. For this purpose there must be room for 18 beads on each rod. Figure 8-9 shows 23,498 on an abacus. It is in its simplest form in (a). It appears in one of many other forms in (b). The second representation is useful either to show the sum of the addition problem

[10] Leonard M. Kennedy and Ruth L. Michon, *Games for Individualizing Mathematics Learning* (Columbus, Ohio: Charles E. Merrill Books, Inc., 1973), pp. 22–29.

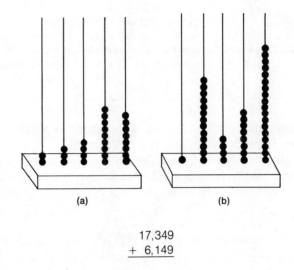

FIGURE 8-9
Abacus representing
23,498—in (a) as 20,000 +
3000 + 400 + 90 + 8 and in
(b) as 10,000 + 13,000 + 400
+ 80 + 18

$$
\begin{array}{r}
17,349 \\
+\ 6,149 \\
\hline
\end{array}
$$

before it is regrouped or to prepare for subtraction using the decomposition (borrowing) method of the problem:

$$
\begin{array}{r}
23,498 \\
-\ 9,129 \\
\hline
\end{array}
$$

Particular attention to numbers with zeros builds readiness for regrouping when such numbers are used in subtraction. If children learn that 204 can be expressed as "20 tens and 4 ones," 3006 as "300 tens and 6 ones," and 40,002 as "4000 tens and 2 ones," they will not be confused by this regrouping:

$$
\begin{array}{rcl}
3006 \longrightarrow & 300 \text{ tens and 6 ones} \longrightarrow & 299 \text{ tens and 16 ones} \\
-\ 2439 \longrightarrow & -(243 \text{ tens and 9 ones}) \longrightarrow & -(243 \text{ tens and } 9 \text{ ones})
\end{array}
$$

The subtraction can begin after one regrouping. This procedure is easier to do and understand than to regroup step by step from the thousands place to the hundreds place, from the hundreds place to the tens place, and finally from the tens place to the ones place. Such a lengthy process is unnecessary for children who can represent numbers in many expanded forms.

**Self-check
of Objective 6**

Explain the difference between a compact and an expanded numeral. Write at least three different expanded notation numerals for 4863.

INTEGERS

The numbers considered so far are used for counting discrete quantities or determining measures of magnitude such as length and volume. There are situations for which these numbers alone are not suitable. For example, measures such as temperature, time, distance, and altitude, and balances in money accounts require numbers that indicate both magnitude and direction. The numbers that do this are the **real numbers.** **Integers** are the part of the set of real numbers that are studied by elementary-school children.

Even though children have limited encounters with situations that require the use of integers, most have had some experience with them by the time they have completed the sixth grade. When primary-grade children learn to use thermometers, they will note that thermometers register temperatures below zero. Older children learn about altitudes above and below sea level, experience or read about gains and losses of yardage in football games, and experience gains and losses in money situations.

The study of integers in the elementary school is largely informal, with children having opportunities to use gamelike activities, stories, and number lines. Stories illustrated with simple drawings are an excellent way to introduce integers. The subject of these stories may be real or fanciful as long as the sequence of ideas can be readily understood. They should end in a way that leads to a discussion of conclusions that enhance children's understanding of these numbers. The following story, accompanied by simple pictures drawn on the chalkboard or projected with an overhead projector, fits all these requirements.

ACTIVITY 8-5   Positive and Negative Numbers

• Read this story:

The Little Hole-Diggers

There was once a group of little hole-diggers. No one is sure how they looked, but some things are certain: the only time the hole-diggers got any joy out of life was when they were digging holes in the ground. They usually made very special holes that gave them very special pleasure. These special holes were straight down into the ground or straight into the side of a mountain, like this. (Display a drawing similar to that included here.)

Not only did the hole-diggers enjoy digging these holes, but they got extra special pleasure out of disposing of the dirt in a particular way. When they dug a hole straight down, the dirt from the first foot of the hole was placed right beside the hole in a pile one foot high. The dirt from the second foot of the hole was piled on top of the first foot of dirt, and so on. Also, they always marked the sides of their holes to show how deep they had been dug and marked the sides of their dirt piles to show how high they had been made. They dug holes into the sides of mountains in about the same way, except that they put the dirt on the ground in front of the hole, as you can see in the picture.

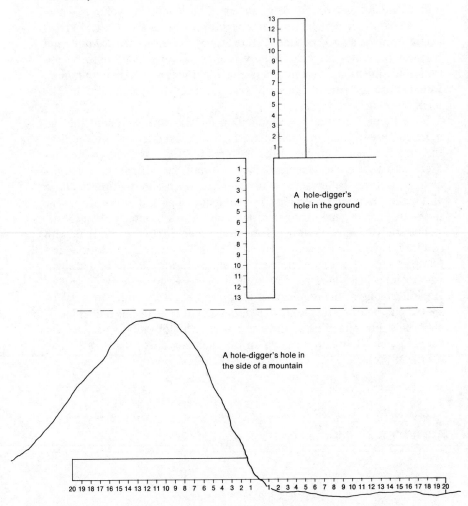

A hole-digger's hole in the ground

A hole-digger's hole in the side of a mountain

- Ask questions: "Which numbers tell how deep the hole is?" "Which numbers tell how high the pile is?" "If we used the same numbers for both the hole and the pile, we might find ourselves getting mixed up as we talk about the hole and the pile of dirt. Can you think of how we could name each of these numbers so we won't get mixed up as we talk about them?" Children might use *above* and *below* for the vertical line (hole) and *right* and *left* for the horizontal line (cave). Some may use *positive* and *negative*. Discuss each of the children's terms. If *positive* and *negative* are not given, you should introduce them, relating *positive* to *above* and *right* and *negative* to *below* and *left*. Put negative signs in front of **negative numbers** and positive signs before the **positive numbers.**

- Use the story situation and drawings to familiarize children with the uses of positive and negative numbers. Have a child locate negative 3 (−3) in the hole and then in the tunnel. Do this with both positive and negative numbers until children can readily locate any number.

Once children have learned the terminology and symbolism, they should practice using integers. David Page uses cricket jumps, and Louis Cohen uses postman stories, as settings for introducing integers.[11] You can adapt their models to make games for practice. A sample of a game for each of these models follows:

GAME Cricket Jumps

- Materials: A number line on adding-machine tape extending from −12 to +12, construction paper crickets for markers, and a pair of dice, one marked −1, −2, −3, −4, −5, and −6 and the other marked +1, +2, +3, +4, +5, and +6.
- Players: 2–4
- Order of Play: Players roll the plus die, with highest number going first, next highest second, and so on.
- Rules: The first player rolls both dice and reads the number on each one. From 0, the player moves a cricket in the positive direction by the number of jumps indicated by the plus die and then in the negative direction by the number of jumps indicated by the minus die. Each player takes a turn in the same way. Play continues until a player is off the board at either end or until a predetermined number of moves have been taken. The player farthest from 0 in either direction is the winner.

GAME Checks and Bills

- Materials: Play money in $1, $5, $10, and $20 denominations and a deck of cards with statements such as: "You receive a rebate of $2.00 from Wrangler jeans." "You get paid $5.00 for yard work." "You pay $5.00 for two hours of time at Waterworld." "You buy a baseball for $6.00."
- Players: 2–4
- Order of Play: Each player draws a card from the deck. Order is determined by value of the cards, highest to lowest.

---

[11] See David A. Page, *Number Lines, Functions, and Fundamental Topics* (New York: The Macmillan Company, 1964), Chapter 6, for a discussion of cricket jumps; and Louis S. Cohen, "A Rationale in Working with Signed Numbers," *Arithmetic Teacher*, XII, No. 7 (November 1965), pp. 563–567 for postman stories.

- Rules: Each player begins with $50.00—5 bills of $1.00, 1 of $5.00, 2 of $10.00, and 1 of $20.00. A bank containing $100.00 is set up. Shuffle the cards and put them face down. The first player draws the top card and tells whether it is a "positive" card or a "negative" card and how much will be gained or lost. For example, "I have a negative card that will cost me $5.00." Players receive money from the bank for positive cards and pay money to the bank for negative cards. Play rotates until one player is out of money or until each player has had a predetermined number of plays. The winner is the player with the most money.

Children should be shown how a **vector,** or directed segment, is a line segment with an arrow at one end to indicate direction on a number line. It represents an integer, or directed number.

ACTIVITY 8-6   Vectors

- Show the vertical and horizontal number lines and point out the vectors on each one. Discuss the fact that each vector indicates both direction and magnitude. Relate the vectors to cricket jumps and money situations. "If a cricket jump is represented by vector **c**, where does the jump begin and end?" "If the vectors represent money situations, what does the vector **h** tell you?"
- Be certain that the children become aware that a vector need not begin at 0.

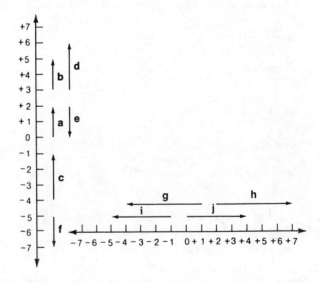

Number lines can also be used to visualize the concepts of *equal to, greater than,* and *less than* with integers. On the whole-number line, the number to the right of another number is always the greater one; a number to the left of another number is always the smaller one. The same properties hold for numbers in the set of integers. When numbers are ordered on a number line, their comparative sizes can be determined by their locations. Zero and all positive numbers are greater than all negative numbers. To compare any two negative numbers, children should recognize that they are treated just like whole numbers. The number on the right is always the larger of the two numbers.

Tell a story you can use to introduce children to integers. Show how a number line can represent positive and negative integers.

Self-check of Objective 7

CALCULATORS AND NUMBERS

Calculator activities will contribute to children's understanding of numbers. The first activity that follows helps children to learn about both the calculator and numbers. The second activity requires some knowledge of how to add with a calculator.

ACTIVITY 8-7   Calculator Counting

- Children work singly or in pairs with a calculator.
- Tell the children that they are to figure out how to make the calculator count by ones. When the children have determined how to do this, have them count by twos, fives, and tens.
- Challenges: (1) "Can you count by fives to 500 in a minute?" (Have one child time another with the second hand of the classroom clock or with a digital timer.) (2) Give children problem cards with activities like the following: [12]

---

[12] Adapted from Project Impact, *Problem Solving Using the Calculator, Book I* (Cedar Falls, Iowa: Price Laboratory School, University of Northern Iowa, 1982), p. 3.

Find how many cards in this stack. Use the code $1 + 7 = = = ...$

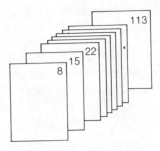

How many cards are in this stack? Try this code: $1 + 9 = = = ...$

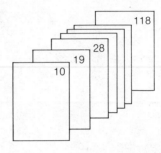

ACTIVITY 8-8   Calculator Addition

- Children work in pairs with a calculator.
- Prepare problem cards with large numbers written with words and a check number. The check number is the sum of the numbers.

CARD 1

Three-hundred forty-five
Eight-hundred twenty-seven
Six-hundred forty
Three-hundred fifty-seven
Six-hundred eight
Seven-hundred eighty-two

Check number
3559

- As one child reads the numbers, the other one punches them into the calculator, pushing + after each one. If the numbers have been read and entered correctly, the check number should appear on the calculator's display.[13]

Demonstrate how to count by five with a calculator. Make up a problem card like the one in Activity 8-6.

Self-check
of Objective 8

SPECIAL STUDENTS AND NUMERATION

1. Learning-Handicapped Children

Children with learning handicaps frequently have problems counting objects in sets larger than 10 or 20 and writing numbers larger than 10. For some, an extension of the time they spend on manipulative activities enables them to progress at a steady pace, which may be slower than their nonhandicapped peers. Others need special help.

   a. Counting Errors   Counting errors occur for some children because they cannot bridge from one decade of numbers to the next. For such children the transition from 19 to 20, 29 to 30, and so on is difficult. Try this with these children.

ACTIVITY 8-9   Counting Using Hundreds Chart

- Count by ten using a hundreds chart. As the children count, emphasize the pronunciation of each number beyond ten: twenty, thirty, forty, and so on. Write the numerals in sequence: 10, 20, 30, 40, 50, 60, 70, 80, 90.
- Locate each number with 9 in the ones place and ask, "What number comes after 29?" "What number follows 49?" Help the children note that in each case, the tens number increases by one.
- Give each child 40 or 50 lima beans to count. Observe each child to note if the transition is made properly.
- Variation: Use a number line instead of a hundreds chart.

---

[13] Adapted from George Immerzeel, *77 Ideas for Using the Rockwell 18R in the Classroom* (Foxboro, Mass.: New Impressions, Inc. 1976), p. 12.

b. Writing Errors   Many children reverse digits when writing two-place numbers; the teens are particularly troublesome for many. When these writing errors persist, special attention should be focused on the number in the tens place. Nancy S. Bley and Carol A. Thornton recommend that color cues be used. After a number like 23 has been represented with sticks or some other device, write the number with a green "2" and a red "3." Tell the children to think of a stop light, in which green means *go* and red means *stop*. Green and red chips can also be used to represent numbers, with green for tens and red for ones. When children write numbers, have them use a green crayon for tens numbers and a red crayon for ones numbers. Color cues should be used until children are able to consistently write numbers correctly.[14]

2. Gifted and Talented Children

Few gifted and talented children experience difficulty with numeration. They form generalizations about the Hindu–Arabic system quite readily. A study of early counting devices and historical and nondecimal numeration systems will interest many of these children and will extend their understanding of numeration. Examples of early counting devices are the quipi, or knots-on-a-cord system, used by the Inca Indians of Peru, the tally used in Europe until the early 1800s (Figure 8-10), and abacuses such as the Chinese suan-pan (Figure 8-11), and the Japanese saroban.[15]

There are several historical numeration systems children can study. The Egyptian, Mayan, and Chinese offer interesting contrasts to our own. Any **nondecimal system** can be studied. Base two is especially interesting to some children because of its use in computers. Children should have opportunities to share their findings with others through bulletin boards, articles in school newspapers, and demonstrations.

The study of number patterns contributes to children's understanding

FIGURE 8-10
Simplified drawing of a tally stick showing a recorded debt of 234 pounds British money

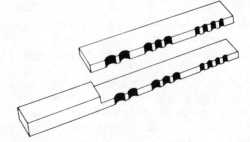

[14]Nancy S. Bley and Carol A. Thornton, *Teaching Mathematics to the Learning Disabled* (Rockville, Md.: Aspen Systems Corporation, 1981), pp. 56–65.

[15]See Florian Cajori, *A History of Mathematical Notation, Vol. I* (LaSalle, Ill.: Open Court Publishing Company, 1926), pp. 30–40; and H.A. Freebury, *A History of Mathematics* (New York: The Macmillan Company, 1961), p. 160 for information about these devices.

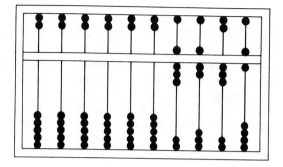

FIGURE 8-11
Chinese *suan-pan* (abacus)
representing the number
8736

of numbers. A calculator takes the drudgery out of processing patterns.
Here is an unusual pattern you can introduce to interested children:

ACTIVITY 8-10   Differences of Squares

- Note this set of subtraction sentences:

$$2^2 - 1^2 = 3$$
$$3^2 - 2^2 = 5$$
$$4^2 - 3^2 = 7$$
$$5^2 - 4^2 = 9$$

- What is the difference for each of these subtraction sentences?

$$6^2 - 5^2 =$$
$$8^2 - 7^2 =$$

- Can you describe the pattern?
- Give answers for the following without using the calculator:

$$51^2 - 50^2 =$$
$$100^2 - 101^2 =$$

- Make up five examples of your own. Write your examples and their
  answers.[16]

Children with access to a computer may be interested in counting programs, such as this one to count by ones to 100:

```
NEW
10  FOR N = 1 TO 100
20  PRINT N
30  NEXT N
40  END
```

Once children have run this program, they can develop variations that
program the computer to count to 1000, or by 2s, 5s, or 10s from one
number to another.

---

[16] Adapted from David Moursund, *Calculators in the Classroom: With Applications for Elementary and Middle School Teachers* (New York: John Wiley and Sons, 1981), p. 130.

**Self-check
of Objectives
9 and 10**

Identify two problems associated with numeration learning-handicapped children frequently experience. Describe at least one way to help children overcome each problem.

Name at least two areas of study for gifted and talented students. Name at least one historical counting device and one historical numeration system.

SUMMARY

Children must have a well-developed understanding of the place-value scheme of the Hindu–Arabic numeration system if they are to be mathematically literate. In addition to understanding one-to-one correspondence, which is the basis for counting, they must understand one-to-many, many-to-one, and many-to-many correspondences, for which numerous applications are found in mathematics. Place-value devices, such as beansticks and bundled sticks, and commercial materials, such as Cuisenaire rods, Dienes blocks, and Unifix cubes, are useful for clarifying the meaning of the Hindu–Arabic and other place-value numeration systems. Numerals can be written in both compact and expanded forms. Expanded forms are useful for explaining place value and algorithms for such operations as addition and subtraction.

Skip-counting is a useful process for counting money, vote tallies, and grouped items. Children who are introduced to integers should learn about them through stories and activities that are meaningful to them. Calculator activities, like counting by ones, fives, and tens, and punching in dictated numbers, enhance children's understanding of larger numbers. Children with learning handicaps frequently need special help with counting more than ten or twenty objects and with writing numbers greater than ten. Gifted and talented children can study early counting devices, historical numeration systems, nondecimal systems, and number patterns to increase their understanding of numeration.

STUDY QUESTIONS AND ACTIVITIES

1. A number of different devices for teaching the meaning of place value are described in this chapter. You should be familiar with each one so that you use it properly with children. Show the meaning of each of the following numbers with Cuisenaire rods or Dienes multibase blocks, beansticks, tongue depressors, and an abacus. (If the devices are unavailable, make drawings to show the representation of each number.)

(a) 136   (b) 95   (c) 308

2. Different forms of expanded notation are described in this chapter. A simple form, "1 ten + 6 ones," is used as first graders learn the meaning of place value. A form using exponents is introduced to older children. Write each of the following numbers in four different expanded forms. Begin with the simple form, then use two intermediate forms, and end with the exponential form.

(a) 2346   (b) 62,894   (c) 40,203

3. Sample statements for the Checks and Bills game cards are given in the directions for this game. Write 12 statements for positive cards and 12 statements for negative cards. Put your statements on cards and make dice and money for this game; add it to your collection of teaching–learning aids, if you wish.

4. There are other place-value and integer games in this chapter and in articles in the chapter's reading list. Make some of these to add to your collection of teaching–learning aids.

5. Daniel Hardin's article (see reading list) contains an intriguing description of how notches in pig's ears can be used to acquaint children with the base-three system of numeration. Read his article and explain in your own words how the ear-notching system is used. Draw pictures to show notches for the fifth pig in a year's third litter and the twelfth pig in a year's eighth litter.

KEY TERMS

Hindu–Arabic numeration system
one-to-one correspondence
one-to-many correspondences
many-to-one correspondences
many-to-many correspondence
place value
abacus
skip-counting

expanded notation
real numbers
integers
negative numbers
positive numbers
vector
nondecimal system

FOR FURTHER READING

Anderson, Alfred L. "Why the Continuing Resistance to the Use of Counting Sticks?" *Arithmetic Teacher*, XXV, No. 6 (March 1978), p. 18. Children who use counting sticks (popsicle sticks) in conjunction with abstract numbers and pictorial representations in textbooks and work sheets performed with more understanding than those restricted to workbooks, work sheets, finger counting, and other methods of tallying.

Ashlock, Robert B., and Tommie A. West. "Physical Representations for Signed-Number Operations," *Arithmetic Teacher*, XIV, No. 7 (November 1967), pp. 549–554. Presents the number line, several simple story situations, and their uses for helping children learn about integers. An extensive bibliography, with brief annotations, is included.

Brennan, Alison D. House. "Mr. Ten, You're Too Tall," *Arithmetic Teacher*, XXV, No. 4 (January 1978), pp. 20–22.
A set of materials to help children make the transition from the conceptual stage to the computational stage of thought when performing operations with base-ten numbers is described. The materials are both proportional and nonproportional and can be used to introduce place-value concepts and then to teach computational processes.

Brumaugh, Frederick L. "Big Numbers in a Classroom Model," *Arithmetic Teacher*, XXIX, No. 3 (November 1981), pp. 18–19.
A model of the solar system, scaled to metric units and small enough to fit in a classroom, gives children practice in reading large numbers as they deal with distances and diameters.

Cajori, Florian. *A History of Mathematical Notations*, Vol. I (LaSalle, Ill.: Open Court Publishing Company, 1928). The history of symbols and notation for many ancient systems is presented in Chapter 2. Of special interest is a section on fanciful hypotheses about the origins of the symbols for the Hindu–Arabic system.

———. *A History of Mathematics* (New York: The Macmillan Company, 1919). In the early chapters, the history of many numeration systems and mathematics in the countries where the systems had their origin is presented; included are Babylonian, Egyptian, Greek, Roman, Mayan, and Hindu–Arabic numeration systems.

Cohen, Louis S. "A Rationale in Working with Signed Numbers," *Arithmetic Teacher*, XII, No. 7 (November 1965), pp. 563–567. Cohen suggests using stories involving a postman and his delivery and picking up of checks and bills as means of involving children in situations that require the addition and subtraction of directed numbers.

———. "A Rationale in Working with Signed Numbers—Revisited," *Arithmetic Teacher*, XIII, No. 7 (November 1966), pp. 564–567. The postman stories are extended to include the operations of multiplication and division.

Coplestone-Loomis, Lenny. "The Big Pumpkin Count," *Arithmetic Teacher*, XXIX, No. 2 (October 1981), p. 36.
Dried seeds removed from a Halloween pumpkin provide counting and grouping activities. When counted in groups of ten and glued to cards, they can be mounted in sets of 100 on a bulletin board to help children count the total number of seeds.

Freebury, H. A. *A History of Mathematics* (New York: The Macmillan Company, 1961). In a rather brief, but very interestingly written book, Freebury describes the origins of the Hindu–Arabic and other numeration systems.

This book is especially recommended for the elementary school teacher's library.

Fremont, Herbert. "Pipe Cleaners and Loops—Discovering How to Add and Subtract Directed Numbers," *Arithmetic Teacher*, XIII, No. 7 (November ,1966), pp. 568–572. Fremont presents a full discussion of pipe-cleaner loops and their uses to help children visualize the meaning of addition and subtraction with directed numbers.

Hardin, Daniel D. "Teaching Base Three? In a Pig's Ear," *Arithmetic Teacher*, XXVII, No. 1 (September 1979), pp. 48–49.
Hog breeders use a uniform system of notching pigs' ears to keep records of each pig's time of birth. The system employs a base of three; it can be used to introduce the system to children.

Lappan, Glenda, Elizabeth Phillips, and M.J. Winter. "Powers and Patterns: Problem Solving with Calculators," *Arithmetic Teacher*, XXX, No. 2 (October 1982), pp. 42–44.
Children use calculators to work with patterns that result from use of powers of numbers and patterns that are generated. Older children get much practice using exponents and reading large numbers.

Makurat, Phillip A. "A Look at a Million," *Arithmetic Teacher*, XXV, No. 3 (December 1977), p. 23. A computer printout of a million "$" signs is relatively easy to acquire—much easier than a million bottle caps. With such a printout children can determine how long it would take each one to print a million dots. Other possible activities are suggested.

March, Rosemary. "Georges Cuisenaire and His Rainbow Rods," *Learning*, VI, No. 3 (November 1977), pp. 81–82, 84, 86. Gives a brief account of the man and how he became inspired to develop the Cuisenaire rods. Describes the struggle to gain acceptance of the rods and includes testimonials to their value.

Page, David A. *Number Lines, Functions, and Fundamental Topics* (New York: The Macmillan Company, 1964). Part II discusses in detail various ways children can learn about negative numbers and operations on them.

Ronshausen, Nina L. "Introducing Place Value," *Arithmetic Teacher*, XXV, No. 4 (January 1978), pp. 38–40. Explains carefully sequenced steps for teaching place value. Although they were developed in one-to-one tutorial situations, the author claims the activities are suitable for small group work, too.

Skokoohi, Gholam-Hossein. "Manipulative Devices for Teaching Place Value," *Arithmetic Teacher*, XXV, No. 6 (March 1978), pp. 48–51. Acorns and glasses provide the means for developing the place-value concept as children record the count of passing cars by one-to-one correspondence. What to do when the first glass is full becomes the basis for determining that a second glass is needed, and the place-value concept is introduced.

Smith, David Eugene. *History of Mathematics*, Vol. II (Boston: Ginn and Company, 1953). The second chapter presents excellent material about the history of numeration systems.

————, and Jekuthial Ginsburg. *Numbers and Numerals* (Washington, D.C.: The National Council of Teachers of Mathematics, 1937). This is one of the early publications of the National Council; it is a highly readable account of numeration, including its history, suitable for older children as well as teachers.

Van Arsdel, Jean, and Joanne Lasky. "A Two-dimensional Abacus—the Papy Minicomputer," *Arithmetic Teacher*, XIX, No. 6 (October 1972), pp. 445–451. The Papy Minicomputer is a simple, easily made device. It is useful for teaching place value in base ten and other bases and for performing addition, subtraction, multiplication, and division.

West, Mike, and Ken Hass. "It's Neat Being Surrounded by Peanuts," *Arithmetic Teacher*, XXVI, No. 1 (September 1978), p. 22. Mike, a ten-year-old student, bought a 100-pound bag of peanuts and held a contest; fellow students guessed the number of peanuts. To determine the number, Mike and a few friends counted the peanuts, grouping by tens and powers of tens—there were 16,870. Guesses ranged from as low as 800 to well over a billion, prompting Ken, the teacher, to observe that even some high-school students who made estimates lack good number sense.

9

Introducing Addition and Subtraction

Upon completion of Chapter 9 you will be able to:

1. Give a definition of addition and subtraction, and name the parts of addition and subtraction sentences.

2. Define a basic addition fact and a basic subtraction fact.

3. Name four real-life situations that give rise to subtraction.

4. Describe at least two types of activities that can be used with young children to develop readiness for addition and subtraction.

5. Describe procedures that can be used to introduce addition and subtraction and the number sentences for these operations.

6. Describe some manipulative materials that should be available for children to use during the beginning stages of work with addition and subtraction.

7. Distinguish between the sentence and vertical forms of writing addition and subtraction combinations, and illustrate at least one procedure for making the transition from the sentence to the vertical form.

8. Illustrate the meaning of addition and subtraction on a number line.

9. Describe at least four strategies for learning basic facts.

10. Demonstrate with markers and other devices how to introduce and develop the commutative and associative properties and the identity for addition so that their meanings are clear to children.

11. Describe two procedures for helping learning-handicapped children cope with basic facts of addition and subtraction.

Chapter 2 contains steps for subtraction with whole numbers and a discussion of the importance of establishing and following a hierarchy of steps for each topic. This chapter and the one that follows discuss ways to present addition and subtraction to children. You should refer to the subtraction hierarchy in Chapter 2 and the one for addition that follows (Figure 9-1) as you read the chapters to see how the procedures and materials for learning about these operations fit in with the steps of each operation's hierarchy.

A considerable amount of the time devoted to mathematics in the elementary school is spent on the operations of addition and subtraction and the development of understanding of an algorithm for computing each operation. Addition is described as the operation used to assign a **sum** to an ordered pair of numbers, which are called **addends.** Subtraction is described as the inverse of addition and is defined as the operation used to find a missing addend when a sum and the other addend are known. These definitions give us useful ways of summarizing addition and subtraction at the abstract level. However, they are not useful definitions for children, who need concrete ways of visualizing the two operations.

Numbers that are added are called *addends,* and their answer is a *sum.* When **subtraction** is defined in terms of addition, the numbers are a sum, a known addend, and a missing addend. There are special names for each of the numbers when they are used in subtraction. The **minuend** is the same as the sum, while the **subtrahend** is the known addend, and the *difference,* or **remainder,** is the missing addend.

BASIC FACTS

A **basic addition fact** is an ordered pair of whole number addends, each smaller than 10, and their sum. Altogether there are 100 addition facts that include all of the possible combinations using pairs of numbers less than 10 and their sums. Every addition fact has a **subtraction fact** that is its inverse, that is, one that reverses the action done by adding, so there are also 100 subtraction facts. Ultimately each child who is capable of doing so must commit each of the facts to memory for immediate recall. Otherwise the child will be handicapped when working with an algorithm for each of the operations.

ADDITION AND SUBTRACTION SITUATIONS

There is only one type of real-world situation that gives rise to addition: the joining of two or more groups of objects. Subtraction, however, arises

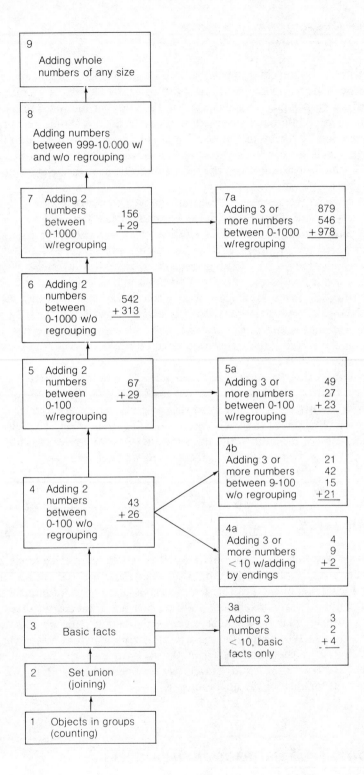

FIGURE 9-1
Hierarchy of steps for learning to add whole numbers

from several kinds of situations. Children should have experiences with these types:

- Subtraction is used when part of a set is removed. This is illustrated by the following situation: "A merchant began a sale with 396 boxes of greeting cards. During the first day she sold 218 boxes. How many boxes did she have left?" This situation is a take-away type and is the one most frequently encountered by children.

- Subtraction is used to compare the sizes of two sets. In this situation subtraction is used to find out how much larger or smaller one set is than another. "There are two schools in town. One school has 684 students, and the other has 478 students. The second school is how much smaller than the first?" (Or "The first school is how much larger than the second?")

- Subtraction is used to determine the size of a set to be united with another set of known size to make a third set of known size. "Mr. Jones is filling his trading-stamp book. It holds 1200 stamps when filled. After putting in his loose stamps, Mr. Jones has 700 stamps in his book. How many more stamps does he need to fill his book?"

- Subtraction is used to determine the size of a group within a set. "A school with 537 pupils has 249 boys. How many girls attend the school?"

Naturally you will not use such large numbers for children's first experiences with subtraction. However, children should have frequent experiences with problem situations that deal with all four types.

Define addition, and name the parts of an addition sentence. Do the same for subtraction. Why are these definitions unsuitable for young children?

Define a basic addition fact, and give an example. Do the same for subtraction.

Identify each type of real-life situation that gives rise to subtraction. Make up a simple problem for each situation.

Self-check of Objectives 1, 2, and 3

DEVELOPING READINESS FOR ADDITION AND SUBTRACTION

Activities that develop children's intuitive understanding of addition and subtraction can be an integral part of their work as they learn to count to ten. As children learn to count with concrete materials, ask questions to stimulate their thinking about addition and subtraction situations:

- "You have six clothespins on that card. If I give you two more, how many do you think you will have? Put these two on, and check to see if there are eight."

- "There are five acorns in your basket. If you take three of them from the basket, how many do you think will be left? Take out three, and see if two are left."

- "You have six golf tees in the holes in that board and four in the holes in the other board. Which board has fewer tees in it? How can you tell? How many fewer tees does it have?"

Children can use a walk-on number line for readiness activities. When the sequence of numbers 0 through 9 has been learned, children can play train on the walk-on line. Each numeral card is a "station."

- "Begin at station 0 and walk to station 3. Now walk four more steps. What station are you on now?"

- "Begin at station 8 and walk four steps toward station 0. What station are you on now?"

Self-check of Objective 4

Two different types of activities for developing readiness for addition and subtraction are described. Explain how each can be used with kindergartners and first graders. Can you think of other activities for developing children's readiness for these activities?

TEACHING ADDITION AND SUBTRACTION

1. Introducing Addition and Subtraction

All children are not ready to be formally introduced to addition and subtraction at the same time. Those who are ready should not be delayed because of less mature classmates. When you have a group of children who are ready for this new work, introduce addition by using a concrete situation.

ACTIVITY 9-1   Introducing Addition

Begin with familiar objects such as a set of two dolls and a set of three dolls.

- Have children identify the number of dolls in each set.
- Put the two sets together and have the children identify the total number.
- Repeat with other objects such as toy cars, books, blocks, and paper plates.

These early experiences are designed to teach the meaning of addition in terms of joining sets of objects. They also offer opportunities for oral descriptions of addition situations and development of terminology: "A set of two dolls joined with a set of three dolls make a set of five dolls." "Two dolls and three dolls make five dolls." "Two plus three is five." "Two and three equal five."

After developing understanding and vocabulary using realistic objects, children can use materials they can manipulate on a magnetic or flannel board and at their desks to learn about addition sentences.

ACTIVITY 9-2   The Addition Sentence

- Put a set of two disks and a set of three disks on a flannel or magnetic board.

$$2 + 3 = \square$$

- Introduce the addition sentence 2+3=5 by using felt or magnetic symbols. Discuss the meaning of each numeral and the + and = signs in the sentence by having children relate each one to actions with markers on the flannel or magnetic board.
- Repeat with other combinations having sums less than 9.

As children use realistic objects and markers they will build up mental images of addition situations and the related numbers sentences. A child with a good store of mental images will have little difficulty in writing **mathematical sentences** when confronted by similar but not identical situations at a later time.

Children need not be working with all of the possible combinations of number pairs having sums through 9 before they are introduced to subtraction. Use concrete materials and begin with a take-away situation.

ACTIVITY 9-3   Introducing Subtraction

- Begin with six books. "Here are six books, I am going to give two of them to Billy. How many books will I have left?"
- Have the children count the original set to confirm that there are six books. Give two books to Billy. Many children will know that you have four books left. Even so, either a single child or the group in unison should count them.
- Repeat with other collections of objects and different combinations.

During introductory lessons children need not use the sentence for subtraction. Neither is it necessary to use the terms *sum, addend,* and *missing addend.* It is better first to establish an understanding of the meaning of the take-away situation. Once children recognize the meaning of take-away subtraction and can distinguish it from addition, the subtraction sentence can be introduced.

ACTIVITY 9-4   The Subtraction Sentence

- Put a set of seven markers on a flannel or magnetic board. "If I take four of these disks off the board, how many will be left?"
- Put a felt or magnetic "7" beneath the seven disks.
- Take four disks off the board. After children give the answer, put the complete sentence "7 − 4 = 3" beneath the remaining disks. Relate the parts of the sentence to the concrete model. Children should see that the "7" represents the original set, the "4" represents the disks that were removed, and the "3" represents the remaining disks. Tell them that the "−" sign is read as "minus."
- Repeat with other sets containing nine or fewer objects.

---

2. Using Manipulative Materials to Reinforce the Meaning of Addition and Subtraction

You should help children reinforce their understanding of addition and subtraction by having them engage in activities with a variety of concrete materials. Teachers who provide opportunities for children to do this report that many children need fewer drill-and-practice exercises at a later time, because of their greater understanding and because they commit many of the facts to memory as they manipulate the objects. Activities like these are examples:

ACTIVITY 9-5 Adding with Beads

- Give a child a 9-inch by 12-inch card with beads strung across the face. The child separates the beads into two groups and writes the addition sentence that describes the arrangement of beads.

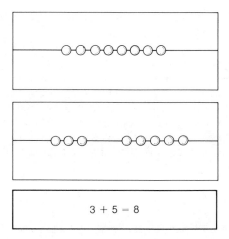

- Separate the beads other ways and use cards with other sets of beads.[1]

ACTIVITY 9-6 Adding Objects to a Container

- Drop six objects into a margarine tub.
- Write a large six on the tub.

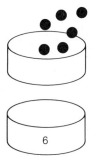

[1] Adapted from Mary Baratta-Lorton, *Workjobs* (Menlo Park, Cal.: Addison–Wesley Publishing Company, 1972), pp. 200–201.

- Drop another object into the container. "How many in the tub now?" "What addition fact should we use to tell how many objects in all?" Write the sentence: "6 + 1 = 7" on the chalkboard.
- Repeat with unmarked tubs and combinations with sums less than ten.[2]

ACTIVITY 9-7   Subtracting with Blocks

- Give a child an aluminum pie tin and several wooden blocks.
- The child chooses a number, say 6, and puts that many blocks into the tin. The child removes a few of the blocks, puts the tin upside down over them, and puts the remaining blocks on top of the tin.
- The child writes two number sentences for the tin. If two blocks are covered, the sentences are 6 − 4 = 2 and 6 − 2 = 4.
- Repeat with different combinations of six blocks and with more or fewer than six blocks.[3]

ACTIVITY 9-8   Dropping Beads

- Enclose seven small wooden beads in your hand. Open your hand so the children can count the beads. Close your hand.
- Drop a bead from your hand onto the table. "How many beads in my hand now?" Drop another bead. "How many beads in my hand now?" "How many beads did I drop?" Confirm both numbers by having children count the beads in your hand and on the table.
- Write the subtraction sentence: "7 − 2 = 5" on the chalkboard and discuss its meaning.
- Repeat with other combinations of seven and other quantities of beads.[4]

ACTIVITY 9-9   Cuisenaire Trains

- Give a child Cuisenaire rods.
- The child selects a rod, say a 6 rod, and makes all of the trains for six.
- The child writes a sentence for each train: 1 + 5 = 6, 2 + 4 = 6, 3 + 3 = 6, 4 + 2 = 6, and 5 + 1 = 6. (0 + 6 = 6 and 6 + 0 = 6 may also be written.)

---

[2] Adapted from Larry Leutzinger, *Strategies for Learning the Basic Facts* (Cedar Falls, Iowa: Iowa Council of Teachers of Mathematics, 1981), p. 6.

[3] Adapted from Mary Baratta-Lorton, pp. 198–199.

[4] Adapted from Larry Leutzinger, p. 14.

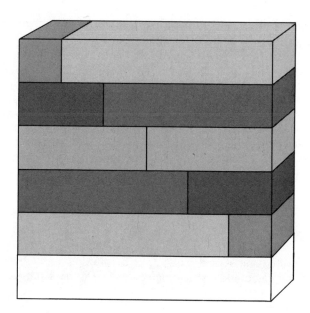

- Repeat with other rods.

Activity 9-10 deals with addition and the comparison situation for subtraction.

ACTIVITY 9-10   Addition and Subtraction

- Have each child take a couple of handfuls of Unifix cubes of four different colors. Tell them to sort and join all cubes of the same color.
- Ask questions:

  - "Which color do you have most of?" Have each child hold up his or her longest link. "Who has the most?"

  - "Which color do you have the fewest of?" Have each child hold up his or her shortest link. "Who has the fewest?"

  - "How many more do you have in your longest link than in your shortest link?"

  - "Can you find two smaller links that together make one as long as the longest?"[5]

---

[5] Adapted from A. Dean Hendrickson, *Mathematics the Piaget Way* (St. Paul: Minnesota Council on Quality Education, 1980), p. 9.

Examples of real-world situations for introducing the how-many-more-are-needed and set-within-a-set situations are

- "Sally is saving the inner seals from the lids of her favorite soft drink for a free kite. She must have nine seals for the kite she wants. She has six seals now. How many more seals does she need?"

- "Billy watched eight airplanes fly overhead. Before they disappeared from sight he saw that four of the planes were red. How many of the planes were not red?"

**Self-check
of Objectives 5 and 6**

Demonstrate with manipulative materials or by drawing a sequence of pictures how to introduce addition and its sentence. Do the same for subtraction.

Explain why a wide variety of manipulative materials should be available to children who are learning addition and subtraction. Describe some of these materials.

3. Introducing the Vertical Notation Form

The mathematical sentence, rather than the **vertical notation** form, is most often used when children are introduced to addition. There are at least two reasons for this:

- It can be considered a shorthand form of the longer word sentence; hence its meaning is more easily recognized.

- It gives children a means of interpreting real-word situations that involve numbers.

However, children must also learn to use the vertical notation form because it is used in algorithms for addition, subtraction, and multiplication. One way to introduce vertical notation is with clothespins on a card.

ACTIVITY 9-11   Addition Sentence Versus Vertical Form

- Arrange two groups of clothespins along the edge of a large card.

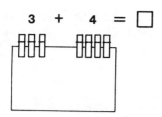

- Hold the card so the pins are along the top. Put the card against the chalkboard and write the addition sentence.
- Turn the card so the pins are along the right edge, hold it against the board, and write the vertical form.

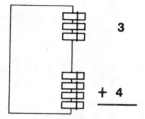

- Discuss the ways the two forms are alike and the way they are different.
- Repeat with other sets of pins.

Once children are familiar with the vertical form for addition use a similar activity to introduce the vertical form for subtraction.

Write examples of the sentence and vertical form for addition involving the addends 6 and 3 and their sum. Demonstrate with materials or illustrate with a sequence of pictures how you can help children make the transition from the sentence to vertical form.

Self-check of Objective 7

4. Addition and Subtraction Facts with Sums Greater Than Nine

An understanding of tens and ones in base-ten numeration is a foundation for understanding addition facts having sums greater than 9. First help children learn the basic facts that involve pairs of addends with a sum of 10 by using objects, markers, and charts showing patterns that make them easy to learn.

Arrange markers on a flannel or magnetic board to show patterns of combinations that make 10. After work with markers, use Activity 9-12 to prepare a chart for future reference as facts with sums from 11 through 18 are learned.

ACTIVITY 9-12   Addition Chart

- Begin with a chart containing pairs of addends at the left, ten empty circles in each line, and the numeral 10 on each line at the right.
- Discuss the first combination: $10+0$. Then have a child color ten of the circles.
- Consider the combination $9+1$. Have a child color 9 of the circles. Discuss the fact that 9 colored and 1 plain circle make 10 circles.
- Do the same for each combination until the chart is completed.

10+0	● ● ● ● ● ● ● ● ● ●	10
9+1	● ● ● ● ● ● ● ● ● ○	10
8+2	● ● ● ● ● ● ● ● ○ ○	10
7+3	● ● ● ● ● ● ● ○ ○ ○	10
6+4	● ● ● ● ● ● ○ ○ ○ ○	10
5+5	● ● ● ● ● ○ ○ ○ ○ ○	10
4+6	● ● ● ● ○ ○ ○ ○ ○ ○	10
3+7	● ● ● ○ ○ ○ ○ ○ ○ ○	10
2+8	● ● ○ ○ ○ ○ ○ ○ ○ ○	10
1+9	● ○ ○ ○ ○ ○ ○ ○ ○ ○	10
0+10	○ ○ ○ ○ ○ ○ ○ ○ ○ ○	10

The addition combinations with sums greater than 10 need to be introduced with markers and not with pictures alone. Figure 9-2 illustrates the sentence $8+4=12$ with disks. Children can rearrange the disks to show that other combinations also equal 12: $9+3=12$, $7+5=12$, $6+6=12$, $5+7=12$, $4+8=12$, and $3+9=12$. In each case there is a set of 10 plus 2 more disks. (The combinations $10+2$, $11+1$, $1+11$, and $2+10$ also equal 12, but are not basic facts.)

Subtraction with minuends 11 through 18 can be directly related to the addition facts with sums greater than 10. After markers have been

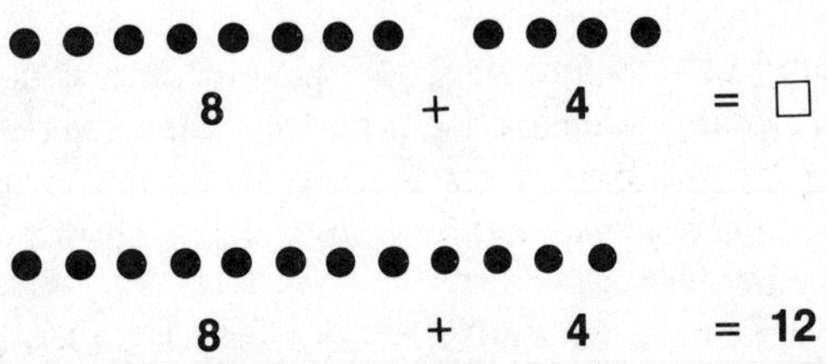

FIGURE 9-2
Sets and sentences illustrating the steps in addition for $8+4=\square$

● ● ● ● ● ● ● ●   ● ● ● ●
    8   +   4   = □

● ● ● ● ● ● ● ● ● ● ● ●
    8   +   4   = 12

used to show sentences such as $8+4=12$ and $6+9=15$, use them to show $12-4=8$ and $15-9=6$. Children need manipulative experiences with all combinations with sums through 18 before beginning paper-and-pencil practice activities.

5. Using the Number Line to Learn Facts

A chalkboard number line is useful to reinforce children's understanding of addition and subtraction and to build mental images of the operations. Some teachers use the idea of a cricket or frog jumping along the line to introduce a chalkboard number line. To illustrate the sentence $3+4=\square$, children can see the cricket or frog start at 0 and jump to 3, and then jump four more units to 7, as shown in Figure 9-3.

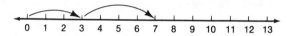

FIGURE 9-3
Number line showing how to illustrate the sentence $3+4=7$

The number line is also useful for showing the relationship between addition and subtraction. First, use an addition sentence. The sentence $6+3=9$ is illustrated in Figure 9-4(a). Children should think of ways the number line can show subtraction. Those who have suggestions should have an opportunity to present their ideas to the class. The procedure illustrated on the number line in Figure 9-4(b) follows logically from the use of the "jumps" in addition. Children should note that the jump showing the number to be subtracted begins at the point that indicates the number from which it is to be subtracted and moves to the left. The fact that subtraction jumps move to the left and addition jumps move to the right should be stressed.

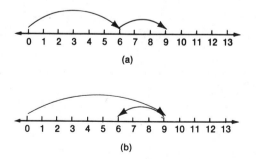

(a)

(b)

FIGURE 9-4
Number lines used to illustrate the inverse relationship between addition and subtraction. (a) The addition sentence $6+3=9$. (b) The subtraction sentence $9-3=6$.

The number line can help children understand the meaning of basic addition facts with larger sums. A sentence, such as $7+8=\square$, should be displayed. Call a child to the number line to show the first addend using a cricket jump. Then the second addend should be shown with a second

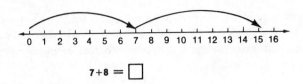

FIGURE 9-5
Number line showing the addition $7 + 8 = \square$

$7+8 = \square$

jump of eight units (Figure 9-5). The addition sentences should be written on the chalkboard as the steps are shown on the number line.

Self-check of Objective 8

Draw two number lines from 0 to 10. Illustrate the addition sentence $4 + 5 = \square$ with cricket jumps on one. Illustrate the subtraction sentence $8 - 3 = \square$ with cricket jumps on the other.

REINFORCING THE LEARNING OF BASIC FACTS

All children who are capable of doing so should commit the basic facts to memory for immediate recall. Rather than giving children random practice-and-drill activities, you should help them by presenting strategies for understanding and remembering the facts. Several effective strategies are presented here.

1. Using Families to Learn the Facts

Addition and subtraction facts can be organized by *families*. Addition and subtraction facts are grouped by families in these two ways:

- All sentences for a given sum are grouped together: $3 + 0 = 3$, $2 + 1 = 3$, $1 + 2 = 3$, $0 + 3 = 3$, and $3 - 0 = 3$, $3 - 1 = 2$, $3 - 2 = 1$, $3 - 3 = 0$.

- Or, the four combinations involving a given pair of addends and their sum are grouped together: $6 + 2 = 8$, $2 + 6 = 8$, $8 - 2 = 6$, and $8 - 6 = 2$.

2. Using Doubles and Near Doubles

Doubles are combinations with like addends; **near doubles** are combinations with numbers that differ by one or two. Most students have little difficulty learning the doubles. Once these have been learned, the near doubles can be learned.

ACTIVITY 9-13   Near Doubles

• Have each child make a set of double cards.

$$4+4 \qquad 5+5 \qquad 6+6$$

• Hold up a near-double card, such as one with the combination $5+6$. Ask, "Which double card will help us with this addition?" Some children will hold up $5+5$, while others may hold up $6+6$. The first card shows a "double plus one" combination, while the second shows a "double minus one" combination. Either strategy is a useful one, and children should be encouraged to consider both of them.
• Repeat with other combinations of numbers.
• Reinforce with a worksheet containing examples like this:
"Ring the doubles you could use to solve the combination on each truck."[6]

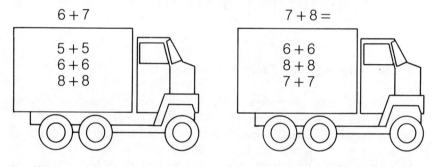

$$6+7 \qquad\qquad\qquad 7+8=$$

$5+5$	$6+6$
$6+6$	$8+8$
$8+8$	$7+7$

3. Adding One Less Than Ten

Children's knowledge of adding a single number to 10 can be used to help learn addition with 9. Present orally combinations with ten, such as $10+3$, $10+8$, and $10+9$. Follow with this activity where children add one less than 10:

ACTIVITY 9-14   Adding One Less Than Ten

Present oral problems. The first should contain a 10 as one addend; the second has the 10 replaced by 9: "$10+5=$? (15) $9+5$ is one less or ?" (14)   "$10+7=$? (17) $9+7$ is one less or ?" (16)[7]

---

[6] Adapted from Larry Leutzinger, pp. 24–25.

[7] Adapted from Larry Leutzinger, p. 29.

+	0	1	2	3	4	5	6	7	8	9
0	0	1	2	3	4	5	6	7	8	9
1	1	2	3	4	5	6	7	8	9	10
2	2	3	4	5	6	7	8	9	10	11
3	3	4	5	6	7	8	9	10	11	12
4	4	5	6	7	8	9	10	11	12	13
5	5	6	7	8	9	10	11	12	13	14
6	6	7	8	9	10	11	12	13	14	15
7	7	8	9	10	11	12	13	14	15	16
8	8	9	10	11	12	13	14	15	16	17
9	9	10	11	12	13	14	15	16	17	18

FIGURE 9-6
An addition table helps children master the addition and subtraction facts.

4. Using the Addition Table to Learn Facts

Sometime during their work with addition and subtraction, children should see the facts organized in a table (Figure 9-6). The table should not be presented already filled in; neither should the children simply fill it in as a seat-work activity. Rather, children should complete it as part of a group lesson during which you discuss with them features that will help them master the facts. Among the ideas to be stressed are these:

1. The first row at the top and the first column at the left contain facts involving zero—the identity for addition. (Ways of teaching the addition identity are discussed later in this chapter.) These facts are easily mastered.

2. The second row and second column contain sums for facts involving 1 as an addend. The sums in each row and column result from adding 1 to the other addend.

3. Sums for facts involving 2 and 3 as addends are in the third and fourth rows and columns, respectively.

4. The diagonal from the upper-left to lower-right corners contains the sums of the doubles, that is, pairs of like addends.

5. The diagonals immediately above and below the one containing doubles contain the near doubles. Sentences like $5 + 6 = 11$ and $7 + 8 = 15$ are near doubles. Once children have mastered the doubles they can use them to learn the near doubles.

6. By now most of the table has been filled in and there remain only a few facts to consider. These are the combinations that give children the most difficulty. Most children will be impressed with how few difficult combinations there are. These should be identified and put on flashcards for future practice.

7. Because subtraction is the inverse of addition, the table also contains the subtraction facts. Instead of using the numbers in the top row and left column as addends to determine sums, use a sum and addend to find a missing addend. To find the answer to $9 - 6 = \square$, locate 9 opposite 6 in the left column and go to the top of the column containing 9; the answer—3—is located at the top of the column. For $9 - 3 = \square$, locate 9 opposite 3 in the left column and go to the top of the column to locate the answer—6.

8. Point out the roles of 0 and 1 in subtraction; discuss the doubles and near doubles in a manner similar to the discussion of them in addition; this will help children master them for subtraction.

Four strategies for helping children learn the addition and subtraction facts have been described. Give an example of each strategy.

Self-check of Objective 9

PRACTICING THE BASIC FACTS

Children's first experiences with addition and subtraction should be with activities that develop understanding of the operations and present the basic facts. Committing facts to memory is not a significant part of the initial learning, but when you are sure that children understand their meanings, provide opportunities for them to memorize each fact.

Five generalizations regarding practice in mathematics are given here:

1. Practice and understanding go hand in hand.

2. The reasons for practice must be clear to children.

3. The kind and amount of practice are not likely to be the same for all children at the same time.

4. The practice sessions should be brief and occur often.

5. A variety of materials and procedures should be used.

In addition to these generalizations, which govern the way practice sessions are organized, there are principles that are helpful for guiding specific strategies during practice sessions.[8] During drill sessions, stress memorization. If children hesitate when shown a flashcard or given a combination orally, do not give an explanation or allow time for them to count on their fingers. Instead, show or name the answer. Then show the flashcard, or repeat the combination orally, and have the child respond immediately. Provide practice with only a few combinations at a time; give frequent review of previously learned combinations. Provide constant encouragement and recognition of progress through verbal praise and individual record charts.

Practice materials are available from many sources. Most commonly used are the practice pages from workbooks. These materials have a place in the program but should not be used to the exclusion of other materials. Cassette tape programs provide one means for individuals and small groups to practice on the specific facts with which they need help. Examples of tape programs are:

- *Arithmetricks*—a set of twelve tapes for the primary grades. Coronet Media, 65 E. South Water Street, Chicago, IL 60601.

- *Skillseekers*—a set of three separate kits, each with twelve tapes and practice cards. Addison–Wesley Publishing Company, Reading, MA 01867.

Many computer courseware programs include exercises for practicing basic facts. The *Prescriptive Math Drill* program from Hartley Courseware and *Milliken Math Sequences* from the Milliken Publishing Company are described in Chapter 6. You should consult catalogs of companies that develop mathematics software for their current programs. (Appendix B contains names and addresses of companies to which you can write for catalogs.) Preprogrammed devices such as Texas Instruments' "Little Professor" and the one illustrated in Figure 6-4 provide a variety of practice activities.

Calculators can be used for practicing basic facts. One way to do this is for one person to show a basic fact combination or to name one orally and then punch it into the calculator to determine the answer. Other children attempt to name the sum or difference before the child using the calculator shows it on the machine's display.

Games provide practice for both small and large groups. The teacher's manuals for mathematics series and mathematics games books contain directions for many games.[9]

---

[8] These principles are adapted from Edward J. Davis, "Teaching the Basic Facts," *Developing Computational Skills*, 1978 Yearbook of the National Council of Teachers of Mathematics, 1978, pp. 52–58.

[9] See, for example, Leonard M. Kennedy and Ruth L. Michon, *Games for Individualizing Mathematics Learning* (Columbus, Ohio: Charles E. Merrill Books, Inc., 1973), pp. 31–54;

Addition bingo is an example of a large group game. Each child is given one or two bingo cards on which numerals from 0 to 18 are printed (Figure 9-7). A numeral may appear more than once on a card. One at a time you show cards containing an addition combination or name the combination orally. Children cover the numeral that names the sum for the combination. Only one numeral is covered for each combination. A winner is declared when a child has five markers in a row, column, or diagonal. Bingo cards for all operations are available commercially or may be made by the teacher.

0	6	18	9	15
4	3	11	8	7
5	7	Free	17	16
6	15	13	2	4
10	1	12	14	6

FIGURE 9-7
Sample card for addition bingo

TEACHING SOME PROPERTIES OF ADDITION AND SUBTRACTION

Less emphasis is placed on properties of addition and subtraction today than at a former time. The commutative and associative properties and identity element for addition need not be stressed in highly formal ways; however, their meanings and applications should be developed informally.

1. The Commutative Property

The following procedure is one of the many effective ways to informally introduce the **commutative property.**

ACTIVITY 9-14   Commutative Property

- Give each child a paper plate that is divided into halves with a line, and a handful of markers.
- Have each child put a few markers in each half of the plate. Each child writes the addition sentence for the markers on the plate.

---

and Mary E. Platts, ed., *Plus*, rev. ed. (Stevensville, Mich.: Educational Services, Inc., 1975), pp. 69–122.

• Have each child turn the plate half way around, so that the two sets of markers are reversed. Each child writes a new sentence for the markers.

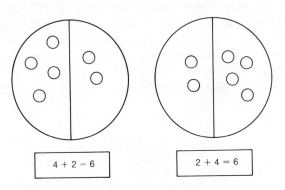

$$4 + 2 = 6 \qquad 2 + 4 = 6$$

• Discuss each of the sentences.

Other examples of how to help children learn the commutative property of addition are:

• Put two sets of clothespins on the edge of a large card. Hold the card against the chalkboard and write the sentence, including the sum, above the card. Turn the card so the order of the sets is reversed and write the new sentence.

• Use beads on pieces of stiff wire like those shown in Figure 9-8. Show the sets (a) and then reverse their order (b).

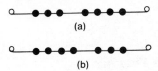

FIGURE 9-8
Beads on a wire to show sentences (a) $3 + 4 = \square$ and (b) $4 + 3 = \square$

• Use Cuisenaire rod trains. Put a train of a 3 rod and a 4 rod next to one made of a 4 rod and a 3 rod (Figure 9-9).

FIGURE 9-9
A Cuisenaire-rod train illustrates the commutative property.

• Use a number line such as the one shown in Figure 9-10.

FIGURE 9-10
Number line used to show the commutative nature of addition

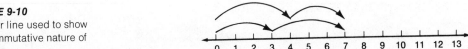

2. The Associative Property

The **associative property** of addition is used when three or more addends are added. Because addition can be done with only two addends at a time (it is a binary operation), it is necessary to select two of the three addends to add first; then the third number is added to the sum of the first two.

Addition using three addends is usually introduced before all the 100 basic addition facts have been introduced. No specific number of basic facts is a prerequisite, but children must previously have worked with all the basic facts they will use when they first work with three addends. As with other new topics, this one should be introduced by activities with sets of manipulative materials. During their first experiences with three addends, children should add them in order, reading from left to right.

- Use clothespins on a card. Put three sets of pins on one edge of the card. Place the card against the chalkboard, and write the addition sentence above the pins. Combine the pins in the two sets to the children's left; then unite the third set with the combined set.

- Use sets of beads on a wire, following the procedure for clothespins on a card.

- Use Cuisenaire rod trains. Make a 3-car train. Have children consider first the two rods on the left and then the third rod.

After children have learned to add in this manner, the associative property of addition can be introduced through a situation such as this:

ACTIVITY 9-15   Three Addends

- Arrange three small sets horizontally across a magnetic or flannel board, and put the mathematical sentence describing the situation beneath the markers.

$$\begin{array}{c} \circ\,\circ\,\circ \quad \circ\,\circ \quad \circ\,\circ\,\circ\,\circ \\[4pt] 3 \;+\; 2 \;+\; 4 \;=\; \square \end{array}$$

- Have a child join the first two sets of markers, and have the children think of the resulting addition sentence,

$$3+2=5$$

Put this sentence beneath the original sentence. Have the children note that there is a set of 4 to be joined with the new set of 5. Put the new sentence $5+4=\square$ beneath the others.

- When all of the steps are completed, these sentences will be on the board:

$$3+2+4=\square$$
$$3+2=5$$
$$5+4=\square$$
$$5+4=9$$

- Review the meaning of each of the sentences.
- Arrange the sets as they originally appeared on the board.
- Have a child join the second and third sets, and have the children discuss the resulting addition sentence, $2+4=6$. Put this sentence beneath the original sentence. Have the children note that there is now a set of 3 to be joined to the set of 6. Put the new sentence $3+6=\square$ beneath the others.
- When all of the steps are completed, these sentences will be on the board:

$$3+2+4=\square$$
$$2+4=6$$
$$3+6=\square$$
$$3+6=9$$

- Review the meaning of each sentence. Then compare them with the first group of sentences.
- Repeat with other sets.

Children in the third grade and beyond can refine their thinking about the two properties through work with examples like these:

$$246+398+2=\square$$

Consider the sum for this example without using paper and pencil. Do the children realize that they can add the 398 and 2 first to get the sum 400 and then add the 246 to 400? Other examples can combine the two properties:

$$696+241+4=\square$$
$$10+367+590=\square$$
$$16+83+7+4=\square$$

3. The Identity Element of Addition

Children who understand the meaning of zero will have little difficulty learning its role in addition. As they deal with markers to learn about

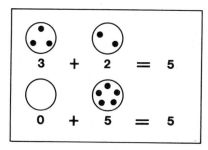

FIGURE 9-11
Sets illustrating addition sentences $3 + 2 = 5$ and $0 + 5 = 5$

addition, they will realize that when zero is an addend, there will be no markers representing that number. To make this more obvious, some primary-grade teachers prefer clearly identifying each group by putting a ring around the markers on a display board. The two addition sentences illustrated in Figure 9-11 are represented by ringed markers. The ring above the 0 in the second sentence indicates the absence of markers when zero is an addend.

Eventually children will see that when zero is one of a pair of addends, the sum is always the number of the other addend. Zero is the **identity element** for addition.

During work with subtraction children should be given opportunities for the role of zero to become clear to them. They should see that when zero is subtracted from another number, the answer is always the other number. And when a number is subtracted from itself, the answer is always zero.

Demonstrate with manipulative materials or in another suitable way how each of these number properties for addition can be demonstrated: commutative, associative, and identity.

Self-check of Objective 10

SPECIAL STUDENTS AND BASIC FACTS

Gifted and talented students seldom have difficulty understanding the meaning of addition and subtraction and learning the basic facts. They do need experiences with concrete materials as meanings are developed, but you are cautioned not to have them spend time on manipulative and drill-and-practice activities they do not need.

On the other hand, children with learning handicaps often have difficulty learning the facts. These children frequently need special activities in addition to the concrete activities they share with others. Highly structured procedures for performing computation have been developed for children with learning problems. *Oregon Math Computation* was developed for children of any age who have severe learning problems. It uses instructional methods that employ visual, auditory, and kinesthetic modes of presenting concepts and having children respond.[10]

In *Oregon Math* children learn verbal and visual cues that direct their actions and to add and subtract by counting on their fingers. For example, when addition is done, a lesson proceeds this way:

1.
3	6	8	5
+2	+2	+1	+2

2. TODAY WE ARE GOING TO ADD.
   Point to the + sign and say:
   THIS SIGN SAYS PLUS. IT TELLS US TO ADD.
3. THE BOTTOM NUMBER TELLS US HOW MANY FINGERS TO PUT UP.
   Point to the number 2 in the first problem.
4. HOW MANY FINGERS DO WE PUT UP?
   Tap the 2. Students respond in unison, "2." (If students do not respond in unison, say WAIT FOR THE SIGNAL.)
5. SHOW ME.
   Put up two fingers as students each put up two fingers.
6. THE TOP NUMBER TELLS US WHERE TO START COUNTING.
   Point to the number 3 in the first problem.
7. WHERE DO WE START COUNTING?
   Tap the 3 as students respond in unison, "3."
8. *Tap* the 3 on the board, saying:

$$3, \ . \ . \ . \ .$$

With students, touch one finger and put it down, saying:

$$4$$

And then the other finger, saying:

$$5$$

9. ARE ALL THE FINGERS GONE?
   Tap. Students respond in unison, "Yes."
10. WHERE DID WE STOP COUNTING?
    Tap. Students respond in unison, "5."
11. WHAT IS THE ANSWER?
    Tap. Students respond in unison, "5."
12. ⑤
13. Repeat steps 3–12 for remaining problems.[11]

---

[10] Lynn C. Weigel and Gerald A. Weigel, *Oregon Math Computation*, Speciman Set (Tigard, Ore.: C.C. Publications, 1979), p. 1.

[11] Lynn C. Weigel and Gerald A. Weigel, p. 1. (Used by permission.)

Although *Oregon Math* is designed for students with severe learning problems, it has features that can be adapted for students in any classroom who experience problems learning basic facts.

Terence Kramer and David A. Krug[12] discuss a different procedure they have used with educable mentally retarded students. It uses fixed reference points on each of the numerals. Students look at a numeral and imagine the points; then they touch or make small marks and count the points. Figure 9-12 shows each of the numerals with its reference points.

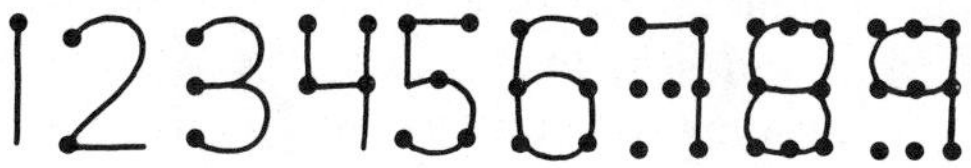

FIGURE 9-12
Reference points for numerals 1 through 9

Once children understand the pattern for each number, they are ready to use them for adding. Figure 9-13 shows the sequence of steps. First the pattern is put on each addend, then they are counted and the sum is recorded.

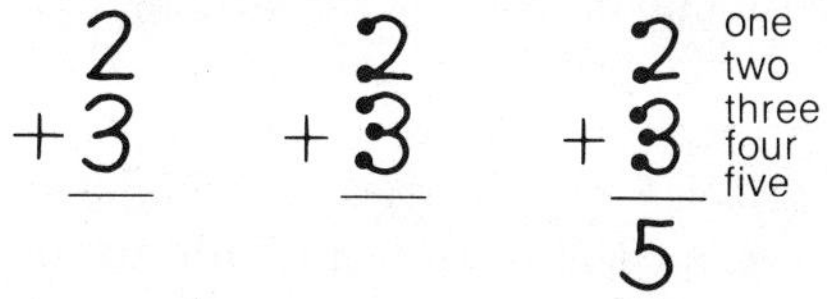

FIGURE 9-13
Sequence of steps for adding with reference points

A second way of adding is for the child to say the first addend—"2"—and then count on the second addend—"3, 4, 5."

Subtraction is done as shown in Figure 9-14. The child marks the points for the minuend. One point is marked out for each point in the subtrahend. The points that remain unmarked are the difference between the two numbers.

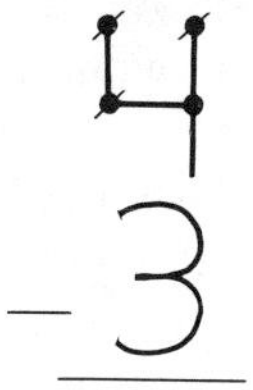

FIGURE 9-14
Subtraction with marked-out reference points

SUMMARY

Addition and subtraction are usually introduced during the first grade; and once each is introduced, they are usually studied simultaneously.

[12]Terence Kramer and David A. Krug, "A Rationale and Procedure for Teaching Addition," *Education and Training of the Mentally Retarded*, VIII, No. 3, (October 1973), pp. 140–145

There are 100 basic addition facts, which are all the possible combinations of pairs of addends smaller than 10 and their sums. Each addition combination has a corresponding subtraction fact. The real-life situation that gives rise to addition is the joining of two or more sets having no members in common; there are four situations that give rise to subtraction.

Children develop readiness for addition and subtraction as they learn to count using concrete materials and the number line. Working in the concrete–manipulative mode with real objects and markers gives children opportunities to join and separate sets of objects; this is the basis for understanding the meaning of addition and subtraction and the use of abstract sentences.

Once children know the meaning of addition and subtraction, they need to learn strategies for learning the facts and to engage in activities that will help them commit each fact to memory. Strategies that use families of facts, doubles and near doubles, adding one less than ten, and the addition table should be used. Practice pages in workbooks, taped and computer courseware programs, calculator activities, and games provide a variety of practice experiences. Children's understanding of the commutative and associative properties and the identity element for addition should be developed through work with manipulative materials.

Children who have difficulty memorizing the basic facts often need a structured way of dealing with the facts. *Oregon Math* and a scheme using reference points on numbers are two ways learning-handicapped children might use to cope with the addition and subtraction facts.

STUDY QUESTIONS AND ACTIVITIES

1. Addition and subtraction are inverse operations. One way for children to grasp the meaning of inverse operations is to consider doing and undoing operations in everyday, nonmathematical situations. Opening, then closing a door is an example. Name five similar situations that are suitable for primary-grade children. Name at least two other pairs of mathematical inverse operations besides addition and subtraction.

2. An activity similar to the one described above can be used to make the commutative property of addition clearer to children. In some instances a sequence of actions lead to the same result no matter the order in which they are done. You can add milk to cocoa or cocoa to milk to make a cocoa drink. In other instances the results are dramatically different when the sequence is reversed. Opening a door and walking through leads to a far different result than walking through the door before opening it. List five pairs of actions that are commutative and five pairs that are not.

3. Some strategies for helping children learn basic addition and subtraction facts are presented in this chapter. Read appropriate articles from this chapter's reading list to identify other strategies. Write a brief description of each strategy.

4. Speed drills in which children furnish sums or differences for a set of addition or subtraction facts while being timed by their teacher are commonly used to help them commit the facts to memory. Write a paragraph in which you present a rationale that either argues for or against this practice.

5. Add games and activities suitable for developing children's mastery of the basic addition and subtraction facts to your file. Include both group and individual as well as self-correcting and teacher-corrected types of games and activities. If possible, find at least one game and activity that serves each of these purposes: helps develop a child's understanding of addition or subtraction, provides practice, and helps evaluate a child's understanding of addition or subtraction.

KEY TERMS

sum	mathematical sentences
addends	vertical notation
subtraction	doubles
minuend	near doubles
subtrahend	commutative property
remainder	associative property
basic addition fact	identity element
subtraction fact	

FOR FURTHER READING

Ashlock, Robert B. "Teaching the Basic Facts: Three Classes of Activities," *Arithmetic Teacher*, XVIII, No. 6 (October 1971), pp. 359–364. According to Ashlock, three classifications of activities are involved in learning the basic facts: understanding the facts, relating the facts, and mastering the facts. Illustrated examples of activities at each level are given.

————, and Carolynn A. Washbon. "Games: Practice Activities for the Basic Facts," *Developing Computational Skills*, 1978 Yearbook of the National Council of Teachers of Mathematics (Reston, Va.: The Council), pp. 39–50. Describes the role of practice activities and guidelines for selecting and preparing them, along with examples of games. A short list of steps for creating games helps the teacher design his or her own games.

Campbell, Patricia F. "What Do Children See in Mathematics Textbook Pictures," *Arithmetic Teacher*, XXVIII, No. 5 (January 1981), pp. 12–16.
The author interviewed first-grade children to get their interpretations of pictures portraying addition and subtraction situations. She found four levels of interpretation, ranging from no understanding to full understanding. She concludes that teachers need to know each child's level of understanding.

Hutchinson, James W., and Carol E. Hutchinson. "Homemade Device for Quick Recall of Basic Facts," *Arithmetic Teacher*, XXV, No. 4 (January 1978), pp. 54–55. An overhead transparency using a grid of random digits and paper shields that reveal rows and columns of digits offers opportunity for several skill-development activities; for example, recall of basic facts (sums and products), comparing numbers, reading two- and three-place numbers.

King, Julia A. "Missing Addends: A Case of Reading Comprehension," *Arithmetic Teacher*, XXX, No. 1 (September 1982), pp. 44–45.
Children are frequently confused by simple missing addend sentences. The author contends that it is a reading problem not a mathematics problem. A game, "Are You Kidding," is recommended as one way to help children who have this problem.

Myers, Ann C., and Carol A. Thornton. "The Learning Disabled Child—Learning the Basic Facts, *Arithmetic Teacher*, XXV, No. 3 (December 1977), pp. 46–50. Even though the title of the article refers to learning-disabled children, the strategies for helping children master the basic addition and multiplication facts and applying them to work with larger numbers are applicable to all children. Explains examples of five different strategies.

Rathmell, Edward C. "Using Strategies to Teach the Basic Facts," *Developing Computational Skills*, 1978 Yearbook of the National Council of Teachers of Mathematics (Reston, Va.: The Council), pp. 13–38. Presents strategies for organizing basic facts for aiding children's understanding and retention. Includes many illustrations.

Thompson, Charles S., and William P. Dunlop. "Basic Facts: Do Your Children Understand or Do They Memorize?" *Arithmetic Teacher*, XXV, No. 3 (December 1977), pp. 14–16. Discusses two simple procedures for diagnosing and analyzing children's knowledge of basic facts, level of understanding, and rate of learning facts. Both require materials easily and inexpensively made by a teacher.

Thompson, Charles S., and John Van de Walle. "Paper Dot Plates Give Numbers Meaning," *Arithmetic Teacher*, XXVIII, No. 1 (September 1980), pp. 3–7.
Paper plates containing round dots serve to introduce counting, matching, addition and subtraction sentences, and other concepts.

Van de Walle, John, and Charles S. Thompson. "A Poster-Board Balance Helps Write Equations," *Arithmetic Teacher*, XXVIII, No. 9 (May 1981), pp. 4–8.
A simple poster-board model of a balance scale attached to the chalkboard serves as a means of helping children understand the meaning of *equals*. Either dots or numerals are used in the pans to develop the concept.

10

Extending the Operations of Addition and Subtraction

Upon completion of Chapter 10 you will be able to:

1. Explain the meaning of higher-decade addition, and describe a minimum of two materials and procedures for helping children understand and perform it accurately.

2. Demonstrate with place-value devices, such as a pocket chart, beansticks, and an abacus, how to represent the addition of two numbers greater than 10 when regrouping (carrying) is not required and when it is.

3. Explain two different algorithms for subtracting when regrouping (borrowing) is necessary, and demonstrate with materials and procedures how to make each process meaningful to children.

4. Demonstrate a one-step process for subtraction involving minuends that contain zeros, such as in the example

    6002
    −4365

5. Use a number line to represent the meaning of addition and subtraction of integers.

6. Describe briefly four addition and subtraction activities for the calculator.

7. Describe common errors committed by children who experience difficulty with addition and subtraction algorithms.

8. Explain low-stress algorithms for addition and subtraction, and tell for whom they are useful.

9. Explain three challenges dealing with addition and subtraction for gifted and talented students.

Materials and procedures for introducing addition and subtraction and their properties are discussed in Chapter 9. The present chapter extends the discussion to include addition and subtraction of larger whole numbers and small integers.

TEACHING HIGHER-DECADE ADDITION

Higher-decade addition is adding a number smaller than 10 to a number between 9 and 100. Examples are $23 + 6 = 29$ and $46 + 9 = 55$. The importance of being able to add such numbers in a single step, with no regrouping, is evident when you consider these situations:

- You are adding $8 + 9 + 7 + 8$. After you add 8 and 9, you add 7 to 17 and then you add 8 to 24.

- You are multiplying 96×48.

$$\begin{array}{r} 48 \\ \times 96 \\ \hline \end{array}$$

After you multiply 6 times 8, you record "8" and "carry" 4. The product of 6 times 4, 24, is added to the 4 that you carried. As the multiplication of 90×48 is completed, you add 7 to 36.

In both cases a person who can complete addition of the two numbers in one step has an advantage over one who must do the addition in stages. Children need special instruction in adding these numbers.

Skip-counting, which is discussed in Chapter 8, contributes to children's background for this addition; but it will not lead to a high level of proficiency, because it deals with patterns rather than random situations, as occurs in the previous examples of addition and multiplication. Third- and fourth-grade children should have introductory and practice activities like the following so they will understand higher-decade addition:

ACTIVITY 10-1   Higher-Decade Addition

- Use a hundreds chart (see Activity 8-4).
- For a sentence like $45 + 6 = \square$, call the children's attention to 45 on the chart; then have them count on 6. "Where did the count stop?" "If you begin at 55, where will the count stop?" "What is $65 + 6$? $75 + 6$? $85 + 6$?"
- Repeat with other numbers.
- Variation: Use a number line rather than a hundreds chart.

After children understand higher-decade addition, they need practice so they can do it as a one-step process. Here are samples of both written and verbal exercises:

- List addition sentences on a worksheet according to a pattern:

$$5+3=\square, \ 15+3=\square, \ . \ . \ . \ 95+3=\square$$
$$7+8=\square, \ 17+8=\square, \ . \ . \ . \ 87+8=\square$$

- List addition sentences on a worksheet in random order:

$$14+9=\square, \ 35+7=\square, \ 64+8=\square$$

- Dictate sentences to which children give oral responses: "Add 6 to 45." "Add 4 to the product of 8 and 7."

***Self-check
of Objective 1***

Explain the meaning of higher-decade addition, and describe at least one situation in which it is used. What materials and procedures can you use to help children understand this type of addition and perform it rapidly?

TEACHING ADDITION OF LARGER WHOLE NUMBERS

Children who have a good understanding of whole numbers and place value are ready to start adding tens and hundreds numbers. This work frequently begins in the late first grade. A first lesson should begin with a common problem situation and proportional place-value models such as a place-value pocket chart or beansticks with which children are familiar.

ACTIVITY 10-2   Adding Tens

- Tell a story. "Yesterday John had thirty baseball trading cards. He got twenty more today. How many cards does he have now?"
- Allow time for children to determine the answer by individual methods.
- When children have determined their answers, write the addition sentence:

$$30+20=50$$

- Write the same problem in vertical form:

$$\begin{array}{r} 30 \\ +20 \\ \hline \end{array}$$

- Have a child represent the addends in a place-value pocket chart.

Tens	Ones
⊟⊟⊟	
⊟⊟	

$30 \longrightarrow$ 3 tens

$+\,20 \longrightarrow +2$ tens

- Have another child combine the 3 tens bundles and the 2 tens bundles and put them in the chart's bottom pocket. Discuss the fact that there are a total of 5 tens, or 50.
- Put the answer in the algorithm.
- Repeat with similar situations and numbers until the process is clear.
- Variations: Children can show the 3 tens and the 2 tens with beansticks, Cuisenaire rods, Unifix cubes, or Dienes blocks.

In lessons that follow, children can use worksheets that contain pictures of the place-value pocket chart or another place-value model. Instead of using markers (concrete mode), they use pictures of them (semiconcrete mode). Figure 10-1 illustrates an example of the type of work children might complete on a worksheet. To illustrate $40 + 30 = \square$, a child draws markers to show the 4 tens in one addend and the 3 tens in the other. Then the child writes numerals at the bottom to indicate the total number of tens—7—and ones—0. Six or eight examples can be put on one worksheet.

Tens	Ones
⊟⊟⊟⊟	
⊟⊟⊟	
7	0

FIGURE 10-1
Child's worksheet showing that $40 + 30 = 70$

Addition of only multiples of ten will not present any special problems to most children. This should be soon followed by addition of numbers without zero in the ones place. Most textbooks introduce the addition of these numbers with examples that do not require regrouping, or "carrying," as the numbers are added. Some authorities believe children should begin regrouping right away. Their argument states that when children add two numbers, such as 23 and 45, using the conventional algorithm form

$$\begin{array}{r} 23 \\ +45 \\ \hline \end{array}$$

they can begin their addition in either the tens or the ones place and get the correct sum either way. Thus they do not learn the value of beginning addition in the ones place. If an addition requires regrouping, as

$$\begin{array}{r} 28 \\ +47 \\ \hline \end{array}$$

does, they will learn from the beginning that it is convenient to start the addition in the ones place and then go to the tens place. You will probably decide which kind of example to use on the basis of what the textbooks used in the classroom include. This is reasonable in most cases, because the textbook will provide most of the practice materials the children will use once they have been introduced to the new work. Of course it is not necessary to introduce a topic according to the text's order of presentation. If your children have a good understanding of numbers and the simpler addition processes, you may choose to use examples that require regrouping regardless of the text's order of progression. Then addition practice with and without regrouping can proceed as you select material from the textbook as needed.

When addition with **regrouping** is introduced, beansticks are useful for making regrouping meaningful. The following situation might begin a lesson:

ACTIVITY 10-3 Regrouping

- Tell a story. "Sally has twenty-six marbles. Her grandmother brings her seventeen more. How many marbles does she now have?"
- Have the children determine the addition sentence for this problem:

$$26 + 17 = \square$$

- Have each child show the two numbers with beansticks.

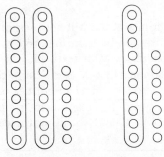

- Each child combines the loose beans and determines how many there are. "Are there more than 9 loose beans?" (Yes.) "What do you do if there are more than 9 loose beans? (Exchange 10 of them for a tens stick.) Have each child do this.

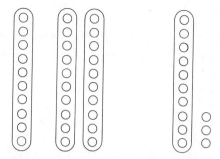

- Each child combines the tens sticks. "How many tens sticks do you have?" (There are 4 tens sticks.) "How many tens and how many ones do you have?" (There are 4 tens and 3 ones.)

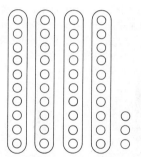

- Repeat with similar stories and numbers.

Children should have enough activities with place-value materials to make the process clear before an algorithm is introduced. When you introduce an algorithm, relate each of its steps to each step on the place-value model. Using the problem in Activity 10-3 as an example, children will work with this algorithm:

$$\begin{array}{r} 26 \\ +17 \\ \hline \end{array}$$

They should associate the addition of 6 and 7 with the combining of the loose beans. The 3 in the ones place is associated with the 3 loose beans. The 1 that is "carried" in the algorithm should be associated with the exchange of 10 loose beans for 1 tens stick; and the addition of the 1, the 2, and the 1 should be associated with the combining of the tens sticks.

Some children are helped by seeing the algorithm's numerals expressed in expanded notation:

$$26 = 2 \text{ tens and } 6 \text{ ones}$$
$$+17 = \underline{1 \text{ ten and } 7 \text{ ones}}$$

Now when they add 6 and 7, they see that they have 13 ones. When ten of these are regrouped as 1 ten, they can add the ten to the 2 tens and 1 ten, giving a total of 4 tens.

As children proceed through the grades, you should review the meaning of regrouping with larger numbers. A good way to do this is with an abacus. This nonproportional device can show the larger numbers and illustrate each step in the algorithm.

To use the abacus to illustrate addition, put an example such as

$$4358$$
$$+2926$$

on the chalkboard and go through the steps shown in Figure 10-2. Ask a child to set beads on the abacus to represent the addend in the lower portion of the algorithm, 2926. Then the other addend, 4358, can be

FIGURE 10-2
Abacus illustrating steps in addition. (a) The two addends. (b) Addition and regrouping in the ones place. (c) Addition in the tens place and addition and regrouping in the hundreds place. (d) Addition in the thousands place.

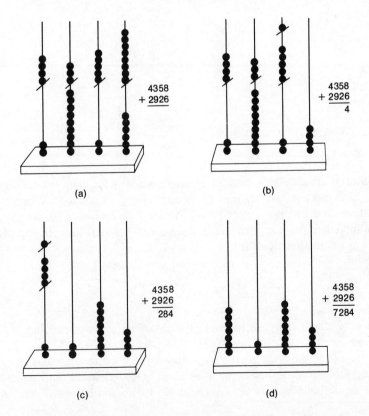

represented with beads at the top of the abacus. In the figure, small clips, such as tiny plastic clothespins, separate the beads on the wires, to illustrate the two addends. The abacus would appear as shown in (a). The meaning of the beads and their relationship to the addends in the algorithm should be discussed. Next, a child should unite the beads on the ones wire by removing the clip between the two sets (b), while a second child works with the algorithm on the board. The regrouping of the sum in the ones place is demonstrated as ten beads from the ones wire are exchanged for one bead on the tens wire. (The one bead on the tens wire is separated from the others by a clip.) The beads on the tens wire are then combined, and the numbers in the tens place of the algo-rithm are added. The process continues as the beads on the hundreds wire are united. Again the regrouping is shown as ten beads from the hundreds wire are exchanged for one bead on the thousands wire (c). The process is completed as the beads on the thousands wire are com-bined and the algorithm is finished (d). The addition of pairs of numbers having sums to 9999 can be shown on a four-wire abacus. For larger numbers an abacus with more wires is needed.

Select any two place-value models described in this chapter and demon-strate how to use them to represent the addition examples in the margin. (Use a sequence of pictures to represent the steps if the two models are unavailable for your demonstrations.) Write the steps as they appear in the algorithm for the sequence of actions with the models.

Self-check of Objective 2

64	74
+33	+87

INTRODUCING SUBTRACTION OF LARGER WHOLE NUMBERS

Introductory work with subtraction of larger whole numbers should par-allel introductory work for addition. That is, first work should be with realistic situations and adequate time for children to explore the opera-tion's meaning. "A rope 70 feet long is being cut into smaller jump ropes. If 40 feet of rope have been cut from it, how many feet remain to be cut?" After children have used their own methods to determine the an-swer, have different ones share their procedures. Place-value models should be brought into the discussion either by a child or by you. Bean-sticks are illustrated here, but any of the models can be used. In Figure 10-3 (a) the 70 feet of rope is represented by 7 ten sticks. The removal of 40 feet of rope is indicated by removing 4 of the ten sticks. The an-swer, 30 feet of rope, is represented by the 3 ten sticks that remain (b).

Other similar problem situations should be illustrated with models un-

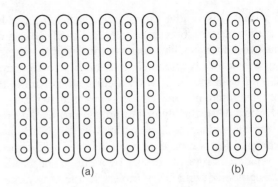

FIGURE 10-3
Beansticks showing the meaning of $70 - 40 = 30$

til the meaning of the subtraction is clear. The children should also represent situations by drawing markers on place-value models illustrated on worksheets. Figure 10-4 illustrates an example of how a child can show the subtraction $80 - 50 = \square$ on a picture of a place-value pocket chart. In (a), the 80 is represented by 8 bundles of ten markers drawn on the chart. In (b), 5 bundles have been marked out to indicate the subtraction of 50, leaving the 3 bundles that represent the answer. The algorithm form

$$\begin{array}{r} 60 \\ -20 \\ \hline \end{array}$$

should be introduced only after children indicate that they are ready for it. Check the children's understanding from time to time by having them illustrate further examples with place-value models and drawings of them.

Tens	Ones
⊞⊞⊞⊞⊞⊞⊞⊞	

(a)

FIGURE 10-4
Child's worksheet showing that $80 - 50 = 30$

Tens	Ones
⊠⊠⊠⊠⊠⊞⊞⊞	

(b)

TEACHING SUBTRACTION WITH REGROUPING

Subtraction with regrouping has been the subject of much debate: which of two methods of computation should children be taught?[1] The decomposition method is most commonly used, but there are many advocates for the equal-additions method.

1. The Decomposition Method

The **decomposition method** of subtraction is generally favored because children easily rationalize its process of regrouping as they use a place-value model. The relationship between subtraction and addition is emphasized by this method, because the steps of subtraction by decomposition are the reverse of those for addition by regrouping.

A good understanding of place value and addition of larger whole numbers, with and without regrouping, is a prerequisite of the decomposition method of subtraction. An understanding of expanded notation is also important. For example, children should know that the number 36 can be expressed as "36," "3 tens and 6 ones," "30 + 6," and "20 + 16."

The following activity will introduce children to subtraction using decomposition:

ACTIVITY 10-4 Decomposition

- "There were eighty-two boxes of apples at a fruit stand when it opened. During the day fifty-three boxes were sold. How many boxes were left at the end of the day?"
- Children should determine the mathematical sentence:

$$82 - 53 = \square$$

- Have a child show the number of boxes at the beginning of the day in a place-value pocket chart.

---

[1] Actually there are more than two processes. Not commonly used in school mathematics programs and subject to less debate are those described by Hitoshi Ikeda and Masui Ando, "A New Algorithm for Subtraction?" *Arithmetic Teacher*, XXI, No. 8 (December 1974), pp. 716–719, and by Paul R. Neureiter, "The 'Ultimate' Form of the Subtraction Algorithm," *Arithmetic Teacher*, XII, No. 4 (April 1965), pp. 277–281.

Tens	Ones
⊟⊟⊟⊟⊟⊟⊟⊟	▯▯

- Discuss the fact that there are not enough ones in the chart to take away 3. "What can we do to get enough ones?" (Regroup one of the tens as 10 ones.) Have a child do this.

Tens	Ones
⊟⊟⊟⊟⊟⊟⊟	▯▯▯▯▯▯▯▯▯▯▯▯

- Remove 3 of the ones markers. "How many ones are left?"

Tens	Ones
⊟⊟⊟⊟⊟⊟⊟	▯▯▯▯▯▯▯▯▯

- "We still have to take away five of the tens bundles. Will you do that, Juan? How many tens bundles are left?"
- "How many boxes of apples were left at the end of the day?"

Tens	Ones
⊟⊟	▯▯▯▯▯▯▯▯▯

- Repeat with other similar problems.
- Variations: Children can use individual sets of beansticks, Cuisenaire rods, Unifix cubes, or Dienes blocks.

After the regrouping process has been made clear, children should be introduced to the algorithm. Again it is important to relate each step in the algorithm to each step with the place-value model. These are the steps for the apple problem in Activity 10-4:

$$
\begin{array}{r}
82 \\
-53 \\
\end{array}
\qquad
\begin{array}{r}
{}^{7\,1}\!\not82 \\
-53 \\
\end{array}
\qquad
\begin{array}{r}
{}^{7\,1}\!\not82 \\
-53 \\
\hline
29 \\
\end{array}
$$

First the original problem is shown. Next the regrouping of 1 ten as 10 ones is shown by the marked-out eight, the small seven, and the 12 ones. The work is then completed with subtraction of 3 from 12 and subtraction of 5 from 7. The line through the 8, the small 7, and the 1 beside the 2 are memory aids that help children keep track of each step as they compute. Children should be encouraged to discontinue using these aids whenever dropping them will not interfere with their ability to compute accurately.

Once children understand the decomposition process with the algorithm for numbers with tens and hundreds, they should be able to subtract with still larger numbers. An abacus with twenty beads on each rod can be used to review the process with larger numbers for children in the middle grades. The process is illustrated in Figure 10-5 for the example in the margin. Only the minuend, 6342, is shown on the abacus in (a). The steps taken to show decomposition on an abacus are comparable to those used with a place-value pocket chart.

In the middle grades, subtraction involving 0 in the minuend should receive special attention, because problems such as

$$
\begin{array}{r}
306 \\
-148 \\
\end{array}
\qquad \text{and} \qquad
\begin{array}{r}
6003 \\
-4298 \\
\end{array}
$$

are difficult for some children. There are two ways decomposition can be done with examples of this type. To subtract 148 from 306, the thinking

$$
\begin{array}{r}
6342 \\
-3528 \\
\end{array}
$$

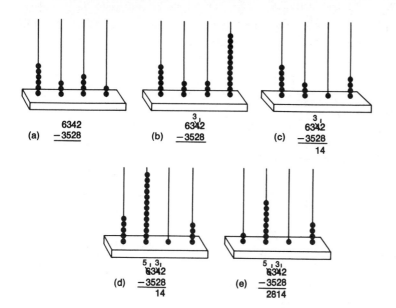

(a) $\begin{array}{r} 6342 \\ -3528 \\ \end{array}$

(b) $\begin{array}{r} {}^{3}6\cancel{3}42 \\ -3528 \\ \end{array}$

(c) $\begin{array}{r} {}^{3}6\cancel{3}\cancel{4}2 \\ -3528 \\ \hline 14 \\ \end{array}$

(d) $\begin{array}{r} {}^{5\ \ 3}\cancel{6}\cancel{3}\cancel{4}2 \\ -3528 \\ \hline 14 \\ \end{array}$

(e) $\begin{array}{r} {}^{5\ \ 3}\cancel{6}\cancel{3}\cancel{4}2 \\ -3528 \\ \hline 2814 \\ \end{array}$

FIGURE 10-5

Abacus and algorithm showing decomposition for the subtraction sentence 6342 − 3528 = 2814

might be: "There are no tens, so go to the hundreds. Regroup one of the hundreds as 10 tens, leaving 2 hundreds. Then regroup one of the tens as 10 ones, giving a total of 16 ones and 9 tens." The subtraction can then be done. The same procedure would be used for the number 6003, except that more regroupings would be required.

$$\begin{array}{r} \overset{2\,9\,1}{\cancel{306}} \\ -\,148 \\ \hline 158 \end{array}$$

Children who have a good understanding of numbers can use another method: 306 can be considered as 30 tens and 6 ones. When the regrouping is done, 1 ten is taken from the 30 tens, leaving 29 tens. The 1 ten is renamed as 10 ones and is added to the 6 ones in the ones place. In one step, all of the required regrouping is completed. If the regrouping is indicated in the algorithm, it appears as shown in the margin. To subtract 4298 from 6003, the regrouping is also done in one step. The number 6003 is thought of as 600 tens and 3 ones. When 1 ten is renamed as 10 ones, there are 599 tens left. The algorithm in the margin shows how the regrouping might be indicated. By the time children are in the fifth or sixth grade, they should be able to subtract using zeros in this more mature way.

$$\begin{array}{r} \overset{5\,9\,9\,1}{\cancel{6003}} \\ -\,4298 \\ \hline 1705 \end{array}$$

2. The Equal-Additions Method

The **equal-additions method** of subtraction is based on the mathematical concept that there is an infinite number of equivalent subtraction problems for a given remainder. The sentences $68 - 14 = \square$ and $70 - 16 = \square$ are equivalent, because the answer, or remainder, is the same for both. The strength of the equal-additions method of subtraction is the ease and speed with which computation can be done once the process has been mastered. The weakness of this method is that many children find it difficult to understand.

If the equal-additions method is taught, it should be preceded by activities to show that the same number can be added to both subtrahend and minuend without changing their difference.

ACTIVITY 10-5   Equal-Additions

- Use a flannel or magnetic board and markers. Show two sets that are to be compared, such as 13 and 7.
- Write the sentence, $13 - 7 = \square$, and determine the answer.

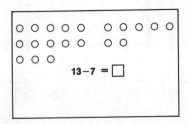

- Put 6 more markers with the larger set, making it a set of 19.

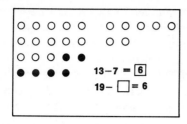

- Ask, "What must we do to the second set so that the difference remains the same?" Help the children realize that 6 markers must also be put with the second set.
- Complete the second sentence, $19 - 13 = 6$.

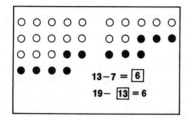

- Repeat with other sets.

The number line is another useful aid for discovering this principle, as Figure 10-6 shows. Write a subtraction sentence, such as $19 - 13 = \square$, and represent the minuend on the number line with an arrow extending from 0 to 19 and the subtrahend by an arrow extending from 19 backward thirteen steps to the 6, as in (a). Then increase the minuend by a given amount, say 6, so it becomes 25. Show the new minuend on the

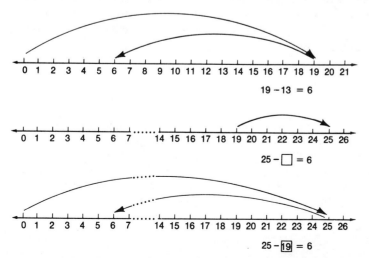

FIGURE 10-6
Number line and sentences showing that the same number must be added to both minuend and subtrahend if the difference is to remain unchanged

number line (b). The children can then discuss what must be done to the subtrahend so the difference, 6, will remain unchanged. An arrow drawn from the new minuend and extending backward to 6 on the line will show the new subtrahend. A look at this arrow reveals that the new subtrahend is the number of the old subtrahend increased by the same amount as was the original minuend (c).

In addition to understanding that the difference remains the same if a given number is added to both minuend and subtrahend, an understanding of place value is also essential before the equal-additions method of subtracting should be introduced. Once an adequate background for the process has been established, proceed as follows. Write a subtraction example on the chalkboard:

$$\begin{array}{r} 632 \\ -216 \\ \end{array}$$

Children see that it is not possible to subtract 6 ones from 2 ones. The subtraction is made possible when 10 ones are added to the 2 ones in the minuend to make 12 ones. The children then subtract 6 from 12 and record a 6 in the ones place of the algorithm. Call the children's attention to the fact that because 10 was added to the minuend, 10 must also be added to the subtrahend. This is done by adding 1 ten to the number in the tens place of the subtrahend. Then 2 tens are subtracted from 3 tens, and the answer is recorded in the tens place. The subtraction is completed by subtracting 2 hundreds from the 6 hundreds. The completed algorithm would appear as shown above in the margin. The sentence $3246 - 1937 = \square$ is shown in the algorithm in the margin. Once children learn the process, the thinking is $16 - 7 = 9$, $4 - 4 = 0$, $12 - 9 = 3$, and $3 - 2 = 1$. When the number in a place-value position in the minuend is smaller than the number in the same place-value position of the subtrahend, it is automatically increased by 10, and the subtraction for that position is completed. Each time this is done, the number in the subtrahend in the place-value position to its immediate left is increased by 1. The process becomes automatic when it is well understood and sufficiently practiced. This process presents no particular difficulties with zeros in the minuend.

$$\begin{array}{r} 6\ 3\ ^{1}2 \\ -2\ ^{2}1\ 6 \\ \hline 4\ 1\ 6 \\ \end{array}$$

$$\begin{array}{r} 3\ ^{1}2\ 4\ ^{1}6 \\ -^{2}1\ 9\ ^{4}3\ 7 \\ \hline 1\ 3\ 0\ 9 \\ \end{array}$$

**Self-check
of Objectives 3 and 4**

$$\begin{array}{r} 5\ 0\ 0\ 4 \\ -1\ 3\ 6\ 8 \\ \end{array} \qquad \begin{array}{r} 4\ 3\ 2 \\ -1\ 9\ 6 \\ \end{array}$$

Explain how to perform decomposition and equal-additions processes for the example in the margin. Demonstrate decomposition with a place-value chart, beansticks, or abacus. Describe materials and procedures that can be used to make the equal-additions process meaningful to children.

Show how renaming the number 5004 can be done to permit a one-step regrouping process for the subtraction example.

ADDITION AND SUBTRACTION OF INTEGERS

1. Addition of Integers

When children are introduced to addition and subtraction of integers, they should use a number line on which vectors represent the directed numbers to be added or subtracted. They should recognize that adding a pair of positive numbers is the same as adding a pair of whole numbers. The addition sentence $(^+2) + (^+4) = \square$ is illustrated in Figure 10-7. The two addends are represented by the abutting vectors with the solid shafts, and the sum is represented by the single vector with the broken shaft.

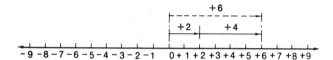

FIGURE 10-7
Number line used to illustrate the addition sentence $(^+2) + (^+4) = \square$

To add a pair of negative numbers, children should note that the vector representing the first addend begins at 0 and goes to the left. The second vector abuts the first and also goes to the left. The sum is represented by the single vector with the broken shaft that begins at 0 and goes to the left for the number of units indicated by the two abutting vectors. The addition sentence $(^-4) + (^-3) = \square$ is illustrated below in Figure 10-8.

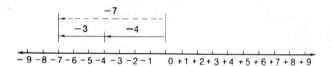

FIGURE 10-8
Number line used to illustrate the addition sentence $(^-4) + (^-3) = \square$

Children should add a sufficient number of pairs of like-directed numbers to understand the meaning of the operation with these numbers before they begin to add pairs of unlike-directed numbers. Then ample opportunities to use vectors on their number lines will permit a clear understanding of the process of addition of numbers with unlike signs. The addition sentence $(^+6) + (^-3) = \square$ is illustrated in Figure 10-9. The two addends are again represented by the vectors with solid shafts, and the sum is represented by the vector with the broken shaft. Three other addition sentences with pairs of directed numbers with unlike signs are

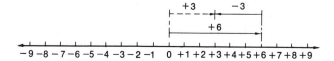

FIGURE 10-9
Number line used to illustrate the addition sentence $(^+6) + (^-3) = \square$

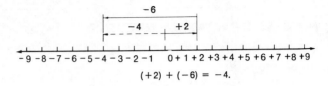

$$(+2) + (-6) = -4.$$

FIGURE 10-10

Number lines used to illustrate three addition sentences

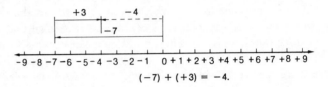

$$(-7) + (+3) = -4.$$

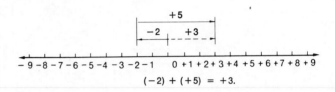

$$(-2) + (+5) = +3.$$

illustrated in Figure 10-10. These three sentences and the one in Figure 10-9 represent different kinds of sentences that occur when pairs of directed numbers are added.

The Checks and Bills game in Chapter 8 can be changed to an addition game. Instead of drawing only one card at a time, each player draws two. Before a move is made, the player determines the sum of the two numbers and then makes the move. For example, if a check for $3.00 and a bill for $5.00 are drawn, a player would add +3 and −5. The sum, −2, indicates a move of 2 in the negative direction.

2. Subtraction of Integers

When whole numbers are subtracted, the minuend must be equal to or larger than the subtrahend. Children discover this when they try to solve sentences like $3 - 5 = \square$. As they use number lines and story situations to learn the meaning of subtraction with integers, children discover that the operation is possible with all pairs of these numbers.

To use vectors on number lines to represent subtraction of directed numbers, children must keep in mind that subtraction is the inverse operation of addition. They should use vectors to represent a sum and a known addend and then determine the direction and length of the vector representing the missing addend. A subtraction sentence is shown with vectors on the number line in Figure 10-11. The original sentence,

FIGURE 10-11

Subtraction sentence $(^-6) - (^+4) = (^-10)$ represented with vectors on a number line

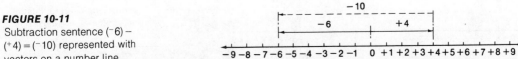

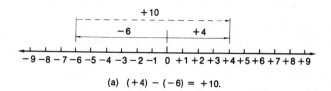

(a) $(^+4) - (^-6) = ^+10$.

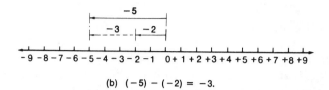

FIGURE 10-12
Number lines used to illustrate three subtraction sentences

(b) $(-5) - (-2) = -3$.

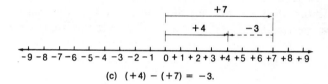

(c) $(^+4) - (^+7) = ^-3$.

$(^-6) - (^+4) = \square$, is rewritten as an addition sentence, $(^+4) + \square = ^-6$, and is read as, "What number is added to $^+4$ to obtain a sum of $^-6$?" The vectors indicate the answer, $^-10$. In Figure 10-12, other subtraction sentences are represented by vectors on number lines. In (a), sentence $(^+4) - (^-6) = \square$ is interpreted after it has been rewritten as $(^-6) + \square = ^+4$. In (b) and (c), the sentences $(^-5) - (^-2) = \square$ and $(^+4) - (^+7) = \square$, respectively, are represented with vectors on number lines.

Checks and Bills can be done with subtraction, too. A player draws two cards as in addition. However, instead of adding them the player subtracts the second card from the first to determine the move. Example: If a player first draws a bill for $6.00 and a check of $3.00, the subtraction is $(^-6) - (^+3)$. Because a check for $3.00 must be given up, or subtracted, the player is that much poorer. The loss of the $3.00 and the bill for $6.00 amount to a total result of negative 9, so the move is 9 in the negative direction.

Make eight number lines for the integers $^-10$ through $^+10$. Use vectors on one line at a time to represent these addition and subtraction sentences: $(^+4) + (^+3) = ^+7$, $(^-3) + (^-3) = ^-6$, $(^+5) + (^-3) = ^+2$, $(^+3) + (^-6) = ^-3$, $(^+6) - (^+3) = ^+3$, $(^-7) - (^-3) = ^-4$, $(^-3) - (^-4) = ^+1$, $(^+3) - (^-6) = ^+9$.

**Self-check
of Objective 5**

THE CALCULATOR AND ADDITION AND SUBTRACTION

There are many interesting activities dealing with addition and subtraction that can be carried out using a calculator. Many children will want to try activities like the ones that follow.

1. Palindromic Numbers

```
  42      421
+ 24    + 124
  66      545
```

A **palindrome** is a number that reads the same backward as forward, such as 232, 46,564, 1,234,321. An interesting investigation involves addition to generate palindromes. Select any whole number. Add that number to the one you get when you reverse its digits. If the sum is a palindrome, the addition is complete, as in the examples in the margin. If the first addition does not give a palindrome, use the sum and its reversed digits as new addends. Add these numbers. If this sum is not a palindrome, repeat the process until a palindrome appears. Note that palindromes can be generated from numbers smaller than 10.

```
  69      596       3
+ 96    + 695     + 3
 165     1291       6
 561     1921       6
 726     3212      12
 627     2123      21
1353     5335      33
3531
4884
```

Interested children will test many numbers. Often the numbers they use will exceed the machine's capacity, so they may revert to paper-and-pencil computation or attempt to devise ways to do the work on the calculator.

2. Magic Squares

Magic squares have a long history.[2] Their mystery has interested professional and amateur mathematicians for centuries. Until now, children who have been interested in magic squares have found the computation required in connection with them so tedious they do not extend their investigations beyond the more simple squares. The calculator provides

---

[2] See William Heck and James Frey, "Magic Squares," *Historical Topics for the Mathematics Classroom* (Reston, Va.: National Council of Teachers of Mathematics, 1969), pp. 80–82.

the means for taking the burden out of the computing, so interested students can investigate much more sophisticated squares. Magic squares with 3×3, 4×4, and 5×5 cells are illustrated in Figure 10-13. Add the numbers in each column, row, and diagonal. If the sum is the same for each group of numbers, you have a magic square. Children should be encouraged to work with these squares and then to generate their own if possible. The book *Adventures With Your Hand Calculator*[3] contains examples of more complex magic squares and a commentary about them.

3. Nim

Nim is an old game that has been played in many ways with a variety of materials. The calculator offers a new means of playing the game. To begin, select a target number, say 50. One player enters a one-digit number into the display. The second player adds a second number to the first. Players alternate adding one-digit numbers until one reaches 50 and is the winner. Different target numbers should be selected. Players should be encouraged to work out a strategy for winning. A variation is to start at a number, say 50, and subtract one-digit numbers to reach 0.

FIGURE 10-13
Magic squares

4. Subtracting to 495

This activity is based on the fact that a series of subtractions involving the largest and smallest numbers created from three digits, with at least one digit different from the other two, will eventually yield the number 495. Try the digits 8, 6, and 4. The largest three-digit number is 864, and the smallest is 468. Subtract 468 from 864: $864 - 468 = 396$; subtract 369 from 963: $963 - 369 = 594$; subtract 459 from 954: $954 - 459 = 495$. Try the digits 9, 8, and 2: $982 - 289 = 693$; $963 - 369 = 594$; $954 - 459 = 495$. Try 8, 9, and 9: $998 - 899 = 99$; $990 - 099 = 891$; $981 - 189 = 792$; $972 - 279 = 693$; $963 - 369 = 594$; $954 - 459 = 495$. Note that zeros are used to make 99 a three-digit number. This practice is followed any time the difference is less than 100. Encourage your children to test two- and four-digit numbers to see if a similar result occurs.

---

[3] Lennart Rade and Burt A. Kaufman, *Adventures With Your Hand Calculator* (St. Louis: CEMREL, Inc., 1977), pp. 9–12, 57.

Describe briefly each of the four addition and subtraction activities involving the calculator.

Self-check of Objective 6

SPECIAL STUDENTS AND ADDITION–SUBTRACTION

1. Learning-Handicapped Children

Students with learning handicaps, such as figure–ground, short-term, and sequential deficiencies, do not always remember the sequence of steps in multiple-step problems. They can do addition and subtraction with small numbers but become confused by the multiple steps that are required when larger numbers are added or subtracted. When these children deal with larger numbers, their addition and subtraction computation needs to be analyzed carefully each day to spot errors. There are common errors children commit when they add and subtract. A few are shown here:

1. Addition
   a. Adding the numbers' digits as though each digit is a separate number:

$$
\begin{array}{r} 32 \\ +65 \\ \hline 16 \end{array}
\qquad
\begin{array}{r} 94 \\ +27 \\ \hline 22 \end{array}
\qquad
\begin{array}{r} 87 \\ +49 \\ \hline 28 \end{array}
$$

   b. Beginning at the left:

$$
\begin{array}{r} 3\,^{2}4\,^{3}2 \\ +9\ 7\ 2 \\ \hline 1\ 1\ 7 \end{array}
\qquad
\begin{array}{r} 4\ 6\,^{3}9 \\ +2\ 7\ 5 \\ \hline 6\ 117 \end{array}
\qquad
\begin{array}{r} 3\,^{1}4\ 2\ 9 \\ +8\ 1\ 5\ 6 \\ \hline 1\ 6,715 \end{array}
$$

   c. Failing to carry:

$$
\begin{array}{r} 342 \\ +972 \\ \hline 12,114 \end{array}
\qquad
\begin{array}{r} 439 \\ +275 \\ \hline 61,014 \end{array}
\qquad
\begin{array}{r} 5798 \\ +6204 \\ \hline 119,912 \end{array}
$$

2. Subtraction
   a. Beginning at the left:

$$
\begin{array}{r} \not{4}\,^{1}7 \\ -2\ 9 \\ \hline 2\ 6 \end{array}
\qquad
\begin{array}{r} \not{7}\ ^{1}\not{3}\,^{1}6 \\ -5\ 8\ 7 \\ \hline 2\ 5\ 9 \end{array}
$$

   b. Subtracting the smaller number in a column from the larger, regardless of where it is in the algorithm:

$$
\begin{array}{r} 47 \\ -29 \\ \hline 22 \end{array}
\qquad
\begin{array}{r} 736 \\ -587 \\ \hline 251 \end{array}
$$

Each of these errors is usually committed by a child who has only a partial understanding of the process. Each error must be detected early and corrected immediately before it becomes habitual. These are general guidelines for correcting such errors:

1. Detect the error pattern.

2. Analyze the child's knowledge and understanding of subordinate concepts and skills.

3. Reteach the processes, beginning with the concrete mode at the level of the hierarchy where the child's lack of knowledge inhibits further growth.

4. Select materials and procedures that provide a slightly different approach from the ones that led to the faulty thinking.

5. Select practice materials carefully. Choose games, puzzles, worksheets, and other materials that emphasize the particular step a child is learning.

6. Provide frequent feedback and recognition of growth.

Special algorithms have been developed for students in grade 6 and beyond who cannot master one of the conventional algorithms. These **low-stress algorithms** do not reduce the number of steps when adding or subtracting. However, they do change the order in which the steps are completed so that the student completes all of one process before moving on to the next. Barton Hutchings, the originator of the algorithms, contends that they can be mastered readily after a brief training period, are performed with less stress than conventional algorithms, and give the learner great computational power in a short time.[4]

a. Addition Algorithm   The addition algorithm is similar to the conventional algorithm, but it has a slightly different form of notation, called half-space notation. The difference is shown in the margin, where the conventional notation for a basic fact is shown on the left, and half-space notation for the same fact is on the right. For a combination having a sum less than 10, the single numeral is written slightly below and to the right of the two addends. In half-space notation the line separating the addends from their sum is omitted in basic facts. The reason for this notation will become clear as the description continues.

The low-stress algorithm is particularly useful for adding when there are three or more addends. The example in the margin shows that all addition is recorded as the work is completed. Each fact in the set of addends has its sum recorded; no mental accumulation of sums is necessary. In the example the process is this: add $8 + 4$, record 12; add $2 +$

$$\begin{array}{r} 5 \\ +7 \\ \hline 12 \end{array} \qquad \begin{array}{r} 5 \\ +_{1}7_{2} \end{array}$$

$$\begin{array}{r} 6 \\ +2 \\ \hline 8 \end{array} \qquad \begin{array}{r} 6 \\ +2_{8} \end{array}$$

$$\begin{array}{r} 8 \\ _{1}4_{2} \\ 6_{8} \\ _{1}9_{7} \\ +_{1}8_{5} \\ \hline 35 \end{array}$$

---

[4] Barton Hutchings, "Low-Stress Algorithms," *Measurement in School Mathematics* (Reston, Va.: National Council of Teachers of Mathematics, 1976), p. 219.

6, record 8; add $8+9$, record 17; add $7+8$, record 15. Now all addends have been added, so record 5 below the line. Count the number of times a ten was recorded at the left of the column; record 3 below the line. The sum for this addition is 35.

Addition with addends greater than 10 is illustrated in the margin. Add $6+4$, 10; $0+8$, 8; $8+9$, 17; record 7 below the line. Count the number of times ten was recorded, then "carry" 2 to the tens column. Add $2+2$, 4; $4+8$, 12; $2+7$, 9; $9+4$, 13. Record 3 below the line. Count the tens (these are actually hundreds since the addition is in the tens column), then record 2 below the line. The answer is 237.

A student who has mastered the process with numbers smaller than 10, and then smaller than 100, can quickly move to addition with quite large numbers and several addends. For an older student who has experienced failure with the conventional algorithm, success with the low-stress computation will perhaps bolster the child's self-esteem and help change a negative attitude toward mathematics to a positive one.

b. Subtraction Algorithm   When doing subtraction, the student completes all regrouping first. The following example illustrates the process. The original combination is shown in (a). The regrouping is placed between the minuend and subtrahend, as shown in the series of steps in (b), (c), and (d).

Finally the subtraction is completed and the answer recorded. Subtraction with zeros in the minuend is done this way:

The original example is shown in (a). In (b) the ones are regrouped, and the 4 in the thousands place is changed to 3, with the zeros being ignored at this point. After this regrouping is completed, each 0 is replaced by a 9, as in (c). Now the subtraction can be completed (d). The process with a larger minuend having zeros is illustrated in the following example, with the original problem shown in (a). In (b) the regrouping of numbers greater than 0 is completed. In (c) each 0 is replaced by a 9; the answer is shown in (d).

The primary advantage of this algorithm for the student is that all of one part of the work, the regrouping, is completed before the next part, the subtraction, is done. This reduces the cognitive load and the possibility of error, because the child does not shift from thinking about regrouping to subtracting, back to regrouping, then subtracting again, and so on. An advantage of both algorithms for the teacher is that it is easy to detect errors. By examining a child's work, one can spot errors with basic addition and subtraction facts, failure to "carry" in addition, and regrouping errors in subtraction.

Identify at least two errors children commonly make as they do addition and subtraction. Give a list of guidelines for helping children overcome systematic errors.

Write an addition example having at least six addends larger than 10. Determine the sum using the low-stress method of computing. Write a subtraction for which both minuend and subtrahend are larger than 1000 and for which regrouping is necessary. Complete it using the low-stress method of subtracting. Indicate for whom these algorithms are especially useful.

Self-check
of Objectives 7 and 8

2. Challenges for Gifted and Talented Students

Gifted and talented students need challenges when working with addition and subtraction. They become bored very quickly if their work is restricted to computation alone. Activities such as the following are recommended:

CHALLENGE 10-1

• You have learned to subtract using the regrouping and equal-additions algorithms. Here is another method of subtracting:

$$7452$$
$$- 873$$

3 from 2 I cannot, but 3 from 10 and 7 remains; which 7 added to 2 gives 9 for a remainder; then I go on, saying, 1 borrowed and 7 make 8, which from 5 I cannot, but from 10, and 2 remain which 2 added to 5 gives 7 for a remainder. . . .

- Can you complete the subtraction? What is the answer?
- Complete these examples using the same process:

$$4526 \qquad 7394$$
$$-1682 \qquad -\ 895$$

- Can you explain why this process works?[5]

CHALLENGE 10-2 [6]

What row has a sum of 390?

```
Row 9 --- 41 42 43 44 45
Row 8 --- 40 39 38 37 36
Row 7 --- 31 32 33 34 35
Row 6 --- 30 29 28 27 26
Row 5 --- 21 22 23 24 25
Row 4 --- 20 19 18 17 16
Row 3 --- 11 12 13 14 15
Row 2 --- 10  9  8  7  6
Row 1 ---  1  2  3  4  5
```

CHALLENGE 10-3

- Teacher: "Give me a five-digit number and I will write it on the chalk-board."
- Student: "My number is 43,682."
- Teacher: "I will ask you for two more five-digit numbers. After each of your numbers I will write a five-digit number. When we are finished, we will add the numbers. Before we add them, I will tell you that the answer is 243,680."
- The following numbers were given, and the addition was completed:

$$43,682$$
$$24,836$$
$$75,163$$
$$84,217$$
$$+15,782$$
$$243,680$$

---

[5] This problem is from Sue Dreiling Brown and Donald E. Brown, "A Look at the Past," *Arithmetic Teacher*, XXVII, No. 5 (January 1980), p. 37.

[6] This problem is from Carole Greenes, et al., *Techniques of Problem Solving: Problem Card Decks* (Palo Alto: Dale Seymour Publications, 1980), Card 192-D.

- Teacher: "Can you figure out what I did? When you think you have it figured out, try it on a classmate."

Three challenges for gifted and talented students are presented. Explain how the first and third are done and give the answer for the second.

**Self-check
of Objective 9**

SUMMARY

When children have a good understanding of place value for numbers through 99 and of the processes of addition and subtraction, they are ready for addition and subtraction of numbers with sums up to 99. Later, addition and subtraction are extended to whole numbers of any size. Skill in adding by endings is important so that children can do certain addition without paper and pencil, as when adding columns of numbers and doing some types of multiplication. Addition of larger numbers will involve some situations where no regrouping ("carrying") is required and other situations where it is. Place-value pocket charts, beansticks, an abacus, and other models will make this addition meaningful to children.

Subtraction of larger numbers can be performed by decomposition, equal additions, and other processes. Decomposition is generally favored by teachers because its meaning can be illustrated with place-value models. Equal addition is performed rapidly by persons who learn to do it. Eventually children learn to use the addition and subtraction algorithms without benefit of manipulative aids.

Not all elementary-school children will learn to add and subtract integers. Children who are ready to learn these operations on integers should use number lines and other activities as they work, rather than learn rote procedures that lack meaning.

The calculator is useful for engaging children in interesting and instructive learning activities and investigations dealing with addition and subtraction. Activities include investigating palindromes and magic squares, a subtraction activity, and the game of Nim.

Students who have learning handicaps should have their daily work analyzed carefully so that errors can be detected and corrective actions taken early to prevent habitual errors from developing. Low-stress algorithms have been developed for older children who cannot master one of the conventional algorithms for adding or subtracting. The number of steps are no fewer in these algorithms, but they are simplified to make it easier for children to remember them. Gifted and talented children need challenges to maintain their interest. An ancient subtraction algorithm, a number pattern problem, and an addition puzzle are three interesting challenges for these students.

STUDY QUESTIONS AND ACTIVITIES

1. Practice with a place-value pocket chart, beansticks, and a classroom abacus until you are proficient in using each aid to illustrate the following examples.

   (a) 23   (b) 68   (c) 203   (d) 688
        +41   +26   +429   +247

2. Use the decomposition and equal-additions methods of subtraction to solve the following problems. Practice each procedure until you become proficient. With which procedure can you subtract most rapidly?

   (a) 62   (b) 436   (c) 943   (d) 4003
        −48   −209   −387   −3829

3. Use a place-value pocket chart, beansticks, and abacus to represent the following examples. Practice until you can represent the decomposition process of subtraction meaningfully.

   (a) 43   (b) 441   (c) 836   (d) 3006
        −19   −236   −447   −1948

4. Practice the low-stress algorithms for addition and subtraction until you are proficient with each one. Make up your own examples, including four or more addends larger than 100 for addition and numbers greater than 1000 and with and without zeros in the minuend for subtraction.

5. Sherrill (see chapter's reading list) compared the performance of children in a third-grade class who learned decomposition subtraction with another group who learned the equal-additions method. What were the results of his study, and what implications do you draw from his report of these children's performances?

6. The article by Beede (see chapter's reading list) describes a game called SAM (Speed and Accuracy in Mathematics). He shows how to make the game for practice with division problems. Prepare this game for children in grades 4 to 6, using appropriate addition and subtraction examples.

7. Add games and activities for addition and subtraction of larger numbers to your collection of mathematics learning materials. Use the guidelines in study question 5 in Chapter 9 as you select your games and activities.

KEY TERMS

higher-decade addition
regrouping
decomposition method
equal-additions method

palindrome
magic squares
Nim
low-stress algorithms

FOR FURTHER READING

Backman, Carl A. "Analyzing Children's Work Procedures," *Developing Computational Skills*, 1978 Yearbook, National Council of Teachers of Mathematics (Reston, Va.: The Council), pp. 177–195. Diagnosis requires more than analysis of tests. Children's daily work—both results and processes—needs to be analyzed, too. Suggestions for doing this and for correcting errors in computation are explained and illustrated.

Battista, Michael T. "A Complete Model for Operations on Integers," *Arithmetic Teacher*, XXX, No. 9 (May 1983), pp. 26–31. The model relies on charged particles which are represented by red and blue poker chips to develop children's understanding of all four operations with integers. Illustrations of situations involving each operation provide appropriate classroom examples.

Beardslee, Edward C. "Teaching Computational Skills with a Calculator," *Developing Computational Skills*, 1978 Yearbook, National Council of Teachers of Mathematics (Reston, Va.: The Council), pp. 226–241. Explains a variety of activities with a calculator dealing with counting, addition and subtraction, multiplication and division, problem solving, pattern investigations, and decimals.

Beede, Rudy B. "Speed and Accuracy in Mathematics," *Arithmetic Teacher*, XXVII, No. 5 (January 1980), pp. 44–45. SAM is a competitive game for two to four children for practicing operations with algorithms. Materials described in the article deal with division, but the game is easily adapted for any operation.

Bennett, Albert B., Jr., and Gary L. Musser. "A Concrete Approach to Integer Addition and Subtraction," *Arithmetic Teacher*, XXIII, No. 5 (May 1976), pp. 332–336. Black chips serve as whole numbers, and red chips represent negative integers for activities that develop the meaning of addition and subtraction with integers.

Bradford, John W. "Methods and Materials for Learning Subtraction," *Arithmetic Teacher*, XXV, No. 5 (February 1978), pp. 18–20. A process for teaching subtraction using white Cuisenaire rods, ten strips, and hundreds and thousands grids shows subtraction's close relationship to addition. The author claims success in helping third and fourth graders overcome systematic errors in subtraction.

Cox, L. S. "Diagnosing and Remediating Systematic Errors in Addition and Subtraction Computations," *Arithmetic Teacher*, XXII, No. 2 (February 1975), pp. 151–157. Identifies and explains systematic errors in addition and subtraction. Describes ways to diagnose and remediate such errors.

Hutchings, Barton. "Low-Stress Algorithms," *Measurement in the Classroom*, 1976 Yearbook, National Council of Teachers of Mathematics (Reston, Va.: The Council), pp. 218–239. Explains low-stress algorithms for all four operations. The processing of multiplication and division facts using the low-stress addition process are also possible.

————. "Low-Stress Subtraction," *Arithmetic Teacher*, XXII, No. 3 (March 1975), pp. 226–322. Discusses the low-stress algorithm for subtraction. Includes several examples and an extensive bibliography dealing with research into the addition and subtraction algorithms.

Logan, Henrietta L. "Renaming with a Money Model," *Arithmetic Teacher*, XXVI, No. 1 (September 1978), pp. 23–24. Children who have difficulty grasping the meaning of subtraction with regrouping may be aided by using dollars, dimes, and pennies as models for place value. First, different ways of representing a given amount of money are practiced, then the money is used as a model for the subtraction algorithm.

Merseth, Katherine K. "Using Materials and Activities in Teaching Addition and Subtraction Algorithms," *Developing Computational Skills*, 1978 Yearbook, National Council of Teachers of Mathematics (Reston, Va.: The Council), pp. 61–77. Explains readiness activities with base-ten blocks, record-keeping activities with mats and blocks, and addition and subtraction activities with the mats and blocks. Activities leading to abstractions of the processes are part of the discussion.

Nichol, Margaret. "Addition Through Palindromes," *Arithmetic Teacher*, XXVI, No. 4 (December 1978), pp. 20–21. There are both words and numbers that are palindromes. Of particular interest are the suggestions for using palindromes to provide addition practice. Also of interest is the fact that it takes 24 steps to change 89 to a palindrome.

Rheins, Gladys B., and Joel J. Rheins. "A Comparison of Two Methods of Compound Subtraction," *Arithmetic Teacher*, II, No. 3 (October 1955), pp. 63–69. Reports the results of a study comparing groups of children taught by two subtraction methods, the decomposition and equal-additions methods. The conclusion is that the decomposition method is a better way to introduce compound subtraction.

Schwartsman, Steven. "A Method of Subtraction," *Arithmetic Teacher*, XXII, No. 8 (December 1975), pp. 628–630. The algorithm employs both regular subtraction and subtraction using complements of numbers. It has been used in a process-oriented way (that is, without structural meaning) with remedial students in upper grades and as enrichment for those who understand the conventional algorithm well.

Sherrill, James M. "Subtraction: Decomposition versus Equal Addends," *Arithmetic Teacher*, XXVII, No. 1 (September 1979), pp. 16–17.

Sherrill compared two groups of third-grade children to determine whether the group that learned the decomposition method or the one that learned the equal-additions method of subtraction performed better at the close of the instructional period. His results confirmed those of many others who have compared the two methods: children who learned the decomposition method worked with greater accuracy and understanding.

Thompson, Charles S., and John Van de Walle. "Transition Boards: Moving from Materials to Symbols in Subtraction," *Arithmetic Teacher*, XXVIII, No. 5 (January 1981), pp. 4–7, 9.

Transition boards provide a nonproportional model for playing trading games, such as the Banker's Game explained in Chapter 8. The authors show how to use the board to help children learn the decomposition method of subtraction.

11

Teaching Multiplication and Division

Upon completion of Chapter 11 you will be able to:

1. Explain how children's knowledge of addition can be used to develop their understanding of multiplication, and demonstrate how the symbolism of multiplication can be explained.

2. Use the terms factor, product, multiplier, and multiplicand properly in connection with a multiplication sentence.

3. Arrange objects or draw pictures to illustrate arrays for sentences such as $6 \times 3 = 18$ and $4 \times 9 = 36$.

4. Tell a story for both a measurement and a partitive situation in division, and demonstrate how manipulative materials can be used to represent each of your stories.

5. Demonstrate at least three strategies that can be used to help children learn the multiplication and division facts.

6. Demonstrate how these properties of multiplication can be made meaningful to children: the commutative, associative, and distribution of multiplication over addition and the roles of one and zero in multiplication.

7. Demonstrate with concrete materials or a series of drawings at least two sets of materials children can use as they learn a multiplication algorithm without regrouping.

8. Make up a real-life story problem for a sentence like $4 \times 16 = 64$. Then demonstrate with markers, a pocket chart, or a series of drawings of one of the devices the meaning of an algorithm for this example.

9. Demonstrate procedures that can be used to introduce multiplication where both factors are greater than 10.

10. Explain processes that help children determine quotients when the conventional division algorithm is introduced.

11. Explain why the ability to multiply by ten and its powers and multiples is an important prerequisite for learning to use the division algorithm, and describe ways these skills can be developed.

12. Demonstrate with concrete materials or a series of drawings how division with quotients greater than ten can be introduced meaningfully.

13. Make up a real-life story involving division with regrouping. Then write a sample dialogue you might use with several children to help them understand an algorithm for the problem.

14. Demonstrate materials and procedures that can be used to help children understand division with large numbers.

15. Describe different problem situations involving remainders, and explain how to deal with each situation.

16. Describe four calculator activities with multiplication and division.

17. Describe a procedure for generating multiplication and division facts with the low-stress addition algorithm.

18. Explain how squared paper and color cues can help certain learning-handicapped children to multiply and divide.

One definition of multiplication states that it is the operation on numbers that assigns a single number called the **product** to an ordered pair of numbers that are called **factors.** Division is defined as the operation used to find a missing factor when one factor and a product are known. Once again we have examples of abstract definitions that are useful at a mature level but which cannot be used with children just beginning work with new operations.

Multiplication is often introduced late in the second grade, although for the majority of children early work with the operation occurs in grade 3. Division is usually introduced in the third grade. Work with the two operations is then extended through the grades, with final work with the most difficult aspects of the two coming in grade 6. Figure 11-1 presents a hierarchy for multiplication, and Figure 11-2 presents one for division. The materials and procedures presented in this chapter follow the sequences of these hierarchies.

INTRODUCING MULTIPLICATION

1. Repeated Addition

One way to introduce multiplication is to relate it to addition. This enables children to use their knowledge of addition as a foundation upon

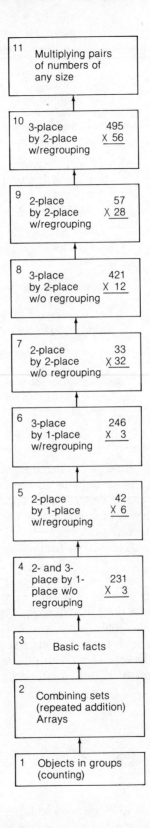

FIGURE 11-1
Hierarchy of steps for
learning to multiply whole
numbers

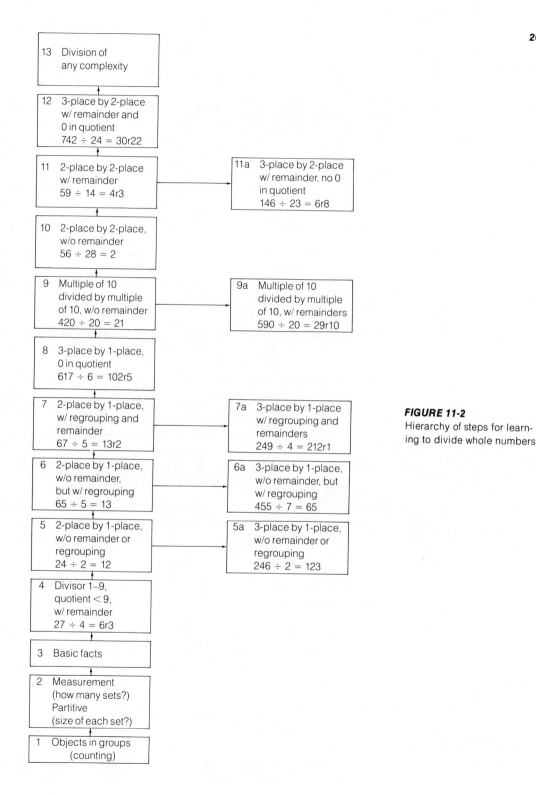

FIGURE 11-2

Hierarchy of steps for learning to divide whole numbers

which to build their understanding of multiplication. For example, when confronted with four sets, each of which contains two objects, children can first determine the answer by adding $2 + 2 + 2 + 2$. They can then be introduced to multiplication by learning that the operation 4×2 can also be used to determine the answer. They are guided to note that $2 + 2 + 2 + 2 = 4 \times 2$; that is, the multiplication sentence $4 \times 2 = 8$ is equivalent to the addition sentence $2 + 2 + 2 + 2 = 8$.

Children's first work must be at the concrete–manipulative level so they will understand multiplication. You should plan lessons to encourage children's use of familiar materials and devices.

ACTIVITY 11-1   Working Out Multiplication

- Begin with this story: "Sally bought gum in packages of seven sticks each. If she bought four packages of gum, how many sticks did she get?"
- Allow time for each child to determine the answer, using actual gum packages, coffee stirrer sticks, or any other materials and procedures. Move among the children to observe their work and encourage promising approaches.
- Discuss what different children did. Let those who used sticks of gum, stirrer sticks, or marks drawn on paper explain their work first. If some children used a mathematical procedure, such as repeated addition or perhaps even multiplication, have their explanations follow the first ones.
- Give other similar problem situations for the children to solve before you introduce the symbolism for multiplication.

Other materials to use to show the repeated addition concept of multiplication include:

- Set cards. Have children organize the combinations for a given number as one factor. For example, with the cards illustrated in Figure 11-3, children can see that one set of 4 is 4, two sets of 4 are 8, and so on.

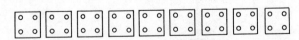

FIGURE 11-3

Set cards used to give children experience with counting by fours. These can be made by sticking adhesive labels to pieces of tagboard or colored railroad board.

- Sets on a magnetic or flannel board. Equal-sized sets of markers can be placed on a magnetic or flannel board, as shown in Figure 11-4.

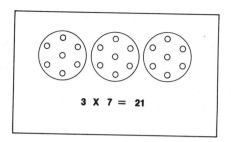

FIGURE 11-4
Markers and symbols used to illustrate the multiplication sentence $3 \times 7 = 21$

- Number lines. Jumps of a predetermined size can be taken on the number line. Figure 11-5 shows 4-unit jumps. Talk about the stopping place for 4 jumps that are 4 units long, and so on.

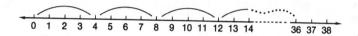

FIGURE 11-5
Counting by fours from 0 to 36 illustrated on the number line

- Unifix cubes. Have the children join a given number of Unifix cubes. Figure 11-6 shows sets with 3 cubes each. Talk about the total number of cubes in 2 sets, in 3 sets, and so on.

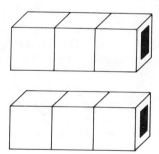

FIGURE 11-6
Unifix cubes linked to show $2 \times 3 = 6$

Once you are satisfied children have the background they need to understand the terms and symbolism used for multiplication, you can introduce them by using an activity that has already been discussed. For the gum situation, the answer might have been determined by using four packages of gum, the addition sentence $7 + 7 + 7 + 7 = 28$, and the addition in the margin. Through discussion, lead children to see common elements in each of the examples: there are four sets of objects, each with seven members, and the addend 7 is used four times. The multiplication sentence $4 \times 7 = 28$ applies to this situation. Both 4 and 7 are factors, and 28 is the product. The 4 indicates the number of sets, the 7 indicates the size of each set, and 28 is the total number of objects. The term **multiplier** applies to the first factor and **multiplicand** to the second factor.

$$\begin{array}{r} 7 \\ 7 \\ 7 \\ + \ 7 \\ \hline 28 \end{array}$$

**Self-check
of Objectives 1 and 2**

Use repeated addition and concrete materials to explain the meaning of the multiplication sentence $3 \times 8 = 24$.

Define each of these terms: *factor, product, multiplier, multiplicand.*

FIGURE 11-7
Four rows of shoe boxes with twelve in each row illustrate a 4×12 array.

Shoes	Shoes	Shoes	Shoes	Shoes	Shoes	Shoes	Shoes	Shoes	Shoes	Shoes	Shoes
Shoes	Shoes	Shoes	Shoes	Shoes	Shoes	Shoes	Shoes	Shoes	Shoes	Shoes	Shoes
Shoes	Shoes	Shoes	Shoes	Shoes	Shoes	Shoes	Shoes	Shoes	Shoes	Shoes	Shoes
Shoes	Shoes	Shoes	Shoes	Shoes	Shoes	Shoes	Shoes	Shoes	Shoes	Shoes	Shoes

2. Arrays

An **array** is an arrangement of items in a number of rows, each row containing the same number of items. An array of shoe boxes is shown in Figure 11-7. In it are 4 rows of boxes, each with 12 boxes, or a total of 48 boxes. Figure 11-8 shows an array of markers. There are 3 rows, with 5 markers in each row. This is a 3 by 5 array, with the "3" designating the number of rows and the "5" the number of objects in each row. The generally accepted sentence for this array is $3 \times 5 = 15$, which is read "3 times $5 = 15$."

FIGURE 11-8
A 3×5 array

In Chapter 17 learning centers are discussed as a setting for children's work in mathematics. Problem cards are mentioned as one way of directing activities in a learning center. You can introduce the concept of array through a series of problem-card activities. Children work singly or in groups of two or three. Each child has a masonite pegboard with 100 holes arranged in ten rows of ten holes each, a box of golf tees, and paper and colored pencils. There should be a set of problem cards for each child or group (Figure 11-9).

Nearly every classroom contains array patterns such as panes of window glass, rows of ceiling or floor tiles, and sets of lights. If your room has no apparent patterns, you can create some by arranging books on shelves, geometric shapes on a wall board, and pictures on a bulletin board. Once children know about arrays, they should search their room and other parts of the school environment for examples. Children's interest can be heightened by challenging them to find unusual arrays in and around their school.

In addition to the problem card-activities, you can have children work with the following materials:

- Adhesive labels. Array patterns made from adhesive labels arranged in rows and columns on colored cardboard provide simple aids for showing arrays. The array for 7×7 is shown in Figure 11-10. In (a), forty-nine labels are arranged in seven rows with seven labels in each row. In (b) an array with seven rows of one label each shows a 7 by 1 array. Have children uncover successive columns to see 7 by 2, 7 by 3, and other arrays. In (c), a 1 by 7 array is shown. Uncovering rows now shows 2 by 7, 3 by 7, . . . 7 by 7 arrays.

- Squared paper. One application of the array concept is to find the area of the plane surface enclosed by a rectangular figure.

MULTIPLICATION ARRAYS   (1)

1. Use 6 red golf tees to make this pattern on your pegboard.

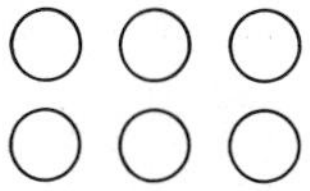

   This pattern has 2 rows of tees, with 3 tees in each row. <u>Altogether there are</u> ___ <u>tees</u>.

2. Make this pattern on your pegboard with green tees.

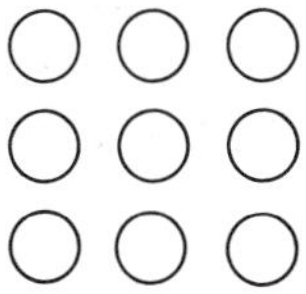

   <u>This pattern has</u> ___ <u>rows of tees, with</u> ___ <u>tees in each row</u>. <u>Altogether there are</u> ___ <u>tees</u>.

3. Make a pattern that has 3 rows, each with 4 yellow tees. Draw the pattern on your paper with a yellow pencil. <u>There are</u> ___ <u>tees in this pattern</u>.

FIGURE 11-9
A series of three problem cards dealing with arrays

274

4. Make a pattern that has 5 rows, with 3 blue tees in each row. Draw the pattern on your paper with a blue pencil. There are ___ tees in this pattern.

5. Each pattern is an <u>array</u> of tees. Another way to write the name of the pattern of blue tees is to call it a 5 by 3 array. <u>The pattern of blue tees is a ___ by ___ array</u>.

6. Use the tees to make these arrays. Draw pictures of arrays on your paper, using any colors you wish.
   a. 2 by 4   d. 5 by 4
   b. 3 by 6   e. 4 by 4
   c. 4 by 5   f. 6 by 2

7. Tell how many tees are in each of the arrays in problem 6.

8. Use your arrays to answer these multiplication sentences:
   a. $2 \times 4 =$ ___   d. $5 \times 4 =$ ___
   b. $3 \times 6 =$ ___   e. $4 \times 4 =$ ___
   c. $4 \times 5 =$ ___   f. $6 \times 2 =$ ___

9. Use colored pencils to draw some arrays of your own on your paper. Write a multiplication sentence for each of your arrays.

10. Look about the room for patterns that form arrays. Make a picture of the arrays you see, then describe each of your pictures. Write a multiplication sentence for each of your pictures.

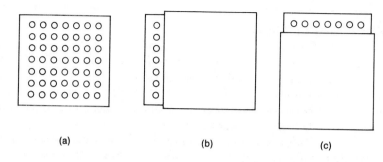

(a)   (b)   (c)

FIGURE 11-10
(a) Card showing a 7 × 9 array. (b) The card is covered to show a 7 × 1 array. (c) The card is covered to show a 1 × 7 array.

Children develop readiness for the area concept by marking arrays on squared paper. A worksheet with printed directions indicating the arrays to be marked can be used to guide children's activities as they complete arrays like those in Figure 11-11.

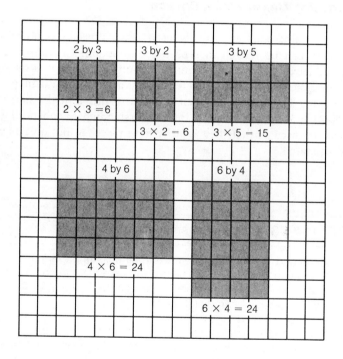

FIGURE 11-11
Samples of arrays drawn on squared paper

Show an array for each of these sentences:

$6 \times 4 = 24$, $3 \times 9 = 27$, $1 \times 8 = 8$, $8 \times 1 = 8$.

Self-check of Objective 3

INTRODUCING DIVISION

Two types of situations give rise to division. In a measurement situation you are to determine the number of equal-sized subsets in a given set. **Measurement division** is illustrated by the following situation: "There are eight eggs. How many servings of scrambled eggs, each using two eggs, can be made with these eight eggs?" In a partitive situation you are given an original set and are to determine the size of each subset when you separate it into a given number of subsets. **Partitive division** is illustrated by this situation: "There are 24 candy bars in a box. If the candy bars are distributed among three children so that each child gets the same number of bars, how many bars will each child get?"

1. Introducing Measurement Division

Measurement situations are usually used when division is introduced, because they can be related to repeated subtraction. Children see that division modeled by repeatedly removing equivalent groups is the opposite of multiplication modeled by repeatedly adding equivalent groups. After studying how young children respond to different division situations, Marilyn Zweng concluded that understanding is enhanced when containers are used so that they actually have places to put objects when sets are separated.[1]

ACTIVITY 11-2   Sharing Beans among Cups

- Give each child 15 to 20 lima beans and nine small paper cups.
- Have each child count out eight beans and hold them in one hand.
- Direct the children to put the eight beans into cups, two at a time, until all of the beans have been distributed.
- "Into how many cups did you put beans?" (4.)
- Repeat with other quantities and groupings of beans. Discuss each situation as it is completed to help the children realize that each time they separate a set of beans into groups of known size, they determine the number of cups into which the beans are put.

Following exploratory lessons, use repeated subtraction to find answers in measurement situations.

---

[1] Marilyn J. Zweng, "Division Problems and the Concept of Rate," *Arithmetic Teacher*, XI, No. 8 (December 1964), pp. 547–556.

ACTIVITY 11-3   Sharing Marbles among Bags

- Use a magnetic or flannel board with circular markers for marbles.
- "Susie has fifteen marbles. She wants to put them into some marble-bags. If she puts five marbles into each bag, how many bags will she need?"
- Show 15 disks, and put a ring around 5 of them. Subtract 5 from 15 to show that 10 marbles are left.

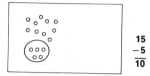

$$\begin{array}{r} 15 \\ -5 \\ \hline 10 \end{array}$$

- Put a ring around another 5 disks, and subtract 5 from 10.

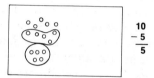

$$\begin{array}{r} 10 \\ -5 \\ \hline 5 \end{array}$$

- Put a ring around the last 5 disks, and show $5-5=0$.

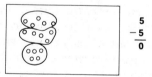

$$\begin{array}{r} 5 \\ -5 \\ \hline 0 \end{array}$$

- Repeat with other quantities of markers and different groupings.

Introduce the division sentence by discussing already completed activities. The sentence $15 \div 5 = 3$ is used for the marble problem. As the sentence is presented, discuss the meanings of its parts. The first numeral in the sentence indicates the size of the original set of marbles (15), the second numeral indicates the size of each of the equal-sized groups of marbles that were removed from the original set (5), and the last numeral indicates the number of groups of marbles (3). The sentence is read: "Fifteen divided by five equals three."

2. Partitive Situations

Introduce partitive situations with a familiar situation, such as this.

ACTIVITY 11-4   Partitive Situation

- Use a collection of paper dolls and a flannel board divided into three sections by horizontal lines representing shelves.
- "Juanita has twenty-four small dolls. She is going to put them in a cabinet that has three shelves. If she puts the same number of dolls on each shelf, how many dolls will be on each shelf?"
- Discuss with the children ways to determine the answer. One way is to distribute the dolls one at a time, putting a doll on each shelf until all are distributed. Children may suggest a faster procedure wherein they place a larger number on each shelf. If dolls are left over, they distribute them one at a time, or perhaps two at a time if the possibility exists and it occurs to them.
- Repeat with other numbers and groupings of dolls.

After children understand partitive situations, help them relate the numbers in a division sentence to such situations. The sentence for the doll problem is $24 \div 3 = 8$. The 24 indicates the size of the original group of dolls, the 3 indicates the number of groups into which the dolls were separated and the 8 indicates the number of dolls in each group.

Children in grades 4 and beyond should learn and use the proper terms when referring to numerals in a division sentence. The first number is the **dividend,** the second number is the **divisor,** and the answer is the **quotient.** The meaning of the dividend never changes: it always tells the size of the original set. However, the roles of the divisor and quotient are interchanged, depending upon the situation. In a measurement situation, the divisor tells the size of each subset, and the quotient tells the number of subsets. In a partitive situation, the divisor tells the number of subsets, and the quotient tells the size of each subset.

Self-check of Objective 4

Compose a word problem that presents a measurement situation; compose one that presents a partitive situation. Describe manipulative materials that are useful for illustrating each of your problems.

REINFORCING THE LEARNING OF THE FACTS

In Chapter 9, strategies for learning addition and subtraction facts are discussed. Similar strategies have been developed for learning multiplication and division facts. Some multiplication combinations are readily learned by most children. For example, children see that multiplying by 2 is the same as doubling the factor that is not 2. Multiplication by five is not difficult for children who have learned to skip-count by fives. Once the principles of multiplying 1 and 0 are understood, children usually have little difficulty with combinations involving them.

1. Using the Multiplication Table

A multiplication table should be used to help children recognize how many facts they already know when the facts with 0, 1, 2, and 5 are mastered.

ACTIVITY 11-5 The Multiplication Table

- Begin with an unfinished multiplication table.

X	0	1	2	3	4	5	6	7	8	9
0										
1										
2										
3										
4										
5										
6										
7										
8										
9										

- Stress these points as the table is completed.
  - The factors for each combination are in the top row and left-hand column.
  - The second row and second column all contain a product of 0 because at least one factor in each combination is 0. There are 19 of these products.
  - The third row and the third column contain products that are the same as the factor that is not 1 (except for 1 itself). These combinations involve the multiplication identity and account for 17 more facts.
  - Altogether, combinations involving either 0 or 1 account for more than one-third of all of the multiplication facts.
  - Combinations for products in the fourth row and fourth column have 2 as one factor. Each product is twice the factor that is not 2. These account for another 15 facts.
  - Products involving 5 as a factor are in the seventh row and seventh column, and account for 13 more facts.

X	0	1	2	3	4	5	6	7	8	9
0	0	0	0	0	0	0	0	0	0	0
1	0	1	2	3	4	5	6	7	8	9
2	0	2	4	6	8	10	12	14	16	18
3	0	3	6	9	12	15	18	21	24	27
4	0	4	8	12	16	20	24	28	32	36
5	0	5	10	15	20	25	30	35	40	45
6	0	6	12	18	24	30	36	42	48	54
7	0	7	14	21	28	35	42	49	56	63
8	0	8	16	24	32	40	48	56	64	72
9	0	9	18	27	36	45	54	63	72	81

- Discuss the idea that facts that include one of these four factors account for nearly two-thirds of all of the multiplication facts.
- Many children also know answers for combinations involving a number multiplied by itself. Point out that the diagonal from top left to bottom right contains products for these numbers.

2. Nine as a Factor

One of the difficult factors is 9. A strategy for dealing with it has two activities:

ACTIVITY 11-6   Nines are Easy

- Begin by discussing these questions:
  - "6 tens are?" (60.) "Six nines will be less; the answer is in the fifties."
  - "4 tens are ?" (40.) "Four nines will be less; the answer is in the thirties."

    Repeat with other tens and nines until the children recognize the pattern.
- Write these combinations on the board:

$$9 \times 6 = 54 \qquad 7 \times 9 = 63$$
$$9 \times 3 = 27 \qquad 8 \times 9 = 72$$
$$9 \times 4 = 36 \qquad 5 \times 9 = 45$$

  "Look at the number in the tens place of each product. How does it compare with the number being multiplied by nine?" (It is one less.)
- Show these combinations:

$$9 \times 4 \qquad 6 \times 9$$
$$7 \times 9 \qquad 9 \times 8$$
$$9 \times 9 \qquad 2 \times 9$$

"What is the number in the tens place for each of these combinations?" (It is one less than the number being multiplied by the 9.)[2]

ACTIVITY 11-7 Products with 9 as One Factor

- Show cards containing numerals such as 4, 3, and 7. "What do we add to each of these numbers to make 9?" (5, 6, and 2.)
- Write some facts with 9 on the chalkboard:

$$9 \times 4 = 36 \qquad 8 \times 9 = 72$$
$$9 \times 7 = 63 \qquad 6 \times 9 = 54$$
$$9 \times 5 = 45 \qquad 2 \times 9 = 18$$

"If we add the digits in each product, what is the sum?" (9.) Tell the children that in the nines facts, the sum of the digits is always 9.
- Show some partially completed facts:

$$9 \times 3 = 2\_ \qquad 7 \times 9 = 6\_$$
$$9 \times 5 = 4\_ \qquad 8 \times 9 = 7\_$$

Point out that the tens digit has been written. "Because the sum of the digits in the product must equal 9, what must be in the ones place of each product?"
- Repeat with all combinations of facts with 9.[3]

Help children to combine the processes in these two activities to determine the product when 9 is a factor. The number in the tens place is one less than the factor being multiplied by 9; the number in the ones place is the number that is added to the tens place number to give a sum of 9. Follow discussions with worksheets to give practice on the facts just considered. Worksheets containing examples like those in Activities 11-6 and 11-7 give practice with multiplying by 9.

3. Strategies for Division

Capitalize on your children's knowledge of multiplication to help them learn division facts. Consider division to be a process of finding a missing

---

[2] This activity is adapted from Larry Leutzinger, *Strategies for Learning the Basic Facts* (Cedar Falls: Iowa Council of Teachers of Mathematics, 1981), p. 48.

[3] Adapted from Larry Leutzinger, p. 50.

factor when a product and one factor are known. Focus on a product and its factors at first:

ACTIVITY 11-8   Missing Factors

- "What numbers do we multiply to get 24?"
  Consider both $4 \times 6 = 24$ and $3 \times 8 = 24$. ($2 \times 12 = 24$ is not a basic fact.)
- "What numbers do we multiply to get 36?"
  Consider both $4 \times 9 = 36$ and $6 \times 6 = 36$. ($3 \times 12 = 36$ and $2 \times 18 = 36$ are not basic facts.)
- Repeat with other numbers that have two factors less than 10.

Next focus on a product and a known factor:

ACTIVITY 11-9   One Missing Factor

- "What is the other factor when we have 56 and 7?" (8.)
- "What is the other factor when we have 48 and 8?" (6.)
- Repeat with other products and known factors.

Use worksheets to give practice with division facts. First show a missing-factor example; then use the related division sentence:

$$36 = 4 \times \square \qquad 36 \div 4 = \square$$
$$49 = 7 \times \square \qquad 49 \div 7 = \square$$
$$63 = 7 \times \square \qquad 63 \div 7 = \square$$

The multiplication table in Activity 11-5 can also be used for learning division facts. To determine the quotient for $56 \div 7 = \square$, locate "56" in the column beneath "7" in the top row of factors; then move across the table to the left column, where the quotient, 8, is located to the left of "56." To find the quotient for $56 \div 8 = \square$, locate "56" in the column beneath "8" in the top row; then move across to "7" in the left column. This use of the table is consistent with the way it is used to learn the multiplication facts.

4. Practice Materials

Flashcards that emphasize the relationships between multiplication and division can be used to provide practice with the basic facts. The card in

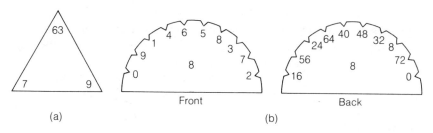

Figure 11-12(a) is used this way: For multiplication, cover the "63" and show the two factors; the child names the product. For division, cover one of the factors and show the other factor and product; the child names the missing factor. The card in Figure 11-12(b) has all the division and multiplication facts in which 8 is one factor. It is used by children working in pairs, one being the "teacher" and the other the "student." The "teacher" puts a pencil in a notch to indicate the number combination to use. When the front is facing the "student" and the pencil is put in the "6" notch, the combination is 6 times 8, to which the "student" responds by giving the product, 48. The answer is on the card's back. For division, the card is turned around so that the "student" sees a product and the "8." Again the "teacher" puts a pencil in a notch to indicate which pair of numbers to consider. The "student" names a factor when shown a product and "8."

Cassette tape and computer courseware programs, like those mentioned in earlier chapters, contain practice exercises dealing with multiplication and division facts. You are advised to check current catalogs of companies producing these materials for information about their latest products.

Demonstrate at least three activities that can be used to provide practice with the multiplication and division facts. If materials for the activities are unavailable, give explanations of the activities.

Self-check of Objective 5

TEACHING SOME PROPERTIES OF MULTIPLICATION AND DIVISION

1. The Commutative Property

The **commutative property of multiplication** is readily observed by children when they use arrays, because many opportunities are available for them to see that changing the order of a pair of factors does not affect their product. For example, the 2-by-3 and 3-by-2 arrays on squared paper in Figure 11-11 show that $2 \times 3 = 6$ and $3 \times 2 = 6$. You can include exercises on problem cards to call children's attention to the commutative property as they work with the pegboards and golf tees and the squared paper and colored pens and pencils.

The number line is a useful aid for understanding the commutative property. When an open sentence with a pair of small factors is displayed, a child can put arrows above the number line to illustrate the sentence and show the product (Figure 11-13). The factors in the sentence should then be reversed and the meaning of the new sentence demonstrated.

FIGURE 11-13
Number line used to show
that $5 \times 3 = 3 \times 5$

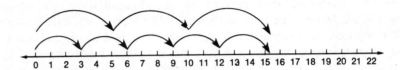

Division is not a commutative operation. Children who understand that multiplication is commutative can see that division is not by examining a few examples such as $72 \div 9 = \square$ and $9 \div 72 = \square$. These examples make it clear that changing the order of the numbers changes the answer.

2. The Associative Property

An introduction to the **associative property of multiplication** should help children recognize its significance. This property frees them to deal with pairs of factors in any way they choose in operations involving three or more factors.

The associative property is of little significance until children begin work with three factors. They will do this when they determine volumes of solid figures, such as rectangular prisms, where numbers indicating length, width, and height are multiplied. The volume of a rectangular prism with a length of 4, a width of 3, and a height of 2 (Figure 11-14) can be determined in several ways:

FIGURE 11-14
A $2 \times 3 \times 4$ rectangular solid

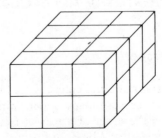

$$3 \times 4 \times 2 = 24$$
$$2 \times 4 \times 3 = 24$$
$$4 \times 2 \times 3 = 24$$
$$3 \times 2 \times 4 = 24$$

(There are still other combinations which you should identify before continuing your reading.) Regardless of which pair of factors is multiplied first, the product is always 24. Work with this type of multiplication is discussed more in Chapter 14. (You should recognize that when the order of the factors is changed, the commutative property is used along with the associative property.)

Another way to show children the usefulness of the associative property is to present combinations such as these:

$$4 \times 9 \times 25 = \square$$
$$36 \times 2 \times 50 = \square$$

In the first example, the product is easily determined when the product of 4×25 is named first; the 100 can then be multiplied by 9. In the second, determine the answer for 2×50, and then multiply 100 by 36.

3. The Distributive Property

The **distributive property of multiplication** over addition can be taught before all the multiplication facts have been introduced. This knowledge provides a useful strategy for studying multiplication facts with larger products. It can be used to find the answer to $4 \times 8 = \square$ if the multiplication fact $4 \times 4 = 16$ is known. The 8 in $4 \times 8 = \square$ can be renamed as $4 + 4$ and the sentence expressed as $4 \times (4 + 4) = \square$. The answer is then determined by completing the sentence

$$4 \times (4 + 4) = \square \rightarrow (4 \times 4) + (4 \times 4) = \square \rightarrow 16 + 16 = 32.$$

Before children can be expected to understand how to apply the property in this way, they should use aids that will make the property meaningful to them. For example, an array can be arranged on a magnetic board for the sentence $4 \times 8 = \square$ (Figure 11-15). Children first verify that

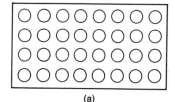

(a)

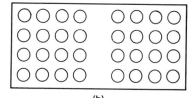

(b)

FIGURE 11-15
Arrays used to illustrate the distributive property. (a) $4 \times 8 = 32$. (b) $(4 \times 4) + (4 \times 4) = 16 + 16 = 32$.

it is a 4-by-8 array (a). Then rearrange the array as in (b), and display it to show

$$(4 \times 4) + (4 \times 4) = \square$$

The children determine the products for the two expressions of 4×4, and the sum of the products is determined. The sequence of steps in the sentence is

$$4 \times 8 = 4 \times (4 + 4) = (4 \times 4) + (4 \times 4) = 16 + 16 = 32,$$

because the second factor, 8, has been renamed $4 + 4$. This sentence now corresponds to the array shown in (b). Finally they should see the original array (a) again and its sentence:

$$4 \times 8 = \square \rightarrow 4 \times 8 = 32.$$

By seeing different arrangements of the 4-by-8 array, children will recognize that 8 can be renamed in other ways, such as $6 + 2$ and $5 + 3$, and that the sentence can be expressed as

$$4 \times (6 + 2) = (4 \times 6) + (4 \times 2) = 24 + 8 = 32$$

and

$$4 \times (5 + 3) = (4 \times 5) + (4 \times 3) = 20 + 12 = 32.$$

4. The Identity Element

An identity element is a number that, when operated on with another number, results in an answer that is the same as the second number. *One* is the identity element for multiplication.

The role of 1 is also important in division. You should provide children with activities that help them generalize that whenever a number is divided by 1, the quotient is always the number that is divided. They should also learn that any number divided by itself results in the quotient of 1, with 0 divided by 0 excepted.

5. The Role of 0 in Multiplication and Division

Zero has a special role in multiplication and division. In multiplication, the product is always 0 when 0 is one of the factors. The role of 0 in division is a special one. When the dividend is 0, the quotient is also 0 if the divisor is a number other than 0. This is illustrated by the example $0 \div 9 = 0$. This sentence is true, because $0 \times 9 = 0$. However, 0 is never used as a divisor. The reasons for 0 not being a divisor can be explained this way: When division is defined in terms of multiplication, $c \div b = a$ if and only if $a \times b = c$. If b is 0 and c is not 0, the sentence $c \div 0 = a$ implies that $a \times 0 = c$. But the product of a and 0 is 0, which means that c could not be a nonzero dividend. This contradiction indicates that the divisor cannot be 0 when the dividend is a whole number other than 0. For the sentence $0 \div 0 = a$, it is implied that $a \times 0 = 0$. Because this latter sentence is true for any whole number a, there is an ambiguity that indicates that 0 cannot be a divisor when the dividend is 0.

Because children are not mature enough to understand the reasons why 0 is never used as a divisor when division is introduced, it is best to exclude discussion of the reasons until later grades. There are mathematically mature children in grades 5 and 6 who can follow an explanation similar to the one given here, but most children in these grades cannot. It is not uncommon, then, for discussion to be delayed beyond the elementary-school years.

Demonstrate at least one procedure, along with materials, that can be used to help children understand these properties of multiplication: commutativity, associativity, distribution of multiplication over addition, and the roles of 1 and 0 in multiplication.

Self-check
of Objective 6

INTRODUCING A MULTIPLICATION ALGORITHM

Historically there have been several algorithms for multiplying pairs of numbers greater than 9. The algorithm shown here is used most often:

$$
\begin{array}{r}
32 \\
\times\ 2 \\
\hline
64
\end{array}
$$

Introduce this algorithm by giving children a problem situation to solve.

ACTIVITY 11-10   Introducing an Algorithm

• Tell this story: "Billy was arranging some books in a new bookcase. He found that twelve books fit on each of the three shelves. How many books did the bookcase hold?"

- Talk about models that can be used to represent the books in this situation. Markers on a magnetic board, a place-value pocket chart, and Cuisenaire rods are shown here.

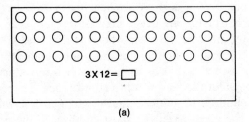

$3 \times 12 = \square$

(a)

$3 \times 12 = 3 \times (10 + 2)$
$(3 \times 10) + (3 \times 2) = 30 + 6 = 36$

(b)

Tens	Ones
H	⊓⊓
H	⊓⊓
H	⊓⊓

(a)

Tens	Ones
HHH	⊓⊓⊓⊓⊓⊓

(b)

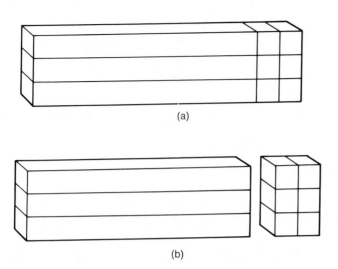

(a)

(b)

- Discuss the multiplication sentence

$$3 \times 12 = 36$$

There is a 3-by-12 array on the magnetic board; the pocket chart shows three pockets, each with a bundle of 10 and 2 single cards; there are 3 sets of Cuisenaire rods, each with 1 tens rod and 2 ones rods. Relate the sentence to each concrete model, making certain that the children see the tens and ones in each model.
- Next show the algorithm form:

$$\begin{array}{r} 12 \\ \times\ 3 \\ \hline \end{array}$$

Show that there is a total of 6 ones in each model, and relate this fact to multiplication of 2 by 3 in the algorithm. Record the answer:

$$\begin{array}{r} 12 \\ \times\ 3 \\ \hline 6 \end{array}$$

- Show that there are 3 tens, or 30, in each model, and relate this to the multiplication of 10 by 3. Record the answer:

$$\begin{array}{r} 12 \\ \times\ 3 \\ \hline 6 \\ 30 \end{array}$$

- Finally talk about the total in each model. Complete the algorithm:

$$
\begin{array}{r}
12 \\
\times\ 3 \\
\hline
6 \\
30 \\
\hline
36
\end{array}
$$

Repeat with other similar problem situations.

Another way to show the algorithm employs expanded notation and may make the work clearer for some children:

$$
\begin{array}{r}
10+2 \\
\times\quad\ 3 \\
\hline
30+6=36
\end{array}
$$

As children work, they see arrays, structured materials, and pocket charts illustrating the meaning of the algorithm. It is recommended that different models be used, because a model that is meaningful to one child may not have the same meaning for another. Under your careful guidance, most children will have the meaning of each step of the algorithm clarified by the models.

After multiplication with numbers like the ones used above, examples that have numbers larger than 100 as multiplicands and require no regrouping can be introduced. No particular difficulties are involved in this multiplication. A few examples like these

$$
\begin{array}{ccc}
123 & 241 & 342 \\
\times\ 3 & \times\ 2 & \times\ 2
\end{array}
$$

can be demonstrated with a pocket chart or structured materials.

Writing numerals in the algorithm in the expanded form should be discontinued once the use of the algorithm for multiplication is understood. Children will realize that the short, or common, form of the algorithm is an efficient way to do multiplication.

Self-check of Objective 7

Demonstrate with one of the place-value models how the multiplication algorithm can be introduced, using $3 \times 12 = 36$ as your example. Show the steps in the algorithm that accompany the sequence of steps with the manipulative materials. (Draw a series of pictures for the model if the materials themselves are not available.)

MULTIPLICATION WITH REGROUPING

Children who understand the meaning of expanded notation and regrouping with addition and subtraction and who also understand simpler multiplication should have no particular difficulties learning to use the algorithm for multiplication with regrouping.

As in all cases when new steps in a process are presented, you should employ meaningful materials to introduce multiplication with regrouping. Children should use these materials as they explore and discuss the meanings of the steps involved in regrouping. The use of the place-value pocket chart and array will be described.

ACTIVITY 11-11   Regrouping in Multiplication

- Put a sentence and algorithm involving 3 and 24 on the chalkboard:

$$3 \times 24 = \square \qquad \begin{array}{r} 24 \\ \times\ 3 \\ \hline \end{array}$$

- Ask each child to make up a problem situation for this multiplication. Example: "There are three boxes of candy bars; each has 24 bars. How many candy bars are in the three boxes?"
- Have a child represent the situation with a place-value pocket chart.

Tens	Ones
日日	∏∏∏∏
日日	∏∏∏∏
日日	∏∏∏∏

- As a child combines the markers in the ones place of the chart, have another child do the multiplication in the ones place of an expanded algorithm.

$$\begin{array}{r} 20 + 4 \\ \times\qquad 3 \\ \hline 12 \end{array}$$

Tens	Ones
日日	
日日	
日日	
日	∏∏

$$
\begin{aligned}
20 + 4 & \\
\times 3 & \\
\hline
60 + 12 & \\
= 60 + (10 + 2) & \\
= (60 + 10) + 2 & \\
= 70 + 2 & \\
= 72 &
\end{aligned}
$$

- Have a child combine the bundles in the tens place while another multiplies 3 times 20 in the algorithm.
- Rename the 12 as $10 + 2$, then add the 10 and 60; complete the addition of the partial products.

Tens	Ones

- Repeat with other pairs of factors.

Arrays are also useful for illustrating multiplication with regrouping. To show the meaning of $7 \times 14 = \square$, prepare two arrays, 7-by-10 and 7-by-4. Place the arrays together to show a 7-by-14 array, as in Figure 11-16(a). Then the array can be separated to show the 7-by-10 and 7-by-4 arrays (b). The sentence and algorithm should be rewritten as

$$7 \times (10 + 4) = \square \qquad \text{and} \qquad \begin{aligned} 10 + 4 \\ \times 7 \\ \hline \end{aligned}$$

FIGURE 11-16
Array used to show the distributive property with the sentence $7 \times 14 = \square$. (a) Array shows the original sentence. (b) Array is separated into two parts to show $7 \times (10 + 4) = (7 \times 10) + (7 \times 4) = 70 + 28 = 98$.

(a)   (b)

The steps to show multiplication with the sentence and algorithm are the same as the ones used in Activity 11-11. Other arrays should be prepared and used in the same manner.

Naturally children should eventually learn the standard algorithm for completing this type of multiplication. Instruction might follow this progression:

$$
\begin{array}{lll}
\begin{aligned}
37 & \rightarrow (30 + 7) \\
\times 2 & \rightarrow \times 2 \\
\hline
& 60 + 14 \\
= & 60 + (10 + 4) \\
= & (60 + 10) + 4 \\
= & 70 + 4 \\
= & 74
\end{aligned}
&
\begin{aligned}
37 \\
\times 2 \\
\hline
14 \\
\underline{60} \\
74
\end{aligned}
&
\begin{aligned}
{}^{1}37 \\
\times 2 \\
\hline
74
\end{aligned}
\\
 (a) & (b) & (c)
\end{array}
$$

In (a) the multiplication is completed using the expanded form, in (b) it is completed with both partial products written in a vertical placement, and in (c) it is completed with the standard algorithm.

Make up a real-life story problem for the sentence $5 \times 13 = 65$. Use markers, a pocket chart, or a series of drawings to illustrate the solution of your problem. Write the sequence of sentences that should accompany your demonstration with markers, pocket chart, or the series of drawings.

Self-check of Objective 8

MULTIPLICATION OF TWO NUMBERS LARGER THAN 10

1. Sequence of Steps

The commonly used algorithm for multiplying two numbers larger than 10 uses the distributive property of multiplication over addition and the associative property of addition. Although these steps are not clear in the algorithm, they can be shown in the sequence of sentences that follow:

$$\begin{array}{r} 53 \\ \times 36 \\ \hline 318 \\ 159 \\ \hline 1908 \end{array}$$

$$
\begin{aligned}
36 \times 53 &= 36 \times (50 + 3) & &\text{Renaming 53} \\
&= (36 \times 50) + (36 \times 3) & &\text{Distributive property} \\
&= [(30 + 6) \times 50] + [(30 + 6) \times 3] & &\text{Renaming 36} \\
&= (30 \times 50) + (6 \times 50) + (30 \times 3) + (6 \times 3) & &\text{Distributive property} \\
&= 1500 + 300 + 90 + 18 & &\text{Multiplication} \\
&= 1500 + 300 + 90 + (10 + 8) & &\text{Renaming 18} \\
&= 1500 + 300 + (90 + 10) + 8 & &\text{Associative property} \\
&= 1500 + 300 + 100 + 8 & &\text{Addition} \\
&= 1500 + (300 + 100) + 8 & &\text{Associative property} \\
&= 1500 + 400 + 8 & &\text{Addition} \\
&= 1908 & &\text{Addition}
\end{aligned}
$$

Such a long series of steps would not be used with a class of fourth- or fifth-grade children; however, you must understand the complete process so you can explain it clearly.

Build on children's knowledge of expanded notation to help them understand the commonly used algorithm for multiplying two numbers greater than 10. When 12 and 14 are factors, the algorithm can be written as

$$\begin{array}{r} 14 \\ \times 12 \\ \hline \end{array}$$

```
    14
  ×12
     8
    20
    40
   100
   168


    14
  ×12
    48
   140
   168


    14
  ×12
    28
    14
   168


    36
  ×48
    48
   240
   240
  1200


  2 ×
    36
  ×48
   288
   144
  1728
```

To multiply these numbers, children should think of the multiplier as 10 + 2. When the multiplication has been completed, there will be four partial products, as shown in the margin. By seeing each of the partial products separately, children are more likely to recognize that there are four separate pairs of numbers to multiply. Later the process is shortened so that only two partial products are written.

When partial products are indicated in the algorithm in the most sophisticated form, the "0" is not written in the ones place of the second partial product. Children must realize that it is omitted only as a time-saving technique (see previous example in margin). The "14" is indented in the second partial product to show that it represents 14 tens, so it is placed with the "4" in the tens place.

2. Regrouping

Multiplication involving numbers greater than 10 that require regrouping, or "carrying," is taught after children understand how to multiply two such numbers with no regrouping. As the first few examples of multiplication with regrouping are encountered, children should complete them by writing each partial product in the algorithm, as in the margin. Then the combined partial products should be written; the 4 tens from the 48 are added to the 24 tens, giving the first partial product of 288. The "carrying" of the 2 hundreds in the second partial product should be noted too. Memory aids, as shown in the example in the margin, might be used in the algorithm to help children remember the numbers that are being regrouped. After it has been used, the "4" is marked out to prevent confusion when the "2" is written later. You should also assign frequent adding-by-endings exercises that involve the products of two numbers smaller than 10 and the numbers 1 through 8. These experiences should include the use of worksheets and oral exercises, as indicated in Chapter 10, to give children practice with the type of addition required in multiplication with regrouping.

Once children understand the process of multiplying two numbers that require regrouping, they can move on to work with larger numbers. The steps in the process are the same as those with numbers expressed by two-digit numerals. You should continually observe children as they work examples involving larger numbers to prevent errors and the formation of incorrect habits.

**Self-check
of Objective 9**

Explain how knowledge of expanded notation can be used to show how the multiplication sentence 11 × 16 = 176 is completed.

ZERO IN MULTIPLICATION

Factors such as 306 and 4,002, especially when they appear in the multiplier, present difficulties to some children. Before multiplying numbers containing 0, multiplication by 10 and its multiples should be mastered. Sets, arrays, the number line, and other aids should be used until children can generalize that when 10 is the multiplier, the product is the multiplicand with a 0 annexed. (An alternate generalization is to think of the process as moving the number one place to the left and placing a 0 in the ones place.) To multiply by a number such as 20 or 30 as in the sentence $20 \times 6 = \square$, children should be able to think "$2 \times 6 = 12$, annex 0 to give 120." Computation with other powers of 10 and their multiples should be taught in a similar manner so that children can generalize about them, too. After they have learned this process, frequent oral exercises reinforce children's ability to use it. Efficient use of this process is important in multiplication and essential before beginning to learn the division algorithm.

$$
\begin{array}{r}
346 \\
\times 209 \\
\hline
3114 \\
6920 \\
\hline
72314
\end{array}
$$

In multiplying the first problem in the margin, children should be able to determine the second partial product by multiplying by the 2 hundreds (or 20 tens) in one step rather than two. There is no reason for children to write the work with three partial products as shown in the second algorithm in the margin.

$$
\begin{array}{r}
346 \\
\times 209 \\
\hline
3114 \\
000 \\
692 \\
\hline
72314
\end{array}
$$

INTRODUCING A DIVISION ALGORITHM

The standard division algorithm for the sentence $138 \div 3 = 46$ is shown in the margin. Before children can perform it with full understanding, they must know and understand certain basic concepts and skills. These include: (1) knowledge of both partitive and measurement division situations, (2) knowledge of the multiplication and division facts, (3) ability to subtract, and (4) ability to multiply and divide by ten and its powers and multiples.

$$
\begin{array}{r}
46 \\
3\overline{)138} \\
12 \\
\hline
18 \\
18 \\
\hline
\end{array}
$$

1. Dividing by Numbers Smaller Than 10

Situations that can be used to promote understanding of the division algorithm abound. A problem such as the following is useful to introduce division by a number smaller than 10:

ACTIVITY 11-12 The Division Algorithm

- "Twenty-eight marbles will be shared equally by six children. How many marbles will each one get?"

- Use 28 real marbles or disks on a magnetic or flannel board. Then form six equal-sized groups. There will be 4 objects in each group, with 4 left over.
- Show an algorithm for this situation:

$$
\begin{array}{r}
4 \\
6\overline{)28} \\
24 \\
4
\end{array}
$$

- Help children develop a strategy for determining quotients without concrete aids. One strategy is to relate division to multiplication. For this example use these facts:

$$6 \times 1 = 6 \quad 6 \times 2 = 12 \quad 6 \times 3 = 18 \quad 6 \times 4 = 24 \quad 6 \times 5 = 30$$

Questions such as "Will each child get at least one marble?" "At least 2 marbles?" "At least 3 marbles?" "At least 4 marbles?" "At least 5 marbles?" help children see that *4 marbles* is the answer. (The four marbles that are left over cannot be divided among 6 children.)
- Repeat with other situations.

Think-back flashcards are helpful for developing children's skills in determining quotients. The card for $8\overline{)79}$ is shown in Figure 11-17. The front of the card (a) shows the division algorithm without the quotient, and the back (b) shows the basic fact associated with the division. A child is shown $8\overline{)79}$ and then thinks back to the related division fact and says, "Seventy-two divided by 8 equals 9." (Avoid the expression "8 goes into 72 9 times.") If a child cannot think back to the correct basic fact, reverse the card so it can be read. Then show the front of the card again and have the child repeat the statement of the basic fact. Group and individual work with think-back cards should be provided frequently until children are skillful in naming quotients.

FIGURE 11-17
Example of a think-back flashcard. (a) Front shows the division algorithm. (b) Back shows the associated basic fact.

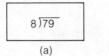

(a)   (b)

Self-check of Objective 10

Explain how multiplication sentences and think-back flashcards are used to help children learn to name quotients when the division algorithm is introduced.

2. Multiplication and Division Patterns

Skill in multiplying and dividing by ten and its powers and multiples is needed in order to estimate quotients or use divisors greater than 10. Patterns such as the following can be used to develop this skill.

$1 \times 1 = 1$	$1 \times 10 = 10$	$1 \times 100 = 100$
$2 \times 1 = 2$	$2 \times 10 = 20$	$2 \times 100 = 200$
$3 \times 1 = 3$	$3 \times 10 = 30$	$3 \times 100 = 300$
.	.	.
.	.	.
.	.	.
$9 \times 1 = 9$	$9 \times 10 = 90$	$9 \times 100 = 900$
$1 \div 1 = 1$	$10 \div 10 = 1$	$100 \div 100 = 1$
$2 \div 1 = 2$	$20 \div 10 = 2$	$200 \div 100 = 2$
$3 \div 1 = 3$	$30 \div 10 = 3$	$300 \div 100 = 3$
.	.	.
.	.	.
.	.	.
$9 \div 1 = 9$	$90 \div 10 = 9$	$900 \div 100 = 9$

- -

$2 \times 1 = 2$	$2 \times 10 = 20$	$2 \times 100 = 200$
$2 \times 2 = 4$	$2 \times 20 = 40$	$2 \times 200 = 400$
$2 \times 3 = 6$	$2 \times 30 = 60$	$2 \times 300 = 600$
.	.	.
.	.	.
.	.	.
$2 \times 9 = 18$	$2 \times 90 = 180$	$2 \times 900 = 1800$
$2 \div 1 = 2$	$20 \div 10 = 2$	$200 \div 100 = 2$
$4 \div 2 = 2$	$40 \div 20 = 2$	$400 \div 200 = 2$
$6 \div 3 = 2$	$60 \div 30 = 2$	$600 \div 300 = 2$
.	.	.
.	.	.
.	.	.
$18 \div 9 = 2$	$180 \div 90 = 2$	$1800 \div 900 = 2$
$2 \div 2 = 1$	$20 \div 2 = 10$	$200 \div 2 = 100$
$4 \div 2 = 2$	$40 \div 2 = 20$	$400 \div 2 = 200$
$6 \div 2 = 3$	$60 \div 2 = 30$	$600 \div 2 = 300$
.	.	.
.	.	.
.	.	.
$18 \div 2 = 9$	$180 \div 2 = 90$	$1800 \div 2 = 900$

Careful development and discussion of these and other patterns help children learn skills for further work with the algorithm. During discussions, note relationships between the sentences in a line, for example, $1 \times 1 = 1$, $1 \times 10 = 10$, and $1 \times 100 = 100$. Also note relationships between a given line of multiplication sentences and the corresponding line of division sentences, such as $2 \times 9 = 18$, $2 \times 90 = 180$, $2 \times 900 = 1800$, and $18 \div 9 = 2$, $180 \div 90 = 2$, $1800 \div 900 = 2$.

You can prepare worksheets that contain multiplication and division patterns like these for children to complete. Discuss their completed worksheets with them to highlight the relationships. Later use oral questions to reinforce written work: "If there are three 9s in 27, how many 9s are there in 270?" "If six 8s are 48, what are six 80s?"

Children's next work is usually with division that yields a quotient greater than ten without regrouping. In the activity that follows, $48 \div 4 = 12$ is the example.

ACTIVITY 11-13   Stamp Display

- "John has forty-eight stamps that he is going to fix for a school display. He will put four stamps on a card. How many cards will he need?"
- Write an algorithm for this situation:

$$4\overline{)48}$$

- Use a dialogue similar to the following to help the children understand the algorithm:

Teacher: "What does the 48 stand for?"
Children: "The number of stamps John has."
Teacher: "What does the 4 stand for?"
Children: "The number of stamps for each card."
Teacher: "Does John need at least ten cards?"
Children: "Yes."
Teacher: "How do you know?"
Children: "Ten cards will hold forty stamps; he has more than forty stamps."
Teacher: "Will he need at least twenty cards?"
Children: "No, twenty cards hold eighty stamps; he doesn't have that many."
Teacher: "After he puts four stamps on each of ten cards, how many stamps are left?"
Children: "Eight."
Teacher: "How many cards will he need for eight stamps?"
Children: "Two."
Teacher: "How many cards does he need for the forty-eight stamps?"
Children: "Twelve."

During the discussion, complete the algorithm step by step:

```
4)48
  40 | 10 × 4
   8
   8 |  2 × 4
```

- Repeat with similar examples.

**Self-check
of Objectives
11 and 12**

State why it is important for children to know how to multiply by ten and its powers and multiples before they begin learning the division algorithm. Describe a procedure that can be used to help children learn these skills.

Make up a real-life division situation and demonstrate a procedure that can be used to make a meaningful introduction of the division algorithm using your example. Tell whether yours is a partitive or a measurement situation.

DIVISION WITH REGROUPING

Regrouping is required when the number in the tens place of the dividend is not a multiple of the divisor.

1. Concrete–Manipulative Model

The division $3\overline{)45}$ requires regrouping because 40 (4 tens) is not a multiple of 3. This example can be worked out for a partitive situation with beansticks. Begin by representing 45 with the sticks, as in Figure 11-18(a). Now the beansticks are to be separated into three groups, each the same size. First consider the tens sticks and separate them into three groups, each containing one stick (b). It is not possible to separate the remaining stick without exchanging it for ten loose beans. This exchange is shown in (c). Finally the 15 single beans are separated into three equal-sized groups, with each group put next to a tens stick (d).

The steps are illustrated in the algorithm in the margin, where the partial quotients are stacked with the divisor at the right.

```
3)45
  30 | 3 × 10
  15
  15 | 3 × 5
  15
```

2. Algorithm Form

The algorithm form should be studied next. The form shown previously, or some variation of it, is frequently used. This form is beneficial because:

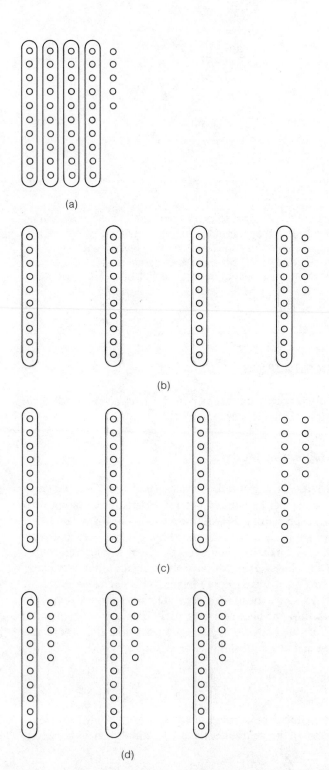

FIGURE 11-18
Division problem $45 \div 3 = 15$
represented with beansticks

1. The parts of the quotient are shown in their complete form; the ten is shown as 10 at the right, rather than as a 1 in the tens place above the dividend.

2. The multiplication is shown in a familiar form, 3×10, rather than in the form

$$\begin{array}{r} 1 \\ 3\overline{)45} \\ 3 \end{array}$$

in which the 1 indicates a ten that is multiplied by 3, the divisor, resulting in a product of 30, which is indicated by a 3 written in the tens place beneath the dividend.

3. The product of 3 and 10 is shown as 30 rather than 3 in the tens place.

Thus the form of the algorithm helps children see the meaning of the steps performed, because the different parts of the algorithm are related to the actions with the beansticks used earlier.

A sufficient number of examples such as the following help make the meaning of the algorithm clear as the children move from the use of manipulative materials to the abstract algorithm:

Teacher: "When we divide 56 by 4, will there be as many as ten 4s in 56?"
Children: "Yes, because $10 \times 4 = 40$; 40 is less than 56."
Teacher: "Will there be as many as twenty 4s in 56?"
Children: "No, $20 \times 4 = 80$; 80 is more than 56."
Teacher: "Let us show [in (a) in the margin] that 10 times 4 equals 40 and then subtract 40 from 56 to see how much is left to be divided. What is 56 minus 40?"
Children: "Sixteen."
Teacher: "What is 16 divided by 4?"
Children: "Four."
Teacher: "We can show that too [in margin example (b)]. Now what is the answer to 56 divided by 4?"
Children: "Fourteen."

$$\text{(a)} \quad 4\overline{)56} \atop \begin{array}{r} 40 \\ \hline 16 \end{array} \Big| 10 \times 4$$

$$\text{(b)} \quad 4\overline{)56} \atop \begin{array}{r} 40 \\ \hline 16 \\ 16 \\ \hline 14 \end{array} \begin{array}{l} 10 \times 4 \\ \\ 4 \times 4 \end{array}$$

Make up a real-life problem involving a division situation that requires regrouping. Write an imaginary dialogue that might involve you and several children as you introduce the algorithm with regrouping.

Self-check of Objective 13

DIVISION INVOLVING LARGER NUMBERS

A good understanding of division with quotients represented by one-digit numerals, including use of the algorithm and the ability to multiply by ten and powers of ten, is a prerequisite to learning division involving larger numbers; without the proper background, children will encounter many difficulties with this kind of division.

1. Two-Digit Divisors and One-Digit Quotients

Children's first work with two-digit divisors is usually done with divisors that are multiples of ten. This is so because patterns can be used to help them develop skill in determining quotients. The patterns illustrated earlier in this chapter lead to this generalization:

$$\underline{\quad}\text{ones} \times \underline{\quad}\text{tens} = \underline{\quad}\text{tens}$$
$$\underline{\quad}\text{tens} \div \underline{\quad}\text{tens} = \underline{\quad}\text{ones}$$

So, for $270 \div 30 = \square$, the 27 tens are divided by 3 tens to determine the quotient, 9.

Answers for examples such as these

$$30\overline{)123} \qquad 30\overline{)98} \qquad 30\overline{)72} \qquad 30\overline{)131}$$

can be determined by using this multiplication pattern:

$$1 \times 30 = 30 \qquad 2 \times 30 = 60 \qquad 3 \times 30 = 90$$
$$4 \times 30 = 120 \qquad 5 \times 30 = 150$$

Because not all divisors are multiples of ten, strategies for estimating quotients for nonmultiples must be learned. A useful strategy is to round the divisor to the nearest ten and use multiples of that number:

THINK

$$32\overline{)129} \longrightarrow 30\overline{)129} \longrightarrow \begin{array}{r} 32\overline{)129} \\ \underline{128}\,|\,4 \times 32 \\ 1\, \end{array}$$

This process will not always yield the correct quotient, as in

THINK

$$33\overline{)129} \longrightarrow 30\overline{)129} \longrightarrow \begin{array}{r} 33\overline{)129} \\ \underline{132}\,|\,4 \times 33 \end{array}$$

so children must be able to adjust the quotient to the correct one by using a smaller number, in this case 3.

2. Two-Digit and Larger Quotients

Problem situations that enable children to visualize the meaning of each term in the algorithm are useful for developing an understanding of division involving larger numbers. Examples like the following should be used.

ACTIVITY 11-14　Bagging Marbles

- Present a problem situation: "288 marbles are to be packaged in bags of twenty-four marbles each. How many bags will it take to hold the marbles?"
- Write the division sentence and an algorithm:

$$288 \div 24 = \square \qquad 24\overline{)288}$$

- Use a dialogue similar to this to help the children solve the problem:

Teacher: "What does the 288 stand for?"
Children: "The total number of marbles."
Teacher: "What does the 24 stand for?"
Children: "The number of marbles to go in each bag."
Teacher: "Will there be at least ten bags of twenty-four marbles each?"
Children: "Yes, because ten times twenty-four is 240. There are more than 240 marbles."
Teacher: "Will there be at least twenty bags of marbles?"
Children: "No, because twenty times twenty-four is 480. There are not that many marbles."

- Show the result of filling 10 bags in the algorithm:

$$
\begin{array}{r}
24\overline{)288} \\
240 \\
\hline
48
\end{array}
\quad 10 \times 24
$$

- Continue the dialogue:

Teacher; "After ten bags have been filled, how many marbles are left to be packaged?"
Children: "Forty-eight."
Teacher: "How many more bags can be filled with the remaining marbles?"
Children: "Two more, because two times twenty-four is forty-eight."

- Complete the algorithm:

$$
\begin{array}{r}
24\overline{)288} \\
240 \\
\hline
48 \\
48 \\
\hline
\end{array}
\begin{array}{l}
\\
10 \times 24 \\
\\
2 \times 24 \\
\hline
12
\end{array}
$$

- Before you leave the algorithm, relate each numeral in it to the problem situation so that children are clear about each one's meaning.
- Repeat with similar problems.

If children have a good understanding of the meaning of division, know how to multiply by tens and powers of ten, and know how to use the algorithm with smaller numbers, the first work they do with two-place and larger divisors need not be restricted to examples that have one-place quotients. In the foregoing example the quotient is larger than 10. Further use of examples with one- and two-digit numerals to represent quotients smaller than 100 will further develop understanding of the algorithm.

3. Estimating Quotients

Skills in determining the quotient must be continuously refined as numbers increase in size. The following strategy can be used.

ACTIVITY 11-15

- Begin with an algorithm:

$$36\overline{)7348}$$

- Ask questions similar to these:

Teacher: "Are there at least ten 36s in 7348?"
Children: "Yes. Ten times thirty-six is 360; that is less than 7348."
Teacher: "Are there as many as one hundred 36s in 7348?"
Children: "Yes. One hundred times thirty-six is 3600; that is less than 7348."
Teacher: "Are there as many as one thousand 36s in 7348?"
Children: "No. One thousand times 36 is 36,000; that is too much."
Teacher: "We know that the answer is more than one hundred but less than one thousand. Will there be as many as two hundred 36s in 7348?"

Children: "Yes. Two hundred times thirty-six is 7200; that is less than 7348."

Teacher: "Can there be as many as three hundred 36s?"

Children: "No, that is too many."

- Show this step in the algorithm:

$$
\begin{array}{r|l}
36)\overline{7348} & \\
7200 & 200 \times 36 \\
\hline
148 &
\end{array}
$$

- Continue the dialogue:

Teacher: "After we multiply thirty-six by two hundred and subtract, we have a remainder of 148. How many 36s in 148?"

Children: "There are four."

- Complete the algorithm:

$$
\begin{array}{r|l}
36)\overline{7348} & \\
7200 & 200 \times 36 \\
\hline
148 & \\
144 & 4 \times 36 \\
\hline
4 & 204
\end{array}
$$

- Review the meaning of each term in the algorithm, including the undivided remainder, 4.
- Repeat with similar examples.

---

4. Shortened Forms

Refinements can be made in the division process so that more mature ways are used with the algorithm to reduce the number of steps and lessen the notation that is written as division is done. For example, to help children decide the number of decimal places there will be in a quotient, place a number of division examples on the chalkboard:

$$39)\overline{4869} \qquad 73)\overline{7421} \qquad 86)\overline{6243} \qquad 23)\overline{78,552}$$

The place value of each quotient figure is revealed by multiplying the divisor by ten and its powers. In the first example this shows that the answer is more than 100 but less than 1000, so there will be a quotient represented by a three-digit numeral. An *x* or something similar can be marked over the place-value position, as shown in the margin. Next, the first quotient figure should be calculated. Because in this example it is known to be some number of hundreds, the exact number of hundreds

$$
\begin{array}{c}
\times \\
\hline
39)\overline{4869}
\end{array}
$$

$$
\begin{array}{r}
\times \\
100 \\
\text{(a) } 39\overline{)4869} \\
3900 \\
\hline
969
\end{array}
$$

$$
\begin{array}{r}
\times 20 \\
100 \\
\text{(b) } 39\overline{)4869} \\
3900 \\
\hline
969 \\
780 \\
\hline
189
\end{array}
$$

$$
\begin{array}{r}
4 \\
\times 20 \\
100 \\
\text{(c) } 39\overline{)4869} \\
3900 \\
\hline
969 \\
780 \\
\hline
189 \\
156 \\
\hline
33
\end{array}
$$

$$
\begin{array}{r}
248r10 \\
32\overline{)7946} \\
64 \\
\hline
154 \\
128 \\
\hline
266 \\
256 \\
\hline
10
\end{array}
$$

is found by multiplying by multiples of 100. Once children can readily discover the first quotient figure, they can begin to shorten the steps used with the algorithm. First, the number of decimal places is decided and marked. Next, the first quotient figure is determined. The number of 39s in 4869 is estimated by rounding 39 to 40 and multiplyihg 40 by multiples of 100. It is more than 100 but less than 200, so "100" is placed in the algorithm, as shown in (a) in the margin. The numeral for the product of 39 and 100 is placed beneath the dividend in the algorithm. The number of 39s in 969 will be about twenty (39 can be rounded to 40 to make the estimate), so "20" is written in the algorithm, as in (b). The product of 20 and 39 is subtracted from 969. Finally, the number of 39s in 189 is estimated by rounding off to 40. The answer, 4, is written in the algorithm, and the numeral for the product of 4 and 39 is written beneath 189. The remainder is then determined. The completed algorithm form is shown in (c).

Some children will continue to reduce the number of written steps until they put just a "1" in the hundreds place, a "2" in the tens place, and a "4" in the ones place, rather than writing "100," "20," and "4." These children may or may not shorten the way products of the quotient figures and divisor are written or the way the subtraction is done. The only reason zeros might be omitted in the algorithm is to save time. However, there is an increased likelihood that mistakes will be made when zeros are omitted, so do not have children leave them out when they are not ready for this step.

Some children will achieve an understanding of the most mature form of the algorithm, explained for the example in the margin. The divisor, 32, is rounded to 30 to give an easier-to-use divisor. The number of 30s in 79 is two. A "2" is recorded in the hundreds place of the quotient because 79 stands for hundreds. The multiplication of 2 and 32 is completed, and the product, 64, is recorded. Sixty-four is subtracted from 79, and the answer, 15, is recorded; the 4 is brought down. Because 32 has been rounded to 30, the second division (that is, 154 divided by 30) gives a quotient of 5. Five is too large, however, and the quotient is reduced to 4. The division is completed by multiplying 4 times 32, recording the 128, subtracting, bringing down the 6, and dividing again to find the number of ones in the quotient. The answer is completed by writing the remainder after the quotient.

Self-check of Objective 14

The division algorithm is difficult for many children to understand when large numbers are involved. Demonstrate your own understanding of the process by making up a real-life problem similar to the one given here, and write a series of questions and answers that might be a dialogue between you and a group of children learning to use the algorithm with large numbers.

DIVISION WITH REMAINDERS

When the divisor is not a whole-number factor of the dividend, a remainder occurs. The way a remainder is treated depends on the nature of the problem situation giving rise to the division. The following situations show different treatments of remainders.

"There are thirty-two children in our class. If we play a game that requires three equal-sized teams, how many players will there be on each team?" In this situation, which is partitive, there will be ten players on each team. The remainder does not actually become a part of the quotient. The answer is that there will be three teams of ten players each.

"Mother baked twenty-six cookies for Sally and her three friends. If the cookies are given to the children so that each child gets an equal share, how many will each one get?" In this partitive situation there will be two cookies left after twenty-four have been shared by the four children. These can be broken into halves, making four halves, one for each child. In this example it makes sense to divide the remainder. The answer, therefore, can be expressed as 6½ cookies per child.

"It costs 79 cents to buy three cans of dog food. If you buy only one can, what will you pay for it?" In this case the division gives a whole-number quotient of 26, with a remainder of 1. Children will understand that the store is not likely to sell one can of dog food for 26 cents because then the price would become three cans for 78 cents. For this example, the answer is changed to 27 when the price of one item is determined.

"A group of fifty-three children is riding to camp in cars. If each car can carry six children, how many cars will be needed?" In this measurement situation the division results in a quotient of 8. There will be a remainder of five children, which means that eight cars are insufficient. Therefore the answer is nine cars, rather than eight.

"Sixty-eight apples must be put in boxes. If each box can hold eight apples, how many boxes can be filled?" For this measurement situation the quotient is eight boxes with four apples remaining. Since these are not enough to fill another box, the answer is eight full boxes.

Starting with third grade, problem situations featuring these different types should be explored periodically to review appropriate ways to deal with remainders. In practice exercises with division involving remainders, there is sometimes no way to determine what the dividends, divisors, and quotients represent. Then the numeral that represents the remainder can be written at the bottom of the algorithm, as in (a) in the margin. It is also correct to write the numeral after the quotient, as in (b), or, as in (c), where the remainder is recorded as $4/9$.

$$(a) \quad 9\overline{)67} \\ \frac{63}{4} \quad {\scriptstyle 7}$$

$$(b) \quad 9\overline{)67} \\ \frac{63}{4} \quad {\scriptstyle 7r4}$$

$$(c) \quad 9\overline{)67} \\ \frac{63}{4} \quad {\scriptstyle 7\,4/9}$$

**Self-check
of Objective 15**

Remainders in division are handled differently depending upon the situation from which they arise. Make up at least three real-life story problems in which the remainder is not 0 and is handled differently in each one. Describe how the remainder should be handled for each problem situation.

THE CALCULATOR AND MULTIPLICATION AND DIVISION

The calculator can be used to help children understand multiplication and division operations and to extend their experiences with these operations beyond the ones usually found in textbooks.

1. Repeated Addition and Subtraction

Relationships between multiplication and addition, division and subtraction, and multiplication and division are readily shown on the calculator. To show multiplication as repeated addition use one factor as an addend and add it as many times as indicated by the other factor. For $7 \times 83 = \square$, use 83 as the addend seven times to get the product 581. Compute by multiplying on the machine to verify the answer.

In a similar way show division as repeated subtraction. Set the dividend into the machine. Subtract the divisor as many times as needed to reach zero or a number smaller than the divisor. Count each time the ⊟ key is pressed to get the quotient. When children alternate these two operations with the same set of numbers, they have another way of seeing that multiplication and division are inverse operations.

2. Multiplying 27

3×27
6×27
9×27
12×27
15×27
18×27
21×27
24×27
27×27
30×27

Complete the products for the examples in the margin. Note the sequence of numbers in the hundreds and ones places of the products and the sequence of numbers in the tens places. Select any product, say 486 (18×27). Rearrange the numerals by putting the "6" before the "48." Is 648 divisible by 27? Put the "4" after "86." Is 864 divisible by 27? Rearrange other products the same ways. Are all of the rearranged numbers divisible by 27?

3. Filling the Holes

Multiplication and division examples such as the following can be given children so they can "fill in the holes." Let each child decide how to proceed without your directions.

```
  364        8 2          4 6
   ×9        ×38    39)17784
  ────       ────    156
  364         76     ─────
  327        261      2 8
 ─────       ────     1 5
 33   4     3136      ───
                       234
                       234
```

4. Russian-Peasant Multiplication

This old multiplication process is made simple by the calculator. The process is illustrated with two examples. In the left-hand column the factor is divided by 2, and the quotient is recorded. (If the calculator shows a decimal fraction quotient, only the whole number portion is recorded.) Divide each successive quotient by 2 until 1 is reached. The factor in the right-hand column is multiplied by 2 and its product recorded beneath it. Each successive product is multiplied by 2. Certain rows are marked out. What criterion is used to determine the rows to mark out? What is done with the remaining numbers in the right-hand column to determine the product?

Encourage children to use calculators to perform multiplication and division of larger numbers in everyday situations. Once children learn the meaning of the operations and are familiar with an algorithm for performing each one, they should not be burdened with practice activities that are designed to develop a high degree of competence with the two algorithms. Rather they should learn to use a calculator to perform this work. The time formerly devoted to practice can be spent working in areas of mathematics for which they might otherwise have no time.

```
 48×--28·      37×   57
 24----56·     18--114
 12---112      9    228
  6--224       4--456
  3    448     2--912
  1    896     1   1824
      ─────        ─────
      1344         2109
```

Demonstrate with a calculator four activities that can be used to extend children's experiences with multiplication and division.

***Self-check
of Objective 15***

COMPUTERS AND MULTIPLICATION AND DIVISION

The discussion of computers in Chapter 6 contains examples of commercial programs that provide drill-and-practice and tutorial materials. The *Milliken Math Sequences* program provides children with help in learning basic facts and multiplication and division algorithms.[4] *The Arithmetic Classroom*, which was developed by the software division of the company that publishes *Scholastic Magazine*, contains programs that deal with multiplication and division facts and operations.[5]

The program that follows uses multiplication and division to answer the question, "How much sleep do I get?"[6] This problem-solving program can be entered into a computer by a child who is familiar with the machine and with the multiplication and division that is used.

```
100   PRINT "HOW MANY HOURS OF SLEEP LAST NIGHT?"
200   INPUT H
300   TH = H * 365
400   D = TH/24
500   W = D/7
600   PRINT "IN ONE YEAR, YOU WILL SLEEP"
700   PRINT W
800   PRINT "WEEKS"
900   END
```

This program tells a student how many hours, days, and weeks are spent sleeping in one year for a given number of hours per night. Students who possess some programming skills can be encouraged to vary the program to reveal the number of minutes slept in a year or the number of hours spent watching TV in the same period of time.

SPECIAL STUDENTS AND MULTIPLICATION–DIVISION

1. Learning-Handicapped Children

Students for whom memorization is hard and who have difficulty with sequencing and spatial organization need special help to learn basic facts. The low-stress algorithm for addition, discussed in Chapter 10, can be used by these children to generate facts. The process works this way, using the facts for 8 as an example:

---

[4]*Milliken Math Sequences* (Milliken Publishing Company, 1100 Research Blvd., St. Louis, MO 63132).

[5]*The Arithmetic Classroom* (Scholastic, Inc., 904 Sylvan Ave., Englewood Cliffs, NJ 07632).

[6]Mary Jean Winter, "Teaching Mathematics with Microcomputers: Middle Grades," *Arithmetic Teacher*, XXX, No. 6 (February 1983), p. 29.

- List nine 8s in a column.

- List sums for the column of 8s, using the low-stress process.

- To determine the product of 4×8, count down four 8s from the top. Note the ones numeral, which is "2." Count the tens from the top down; there are three. The product of 4×8 is 32.

- For 8×8, count eight 8s; note the "4." Count the tens; there are six, so 8×8 is 64.

8
$_1 8_6$
$_1 8_4$
$_1 8_2$
$_1 8_0$
8_8
$_1 8_6$
$_1 8_4$
$_1 8_2$

This same column can be used for determining division facts:

- To determine the number of 8s in 56, count tens downward until you have counted five; look at the ones side to see if there is a "6" alongside the fifth ten. There is, so you have reached 56.

- Count the 8s upward; there are seven, so $56 \div 8 = 7$.

- To determine the answer to $48 \div 8$, count tens downward until you have counted four. There is not an "8" next to the fourth ten, so you will need to go down one more 8 to get "8" on the ones side. Count upward; there are six 8s, so $48 \div 8 = 6$.

The alignment and order of steps in the common algorithms for multiplication and division are sources of difficulty for many learning-handicapped children. One way they can keep numerals properly aligned is to work on squared paper. Green and red color cues will help them to keep the sequence of steps in order. Figure 11-19 shows a multiplication algorithm for $46 \times 29 = \square$. Mark the "6" and the first circle above the "2" green to indicate that multiplication by 6 is done first. The circle is for the "5" that is "carried." Mark the "4" and the second circle red to indicate that multiplication by 4 is done last. Mark the answer space for "174" green and the space for "1160" red.

		2	9
	×	4	6
	1	7	4
1	1	6	
1	3	3	4

FIGURE 11-19
Multiplication done on vertically lined paper helps keep numerals aligned.

The division example in Figure 11-20 also has green and red cues. The "8" and the answer space above it are green; the "30" and the answer space above the "7" are red. The green "8" reminds children where to begin dividing; the green answer box shows where the first quotient figure goes. The red "30" reminds them that it is divided last, and the red answer box shows that the "7" goes in the ones place. It should also help them remember to put a "0" in the tens place of the quotient.[7]

FIGURE 11-20
Vertically ruled paper helps children remember to put zeros in a quotient.

Learning-handicapped children should also learn to use a calculator for multiplication and division.

2. Gifted and Talented Children

Gifted and talented children should have opportunities to learn alternate algorithms for multiplication and division. They can also learn about the origin and rationale for each of the alternate algorithms. Russian-peasant multiplication has already been discussed. The book *Historical Topics for the Mathematics Classroom*[8] contains information about the gelosia, or grating, method of multiplying and the galley method of multiplying and dividing. Napier's rods are also pictured and discussed. The use of Genaille's rods for division is discussed by Elroy Bolduc.[9] The two articles by Charlotte Junge and the one by Kulm in this chapter's reading list describe activities that challenge gifted and talented children.

Tests of divisibility provide another area of study for gifted and talented children. Tests for several numbers are discussed in Chapter 16. H. Laurence Ridge and Joseph S. Renzulli discuss a novel test for divisibility by 11 that is credited to a gifted student.[10]

---

[7] The ideas for using color cues and circles for regrouped numbers in multiplication are adapted from Nancy S. Bley and Carol A. Thornton, *Teaching Mathematics to the Learning Disabled* (Rockville, Maryland: Aspen Systems Corporation, 1981), pp. 244 and 260.

[8] National Council of Teachers of Mathematics, *Historical Topics for the Mathematics Classroom*, Thirty-first Yearbook (Washington, D.C.: The Council, 1969).

[9] Elroy J. Bolduc, "Genaille Division Sticks," *Arithmetic Teacher*, XXVII, No. 5 (January 1979), pp. 12–13.

[10] H. Laurence Ridge and Joseph S. Renzulli, "Teaching the Talented and Gifted," in Vincent J. Glennon, ed., *The Mathematical Education of Exceptional Children and Youth, an Interdisciplinary Approach* (Reston, Virginia: National Council of Teachers of Mathematics, 1981), pp. 226–227.

Use 7s to demonstrate how the low-stress algorithm for addition can be used to generate the multiplication and division facts involving 7.

Mark squares on a paper and show with red and green pencils how color cues can be used for the multiplication $23 \times 48 = \square$ and the division $568 \div 8 = \square$.

Self-check of Objectives 17 and 18

SUMMARY

There are two interpretations of multiplication with which children should become acquainted. Each one can be demonstrated with manipulative materials and story situations to make them meaningful. These interpretations are repeated addition and the array. Repeated addition is used most often to introduce multiplication because it can be related to the already understood addition operation. Arrays are easily represented by objects such as poker chips and dot patterns and are useful for showing basic multiplication combinations that involve a given factor, such as all combinations with a factor of 7.

There are two types of situations that give rise to division, measurement and partitive. Children should be introduced to both types of situations through meaningful real-life problems and manipulative-material activities. Strategies for teaching basic facts and helping children learn them include use of the multiplication table, a special characteristic of multiplying by 9, and relating divisors to multiplication with special practice materials.

The basic properties of multiplication—commutativity, associativity, distribution of multiplication over addition, and the roles of 1 and 0—can be presented through activities with markers, arrays, multiplication tables, number lines, blocks, and other manipulative devices.

Care must be used when children are taught to use algorithms for multiplication and division so the algorithms' meanings and applications will be clear. Materials to use include place value devices, markers for magnetic or flannel boards, arrays, and structured materials. Real-life story problems play an important role in making applications of the algorithms meaningful. Division situations frequently result in answers with remainders other than zero. Children should learn to handle remainders according to the nature of the situation, rather than by rule alone.

The calculator gives children the opportunity to better understand multiplication and division algorithms and to extend their work with these operations.

Learning-handicapped children can use the low-stress algorithm for addition to generate multiplication and division facts. Squared paper and color cues help children to align numerals in algorithms and to sequence steps as they work. Gifted and talented students can be challenged by alternate algorithms and tests of divisibility.

STUDY QUESTIONS AND ACTIVITIES

1. Examine a modern mathematics textbook series to note the different situations involving multiplication that are included. Which one is used during introductory lessons? Are the situations discussed in this chapter included in the series?

2. Examine a modern textbook series to see if both partitive and measurement situations are used as examples of division. Give an example of a word problem for each type of situation if they are both included. Check the teacher's manual to see if it includes a discussion that distinguishes between the two situations. Does the manual suggest procedures for introducing both situations?

3. Compose a word problem for a measurement situation and one for a partitive situation for each of these division sentences: $216 \div 12 = 18$ and $645 \div 15 = 45$. Identify the type of situation each problem represents. Choose one of your measurement problems, and write a dialogue similar to the one in Activity 11-14 to show that you understand how dialogue can be used as children learn an algorithm to solve problems. Do the same with one of your partitive problems.

4. Add materials and games for teaching multiplication and division facts and algorithms to your collection of teaching–learning aids. A set of popsicle sticks, described by Dunkels, could be one of your materials.

5. Read Ashlock's article (see the chapter's reading list). What does he mean by "model switching"? What problems are caused by model switching? How can you overcome this common weakness?

6. Heddens and Lazerick say that lies and half-truths are told to children when the "guzinta" approach to division is used (see the reading list). What is the guzinta approach? What lies and half-truths does it generate? What alternative to this approach do these authors recommend?

KEY TERMS

product
factors
multiplier
multiplicand
array
measurement division
partitive division
dividend
quotient

divisor
commutative property of
   multiplication
associative property of
   multiplication
distributive property of
   multiplication
tests of divisibility

FOR FURTHER READING

Adkins, Bryce E. "A Rationale for Duplication–Mediation Multiplying," *Arithmetic Teacher*, XI, No. 4 (April 1964), pp. 251–253. Explains an old multiplication process, frequently called Russian-peasant multiplication. Some students will enjoy using this procedure to supplement the regular multiplication algorithm.

Ando, Masue, and Hitoshi Ikeda. "Learning Multiplication Facts—More than Drill," *Arithmetic Teacher*, XVIII, No. 6 (October 1971), pp. 359–364. Presents activities that develop understanding of the basic mutiplication facts, ways of organizing the facts in tables and procedures for memorizing them.

Bruni, James V., and Helene J. Silverman. "The Multiplication Facts: Once More, With Understanding," *Arithmetic Teacher*, XXIII, No. 6 (October 1976), pp. 402–409. Several activities and games using arrays provide the means for developing understanding and memorization of the basic multiplication facts.

Ashlock, Robert. "Model Switching: A Consideration in the Teaching of Subtraction and Division of Whole Numbers," *School Science and Mathematics*, LXXVII, No. 4 (April 1977), pp. 327–335. Models are used to help children understand operations and their algorithms. Chips or blocks may be used to represent partitive and measurement division situations. Ashlock cautions teachers to use models consistently so children do not become confused by discrepancies between how a model is used and the problem situation it represents.

Bolduc, Elroy J., Jr. "The Monsters in Multiplication," *Arithmetic Teacher*, XXVIII, No. 3 (November 1980), pp. 24–26.
Ways to help children master the basic multiplication facts are discussed. Finger multiplication and the times table are suggested as two worthwhile activities.

Cacha, Frances B. "Exploring the Multiplication Table and Beyond," *Arithmetic Teacher*, XXVI, No. 3 (November 1978), pp. 46–48. Close study of the multiplication table reveals the properties of multiplication, information about odd and even factors, patterns on diagonals, and digit sums, all of which help children understand and master the facts.

————. "Understanding Multiplication and Division of Multidigit Numbers," *Arithmetic Teacher*, XIX, No. 5 (May 1972), pp. 349–354. Illustrates the use of arrays to interpret the meanings of the multiplication and division algorithms. The illustrations can serve as models for transparencies or magnetic board manipulatives.

Dunkels, Andrejs. "More Popsicle-Stick Multiplication," *Arithmetic Teacher*, XXIX, No. 7 (March 1982), pp. 20–21.
Common popsicle sticks are models for multiplying numbers between 10 and 100. Step-by-step instructions are explained and illustrated.

Fishback, Sylvia. "Times Without Tears," *Arithmetic Teacher*, XXI, No. 3 (March 1974), pp. 200–201. Describes the experiences with multiplication of one teacher and her class. It is an excellent example of how fourth graders can master many multiplication skills with understanding when a teacher is aware of the operation's properties.

Hazekamp, Donald W. "Teaching Multiplication and Division Algorithms," *Developing Computational Skills*, 1978 Yearbook of the National Council of Teachers of Mathematics (Reston, Va.: The Council), pp. 96–128. A variety of manipulative materials—abacus, beansticks, base-ten blocks, and others—serve as models for developing understanding of the algorithms. Many of the activities are illustrated.

Heddens, James W., and Beth Lazerick. "So 3 'Guzinta' 5 Once: So What!" *Arithmetic Teacher*, XXIX, No. 7 (November 1977), pp. 576–578. When the guzinta approach to teaching division is used, half-truths and lies are told children. These half-truths and lies are eliminated when a meaning approach described by the authors is used.

Junge, Charlotte W. "Now Try This—In Multiplication," *Arithmetic Teacher*, XIV, No. 1 (January 1967), p. 47. Explains a process of multiplication based on separating the multiplier into two or more of its factors and multiplying the multiplicand by one factor, that product by another factor, and so on. The procedure is a good enrichment exercise.

————. "Now Try This—In Multiplication," *Arithmetic Teacher*, XIV, No. 2 (February 1967), pp. 134–135. Explains several shortcuts used to multiply certain types of whole numbers. Gives three procedures for multiplying a pair of numbers ending in 5.

Krulik, Stephen. "Painless Drilling—Not Your Dentist, but the History of Mathematics," *Arithmetic Teacher*, XXVII, No. 8 (April 1980), pp. 40–42. Historical "magical" figures and the gelosia method of multiplying are the basis for drill on basic facts. Explanations of processes are given.

Kulm, Gerald. "Multiplication and Division Algorithms in German Schools," *Arithmetic Teacher*, XXVII, No. 9 (May 1980), pp. 26–27.
The German algorithms in this article can be used to challenge gifted and talented children.

Laing, Robert A., and Ruth Ann Meyer. "Transitional Division Algorithms," *Arithmetic Teacher*, XXIX, No. 9 (May 1982), pp. 10–12.
These authors contend that there is a higher percentage of children failing to understand division algorithms today than in the past. They believe that the use of transitional algorithms is to blame and that use of such algorithms should be curtailed in favor of a more direct approach.

Smith, C. Winston, Jr. "Tiger-bite Cards and Blank Arrays," *Arithmetic Teacher*, XXI, No. 8 (December 1974), pp. 679–682. Arrays with "bites" taken from them serve as a basis for children's searches for missing factors when the total (product) and number of rows (given factor) are known. The cards lead to a useful way of investigating the meaning of the division algorithm.

Souviney, Randall J. "Giving Division Some Meaning," *Learning*, V, No. 6 (February 1977), pp. 68–69. The two types of division situations are described and illustrated. Representational materials, in the form of tens strips and small squares, are used to help children understand the meaning of the algorithm for each type of division situation.

Spitler, Gail. "Multiplying by Eleven—A Place-Value Exploration," *Arithmetic Teacher*, XXIV, No. 2 (February 1977), pp. 122–124. Shortcuts for multiplying by eleven are easily learned. The process is of little value, however, unless children use their experiences as a basis for making conjectures about why the process works. They also employ many concepts of place value.

Stuart, Maureen, and Barbara Bestgen. "Productive Pieces: Exploring Multiplication on the Overhead," *Arithmetic Teacher*, XXIX, No. 5 (January 1982), pp. 22–23.
An overhead projector, a transparent grid, and colored transparent rectangles that fit the grid serve to develop children's understanding of multiplication. The materials make a nice tie-in of semiconcrete materials and the abstract multiplication table.

Swart, William L. "A Diary of Remedial Instruction in Division—Grade Seven," *Arithmetic Teacher*, XXII, No. 8 (December 1975), pp. 614–622. Children who fail with a conventional algorithm often will not even attempt to learn to use it when they get older. A new division algorithm and how it was used with two seventh-grade girls who rebelled against the conventional algorithm are described.

Winters, Mary Jean. "Teaching Mathematics with Microcomputers: Middle Grades," *Arithmetic Teacher*, XXX, No. 6 (February 1983), pp. 28–29, and 66. The author describes various programs, including drill-with-tutorial, skill-development, concept-development, and problem-solving programs. Activities for children to program themselves are also described.

Zweng, Marilyn J. "Division Problems and the Concept of Rate," *Arithmetic Teacher*, XI, No. 8 (December 1964), pp. 547–556. This is a report on research done with second graders to determine which types of division situations are easiest for them to understand. Zweng found that measurement-rate situations were the most easily understood.

————. "The Fourth Operation Is Not Fundamental," *Arithmetic Teacher*, XIX, No. 8 (December 1972), pp. 623–627. This article contains a discussion of division. It has good examples of partitive and measurement situations, with sample illustrations.

12

Working with Fractional Numbers—Common Fractions

Upon completion of Chapter 12 you will be able to:

1. Identify at least three different real-world situations that give rise to common fractions, and name an example of a common fraction for each situation.

2. Demonstrate, using geometric regions, number lines, and markers, activities for children who are learning about common fractions.

3. Explain why there are infinitely many fractional numbers between a given pair of fractional numbers, and demonstrate a procedure for helping children develop their intuitive understanding of this fact.

4. Demonstrate activities for children that will enable them to compare fractional numbers.

5. Explain an abstract process that can be used for comparing two or more fractional numbers.

6. Demonstrate at least three systematic procedures for renaming fractional numbers so they are represented by common fractions having the same denominator.

7. Explain what it means to express a fractional number in its simplest form, and demonstrate at least two procedures for helping children to do so.

8. Demonstrate, using unit regions, fraction strips, and number lines, activities involving addition of fractional numbers where denominators are the same, where denominators are different, and where there are mixed numerals.

9. Demonstrate with appropriate materials, activities involving subtraction of fractional numbers expressed as common fractions where denominators are the same, where denominators are different, and where there are mixed numerals.

10. Illustrate situations in which the repeated addition and array interpretations of multiplication apply to fractional numbers.

11. Use manipulative and other materials to represent the meaning of various types of multiplication sentences involving fractional numbers.

12. Explain what cancellation means, and describe how children can learn to do it.

13. Give examples of real-life situations that illustrate partitive and measurement division involving fractional numbers, and illustrate each situation with learning aids.

14. Explain the steps for completing division with fractions by the invert-and-multiply process.

15. Demonstrate with appropriate materials some procedures that can be used to help

children understand ratios and use them in real-life situations.

16. Demonstrate two procedures that can be used to help learning-handicapped children understand common fractions and their numerals.

17. Identify common errors children commit as they compute with fractions.

18. Name and explain two enrichment activities for gifted and talented students.

Children's study of fractional numbers begins as early as kindergarten and continues through elementary school. The fractional numbers treated during the elementary-school period are a part of the set of rational numbers; those that can be expressed in the form a/b, when a is any whole number and b is any nonzero whole number. It is possible to consider such numbers on a purely abstract basis with the meanings of the numbers and operations developed from undefined terms, postulates, or axioms, and the theorems that pertain to them. However, such an approach is not meaningful to elementary-school children, so a concerete approach to the study of fractional numbers must be taken.

The most useful approach is one that allows children to intuitively develop a reasoned understanding of fractional numbers. In all grades of elementary school, many concrete representations of fractional numbers help children to develop a clear understanding of the meaning of these numbers and the way operations with them are performed.

Fractional numbers, like whole numbers, can be expressed in a number of ways. Symbolically they may be expressed in any one of three ways: as common fractions (½ and ⅔), as decimal fractions (0.5 and 0.6666 . . .), and as percent (50% and 66⅔%). Also, any given fractional number has an infinite number of numerals, for example, $1/2 = 2/4 = 3/6 = 4/8 = 5/10 = ...$

THE MEANING OF COMMON FRACTIONS

Common fractions are numerals used to represent fractional numbers and ratios. Historically children have experienced considerable difficulty with the meaning of common fractions, because there are several situations out of which they arise, and these have not always been well understood. If they are to understand common fractions, children must become familiar with each situation and work with it in a mature fashion.

1. Unit Subdivided into Equal-Sized Parts

When a unit of measure, such as an inch, is subdivided into equal-sized parts, common fractions can be used to express the meaning of each subunit. For example, when an inch is subdivided into two equal-sized parts, each part is ½ of an inch. Likewise, when an object such as a cake is first considered as a whole and is then cut into four parts of equal size, the common fraction ¼ can be used to express the size of each part. The parts of a common fraction indicate the nature of the situation from which the numeral arises. In the numeral ½, the 2 indicates the number of equal-sized parts into which the whole, or unit, has been subdivided. This part of the fraction is the **denominator.** The 1 indicates the number of parts being considered at the moment and is called the **numerator.**

2. Set Subdivided into Equal-Sized Groups

Situations that lead to fractional numbers when a set is subdivided into groups of equal size are clearly related to those that involve division. When a set of twelve objects is subdivided into two equal-sized groups, the mathematical sentence $12 \div 2 = 6$ represents the situation. The 6 in the sentence represents one-half of the original set of twelve. The sentence ½ of $12 = 6$ also describes this situation. Children will often engage in activities that involve parts of sets of discrete wholes. To find ⅙ of 18, for instance, children must think of eighteen objects that are to be subdivided into six groups of equal size. The size of each group relates to the size of the original set in such a way that each is ⅙ of the original set. When a common fraction is used to represent this type of situation, the denominator indicates the number of equal-sized groups into which the set is subdivided, and the numerator indicates how many of the groups are being considered.

3. Expression of Ratios

The relationship between a pair of numbers is often expressed as a ratio. Ratios arise from many situations. Examples of common situations are

- A comparison made between the number of children in a classroom and the number of textbooks in the same classroom. If each child has six textbooks, the ratio is 1 to 6 and may be expressed as $^1/_6$ or 1:6. Here the numerals in the ratio expression represent the numbers of objects in two completely different sets.

- A comparison made between the number of blue-covered books in a set and the number of books in the complete set. If there are three blue-covered books in a set of ten books, the ratio is 3 out of 10 and may be expressed as $^3/_{10}$ or 3:10. Here the numerals in the ratio represent the numbers of objects in a set and one of the groups within it.

- A comparison made between the length of two objects. If four pieces of dowel rod, each the same length, are laid end-to-end alongside a second rod and have a total length as long as the second rod, the ratio is 4 to 1 and may be expressed as $^4/_1$ or 4:1. (The length of one short rod is ¼ of the longer rod.) Here the numerals represent the number of shorter objects compared with a single object.

4. Indicated Division

Sentences such as $3 \div 4 = \square$ and $17 \div 3 = \square$ indicate that division is to be performed. A physical model of the first sentence is the subdivision of 3 feet of cloth into four equal-sized parts, with the answer, ¾, indicating the size of each of the four parts. The second sentence might represent a situation in which 17 cookies are shared equally by 3 children, with 5⅔ being each child's share.

5. Expression of Rational Numbers

At a completely abstract level it is possible to think of common fractions as representing the elements in the set of nonnegative rational numbers. Though children in the elementary school will not study rational numbers in this abstract sense, the development of concepts of fractional numbers and common fractions should be consistent with that of concepts of rational numbers.

Common fractions are used when units are subdivided into equal-sized parts, when sets are subdivided into equal-sized groups, when ratios are considered, to represent answers for all division situations, and to give numerals for abstract rational numbers. Give real-life examples for any three of these situations, and write a common fraction for each example. Identify the meaning of each numerator and denominator in your examples.

Self-check of Objective 1

INTRODUCING COMMON FRACTIONS

There are those who advocate that common fractions not be taught in elementary school. They contend that the calculator and metric system will make these fractions obsolete and that children will not need to learn about them. This view is short-sighted for at least two reasons.

First, the preceding discussion shows that common fractions are used in ways unrelated to those the calculator and metric system will replace. Children need to learn these uses, because their importance will not diminish.

Second, the amount of time that will be required to change from the customary system to the metric system of measure is undetermined. Until the transition is complete, children will need to know how common fractions are used in the customary system.

The study of fractional numbers, represented by common fractions, should begin with a variety of geometric regions and markers for children to subdivide into equal-sized parts or sets. Develop each concept carefully so that children understand the meanings of the parts of the whole. Although it is not essential that the equal-sized parts be the same shape, it is easier for young children to understand the meanings of common fractions when the parts are congruent.

1. Using Regions

Children's first work with fractions can be done with pieces of paper that have been cut to show different regular geometric regions.

ACTIVITY 12-1   Geometric Regions

- Give each child several geometric regions and a pair of classroom scissors.
- Let children experiment to see how many ways they can fold and cut each region to show two pieces that are the same size.

- After time for exploration, have children discuss and show what they have done. Help them use the words *one-half, halves,* and *a half* to describe their parts.

- Use a similar lesson to introduce the concept of one-fourth.

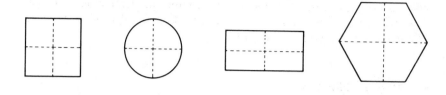

Have children subdivide other regions into equal-sized parts until the meanings of the subdivisions become clear. Some models should be marked by you to show where children should cut. For example, it is difficult for young children to accurately fold and cut blank paper models for thirds and fifths. During children's early work do not introduce numerals for common fractions or the terms *numerator* and *denominator*. Their introduction should be delayed until children thoroughly understand the fraction concept.

From time to time, worksheets containing models like those in Figure 12-1 should be completed by children. In (a) they color one of the three parts in each region to show one-third; in (b) they put an X on the shapes that do not show halves. Workbooks for first and second graders contain a limited number of practice exercises of these types; you can duplicate additional worksheets for children who need further practice with the identification of simple fractional parts of a whole.

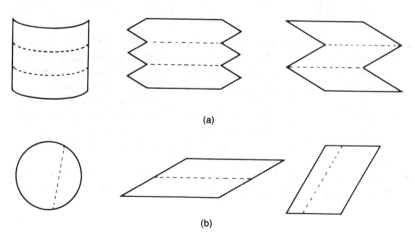

(a)

(b)

FIGURE 12-1
Samples of items to use on worksheets. (a) Color each shape to show one of the three equal-sized parts. (b) Cross out a shape if the two parts are not equal in size.

Once the meanings of the shapes and their parts are clear, introduce common fractions as numerals for fractional numbers. Relate the numerals to shapes that have been cut into two, three, or more parts. At first use only one part of each shape to show the related unit fraction. (A unit fraction is one with a numerator of 1.) Refrain still from using *denominator* and *numerator*. However, do help children understand that the bottom part of the numeral tells the number of equal-sized parts into which a shape has been cut, and the top part tells the number of parts being considered at the moment. Later introduce numerators greater than 1 as children consider ⅔ of a shape cut into three equal-sized parts or ⁵/₆ of one cut into six equal-sized parts.

2. Using a Number Line

Number lines are useful for showing the meaning of common fractions. Children should mark the fractional parts of lines as they work, rather than seeing ready-made lines; so begin with lines that have the same scale and show only whole numbers (see the lines in Activity 12-2).

ACTIVITY 12-2   Number-Line Fractions

- Begin with congruent lines showing whole numbers.

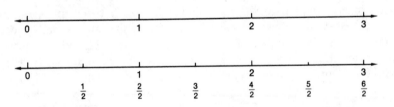

- Mark points midway between the whole numbers on the second line. Help the children note that each whole-number segment has been divided to show two equal-sized segments. Discuss the fact that each of the new segments is one-half the length of the original segment.
- When all of the whole-number segments have been subdivided, have the children count along the line, using halves. There are two ways to do this: one-half, two-halves, three-halves, ... six-halves; and one-half, one, one and one-half, . . . three. And there are two ways of writing the numerals: ½, ²/₂, ³/₂, . . .⁶/₂; and ½, 1, 1½, . . .3.
- Number lines marked with segments showing thirds, fourths, fifths, and so on should be used to extend children's understanding of these common fractions.

When children make measurements, many of the instruments they use have a form of number line on them. For instance a ruler like the one in Figure 12-2(a) has inch units; in (b) the ruler is marked with half-inch units. Other measures, such as measuring cups, have scales with units and parts of units on them.

(a)

(b)

FIGURE 12-2
Rulers marked (a) in inches
and (b) in inches and half
inches

3. Using Sets of Objects

The introduction of the concept of a fractional part of a set can be made
only after children have a good grasp of whole numbers and are skillful
in counting the number of objects in a set. The first work must be handled carefully so that this fraction concept is developed meaningfully.

ACTIVITY 12-3   Developing the Fraction Concept

• Give each child a container with a dozen markers.
• Say: "Count a set of eight markers."

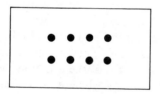

• Have each child separate the 8 markers into two groups, each with the
  same number of markers.

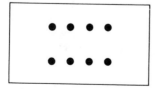

• Discuss what has been done; relate separation of the set into two parts
  of equal size to earlier work with the separation of unit regions into parts
  of equal size.
• Repeat with other sets that can be separated into 2, 3, and 4 equal-
  sized groups.

The association of the new work with previous work is important so that children will realize that when half of a set is to be found, it is necessary to form two groups of the same size. Children find one-half of the set as they separate the markers into two equal-sized groups and then count the objects in one group. The fact that the answer is a whole number rather than a fractional number is sometimes troublesome, so it is necessary to repeat activities with different-sized sets that can be subdivided into equal-sized groups without any objects left over. Discussion of this concept is continued later in the section dealing with multiplication of fractional numbers.

Self-check of Objective 2

Use these materials and demonstrate the meaning of two-thirds of a unit and the meaning of two-thirds of a set: unit regions, number lines, and markers.

COMPARING FRACTIONAL NUMBERS

As children study whole numbers, they learn to compare numbers so that they can tell when one number is greater than, less than, or equal to another. They use sets, number lines, and other means of comparing numbers until the idea is clear. They learn that one number is greater than another if it is to the right of the other on the number line. At the same time they learn that every whole number has an immediate predecessor and an immediate successor. It is always possible to determine the predecessor of a whole number greater than 0 by subtracting 1 from it. The successor of a number is determined by adding 1 to it. As children study fractional numbers, they learn that these numbers can be ordered by size, even though there is no constant value between fractional numbers as there is between every pair of adjacent whole numbers. Children also learn that a fractional number has no immediate predecessor or successor. An infinite number of fractional numbers lie between any pair, so fractional numbers do not have immediate predecessors or successors. This can be demonstrated by the fact that it is always possible to determine a fractional number midway between a pair of fractional numbers. The number midway between $5/8$ and $3/4$ is $11/16$; it determined by expressing $3/4$ as $6/8$ and adding it to $5/8$; $5/8 + 6/8 = 11/8$ and $11/8 \div 2 = 11/16$.

It is possible to compare the sizes of two fractional numbers by multiplying the numerator of the first by the denominator of the second and the denominator of the first by the numerator of the second and comparing the two products. For the two fractional numbers a/b and c/d, when $a \times d = b \times c$, the two numbers are equivalent. The fractional number *a/b* is greater than *c/d* when $a \times d > b \times c$; the fractional number *a/b* is less than *c/d* when $a \times d < b \times c$.

It should be clear that such abstract approaches for ordering and comparing numbers are unsuitable for children. Initial experiences should come through investigations with models of various kinds. Later, abstract procedures can be used with mathematically mature children in the higher grades of the elementary school.

1. Using Congruent Geometric Shapes

Children can use **congruent geometric shapes** cut from construction paper to compare the sizes of fractional numbers.

ACTIVITY 12-4   Congruent Shapes

- Give each child paper cut in circles, squares, or other shapes that they can fold and cut to show halves, fourths, and eighths.
- Children fold one piece to show halves, cut it, and color one half with a crayon. One piece is folded and cut to show fourths, and another is folded and cut to show eighths. One fourth piece and one eighth piece are colored. One unit piece is neither cut nor colored.

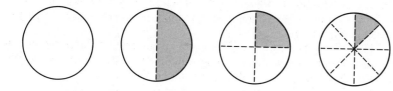

- Have children compare the colored pieces to see that ½ > ¼ > ⅛.
- Shapes cut and colored to show thirds, sixths, ninths, and twelfths, and halves, fifths, and tenths should be used to compare those fractions.

Congruent shapes are also useful for investigations in which children compare nonunit fractions. Models folded and shaded like those in Figure 12-3 help them see that ¾ > ⅔ > ½. As long as the shapes are congruent, children can see and order any fractional numbers that can be conveniently represented with shapes.

FIGURE 12-3
Geometric shapes used to compare the sizes of ½, ⅔, and ¾

2. *Using Fraction Strips*

Fraction strips are also useful for comparing fractional numbers. Cut a set of strips from colored cardboard and attach a magnet on the back of each strip for manipulation on a magnetic board. One useful set is pictured in Activity 12-5.

ACTIVITY 12-5   Fraction Strips

• Arrange the set of strips on the magnetic board.

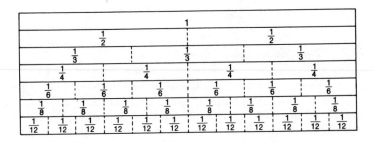

• Ask questions like these:
  ○ How many ½ strips are as long as the 1 strip? How many ⅓ strips are as long as the 1 strip? Which is longer, a ½ strip or a ⅓ strip?
  ○ What is the shortest fraction strip in this set? Which strips are longer than this strip?
  ○ Use the fraction strips to put these common fractions in order, beginning with the largest and ending with the smallest: ⅛, ½, ⅓, ⅙, ¼.
  ○ Which is longer, the ½ strip or two of the ⅓ strips?
  ○ Which is longer, two of the ⅙ strips or one of the ¼ strips?
  ○ Which is shorter, two of the ½ strips or two of the ⅛ strips?
  ○ Use strips to put these common fractions in order, beginning with the smallest and ending with the largest: ⅛, ⅔, 2/4, 3/6, 4/12.

---

3. *Using the Number Line*

Use the number line extensively with children in grades 4 through 6. There is no better device for comparing fractional numbers and helping children to see that there are infinitely many numbers between any pair of fractional numbers.

ACTIVITY 12-6 Number-Line Charts

- Display a chart showing number lines with only the whole numbers named. (Points for fractional numbers are lightly marked to make them easy to locate during the activity.)

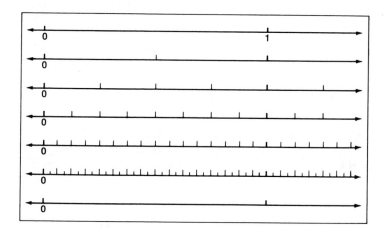

- Direct children's attention to the top line to note the unit segments.
- Go to the next line and mark the point midway between the unit segment. Have the children identify and label the points that show ½ and ²/₂.
- Go to the next line and mark points on it; have the children identify and label these points: ¹/₄, ²/₄, ³/₄, ⁴/₄, ⁵/₄.
- Continue until the line that shows thirty-seconds has been marked and counted.

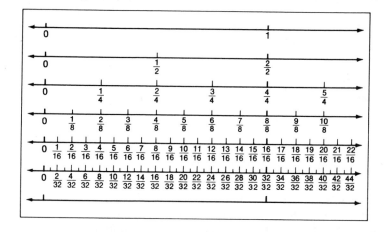

- Ask questions similar to those in Activity 12-5 so children can compare fractions on the number lines.

Use the number-line chart to help children intuitively recognize that subdivision of the line can go on forever and that there are an infinite number of points between any pair of points on the line. Questions like these can be used:

- "If we follow this pattern (the one used in Activity 12-6), what will be the name of the first point on the line at the bottom of the paper?"

- "I have run out of space on the chart for more lines and on the lines for more points. Does this mean there are no fractional numbers between 0 and $1/32$, 0 and $1/64$, 0 and $1/128$ . . . ?"

- "Will the sequence ever end? Why not?"

Children in the fifth and sixth grades can use the number-line chart to learn how to determine fractional numbers that lie midway between any pair of fractional numbers. They can eventually use the averaging process to find the number midway between a pair of fractional numbers.

ACTIVITY 12-7   Midpoints

- Have children locate the points $2/4$ and $3/4$ on the fourths line. Have them locate the point midway between them. "What is the simplest name we can give this point?" If children say "five-eighths," ask how they know. If this answer is not given, call attention to the point located at the same position on the eighths line.
- Use questions like these to focus attention on the averaging process:
  "What will $2/4$ and $3/4$ be called if we express them as eighths?"
  "What will be the sum if we add $4/8$ and $6/8$?"
  "Can you figure out what we can do to the $10/8$ to determine the fraction midway between $4/8$ and $6/8$?" Help children see that the 10 is divided by 2.
- Repeat with other pairs of fractions until the children recognize that by adding a pair of fractional numbers and dividing their sum by 2, they can find a number that lies midway between that pair of fractional numbers.

4. Using Abstract Procedures

Children who have a mature understanding of the procedures for comparing numbers that have already been discussed, who understand the meaning of common fractions, and who can multiply fractional numbers in ways developed later in this chapter, can use the multiplication process explained in the second paragraph following the self-check for Objective 2 to compare fractions. As you explain the process, give children practice pages containing pairs of common fractions and help them relate the abstract process to earlier work with models. This is a useful process for dealing with ratios and proportions and is discussed in this connection later.

Give an explanation of why there are infinitely many fractional numbers between any given pair of fractional numbers. Demonstrate with a sequence of number lines a children's activity that will help them discover this fact.

Self-check of Objectives 3, 4, and 5

Activities for comparing fractional numbers with unit regions, fraction strips, and number lines are described. Demonstrate with at least two activities how children can show that these relations are true: $^1/_5 < ^1/_4 < ^1/_3 < ^1/_2$ and $^6/_7 > ^4/_5 > ^2/_3$.

The abstract multiplication process for comparing fractional numbers can be used with mature elementary-school children. Explain how this process can be used to compare each of these pairs of numbers, and name the greater fractional number in each pair: $^4/_{15}$ and $^5/_{16}$, $^{21}/_{36}$ and $^{19}/_{35}$.

SYSTEMATIC PROCEDURES FOR NAMING EQUIVALENT FRACTIONS

Before children can become proficient in adding and subtracting fractional numbers using common fractions, they must learn to express common fractions so that they have the same denominators. The process for doing this, commonly referred to as changing to a **common denominator,** must be developed carefully so children will understand both the necessity for doing it and how to do it meaningfully. Children should learn that when they use two equivalent common fractions to rename fractional numbers, the value of each number remains unchanged. Children who have had many experiences with various learning aids will have little difficulty with numbers such as ½, ¼, ⅛, ⅓, and ⅙. They will "just know" that ½ can be renamed as $^2/_4$ or $^4/_8$, ¼ as $^2/_8$, and ⅓ as $^2/_6$. However, they should learn systematic procedures for dealing with less familiar numbers.

1. Using Multiples

In some cases the denominator of one fraction is a multiple of another. When this is so, as with $^2/_5$ and $^3/_{20}$, the larger of the two denominators is a common denominator. The following thought process can be used:

- "Twenty is a multiple of 5. By what number do we multiply 5 to get 20?

- "To rename $^2/_5$ with a denominator of 20, multiply both the numerator, 2, and the denominator, 5, by 4. Two-fifths is equal to $^8/_{20}$."

When neither of the denominators is a common denominator, a different procedure must be used. The easiest procedure if denominators are small—for example, ¼ and $^1/_5$ or ¼ and $^1/_6$—is to use successive multiples of the larger denominator until a common denominator has been determined. For ¼ and $^1/_5$, multiples of 5 are used.

ACTIVITY 12-8 Multiples

- "What are the first several multiples of five?" (5, 10, 15, 20, 25, . . .) "Which of these numbers is also a multiple of four?" (20.)
- "Twenty is a common multiple of 4 and 5. By what number is 4 multiplied to give a product of 20?" (5.) "What is ¼ when it is renamed with a denominator of 20?" (5/20.) "By what number do we multiply 5 to give a product of 20?" (4.) "What is $^1/_5$ when renamed with a denominator of 20?" (4/20.)
- "We can rename a common fraction this way:

$$\frac{1 \times 5}{4 \times 5} = \frac{5}{20}$$

- Repeat with other common fractions.

---

2. Using Equivalence Classes

Another procedure for finding common denominators is to list the first several numbers in the **equivalence class** of each number. To add $^1/_6$ and $^3/_8$, the following numerals would be listed:

$$\frac{1}{6}, \frac{2}{12}, \frac{3}{18}, \frac{4}{24}, \frac{5}{30}, \frac{6}{36}, \frac{7}{42}, \frac{8}{48}, \ldots$$

$$\frac{3}{8}, \frac{6}{16}, \frac{9}{24}, \frac{12}{32}, \frac{15}{40}, \frac{18}{48}, \frac{21}{56}, \ldots$$

Guide children to see that in the first list there are names for some fractional numbers with the same denominators as some in the second listing. These should be indicated: $^1/_6 = {^4/_{24}} = {^8/_{48}}$ and $^3/_8 = {^9/_{24}} = {^{18}/_{48}}$. Children can use both pairs of numbers, $^4/_{24}$ and $^9/_{24}$ and $^8/_{48}$ and $^{18}/_{48}$, to complete the addition of $^1/_6 + {^3/_8} = \square$.

$$\frac{1}{6} \rightarrow \frac{4}{24} \rightarrow \frac{8}{48}$$

$$+\frac{3}{8} \rightarrow +\frac{9}{24} \rightarrow +\frac{18}{48}$$

$$\frac{13}{24} \qquad \frac{26}{48}$$

After the sums in the algorithms have been determined, children should note that the answer cannot be simplified when the denominator is 24 (in this example) but can be when it is 48.

3. Using Prime Factorizations

Mature children can determine the **least common multiple** (LCM) for fractional numbers by using the **prime factorization** of their denominators. Processes for factoring numbers are discussed in Chapter 16. For work with fractional numbers, factoring is applied as follows: Determine the prime factorization of the denominators of the two numbers. For example,

$$\frac{4}{15} = \frac{4}{3 \times 5}$$

$$\frac{5}{12} = \frac{5}{2 \times 2 \times 3}$$

Next form the union of the sets of factors used in the prime factorization of the denominators: $2 \times 2 \times 3 \times 5$. This becomes the denominator that is used in renaming the fractional numbers:

$$\frac{4}{15} = \frac{4 \times 2 \times 2}{2 \times 2 \times 3 \times 5}$$

$$\frac{5}{12} = \frac{5 \times 5}{2 \times 2 \times 3 \times 5}$$

The number by which each numerator is multiplied is found by noting the factors by which the original denominator is multiplied to yield the new denominator: for ⁴/₁₅ the factors 2×2 are used, so the numerator is multiplied by 4; for ⁵/₁₂ the factor 5 is used, so the numerator is multiplied by 5.

$$\frac{4}{15} \rightarrow \frac{4}{3 \times 5} \rightarrow \frac{4 \times 2 \times 2}{2 \times 2 \times 3 \times 5} \rightarrow \frac{16}{60}$$

$$+\frac{5}{12} \rightarrow +\frac{5}{2 \times 2 \times 3} \rightarrow +\frac{5 \times 5}{2 \times 2 \times 3 \times 5} \rightarrow +\frac{25}{60}$$

$$\frac{41}{60}$$

**Self-check
of Objective 6**

Use any two of these procedures to show how children can learn to rename fractional numbers so they are represented by common fractions having like denominators: multiples, equivalence classes, and prime factorizations.

RENAMING FRACTIONAL NUMBERS IN SIMPLEST FORM

A fractional number is expressed as a common fraction in its simplest form when the numbers represented by the numerator and denominator have no common factor, or are relatively prime. There are times when the original answers to problems involving fractional numbers are not in their simplest form, and it is desirable to simplify them. Thus after the answer to a subtraction such as ⅝ minus ⅛ has been named as ⁴/₈, it may need to be renamed as ½.

1. Using Number Lines

Number lines are particularly good for helping children learn about expressing common fractions in simplest terms. (You may recognize the process of renaming a fraction in simplest terms as "reducing a fraction to its lowest terms.") During early work with number lines children use them to compare common fractions and learn that a fraction like ½ can be renamed as ²/₄, ³/₆, ⁴/₈, and so on. At that time they are changing fractions to higher terms. Now they use the lines to do the reverse; they will simplify fractions, or express them in lowest terms.

ACTIVITY 12-9 Simplifying Fractions

- Use the set of number lines from Activity 12-6.
- Direct the children's attention to ¹⁶/₃₂ at the bottom. "What names on other lines name the same point as ¹⁶/₃₂?" (⁸/₁₆, ⁴/₈, ²/₄, ¹/₂.) "Which of these has the smallest denominator?" (½.) "Is there a simpler way to name this point?" (No.)
- Discuss the fact that each of the fractions ¹⁶/₃₂, ⁸/₁₆, ⁴/₈, and ²/₄ is expressed in simplest form as ½.
- Repeat with other points on these lines and with lines showing thirds, sixths, ninths, and twelfths, and fifths and tenths.

Fraction strips can be used in ways similar to the ways number lines are used.

2. Examining Numerator and Denominator

One procedure that is commonly used is to examine the numerator and denominator to determine the largest number by which both may be divided. Once a common divisor is found, both numerator and denominator can be divided by it. This procedure is satisfactory as long as the numbers represented by the numerators and denominators are reasonably small and the greatest common divisor can be readily determined, as in $^6/_{12}$ or $^9/_{15}$. However, it may fail to be useful when the numerators and denominators are larger numbers.

3. Using Prime Factorizations

With larger numbers in the numerator and denominator, a better procedure is to find the prime factorization of each one. An example, $^{24}/_{36}$, will be treated in the same way that children should proceed.

Rewrite each term using its prime factorization:

$$\frac{24}{36} = \frac{2 \times 2 \times 2 \times 3}{2 \times 2 \times 3 \times 3}$$

Determine the greatest common factor (GCF) by noting all factors common to both numerator and denominator. (The GCF is made up of the factors in the intersection of the two factorizations. This may be shown with a Venn diagram to help children visualize it. See Activity 16-4.) Both the numerator and denominator of the fraction should be divided by this common factor to rename it in its simplest form:

$$\frac{24}{36} = \frac{24 \div 12}{36 \div 12} = \frac{2}{3}$$

Give an explanation of what is meant by the expression "The common fraction $^2/_3$ represents the fractional number two-thirds in its simplest form." Demonstrate with at least two different materials or abstract processes some activities children can use to learn to simplify fractional numbers.

Self-check
of Objective 7

OPERATIONS WITH FRACTIONAL NUMBERS EXPRESSED AS COMMON FRACTIONS

By the time children begin to perform the operations of addition, subtraction, multiplication, and division with fractional numbers, they have already developed some skill in performing these operations with whole numbers. Armed with this knowledge teachers frequently introduce these operations with fractional numbers by using a series of rules: "If two fractions have the same denominator, their sum can be determined by adding the numerators and placing the sum over the denominator." "If two fractions have different denominators, they must be changed to their least common denominator before they can be added." Rules for renaming fractional numbers with a least common denominator are then listed so children can proceed with the addition. However, teaching these operations by rules alone means that many children will have little or no understanding of what they are doing or why they are doing it.

Procedures that help children visualize operations with fractional numbers are extensions of those used with whole numbers. As children learn to add whole numbers, they learn the meaning of the operation in terms of joining sets. Objects, markers, number lines, and other devices are used so children can discover the meaning of the operation. Children should learn to add fractional numbers in much the same way. Again physical models help extend children's understanding of addition to include fractional numbers.

ADDITION WITH COMMON FRACTIONS

Children's initial experiences with addition should be with familiar situations that are easily represented by physical models.

1. Adding When Denominators Are the Same

The setting in which children work should be stocked with concrete materials with which children are well acquainted: geometric regions left whole and cut into fractional parts, sets of fraction strips, and number-line charts. Present a problem, such as the one in Activity 12-10.

ACTIVITY 12-10   Adding Common Fractions

- "Last night Jim practiced his piano lesson for ¼ of an hour before dinner and ¼ of an hour after dinner. What part of an hour did he practice altogether?"

- Let each child use concrete materials, if necessary, to determine the answer.
- Discuss each child's way of determining the answer. These are possibilities:
  - ○ "I used fourths of the circle to represent each of the two fourth hours. When I put the circles together, I saw that he had practiced for a half hour."

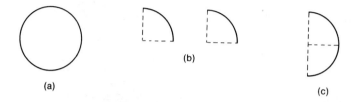

(a)   (b)   (c)

  - ○ "I used two pieces that show fourths in our fraction-strip set. They showed me that two-fourths is the same as one-half."

  - ○ "I used the number-line chart. When I took jumps that are each ¼-unit long, I stopped at ²/₄. That is the same as ½."

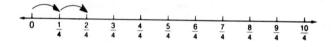

  - ○ Some children may say, "I just know that ¼ and ¼ equal ½." Some of these children may have used the addition sentence ¼ + ¼ = ²/₄ (or ½) to determine the answer.
- Present other, similar problem situations to be solved in the same ways.

After children have determined the answers for several problem situations, display the addition sentence for each one and call attention to them: "What have we done in each of these sentences to determine the answer?"

$$\frac{1}{4} + \frac{1}{4} = \frac{2}{4}$$

$$\frac{1}{3} + \frac{1}{3} = \frac{2}{3}$$

$$\frac{1}{2} + \frac{1}{2} = \frac{2}{2}$$

$$\frac{1}{4} + \frac{2}{4} = \frac{3}{4}$$

Guide the children to see that the sum is found by adding the numerators of the fractional numbers. It will be helpful to children to see the sentences rewritten as

$$\frac{1+1}{4} = \frac{2}{4}, \quad \frac{1+1}{3} = \frac{2}{3}, \quad \frac{1+1}{2} = \frac{2}{2}, \quad \text{and} \quad \frac{1+2}{4} = \frac{3}{4}$$

This emphasizes the fact that the numerators are added. If children have difficulty understanding the process, the examples can be further simplified:

$$
\begin{array}{cccc}
\text{1 fourth} & \text{1 third} & \text{1 half} & \text{1 fourth} \\
+\text{1 fourth} & +\text{1 third} & +\text{1 half} & +\text{2 fourths} \\
\hline
\end{array}
$$

Problems with answers greater than 1 can also be examined through activities with concrete materials.

ACTIVITY 12-11   Answers Greater Than One

- "Josie is making a flag and will need ⅔ of a yard of red material and ⅔ of a yard of white material. How much material will she use for the flag?"
- Fraction strips and number-line charts are useful here, because their properties parallel the linear measure used for determining the amount of material used for the flag.

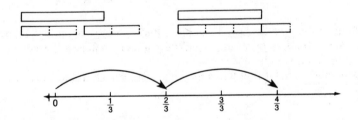

- Write the addition sentence for this situation:

$$\text{²/₃} + \text{²/₃} = \text{⁴/₃}$$

- Show that ⁴/₃ can be renamed as as 1⅓. Emphasize that ⁴/₃, 1 and ⅓ are all names for the same number.
- Repeat with other pairs of fractions.

---

2. Adding When Denominators Are Different

Children should have a good background of skills and understandings before they are introduced to addition of fractional numbers expressed as common fractions with unlike denominators. Included in their background should be

- Understanding of the meaning of addition of whole numbers
- Mastery of the basic addition facts
- Understanding of common fractions and concrete models that represent them
- Understanding of addition of fractions with like denominators
- Understanding that by using equivalent fractions, fractional numbers can be renamed so they have common denominators

---

ACTIVITY 12-12   Adding with Unlike Denominators

- "Making some clothes for her sister, Suzy used ½ yard of material for a skirt and ¼ yard for a blouse. What part of a yard did she use for the outfit?"
- Some children will perhaps "just know" that the answer is ¾ of a yard. Others will probably be uncertain. Use fraction strips as a concrete model of the situation.

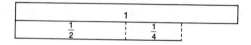

- Write the addition sentence for this situation:

$$½ + ¼ = \square$$

- Discuss what must be done before the addition can be completed. Children who "just know" the answer can perhaps show how the ½ must be renamed as ²⁄₄ before the addition is completed:

$$²/_4 + ¹/_4 = ³/_4$$

- Verify this with the fraction strips by exchanging the half-strip for two of the fourth-strips.

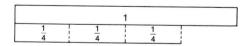

- Repeat with other situations.

The addition sentence $½ + ⅓ = \square$ is illustrated with number lines in Figure 12-4. Children will note that it is necessary to rename both frac-

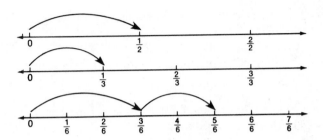

FIGURE 12-4
Number lines showing that
$\frac{1}{2} + \frac{1}{3} = \square$ is renamed as
$\frac{3}{6} + \frac{2}{6} = \square$ to determine the
sum $\frac{5}{6}$.

tional numbers so they have common denominators before the addition
can take place. To do this, they should study the number lines to locate
the line with points that correspond to points on the lines for both thirds
and halves. The number lines indicate that a number line showing sixths
has points that correspond to points on both the halves and thirds lines.
The addition for $\frac{1}{2} + \frac{1}{3} = \square$ is shown when $\frac{1}{2}$ is expressed as $\frac{3}{6}$ and $\frac{1}{3}$
as $\frac{2}{6}$.

Ultimately children who understand least common multiples, or lowest
common denominators, and processes for renaming fractions as equivalent fractions will use mature processes for adding fractional numbers.
Processes for finding common denominators are discussed in the section
of this chapter that deals with systematic procedures for naming equivalent fractions. As children learn these processes, they should also learn
to use them when adding fractions with unlike denominators. By the
time they complete elementary school, many children will handle examples such as

$$
\begin{array}{ccc}
\frac{3}{4} & \frac{3}{8} & \frac{7}{12} \\
+\frac{5}{6} & +\frac{5}{12} & +\frac{11}{15} \\
\hline
\end{array}
$$

without difficulty.

3. Adding with Mixed Numerals

Historically the expression "adding mixed numbers" has described addition situations in which both whole and fractional numbers are involved. An example of this addition is

$$
\begin{array}{r}
1\frac{1}{2} \\
+1\frac{1}{4} \\
\hline
\end{array}
$$

In order to maintain the proper distinction between *number* and *numeral*,
the expression "addition with **mixed numerals**" is a better description of
addition of this kind.

ACTIVITY 12-13   Adding Mixed Numerals

- "Jacques had one and one-half pieces of yellow cardboard and one and one-quarter pieces of blue cardboard. How much cardboard was there when the pieces were put together?"
- Represent the situation with models of rectangles, and write an addition algorithm.

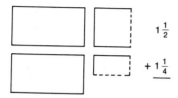

- Have the children note that the fractions have unlike denominators; discuss what to do. Show that the ½ piece can be exchanged for two ¼ pieces; rename the ½ as ²/₄ in the algorithm.

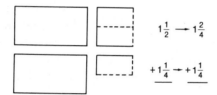

- Combine the pieces in the model; complete the algorithm.

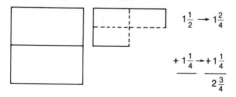

- Repeat with other mixed numerals.

Use at least two different types of learning aids to represent each of these addition sentences: $^2/_5 + ^1/_5 = ^3/_5$, $^1/_3 + ^1/_6 = ^3/_6$, $^1/_4 + ^1/_6 = ^5/_{12}$, and $1^1/_4 + 1^1/_3 = 2^7/_{12}$. (Use a series of illustrations for each example if learning aids are not available.)

Self-check
of Objective 8

SUBTRACTION WITH COMMON FRACTIONS

Subtraction of fractional numbers arises from the same kinds of situations that give rise to subtraction with whole numbers. Over a period of time, children should have numerous experiences with each situation by studying problems like these:

1. "If there is ¾ of a pie in a pan and Billy eats a piece that is ¼ of the original pie, how much pie is left?" This is a take-away situation and is represented by circular regions in Figure 12-5.

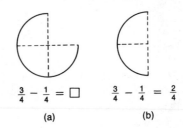

FIGURE 12-5
Circular regions used to represent the subtraction sentence ¾ − ¼ = ²/₄. (a) ¾ of the unit. (b) ²/₄ of the unit.

$$\frac{3}{4} - \frac{1}{4} = \square \qquad \frac{3}{4} - \frac{1}{4} = \frac{2}{4}$$

(a)   (b)

2. "It is ¾ of a mile from Sue's house to school and ⅞ of a mile from Ted's house to school. How much farther is school from Ted's house than from Sue's house?" This comparison situation is represented with a number line in Figure 12-6.

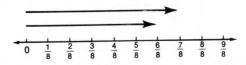

FIGURE 12-6
Number line used to represent the subtraction sentence ⅞ − ¾ = ⅛

3. "Judy is working on a new track layout for her model railroad. She will have a total of 8½ yards of track in the new layout. If she has put down 3½ yards of track, how many more yards of track does she have left to put down?" This situation is represented by a number line in Figure 12-7.

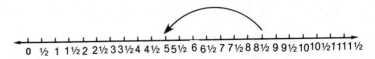

FIGURE 12-7
Number line used to represent the subtraction sentence 8½ − 3½ = 5

4. "Carmen has a mixture of two chemicals that weighs ¹³/₁₆ of a pound. She has ⁷/₁₆ of a pound of sulfur in the mixture. How much of the mixture is made up of the other chemical?" This situation is illustrated by fraction-strip pieces in Figure 12-8.

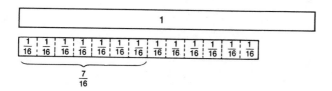

FIGURE 12-8

Fraction strips used to illustrate the subtraction sentence $^{13}/_{16} - ^7/_{16} = ^6/_{16}$

Children already know that subtraction and addition are inverse operations, so they learn to add and subtract fractional numbers simultaneously. You should use the same care to introduce subtraction through situations that are relevant to them. Children's first subtraction should be with fractions having like denominators; problems 1 and 4 illustrate suitable situations and appropriate learning aids. Subtraction with fractions having unlike denominators, as in problem 2, should be introduced along with addition with unlike denominators. In this way the need for renaming fractions so as to result in common denominators will be clear. The renaming process is the same for either operation.

Subtraction with mixed numerals is troublesome for some children, especially when the common fraction part of the minuend is smaller than the common fraction part of the subtrahend. A child may rename the subtrahend as in the margin. Here the child has used the same procedure for renaming the mixed numeral as used earlier for regrouping when subtracting whole numbers, renaming it as $^{11}/_4$, rather than $^5/_4$. To avoid this type of error, begin instruction for this kind of subtraction with situations such as the one that follows.

$$6\tfrac{1}{4} \qquad 5^{11}/_4$$
$$-3\tfrac{3}{4} \qquad -3\tfrac{3}{4}$$

ACTIVITY 12-14 Cake Sale

- "Roberto was in charge of the cake sale at his school's bazaar. At 8:00 he counted 3½ cakes on the table. By 8:30 he had sold 1¾ of these cakes. How many cakes were left at 8:30?"
- Show models of the cakes at 8:00.

$$3\tfrac{1}{2}$$
$$-1\tfrac{3}{4}$$

- Discuss what must be done before 1 and ¾ cakes can be removed; cut 1 cake into fourths and combine it with the half cake, which has also been cut into fourths.

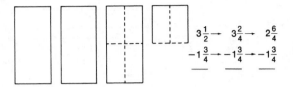

- Remove 1¾ from the model, leaving 1¾; complete the algorithm.

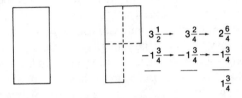

- Relate each step in the algorithm with each step in the model.
- Repeat with similar situations and models.

**Self-check
of Objective 9**

Use suitable learning aids to represent each of these subtraction sentences:
$^5/_8 - ^2/_8 = ^3/_8$, $^7/_8 - ^3/_4 = ^1/_8$, $3^5/_6 - 2^1/_6 = 1^4/_6$, and $2^1/_4 - 1^1/_2 = ^3/_4$

MULTIPLICATION WITH COMMON FRACTIONS

The operations of multiplication and division of fractional numbers are deceptively easy for teachers to teach and children to perform, but their meanings are elusive. Children can be taught rules for performing these two operations, and as long as they remember the rules, they can multiply or divide pairs of fractional numbers with ease. However, if children learn to perform these operations using only rules, they probably will understand very little of the meaning behind them. If you adopt the philosophy of this book, you will use learning aids, not simply the rules, as you explore with children the meanings of the operations.

1. Multiplication of Fractional Numbers by Whole Numbers

Multiplication of fractional numbers by whole numbers is usually used for beginning work, because the examples are easily related to the repeated-addition interpretation of multiplication. When a group of children is ready, use a realistic situation.

ACTIVITY 12-15 Multiplying a Fraction by a Whole Number

- "Sarah practices the piano ¾ of an hour each day. What is the total amount of time she practices in a week?"
- Discuss the meaning of this problem, then have the children give a multiplication sentence:

$$7 \times \text{¾} = \square$$

- Use models to represent the situation. Circular regions, each showing ¾, are good because they can be related to ¾ of an hour on the clock. A number line is another easily handled model.

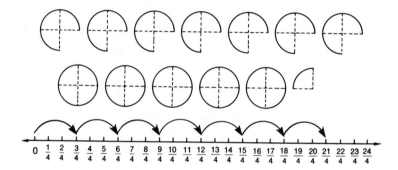

- Complete the multiplication sentence. Rename the answer as a mixed numeral:

$$7 \times \text{¾} = {}^{21}/_4$$
$${}^{21}/_4 = 5\text{¼}$$

- Call children's attention to the fact that the 5¼ represents hours.
- Repeat with similar problems.

2. Multiplication of a Whole Number by a Fractional Number

Many practical situations give rise to the need for finding a fractional part of a whole number. When one cube of butter weighs ¼ of a pound, the weight can be expressed as ¼ of 16 ounces, or 4 ounces. One-third of a foot is the same as ⅓ of 12 inches, or 4 inches; ½ of a dollar is ½ of 100 pennies, or 50 cents. Frequent encounters with these and similar applications enhance children's appreciation of the need for knowing how to perform such multiplication.

ACTIVITY 12-16   Multiplying a Whole Number by a Fraction

- Display a 3-by-6 array of disks. Have the children recall the multiplication sentence for this array: $6 \times 3 = 18$.
- "I want to set ⅓ of this array off to one side. How many disks should I set aside?"

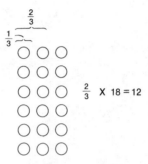

$\frac{2}{3} \times 18 = 12$

- Discuss the fact that to determine ⅓ of the set it is necessary to separate the disks into three equal-sized groups; one of the groups is ⅓ of the 18 disks. "How many disks are in ⅓ of the set?" (6.)
- "How many disks are in ⅔ of the 18 disks?" (12.)
- Repeat with other sets that can be separated into equal-sized groups without remainder.

Once children have used arrays many times, help them learn that the multiplication of a pair of numbers, such as ⅔ and 18, can be completed by either of these procedures:

$$\frac{2 \times 18}{3} = \frac{36}{3} = 12 \quad \text{or} \quad \frac{18}{3} \times 2 = 6 \times 2 = 12.$$

3. Multiplication of Fractional Numbers by Fractional Numbers

A paper-folding learning center can be used to give children an interesting approach to multiplication of one fractional number by another. Problem cards give directions, and paper cut in the shapes of squares, circles, and rectangles provides the materials for investigations. A manila envelope containing a set of shapes and a response sheet for each person makes it easy for a child to begin work. Sample cards are shown in Figure 12-9.

Prepare other cards for activities with thirds, fourths, sixths, and eighths of fractions and for nonunit fractions like two-thirds and two- and three-fourths of units.

```
FINDING PARTS OF PARTS                    (1)

1. Get a square of paper from your envelope.  Fold it
   in half by putting two opposite edges together and
   making a crease in it, like this:
```

```
   The paper on each side of the crease is ___ of
   the square piece of paper.
```

FIGURE 12-9
Sample paper-folding problem cards

```
                                          (2)

2. Fold the paper one more time so that it looks like
   this:
```

```
   Now, the paper is folded so there are ___ sections,
   or parts.  Each part is ___ of the square I began
   with.

3. After your first fold, each section was ___ of the
   square.  When you made the second fold, each
   section was ___ of the square.  This shows that
   1/2 of 1/2 is ___ of the whole piece of paper.
```

When children have completed the center activities, discuss their work with them to help them summarize their findings. Overhead transparencies are useful for a review of the paper-folding activities. The transparencies for the sentence $\frac{2}{3} \times = \frac{3}{4} = \frac{6}{12}$ are illustrated in Figure 12-10. In (a) a unit square is shown. In (b) $\frac{3}{4}$ of the unit is represented by shading on an overlay. In (c) another overlay represents $\frac{2}{3}$ of the unit. Finally,

---

(3)

4. Take out the sheet of paper that looks like this:

Fold on the dotted lines. <u>Each section of the paper is ___ of the whole rectangle.</u>

5. Fold the paper so that you fold the thirds in half. What is the size of each section now? This shows that 1/2 of 1/3 is ___ of the whole piece of paper.

⅔ times ¾ is illustrated when both overlays are placed over the unit region at the same time. The answer, ⁶/₁₂, is represented by the six doubly shaded sections.

FIGURE 12-10
The multiplication sentence ⅔ × ¾ = ⁶/₁₂ illustrated with a series of overhead transparencies

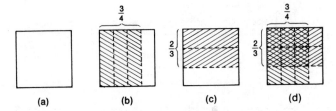

As children work with their various models to gain an understanding of multiplication of fractional numbers, their attention should be directed so they will see the relationship between the fractions' numerators and the product and the denominators and the product. Eventually they should generalize that to multiply fractional numbers, they multiply the numbers represented by numerators and the numbers represented by denominators to get the product. Thus the answer for the sentence ¾ × ⅞ = □ is found by multiplying 3 times 7 to name the numerator of the product and 4 times 8 to name its denominator.

4. Multiplication Involving Mixed Numerals

An extension of multiplication with pairs of whole numbers and pairs of fractional numbers is made when multiplication is done with what are commonly referred to as *mixed numbers*. The phrase "multiplication with mixed numerals" more properly explains this type of multiplication, because it maintains a distinction between number and numeral. An example of this multiplication is $2\frac{1}{2} \times 1\frac{1}{2} = \square$.

ACTIVITY 12-17 Multiplying with Mixed Numerals

* "A cookie recipe calls for one and one-half cups of flour. If you want two and one-half times as many cookies as one recipe makes, how many cups of flour will you need?"
* Discuss the situation and portray the 1½ cups of flour.

* "You want two and one-half times as many cookies as you will get if you make the recipe once. Can you figure out how much flour you will need?" Help the children see that they will need one more 1½ cupfuls, plus ½ that much again, or ¾ of another cup.

* "Altogether, how much flour will you use?" (3¾ cups.)
* Write the multiplication sentence for this situation:

$$2\frac{1}{2} \times 1\frac{1}{2} = \square$$

Rename each mixed numeral as an improper fraction:

$$\frac{5}{2} \times \frac{3}{2} = \square$$

Complete the multiplication:

$$\frac{5}{2} \times \frac{3}{2} = \frac{15}{4} = 3\frac{3}{4}$$

* Use other examples from the same recipe:
  * The recipe calls for 1¼ teaspoons of baking soda. How much is needed for 2½ recipes?
  * The recipe calls for ¾ teaspoon of vanilla. How much is needed for 2½ recipes?

**Self-check
of Objectives
10 and 11**

Make up real-life problem situations showing how each of the repeated addition and array interpretations apply to multiplication with fractional numbers. Use learning aids or picture sequences to illustrate each example and write each situation's number sentences.

Use suitable learning aids to illustrate the meaning of each of these sentences: $4 \times 1/3 = 4/3$ (or $1\frac{1}{3}$), $2/3 \times 12 = 8$, $1/4 \times 2/3 = 2/12$ (or $1/6$), $3 \times 1\frac{1}{2} = 4\frac{1}{2}$, and $2\frac{1}{3} \times 1\frac{1}{4} = 35/12$ (or $2\frac{11}{12}$).

5. Cancellation

(a) $\dfrac{2}{3} \times \dfrac{9}{10} = \square$

(b) $\dfrac{2 \times 9}{3 \times 10} = \square$

(c) $\dfrac{2 \times (3 \times 3)}{3 \times (2 \times 5)} = \square$

(d) $\dfrac{2 \times 3 \times 3}{2 \times 3 \times 5} = \square$

(e) $\dfrac{2}{2} \times \dfrac{3}{3} \times \dfrac{3}{5} = \square$

(f) $1 \times 1 \times \dfrac{3}{5} = \square$

Cancellation is a process of simplifying the common fractions used in multiplication before the work is done rather than after. (Cancellation also works in certain division situations.)

The rationale for the process is given by the examples in the margin. The original multiplication sentence is shown in (a). Rewrite the sentence as in (b). Next, factor the composite numbers as in (c). Application of the commutative property permits rewriting the sentence as in (d). In (e) the sentence is written in a way that emphasizes fractions that are names for one. Finally, two of the fractions are rewritten as ones, and the multiplication is completed.

Children will complete the process without following all of the steps. You will help them recognize that they can cancel when they find a numerator and denominator that are alike, as in the first of the following examples, or when there are numerators and denominators that have common factors as in the other two examples:

$$\frac{4}{5} \times \frac{3}{4} = \square$$

$$\frac{3}{4} \times \frac{8}{9} = \square$$

$$\frac{5}{12} \times \frac{3}{10} = \square$$

**Self-check
of Objective 12**

Explain the meaning of cancellation. List the sequence of steps that illustrate why cancellation can be used in this example: $6/10 \times 12/15 = \square$.

DIVISION WITH FRACTIONAL NUMBERS

1. Situations That Illustrate Division with Common Fractions

Help children relate division with fractional numbers to division with whole numbers and extend their understanding of both partitive and measurement situations to include fractional numbers. As before, early experiences should include work with concrete models to aid in visualizing problem situations and the role of division in their solution. Introductory lessons should begin with a review of a situation used with whole numbers. The examples need not involve large numbers.

ACTIVITY 12-18 Measurement Division with Fractions

- Put fifteen markers on a magnetic board. "If we put these markers into groups that each have three markers, how many groups will there be?" Review the idea that this measurement problem can be solved by repeated subtraction.
- Show a rectangular region and this situation: "I have a piece of lumber three feet long. If I cut it into pieces that are each one-half foot long, how many pieces will I have?"

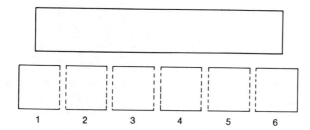

- Help the children see that this is also a measurement situation. Once the board has been cut, the ½-foot-long pieces can be removed one at a time. There are 6 pieces.
- Show a model of ¾ of a cake and present this situation: "I have three-fourths of a cake. When I cut it into pieces that are each one-fourth of the cake, how many pieces will there be?"

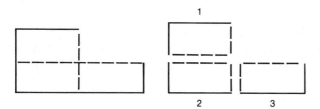

- This is also a measurement situation. Count the ¼-sized pieces as they are removed one at a time. There are 3 pieces.
- Repeat with other situations that yield whole number answers.

A similar series of activities should be used to introduce partitive situations. Use examples like these:

- "There is three-fourths of a pie in Jack's refrigerator. If he cuts it into three equal-sized pieces, what part of the whole pie will each piece be?"
- "A half gallon of ice cream is divided into six equal-sized portions. What part of a gallon is each portion?"

2. Division Algorithms

Two algorithms can be used for dividing with common fractions. Most commonly taught in the elementary school is the **invert-and-multiply** algorithm, which is based on the idea that dividing one number by another is the same as multiplying the number by the reciprocal of the divisor. Dividing 6 by 3 is the same as multiplying 6 by ⅓; $4 \div \frac{1}{2}$ equals 4×2. The algorithm is shown for these two division situations:

$$6 \div 3 = 6 \times \frac{1}{3} = 2$$

$$4 \div \frac{1}{2} = 4 \times \frac{2}{1} = 4 \times 2 = 8$$

The other algorithm requires that both fractions have the same denominator. Division is done by dividing the numerator of the dividend by the numerator of the divisor. To divide $\frac{1}{2}$ by $\frac{1}{4}$, rename $\frac{1}{2}$ as $\frac{2}{4}$ and then divide 2 by 1. This series of steps shows this algorithm.

$$\frac{1}{2} \div \frac{1}{4} = \frac{2}{4} \div \frac{1}{4} = \frac{2 \div 1}{4 \div 4} = \frac{2}{1} = 2$$

Because the invert-and-multiply process is the most widely used algorithm, it is the only one explained in this book for presentation to all children.

a. Reciprocals Before children are introduced to the invert and multiply process they should have an understanding of reciprocals. They can be introduced to this concept through an activity like this:

ACTIVITY 12-19   Finding Reciprocals

- Show the children this list of multiplication sentences:

$$\frac{3}{4} \times \square = \frac{12}{12}$$

$$\frac{6}{7} \times \square = \frac{42}{42}$$

$$\frac{2}{3} \times \square = \frac{6}{6}$$

- Ask these questions:
  - "By what number must we multiply ¾ to obtain the product $^{12}/_{12}$?" ($^4/_3$.)
  - "By what do we multiply $^6/_7$ to obtain a product of $^{42}/_{42}$?" ($^7/_6$.)
  - "By what do we multiply $^2/_3$ to obtain the product $^6/_6$?" ($^3/_2$.)
- After the second factor for each sentence has been determined, ask these questions:
  - "What do you notice about each product in these sentences?" (They are all names for 1.)
  - "What do you notice about the two factors in each example?" (The numerator and denominator of the second are the reverse of the first.)
- "What is the product of each of the following sentences?"

$$\frac{4}{15} \times \frac{15}{4} = \square$$

$$\frac{9}{7} \times \frac{7}{9} = \square$$

$$2 \times \frac{1}{2} = \square$$

- After children know how to determine a reciprocal, help them compose a definition of it. For example, "The reciprocal of a number is the number by which the original number is multiplied to yield a product of one."

---

b. Invert and Multiply   When children can both describe measurement and partitive situations that involve fractions and understand reciprocals, they are ready to learn the invert and multiply algorithm for dividing with common fractions. The algorithms that follow are based on the problems in Activity 12-18.

ACTIVITY 12-20

- Begin with the sentence for the lumber situation in Activity 12-18:

$$3 \div \tfrac{1}{2} = 6$$

- Ask questions like these:
  - "What is the reciprocal of $\tfrac{1}{2}$?" ($\tfrac{2}{1}$, or 2.) "What happens if I multiply 3 by the reciprocal of $\tfrac{1}{2}$?" (The product is 6.)
- Show the sentence for the cake situation:

$$\tfrac{3}{4} \div \tfrac{1}{4} = 3$$

- Use these questions:
  - "What is the reciprocal of $\tfrac{1}{4}$?" ($\tfrac{4}{1}$, or 4.) "What happens if I multiply $\tfrac{3}{4}$ by $\tfrac{4}{1}$ and simplify the answer?" (The product is 3.) Repeat with the other examples you used earlier.
- Help the children see that answers to these division situations are obtained by inverting the divisor and then multiplying. Show the sequence of steps for each situation like this:

$$3 \div \tfrac{1}{2} = 3 \times \tfrac{2}{1} = 3 \times 2 = 6$$
$$\tfrac{3}{4} \div \tfrac{1}{4} = \tfrac{3}{4} \times \tfrac{4}{1} = \tfrac{3}{4} \times 4 = \tfrac{12}{4} = 3$$

Guide the children through as many examples as are necessary for them to relate the invert-and-multiply algorithm to both measurement and partitive situations. When its use is clear, help them state a generalization such as: "To divide fractional numbers, multiply the dividend by the reciprocal of the divisor."

Self-check of Objectives 13 and 14

Describe a real-life partitive situation for this division sentence: $\tfrac{1}{3} \div 4 = \tfrac{1}{12}$. Illustrate your example with an appropriate learning aid. Do the same for this sentence, using a measurement situation: $3 \div \tfrac{1}{4} = 12$.

Write the sequence of steps that illustrate the completion of the division sentence $\tfrac{3}{4} \div \tfrac{1}{2} = 1\tfrac{1}{2}$ by the invert-and-multiply method.

RATIOS

One of the uses of common fractions discussed at the beginning of this chapter is that of indicating **ratios.** When common fractions are used to indicate ratios, they are interpreted differently than when they represent parts of a whole or group. For example, the numerator of a common fraction that represents a ratio may tell the number of elements in one of two sets, whereas the denominator tells the number of elements in the other set. Ratios cannot be added, subtracted, multiplied, and divided like fractional numbers, either. Consequently you must use care when common fractions are introduced as ways of representing ratios so that their meaning is clear.

1. Rate Pairs and Tables

You do not need to delay introduction of ratios until children have mastered all the other uses of common fractions. In fact many children who have only begun work with common fractions as representations of fractional numbers can be introduced to the idea of ratios. A good way to make the introduction is through work with **rate pairs.** A simple example shows how this can be done.

ACTIVITY 12-21   Rate Pairs

- "I bought two pencils for five cents. Will one of you use these play coins and these pencils to show us two pencils and five cents?"
- "How much money will I need in order to buy four pencils at the same price?"
- Through questions and use of common materials, you can help children understand the many-to-many correspondences involved in this situation.
- Show a simple table and discuss how it can be completed.

Number of Pencils	2	4	6			
Cost of Pencils	5¢	10 ¢	15¢			

- Repeat with other common situations and materials.

---

2. Proportions

Proportional relationships are frequently used in problem solving. Consider this situation:

Mary and Sue share a newspaper route. Mary delivers papers 1 day out of every 3; Sue delivers the papers 2 days out of every 3. For every day that

Mary delivers papers, Sue delivers them on 2 days; this is a ratio of 1 to 2. If Sue has delivered papers for a total of 30 days, on how many days has Mary delivered them?

This proportion can be used to solve the problem:

$$1/2 = n/30$$

Help children see that this problem can be solved by determining the number by which 2 is multiplied to get a product of 30 and then multiplying 1 by the same number. Also help children see that the process is the same as they have used to rename fractional numbers to find common denominators.

The missing term in any proportion can be determined by **cross multiplying** and then dividing. To find the value of n in the expression $6/7 = n/42$, multiply 6×42 and then divide by 7. When 42 is multiplied by 6, the product is 252; $252 \div 7 = 36$, so $6/7 = 36/42$. Naturally, more than one example needs to be used so that cross multiplication is clear to children.

The use of proportions in problem solving is discussed further in the next chapter, in which their use in solving percent problems is considered.

*Self-check
of Objective 15*

Several examples of situations involving ratios are described or listed. List two or three of these, and name at least two similar but different examples. Prepare a table that reports data for one of your situations. Use cross multiplication to determine whether the following are expressions of proportion: $15/35 = 45/105$ and $72/120 = 18/32$

SPECIAL CHILDREN AND COMMON FRACTIONS

1. Learning-Handicapped Children

Learning-handicapped children frequently experience difficulties as they learn about common fractions. Children with visual discrimination or figure–ground weaknesses often find it hard to distinguish a part from the whole when a geometric region represents a part-of-a-whole situation and a set of disks represents a part-of-a-set situation. The parts of a common fraction numeral are equally baffling for many of these children. Children with memory deficits cannot always retain information acquired during work with concrete models long enough to transfer it to a symbolic form as they learn about numerals for common fractions. Integrative problems lead to difficulties with computational processes with common fractions.

Specially prepared materials and the careful development of their meanings will help lessen the difficulties these children experience. Each algorithm must be introduced through situations and with models that are clear to each child. An early and careful analysis of children's written computational procedures will enable you to deal with problems as they arise and prevent faulty procedures from becoming habitual.

Models like those used throughout this chapter are less confusing for many children than the ones used in many textbooks. In this book the region or strip that represents a whole is outlined with a solid line, and the parts into which the region or strip is separated are shown with broken lines. This model is easier for children to visualize than when solid lines are used alone. When these models are combined with the use of color cues, as suggested by Nancy Bley and Carol Thornton[1], children can see the sequence to follow as they interpret the model and write the fraction's numeral. The model and numerals in Figure 12-11 might be used. The original geometric figure and the number of parts into which it is separated are colored red, and the parts being considered are green. The box in the numerator position is green, and the denominator box is red. The child counts the green parts and writes a "3" in the green box. Next all of the parts are counted, and a "5" is written in the red box. Finally the "3/5" is written.

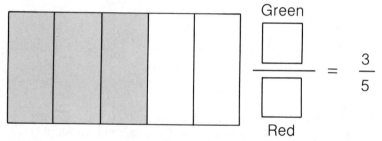

FIGURE 12-11
Geometric model and colored boxes for learning to interpret a common fraction

Numerals that represent fractional numbers as common fractions are confusing for many learning-handicapped children. Whole-number numerals are written horizontally, beginning at the left and ending at the right, but common fractions are written with one numeral above another. Mixed numerals are especially confusing for some. Sandpaper or felt numerals and flat boxes with wet sand, as suggested in Chapter 7 for children who have difficulty writing the numerals for whole numbers, are useful now. As a child traces a mixed numeral, the fraction it represents should be named by the child. Then the numeral should be copied with chalk on a chalkboard or with pencil on paper. An adult or another student can work with a learning-handicapped child to direct the work and determine the correctness of responses.

Once children begin computing with common fractions, their work should be analyzed carefully so that errors caused by misunderstandings can be spotted and corrected immediately. The errors that follow occur frequently and require immediate attention:

[1] Nancy S. Bley and Carol A. Thornton, *Teaching Mathematics to the Learning Disabled* (Rockville, Md.: Aspen Systems Corporation, 1981), p. 312.

1. Addition
   a. Adding both the numerators and denominators:

   $$^7/_8 + ^3/_8 = ^{10}/_{16}, \qquad ^5/_6 + ^4/_8 = ^9/_{14}.$$

   b. Failing to rename one fraction when there are unlike denominators:

   $$^2/_3 + ^1/_6 = ^3/_6, \qquad ^4/_5 + ^3/_{10} = ^7/_{10}.$$

2. Subtraction
   a. Subtracting both numerators and denominators:

   $$^3/_8 - ^1/_4 = ^2/_4, \qquad ^2/_5 - ^1/_3 = ^1/_2.$$

   b. Failing to subtract whole numbers when there are mixed numerals:

$$
\begin{array}{cc}
4^1\!/_3 \rightarrow {}^4/_{12} & 5^5\!/_6 \rightarrow {}^{10}/_{12} \\
-2^1\!/_4 \rightarrow {}^3/_{12} & -2^1\!/_3 \rightarrow {}^4/_{12} \\
\hline
{}^1/_{12}, & {}^6/_{12}.
\end{array}
$$

3. Multiplication
   a. Renaming with common denominators, multiplying numerators only:

   $$^3/_4 \times ^1/_8 = ^6/_8 \times ^1/_8 = ^6/_8.$$
   $$^5/_6 \times ^2/_3 = ^5/_6 \times ^4/_6 = ^{20}/_6.$$

   b. Inverting and multiplying:

   $$^2/_3 \times ^1/_4 = ^2/_3 \times ^4/_1 = ^8/_3.$$
   $$^5/_6 \times ^2/_3 = ^5/_6 \times ^3/_2 = ^{15}/_{12}.$$

4. Division
   a. Dividing both numerator and denominator (disregarding order when divisor number is larger than dividend number):

   $$^4/_6 \div ^1/_3 = ^4/_2, \qquad ^1/_2 \div ^1/_4 = ^1/_2.$$

   b. Failing to invert:

   $$^1/_2 \div ^1/_4 = ^1/_2 \times ^1/_4 = ^1/_8.$$
   $$^3/_8 \div ^3/_4 = ^3/_8 \times ^3/_4 = ^9/_{32}.$$

In addition to computational problems like the ones above, learning-handicapped children may be unable to organize numerals in algorithms properly. Bley and Thornton recommend that a preformatted page be used.[2] Figure 12-12(a) shows a model for adding when there are mixed numerals with like denominators. The whole number for each addend is placed in the box; the numerator for the fraction goes above the line and the denominator below the line. A page of eight or ten models is given to a child who cannot align numerals in an algorithm. Each example from an assignment is copied in one of the models before any answers are determined. The second model (b) is for adding mixed numerals with unlike denominators. These same models can be used for subtraction,

---

[2] Bley and Thornton, p. 305.

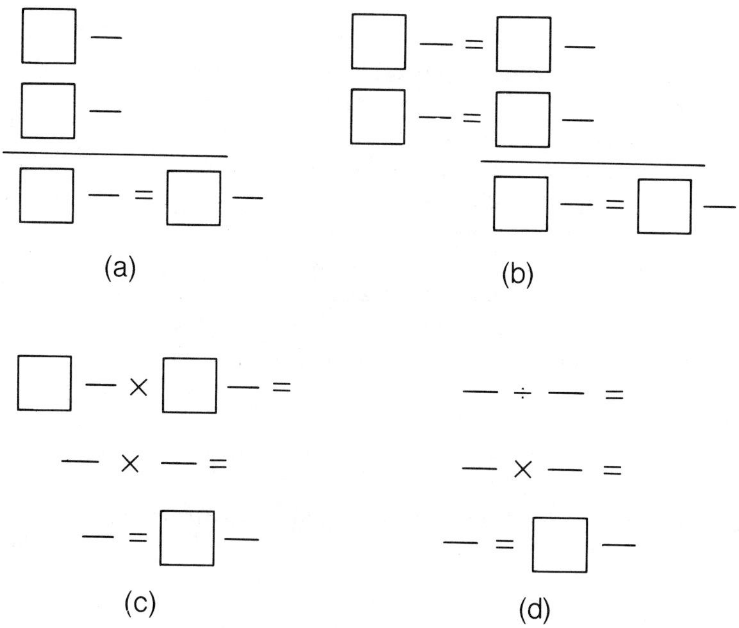

(a)   (b)

(c)   (d)

FIGURE 12-12
Patterns for computing with fractional numbers

also. The models in (c) and (d) are for multiplying mixed numerals and dividing fractions, respectively.

2. Gifted and Talented Children

There are topics that can be presented to gifted and talented children to extend their understanding of common fractions and operations with them. One challenging topic is the study of Egyptian fractions, which were used as early as 1650 B.C. Information about these fractions was found in *The Rhind Mathematical Papyrus*, which was written about 1650 B.C. Egyptians used only unit fractions, that is, fractions with a numerator of 1. They also chose to express fractions as the sum of unlike fractions. Thus ¾ was written as the sum of ½ and ¼ rather than ¼ + ¼ + ¼. The simplist interpretation of ½ is with ¹/₆ and ⅓. (A sign for addition was not used between the two numerals.) The list that follows illustrates other expressions of common fractions as Egyptians would name them. Study them carefully to find a pattern for naming the fractions.

$$1/4 = 1/6 + 1/12$$
$$1/6 = 1/9 + 1/18$$
$$1/8 = 1/12 + 1/24$$
$$1/16 = 1/24 + 1/48$$

Egyptian symbols were not like ours, and children should not be expected to learn them. Rather they can use ours to show how the Egyptians would write these fractions:

$$1/10 \qquad 1/12 \qquad 1/16 \qquad 1/24 \qquad 1/32$$

In a brief article in *Enrichment Mathematics for the Grades*, Julia Adkins discusses Egyptian fractions and other activities dealing with unit fractions that are ideal for gifted and talented students.[3]

The common-denominator method of dividing with common fractions is another area of work that is suitable for gifted and talented children. This method is not difficult to learn, but once it is learned, it gives children the opportunity to choose between it and the invert-and-multiply procedure. This method is based on the idea that once the denominators in the dividend and divisor have been renamed with common denominators, the division can be completed by dividing the numerator of the dividend by the numerator of the divisor. To divide ¾ by ⅛, the following process is used:

$$3/4 \div 1/8 = 6/8 \div 1/8 = 6 \div 1 = 6$$

In the case of $2 \div ¾ = \square$, the algorithm can be completed like this:

$$2 \div 3/4 = 2/1 \div 3/4 = 8/4 \div 3/4 = 8 \div 3 = 2\,2/3$$

After children have completed several examples, they should examine their work and determine why this algorithm works.

---

[3] Julia Adkins, "Unit Fractions," in National Council of Teachers of Mathematics, *Enrichment Mathematics for the Grades*, 27th Yearbook (Washington, D.C.: The Council, 1963), pp. 221–226.

Self-checks of Objectives 16, 17, and 18

Describe two procedures for helping learning-handicapped children understand common fractions and to write their numerals.

Examples of common errors committed by children as they compute with common fractions are given. Explain how a child would compute each of these examples if that child used one of the erroneous ways of computing:

$$1/4 + 1/2 = \square \qquad 5/8 - 1/2 = \square$$
$$4/5 \times 1/3 = \square \qquad 5/8 \div 1/4 = \square$$

Explain how Egyptians used unit fractions to express common fractions; then express these fractions as the Egyptians would:

$$1/18 \qquad 1/36 \qquad 1/42$$

Show how the common denominator method of dividing with common fractions works with this division sentence:

$$4/5 \div 1/2 = \square$$

SUMMARY

Common fractions have several meanings, depending upon the situation in which they are used. Children need experience with concrete and semiconcrete models that represent all of the meanings. Geometric regions, fraction strips, markers, and number lines are used during investigative activities designed to make the common-fraction representation of fractional numbers meaningful. Children learn that common fractions are used to express parts of a unit or set of objects that has been subdivided into equal-sized parts or subsets, to express ratios, to indicate division, and to express abstract fractional numbers. These same materials, along with certain abstract procedures, help children learn to compare fractional numbers, to rename them as common fractions in their simplest form, and to rename two or more fractional numbers so they are expressed by common fractions having the same denominator.

Operations with fractional numbers expressed as common fractions require the same careful development that is made for operations with whole numbers. Even though children are older when operations with fractional numbers are developed, it is still necessary that the processes be developed through carefully sequenced activities with appropriate learning aids rather than by rules alone. Real-life problems can illustrate situations that give rise to addition, subtraction, multiplication, and division with fractional numbers. Geometric regions, fraction strips, markers, and number lines should accompany the real-life problems to give further meaning to the operations. References to similarities that exist between the operations with whole numbers and those with fractional numbers should be stressed whenever it is appropriate.

There are procedures for developing children's understanding of how cancellation is done when multiplying fractional numbers. Uses of common fractions to express ratios can be introduced early in the program and be developed through simple examples at first, with more complex examples introduced as children mature.

Learning-handicapped children often experience difficulty with common fractions, because models and numerals are not always understood. Models that use color cues, sandpaper and felt numerals, and wet-sand boxes for writing numerals are useful aids for these children. There are common errors committed by children as they compute with common fractions. The errors must be detected and corrected early so they do not become habitual. Egyptian fractions and the common-denominator method of dividing with common fractions are examples of enrichment topics for gifted and talented students.

STUDY QUESTIONS AND ACTIVITIES

1. Several of the articles in this chapter's reading list describe activities with games and concrete materials that contribute to children's understanding of common fractions. Add some of these to your collection of teaching–learning aids.

2. Read Usiskin's article (see the reading list) and summarize his argument that the need for common fractions will not diminish in the future. Indicate your position and tell in what way(s), if any, your point of view differs from Usiskin's.

3. Word problems are used frequently in this chapter to present situations that lead to operations with common fractions. One way to test children's understanding of sentences that you present is by having them make up a word problem for each sentence. Seven sentences are given here. Make up a word problem for each one to show that you understand the type of situation that gives rise to each one.

   (a) $3/8 + 3/8 = 6/8$

   (b) $1 1/2 + 1/4 = 1 3/4$

   (c) $7/8 - 3/8 = 4/8$

   (d) $2 \times 3/8 = 6/8$

   (e) $2/3 \times 18 = 12$

   (f) $6 \div 1/2 = 12$

   (g) $1/3 \div 2 = 1/6$

4. Another indication of a child's understanding of operations with fractional numbers is the ability to represent a word problem and sentence with concrete materials or pictures. Use drawings of classroom learning aids to illustrate each sentence in study question 3. When a sequence of illustrations is used, indicate their order by labeling them (a), (b), (c), . . .

5. Examine a current mathematics textbook series to determine at which grade level children are introduced to the concept of ratio. What are some of the situations used to introduce this concept? When is the concept of proportion introduced? What situations illustrate this concept?

KEY TERMS

common fractions
denominator
numerator
congruent geometric shapes
common denominator
equivalence class
least common multiple
prime factorization

mixed numerals
cancellation
invert-and-multiply
ratios
rate pairs
proportional relationships
cross multiplying

FOR FURTHER READING

Brown, Christopher N. "Fractions on Grid Paper," *Arithmetic Teacher*, XXVII, No. 5 (January 1979), pp. 8–10.

Describes and illustrates grid-paper activities to develop fundamental concepts of common fractions and visual recognition of parts and wholes and to give students experiences with equivalent fractions.

Bruni, James V., and Helene J. Silverman. "An Introduction to Fractions," *Arithmetic Teacher*, XXII, No. 7 (November 1975), pp. 538–545.

Fractions are introduced through a series of games and related tables. Geometric regions cut from oaktag, outlines of regions, and spinners serve as the playing pieces.

———. "Using Rectangles and Squares to Develop Fraction Concepts," *Arithmetic Teacher*, XXIV, No. 2 (February 1977), pp. 96–106.

Explains and illustrates a variety of activities, including paper folding and cutting, coloring regions, and a fraction game.

Carlisle, Earnest. "Fractions and Popsicle Sticks," *Arithmetic Teacher*, XXVII, No. 6 (February 1980), pp. 50–51.

Natural and colored popsicle sticks serve as models for multiplying and dividing with common fractions. Examples are described and illustrated.

Easterly, Nancy J., and Roy M. Bennett. "Teaching Fractions with Dominoes," *School Science and Mathematics*, LXXVII, No. 2 (February 1977), pp. 117–121.

A teacher-made set of 28 dominoes becomes a game for adding with common fractions. A description of the dominoes, rules, and a simulated game are included.

Ellerbuck, Lawrence W., and Joseph W. Payne. "A Teaching Sequence from Initial Fraction Concepts through the Addition of Unlike Fractions," *Developing Computational Skills*, 1978 Yearbook of the National Council of Teachers of Mathematics (Reston, Va.: The Council), pp. 129–147.

The sequence includes initial work with common fractions using objects and diagrams and leading to oral names and fraction symbols. The concepts are extended to include work with equivalent fractions, comparing, and renaming. Addition of like and unlike fractions is described briefly.

Green, George F., Jr. "A Model for Teaching Multiplication of Fractional Numbers," *Arithmetic Teacher*, XX, No. 1 (January 1973), pp. 5–9.

Green lists five characteristics of a satisfactory model for teaching a mathematical concept. Then he identifies a model for teaching multiplication with fractional numbers that has the five characteristics.

Moulton, J. Paul. "A Working Model for Rational Numbers," *Arithmetic Teacher*, XXII, No. 4 (April 1975), pp. 328–332.
The model is a balance beam scaled to show common fractions with denominators of 1, 2, 3, . . . , 20 and large paper clips. It shows equivalent relations and addition and subtraction with common fractions.

Souviney, Randall J. "Seeing Through Fractions," *Learning*, V, No. 7 (March 1977), pp. 66–67.
Regions cut from colored transparent acetate serve as models for developing the meaning of common fractions. Later they are used to give meaning to addition, subtraction, and multiplication with common fractions.

Swart, William L. "Fractions vs. Decimals—the Wrong Issue," *Arithmetic Teacher*, XXIX, No. 2 (October 1981) pp. 17–18.
Swart argues that a greater emphasis needs to be placed on concepts of fractions and less on computation with them. He uses an interesting problem to present his case.

Thompson, Charles. "Teaching Division of Fractions with Understanding," *Arithmetic Teacher*, XXVII, No. 5 (January 1979), pp. 24–27.
Illustrates and explains a set of materials and a sequence of steps for teaching the common-denominator method of dividing with common fractions.

Usiskin, Zalman P. "The Future of Fractions," *Arithmetic Teacher*, XXVII, No. 5 (January 1979), pp. 18–20.
Usiskin refutes the argument that common fractions will become obsolete by exploring uses of fractions that will persist regardless of the import of either the calculator or the metric system.

Van de Walle, John, and Charles S. Thompson. "Fractions with Counters," *Arithmetic Teacher*, XXVIII, No. 2 (October 1980), pp. 6–11.
Sets of teacher-made unit holders and markers form the basis for activities that develop understanding of common fractions, equivalent fractions, and addition and subtraction of fractions.

13

Fractional Numbers—
Decimals and Percents

1. Demonstrate the uses of at least two different learning aids for activities dealing with the meaning of decimal fractions.

2. Demonstrate a procedure for extending children's understanding of place-value notation to include positions to the right of the ones place.

3. Write two different expanded-numeral forms for representing fractional numbers expressed as decimal fractions.

4. Describe real-life situations involving addition and subtraction with decimal fractions, and demonstrate learning aids children can use to develop an understanding of this type of addition and subtraction.

5. Make up story problems for multiplication sentences such as $4 \times 0.3 = 1.2$, $0.5 \times 10 = 5$, and $0.2 \times 0.4 = 0.08$, and use suitable learning aids to show the meaning of each sentence.

6. Explain two procedures that can be used to determine the number of places to the right of the ones place in the product of multiplication involving decimal fractions.

7. Demonstrate with appropriate learning aids activities that extend partitive and measurement division situations to include fractional numbers represented by decimal fractions.

8. Explain two ways of determining where to put the decimal point in quotients for division involving decimal fractions.

9. Define percent, and describe a real-life situation involving it.

10. Distinguish between percent (rate), base, and percentage, and give an example of each in a real-life situation.

11. Describe materials that are suitable for children's investigations into the meaning of percent.

12. Rename common and decimal fractions as percents, and rename percents as common and decimal fractions.

13. Use the proportion method for solving percent problems.

14. Describe four activities with the calculator dealing with decimal fractions.

15. Rename common fractions as decimal fractions and vice versa, and identify which kinds of common fractions re-sult in terminating fractions and which result in repeating decimals.

The need for knowledge of decimal fractions is greater than ever. The calculator and the movement toward use of the metric system in the United States place a greater premium on knowledge of this way of representing fractional numbers than in the past. A good understanding of decimal fractions is needed if an individual is to be mathematically literate. This chapter discusses materials and procedures for helping children learn about decimal fractions and percent.

INTRODUCING DECIMAL FRACTIONS

Decimal fractions are one of three ways to represent **fractional numbers.** Studying them should be related to what has been learned about common fractions and the Hindu–Arabic numeration system. Models for decimal fractions should be similar to those used to learn about common fractions so that relationships between the two ways of representing fractional numbers can be emphasized. In many instances middle-grade children can learn about common and decimal fractions simultaneously, using the same models. This approach has two benefits. First, children learn that common fractions and decimal fractions both represent fractional numbers rather than viewing them as being unrelated, as is often the case when they are studied separately. Second, it saves time, because many of the same concrete and semiconcrete materials can be used simultaneously to develop an understanding of both types of fractions.

You should also make clear that decimal fractions are an extension of the already familiar base-ten numeration system.

Once it is clear that children are ready to learn about decimal fractions, familiar concrete aids should be used for developing their understanding. Cuisenaire rods or Dienes multibase blocks are useful if they are available. Children who are accustomed to these materials will know that any particular piece can be named as a unit. Therefore they can use a tens flat from a Cuisenaire or Dienes set as a unit. Ten rods cover a flat, so each rod is a tenth of the flat; while 100 small unit squares cover a flat, and each one is a hundredth of a flat.

Squared paper with centimeter squares can be cut to make an activities kit. A kit, which each child can make, consists of squares that are ten units along each side, at least ten strips that are ten units long, and 100 small unit squares. If squared paper is not available, you can draw a kit's pattern on duplicating masters and make copies of the parts for each child.

1. Tenths

When a group of children is ready for work with decimal fractions, give each child a kit of materials containing either structured materials such as Cuisenaire or Dienes flats and rods or squared-paper materials.

ACTIVITY 13-1   Tenths

- Discuss the fact that the Cuisenaire flat is a unit piece that represents 1.
- Have the children lay 10 rods on top of the flat. After the children have counted the rods, point out that each rod is one-tenth of the unit.

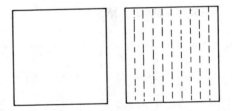

- Ask: "What common fraction do we use to indicate the size of each tenth piece?" ($^1/_{10}$.) Write "$^1/_{10}$" on the board, then put "0.1" next to it. Tell the children that "0.1" is another way to write "$^1/_{10}$."
- Develop the meaning of 0.2, 0.3, 0.4, . . . 1.0 in the same way. Pay particular attention to "1.0" so children see that it represents a unit region that has been separated into 10 congruent parts.

After children are acquainted with notation for tenths, associate tenths with common real-life uses such as automobile odometers, gasoline fuel pumps, and the metric system.

Some teachers use the United States currency system as an example of decimal notation. However, there are sound arguments against its use during introductory lessons. Many children do not think of a dollar as the unit of which pennies and dimes are fractional parts; instead they think the penny is the unit from which other coins and bills of greater value are built. Also, any discussion of the different coins—pennies, nickels, dimes, quarters, and half dollars—requires that hundredths as well as tenths be discussed. Children should understand tenths and their decimal notation before they begin to study hundredths and their notation.

Other learning aids can be used before children begin their study of tenths. For example:

- *Geometric shapes.* Shapes other than squares can be separated into ten congruent parts. The parts should be identified and represented by decimal-fraction notation (Figure 13-1).

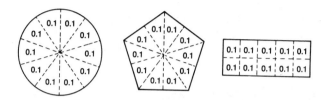

FIGURE 13-1
Geometric shapes separated into ten congruent parts to illustrate tenths

- *Fraction strips.* Use a unit strip and a strip separated into ten congruent parts. Children will note that decimal-fraction notation represents tenths (Figure 13-2).

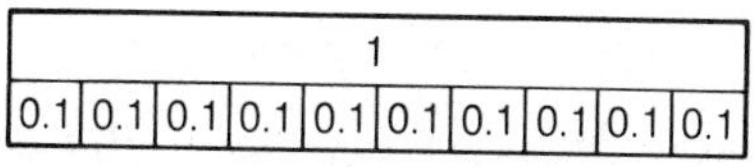

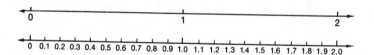

FIGURE 13-2
Fraction strips showing the decimal-fraction representation of tenths

- *Number lines.* You can use number lines to develop understanding of decimal fractions. Begin with a line that shows only unit segments. On a second line show each unit marked into ten congruent segments. The children should identify and name each point on the line as its meaning is discussed (Figure 13-3).

FIGURE 13-3
Number lines used to illustrate units and tenths

2. Hundredths

Develop children's understanding of the decimal-fraction representation of hundredths through extension of activities with tenths.

ACTIVITY 13-2 Hundredths

- Display a unit region. Separate it into ten congruent parts; review the notation for decimal tenths.
- Separate each tenth into 10 congruent parts so there are 100 parts.

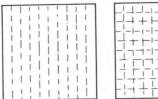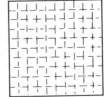

- Discuss the fact that there are now 100 congruent parts. Introduce the notation for one hundredth: "0.01."
- Have the children count a few of the parts; display this sequence of numerals as they count:

0.01, 0.02, 0.03, ...

- Name decimal fractions for children to represent with kit materials: 0.15, 0.36, 0.98, and so on.
- Show representations of decimal fractions with models; have the children name each fraction.

A number line with units separated into 100 congruent segments also helps develop an understanding of hundredths (Figure 13-4). Even though it may be impractical to write the numeral for each point on the line, children can recite their names as they indicate numbers in sequence. Fraction strips separated into 100 congruent parts are also useful learning aids. The fact that ten-hundredths are equivalent to one-tenth should be emphasized as these materials are used.

FIGURE 13-4

Number line with a unit segment separated into 100 congruent parts to illustrate hundredths

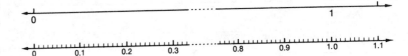

3. Other Decimal Fractions

Learning aids for representing fractional numbers smaller than hundredths are difficult to make in sizes that are practical for children to manipulate. A unit region that shows 1000 or more congruent parts can be made on a large sheet of tagboard for children to use during discussion of decimal fractions smaller than hundredths. It is not unreasonable for children to *imagine* that such a unit has been cut into 1000, or 10,000, or even 100,000 parts as they deal with the smaller decimals.

**Self-check
of Objective 1**

Select any two learning aids and demonstrate how they are used to show the meaning of decimal fractions.

EXTENDING PLACE VALUE TO INCLUDE FRACTIONAL NUMBERS

Kits of structured or squared-paper materials provide a basis for developing the concept of decimal fractions as numerals for fractional numbers. By using these kits, children will learn that $2/10$ and 0.2, $13/100$ and 0.13, and $1^3/10$ and 1.3 are pairs of numerals for naming three different numbers. Children's work must go beyond the simple fractions studied through activities with manipulative materials so that they can see how decimal fractions fit into the Hindu–Arabic numeration system. Children must see how decimal fractions provide place positions to the right of the ones place to accommodate numbers smaller than one.

1. Using Place-Value Pocket Charts

A place-value pocket chart is useful for developing children's understanding of how decimal fractions are an extension of the already familiar decimal notation scheme.

ACTIVITY 13-3   Decimal Fractions

- Display a pocket chart and a squared-paper model of the number it portrays.

Ones	Tenths
⊓⊓⊓	⊓⊓⊓⊓

- Point out that three markers in the ones pocket represent three unit squares, whereas four markers in the tenths pocket represent tenths pieces in the model. Write the numeral "3.4" on the chalkboard, and discuss its meaning.

- Repeat with other decimal fractions, using models as well as the pocket chart to represent each one.
- Add a pocket to the right of the tenths place to represent hundredths; use models and markers in the chart to show hundredths.
- Dictate or give written decimal fractions for children to represent in the pocket chart.
- Show representations of numbers in the pocket chart for which children write numerals.

2. Using an Abacus

When an abacus is used, a rod other than the one on the extreme right represents the ones place. Put a small tag with a dot on it to the right of the rod used to indicate the ones place. The abacus in Figure 13-5 represents the number 234.062. Use exercises such as the ones mentioned above to reinforce children's understanding of place-value positions represented on an abacus.

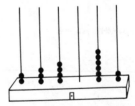

FIGURE 13-5
The number 234.062 represented on an open-end abacus

Pocket-chart and abacus work should be followed by an activity that helps children summarize ideas about place value. Emphasize that it is the ones place, not the decimal point, that is the point of symmetry for place value in the Hindu–Arabic numeration system. Also, each place-value position has a value that is ten times that of the position to its right and one-tenth that of the position to its left, regardless of where it is in relation to the ones place. A chart like the one shown in Figure 13-6 clearly shows that the ones place is central to the system; it stands alone. Other

FIGURE 13-6
Place-value positions of a number indicated on a chart

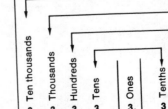

positions such as tens and tenths are positioned to the left and right, respectively, an equal number of places from the ones place.

As children work with whole numbers, they learn to use expanded notation to interpret the meaning of different numbers. First they learn that a whole number such as 6382 can be expressed as $6000 + 300 + 80 + 2$. By the end of elementary school they should refine the interpretations to include these:

$$(6 \times 1000) + (3 \times 100) + (8 \times 10) + 2.$$
$$(6 \times 10 \times 10 \times 10) + (3 \times 10 \times 10) + (8 \times 10) + 2.$$
$$(6 \times 10^3) + (3 \times 10^2) + (8 \times 10) + 2.$$

They should also learn to use expanded notation with decimal fractions.

Initial exercises such as the following should involve filling in the blanks:

$2.36\ =$ ____ ones ____ tenths ____ hundredths.
$0.46\ =$ ____ ones ____ tenths ____ hundredths.
$2.482 =$ ____ ones ____ tenths ____ hundredths ____ thousandths.

Later exercises should stress more abstract symbolism:

$4.68\ = 4 + ($ ____ $\times 0.1) + ($ ____ $\times 0.01).$
$2.43\ = 2 + (4 \times$ ____ $) + (3 \times$ ____ $).$
$2.006 = 2 + ($ ____ $\times 0.1) + ($ ____ $\times 0.01) + ($ ____ $\times 0.001).$

Finally, by the end of grade 6, some children will be ready to use exponential notation to represent decimal fractions:

$$343.68 = (3 \times 10^2) + (4 \times 10) + 3 + (6 \times {}^1/_{10}) + (8 \times {}^1/_{10_2})$$
$$241.32 = (2 \times 10^2) + (4 \times 10) + 1 + (3 \times {}^1/_{10}) + (2 \times {}^1/_{10_2})$$

The following form may be used by children who have a mature enough understanding of negative numbers to make the use of exponents in this notation clear:

$$343.68 = (3 \times 10^2) + (4 \times 10^1) + (3 \times 10^0) + (6 \times 10^{-1}) + (8 \times 10^{-2})$$

Use a place-value pocket chart or an abacus to show how each of these numbers can be represented: 23.4, 36.50, 42.031, and 40.36.

Write two different expanded numerals for each of these decimals: 246.48, 304.06, and 0.342.

Self-check
of Objectives 2 and 3

ADDING AND SUBTRACTING WITH DECIMAL FRACTIONS

Children who have developed a good understanding of fractional numbers and their decimal-fraction representations will have little difficulty adding and subtracting them. Fractional numbers expressed with decimals are added and subtracted just like whole numbers expressed with Hindu–Arabic numerals. Begin addition and subtraction activities with word problems to help children relate decimal fractions to realistic situations.

ACTIVITY 13-4 Odometer

- "Judy uses her bicycle for errands. She keeps track of distance with a metric odometer (which measures kilometers) attached to her bicycle. One day she recorded these distances: 0.7, 0.3, and 0.8. How many kilometers did she ride that day?"
- Have children write a mathematical sentence for this situation:

$$0.7 + 0.3 + 0.8 = \square$$

- If necessary have children use materials to represent the decimal fractions. A number line is illustrated here.

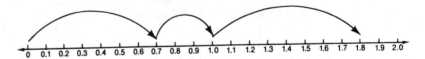

$$
\begin{array}{r}
0.7 \\
0.3 \\
+0.8 \\
\end{array}
$$

$$
\begin{array}{r}
0.7 \\
0.3 \\
+0.8 \\
\hline
1.8 \\
\end{array}
$$

- Write an algorithm, as in the margin.
- Add the numbers shown in the algorithm.
- Repeat with similar problem situations.

Addition with hundredths can be illustrated in similar ways. In Figure 13-7 the addition sentence $0.26 + 0.49 = \square$ is represented with parts of

FIGURE 13-7
The addition sentence $0.26 + 0.49 = 0.75$, illustrated with parts of a unit region

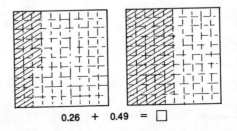

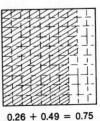

0.26 + 0.49 = $\square$ 0.26 + 0.49 = 0.75

a unit region. First, twenty-six of the 100 congruent parts are shaded to represent the first addend; then forty-nine parts of another square are shaded to represent the second addend. When the two sets of shaded parts are considered together, they indicate the sum, 0.75.

Addition with decimal fractions can be represented with place-value pocket charts and an abacus, also. These devices are used with decimal fractions in the same way as with whole numbers. Procedures with whole numbers are described in Chapter 10.

2. Subtracting with Decimal Fractions

Two subtraction algorithms for whole numbers are discussed in Chapter 10. Either of the processes can be used with decimal numbers. Whichever algorithm your children have mastered is the one they should use now. It is still important to use problem situations so children will learn about real-world applications of the new subtraction.

ACTIVITY 13-5 Subtracting Decimal Fractions

- "A piece of jewelry wire is 63.24 centimeters long. A piece that is 12.69 centimeters long is cut from it. How long is the remaining piece?"
- Have the children give the subtraction sentence for this situation:

$$63.24 - 12.69 = \square$$

- Write an algorithm:

$$
\begin{array}{r}
63.24 \\
-12.69 \\
\hline
\end{array}
$$

- Discuss the fact that it is not possible to do decomposition subtraction without regrouping in the ones and tens places.
- Complete the algorithm:

$$
\begin{array}{r}
{\scriptstyle 2\ 11\ 1} \\
6\cancel{3}.\cancel{2}4 \\
-12.69 \\
\hline
\end{array}
$$

- Repeat with similar problems.

***Self-check of
Objective 4***

Describe real-life problem situations for each of these sentences: $0.4 + 0.5 + 0.7 = 1.6$ and $1.4 - 0.8 = 0.6$. Demonstrate with suitable learning aids how children can learn the meaning of the algorithms for these two sentences. (Use illustrations if the learning aids are unavailable.)

MULTIPLYING WITH DECIMAL FRACTIONS

Because fractional numbers expressed as decimal fractions are multiplied using the same algorithm form as whole numbers, you should guard against having this process become mechanical for your children. Introductory work with such multiplication should be presented within a familiar context relevant to other aspects of the children's lives.

1. Multiplication Situations

There are three possible combinations of factors in which decimal fractions are multiplied: a fractional number is multiplied by a whole number, a fractional number is multiplied by a fractional number, and a whole number is multiplied by a fractional number. Each of these situations is illustrated in one of the activities that follow.

ACTIVITY 13-6 Multiplying Decimal Fraction by Whole Number

- "Jack is repairing his railroad track layout. He has found that he will need six pieces of wire, each 0.6 of a meter long. How much wire will he need altogether?"
- Point out that this is a repeated-addition situation; the multiplication sentence is:

$$6 \times 0.6 = \square$$

- Use a number line to illustrate this multiplication:

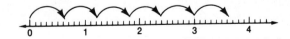

- Discuss the meaning of the answer: 3.6 meters.
- Repeat with similar situations.

ACTIVITY 13-7 Multiplying a Decimal Fraction by a Decimal Fraction

- "A sheet of art foil is 10 centimeters square. Sarah has 0.7 of a full sheet. If she uses 0.3 of this piece for an art project, what part of the entire sheet will she use?"
- Use a square to represent this situation. First show the 0.7.

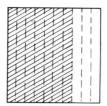

- Separate each of the tenths into ten congruent parts, and shade the top three tenths to show that 0.3 are used.

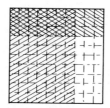

- The answer is represented by the 21 parts that are shaded twice. Each of the 21 parts represents one of the 100 parts into which the entire unit has been separated; so the product is 0.21.
- Repeat with similar problem situations.

ACTIVITY 13-8 Multiplying Whole Number by Decimal Fraction

- "A piece of ribbon that is 4 meters long is cut so that 0.2 of it is removed. What is 0.2 of 4 meters?"
- Write the multiplication sentence:

$$0.2 \times 4 = \square$$

- Illustrate with a piece of adding-machine tape.
- Mark the tape to show ten congruent pieces; each piece is 0.1 of the tape.
- Shade two of the pieces.

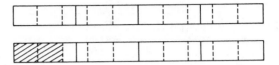

- Measure the two shaded parts to show that 0.8 is removed.
- Repeat with similar problem situations.

2. Placement of the Decimal Point in a Product

After visualizing the meaning of multiplication of decimals with the help of learning aids, children should learn where to place the decimal point in a product. Eventually they should be guided to generalize that the number of **decimal places** in a product equals the sum of decimal places to the right of the ones place in the factors.

Estimation is a useful way to learn how to put decimal points in a product. In the sentence $0.9 \times 2.1 = \square$ the product will be about 2, because 0.9 is almost 1, and the 2.1 is only slightly larger than 2. After the multiplication has been completed, children can use the estimated answer to determine that the 1 in the product will be in the ones place; so the answer is 1.89. The sentence $11.2 \times 23.4 = \square$ can be estimated by thinking: 10 times 25 equals 250; so 11.2 times 23.4 will be about 250. The product of the sentence should then be determined to be 262.08.

After children understand how to determine the placement of the decimal point, give them practice with exercises similar to the following. Have them underline the numeral that names the correct product for each pair of factors.

$2.4 \times 6.8 =$	16.32	1.632	163.2	1632
$10.6 \times 3.68 =$	3900.8	390.08	39.008	3.9008
$9 \times 2.98 =$	2682	268.2	2.682	26.82

After children have completed exercises such as these, ask questions to help them discover the generalization about determining the number of decimal places in a product. "How many decimal places are there following the one in the first factor of this sentence?" "How many are there in the second factor?" "What is the sum of the number of places to the right of the ones in both factors?" "How many decimal places are there to the right of the ones place in the product?" "Look at the next sentence. What do you notice about the number of decimal places to the right of the ones place in both of its factors and in its product?" "Now look at the remainder of the sentences. What do you notice about them?" "Can anyone tell how to determine where to put the decimal point in a product when the factors are decimal fractions?"

Describe a real-life problem situation for each of these sentences: $4 \times 0.3 = 1.2$, $0.5 \times 10 = 5$, and $0.2 \times 0.4 = 0.08$. Demonstrate with suitable learning aids ways children can learn the meanings of these sentences. (Use illustrations if the learning aids are unavailable.)

Self-check of Objectives 5 and 6

Explain how the two procedures described in the preceding paragraphs can be used to determine the number of decimal places to the right of the ones place in the product of each of these multiplication examples: $0.8 \times 0.9 = \square$, $3.1 \times 15.14 = \square$, and $11 \times 4.92 = \square$.

DIVIDING WITH DECIMAL FRACTIONS

Division involving decimal fractions determines either the size of each group when a set is divided into a given number of groups or the number of groups when a set is subdivided into groups of a given size, just as it does in division of whole numbers. The first of these is a partitive situation; the second is a measurement situation. The algorithm forms used for division of whole numbers are also used for division of fractional numbers expressed as decimal fractions. The concepts and algorithms are the same for division of both kinds of numbers. The new element is the treatment of the decimal point in the quotient. A logical explanation, not a memorized rule, is needed to help children learn to place it properly.

1. Division Situations

This activity introduces a partitive situation.

ACTIVITY 13-9   Partitive Division

- "A rope is 16.4 meters long. If Jane cuts it into four pieces of equal length, how long will each piece be?"
- Adding-machine tape is a good model to use. Cut a piece that is 16.4 meters long. Discuss the problem to determine what is to be done, and write a division sentence and an algorithm:

$$16.4 \div 4 = \square \qquad 4\overline{)16.4}$$

- "Will each piece be at least one meter long? (Yes.) "Two meters long?" (Yes.) "Three meters long?" (Yes.) "Four meters long?" (Yes.) "Five meters long?" (No.)

- Show the division of 16 by 4 in the algorithm:

$$
\begin{array}{r}
4 \\
4\overline{)16.4} \\
16.0 \\
\hline
4
\end{array}
$$

- "After we have divided 16 by 4, what is left to be divided?" (0.4.)
- Show this division in the algorithm:

$$
\begin{array}{r}
4.1 \\
4\overline{)16.4} \\
16.0 \\
\hline
4 \\
4 \\
\hline
0
\end{array}
$$

- Fold the adding-machine tape into four congruent parts. Measure one part to show that it is 4.1 meters long.
- Repeat with other partitive situations.

Children should also have experiences with measurement situations.

ACTIVITY 13-10   Measurement Division

- "A relay team is to run a 27.5-kilometer cross-country race. Each member of the team will run 5.5 kilometers. How many team members are there?"
- A number line is useful to illustrate this situation. Begin at 27.5 and make jumps toward zero; each jump is 5.5 units long.

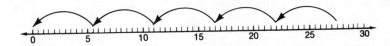

- The answer is represented by the five jumps.
- Point out that repeated subtraction can be used to determine the answer:

$$
\begin{array}{ccccc}
27.5 & 22.0 & 16.5 & 11.0 & 5.5 \\
-\ 5.5 & -\ 5.5 & -\ 5.5 & -\ 5.5 & -5.5 \\
\hline
22.0 & 16.5 & 11.0 & 5.5 & 0
\end{array}
$$

- Complete the algorithm:

$$\begin{array}{r} 5 \\ 5.5\overline{)27.5} \\ \underline{27.5} \\ 0 \end{array}$$

- Repeat with other measurement situations.

---

2. Placement of Decimal Point in Quotient

Understanding the following ideas helps children learn how to place the decimal point in quotients.

- Estimation is a way to determine the number of decimal places in a quotient. To divide a pair of numbers, as in the sentence $2.36 \div 0.9 = \square$, children should think "2.36 is a little larger than 2, and 0.9 is a little smaller than 1. Since $2 \div 1 = 2$, 2.36 divided by 0.9 will be about 2." When the quotient is determined, children should place the decimal point so that 2 is in the ones place. An exercise such as the following provides practice in estimating. Each sentence becomes a true statement only when the decimal point is correctly placed.

$$\begin{array}{l} 69.3 \div 3 \;\; = 231 \\ 811.8 \div 22 = 369 \\ 20.74 \div 3.4 = 61 \end{array}$$

- Children who know that common fractions can be used to express division can rewrite a decimal fraction, such as $0.3\overline{)6.3}$, as a common fraction: $^{6.3}/_{0.3}$. When both numerator and denominator are multiplied by 10, it becomes $^{63}/_3$. This can then be rewritten in algorithm form $3\overline{)63}$ so the division can be completed. This is the mathematical justification for the caret method of placing the decimal point in a quotient. If both divisor and dividend are multiplied by 10 or a power of 10 so that the divisor is changed to a whole number, the decimal point in the quotient can be placed immediately above the decimal point in the changed dividend. This is illustrated in the margin; a caret ($\wedge$) indicates the new position of the decimal point in the divisor and dividend. Children should use this procedure after its rationale has been made clear to them.

$$\begin{array}{r} 4.98 \\ 6.3_\wedge\overline{)31.3_\wedge 74} \\ \underline{252} \\ 617 \\ \underline{567} \\ 504 \\ \underline{504} \end{array}$$

Eventually children should be guided to make this generalization: The number of **decimal places** to the right of the ones place in a quotient is the difference between the number of places to the right of the ones place in the dividend and the number there are in the divisor. Once they have stated this generalization, have children compare it with the generalization about how to determine the number of decimal places in a product. They should observe that the operations indicated by the two generalizations are the inverse of each other.

**Self-check
of Objectives 7 and 8**

Make up a story problem for partitive division involving this sentence: $1.2 \div 4 = 0.3$. Use an appropriate learning aid to illustrate the sentence's meaning. Describe a measurement situation for this sentence: $4 \div 0.5 = 8$. Use an appropriate learning aid to illustrate this sentence's meaning.

Explain how the two procedures described in the preceding paragraphs can be used to determine where to put the decimal point in the quotients for these division examples: $15.6 \div 3 = \square$, $0.45 \div 0.09 = \square$, and $64.8 \div 0.8 = \square$.

PERCENT

In a sense, activities with percent in the sixth grade are a capstone for the work with comparisons that began in the first year of school. A part of children's first activities in mathematics is concerned with comparing sets to determine which one is larger or smaller or whether they are equivalent, and with comparing the length of two objects to find out which is longer or shorter or whether they are the same length. Later, children count discrete objects, measure continuous objects, and use subtraction to compare the sizes of sets or measures of objects. As their knowledge of mathematics increases, they use common and decimal fractions for making comparisons. Work with percent gives children yet another way of dealing with comparisons.

1. Meaning of Percent

When percent is used, the comparison is expressed as a ratio between some number and 100. For example, when 15 is used as a percent, it is an expression of the ratio between the numbers 15 and 100; it is symbolized as 15%. The symbol % expresses a denominator of 100; the word **percent** names the symbol and means *per hundred*, or *out of 100*.

In practice percent is used in various ways, and its applications in business, government, science, industry, and other aspects of our lives are numerous. For example, a store reports that 16% of its sales are made in its garden department. This indicates that for every 100 dollars of sales, 16 are in the garden department. The complete report will contain information that tells the portion of sales made in the store's other departments, with the total amount of sales equaling 100%.

Some states use a sales tax as a means of raising revenue for part of their annual budget. A tax of 5% means that for every 100 cents (1 dollar) of the purchase price of an article, a tax of 5 cents (0.05 of a dollar) must be collected. This situation provides the setting for a discussion of terms used in connection with percent and consideration of a point of confusion that often arises during the study of percent.

For a number of years the state of California used a 5% sales tax as a means of collecting a part of the money needed for its budget. When a $10.00 sale was made, 50¢ was collected for the sales tax. Three words are used to describe the different numerals in this situation. The 5% is the **rate**, $10.00 is the **base**, and 50¢ is the **percentage**.

When children encounter a statement such as the following, which might appear in a social studies textbook, they need to know how to interpret it so it will have meaning: "The imports of grain are 36% of the country's imports. The total value of all imports for one year was $236,000,000." In this statement, 36% is the rate and $236,000,000 is the base. Children must analyze the statement by thinking somewhat as follows: "I know that 36% represents a rate of $36 out of every $100. This means that about ⅓ of all the money value of the imports is for grain. One-third of $236,000,000 is about $80,000,000. The country imports about $80,000,000 worth of grain." Thus $80,000,000 is the estimated percentage of grain among all imports.

Percent and *percentage* are often confused, and many children (and adults, as well) are uncertain about the distinction between them. Because confusion is likely, you must make it clear that percent indicates the *rate* (of sales in a store's department, or of sales tax), whereas percentage indicates the *quantity*, or *amount* (of sales or of tax). Thus a base and a percentage always represent numbers that refer to the same thing, for example, numbers of dollars of sales made or the weights of different ingredients in a mixture; and percent is the rate by which the percentage compares with the base. The potential for confusion is great enough to justify delayed use of the word *percentage* during elementary school, leaving it for teachers in higher grades to introduce. Its omission will not interfere with children's understanding of the basic ideas involved.

The California state sales tax provides the basis for discussion of another potential point of confusion. On the first of July, 1973, the sales tax rate was changed from 5% to 6%. This was a very unpopular change, because at the time the state's treasury had a budget surplus of nearly 600 million dollars. Later the legislature passed and the governor signed into law a bill that rescinded the increase for 6 months beginning October 1, 1973. Was the *rate* (percent) of decrease the same as the rate of increase? In both cases the *amount* was the same. The increase was 1¢ for every dollar spent, and the decrease was also 1¢ for every dollar spent. However, the rate of decrease was not the same as the rate of increase.

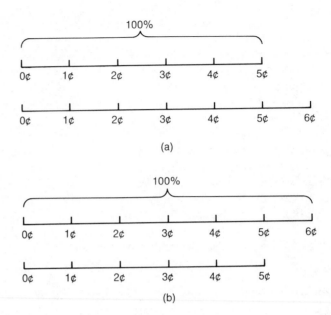

FIGURE 13-8
Number lines showing: (a)
When a sales tax is increased
from 5¢ to 6¢, the rate of increase is 20 percent. (b)
When the tax is decreased
from 6¢ to 5¢, the rate of decrease is 16⅔ percent.

The number-line graphs in Figure 13-8 show why the rates in this in-crease–decrease situation are different, even though the amounts are the same. In (a) the original sales tax, which was 5¢ for every dollar spent (5%), is represented by the first line and is shown as 100%, because 5¢ was the whole amount of tax for each dollar before the increase. The second line in (a) shows the sales tax after it was changed to 6%. The amount of increase in the length of this line is the same as the length of one of the five parts of the original line. One of five is 20% of the whole; so the rate of increase was 20%.

In (b) the new sales tax is represented by the top line. It now repre-sents 100%, because the rate was 6¢ for every dollar spent. The amount of decrease in the length of the second line is the same as the length of one of the six parts of the top line. One of six is 16⅔% of the whole; so the rate of decrease was 16⅔%.

**Self-check
of Objectives
9 and 10**

Give a definition of the meaning of percent. Describe a real-life situation that involves it.

Describe a real-life situation in which percent (rate), percentage, and base are used. Identify each term in your example.

2. Introducing Percent

Before children begin work with percent, they must have a clear understanding of fractional numbers and decimal-fraction representations of them because of the relationship between decimal hundredths and percent. There are many elementary-school children who fail to understand their work with percent, because they lack the necessary background. Do not start activities with youngsters whose backgrounds are inadequate, even if it means delaying their work until after their elementary-school years.

You can introduce percent to children who are ready through activities with learning aids used for other topics. The key point to make during early work is that *percent* means *per 100*, or *out of 100;* so it is necessary to use materials that show a unit, or whole, that can be readily subdivided into 100 parts or easily compared with that many parts. Especially helpful are magnetic materials, such as sets of poker chips with magnets attached, a hundreds board (such as the one in Activity 8-4), structured materials, and square-paper decimal fraction kits.

In most instances you will introduce percent to the mathematically mature children in your class who are ready for it and not to the entire class. Therefore problem cards are a useful means of guiding these children's work.

ACTIVITY 13-11   Introducing Percent

- Give each individual a flat, five orange rods, and 100 white cubes from a Cuisenaire set. Children work alone or in small groups to complete the work on a set of problem cards; answers are recorded on a response sheet.

When children have completed activities such as the ones on the problem cards, discuss the meaning of the word *percent* and the % symbol. Follow-up activities, such as naming the percent of blue, red, and white chips in sets of 100 poker chips, are useful. (After children have used poker chips for three or four examples, you can give them pictured sets for practice.) Other activities include naming the percents of numbers blocked off on a hundreds board and naming the percents of shaded or colored squares in 10-by-10 arrays. A variation of these activities that children enjoy is one in which they make colored designs in 100-square sections of squared paper. Children can mark off their own blocks of 100 squares. The blocks do not need to be 10-by-10 arrays but can be any arrangement that contains 100 squares. Have each child leave enough space between blocks to write the percents for the different colors used in each of the designs.

PERCENT   (1)

Use your flat, orange rods, and white cubes to do these activities:

1. Lay your flat on your desk. Put 5 orange rods side by side on top of it. Write a statement on your response sheet using a common fraction to tell how much of the flat is covered by the 5 rods. Write a decimal fraction that tells how much of the flat is covered by the rods.

2. Cover the rest of the flat with white cubes. Count the white cubes, and then write a statement on your response sheet telling how many there are. Write another statement using a common fraction to tell what part of your flat is covered by the white cubes. Write a decimal fraction that tells how much of the flat is covered by white cubes.

3. Cover your flat completely with white cubes. Write a statement that tells how many white cubes cover one flat.

4. Some sets of white cubes are listed below. Use one set at a time, and put the cubes on your flat; then use both a common and a decimal fraction to tell the part of the flat that is covered by each set. The picture on the next card shows how to do the first one.
   a. 6 cubes   e. 63 cubes
   b. 15 cubes   f. 94 cubes
   c. 23 cubes   g. 36 cubes
   d. 45 cubes   h. 1 cube

(2)

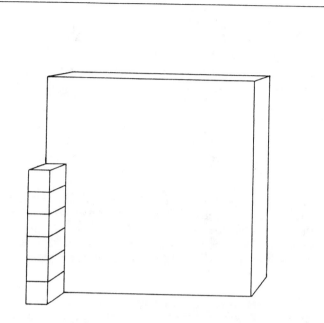

Six cubes cover 6/100, or 0.06, of the flat.

5. So far you have used common and decimal fractions
   to tell what part of the flat is covered by rods
   and cubes. There is another way you can write your
   answers. You will learn about <u>percent</u> so you can
   use this new way.

   In problem 1 you put 5 orange rods on the flat.
   Your statement with a common fraction could have
   used either 1/2 or 5/10 to tell how much of the
   flat was covered by orange rods. Your decimal
   answer could have been either 0.5 or 0.50.

(3)

In problem 2 you put 50 white cubes on the rest of the flat. Your statement with common fractions is correct if you used 1/2, 5/10, or 50/100 in it. Your decimal fraction can be either 0.5 or 0.50.

Another way to tell how many orange rods or white cubes cover half of the flat is with <u>percent</u>. Write <u>50 percent</u> on your response sheet in the space you left blank earlier.

6. In problem 3 you used 100 white cubes to cover the flat. These cubes cover <u>100 percent</u> of the flat. One hundred percent means that all of the flat was covered by white cubes. What do you think 50 percent means? Write your answer on your response sheet.

7. In problem 4 you used eight different sets of cubes and wrote common and decimal fractions to tell what part of the flat was covered by each set. The answer for the set of 6 cubes was written as 6/100 and 0.06. Another way to answer is to say that the cubes cover <u>6 percent</u> of the flat.

Use the rest of the spaces in problem 4 to tell what percent of the flat is covered by each of the sets of cubes.

PERCENT RESPONSE SHEET

Name _____

1. _____
   _____
   _____
   _____ Decimal fraction _____

2. _____
   _____
   _____
   _____ Decimal fraction _____
   _____ (Leave this line blank for now.)

3. _____
   _____

4. a. ___ ___   e. ___ ___
   b. ___ ___   f. ___ ___
   c. ___ ___   g. ___ ___
   d. ___ ___   h. ___ ___

   (Leave these lines blank for now.)

   ___ ___   ___ ___
   ___ ___   ___ ___
   ___ ___   ___ ___
   ___ ___   ___ ___

   _____
   _____
   _____

Describe at least two learning aids children can use to learn the meaning of percent. Explain why problem-card activities are well suited for children who are learning about percent.

3. Extending Understanding of Percent

The problem cards in Activity 13-11 contain activities that acquaint children with the idea that percent is an extension of the common and decimal-fraction forms of representing comparisons. Subsequent work with poker chips, hundreds boards, and other manipulative and pictorial materials should continue to emphasize the relationships among common and decimal fractions and percents. Once the relationships are clear, children are ready to move to more abstract levels of work. They can begin to name the equivalents for different fractions that are given in one or another of the three numerals. An activity sheet that contains several sections can be prepared. Each section has expressions of one type, which are to be changed to another form (Figure 13-9).

FIGURE 13-9

Sample activity sheet for renaming common and decimal fractions and percents

1. Rename each decimal fraction as a percent:
   a. 0.50 = ___   c. 0.14 = ___   e. 0.79 = ___
   b. 0.03 = ___   d. 0.19 = ___   f. 0.83 = ___

2. Rename each common fraction as a decimal:
   a. 1/4 = ___   c. 1/2 = ___   e. 2/10 = ___
   b. 3/4 = ___   d. 1/10 = ___   f. 9/10 = ___

3. Rename each common fraction as a percent:
   a. 1/4 = ___   c. 1/2 = ___   e. 2/10 = ___
   b. 3/4 = ___   d. 1/10 = ___   f. 9/10 = ___

4. Rename each percent as a decimal fraction:
   a. 13% = ___   c. 69% = ___   e. 4% = ___
   b. 45% = ___   d. 21% = ___   f. 1% = ___

Not all percents arise from situations in which 100 is conveniently present as the quantity against which another number is compared, as in the introductory situations given above. Therefore, once the basic concept is well established, children's work should focus on activities that deal with groups other than 100. For example, if you begin with a set of ten chips, four of which are blue and six white, what percent of the entire set is the group of blue chips?

ACTIVITY 13-12   Percent

- Begin by showing ten magnetic chips, four blue and six white, on a magnetic board.

- Note that there are a total of ten chips, "What part of the set is blue?"($^4/_{10}$ or 0.4.) "Can anyone tell what percent of the chips is blue?" (40%.) If a child gives the answer, ask for an explanation of how it was determined. If no answer is given, ask, "What must we do to change $^4/_{10}$ to a fraction with a denominator of 100?" (Multiply both numerator and denominator by 10.) "When we do this, what fraction is equivalent to $^4/_{10}$?" ($^{40}/_{100}$.) "$^{40}/_{100}$ is what percent?" (40.)
- Show a set that has 8 blue chips out of 20. "Are the blue chips in this set 40% of the set?" (Yes.) Discuss what is done to confirm the answer. (Multiply both numerator and denominator by 5.)

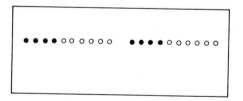

- Repeat with other sets that have the same ratio of blue chips to total chips.
- Complete a table with other fractions that are equivalent to $^4/_{10}$ to show that in each case the blue chips are 40% of all of the chips.

4	8	12	16	20	24	28	32	36	40
10	20	30	40	50	60	70	80	90	100

- Repeat with other sets wherein the total number of chips is a divisor of 100 to make the renaming of fractions with denominators of 100 easy.

Use whatever additional activities are necessary to make certain that children can find what percent one number is of another in situations in which the comparison is made with both 100 and numbers other than 100. When numbers other than 100 are used, they should be those for which the equivalent ratio containing 100 can be easily determined. A ratio of 4 out of 10 is suitable, but a ratio of 7 out of 13 is not. In the elementary school, percents less than 1 and greater than 100 are seldom used.

Self-check of Objective 12

Rename each of these common and decimal fractions as a percent: $^{31}/_{100}$, $^{3}/_{100}$, $^{6}/_{50}$, $^{2}/_{6}$, 0.51, and 0.05. Rename each of these percents as both a common and a decimal fraction: 75%, 83%, 90%, and 6%.

4. Working Percent Problems

Children who successfully complete the activities already discussed are ready for percent problems. There are three methods of solving percent problems: the proportion method, the case method, and the unitary analysis method. The proportion method is used most widely in elementary-school programs and is the only one included in this book.

The proportion method has gained favor in recent years because it is easier for most children to learn and use. It is based on the idea that a single expression can be used to show each of the three types of percent problems. Children must understand the meanings of percent (rate), percentage, and base and how to express these as a proportion. The proportion expression is

$$\frac{\text{rate}}{100} = \frac{\text{percentage}}{\text{base}}$$

Children will have encountered other proportion expressions if they have completed activities such as those described in Chapter 12, where tables are developed and markers used to illustrate proportion situations. A parking lot that contains fifty cars, with eighteen of the cars foreign-made, will serve as a setting for considering the proportion method of solving percent problems. The eighteen foreign cars are 36 percent of the total number of cars.

When the percent and total number of cars are known, we can determine the percentage by putting the two known terms in the proportion expression and solving for the percentage.

$$\frac{36}{100} = \frac{\text{percentage}}{50}$$

When the number of foreign-made cars and the total number of cars are known, fill in the expression with the two known terms and solve for the unknown term:

$$\frac{\text{percent}}{100} = \frac{18}{50}$$

In the third situation the percent and percentage are known, and the base is to be determined; so the expression becomes

$$\frac{36}{100} = \frac{18}{\text{base}}$$

In the examples used here the solution is not difficult. For $^{36}/_{100} = n/50$, children will know that 100 is divided by 2 to give 50; so they know that 36 divided by 2 will give the answer, 18. For $n/100 = {}^{18}/_{50}$, they will know that 2 times 50 is 100; so the answer can be found by multiplying 2 times 18. And for $^{36}/_{100} = 18/n$, 36 is divided by 2 to give 18; so 100 is divided by 2 to give 50.

Not all proportion problems can be solved as easily as these. Therefore children should become familiar with the procedures explained in Chapter 12, so they can use the more mature methods to solve all types of percent problems, as well as the simple ones used here.

Show how the proportion method is used to solve each of these percent problems: 25% of 160 = □, □ of 160 = 40, and 25% of □ = 40.

Self-check of Objective 13

THE CALCULATOR, DECIMALS, AND PERCENT

The calculator offers many oppportunities for children to extend their understanding of decimal fractions and to solve problems involving percent. The examples that follow are samples of the type of work children can do with their machines in these areas of study.

1. Reading Words for Decimal Fractions

Children can check skill in translating decimals expressed in words with activities such as this one:

Enter each of the following decimals in your calculator. Press the ⊞ key after each entry. Your work is correct if the display matches the numeral at the bottom of each list of words.

two and five tenths	sixty-one and forty hundredths
four and three tenths	seventy-five and sixty-seven hundredths
six and nine tenths	four and twenty-one hundredths
five and seven tenths	ninety-six and nine hundredths
19.4	237.37

2. Placing Decimal Points

Estimate where to put the decimal point in each product or quotient. Check your answers by computing each example on your calculator.

$$\begin{array}{cccc} 21.3 & 0.78 & 0.789 & 3.621 \\ \times 4.8 & \times 4.3 & \times 26.3 & \times 0.4 \\ \hline 10224 & 3354 & 207507 & 14484 \end{array}$$

$$\begin{array}{cccc} 263 & 654 & 0051 & 632 \\ 0.3)\overline{7.89} & 3.6)\overline{235.44} & 9)\overline{0.459} & 0.27)\overline{170.64} \end{array}$$

3. Checking Products

Below are 22 multiplication combinations. Put a check mark in front of each combination you think has a product of 3.6. Check your work by computing each one on your calculator.

3.6×1	0.4×9
0.12×30	1.8×2
1.0×36	0.04×0.9
9×0.04	0.3×12
120×0.03	6×0.6
18×0.02	40×0.09
3×1.2	60×0.6
2×1.8	0.05×720
4×0.9	18×0.2
0.6×0.6	36×0.1
72×0.5	360×0.01

4. Batting Averages

A baseball player's seasonal batting average is determined by dividing the number of hits made by the number of times the player was officially at bat during the season. The division is carried to three decimal places. Which of these ball players had a batting average of more than .300?

Player	Hits	At Bat	Average
Oliver	199	594	
Madlock	180	565	
L. Smith	178	578	
Knight	177	591	
Kennedy	161	538	
Baker	163	545	

Describe four calculator activities that deal with decimals.

**Self-check
of Objective 14**

SPECIAL STUDENTS AND DECIMAL FRACTIONS AND PERCENT

1. Learning-Handicapped Children

Children with learning handicaps often encounter difficulties with decimal fractions and percent. They sometimes lack a firm understanding of whole numbers upon which to anchor their work with the new concepts. In addition, decimal and percent concepts are more complex than whole-number concepts. Nancy Bley and Carol Thornton believe that decimal fractions should be related to common fractions when they are introduced rather than developed through an approach that presents them as an extension of whole numbers.[1] They recommend materials and procedures similar to the ones discussed in this chapter, with a heavy emphasis on concrete materials, both real and pictured. They also suggest using dimes and pennies after the children thoroughly understand place value for decimals to hundredths and writing decimal numerals.[2]

2. Gifted and Talented Students

Gifted and talented students will benefit from activities that extend their understanding of decimal fractions and percent. The first activity introduces them to repeating and terminating decimals, and the second one gives a process for renaming decimal fractions as common fractions.

[1] Nancy S. Bley and Carol A. Thornton, *Teaching Mathematics to the Learning Disabled* (Rockville, Md.: Aspen Systems Corporation, 1981), p. 267.
[2] Bley and Thornton, p. 271.

a. Repeating and Terminating Decimals

ACTIVITY 13-13 Repeating and Terminating Decimals

- Give children a worksheet containing two columns of common fractions:

<table>
<tr><td>¹/₂</td><td>¹/₃</td></tr>
<tr><td>¹/₄</td><td>²/₃</td></tr>
<tr><td>³/₄</td><td>¹/₆</td></tr>
<tr><td>¹/₅</td><td>⁵/₆</td></tr>
<tr><td>²/₅</td><td>¹/₇</td></tr>
<tr><td>³/₅</td><td>²/₇</td></tr>
</table>

- Instruct the children to rename each common fraction as a decimal fraction.
- Have the children compare the answers in the first column with those in the second column. Help them to observe that in the first column division of the numerator by the denominator results in a **terminating decimal;** division is complete when either a 0 or 5 appears in the quotient. The common fractions in the second column result in **repeating decimals;** there is always a remainder, no matter the number of decimal places to which the division is extended.
- Show a chart displaying terminating and repeating decimals.

Terminating decimals	Repeating decimals
$\frac{1}{2}$ = 0.5	$\frac{1}{3}$ = 0.333...
$\frac{1}{4}$ = 0.25	$\frac{2}{3}$ = 0.666...
$\frac{3}{4}$ = 0.75	$\frac{1}{6}$ = 0.1666...
$\frac{1}{5}$ = 0.2	$\frac{5}{6}$ = 0.8333...
$\frac{2}{5}$ = 0.4	$\frac{1}{7}$ = 0.142857142857...
$\frac{3}{5}$ = 0.6	$\frac{2}{7}$ = 0.285714285714...
$\frac{4}{5}$ = 0.8	$\frac{3}{7}$ = 0.428571428571...
$\frac{1}{8}$ = 0.125	$\frac{4}{7}$ = 0.571428571428...
$\frac{3}{8}$ = 0.375	$\frac{5}{7}$ = 0.714285714285...
$\frac{5}{8}$ = 0.625	$\frac{6}{7}$ = 0.857142857142...
$\frac{7}{8}$ = 0.875	$\frac{1}{9}$ = 0.111...
$\frac{1}{10}$ = 0.1	$\frac{2}{9}$ = 0.222...
$\frac{3}{10}$ = 0.3	$\frac{3}{9}$ = 0.333...
$\frac{7}{10}$ = 0.7	$\frac{4}{9}$ = 0.444...
$\frac{9}{10}$ = 0.9	$\frac{5}{9}$ = 0.555...
$\frac{1}{20}$ = 0.05	$\frac{6}{9}$ = 0.666...

- Help the children find a rule for determining which common fractions result in terminating decimals and which result in repeating decimals. Ask questions like these:
  - ○ "If you write the prime factorization for the denominator of each fraction in the first column, what prime numbers do you get?" (They are always 2s or 5s, or combinations of 2s and 5s.)
  - ○ "What prime numbers do you get in the factorization of the numbers in the second column?" (They may contain 2s and 5s, but there is always at least one prime number other than 2 and/or 5.)

- Give the children common fractions that are not on the chart so they can determine which are terminating and which are repeating. Examples: $5/16$, $7/32$, $8/15$, $4/22$, $3/50$, $21/40$.

b. Renaming Decimal Fractions as Common Fractions   Mathematically mature children should also learn to rename decimal fractions as common fractions. Fractional numbers expressed as terminating decimal fractions can be readily renamed as common fractions: 0.5 is equivalent to $5/10$, which in simplest form is $\frac{1}{2}$; 0.75 as $75/100$, simplified to $\frac{3}{4}$; and 0.125 as $125/1000$, simplified to $\frac{1}{8}$.

A fractional number expressed by a repeating decimal cannot be renamed as a common fraction in such a direct manner. A different procedure must be used. Use n to represent the repeating fraction 0.121212 . . . in an equation: $n = 0.121212$. . . . Then multiply both terms of the equation by 100. One hundred is used in this case because the pattern of repetition is a block of two digits; if the pattern consists of one digit, multiply by 10; if the pattern consists of three digits, multiply by 1000; and so on. Subtract the first equation from the second, as shown in the margin. Finally divide both terms of the new equation by 99 to determine the value of n expressed as a common fraction. The common fraction $12/99$ is equivalent to the repeating decimal 0.121212. . . . When expressed in its simplest form, $12/99$ becomes $4/33$. Children should verify their work by expressing $4/33$ as a repeating decimal by dividing 4 by 33.

$$100\,n = 12.121212 \ldots$$
$$-\quad n = 0.121212 \ldots$$
$$\overline{99\,n = 12.000000 \ldots}$$

An ellipsis (. . .) is used in each repeating decimal on the chart in Figure 11-15. It is one of several ways to show repeating decimals and is convenient for decimals such as 0.333 . . . and 0.1666 . . . , where only one numeral is repeated. It is less convenient for a decimal such as 0.142857142857 . . . , because so many numerals are repeated. For decimals of this type a simpler, alternate procedure may be used. At least two are generally acceptable: $0.\dot{1}4285\dot{7}$ and $0.\overline{142857}$.

Rename each of these common fractions as a decimal fraction: $8/75$, $3/50$, $4/15$, and $27/200$. What distinguishes the denominators of common fractions that result in terminating decimals from those that result in repeating decimals?

Self-check of Objective 15

SUMMARY

The fractional number system includes all of the positive and negative integers and numbers between integers that can be expressed in the form a/b, where a is any integer and b is any integer other than 0. Fractional numbers can be expressed with common fractions, decimal fractions, and percent. Fractional numbers greater than 0 are included in the elementary curriculum. Ways to introduce decimal and percent representations are presented in this chapter, along with ways of teaching operations with decimal fractions.

Work with decimal fractions and percent extends the understanding of fractional numbers and ways to express them. Decimal fractions express numbers smaller than 1 that have a denominator of ten or a power of ten. The denominator is not written but is indicated by how many numerals there are to the right of the ones place in a decimal numeral. Structured materials, unit-region kits, and number lines are aids children use to learn the meaning of decimal fractions. Once the meaning of decimal fractions is understood and children can write decimal numerals accurately, they are ready to learn to add, subtract, multiply, and divide fractional numbers expressed as decimals. The algorithms for these operations are like those for whole numbers. Real-life situations and work with learning aids will help children extend their use of the algorithms to include decimals. Carefully developed procedures for determining where to put the decimal points in answers should be used rather than teacher-dictated rules.

Percent is used to express a ratio between some number and 100. Carefully sequenced activities will help mature elementary-school children understand its meaning. Special attention needs to be given to the meanings of percent (rate), base, and percentage. The proportion method of solving percent problems is described in this book. Instruction about it can be related to work with rate pairs and proportion completed during earlier problem-solving activities.

The calculator offers opportunities for children to extend their understanding of decimal fractions. Children can use it for computing problems and for playing games dealing with this way of expressing fractional numbers. Learning-handicapped children can learn about decimal fractions and percent when care is taken to relate the new work to common fractions through activities with familiar materials. Work with terminating and repeating decimals and a process for renaming decimal fractions as common fractions are suitable for extending gifted and talented students' understanding of decimal fractions.

STUDY QUESTIONS AND ACTIVITIES

1. Carpenter and his associates (see chapter's reading list) evaluated children's work on the decimal-fraction portion of the National Assessment of Educational Progress test and identified weaknesses. They indicated the implications of the test results for teachers. What do they say is needed to improve instruction about decimal fractions? Describe materials you believe should be available so children can overcome the weaknesses identified by these authors.

2. Estimation is recommended as one way to help children to place decimal points properly in products and quotients. Use estimation to place a decimal point in the answer for each of these examples:

(a)
$$\begin{array}{r} 4.8 \\ \times 2.3 \\ \hline 1104 \end{array}$$

(b)
$$\begin{array}{r} 36.2 \\ \times 1.08 \\ \hline 39096 \end{array}$$

(c)
$$\begin{array}{r} 48.36 \\ \times 51.28 \\ \hline 24799008 \end{array}$$

(d) $3.2\overline{)21.824}$ with answer 682

(e) $0.33\overline{)9.966}$ with answer 302

Why is the estimation process not useful for these examples?

(a)
$$\begin{array}{r} 0.341 \\ \times\ 0.682 \\ \hline 232562 \end{array}$$

(b) $0.036\overline{)0.0072}$ with answer 2

3. Fisher (see reading list) describes games for "Deci-Deck" cards. Make a set of cards and transcribe a set of directions for each game to add to your collection of teaching–learning aids.

KEY TERMS

decimal fractions
fractional numbers
decimal places
percent
rate

base
percentage
repeating decimals
terminating decimal

FOR FURTHER READING

Carpenter, Thomas P., et al. "Decimals: Results and Implications from National Assessment," *Arithmetic Teacher*, XXVIII, No. 8 (April 1981), pp.

34–37. The latest NAEP test indicates that children lack a clear understanding of decimal fractions. This and other weaknesses are reported, along
with implications of the test's results for classroom teachers.

Cole, Blaine L., and Henry S. Weissenfluh. "An Analysis of Teaching Percentage," *Arithmetic Teacher*, XXI, No. 3 (March 1974), pp. 226–228. Describes the relationship between the ratio method and the case method of
solving percent problems. Explains the ratio method and gives a brief outline of the background for understanding it.

Firl, Donald H. "Fractions, Decimals, and Their Futures," *Arithmetic Teacher*,
XXIV, No. 3 (March 1977), pp. 238–240. The author predicts an increasing emphasis on decimal fractions, because of the advent of the calculator
and greater use of the metric system. The role of common fractions will
diminish, but they cannot be eliminated entirely. Even after total metrication there will be a continuing need for certain common fractions.

Fisher, John W. "Deci-Deck," *Arithmetic Teacher*, XXII, No. 2 (February 1975),
p. 149. The deci-deck card game provides practice in naming equivalent
common fractions, decimal fractions, and percent. Several card games are
possible with the deck.

Lichtenberg, Betty K., and Donovan R. Lichtenberg. "Decimals Deserve Distinction," in *Mathematics for the Middle Grades (5–9)*, 1982 Yearbook of
the National Council of Teachers of Mathematics (Reston, Va.: The Council), pp. 142–152.
Materials and procedures for teaching decimal fractions to fifth-grade and
older children are illustrated and described. Processes for comparing and
rounding decimal fractions are included.

Schmalz, Rosemary, S. P. "A Visual Approach to Decimals," *Arithmetic Teacher*,
XXV, No. 8 (May 1978), pp. 22–25. Dienes multibase arithmetic blocks,
with a cardboard shape ten times the area of a flat, serve as a model for
decimal representation of fractional numbers. Procedures for their use are
described.

Vance, James H. "An Opinion Poll: A Percent Activity for All Students," in
Mathematics for the Middle Grades (5–9), 1982 Yearbook of the National
Council of Teachers of Mathematics (Reston, Va.: The Council), pp. 166–
171.
Children work in pairs to poll individuals on their preference for foods,
cars, sports, and so forth. They compile and organize their data, using
charts and graphs. Percents are used to compare preferences in each chart.

14

Measures and the Processes of Measuring

Upon completion of Chapter 14 you will be able to:

1. Explain the meaning of measurement.

2. Trace briefly the historical development of the metric system.

3. List the seven basic and two supplementary units of the International System of Units (SI).

4. Identify at least two characteristics of the metric system.

5. List at least four advantages of the metric system over the English (customary) system.

6. Identify the grade levels at which it is recommended that standard units for these measures be introduced: length, weight, capacity, volume, area, time, and temperature.

7. Identify and demonstrate activities for building a preoperational-level foundation for measurement.

8. Describe activities for introducing underlying concepts of measurement using non-standard units.

9. Define the meaning of linear measure, and demonstrate procedures children can use to understand it and to measure lengths directly and by estimation.

10. Identify the commonly used units of weight (mass) measure, and name two types of scales children should learn to use.

11. Define the meaning of area measure, and describe materials and activities for learning how to measure the area of squares, rectangles, parallelograms, and triangles.

12. Define the meaning of perimeter, and explain how to prevent confusion between perimeter and area.

13. Describe the meaning of volume measure, and demonstrate a procedure children can use to understand it and to determine how to find the volumes of space figures such as cubes and rectangular prisms.

14. Describe activities to help children learn the meaning of time and how to tell time on a clock.

15. Describe a set of materials for helping children learn the value of coins, and explain at least three activities with these materials.

16. Summarize the important measurement concepts included in the elementary-school program.

17. Describe an application of the three-level enrichment model for gifted and talented students that involves the use of specialized measuring instruments.

On December 23, 1975 President Gerald Ford signed the Metric Conversion Act of 1975. This act (Public Law 94-198) was designed to change the official system of measure in the United States from the English (customary) to the metric system. Changeover was not mandated by this act; it was to be voluntary. Even so, it was anticipated that business and industry, governmental agencies, and the population in general would accept the plan so that conversion would be complete within a few years. The Federal Highway Administration planned to change distance markers to kilometers and speed limits to kilometers per hour by July 1, 1978. The National Weather Service planned to report temperatures, windspeed, precipitation, and air pressure in metric units by January 1, 1979. Companies in the private sector, such as Black and Decker, IBM, Coca Cola and Seven-Up, Butterick and Simplicity, and Chrysler, Ford, and General Motors, changed entirely or partially to the metric system. It seemed that the United States, the last major nation not yet metricated, would join other countries of the world as a metric nation.

The hopes and expectations of those who supported the move to metrication have not materialized. Public resistance was great enough to thwart plans to indicate distances, speed limits, and weather information in metric units. The U.S. General Accounting Office reported that the benefits may not be as great as were anticipated and recommended that immediate conversion not be undertaken. On September 30, 1982 the United States Metric Board, established in 1975 to oversee the conversion process and provide guidance to governmental, business, industrial, and educational institutions, was disbanded. Metrication in the private sector has not continued at the pace seen in the years immediately following passage of the conversion act.

The slowdown of conversion plans means that the customary system of measures will continue as the predominant system in the United States for the foreseeable future. Changes already in place will probably remain, but further large-scale changes are unlikely for the present time. Therefore children need to develop an understanding of both the metric and the customary systems and to become skillful users of measuring instruments for both systems.

This chapter includes a discussion of the meaning of measurement, a brief history of the metric system, the metric system's characteristics, and examples of activities for teaching about measures and measuring processes. The metric system serves as the example for each activity. However, the customary system is taught in identical ways, so its units could be substituted wherever metric units are used.

WHAT IS MEASUREMENT?

The distinction between discrete and continuous objects is made in Chapter 7, in which children's early mathematical experiences are discussed. Discrete objects are those that can be counted, whereas continuous objects are measured. Measurement is the process of attaching numbers to the physical qualities of **length, area, volume, weight** (mass), or **temperature.** (Time is also measured, but it lacks a physical quality.) Each physical quality can be measured by means of one or more units. For example, the **meter**[1] is the basic unit for referring to an object's length, but units larger and smaller than the meter are used for finding the length of objects for which the meter is inappropriate.

1. Two Types of Measuring Processes

Two types of measuring processes exist: **direct measure** and **indirect measure.** The processes for determining most measures of length and capacity are direct, made by applying the appropriate unit directly to the object being measured. This direct process is referred to as **iteration.** Iteration is illustrated by the use of a meter stick to measure a room's length. The length is measured by placing the zero end of the stick against one wall, marking a spot on the floor at the other end, moving the stick to put the zero end at the mark, and repeating the process until the opposite wall is reached. All the while, the number of times the stick is moved is counted. This number is the room's length expressed in meters.

Weight (mass), temperature, and time cannot be measured in the direct fashion just described. The characteristics, or properties, of weight, temperature, and time require an instrument that measures each one by translating the measurable property into numbers indirectly. Thus one type of weather thermometer has a number scale aligned with a tube containing a liquid. The liquid expands (and rises) when it is warmed as the surrounding air becomes hotter; it contracts (and goes down) when it is cooled as the air becomes colder. The temperature at a given time is

---

[1] *Meter* is the accepted spelling in the United States for the basic unit of length, and *liter* is the spelling for the basic unit of capacity (volume). Children should also learn the alternate spellings for these words—*metre* and *litre*.

determined indirectly by reading the numeral on the scale that indicates the height of the column of liquid at that time.

There are indirect processes for determining length (height, width, distance, and so on). These processes are too technical for most elementary-school children and are not considered in this book.

2. Measurement Is Approximate

Although the counting of discrete objects is exact, all measurement is approximate. The **approximate nature of measurement** stems from the fact that for any particular unit of measure there is, theoretically at least, one that is more precise. If a city block is measured with a meter stick, it might be found to be 100 meters long. However, if a unit one-tenth of a meter—a decimeter—is used to measure the same block, it might be found to be 998 decimeters long, or slightly less than 100 meters. Even more precise measurements could be made using centimeters or millimeters, although in most instances this would be impractical and unnecessary.

Give a brief explanation of the meaning of measurement.

Self-check
of Objective 1

THE METRIC SYSTEM

The **metric system** has assumed a more prominent role in the United States, in spite of setbacks in the conversion plan, and children must learn to understand and use it. This section gives a brief overview of the history of this system, discusses its key characteristics, and presents its advantages over the **English (customary) system.**

1. Brief History of the Metric System

The earliest proposal for a worldwide decimalized system of measure was made in France in the late 1600s, but a century passed before serious attention was given to such a system. Then in 1790, the National Assembly of France asked the French Academy of Sciences to devise a system having an invariable standard for all measures. The academy derived its unit of length from a portion of the earth's circumference. This standard, which is called a meter, was one ten-millionth of the distance from the equator to the north pole along the meridian running near Dunkirk in France and Barcelona in Spain and was represented by a prototype measure made of platinum.

Other units were derived from the meter (m). The units of linear measure are decimal parts or multiples of the meter based on powers of ten. A **decimeter** (dm) is $1/10$ of a meter, a **centimeter** (cm) is $1/100$ of a meter, and a **millimeter** (mm) is $1/1000$ of a meter. A **dekameter** (dam) is 10 meters, a **hectometer** (hm) is 100 meters, and a **kilometer** (km) is 1000 meters.[2]

Basic units for capacity (volume), weight (mass), and area were established at the time the base unit for linear measure was established. A **liter** (L),[3] the basic unit for capacity, is the volume of one cubic decimeter (dm^3). A **kilogram** (kg) is the basic unit of weight (mass) and was originally determined to be one cubic decimeter of water at $4°C$, the temperature at which water is at its greatest density. Today's international prototype of the kilogram is a platinum–iridium solid maintained at Sèvres, France. For measuring land, the basic unit is the **are** (a), which is 100 square meters (m^2). A **hectare** (ha) is 100 ares. Volume is also measured in cubic meters (m^3) and cubic centimeters (cm^3).

In 1960 the Eleventh General Conference of Weights and Measures adopted the **International System of Units (SI).** There are seven basic units and two supplementary units, as shown in Tables 14-1 and 14-2. The SI system is accepted worldwide with nearly full agreement among nations on the units, their values, names, and symbols. An exception to full agreement is the use of L as the symbol for liter in the U.S., whereas l is the SI symbol.

TABLE 14-1   Base units in the international system of units (SI)

Quality to be Measured	Unit	Symbol
Length	meter	m
Weight (mass)	kilogram	kg
Time	second	s
Electric current	ampere	A
Thermodynamic temperature	kelvin	K*
Amount of substance	mole	mol**
Luminous intensity	candela	cd

*Degrees Celsius is an acceptable alternate unit for measuring temperature.

**Some listings contain only six units, omitting the mole. See M. J. B. Jones, *A Guide to Metrication* (Oxford, England: Pergamon Press Ltd., 1969), p. 15.

---

[2] There are smaller subdivisions and larger multiples of the metric system's basic units, but they are seldom used outside the field of science and are not included in the elementary school curriculum.

[3] A capital L is used in the United States as the symbol for liter. This avoids the possibility of confusing the symbol with the numeral 1. The use of the script *l* has been discarded, because of its unavailability on typewriters and other printing devices.

TABLE 14-2 Supplementary SI units

Quality to be Measured	Unit	Symbol
Plane angle	radian	rad
Solid angle	steradian	sr

One detail of interest coming from the 1960 conference was a redefinition of the meter. It is approximately the same length as the original meter but is now defined as 1 650 763.73[4] wavelengths in vacuum of the orange-red line of the spectrum of the krypton-86 atom. This standard was adopted because it is unvarying and indestructible and can be reproduced in any laboratory possessing the proper equipment.

The SI system is highly technical, and only the parts dealing with length, mass, and temperature and certain non-SI metric units dealing with time, area, and volume are studied by elementary-school children.

2. Characteristics of the Metric System

One significant characteristic of the metric system has already been mentioned—the fact that measures of capacity, weight, and area are all based on the meter.

Another important feature is that the metric system is a decimal system. This means that for each type of measure there is an interrelationship of units based on multiplication or division by 10. This scheme is essentially the same as the Hindu–Arabic numeration system, a fact that should be capitalized on to help children develop their understanding of the metric system. Table 14-3 shows the relationship between the metric system and the Hindu–Arabic numeration system and certain portions of our monetary system. Only certain of the measures shown in Table 14-3 are commonly used: the meter, kilometer, centimeter, and millimeter; gram, kilogram, and milligram; and liter and milliliter. These, along with certain units for area (square meter and square centimeter), volume (cubic meter and cubic centimeter), time (year, day, hour, minute, and second), and temperature (degrees Celsius), are the units most elementary-school children will use during their study of the metric system and are the units considered in this book.

---

[4]The comma is omitted from numerals for large and small numbers in SI. Large numbers appear as indicated here, and small ones appear as 0.362 45. This practice is followed because the comma serves as a decimal point in some countries.

TABLE 14-3 Relationship between parts of the metric system and the Hindu–Arabic numeration system and pertinent parts of our monetary system

	1000x (10³)	100x (10²)	10x (10¹)	Base	1/10X (10⁻¹)	1/100X (10⁻²)	1/1000X (10⁻³)
Hindu–Arabic system	thousands	hundreds	tens	ones	tenths	hundredths	thousandths
Monetary system	$1000.00	$100.00	$10.00	$1.00	$0.10 (10¢)	$0.01 (1¢)	$0.001 (mill)
Metric prefix	kilo-	hecto-	deka-		deci-	centi-	milli-
Length	kilometer (km)	hectometer (hm)	dekameter (dam)	meter (m)	decimeter (dm)	centimeter (cm)	millimeter (mm)
Capacity	kiloliter (kL)	hectoliter (hL)	dekaliter (daL)	liter (L)	deciliter (dL)	centiliter (cL)	milliliter (mL)
Weight (mass)	kilogram* (kg)	hectogram (hg)	dekagram (dag)	gram (g)	decigram (dg)	centigram (cg)	milligram (mg)

*The kilogram is the basic unit for weight. Therefore it is a contradiction of the idea that the base units stand without a prefix.

3. Advantages of the Metric System

The following advantages of the metric system are reported in "1 . . . to get ready"[5]:

1. The metric system is simple and logically planned and is a decimal system like our numeration and monetary systems.

2. The basic unit, the meter, is always reproducible from natural phenomena.

3. A single set of prefixes is used to designate all subdivisions and multiples of units for all types of measures. This simplifies the process of converting from one unit to another.

4. Uses of common fractions will be reduced, which means that less time will be required for children to understand the common fractions they will need. The time gained can be devoted to other important topics.

5. Familiarity with the meter, gram, and liter and their subdivisions and multiples will be sufficient for most persons. Extension of the study of the International System of Units can be made by those persons who need a deeper understanding of the system.

6. The metric system is the universal measuring language.

---

[5]"1 . . . to get ready" is a selected bibliography on metrication issued in April 1973 by a Joint Committee of the American Association of School Librarians and the National Council of Teachers of Mathematics. Copies are available from the AASL, 50 East Huron Street, Chicago, Ill. 60611.

Give a brief statement in which you trace the history of the metric system.

The International System of Units (SI) has seven basic and two supplementary units. List these units, and identify whether each is basic or supplementary.

Two characteristics of the metric system are described. Give an oral or written explanation of them.

The AASL/NCTM publication quoted lists six advantages of the metric system over the English (customary) system. List at least four of these advantages.

Self-check of Objectives 2, 3, 4, and 5

CHILDREN'S READINESS FOR MEASUREMENT ACTIVITIES

Piaget's research and its general implications for teaching mathematics are discussed in Chapter 2. The section dealing with this research should be reviewed now, because the contents of that discussion are important in the planning of measurement activities. That discussion is now extended to introduce additional information dealing with children and **conservation.**

To study children's ability to conserve length, a pair of rods or sticks of equal length can be used. Initially, place the rods side by side on a table with their ends an equal distance from one edge, as in Figure 14-1(a). Ask the child if the rods are of equal length. A child who understands the question will usually agree that they are. Next, move one stick so it is farther from the table's edge (b) and repeat the question. A child who is not a conserver of length will say that the sticks no longer have equal lengths. A conserver recognizes that the length of either rod is not altered by changing the position of one of them. Generally, children are unable to conserve length until they are about eight years of age.

A similar test can be used to determine whether a child is a conserver

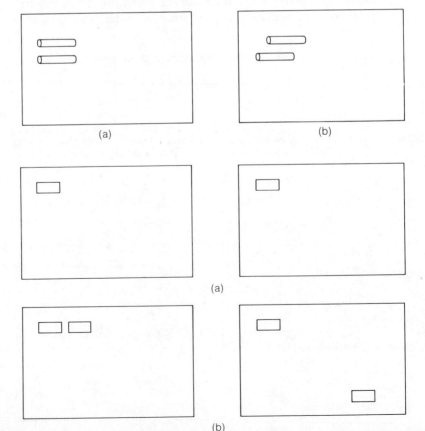

FIGURE 14-1
Test for determining a child's ability to conserve length

(a)   (b)

FIGURE 14-2
Test for determining a child's ability to conserve area

(a)

(b)

of area. A pair of "fields," represented by equal-sized pieces of green paper, and "buildings," represented by smaller equal-sized pieces of brown paper, are used. Place the fields side by side with a building in place on each, as in Figure 14-2(a). Ask the child if one building covers the same amount of land as the other. Next, place an additional building on each field, as shown in (b), and rephrase the question. A nonconserver will say that the buildings on one field cover more land than those on the other. The conserver recognizes that an equal number of equal-sized buildings cover the same amount of land (area) regardless of their positions. Children generally do not conserve area until around eight years of age.

Neither of these tests alone is sufficient to determine whether a child is a conserver of area or length. Several tests using similar materials and techniques should be used before a firm decision about a child's status can be reached.[6]

Children's reactions to these and similar tests give curriculum planners and teachers a basis for establishing the proper scope and sequence of

Activities	Measurement	Grade Levels
		K 1 2 3 4 5 6
Exploratory pouring matching balancing ordering sorting comparing	length weight capacity (L, mL) time area temperature	
Nonstandard Units pouring matching balancing ordering sorting comparing measuring estimating recording	length weight capacity (L, mL) volume (m³, cm³) time area temperature angle	
Standard Units measuring estimating recording choosing converting describing applying	length weight capacity (L, mL) volume (m³, cm³) time area temperature angle	

FIGURE 14-3

A suggested scope and sequence for measurement in elementary schools. Adapted from Mathematics Education Task Force, *An Introduction to the SI Metric System* (Sacramento: California State Department of Education, 1975), p. 15.

[6] For additional discussion of conservation of length and area, and examples of other tests, see Richard W. Copeland's *Math Activities for Children* (Columbus, Ohio: Charles E. Merrill Publishing Company, 1979), Ch. 4.

activities dealing with measurement. It is generally agreed that children's early experiences should be exploratory, with first activities being play-like in nature. Nonstandard units, such as cans and jars, acorns, paper clips, and 3 by 5 cards, are used to introduce the underlying concepts of measurement once it is determined that children are conservers. Finally, standard units are introduced. Figure 14-3 illustrates a suggested scope and sequence for measurement in elementary schools.

The scope-and-sequence chart in Figure 14-3 cannot be applied directly as a means of establishing a program for your children. Variations in children's levels of cognitive development, particularly with reference to conservation, their abilities to comprehend mathematical concepts, and previous experiences with measurement, must be considered as you plan their activities.

Self-check of Objective 6

These types of measures are included in the elementary-school program: length, capacity, area, time, temperature, and weight. List each one, and write the grade level that is recommended for its introduction.

EXPLORATORY ACTIVITIES

Children who are still in the preoperational stage of development and who are not yet conservers should not be given activities dealing with standard units of measure. Rather they need a variety of activities that build a foundation for later work. In addition to those in the readiness section of Chapter 7, the following types of activities should be made available to young children.

ACTIVITY 14-1   Capacity

- The purpose of this activity is to provide a background for understanding capacity.
- Prepare plastic or glass containers of various sizes by gluing rubber bands around them at different levels. Put 2 to 6 pounds of rice, a funnel, and a scoop in a plastic tub or large cardboard box.
- Children use the scoop and funnel to fill each container to the rubber-band level.
- This exploratory activity is not designed for children to count the number of scoops required to fill each container. However, some children may be able to do this, so provide squares of paper for them to record

their counts. Encourage children to order the containers from least to most amount of rice.[7]

ACTIVITY 14-2 Heavier and Lighter

- A balance beam, either commercial or teacher-made, gives children opportunities to compare pairs of objects to determine which is heavier or lighter.

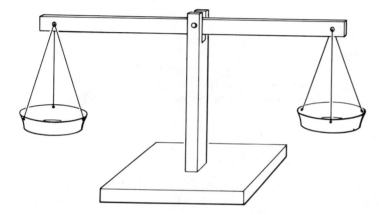

- Children's first work with a balance beam should be exploratory. They will learn to make it balance by putting an object in one pan and other objects in the second pan until the crossbar is level. They also see the crossbar go down at one end when the object in one pan is heavier than the object in the other pan.
- Set up pairs of objects—toy car and wooden block, chalkboard eraser and small bag of rice, small rubber ball and box of pencils—so children can determine which object is heavier and which is lighter. They can place the objects on a mat having the headings *lighter* and *heavier* separated by a line down the middle.

Lighter	Heavier

[7] Mary Baratta-Lorton, *Workjobs* (Menlo Park, Cal.: Addison–Wesley Publishing Company, 1972), pp. 22–23.

ACTIVITY 14-3   Passage of Time

- This teacher-led activity gives children an experience dealing with the passage of time.
- Use four or five cans alike both in shape and size. Punch a hole in the bottom of each: a small hole in one, a large hole in another, and in-between sizes in the others. Paint each can a different color. Put water or clean, fine-grained sand in a plastic tub.
- Have a child select a can, fill it, and hold it so the water or sand drains through the hole. Have children watch carefully as each can is filled and drained.
- Ask questions about what they observe:
  - "Does the red can empty quickly or slowly?"
  - "Which can drains more slowly, the red one or the blue one?"
  - "What is the color of the can that drains fastest?"
  - "Can you put the cans in order from fastest to slowest?"
  - "What can you tell me about the size of a hole and how fast a can drains?"

ACTIVITY 14-4   Temperature

- Outdoors on a sunny day provides a setting for an investigation and discussion about temperature. Choose a location where there is a sidewalk, some grass, and a patch of bare ground, and select a time when one part of each is in sunlight and another part is in shade.
- Have children remove their shoes and socks and walk on the sunny sidewalk. Talk about how it feels. Have them walk on the shady sidewalk and compare its feel with that of the sunny walk.
- Have the children walk on the sunny and shady portions of the other surfaces. Discuss differences in temperature, if any, between each spot and the others. Can the children order the six locations from warmest to coolest?

**Self-check
of Objective 7**   Describe materials and activities for helping preoperational-level children build backgrounds for capacity, weight, linear, time, and temperature measures.

NONSTANDARD UNITS

Children's understanding of measure begins as they engage in activities such as those already described. Continue with these activities until you see evidence that some children are able to conserve length, volume, and so on. After simple tests show which children are able to conserve length, for example, group them for their first work with **nonstandard units.**

1. Purposes of the Activities

Activities with nonstandard units bridge the gap between exploratory work and the introduction of standard units. Two goals of these activities are to help children recognize the need for a uniform set of measures and to lay the groundwork for their appreciation of the simplicity of the metric system.

2. Suggested Activities

The activities that follow are examples of those dealing with nonstandard units for the various types of measures.

For their first work with linear measure children should use such things as new pencils as nonstandard units.

ACTIVITY 14-5   New-Pencil Measurements

- New pencils serve as units of measure in this introduction to linear measure. Select an object such as a desk top to measure. Demonstrate how to put pencils end to end to find the length and width of the desk in pencil-units. Stress the importance of not leaving gaps or letting pencils overlap and of counting the pencils carefully.
- Use problem cards as a means of giving directions to individual and small group activities.

MEASURING WITH PENCILS

Use new pencils from the box to answer these questions.

1. How long is the reading table?

2. How wide is the reading table?

3. Can you figure out a way to find out how high the table is? If you can, tell how high it is.

Write each of your answers in a complete sentence.

When a single object, rather than many, is used to measure the length of an object, the iteration process is used. (Iteration is explained earlier in this chapter.) A child's cutout foot provides a useful nonstandard unit of measure for introducing the process of iteration.

ACTIVITY 14-6 Foot Units

- Have each child make an outline of his or her foot on a piece of paper and cut it out.
- Demonstrate how to use the cutout foot to measure the length and width of a desk or table top.
- Give the children a list of objects to measure with their "foot" units such as the length of the chalkboard chalk tray, the length and width of file cabinet, and the width of room. Add others of your own choosing.
- Children should record each measure in "foot" units.
- During a class discussion talk about the children's measures for each object. When the number of units that are reported for a given object, such as a chalkboard tray, are not the same, stress that when nonstandard units are used, differences may occur because their "foot" units are not all the same length.
- Make a chart on which the children's "foot" measures are ordered from shortest to longest.

An extension of exploratory activities with a balance beam provides experiences with nonstandard units for weighing objects.

ACTIVITY 14-7 Nonstandard Weights

- Provide objects such as walnuts, wooden blocks, Unifix cubes, and small bags of rice, as units of measure.
- Use problem cards and answer sheets for children's responses. Questions like these can be used on problem cards:
  - How many Unifix cubes balance the red bag of sand?
  - How many walnuts balance one block?
  (Add other questions to fit your objects.)

Water- or sand-table activities can also be extended to include experiences with nonstandard units for measuring capacity.

ACTIVITY 14-8 Colored-Can Units

- Select cans so that one has four times the capacity of another, one has a capacity twice another, and so on. Paint all cans with the same capacity a given color.
- Direct children's activities with problem-card questions:
  - "How many blue cans does it take to fill one red can?"
  - "How many green cans can you fill from one yellow can?"
  (Prepare other questions based on the cans at your table.)

Glass sand-filled timers can be used as nonstandard time-measuring units. Get as many different timers as possible. Children can observe that the sand transfers more quickly from one than from another and that the sand in two differently sized timers can transfer in the same amount of time.

Squares cut from corrugated boxes can be used to introduce children to the concept of area. The idea to be developed during early activities is that area is the measure of a surface enclosed by a closed plane figure. Under your direction children can cover desk and table tops, sections of carpet, and other surfaces with cardboard squares and count the squares covering each one. Answers should be labeled as "square units of cardboard."

Nonstandard units for length, capacity, time, and area have been described. Name at least one nonstandard unit for each type of measure and explain its use by children.

***Self-check
of Objective 8***

STANDARD UNITS OF MEASURE

It has already been said that children need to learn both the metric and the customary systems of measure. The premise of this book is that children learn about measurement best when they have frequent opportunities to measure objects. Rather than reading about a measuring process, such as linear measure, children should use an appropriate measuring instrument to actually measure objects. As they work, they learn that there are 10 decimeters in a meter or 12 inches in a foot. Once children are familiar with units for one system, they can learn the comparable units for the other system.

The time spent on learning both systems need not be extensive. Children who understand the basic concepts of measure and who learn to use measuring instruments properly can learn units of measure in both systems simultaneously.

It is recommended that children not be asked to convert measurements from customary units to metric units and vice versa. Beyond learning that a meter is slightly longer than a yard, a liter is a little more than a quart, and a kilogram is about 2.2 pounds, there is little to be gained from having children compare units in the two systems. Heavy doses of conversions weaken children's interest in measurement and may lead to a negative attitude toward it.

The remaining sections of this chapter are focused on the metric system except for the parts dealing with time and money. Teachers who want to introduce customary units first can use the information from these sections as a guide for planning activities by substituting customary units for their metric counterparts.

The progression from working with nonstandard units to standard units goes smoothly for children experienced in working in a laboratory setting. Instead of pencil or cutout-foot units for linear measure, they now use centimeter and meter rulers. Sets of kilogram weights replace walnuts and blocks, and liter containers replace cans.

1. Linear Measures

The commonly used units of linear measure are the meter, centimeter, millimeter, and kilometer. By the time children complete the sixth grade, they should demonstrate their knowledge of these units by being able to show a reasonable approximation of each and use devices for measuring meters, centimeters, and millimeters accurately. They should also be able to name the other units of linear measure—decimeter, dekameter, and hectometer—and identify the relationships between these and the more common units.

Children will generally begin work with the centimeter. When introduced to this unit, children should use rulers marked only in units, that is, the units should not be marked with numerals (Figure 14-4). Children are forced to count units as they use these rulers; thus their understanding of the meaning of linear measure is reinforced as they work. If such rulers cannot be bought, they can be easily duplicated on tagboard.

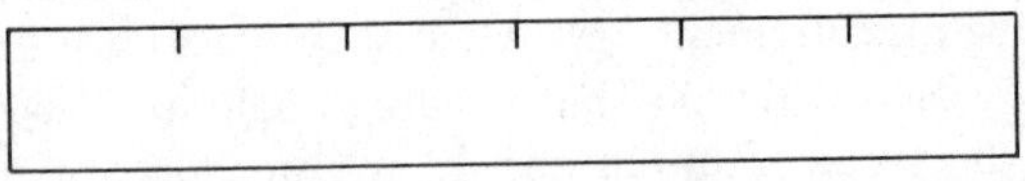

FIGURE 14-4
Ruler for use by youngsters. Only unit segments are marked.

Objects whose lengths are a whole number of centimeters should be measured first. This can pose a problem because many familiar objects do not possess this dimension. You can locate appropriate articles for children to measure by looking around the classroom and your home. For instance, a role of 35 millimeter film is packaged in a box that is 4 centimeters wide and 6 centimeters long. A Parker ballpoint pen is 1 centimeter thick and 13 centimeters long. You can also cut sticks, sharpen pencils, and trim paper edges so they have centimeter dimensions.

As children's activities continue, you will want them to measure things that have not been preselected. As they do, they will encounter objects whose dimensions are not a whole number of centimeters. Children will note that one pencil is a little more than 4 centimeters long, and another is a little less than 4 centimeters long; Figure 14-5 is an example of this. Even so, each pencil is 4 centimeters long to the nearest whole unit.

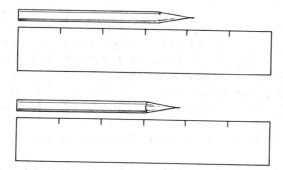

FIGURE 14-5
Unit rulers are used to measure the length of two pencils. Each pencil has a measurement of 4 units.

When the end of an object falls near the midpoint between two units, children must make a judgment about the measurement to be recorded as its length (Figure 14-6). It should be clear that different individuals may record either of two different measurements for this pencil. The measurement might be recorded as 5 centimeters by one child and 6 centimeters by another. Both of them are considered correct.

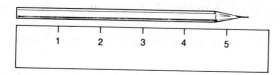

FIGURE 14-6
This pencil might be recorded as having a measurement of 5 units by some children and 6 units by others.

The ruler in Figure 14-6 has units indicated by numerals. Now a measure can be determined by noting the numeral rather than counting the units.

Work with the meter follows the centimeter. The first meter stick should be one that has no subdivisions. Inexpensive pine molding from a lumber yard cut into meter lengths is a convenient source of such sticks. Have children measure the width, length, and height of their classroom, the distance from the classroom door to the cafeteria door, the length of the sidewalk from curb to front door, and so on.

A wheel having a circumference of 1 meter attached to a handle so it rolls easily across flat surfaces is handy for measuring longer distances. Such a device is called a trundle wheel and can be purchased or the parts cut from plywood by a teacher and assembled by children.

Eventually children should work with meter sticks subdivided into decimeters and centimeters. Metric measuring tapes and millimeter rulers should also be available. Now children will measure all sorts of objects, including themselves. Measurements will be recorded in different ways depending upon children's maturity. For instance a child's height might be recorded as 148 cm or 1.48 m. Mixed units are not used to record measurements. The above height measurement would not be recorded as 1 m 48 cm.

As their understanding of the metric system matures, children should be guided toward recognition of the fact that a given measurement can be converted from one unit to another by shifting the decimal point in one direction or the other. Moving the decimal point one position to the left is the same as dividing by 10, moving it two positions to the left is the same as dividing by 100, and so on. Moving the decimal point to the right one position is the same as multiplying by 10, two positions is the same as multiplying by 100, and so on. To change 148 centimeters to meters, divide 148 by 100 (there are 100 centimeters in 1 meter). The answer is 1.48; hence, 148 cm = 1.48 m. To change 3.26 meters to millimeters, multiply 3.26 by 1000. The answer is 3260, so 3.26 m = 3260 mm.

One objective of activities dealing with linear measure is that children be able to show reasonable approximations of the meter, decimeter, millimeter, and kilometer. One way to help them do this is to give them opportunities to estimate lengths and distances as well as measure them. Identify a list of objects to be measured. Have each child first record an estimate of the length of each object; then have the child measure the objects and compare the two sets of figures.

Another way to meet this objective is to help children establish references based on familiar objects. A dime is approximately 1 millimeter thick. The width of the nail on a person's little finger is about 1 centimeter. The chalk rail in many classrooms is about 1 meter above the floor.

The best way for children to gain a "feeling" for the kilometer is for them to walk the distance several times. Locate landmarks that are about a kilometer from a given point at school—a child's house, a store, a playground, a bridge. As children walk from the point at school to a point at each landmark, have them count their paces. By doing this several times, the children can determine the average number of paces they take while walking a kilometer.

Self-check of Objective 9

Describe materials and activities that will help children to understand linear measure and to make accurate measurements and reasonable estimates of length.

2. Weight (Mass) Measures

Technically, weight and mass are not the same. Weight is the force exerted on an object because of gravity, whereas mass is the quantity of matter of which the object is composed. Thus a given object will weigh less on the moon, where the force of gravity is less, than it will weigh on Earth. It will have the same mass in either place, because the quantity of matter remains the same. Even though this technical difference exists, it is common practice to consider weight and mass to be the same. Therefore the term that is commonly used—weight—will be used in the rest of this chapter.

The basic unit of weight in the metric system is the kilogram. As pointed out earlier, this unit contradicts the notion that basic units have no prefixes. The commonly used units are

$$1 \text{ metric ton} = 1000 \text{ kilograms}$$
$$1 \text{ kilogram} = 1000 \text{ grams}$$
$$1 \text{ gram} = 1000 \text{ milligrams}$$

By the time children complete the elementary school, they should be able to name these as commonly used units and identify familiar objects that weigh about 1 kilogram or 1 gram. They should also be able to name the less commonly used units, that is, hectogram, dekagram, decigram, and centigram, and state the relationships between each unit and those that are larger or smaller.

Two types of scales should now be available, balance scales and spring scales. In order to weigh objects on a balance scale, a set of weights is needed. A commercial set may contain these weights: one 1-kilogram, two 500-gram, two 250-gram, two 100-gram, two 50-gram, four 10-gram, two 5-gram, and five 1-gram. You can duplicate most of these by filling cloth bags with the appropriate amount of sand or rice. Lead fish weights can be used for the smaller ones. Kitchen-type spring scales, weighing to 5 kilograms, and platform (bathroom) spring scales are both needed.

ACTIVITY 14-9   Weighing Produce

- Provide a balance scale, set of metric weights, and bags of fresh produce commonly sold by weight.
- Give each child a worksheet that lists the items and provides spaces for recording their weights.
- Children weigh the bagged produce and record their weights, using grams as the unit of measure.
- Children should also have opportunities to weigh the same or similar items using a spring scale.

Three commonly used units and two types of scales are discussed. Name the units and identify the two types of scales.

3. Capacity Measures

The liter is the basic unit of capacity measure in the metric system. It is a derived unit based on a part of the meter—the centimeter. A cube with inside dimensions of 1 decimeter has a volume of 1 cubic decimeter (dm^3), or 1000 cubic centimeters (cm^3); this is 1 liter. Any container having a volume of 1 cubic decimeter has a capacity of 1 liter. Plastic containers of various sizes are inexpensive and can be purchased for classroom investigations. The metric containers in which soft drinks, wine, medicines, and similar products are sold should not be overlooked. By choosing carefully, you can accumulate a collection of graduated containers for your children.

ACTIVITY 14-10   Liters

- Set up a center that has a liter container and other containers, such as soft drink, detergent, and vinegar bottles. Have some bottles that hold less and some that hold more than a liter. Label one container *A*, another *B*, and so on; do not label the liter container.
- Provide a problem card and answer sheet:
  - Guess which containers hold less than a liter; list their letters under the heading *Less than a liter*. Guess which containers hold more than a liter and list their letters under *More than a liter*.
  - Fill the liter container with water. Fill the *A* container with water from the liter container. Was your guess about the size of that container a correct one? If your guess was not correct, mark out the letter *A* on your answer sheet and put it under the correct heading.
  - Fill each of the other containers from the liter container to determine whether or not your guess for it is a correct one. Mark out any letter that is under the wrong heading and write it under the correct heading.

Other centers can provide opportunities for work with milliliters. Specially prepared milliliter containers are available from school supply houses. Small plastic medicine containers cost little or nothing. Children can use these containers to determine the capacity of small bottles, such as those that hold spices and food colors.

4. Area Measure

The units of measure for the area of the interior region bounded by a closed plane figure are derived from linear units. The metric units elementary-school children learn are derived from the centimeter and the meter. A square unit with 1-centimeter sides is used for determining the area of small plane figures. It is a centimeter square and is designated by the symbol cm². A square with 1-meter sides is used for determining areas of larger regions. Its symbol is m². Goals of instruction are for children (a) to be able to name these common units and (b) to be able to measure area directly by using square centimeter grids and indirectly by first measuring the edges of regions with centimeter and meter rulers and then applying the formula $l \times w = A$.

ACTIVITY 14-11   Finding the Area

- Give each child a piece of tissue or plastic that has a grid of centimeter squares marked on it and a page with outlines of rectangular regions on it. Use regions that have a whole number of centimeters along each side.
- Show the children how to align the tissue or plastic grid on top of a rectangle so that the number of square units contained in its interior can be counted.

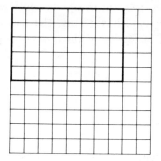

- Children will measure each of the regions and record its measure.

Squares of corrugated cardboard cut with 1-meter edges can be used to measure larger regions. Children can take their squares to the playground or multipurpose room to cover and measure the interiors of game-playing regions bounded by lines painted on the hardtop or floor.

Not all regions can be measured in an exact number of square centimeter or meter units. A square centimeter grid can be used to give an estimate of the measure of such a region's interior. The situation is illustrated in Figure 14-7. First, children should count the units entirely within

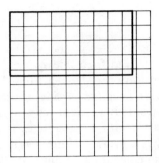

FIGURE 14-7
Grid used to estimate a region's area

the bounds of the region—there are 32; then they should count those entirely or partially within the region's bounds—there are 45. The region's measure will be greater than 32 but less than 45; a good estimate is 38.

The next experiences should enable children to state the general formula for finding the measure of any rectangular region using square units: $A = l \times w$ (A represents the measure of the area; l and w represent the measure of length and width, respectively). As they use their grids to measure regions, children should be guided to note that each time they measure a region by counting, they are counting the units in an array. By now the children should know that the product of an a-by-b array is the product of a times b. If a 1-centimeter unit is used to measure the length and width of a rectangular region, the two measures indicate the array of square units for that region. The picture for Activity 14-11 shows a 5-by-8 array; the measurement in square centimeters is 40.

Once children understand how to find the area of rectangular regions, they should determine formulas for the areas of regions bounded by parallelograms.

ACTIVITY 14-12   Area of a Parallelogram

- Give each child a piece of paper cut in the shape of a parallelogram similar to the one shown in (a).
- Instruct the children to fold one end of the parallelogram as in (b).
- Show the children how to cut off the folded end and put it at the other end to make a rectangle, as in (c).

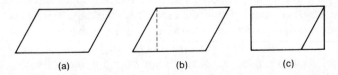

(a)   (b)   (c)

Review the formula for determining the area of a rectangle, and point out that it can be used to determine the area of a parallelogram. (The formula for a parallelogram is sometimes stated as $b \times h = A$, where b represents base, h height, and A area.)

Children also should explore with triangular-shaped regions. Two congruent triangular regions can be placed side by side to form a parallelogram-shaped region (Figure 14-8). The measure of this area is determined by the formula $A = b \times h$. Because the area for only one triangular region is to be determined, the product of $b \times h$ must be divided by 2; this can be expressed by the formula

$$A = \frac{b \times h}{2}$$

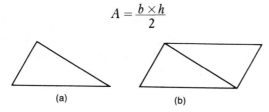

(a)   (b)

FIGURE 14-8
Two congruent triangular regions can form the shape of a parallelogram, a fact that can help children derive the formula for determining the area of a triangle.

Describe materials and activities that will help children understand the meaning of area measurement for each of these plane figures: square and rectangle, parallelogram, and triangle.

***Self-check
of Objective 11***

5. Perimeter Measure

The perimeter of a plane figure is determined by finding the measure of each of the figure's segments and adding the numbers. Children frequently confuse **perimeter** with area and use a formula for determining area when working with perimeter or vice versa. One way to prevent this confusion is to relate the word *perimeter* to the word *periscope*. Nearly all fifth- and sixth-grade children know that a submarine's periscope is used to look around the surface of a body of water. Point out that the prefix *peri-* means *around,* so perimeter means "to measure around." Once the meaning is clear, children can use centimeter rulers to determine the perimeters of book covers, desk tops, and other small regions. The perimeters of classrooms, playing areas marked on the playground, and larger regions can be determined by using meter tapes or a metric trundle wheel.

Explain the meaning of perimeter, and describe a way to prevent children from confusing perimeter with area.

***Self-check
of Objective 12***

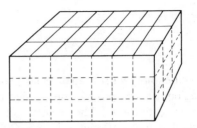

FIGURE 14-9
A rectangular solid (box) filled with cubes helps children learn the formula for finding the volume of the solid.

6. Volume Measure

Fifth- and sixth-grade children should learn about the measure of closed three-dimensional figures by making direct measurements of small containers with Cuisenaire cubes that have edges 1 centimeter long (Figure 14-9). Each cube has a volume of 1 cubic centimeter; the symbol for this measure is cm³. Children should also see a model of a cubic meter. They can make one of corrugated cardboard cut from large boxes.

Their experiences with centimeter cubes should enable them to see that indirect measurement can be used to determine the volume of a solid. This is done by determining the measure of the length, width, and height of a solid and multiplying the three numbers. The formula that is usually associated with volume is $l \times w \times h = V$. Children who have learned to determine areas of rectangles and triangles can use that knowledge to apply the formula $V = B \times h$, where B designates the area of the base, to determine volumes of rectangular and triangular prisms (Figure 14-10).

FIGURE 14-10
Children can find the volume of a simple geometric solid by using the formula $V = B \times h$.

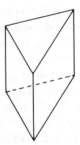

Self-check of Objective 13

Tell what is meant by the volume of a geometric solid. Describe investigations for children that will help them develop their understanding of the concept and the formulas for finding the volumes of such figures as rectangular and triangular prisms (boxes), and cylinders.

7. Mini-Olympics

A mini-olympics is an entertaining way to provide practice with metric measuring instruments. The activity can be conducted indoors or outdoors and with one or more classes. Establish the events, prepare a large chart to record results, and determine what, if any, prizes will be awarded.

Events can be imitations of real olympic contests or can be invented just for your mini-olympics. Mock events include such things as a *cotton-ball put* (a cotton ball is put like a shot), a *straw throw* (a soda straw is thrown like a javelin), and a *paper-plate throw* (a paper plate is thrown like a discus). There also could be a standing broad jump and a reaching high jump (a reaching jump is made beside a wall, with the highest point marked by a piece of chalk held in the jumper's upstretched arm). Each event is measured from the beginning point to the ending point with a centimeter measuring tape.

Weight-lifting events can be a part of two bridge-building activities. For the first event children work in pairs. Each pair measures a 50-gram piece of plasticine clay; a judge verifies the weight before the bridge is built. The bridge is made by rolling the clay into a long snakelike shape. The winning team is the one that makes the longest bridge that remains intact for at least 10 seconds when stretched between two chairs with no more than 5 centimeters of each end on a chair.

Bridges for the second event are made in advance of the contest. Each team is given 50 soda straws, some pieces of cardboard, and some white glue to make a soda-straw bridge. Each team chooses a style for its bridge, subject to two conditions: the bridge must be at least 75 centimeters long and have a cardboard "roadway" that is 20 centimeters wide extending from end to end. A 10-centimeter square is marked at the midpoint of each bridge. On olympic day each bridge is placed between two chairs, with no more than 5 centimeters of either end on a chair. Weights are stacked in the square on each bridge. The winner is the team that constructs the bridge that supports the most weight.

8. Measuring Temperature

Children in the second and third grades will learn to use thermometers by reading them and recording temperatures during daily activities connected with weather study. In the higher grades there are opportunities for children to use thermometers as they engage in science studies. By the end of elementary school, children should read temperatures indicated on a Celsius thermometer, know that the freezing point of water is 0°C and the boiling point is 100°C, and identify some temperatures associated closely with their lives—normal body temperature is approximately 37°C, an outdoor temperature of 10°C indicates a cool day, a temperature of 30°C indicates a warm day, and 40°C indicates a hot day.

Primary-grade children should use large, easy-to-read alcohol thermometers. You can make a demonstration thermometer by printing the scale on a large piece of stiff cardboard or masonite painted a light color. The alcohol is represented by a strip of red cloth, made by sewing a strip of red cloth to a strip of white cloth, inserting the ends into slits at the top and bottom of the scale, and sewing the two ends together so the band is taut (Figure 14-11). After one child has read the temperature from the real thermometer, another should show the temperature on the demonstration thermometer so it can be read by the rest of the class.

FIGURE 14-11
Demonstration thermometer
to help children learn how
temperature is determined

LEARNING ABOUT TIME

Instruction about **time** deals with two aspects of the subject: the concept of time, which includes an understanding of the duration of time and the sequence of events, and the mechanics of reading calendars and telling time on a clock. Piaget's research indicates that some children are ready to develop a full understanding of time by the age of nine, and others are not ready until ten or eleven.[8] Before this time, children have a poor

[8] Richard W. Copeland, *How Children Learn Mathematics, Teaching Implications of Piaget's Research*, Third Edition (New York: Macmillan Publishing Company, Inc. 1979), p. 209.

sense of duration of time and many misconceptions about the sequence of events. Activities with sand or water flowing through holes in cans and with sand-filled timers, described earlier, are aids for developing a sense of duration. An activity with shadows cast on a simple sundial aids in developing understanding of both the duration and sequencing concepts.

ACTIVITY 14-13   Sundial

- Prepare a sundial by attaching a pencil to a square piece of cardboard with plasticine clay.

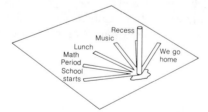

- Set the sundial in a south-facing window (or outdoors) when a school day begins. Periodically observe the sundial to note the position of the pencil's shadow. Have a child mark the shadow's position at each observation.
- Note the event that occurs just before or after each observation: "school begins," "math class begins," "recess," "lunch time," and so on.

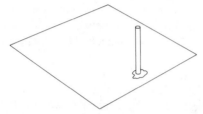

- Repeat the activity each day for a week; be certain observations are made at the same time.
- Repeat the activity for a second week but make each observation on-the-hour each day. Mark shadows and the time.

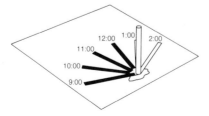

Follow up the sundial activities with discussions that deal with the order of events, and later, with the sequence of hours.

- "This morning we did some work with subtraction, and we made some paper-bag puppets. Which did we do first?"

- "We did three different things this afternoon. Who can tell me what we did first?" (Listened to a story.) "What did we do next?" (Played a math game.) "What was the last thing we did?" (Saw a film about animals.) "The game came after the story, and the film came after the game. Did the film come before or after the story?" (This latter question helps children see that if event *B* follows *A*, and *C* follows *B*, then *C* follows *A*. This deals with **transitivity,** a difficult concept for young children to understand.)

- "What is the first hour marked on our sundial?" "What is the last hour?" "What hours are in between?" "Let's name the hours in sequence." (9 o'clock, 10 o'clock, 11 o'clock, . . . 2 o'clock.)[9]

Duration and sequence are also features of children's study of the calendar. They learn that calendars indicate days of the week, the number for each day, and the month of the year, as well as the year itself. Many teachers like to incorporate the calendar into seasonal bulletin board arrangements. For the month of February, birthdays of famous Americans and Valentine's Day can be featured. Calendars such as the one in Figure 14-12, which you can make or buy, can be the basis for daily discussion; as a new date is posted, children should talk about such things as the year, month, day of the week, number of the day, number of days of the month that have already passed, and special days.

Children's understanding of time can be enhanced by having them view an entire calendar as one continuous number line. Cut up a large

FIGURE 14-12
Classroom calendar with removable tabs for recording dates

March						
Sun.	Mon.	Tues.	Wed.	Thur.	Fri.	Sat.
–	1	2	3	4	5	–
–	–	–	–	–	–	–
–	–	–	–	–	–	–
–	–	–	–	–	–	–
–	–	–	–	–	–	–
–	–	–	–	–	–	–
–	–					

[9] This activity is adapted from Charles S. Thompson and John Van de Walle, "A Single-Handed Approach to Telling Time," *Arithmetic Teacher*, XXVIII, No. 8 (November 1981), pp. 4–9.

calendar and glue or staple the strip for each week in sequence to a long piece of adding machine tape. Do not leave a gap between the last day of one month and the first day of the next. Affix this new calendar to the walls above chalkboards, with the name of each month centered above its weeks. Labels for each child's birthday and for significant school days and holidays provide a basis for discussion of past and upcoming events. Compare the number of days between Thanksgiving and Christmas and between Christmas and Easter, count the days until the next birthday, and so on.

Instruction about telling time should be built around activities with traditional clocks. Telling time with a digital clock should be learned but not at the expense of learning about regular clocks. A clock or watch does more than tell time; it helps us determine how much time has passed since, or is left before, a certain event. A person who says, "A half hour has passed since we began our walk at 3:00," has noted that the minute hand has moved half way between 3:00 and 4:00. "It is 2:00; we have 45 minutes before the bus leaves at 2:45." A clock face makes it easy to see that 45 minutes remains before the bus leaves.

One recommended sequence of activities for learning to tell time has this order:

- Begin with a clock marked with black hour numerals. Talk about the sequence of numbers. Children should note that 12 is at the top and 6 is at the bottom. The numbers between 12 and 6 and between 6 and 12 should be noted. Prepare a worksheet with one large clock face but no numerals. Children write the numerals at each hour mark (Figure 14-13).

FIGURE 14-13
Clock without hands for introducing clocks to children

- Add a black hour hand to the clock. Point it at the 12. Tell children that when the black hand points directly toward a num-ber, it tells the hour. Point it at different numbers and have chil-dren name the hour (Figure 14-14).

FIGURE 14-14
Clock face showing hour
hand only

- Show a clock that has black hour numerals and a black hour hand, red minute marks, and a red minute hand. Have children point out differences between this and the first clock. Tell them that when the hour hand points to a numeral and the minute hand points to 12, the time is the hour shown by the hour hand. Set the clock at different times to indicate hours; have children name each hour. Show and discuss two ways of writing time to the hour: 9:00 and 9 o'clock.

- Use a clock with synchronized hands to show the direction the hands move. (Demonstration clocks are available from school supply businesses. Inexpensive mechanical alarm clocks can be used, too.) Start with both hands at 12. Have children watch the hands as you turn them. Discuss the fact that while the minute hand makes one complete turn, the hour hand moves from 12 to 1. Repeat, beginning at other hours.

- Practice reading time to the half hour. Emphasize the fact that the minute hand always points to 6 and the hour hand is halfway between two numerals. Set the clock hands at different half-hour positions for children to read.

- Introduce reading time at 5-minute intervals. The ability to count by fives is a useful skill that will make it easier for children to learn to tell time to these intervals. Also point out that 5 minutes pass as the big hand moves from 12 to 1, 1 to 2, and so on. To help children realize this and to grasp the meaning of 5 minutes, have them watch the classroom clock. Remind them often to keep their eyes on the big hand as it moves from one numeral to the next as 5 minutes pass. Tell children how to read the clock when the big hand points to a numeral other than 12 or 6, and show them how to write the time, for example, 6:20 and 8:45. To simplify the time-telling process, eliminate expressions like "a quarter past 5," "half past 9," and "a quarter to 10." These times can be expressed as "5:15," "9:30," and "10:45," and read as "five-fifteen," "nine-thirty," and "ten-forty-five," respectively. Time is expressed in figures like these in timetables, TV guides, and other written materials that mention times.

- Introduce times to the minute, using procedures like the ones already mentioned.

Worksheets such as the one illustrated in Figure 14-15 should accompany lessons during which children learn to tell and write times.

Children in the middle grades should continue to practice until they learn to tell time accurately. Some will need to use demonstration clocks and worksheets until they can tell time correctly; others will need no special help. Class activities in the middle grades should also include such topics as the establishment of uniform time zones around the world,

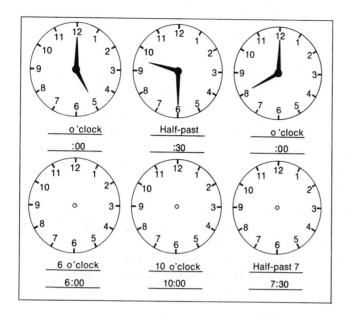

FIGURE 14-15
Worksheet for primary-grade children learning to tell time to the hour and half hour

the history of telling time, and precision instruments, such as electronic timers, that record time.

Games are useful for helping children to tell time accurately once they have learned the basic skills. Games are particularly useful for older children whose skills have not been fully developed. Calendar Bingo [10] helps develop understanding of days, weeks, months, years, A.D., B.C., and significant and less well-known holidays and birthdates of famous people. Clyde Corle's book *Skill Games for Mathematics* [11] contains four games, and *Games for Individualizing Mathematics Learning* [12] has two.

[10] Nikki Bryson Schriener, *Games & Aids for Teaching Math* (Hayward, Calif.: Activity Resources Company, 1972), pp. 37–58.

[11] Clyde C. Corle, *Skill Games for Mathematics* (Danville, N.Y.: The Instructor Publications, 1968), pp. 35–39.

[12] Leonard M. Kennedy and Ruth L. Michon, *Games for Individualizing Mathematics Learning* (Columbus, Ohio: Charles E. Merrill Books, Inc., 1973), pp. 109–112.

Describe two different aspects of time children need to learn. Explain at least one activity for dealing with each one.

Self-check of Objective 14

LEARNING ABOUT MONEY

Children receive allowances and spend money at early ages. They need to know the value of each coin and bill in order to use their money properly. Instruction begins in grade one with activities designed to acquaint children with small coins. By the end of grade three, children have experiences with all coins and small bills. Textbooks for these grades often contain realistic pasteboard models of coins. They also contain pages of exercises for which children write the amounts of money represented by pictured coins and indicate amounts of change for simulated purchases.

Even though children work with realistic models and workbook pages, they do not always grasp the relationships between pennies and nickels, nickels and dimes, and so on. These many-to-one and many-to-many matchings are confusing, because there is no physical relationship between one coin and another to make their values clear. The set of proportional materials described here offers one way to show relationships between all coins and a dollar.

- Cut a square with 30-cm sides from tagboard. Mark a 10-by-10 grid on it. Label this large square $1.00.

- Cut these pieces: ten small squares, 3 cm by 3 cm; five rectangles, 3 cm by 15 cm; five rectangles, 6 cm by 15 cm; four squares, 15 cm by 15 cm; and 2 rectangles, 15 cm by 30 cm. Use cutout pictures of coins or coin stamps to mark the small pieces. A penny goes on each small square, a nickel on each 3-by-15 piece, a dime on each 6-by-15 piece, a quarter on each large square, and a half dollar on each large rectangle.[13]

Use these proportional models for developing an understanding of each coin's value and of relationships among coins and for change-making activities. Prepare activities that include these types of experiences:

- Cover larger coin pieces with smaller pieces. "How many pennies cover a nickel?" "How many nickels cover a dime?" "What different combinations will cover a quarter?"

- Use the pieces to represent different amounts of money. "Show me seven cents." "Show me thirty-two cents." "What are the fewest coins you can use to make sixty-seven cents?"

- Introduce numerals for naming the values of different coins: 1¢, 5¢, 10¢, 25¢, and 50¢. (The decimal forms, .01, .05, .10, .25, and .50, are not introduced until values greater than $1.00 are

---

[13] This set of materials is described by Stephen J. Ginaitis in "Sense with Cents," *Arithmetic Teacher*, XXV, No. 4 (January 1978), p. 43. Some of the activities that follow are adapted from this article.

learned.) Show an amount of money, say 53¢. Have children show that amount with the smallest number of pieces.

- Use the $1.00 mat and coin pieces for change-making activities. Display a picture of a small toy and a price. If the toy's price is 35¢, the children put 35¢ worth of pieces in the upper left corner of the mat. The amount of change to receive from a dollar is the value of the uncovered portion of the mat. If the purchase is made with a half dollar, use only the half of the grid in which the coin pieces are located.

- Gradually abandon the grid pieces in favor of real coins or models as children show they are ready to change.

Children who are familiar with coins and small bills need to maintain and expand their understandings by regularly engaging in real or contrived activities that require the use of money. These are typical of the activities that are recommended for older children:

- Give each child a real or simulated menu from a favorite fast-food restaurant. An activity sheet with directions such as these can guide children's work:

  ○ Choose your favorite lunch. List each item and its cost. What is the cost of your favorite lunch?

  ○ If you pay for your favorite lunch with a $5.00 bill, how much change will you get back?

  ○ What combinations of three items can you get for less than $1.00?

  ○ Variations: Use mail-order catalogs or grocery or sporting-goods store ads.

- Older children can set up and operate a school supplies business. Pencils, paper, notebooks, erasers, school T-shirts, and so forth can be stocked and sold.

- One teacher of the author's acquaintance helped children organize a corporation for which they sold stock to purchase hot-food dispensers for the school's adult lunchroom. The children learned about time purchases, accounting procedures, profits and losses, inventory control, stock dividends, and other aspects of running a business.

Describe a set of proportional materials for teaching children the value of money, and explain three activities with these materials.

**Self-check
of Objective 15**

SUMMARY OF MEASUREMENT CONCEPTS

As children progress in their study of measurement, they should period-ically summarize the concepts they have learned. By the time children have completed the elementary school, most will have mastered these concepts:

1. The process of measuring means selecting a unit of measure and applying it to whatever is being measured. The result gives a comparison between the unit and the item being measured. The number of times the unit can be laid end to end with no over-lapping or gaps (in the case of linear measure) is its measure. When the unit of measure is named, for example, 6 centimeters, the item's measurement is stated.

2. Measurements are determined for quantities that are continuous rather than discrete. Because the quantities are continuous, all measurements are *approximate* rather than exact.

3. Units of measure must be of the same nature as what is being measured. For example, line segments are units used for deter-mining linear measurements, and square regions are units for determining area measurements.

4. Units of measure must be uniform wherever they are used. A government establishes standards that guarantee uniformity throughout the country.

5. A measuring instrument is selected on the basis of the job to be done. Generally, the smaller the object to be measured, the more precise the instrument. A meter stick or trundle wheel is suit-able for measuring a school yard, whereas a centimeter ruler is used to determine the dimensions of a desk top.

**Self-check
of Objective 16**
Give a summary of the important measurement concepts included in the elementary-school program.

SPECIAL STUDENTS AND MEASUREMENT

1. Learning-Handicapped Children

Handicaps that make it difficult for some children to learn about whole and fractional numbers and to perform operations with them make it difficult for these same children to understand measurement and time concepts, to use measuring instruments, and to learn about money. Students with impaired vision or those whose visual discrimination, figure-ground, and auditory-memory skills are weak cannot always make proper distinctions between units of measure, different coins, and the minute and hour hands on a clock. Even when they can properly distinguish a penny from a nickel, they cannot always identify the value of each and specify which is worth more.

Special care is needed to provide a progression of activities and to pace them so these children can meaningfully assimilate topics as they are presented. The three-step progression recommended in this chapter—exploratory activities, work with nonstandard units, and finally work with standard units—is critical for learning-handicapped children. The exploratory materials and large nonstandard units provide experiences that help children develop motor skills; learn to discriminate on the basis of size, shape, and color; sequence materials; and develop other prerequisite skills for understanding measurement, time, and money.

When you introduce standard units of measure, use measuring instruments that are uncluttered. A centimeter ruler should contain only centimeter units; a foot ruler should have only inch units. A spring scale should contain either kilograms or pounds, with no marks for in-between units. Carefully select the objects that the children are to measure so that they can easily find the whole-unit measure of each one. An object can have a measure that is a little less or a little more than a whole unit, but it should not have one that is about halfway between two units. Be sure your children are able to measure to the nearest whole unit accurately before you introduce subdivisions. When a child is ready for subdivisions, a ruler with millimeter or half-inch marks can be introduced. Meter, foot, and other larger units should be introduced according to individual children's readiness to deal with them. Not all learning-handicapped children will learn about and use the same units of measure.

The money and time activities discussed earlier are important life skills for many learning-handicapped children. The sequence that is presented here is appropriate for these children. When activities are presented at a suitable pace, many learning-handicapped children will develop an understanding of time and money that is comparable to that of their classmates. Nancy S. Bley and Carol A. Thornton describe materials and procedures for children who need intensive special help in Chapter 3 of *Teaching Mathematics to the Learning Disabled*.[14]

2. Gifted and Talented Students

Work with measurement offers an opportunity to use the **three-level enrichment plan** for enriching the experiences of gifted and talented children described in Chapter 3. For the *first level* of work, you can set up

---

[14]Nancy S. Bley and Carol A. Thornton, *Teaching Mathematics to the Learning Disabled* (Rockville, Maryland: Aspen Systems Corporation, 1981).

an exploratory center that deals with an occupation that uses specialized measuring instruments. For example, civil engineers use specialized instruments for making land surveys for construction projects. A center can contain pictures and models of transits and other measuring devices used by surveyors. Books about the work of civil engineers; about special projects, such as the Egyptian pyramids or present-day dams, highways, and bridges; and about famous engineers, such as Colonel George W. Goethals, who worked on the Panama Canal, should be at the center. A highway department or construction company engineer can come in to talk about engineering work and explain some of the instruments used. Allow all children to examine materials at the center and to listen to the engineer.

Encourage gifted and talented children, and perhaps others who exhibit a strong interest, to advance to the *second level* of work. These children will spend time reading about the civil engineer's work, famous historical and modern engineering projects, and learn to operate an engineer's transit, which is used for measuring angles, determining bearings, and making other construction-site measurements. Some students might do research on the pyramids and make models of measuring instruments used in their construction.

Move these students to the *third level* by giving them responsibility for planning and laying out a baseball diamond, soccer field, or some other game space for the playground or multipurpose room. Students who studied the pyramids can demonstrate the model instruments and share information about the pyramid's construction orally or with a mural or some other means of visual presentation.

Self-check
of Objective 17

You have just read a description of one way to apply the three-level enrichment model to work with measurement for gifted and talented students. Select an occupation similar to the one used here and describe how it might be used in the model.

SUMMARY

At the time the Metric Conversion Act was signed by President Ford in 1975 it was anticipated that within a few years the United States would become a metric nation. Plans were established for federal agencies to change to metric measures for highway markers, speed limits, and weather reports. Private-sector responses in the automobile and other industries were positive. However, public acceptance of the plan was poor, and because the law was not mandatory, the strong resistance resulted in virtual abandonment of the plan to change from the customary to the metric system. The U.S. Metric Board was abolished, and change in both governmental and private organizations has become nil. For the foreseeable future, children in schools will need to learn about and become skillful in using both the metric and the customary system of measures.

Children's first activities should be exploratory; they should pour water, sand, and rice from one container to another, feel temperature differences, put objects on balance scales, and order objects by length, height, capacity, and size in order to build background for understanding linear, weight, capacity, area, time, and temperature concepts. Nonstandard units are used to introduce the meanings of different measures—linear, weight, capacity, area, and time. Later various commonly used metric and customary units are introduced, and children learn the instruments and processes for using each one. Learning-center activities guided by problem-card directions are useful for giving children measuring experiences. By the time children complete the elementary school, they should be able to name commonly used metric and customary units, describe the structure of the metric system, and use measuring instruments accurately. Special units are used to acquaint children with time concepts, to read time from a clock, and to understand and use money effectively.

Children with learning disabilities learn measurement, time, and money concepts in the same ways that other children do; but care must be taken to assure that materials and procedures for teaching concepts and the amount of time for learning them are appropriate for these children. The three-level model for enrichment of learning for gifted and talented students can be used to extend these children's knowledge and understanding of measurement. An example is the study of the work done by civil engineers and their special measuring instruments.

STUDY QUESTIONS AND ACTIVITIES

1. John Bradford's article in this chapter's reading list contains a description of a way to use Cuisenaire rods and plastic grids to help children learn the value of each coin. Read Bradford's article. Compare his materials and procedures with the tagboard grid described in this chapter. What are the strengths and weaknesses of each set of materials? Which of the materials would you prefer to use with a group of first- or second-grade children? Why? Do you think one set of materials would be superior for working with older children who have not learned the value of each coin and how to make change? If so, which set? Why?

2. Many books dealing with the metric system have been written for children in recent years. Read at least eight of these books. Write a short review of each one. Include author, title, publisher,

date, a brief review of the contents, and age of children for whom it is intended. Rate the books on a scale of 1 to 5, where 1 is best. Tell why the book at the top and the book at the bottom of your list are where they are.

3. Several articles in this chapter's reading list contain games and puzzles for teaching about the metric system, time, and money. Use these and articles from other publications to locate materials to add to the collection of teaching materials you accumulate.

4. Devise rules and prepare materials for a bingo game for helping intermediate-grade children learn the metric prefixes and their values and the metric measures and their abbreviations. Hint: Each prefix has a value that relates to a basic unit, for example, *milli-* stands for $1/1000$ and *kilo-* stands for 1000. Also each unit has a standard abbreviation: the abbreviation for liter is L, and that for millimeter is mm.

5. List at least five occupations in which specialized measuring instruments are used. Identify the special instrument(s) associated with each one. Which of these occupations are appropriate for inclusion in the three-level model for enriching the learning of gifted and talented children?

KEY TERMS

length	dekameter
area	hectometer
volume	kilometer
weight	liter
temperature	kilogram
meter	are
direct measure	hectare
indirect measure	International System of Units (SI)
iteration	conservation
approximate nature of measurement	nonstandard units
metric system	perimeter
English (customary) system	time
decimeter	transistivity
centimeter	three-level enrichment plan
millimeter	

FOR FURTHER READING

Bradford, John W. "Making Sense Out of Dollars and Cents," *Arithmetic Teacher*, XXVII, No. 7 (March 1980), pp. 44–46.

Cuisenaire rods and plastic hundred-grids serve as models for coins and $1.00. Procedures for moving from the concrete models to a written code for representing money are described.

Brougher, Janet Jean. "Discovery Activities with Area and Perimeter," *Arithmetic Teacher*, XX, No. 5 (May 1973), pp. 382–385.
Presents discovery activities dealing with geometric figures having constant perimeters and varying areas and having constant areas and varying perimeters. These activities can serve as the basis for teacher-made problem cards dealing with area and perimeter.

Carr, Karen D. "A Common Cents Approach to Mathematics," *Arithmetic Teacher*, XXVI, No. 2 (October 1978), pp. 14–15.
A sixth-grade class banking project, complete with forms and simulated life experiences, provides a study of the economics of daily living and how to cope with management of checking and savings accounts.

Cooper, Martin. "Leap Years and Such," *Arithmetic Teacher*, XXVII, No. 5 (January 1980), pp. 26–27.
Not every fourth year after 1984 is a leap year! Cooper tells why and describes activities about the history of the calendar for children. This work is for interested older children. It offers practical calculator exercises.

Daane, C.J. "Primary Coin Activity Cards," *Arithmetic Teacher*, XXVII, No. 6 (February 1980), pp. 34–36.
Coin sheets and a coin trading board are the materials needed for six games, with emphasis on pennies, nickels, dimes, and quarters.

Elliott, Portia A. "Money Changer's Bingo," *Arithmetic Teacher*, XXVII, No. 1 (September 1979), pp. 50–51.
Money Changer's Bingo is for upper-grade children who need practice in making and counting change. The rules and materials for the game are described.

Ginaitis, Stephen J. "Sense with Cents," *Arithmetic Teacher*, XXV, No. 4 (January 1978), p. 43.
Describes procedures using a 10×10 hundreds board and smaller regions to represent dollars and cents. Activities with the materials aid children in learning coin values and change-making skills.

Lindquist, Mary M., and Marcia E. Dana. "The Neglected Decimeter," *Arithmetic Teacher*, XXV, No. 1 (October 1977), pp. 10–17.
The decimeter is more suitable than either the centimeter or meter for introducing children to standard units of linear measure, claim these writers. Five types of activities with many examples of each are presented.

Nelson, Glenn. "Teaching Time-Telling," *Arithmetic Teacher*, XXIX, No. 9 (May 1982), pp. 31–34.
The author's approach to teaching time is one that simplifies the process by eliminating many of the confusing terms that inhibit learning. His simplified materials and terminology, along with a sequence for teaching time-telling, are illustrated and discussed.

Riley, James E. "It's About Time," *Arithmetic Teacher*, XXVIII, No. 2 (October 1980), pp. 12–14.
Activities dealing with duration and sequence of time are described.

Ropa, Adrienne. "Roll Out the Meters," *Instructor*, LXXXVI, No. 9 (May 1977), pp. 78–79.

Self-adhesive meter and dekameter strips, each a different color, serve as a means for building children's understanding of meter, dekameter, hectometer, and kilometer. Both indoor and outdoor activities are described.

Steffe, Leslie P. "Thinking about Measurement," *Arithmetic Teacher*, XVIII, No. 5 (May 1971), pp. 332–338.

Piaget's theories of cognitive development and some of their applications to learning the meaning of measurement are discussed in this thought-provoking article.

Strangman, Kathryn B. "Grids, Tiles, and Areas," *Arithmetic Teacher*, XV, No. 8 (December 1968), pp. 668–672.

Instructing children about area-measurement processes using grids and irregularly shaped regions is discussed. The process enables children to formulate generalizations of the important concepts involved.

Thompson, Charles S., and John Van de Walle. "A Single-Handed Approach to Telling Time," *Arithmetic Teacher*, XXVIII, No. 8 (April 1981), pp. 4–9.

Sundials and one-handed clocks provide the basis for activities to introduce children to time concepts and how to read clocks.

Walter, Marion. "A Common Misconception about Area," *Arithmetic Teacher*, XVII, No. 4 (April 1970), pp. 286–289. The common misconception is that figures with common perimeters will have the same area regardless of the measures of their sides. The examples given here can serve as the basis for several problem cards to challenge mathematically mature fifth and sixth graders.

Williams, David E., and Brian Wolfson. "Play Metric—Games to Help Kids Think Metric," *Instructor*, LXXXVI, No. 8 (April 1977), pp. 62–63, 66. Three games—Shuffleboard, Roll a Meter, and Metric Bet—are described and illustrated. All are teacher-made.

Yvon, Bernard R. "Metrics with Marcel and Marcette," *Arithmetic Teacher*, XXV, No. 1 (October 1977), pp. 26–27. Marcel and Marcette are meter-long cloth snakes. Instructions are given for making them and some of the ways they can be used by young children to learn about the meter.

Zalewski, Donald. "Some Dos and Don'ts for Teaching the Metric System," *Arithmetic Teacher*, XXVI, No. 4 (December 1978), p. 17. Briefly discusses a list of six "dos" and two "don'ts" to consider while teaching the metric system.

15

Informal Geometry

Upon completion of Chapter 15 you will be able to:

1. Distinguish between a topological and a Euclidean view of space.

2. List four important topological relations included in the early school program, and describe children's activities for learning about them.

3. Demonstrate activities at both the primary and the intermediate levels for learning about plane figures.

4. Identify geometric figures associated with lines and line segments.

5. Describe and demonstrate activities dealing with points and lines.

6. Discuss activities that can be used to develop children's understanding of space figures.

7. Distinguish between congruent and similar figures, and describe materials and activities children can use to develop their understanding of both kinds of figures.

8. Give a definition of symmetry, and describe materials and activities children can use to learn about it.

9. Describe and demonstrate activities for helping children learn about coordinate geometry.

10. Illustrate with appropriate models three transformations: translations (slides), rotations, and reflections.

Geometry has been a part of the elementary-school curriculum for many years. For a long time children have learned to recognize and name simple common plane and space figures. Since the late 1950s educators have recognized that a more comprehensive study of geometry is beneficial to children. At first there was wide divergence of opinion about which aspects of the topic should be included in new programs. Although edu-

TABLE 15-1 The grade level at which various geometry topics are introduced in four different textbook series.

Topic	Textbook series			
	A	B	C	D
Common plane figures	1	1	1	1
Circle	1	1	1	1
Segments	4	3	2	1
Angles, rays	4	3	3	4, 5
Symmetry	2	2	4	1
Congruence, similarity	2	3	2	1
Coordinate graphing	3	3	5	1
Parallel, perpendicular, intersecting lines	4	4	5	4

cators agreed on the need for more geometry, they did not agree on the particulars.

There is greater agreement today, and some topics are common to most contemporary mathematics textbook series. Table 15-1 lists nine topics and the grade level at which each one is introduced in four current series. There is still not agreement about the grade levels at which certain topics should be introduced. Only circles and common plane polygons are introduced in the same grade in all series. Series D introduces six of the eight topics in grade 1, whereas each of the other series introduces only plane figures in that grade. Coordinate geometry is introduced in grade 1 in series D, but it is delayed until grade 5 in series C.

P. van Heile, a Dutch mathematician, has studied the mental development of students with respect to geometry and has concluded that there are five levels of knowledge through which individuals pass as they learn the subject. Instruction in elementary-school geometry should be organized to deal with the first three of van Heile's five levels. Children first learn to recognize common shapes such as square, circle, triangle, and rectangle. Next they determine each shape's general characteristics, such as the number of sides in a square, triangle, or rectangle. By the end of grade 6, children should have third-level knowledge. They then should be able to classify common figures according to their characteristics (for example, all four-sided figures are quadrilaterals) and should be able to explain why a square is both a rectangle and a parallelogram.[1] The elementary-school program must be informal so children can move through the three levels with an understanding of the geometry they learn. A deductive study of geometry, which is van Heile's fourth level of understanding and is probably familiar to you from your study of the subject in high school and college, must be delayed until students are mature enough to cope with it.

A comprehensive discussion of materials and procedures for teaching

---

[1] For a discussion of van Heile's five levels, see Izaak Wirzup, "Breakthroughs in the Psychology of Learning and Teaching Geometry," in *Space and Geometry*, J. Larry Martin, ed. (Columbus, Ohio: ERIC Information Analysis Center for Science, Mathematics, and Environmental Education, 1976), pp. 76–79.

geometry is beyond the scope of this book. The topics that are discussed are from Table 15-1. Before presenting information about teaching these topics, there is a brief discussion of the implications of Piaget's research about children's mental development for teaching geometry.

TOPOLOGICAL VERSUS EUCLIDEAN CONCEPTS OF SPACE

You will recall that Piaget stated that each individual progresses through four stages of mental development during maturation:

1. The sensorimotor stage (zero to two years).

2. The preoperational stage (two to seven years).

3. The concrete operations stage (seven to eleven years).

4. The formal operations stage (eleven years and older).

Piaget said that children's first concepts about the world (space) around them are topological rather than Euclidean. A **topological** view does not require that figures maintain a fixed shape, as they must in **Euclidean geometry.** In topology a shape may be altered so that it assumes a new configuration, much as it would if drawn on a rubber sheet where it can be pulled in different directions. For example a square may assume the shape of a circle or some other simple closed curve. Or an open figure, such as one shaped like the letter *C*, can be reshaped to look like the letter *S*. Even though the shapes' configurations change, certain characteristics are unchanged. The shape that was once the square remains a simple closed curve, and the open figure remains open with only two end points. In Euclidean geometry all figures, whether line, plane, or space, remain rigid and unchanged.

According to Piaget very young children do not view people and objects as being rigid and unchanging but view them in the topological sense. To children in the sensorimotor stage the appearances of people and objects change as the positions from which they are viewed change. This topological way of viewing things continues into the preoperational stage. During preschool and kindergarten children should have experiences that deal with four important topological (spatial) relations: proximity, separation, order, and enclosure. As children move from the preoperational to the concrete operational stage of development, their study of geometry can change from topological to Euclidean.

1. Proximity

Proximity refers to the nearness of one object to another. Naturally, very young children are interested in things near to them, because they can touch and manipulate them. Things that are out of their reach are usually of little interest, unless the child sees something that is eye-catching such as a shiny part of a swinging mobile. Objects that are out of sight do not exist in the mind of the sensorimotor child.

Gradually children engage in activities that help them recognize that out-of-sight objects exist and clarify the distinction between near and far and the relationships of objects in terms of their nearness to each other. The prenumber activities discussed in Chapter 7, particularly the ones dealing with classification and spatial relationships, provide experiences that help develop children's understanding of proximity. Once children have classified a set of materials or arranged a set of beads to form a pattern on a string, you can ask such questions as: "Which red car is nearest to the green car?" "Which black bead is farther from the blue bead?"

ACTIVITY 15-1   Near and Far

- Set up a flannel board that displays colored felt cars, airplanes, and train engines.

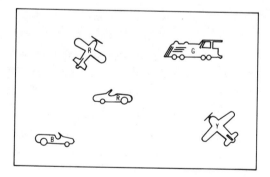

- Ask questions like these:
    - "Which is nearer the red airplane, the red car or the green train engine?"
    - "Which object is farthest from the green train engine?"
    - "Sally, will you move the blue car so that it is nearer to the train engine than it is to the yellow airplane?"
- Variations: Use magnetized objects on a magnetic board. Use objects such as apples, oranges, and bananas placed on a table top. Have children go to places in the room that are near or far from tables, cabinets, doors, and so on.

2. Separation

Until children achieve an understanding of **separation,** they cannot clearly visualize an object as having separate parts or a collection as being made up of separate objects. All of the parts run together in the child's mind. Children's drawings provide a good indication of their understanding of separation. Drawings of human figures are particularly enlightening. A child who understands separation will put the arms and legs in place with the body properly separating them, and the eyes will be in their proper position on the face with the nose separating them.

ACTIVITY 15-2 Separation

- Arrange two sets of felt shapes about six inches apart on a flannel board with a piece of yarn stretched from top to bottom separating them.
- Have the children describe what they see. During the discussion, say that the yarn separates one set from the other.
- Move the sets about, putting them closer together or farther apart, with the yarn still between them. After each move, ask if the yarn still separates the sets.
- Move both sets to the same side of the yarn. "Does the yarn still separate the two sets?"

---

3. Order

Activities that deal with continuous and discrete objects, classification, and patterns, such as the ones described in Chapter 7, contribute to children's understanding of **order.** Children will see order in the way attribute blocks are organized and the way beads or pegs are put into patterns on cords or pegboards. During early work children may be able to copy patterns directly from models, but they may not be able to reverse the order. They will eventually be able to do this if they are given enough unhurried pattern-card activities. When they can reverse a pattern's order, they demonstrate that they have a clear understanding of order.

4. Enclosure

Enclosure includes the positioning of one point between two others on a line, a point within a closed curve on a plane, and a point within a closed space figure. Enclosure on a line is important because it is a relation children encounter frequently in mathematics. For example they will talk about a number being between two other numbers. (A number that is between two numbers can be said to be enclosed by the numbers.) Children's first work with enclosure should be at the concrete-operations level. Activity 15-3 is for developing children's understanding of enclosure on a line.

ACTIVITY 15-3   Enclosure on a Line

- Put three different beads on a string.
- Have children describe what they see. If they have already considered separation, they can mention that the center bead separates the other two.
- Point out that the two outside beads enclose the bead in the middle. Help them see that the middle bead cannot be taken off without removing one of the two outside beads.
- Variations: Have children stand so one is enclosed by others on either side. Use a play clothesline and discuss items of clothing that are enclosed by other clothing on the line. Discuss how some chairs are enclosed by others in a row of chairs.

Toys and pictures can be used to develop children's understanding of enclosure on a plane. The rural setting in the following activity is one way to use toys.

ACTIVITY 15-4   Enclosed by a Fence

- Set up a scene with plastic fences, horses, cows, barns, and so on. Have some animals inside a closed fence and some outside of it.
- Ask questions similar to these:
  - "Who can show me some animals that are inside the fence?"
  - "Is the brown horse inside or outside of the fence?"
  - "Is the barn inside or outside of the fence?"
- Point out that the things inside the fence are enclosed by the fence. As long as the gate is closed, they cannot get out, and the animals that are outside cannot get in.
- Variations: (1) Felt animals and a yarn loop can be used on a flannel board. (2) Young children's playgrounds are often separated from those for older children by a fence. Some pieces of play equipment are permanently placed inside the fence, whereas wagons and other wheeled toys are not. Discuss these pieces of equipment in terms of whether or not they are permanently enclosed by the fence.

Have a wide assortment of boxes and bottles that are opaque and clear to build children's understanding of enclosure in space. An activity like this can be used.

ACTIVITY 15-5   Enclosed in a Jar

- Put a colored marble or small rubber ball in a clear jar with a lid and another one in an open jar.
- Have the children explain the differences between the two bottles.
- Ask: "Can I take the marble out of the jar with the lid without removing the lid?" "Can I take the marble out of the other jar without doing anything to the jar?"
- Discuss the fact that the closed jar encloses the marble so it cannot be taken out and other marbles cannot be put in without removing the lid.
- Put a cotton ball in a lidded opaque box.
- Shake the box; then ask, "Do you think the cotton ball is still in the box?" "Does the box enclose the cotton ball?"
- Repeat with other objects in both open and closed boxes and bottles. Be sure children understand that when an object is enclosed in a box or bottle, it cannot be taken out without opening the container.

Self-check of Objectives 1 and 2

Give a statement in which you distinguish between a topological and a Euclidean view of space. List four topological relations included in the primary program, and describe at least one activity dealing with each relation.

ACTIVITIES WITH PLANE FIGURES

Plane figures, including circles and closed figures composed of line segments—triangles, squares, and rectangles—are commonly introduced in the first grade. In each succeeding grade children study these and other figures more thoroughly until by the time they leave the sixth grade they can classify figures by their common characteristics, or attributes. The activities that follow are based on the belief that children's experiences should be at the concrete-manipulative mode of learning. The activities for each material are not exhaustive but are representative of things children can do with the material.

1. Shapes and Posting Holes

Shapes cut from plywood, masonite, or heavy art paper such as colored railroad board are easily made. If they are cut carefully, you will have not only the shapes, as shown in Figure 15-1(a), but also their outlines in the pieces of material from which they were cut (b). These holes are called **posting holes.** Children use the models to get the "feel" of each

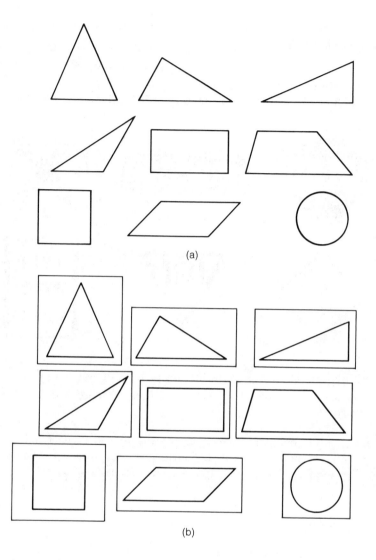

FIGURE 15-1
(a) Common geometric shapes. (b) Posting holes for the shapes.

shape by running their fingers around the outside of the shapes and the inside of their posting holes. Have children count the sides (edges) and corners of each shape and talk about the way corners feel: they will feel "sort of flat," "sharp," or "square." Children can also talk about the differences in the feel of the edges of polygons compared with a circle.

Once they are familiar with some shapes, primary-grade children should search their environment for examples of the ones they know. Activities such as the following are interesting to most children.

- Children can look around the classroom to find things that have shapes similar to the geometric figures they have been studying. Many of the figures will be represented by objects already in the room. You should prearrange the room to contain representative objects of certain shapes not usually present, particularly spheres and circles.

- During their study of safety, children can be guided to recognize the different shapes of signs used along streets and highways (Figure 15-2). Replicas or pictures of them should be available.

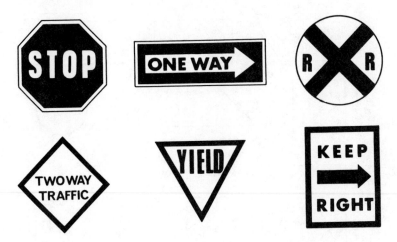

- Children can look in magazines for pictures of objects of different geometric shapes. The pictures can be displayed on bulletin boards.

Later, fifth and sixth graders can use the cut-out models and posting holes to learn more advanced geometric ideas. An investigation that uses these materials to learn about symmetry is discussed later.

2. Geoboards

A **geoboard** is a square piece of wood or plastic in which pegs are arranged in some orderly fashion. Arrangements in common use have nine, sixteen, twenty-five, or thirty-six pegs ordered in 3-by-3, 4-by-4, 5-by-5, and 6-by-6 patterns, and some have circular patterns (Figure 15-3). Boards with 100 pegs arranged in a 10-by-10 pattern are also useful because they have room for the outlines of several plane figures at one time. Rubber bands are used to make figures on the boards. Paper covered with rows and columns of evenly spaced dots should be available so children can copy figures from their geoboards. Geoboards and dot paper are produced commercially by a number of companies. Many teachers make geoboards with plywood and small finishing nails, and dot paper with the copy machine.

Geoboards make possible a wide range of investigations. In the primary grades children can use them to investigate and gain an intuitive understanding of plane figures, both open and closed, and of points and line segments. Older children can use them to study different types of triangles, quadrilaterals, and other figures and to learn about regular and irregular figures, concave and convex figures, and other more mature concepts.

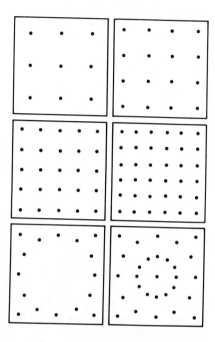

FIGURE 15-3
Examples of commonly used geoboards

ACTIVITY 15-6   Three-Sided Figures

- Have children work singly or in pairs.
- Show them how to make a three-sided figure with one rubber band.
- Have the children compare their triangles.
- Ask: "Are all of the figures alike?"
- Discuss the ways any of the figures are different.
- If the term *triangle* is unknown, introduce it now. Tell the children that each of the figures they made is a triangle.
- Repeat with four-sided figures made with one rubber band.

ACTIVITY 15-7   Polygons

- Have children make a series of figures, each one having one more side than its predecessor. (Ten-by-ten boards are good for this activity. If smaller ones are used, children will probably need to copy each figure on dot paper before a new one is made. Do not do this activity unless your children are mature enough to make accurate copies.

- Have the children compare their figures with those of their neighbor to see the differences, if any, in each kind.
- Talk about changes in the figure's shapes as more sides are used.
- Some children will probably make concave as well as convex figures. The figure on the left in the illustration is concave, and the one on the right is convex. Accept these as long as children recognize that they are closed figures and have the number of sides claimed by their makers.

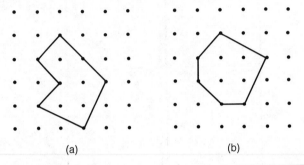

(a)   (b)

ACTIVITY 15-8   Open and Closed Curves

- Have children make open and closed curves. Open curves can be made by stretching a rubber band between two or more pegs, either in a straight line or going around a corner.

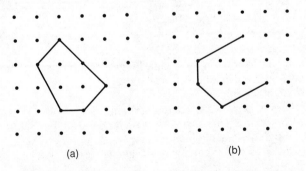

(a)   (b)

- Discuss differences in the children's figures.
- Extend children's understanding of enclosure by considering pegs located inside both closed and open figures. Discuss the fact that another rubber band cannot be stretched between a peg inside the closed figure and one outside the figure without crossing the figure itself.

There are geoboard activities to help older children extend their knowledge of plane figures to van Heile's third level of knowledge. The ones that follow are examples of some you can give orally or present with problem cards.

ACTIVITY 15-9 Four-Sided Figures

- Have children make these four-sided figures on their geoboards:

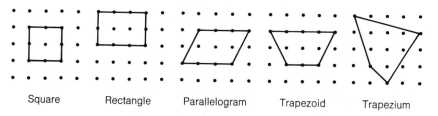

| Square | Rectangle | Parallelogram | Trapezoid | Trapezium |

- Discuss each figure to point out the similarities and differences.
- Organize information about each figure in a table.

Figure	Angles	Sides
Square	four right (90°)	Congruent, parallel
Rectangle	four right (90°)	Opposite sides congruent and parallel
Parallelogram	Opposite angles congruent	Opposite sides congruent and parallel
Trapezoid	May have adjacent angles con-gruent	One pair of parallel sides, nonparallel sides may be congruent
Trapezium	May have two adjacent angles congruent	No parallel sides, may have two adjacent sides congruent

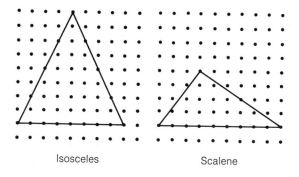

| Isosceles | Scalene |

FIGURE 15-4
Two triangles classified by the characteristics of their sides are shown on a 7-by-7 geoboard.

Models of some triangles classified by their sides can be made on larger geoboards, such as 10-by-10 boards (Figure 15-4). During a study of

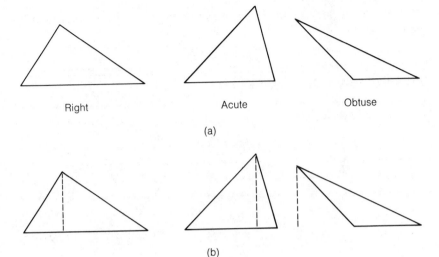

Right　　　　　Acute　　　　　Obtuse

(a)

FIGURE 15-5
Three triangles classified by
characteristics of their angles
(a) and their altitudes (b) are
represented on geoboards.

(b)

these models children will learn to classify triangles as **isosceles,** which
have two congruent sides, and **scalene,** which have no congruent sides.
Children can also learn that triangles are classified according to the types
of angles they have, as shown in Figure 15-5. In (a) the three types of
triangles classified by angles are illustrated. A right triangle has one **right
angle;** an acute triangle has three **acute angles;** an obtuse triangle has
one **obtuse angle,** which is an angle that is greater than 90°. These models
can also be used to illustrate the meaning of a triangle's **altitude** (b). For
the right and acute triangles, a rubber band (shown by the broken line
and representing the altitude) is inside of the triangle; it is outside of the
figure when the triangle is obtuse. (If the obtuse triangle is placed with
the longest side at the bottom, the altitude can be shown by a broken
line in its interior.)

3. Other Activities

Turtle geometry, which is available through the Logo computer programming language, provides opportunities for children to investigate
many types of plane figures, as well as more fanciful figures. Instructions
for using this language to make a square are listed in Chapter 6.

By the end of sixth grade, children should be familiar with the common figures shown in Figure 15-6. They should also be able to explain
how each closed figure separates a plane into three distinct sets of points—
the set that is the polygon itself, the set within the polygon (enclosed by
the polygon), and the set outside the polygon. When children find the
area of a region, they actually determine the measure of that part of the
plane enclosed by the simple closed curve. When they find the perimeter, they determine the measure of the line segments (or the curved line)
that comprise a simple closed curve.

The final activity is one for which children must use several problem-

Polygon	Name of Polygon	Number of sides	Name of Region
△	Triangle	3	Triangular
□	Quadrilateral	4	Quadrilateral
⬠	Pentagon	5	Pentagonal
⬡	Hexagon	6	Hexagonal
⬡	Heptagon	7	Heptagonal
⬡	Octagon	8	Octagonal

FIGURE 15-6
Chart to classify polygons

solving strategies. They can make shapes of common plane figures and show the number of diagonals for each on geoboards. A **diagonal** is a segment that connects two nonadjacent corners. Then they should organize their data in a table.

ACTIVITY 15-10 Diagonals

- Have the children make each of these figures and show its diagonals on a geoboard.

- State the name for each figure and count its diagonals. Put the data in a table.

Figure	Angles	Diagonals
Triangle	3	0
Quadrilateral	4	2
Pentagon	5	5
Hexagon	6	9
Heptagon	7	14

- Examine the table to determine how the number of diagonals changes as the diagonals for each succeeding figure are made. Write the pattern on the chalkboard: 2, 3, 4, 5, . . .
- Have the children predict the number of diagonals in an 8-sided and a 9-sided figure. Check their predictions by making 8- and 9-sided figures and their diagonals.
- Challenge children to determine a formula for finding the number of diagonals in an *n*-sided figure.

Demonstrate one activity for work with plane figures at the primary level and one at the intermediate level using these devices: shapes and posting holes and geoboards.

ACTIVITIES WITH POINTS AND LINES

The very nature of geometric points and lines makes them difficult for children to conceptualize. Piaget recommended that study of these figures be postponed until children are eight or nine years old, which means at least the third grade of elementary school. By this time most children will have a background of earlier experiences upon which to build their understanding. Once points and lines are introduced, children will study them and plane and solid figures in such a way that work with one type of figure will extend and reinforce their understanding of the others.

ACTIVITY 15-11   Segments and Rays

- Hold a piece of string with one end in each hand; draw the string taut against the chalkboard. Tell the children that the string represents a part of a line that could go clear across the chalkboard. Discuss the fact that the line could extend forever in both directions from the board. Tell them that a part of a line is called a **segment.**
- Draw a picture of a segment on the board that is as long as the taut string. Label it to show how line segments are named.

- Draw a picture of a line on the board and show how it is labeled. Explain that the arrow heads at each end are used to show that the line goes on without end.

- Draw a picture of a **ray** on the board. Explain that a ray includes an end point and all points extending in one direction from that point. Ask: "Why is there only one arrowhead on a ray?"

ACTIVITY 15-12   Closed Curves

- Give each child a 50-cm length of yarn.
- Show a picture of each of these shapes and have the children copy them with their yarn.

- Discuss the fact that the first figure is a simple closed curve. It begins and ends at the same point. The other two figures are not simple closed curves; one crosses itself and the other does not begin and end at the same point.
- Have the children make other figures of both types. Discuss their figures to help them distinguish between the two.

An infinite number of lines pass through a point. One way to illustrate this is with an overhead projector and a series of transparent overlays (Figure 15-7). Show a single line passing through a point on the first overlay (a). Show a second overlay that contains more lines passing through the point (b). With each successive overlay show more lines passing through the point. Point out that there are also other lines passing through the point in directions other than those that are on the plane; these cannot be shown on the transparencies.

Perpendicular and **parallel** lines are commonly introduced to children in grades 4 through 6. Your classroom provides models for both kinds of lines. The line segments formed where a wall joins the floor and the ceiling provide a model of parallel lines. Children can imagine that if the

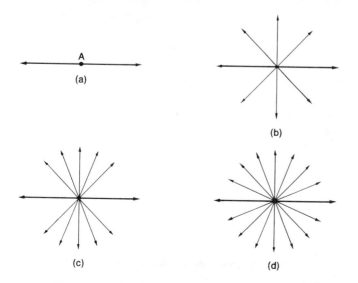

FIGURE 15-7

By using transparencies and overlays one can show that many lines pass through a point.

two lines were extended infinitely in both directions, they would never meet. The line formed by two walls joining at a corner and the line formed by the floor and one wall serve as models for perpendicular lines. Your children should be challenged to find other models of these two line relations in and out of the classroom.

**Self-check
of Objectives 4 and 5**

Define and illustrate models of each of these figures or relations: line, line segment, ray, closed curve, parallel lines, and perpendicular lines.

Describe an activity that can be used by children to learn about the meaning of each term above.

SPACE FIGURES

We live in a three-dimensional world, and children's experiences inside and outside the home are with objects that have three dimensions. It is recommended that children work with three-dimensional models of the space figures in school.

1. Play Activities

Commercial materials such as Geo Blocks[2] and the attribute materials mentioned in Chapter 7, the colored wooden or plastic blocks, commonly found in preschool and kindergarten classrooms, and boxes and cardboard tubes of all shapes and sizes should be available for children's play. Initial activities should give children freedom to construct whatever they like. They will design and create many imaginative structures; some will show a surprising amount of creativity. Many children have a natural inclination to make patterns and structures that balance or are symmetrical. Though you do not need to develop the notion of symmetry during early play activities, you can comment on the way two sides of a pattern look almost alike or are the same.

Another activity that interests children is making their own structures to take home. Give children a collection of various-sized boxes and tubes, some glue, and tempera paint; then allow them freedom to make a truck, railroad engine, steamship, or whatever strikes their fancies. Again call attention to the way two sides look alike (if they do) and any other interesting aspects of their creations.

---

[2] A set of Geo Blocks contains more than 100 hardwood pieces cut into a wide variety of shapes having edges up to 4 inches long. In addition to the blocks, there are a *Teacher's Guide for Geo Blocks* and *Problem Cards for Geo Blocks*. All are produced by the Webster Division of the McGraw–Hill Book Company, Manchester Road, Manchester, MO 63011.

2. Examination and Discussion of Solid Figures

During play activities children gradually learn some of the terminology for parts of space figures—corner, edge, square, triangle, circle. You should encourage them to use these words but do not force the specialized names and definitions too soon. As children indicate their interest by asking for names of a figure's parts, organize them into small groups to examine and talk about their models. Work with each group until children are making the proper associations of terminology and parts. Later you can make problem cards to guide their work in a classroom learning center. Use plastic or tagboard models, if possible, because children can conceive of the figure itself and its inside and outside more easily with hollow and, especially, transparent models than with wooden or other solid figures.[3]

ACTIVITY 15-13   Planes and Solids

- Give each child or pair of children a plastic model of a cube, pyramid, prism, or cylinder.
- Discuss the plane figures associated with the models—square, triangle, rectangle, and circle—and the edges and corners. Discuss the fact that each figure has an inside and an outside.
- Count the shapes of a particular kind in a model. "How many squares are there in your model? Are there any other shapes in it? What are they? How many are there? Are they all the same size?"
- "How many edges are there in each model?"
- "How many corners are there in each model?" (*Vertex* is the proper mathematical term for corner, but reserve its use for older children. Later, children will learn more precise definitions for each part of the space figures with which they work.)
- "Which models roll easily? Which don't roll? Which slide when they are pushed? Which roll when placed one way but slide when placed the other way?"

Other activities for young children include these:

- Have children locate and name objects in the room and around school that look like the solid figures they have studied. Discuss reasons why a particular figure is used in a given situation.

- Have children complete work sheets by matching or drawing lines between pictures of similar objects (Figure 15-8).

---

[3] See Leonard M. Kennedy, *Models for Mathematics in the Elementary School* (Belmont, Cal.: Wadsworth Publishing Company, 1967); pp. 158–173, for patterns and directions for making fourteen inexpensive clear plastic models.

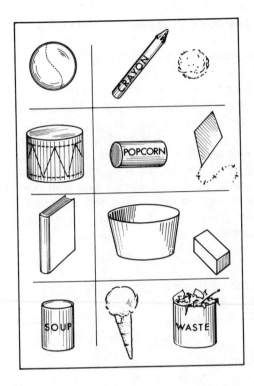

FIGURE 15-8
Sample work page for shape recognition by primary-grade children

- Have children make a bulletin board or individual booklets with magazine pictures of objects that look like the space figures they have studied.

The following activities are appropriate for children in grades 4 through 6. The first one helps them clear up the confusion that often surrounds textbook illustrations of space figures. They do this by drawing their own pictures of simple solid figures, such as the ones in Activity 15-14. Two different types of drawings are used in books, so children should draw some of each kind.

ACTIVITY 15-14   Solid Perspectives

- Have several children draw a picture of the same figure, such as a rectangular prism, each from a different perspective.

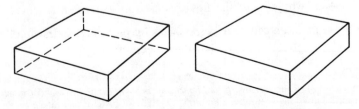

- Give their pictures and the model to another group of children who are to arrange the pictures according to the perspective from which each was drawn.
- Repeat with different figures until each child can draw each model from different perspectives and can arrange pictures accurately.

Clear plastic models are ideal for older children's analysis of space figures such as **prisms** (Figure 15-9) and **pyramids** (Figure 15-10). They should learn that a right prism has two parallel bases that are congruent polygons and sides (faces) that are rectangles. If the bases are regular polygons, such as squares or equilateral triangles, the faces will be congruent rectangles. If the bases are not regular, such as a rectangle or an isosceles triangle, not all of the rectangular faces will be congruent. In a right prism the faces are perpendicular to the bases so that they form right angles where they meet.

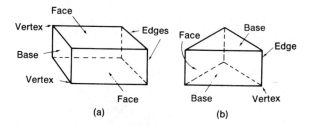

(a)

(b)

FIGURE 15-9

Identification of the parts of (a) a rectangular prism and (b) a triangular prism

Pyramids have one base and triangular faces that meet at a point at the top, or apex. The pyramids studied in the elementary school usually have regular polygons as bases, although polygons that are irregular are also found in pyramids. Both prisms and pyramids are named according to the polygon that forms their bases. In Figure 15-9 there are (a) rectangular and (b) triangular prisms, and in Figure 15-10 there is a pentagonal pyramid. Polygons with any number of sides can form the bases of these figures.

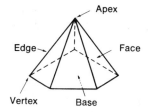

FIGURE 15-10

Identification of the parts of a pentagonal pyramid

During their study, children should learn the proper names for each figure and its parts. The parts named in Figures 15-9 and 15-10 are names children should learn. They should also learn that these figures are polyhedrons. A polyhedron is a closed figure formed by the union of four or more polygons and their interiors.

The solid figures associated with the circle—sphere, cylinder, and cone—should also be studied (Figure 15-11).

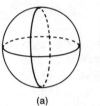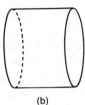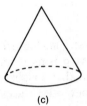

FIGURE 15-11
Common geometric solids associated with the circle

(a)   (b)   (c)

Commercial or teacher-made clear plastic models of these figures should be used rather than solid ones, if possible, so that children can visualize points on, inside, and outside each model (Figure 15-12). They can grasp the idea that polyhedrons or figures associated with the circle separate space into three distinct sets of points: the set of points that are a part of the figure itself; the set of points that occupy the interior of the figure; and the set of points found outside of the figure.

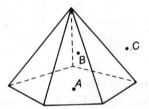

FIGURE 15-12
A polyhedron separates space into three distinct sets of points. Point A is on the pyramid itself, point B is inside the pyramid, and point C is outside the pyramid.

Here are other investigations with solid figures for older elementary-school children. Directions for each of these can be put on problem cards to make interesting learning center activities.

There are five figures called **Platonic solids** that are formed by the union of four or more congruent regular polygons and their interiors. These are the regular tetrahedron, cube (or regular hexahedron), regular octahedron, regular dodecahedron, and regular icosahedron (Figure 15-13). Give children models of these and some nonregular solids and

FIGURE 15-13
The five Platonic solids: (a) regular tetrahedron, (b) cube (regular hexahedron), (c) regular octahedron, (d) regular dodecahedron, and (e) regular icosahedron.

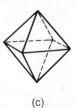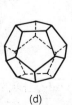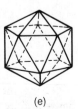

(a)   (b)   (c)   (d)   (e)

the above definition. Challenge them to identify the Platonic solids and to match each one with its name. (The names of many polyhedrons are combinations of the Greek word for the number of faces and *hedron*, which means "closed figure." *Polyhedron*, for example, means "many-sided closed figure.") Have children name the plane figures associated with each Platonic solid.

Many different types of models should be available for children to study. Children can make some themselves. Plasticine clay or Play-Doh can be used for nonhollow figures. These models are especially good to have on hand when children investigate symmetry of solid figures. (Symmetry is considered later in this chapter.) Soda straws connected with pipe cleaners and glue make good skeleton models (Figure 15-14). Skeleton models can also be made by joining lengths of pipe cleaners. Tagboard figures can be made from printed patterns that are cut and assembled by the children. As children make their own figures, they learn about edges, corners, the interiors of plane figures, and other parts of solid figures.

FIGURE 15-14
Soda-straw geometric solids

An interesting aspect of work with tagboard models is the study of nets of solid figures. A net is made by cutting some of the edges of a figure so that it will lie flat or by drawing the outline of a figure and cutting it out. Two nets for a cube are shown in Figure 15-15. To begin, give children cardboard models to cut. Cut-down milk cartons, either with a part of one side left to form a sixth face or with an open top and only a base and four sides, give a plentiful supply of cubes. The nets in Figure 15-15 are for complete cubes. Challenge children to see how many ways they can cut the cartons to form different nets. A related activity is to give children a worksheet that contains nets so they can identify the

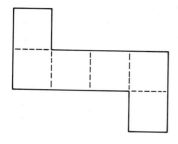 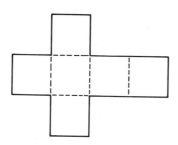

FIGURE 15-15
Two nets for a cube

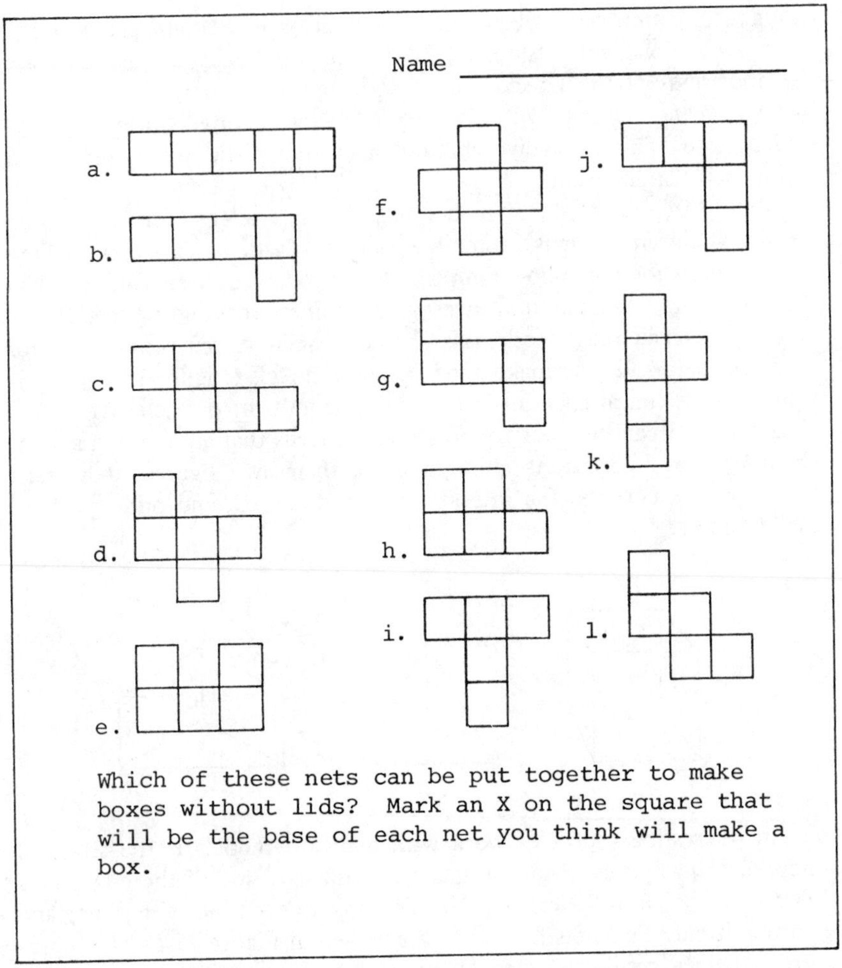

FIGURE 15-16

Worksheet for making boxes without lids from five-square nets

Name _____

a.

b.

c.

d.

e.

f.

g.

h.

i.

j.

k.

l.

Which of these nets can be put together to make boxes without lids? Mark an X on the square that will be the base of each net you think will make a box.

ones that can be cut out and assembled to form a cube (Figure 15-16).[4] After children have marked their papers, they can cut out the nets and try to assemble them to make boxes to check their answers.

Nets for other figures—pyramids, the five Platonic solids, other polyhedrons, and models of spheres, cylinders, and cones—should be included in the children's investigations, too. Children will find that a sphere cannot be flattened. They will also find that if the top and bottom of a cylinder are removed and the side is cut straight down from one edge to the other, a rectangle is formed when the figure is flattened, as in Figure 15-17(a), but if the cut is an oblique one, the flattened figure is a parallelogram as in (b).

[4]This worksheet is adapted from Marion I. Walter, *Boxes, Squares and Other Things* (Washington, D.C.: The National Council of Teachers of Mathematics, 1970), p. 9. (Used by permission.) This book contains a number of investigations dealing with solid figures and their patterns, symmetry, tessalation, and geometric transformations.

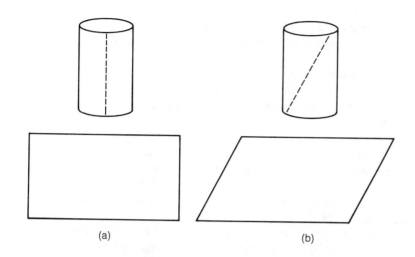

FIGURE 15-17
(a) A cylinder cut square with the edges gives a rectangle when it is flattened. (b) When the cylinder cut is oblique, flattening gives a parallelogram.

(a)   (b)

Activities with space figures are discussed. Describe at least three of these activities and tell the age of children for whom each is intended.

Self-check
of Objective 6

CONGRUENCE AND SIMILARITY

Two line segments are **congruent** when all points on one segment coincide exactly with all points on the other. Similarly, two plane figures or two space figures are congruent when all points of one figure coincide exactly with all points on the other. This is the concept on which standardized measurement, with its units for linear, area, and volume measures, is based.

Two figures are **similar** when they have the same shape and all of their corresponding parts are proportional. Thus all squares, except those that are congruent, are similar, whereas not all rectangles are. Other similar shapes are equilateral triangles, regular pentagons, hexagons, and circles, except when two like shapes are congruent. Two drawings of a room's floor plan are also similar if they are drawn to different scales.

1. Congruence

You can use several types of activities to introduce congruence or extend children's understanding of it. Problem cards can be prepared for many of them.

a. Pattern Blocks Give pairs of children sets of pattern blocks. Have one child choose and put together a pattern for the other child to copy.

b. Attribute Blocks Have children separate a set of attribute blocks into groups of congruent blocks.

c. Geoboards You can set up a geoboard with line segments, angles, and open and closed figures for children to copy. Leave enough space next to each figure for a child's copy of it, or give children individual boards.

d. Tracings Cut out line-drawing figures of animals, automobiles, other objects, and plane figures and glue them on cards, or draw simple line figures on cards for children to trace. Use either lightweight paper or clear plastic for the tracings. Figure 15-18 shows a triangle *ABC* and its tracing *MNO*. Tracings can also be used to show that two figures are not congruent. In Figure 15-19, the tracing of *XYZ*, represented by the broken lines on *DEF*, shows that the two angles are not congruent.

FIGURE 15-18
A triangle *ABC* and its tracing *MNO*

FIGURE 15-19
The tracing of ∠*XYZ* placed over ∠*DEF* shows that the two angles are not congruent.

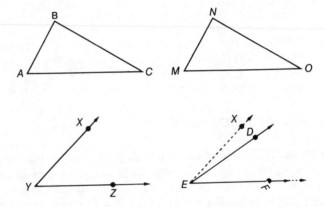

ACTIVITY 15-15 Similarity

- Give each child a geoboard and several rubber bands.
- Show a right triangle on your geoboard. Instruct the children to make one that is like yours but with sides only half as long.

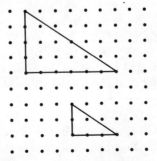

- Discuss the differences between your triangle and those of the children. Make certain that the children realize that each side of their triangle is half as long as the corresponding side on yours.
- Now have the children make a triangle with sides one and one-half times as long as yours.

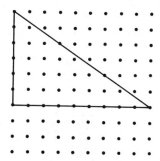

- Compare this triangle with the other two.
- Tell the children that two figures which look alike but are not the same size are *similar* figures.
- Repeat with other figures: squares, rectangles, parallelograms, and so on.

Give a statement distinguishing between congruent and similar figures. Describe at least three different investigations for developing children's understanding of congruence and similarity.

Self-check of Objective 7

SYMMETRY

Symmetry is found in both natural and human-made objects. Many geometric figures are symmetrical. Investigations in this area of geometry refine children's understanding of concepts such as congruence and the nature of plane figures. They also help children develop an appreciation of some applications of symmetry in art. The activities that follow will acquaint you with ways to introduce the concept of symmetry and broaden children's understanding of it.

ACTIVITY 15-16   Symmetry

- Select two children who are the same sex and about the same size.
- Tell them to stand on a table at the front of the room, face each other, and join hands. Give them these instructions: "Raise your hands high above your heads." "Keep your hands joined above your heads as you bend your knees until they touch." "Now let go of your hands and turn around so your backs are touching. Put your hands straight out in front of you, then push against each other and slowly move your feet forward so you look as though you are going to sit down."

- Have the pair of children model other similar types of motions.
- Have children from the class tell you what they noticed each time the positions changed. These responses might be expected: "Each one looked like the other after they moved." "They always did the same thing." "It looked like one was in front of a mirror and we saw her image in it."

ACTIVITY 15-17   Symmetrical Blobs

- Give each child a piece of white art paper and access to several pots of colored tempera paint.
- Instruct the children to fold their papers in half. (The fold can be made either the long or the short way.)
- Have the children open their papers, put blobs of different colored paint on one side, and fold the clean side over the paint. Smooth the two halves so the paint is spread evenly on both halves.
- When the paint is dry, mount the papers on a bulletin board.
- Discuss the fact that one side is the mirror image of the other; the two sides are symmetrical.

Once the concept of symmetry is understood, you can introduce activities dealing with lines and points of symmetry. Paper-folding and posting-hole activities are interesting to children in grades 4 through 6.

ACTIVITY 15-18   Lines of Symmetry

- Give each child a model of a square, rectangle, equilateral triangle, isosceles triangle, regular pentagon, and other regular polygons to cut from plain paper.
- Begin with the square and ask: "How many different ways can you fold it so that one half completely covers the other half?"

 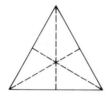

- Begin a chart by writing *square* on the chalkboard and listing the number of times the figure can be folded.
- Tell the children that each fold is called a *line of symmetry*. There are four such lines in a square.
- Repeat with each of the other figures.
- Do the children see any relationship between the number of sides and number of lines of symmetry in regular polygons?

ACTIVITY 15-19   Rotations

- Give each child a posting hole and its insert. Have each child number the corners of the insert, as shown in the first picture for each figure below.

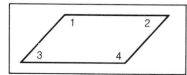 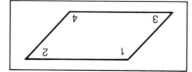

- Beginning with insert in the upright position, have each child count the different ways it can be placed in the posting hole.
- Make a chart of the figures and the number of posting-hole positions for each one.
- Compare the table with the one made for Activity 15-18.

ACTIVITY 15-20 Rotational Symmetry

- Collect square, rectangular, round, and hexagonal boxes with lids for investigations of rotational symmetry. (A figure has rotational symmetry if it can be rotated part way around a point at its center and appear not to have been moved.)
- Have the children with square boxes count the ways a lid can be put on the box. A lid for a square box can be put on four ways: a square has fourfold rotational symmetry. Compare this with the number of times a square piece of paper can be folded and the insert for a square posting hole can be set in place.
- Repeat with other boxes. Discuss the number of ways each lid can be placed on its box and compare with paper-folding and posting-hole activities for each shape.

Other symmetry activities can be organized around these materials:

- Children can collect and prepare pictures of symmetrical natural and human-made objects for a bulletin board.

- Number patterns are frequently symmetrical. There is symmetry along the line drawn from the upper left to the lower right in the addition table (Figure 9-6) and the multiplication table (Activity 11-5). It is the symmetry of these tables that makes it possible to show that the commutative property applies to each one. Many interesting investigations can be done with Pascal's triangle (Figure 15-20).

FIGURE 15-20
Pascal's triangle

```
            1
          1   1
        1   2   1
      1   3   3   1
    1   4   6   4   1
  1   5  10  10   5   1
1   6  15  20  15   6   1
```

- Block letters can be investigated for line and rotational symmetry. Consider all letters and note that certain ones are symmetrical along a vertical line (A and T are examples), along a horizontal line (B and C are examples), or both ways (I and O are examples). The latter two letters also have rotational symmetry.

Define symmetry. Describe several investigations that will help children understand symmetry.

Self-check of Objective 8

COORDINATE GEOMETRY

Rene Descartes (1596–1650) is credited with the development of **coordinate geometry.** Elementary-school children can be introduced to the coordinate plane through activities that are both practical and fun. A prerequisite skill is that children be familiar with number lines. You can introduce the coordinate plane to children who have no knowledge of negative numbers, although knowledge of them is necessary to work with the complete coordinate grid. The first activity is designed to develop children's understanding of the plane. It begins with the whole-number line, which it uses as the basis for constructing the coordinate system. Other activities suggest ways children's understanding and use of the system can be extended.

ACTIVITY 15-21 The Coordinate Plane

- Make a horizontal drawing of a whole-number line on the chalkboard. Mark the points 0–10.

- Review the way counting is done on a number line.
- Draw a vertical number line that has the same origin as the first line, and name its points.

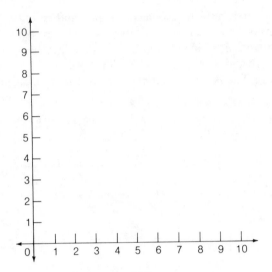

- Have the children demonstrate how counting is done on this line.
- Tell the children that the horizontal line is the first axis and the vertical line is the second axis.
- Introduce the concept of ordered pairs by drawing a star, square, circle, or other simple figure on one of the points of the plane, say (2,3). Point out to the children that the first number of the pair, called the coordinates of the point, indicates the number of units to count on the first, or horizontal, axis, and the second number indicates the units to count on the second axis. Mark a dark line on your coordinate plane to show the sequence of steps for locating a point.

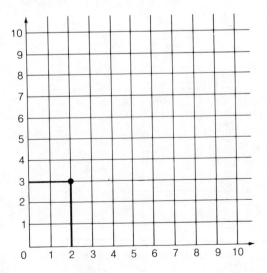

- Locate other points on the plane and have children identify each one's coordinates.
- Name coordinates and have individuals come to the board to show the order of steps for locating each one and then indicate each one's position.
- Variation: If your children have knowledge of integers, begin work with the coordinate plane by using all four quadrants during the introductory lesson.

Each of the following suggestions is representative of activities you can design or find in journals such as *Arithmetic Teacher* and in teacher's and resource manuals and children's workbooks.

- Use a geoboard for a coordinate plane by locating the intersection of the horizontal and vertical axes in the lower left corner. Children can demonstrate understanding by putting small washers on points for coordinates you name. They can put rubber bands on the board to represent simple pictures. Figure 15-21 shows a duplex that was made using a rubber band to connect coordinates.

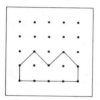

FIGURE 15-21
Duplex constructed using geoboard as the coordinate plane

- Children can locate points on dittoed grids and connect them with line segments to make pictures. The Christmas tree in Figure 15-22 is made by connecting the coordinates named next to it.

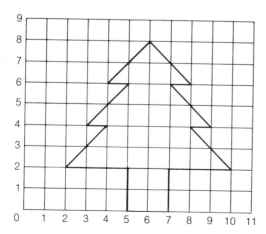

FIGURE 15-22
Christmas tree constructed on a coordinate plane, using the coordinates: (5,0) (7,0) (7,2) (10,2) (8,4) (9,4) (7,6) (8,6) (6,8) (4,6) (5,6) (3,4) (4,4) (2,2) (5,2) (5,0)

- Children can use the coordinate system to make similar figures. Give a set of coordinates to make a right triangle, as in Figure 15-23(a). Then give a set that will enlarge the triangle's size, as in Figure 15-23(b). Discuss the fact that the two triangles are similar. Repeat with other figures.

FIGURE 15-23
(a) A right triangle on a coordinate plane, with coordinates (0,0) (3,0) (0,3) (b) An enlarged right triangle on a coordinate plane, with coordinates (0,0) (4,0) (0,4)

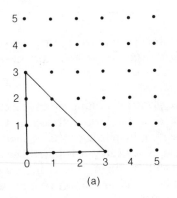

(a)

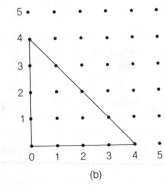

(b)

Self-check of Objective 9

Explain how both a geoboard and coordinate grid paper can be used to help children learn about coordinate geometry.

GEOMETRY AND SPECIAL STUDENTS

Many geometric concepts are difficult for learning-handicapped children. Visual perception problems make some of the more abstract concepts difficult or impossible for them to comprehend. Even simple work with a geoboard or with a straightedge and pencil is laborious for a child with motor deficits. These difficulties do not mean that these children cannot learn any geometry. On the contrary, many geometry activities are beneficial to them.

The topological activities described at the beginning of this chapter will help learning-handicapped children develop readiness for both the mathematics activities that follow and for reading and writing. As children copy bead patterns and deal with enclosure on a line, examine open and closed figures, and deal with enclosure on a plane, they develop an understanding of open, closed, inside, outside, and around, which are skills essential for learning about the order of numbers and the config-urations of numerals and letters. Frequent activities dealing with prox-imity help these children learn to identify and use relations such as near, far, close to, next to, and so on.

Later, as Euclidean concepts are introduced, children with visual per-ception, discrimination, and motor deficits, can use extra-large posting holes and inserts, geoboards, plane and space models, and large-scale graph paper for learning concepts included in a contemporary geometry program. Special provisions for the recording or indicating of responses to activities may be necessary. For example, it may not be possible for a learning-handicapped child to copy a geoboard figure on dot paper. You may need to inspect the child's work while it is still on the board, rather than evaluating a set of copied dot-paper figures. You may need to allow time for the student to make an oral rather than a written description of the work. It may also be necessary to allow these children more time to complete their work than is given their classmates.

There are many aspects of work with geometry that can be extended to challenge gifted and talented children. For example, the study of space figures can include an intensive study of the five Platonic solids (Figure 15-18) and the **Archimedean solids.** There are thirteen Archimedean sol-ids, which are semi-regular rather than regular like the Platonic solids. They are formed by combinations of triangles, squares, and pentagons which have congruent sides. Library research about Plato and Ar-chimedes and construction and investigation of the space figures associ-ated with these men can be undertaken by interested students.[5]

Transformational geometry is an area of study that will intrigue many students. It deals with three basic motions that can be applied to geo-metric and other figures: translations, or sliding motions; rotations, or turning motions; and flipping motions. Each motion is defined as a rigid motion, because it follows certain rules. Only when a motion adheres to these rules does a transformation occur. The figure obtained as a result of a transformation is congruent with the original figure and can be called a congruency transformation. The figure that comes from a transforma-tion is also an image of the original figure.

Children's first experiences should be exploratory, with investigations that refine their understanding of concepts of congruency, symmetry, parallelism, and the nature of plane figures. Slide and turn motions can be visualized with a piece of tissue paper on which figures are traced and then moved; flip motions can be visualized with wire models of plane figures.

- Slide motion. A **slide motion** occurs when a geometric figure moves along a plane so that the distance between all correspond-

---

[5] See Magnus J. Wenninger, *Polyhedron Models for the Classroom* (Washington, D.C.: Na-tional Council of Teachers of Mathematics, 1966) for pictures and patterns for these and other space figures.

ing points on the two figures remains the same. A slide motion involving a triangle is illustrated in Figure 15-24. The original triangle ABC has been transformed to triangle $A'B'C'$ by the slide motion represented by the dotted lines.

FIGURE 15-24
The slide of triangle *ABC* transforms it into triangle *A'B'C'*.

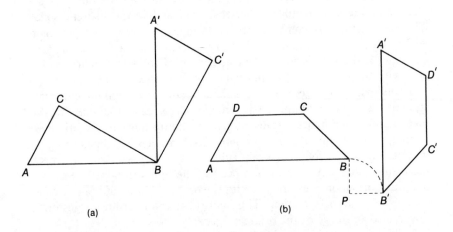

- Turn motion. A **turn motion** occurs when a figure is rotated around a point at the center of the turn as in Figure 15-25. The turn motions easiest for children to understand are those with the point on the figure, as in (a), or outside the figures, as in (b), where the turn is around point P.

FIGURE 15-25
A turn may be made (a) around a point on the figure or (b) around a point *P* away from the figure.

(a)   (b)

- Flip motions. **Flip motions** create a reflection of the original figure. During their examination of these motions children will extend their understanding of symmetry and of regular plane figures. A flip action may take place in relation to a point or a line. In Figure 15-26(a) parallelogram $A'B'C'D'$ is the reflection of parallelogram $ABCD$. The line between the two parallelograms is equidistant from each and is the line of symmetry, or *flip axis*. In (b) the reflection is in respect to a point at the center of the figure. Children should be guided to observe that symmetry of the type considered here is found frequently in nature. The two halves of a butterfly have line symmetry; the parts of many flowers have point symmetry. Children should use mirrors to deter-

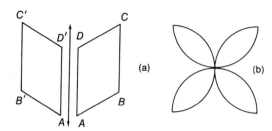

mine symmetry of figures. When a mirror is placed along the line in (a) and between halves of the drawing in (b), it will reflect figures that duplicate the originals.

Some figures, for example, the equilateral triangle in Figure 15-27, have both point and line symmetry. Each point on the left half of the triangle has a corresponding point on the right half that is equidistant from the point at the center. Each point on one half also has a corresponding point that is equidistant from the line that is the perpendicular bisector of the triangle's base.

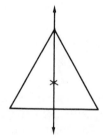

FIGURE 15-27
An equilateral triangle has both point symmetry and line symmetry.

A flip action will help children further their understanding of the meaning of perpendicular lines. Two lines are perpendicular to each other when the reflection of one remains unchanged after it has been flipped along the axis of the other line (Figure 15-28). Children can demonstrate this with pieces of wire bent in the shape of angles (Figure 15-29). The

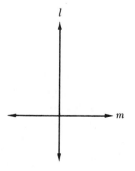

FIGURE 15-28
Two lines are perpendicular if the line *m* is invariant when a flip is made on the line *l*.

FIGURE 15-29
Pieces of wire can be used to determine whether two lines are perpendicular. In (a) the tracing indicates that the lines are perpendicular; in (b) they are not.

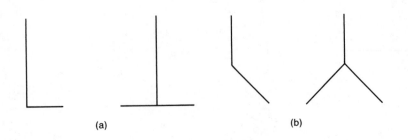

(a)   (b)

wire should be placed on a piece of paper so a tracing can be made of it. Then it should be flipped along one axis and another tracing made. When the line that is not the axis continues as a part of the original nonaxis line, the two lines are perpendicular (a). When the line does not continue as a part of the same line, they are not perpendicular (b).

**Self-check
of Objective 10**

Demonstrate each of these geometric transformations with appropriate materials: translation (slide), rotation, and reflection.

SUMMARY

Geometry is a part of contemporary mathematics in the elementary school. There is substantial agreement that children do profit from work with it. Piaget's research indicates that children first have a topological view of their world rather than a Euclidean view. Topologically oriented activities are recommended for preoperational-level children. Four topological concepts are discussed: proximity, separation, order, and enclosure. P. van Heile has determined that individuals pass through five levels of knowledge before they develop an understanding of Euclidean geometry. The first three of his five levels are of concern to elementary-school teachers. They deal with recognition of simple geometric figures, recognition of each figure's major characteristics, and classification of figures according to their attributes.

All work should be informal; investigations with models of figures predominate. Children learn about plane and space figures, as well as those associated with the line. They become acquainted with concepts of similarity, congruency, and symmetry.

Activities dealing with topological concepts help learning-handicapped children acquire some of the skills and understandings they need to work with other areas of mathematics and with numerals, letters, and words. They can learn many of the geometric concepts included in contemporary mathematics programs as long as materials and procedures accommodate their handicaps. Gifted and talented children profit from studying geometric concepts in greater depth. Platonic and Archimedean solids and geometric transformations are examples of areas of study for these children.

STUDY QUESTIONS AND ACTIVITIES

1. Directions for many activities in geometry can be placed on problem cards or individual worksheets to guide children's work in laboratories or learning centers. Select one of these areas of study and design a set of problem cards or worksheets suitable for children in grade 4, 5, or 6: symmetry with Pascal's triangle, symmetry with block letters, coordinate activities on a geoboard, or similar figures on the coordinate plane.

2. Glenda Lappan and Mary Jean Winter (see chapter's reading list) discuss a sequence of activities for improving children's spatial visualization skills. Use their article as the basis for designing a spatial visualization unit for fourth, fifth, or sixth graders.

3. Glenn Nelson and Larry P. Leutzinger (see chapter's reading list) recommend that children learn about geometry by taking a "geometry" walk. Read their article; then take a walk around an elementary school or your university classroom building to plan a geometry walk. The article includes suggestions about the types of questions you can ask during your walk. Write questions and possible responses in the same manner as that of the article's authors.

4. Add materials for helping children learn about lines, segments, plane, and space figures to your collection of teaching–learning aids.

5. Make a collection of pictures that illustrate symmetrical figures for a classroom bulletin board. Include illustrations of both plane and space figures having point symmetry, line symmetry, and plane symmetry.

KEY TERMS

topological   enclosure
Euclidean geometry   plane figures
proximity   posting holes
separation   geoboard
order   isosceles

scalene
right angle
acute angles
obtuse angle
altitude
diagonal
segment
ray
perpendicular
parallel
prisms

pyramids
Platonic solids
congruent
similar
symmetry
coordinate geometry
Archimedean solids
transformational geometry
slide motion
turn motion
flip motions

FOR FURTHER READING

Arithmetic Teacher, XXVI, No. 6 (February 1979).
   Five articles in this issue deal with geometry. Activities and materials for all grade levels are included.

Battista, Michael T. "Distortions: An Activity for Practice and Exploration," *Arithmetic Teacher*, XXIX, No. 5 (January 1982), pp. 34–36.
   Morris the cat serves as the basis for a study of the plane coordinate system. He is first drawn on a normal grid. Then a variety of grids that distort the cat's appearance focus attention on different grid forms and the transformations that occur on them.

Bright, George W. "Using Tables to Solve Some Geometry Problems," *Arithmetic Teacher*, XXV, No. 8 (May 1978), pp. 39–43.
   Describes and illustrates five problems dealing with shapes contained in square and triangular grids. Each one uses a table to organize data and reveal patterns that can be extended beyond the materials themselves.

Burger, William F. "Graph Paper Geometry," *Mathematics for the Middle Grades (5–9)*, 1982 Yearbook of the National Council of Teachers of Mathematics (Reston, Va., The Council), pp. 102–117.
   Activities with the coordinate plane introduce coordinates, patterns of shapes and tessellations, and symmetry and motions. Coordinates for nine different activities are given.

Dana, Marcia E., and Mary M. Lindquist. "Let's Try Triangles," *Arithmetic Teacher*, XXVI, No. 1 (September 1978), pp. 2–9. Triangle puzzles provide the basis for a variety of geometry activities. Besides triangles, children deal with rhombuses, parallelograms, hexagons, trapezoids, symmetry, and even metric measurement.

———. "The Surprising Circle," *Arithmetic Teacher*, XXV, No 4 (January 1978), pp. 4–10. Eight ideas, one for each grade from first through eighth, show how children can investigate circles. Each idea involves children in manipulative activities.

Holcomb, Jean. "Using Geoboards in the Primary Grades," *Arithmetic Teacher*, XXVII, No. 8 (April 1980), pp. 22–25.
   Kindergarten and first-grade children use geoboards to make designs and

patterns, explore three- and four-sided figures, practice making block letters, and learn about open and closed figures. Examples of activities are explained and illustrated.

Horak, Virginia M., and Willis J. Horak. "Using Geometry Tiles as a Manipulative for Developing Basic Concepts," *Arithmetic Teacher*, XXX, No. 8 (April 1983), pp. 8–15.
Geometry tiles are squares cut from heavy cardboard or flexible floor tiles that are used for developing geometric concepts. Directions for making tiles and for using them are explained.

Jensen, Rosalie, and David R. O'Neil. "Informal Geometry Through Geometric Blocks," *Arithmetic Teacher*, XXIX, No. 9 (May 1982), pp. 4–8.
A set of teacher-made blocks (illustrated in the article) are used to develop geometric concepts and skills appropriate for kindergarten through grade 3. Shape-comparison, classifying and naming, tracing, and measuring activities and discussions of properties are described.

Lappan, Glenda, and Mary Jean Winter, "Spatial Visualization," *Mathematics for the Middle Grades*, 1982 Yearbook of the National Council of Teachers of Mathematics (Reston, Va., The Council), pp. 118–129.
Children are introduced to "buildings" made of blocks placed on mats. Perspective drawings are used to help visualize each building. Activities for drawing plans, constructing buildings from plans, measuring and designing buildings, and making three-dimensional drawings are included.

Nelson, Glenn, and Larry P. Leutzinger. "Let's Take a Geometry Walk," *Arithmetic Teacher*, XXVII, No. 3 (November 1979), pp. 2–4.
A geometry walk helps children learn the relevance of geometry to their lives. Suggestions of things to view and questions to ask during a walk are presented.

Raines, Bob G., and Ruth G. Sheffield. "Geometry," *Practical Ways to Teach the Basic Mathematical Skills* (Richmond, Va.: The Virginia Council of Teachers of Mathematics, 1978), pp. 84–104.
Suggests a variety of commercial and teacher-made materials for teaching basic plane and space figures, congruence and similarity, and symmetry.

Thornton, Carol A. "Geometry: Perceptual-Motor Help for Many Handicapped Learners," *Arithmetic Teacher*, XXVII, No. 2 (October 1979), pp. 24–26.
The author believes that the benefits of geometry activities for handicapped learners are too great to be ignored. She indicates some activities for enriching children's perceptual awareness.

Van de Walle, John, and Charles S. Thompson. "Concepts, Art, and Fun from Simple Tiling Patterns," *Arithmetic Teacher*, XXVIII, No. 3 (November 1980), pp. 4–8.
Tessellations are repeating patterns formed with one or more plane geometric shapes. The shapes in this article are two different rectangles, a triangle, and a parallelogram. Basic patterns and the educational payoffs from work with them are described.

———, "A Triangle Treasure," *Arithmetic Teacher*, XXVIII, No. 6 (February 1981), pp. 6–11.
Games and activities that use a set of triangle pieces (described in the article) give children experiences in comparing likenesses and differences, studying and measuring angles, making quadrilaterals from triangles,

measuring perimeters, working with symmetry, generating solids, and making tessellations.

Walter, Marion. "Frame Geometry: An Example in Posing and Solving Problems," *Arithmetic Teacher*, XXVIII, No. 2 (October 1980), pp. 16–18.
A set of 3-cm, 5-cm, and 8-cm sticks, representing materials for picture frames, is used to pose a problem about the number of different frames that can be constructed with them. The article outlines the paths different children might take as they work at solving the problem.

Wenninger, Magnus J. *Polyhedron Models for the Classroom* (Washington, D.C.: National Council of Teachers of Mathematics, 1966).
Presents illustrated directions for making polyhedron models. Includes many line drawings and photographs.

Young, Jerry L. "Improving Spatial Abilities with Geometric Activities," *Arithmetic Teacher*, XXX, No. 1 (September 1982), pp. 38–43.
Suggests ways to enhance children's visualization of space by associating objects with their pictures or drawings, working with tangrams, seeing a shape as part of a larger figure, and using perspective and hidden lines.

16

Elementary Number Theory, Probability, and Statistics and Graphs

Upon completion of Chapter 16 you will be able to:

1. Present three reasons for including some number theory in the elementary mathematics program.

2. Define odd and even numbers, and describe at least one activity with these numbers for primary and intermediate levels of the elementary school.

3. Distinguish between prime and composite numbers.

4. Demonstrate an activity that can be used by children to discover the meanings of prime and composite numbers.

5. Describe the modernized sieve of Eratosthenes, and explain how it is used to determine prime numbers.

6. Use at least three processes for changing composite numbers so they are represented in prime factor form.

7. Give a definition of the greatest common factor for two or more numbers, and determine the GCF for two numbers in at least two different ways.

8. Demonstrate at least two procedures for finding the least common multiple for two or more numbers.

9. Use tests of divisibility to determine numbers that are divisible by 2, 3, 4, 5, 6, 7, 8, 9, 10, or 11.

10. Demonstrate at least two probability experiments for children.

11. Define commonly used probability terms, give appropriate examples of each one, and cite examples of ways these terms can be introduced to children.

12. Describe four types of graphs used by elementary-school children, and identify at least one source of data for each one.

13. Describe five activities for the calculator that extend children's understanding of number theory, probability, and statistics and demonstrate the calculator's application for each.

14. Explain why many topics in this chapter are especially beneficial to gifted and talented students.

Number theory, probability, and statistics and graphs are relatively new topics in the elementary mathematics program. Reasons for including these topics are given in Chapter 1. If you have forgotten them, read the sections that deal with them again.

ELEMENTARY NUMBER THEORY

According to Dantzig **number theory** was developed before the theory of arithmetic.[1] Long before efficient ways to use algorithms were worked out, people began to study the relationships among numbers. Number lore, the study of prime and composite numbers, tests of divisibility, and other aspects of number theory have a long history. Even so, ". . . the theory of number is the branch of mathematics which has found the least number of applications. Not only has it so far remained without influence on technical progress, but even in the domain of pure mathematics it has always occupied an isolated position only loosely connected with the general body of the science."[2]

Today number theory has achieved a new position in the elementary-school program. Where formerly the study of number theory was incidental and haphazard, if it existed at all, now it is planned and organized to lead children to discover certain elementary generalizations about numbers. There are at least three reasons for its present position:

1. The study helps children understand that number theory can be useful in other areas of mathematics. Children who know about prime and composite numbers can use them to factor composite numbers and find the *greatest common factor* (GCF) and the *least common multiple* (LCM) of two or more numbers. Later they can use this knowledge to find common denominators and to simplify, or reduce to *lowest terms*, common fractions that represent fractional numbers.

---

[1] Tobias Dantzig, *Number, the Language of Science*, 4th ed. (New York: Doubleday & Company, Inc., 1954), p. 38.

[2] Dantzig, p. 38.

2. Many children find that work with number theory is interesting and fun. Some find that work with prime and composite numbers leads to many interesting areas of investigation.

3. During the study of different aspects of number theory many opportunities arise to work with the basic facts of the four operations, to practice computational skills, and to further develop a mathematics vocabulary. For example, the process of factoring numbers involves factors, or divisors, and multiples of numbers.

Many topics dealing with number theory are well suited for learning centers, with directions for activities on problem cards or tapes for playback on cassette recorders. Activities and materials, some in a problem card format, are suggested in this chapter.

Give three reasons for including some number theory topics in today's mathematics program.

***Self-check
of Objective 1***

2. Odd and Even Numbers

Investigations that deal with whole numbers to give children an understanding of **odd and even numbers** can begin in the primary grades. Children can use disks, cubes, or other objects as manipulative materials to complete an activity like the following.

ACTIVITY 16-1   Even and Odd

- Have children work in pairs, using disks.
- Tell them to arrange 8 disks in two rows, with the same number in each row. Count the number in each row.

- Repeat with 10, 2, 6, 14, 30, 18, and other even numbers.
- Have children make other sets that have two rows with an equivalent number in each row.
- Have children arrange 5 disks in two rows so that one row contains an extra disk. Emphasize that the rows do not contain the same number of disks.

- Repeat with 7, 11, 15, 21, 1, and other odd numbers. Emphasize that the rows never contain the same number of disks.
- Have children make other sets that cannot be put in rows with the same number of disks in each row.
- Have children identify the numbers that formed two equivalent sets (2, 4, 6, . . .) and those that have an extra disk in one row (1, 3, 5, . . .). Tell them that the numbers 2, 4, 6, . . . are even numbers and the numbers 1, 3, 5, . . . are odd numbers.

Follow this activity with investigations on the number line. Have children locate odd and even numbers on the line and then count by twos beginning at an even or an odd number and going forward or backward. The forward count can go to the end of the line or to a designated number such as 14 or 19. The backward count can go to 0 or 1 or to any designated number such as 3 or 6.

A hundreds chart offers many opportunities for children to extend their experiences with odd and even numbers (see, for example, Activity 16-3). Counting activities similar to those done with the number line can be done with the chart. These observations are among the ones children will make:

- Beginning at 2, every other number is an even number; beginning at 1, every other number is odd.

- The column on the left side of the chart contains all odd numbers ending in 1. Each alternate column across the chart contains odd numbers ending in 3, 5, 7, and 9.

- The second column from the left contains all even numbers ending in 2. Each alternate column across the chart contains even numbers ending in 4, 6, 8, and 0.

- The even numbers are multiples of 2.

Intermediate-grade children can study odd and even numbers at a more abstract level. These generalizations can arise from their investigations:

- If an even number is designated by $2n$, then its successor is $2n + 1$ and is an odd number. ($2n$ is used to designate an even number, because every even number has 2 as a factor; therefore 2 times any number must be even.)

- Zero is an even number.

- When two even numbers are added, their sum is an even number: $2n + 2n = 4n$. When two odd numbers are added, their sum is an even number: $(2n + 1) + (2n + 1) = 4n + 2$. When an even number and an odd number are added, their sum is an odd number: $2n + (2n + 1) = 4n + 1$.

- When two even numbers are multiplied, their product is an even number: $2n \times 2n = 4n^2$. When two odd numbers are multiplied, their product is an odd number: $(2n + 1) \times (2n + 1) = 4n^2 + 4n + 1$. When an even and an odd number are multiplied, their product is an even number: $2n \times (2n + 1) = 4n^2 + 2n$.

Define an even and an odd number. Demonstrate with materials an activity suitable for introducing odd and even numbers to primary-grade children. Describe an activity with these numbers for intermediate-grade children. Tell how these activities will help these children understand addition and multiplication better.

Self-check of
Objective 2

2. Prime and Composite Numbers

Intermediate-grade children can investigate the nature of **prime and composite numbers.** Activities with poker chips or other disks allow children to investigate different array patterns. The following activities can be presented in a series of teacher-directed lessons.

ACTIVITY 16-2   Prime and Composite Numbers

- Arrange sets of 4, 6, 8, 9, 10, 15 disks into all of their possible arrays. (The arrays for 6 disks are shown.)

```
 o o o     o o     o      o o o o o o
 o o o     o o     o
           o o     o
                   o
                   o
                   o
```

- Keep a record of the arrays for each set of disks.

Whole Number	Arrays	Number of Different Arrays
6	2 by 3, 3 by 2, 6 by 1, 1 by 6	4

- Make arrays for sets of 2, 3, 5, 7, 11, 13, and 17 chips and record the results. (The arrays for 7 disks are shown.)

- Determine the array for 1 disk and record it.
- Have the children examine the chart for generalizations about different arrays and factors for the numbers. The following chart helps children make these generalizations:

Whole Number	Arrays	Number of Different Arrays
1	1 by 1	1
2	1 by 2, 2 by 1	2
3	1 by 3, 3 by 1	2
4	2 by 2, 1 by 4, 4 by 1	3
5	1 by 5, 5 by 1	2
6	2 by 3, 3 by 2, 6 by 1, 1 by 6	4
7	1 by 7, 7 by 1	2
8	2 by 4, 4 by 2, 8 by 1, 1 by 8	4
9	3 by 3, 9 by 1, 1 by 9	3
10	2 by 5, 5 by 2, 10 by 1, 1 by 10	4

- Some whole numbers—2, 3, 5, and 7—have only two arrays; these form a straight line rather than a rectangular pattern. The numerical description always contains a 1 and the numeral that tells the total number of markers in the array.
- Some whole numbers—4, 6, 8, 9 and 10—have more than two arrays. They can be arranged in one or more rectangular patterns (square in

the case of 4 and 9). Numerals other than 1 and the numeral that names the number of markers in the set are used in the numerical expressions for these arrays.

o Only one whole number—1—has exactly one array.

These generalizations open the way to further work with prime and composite numbers. Leave room on the chart to record other arrays, perhaps for all sets up to and including thirty chips. Children can then list all the prime numbers between 1 and 31. By the time children complete this activity, they should be able to give a suitable definition of prime and composite numbers: "A prime number has only two different whole-number factors: 1 and the number itself." "A composite number has three or more different whole-number factors." The special characteristics of the number 1 should be stressed: it has only one factor—itself—and it is a factor of every other number. Make it clear that it is a special number that is neither prime nor composite. It is treated as a *unit*.

Work with prime and composite numbers extends understanding of factors, divisors, and multiples. Children have already encountered these terms in connection with their earlier study of multiplication and division. Now they should learn that the terms *factor* and *divisor* can be used interchangeably. When two whole numbers are multiplied, they yield a product; they can be called either factors or divisors of their product. (An exception to this statement is that 0 can be a factor but not a divisor.) The product of a pair of numbers can also be called a multiple of the two numbers. Thus 5 and 7 are factors or divisors of 35; 35 is a multiple of both 5 and 7.

a. The Sieve of Eratosthenes Another activity for intermediate-grade children is an investigation of the **sieve of Eratosthenes** (see facing page). Eratosthenes was a Greek astronomer–geographer who lived in the third century B.C. He devised a scheme for separating any set of consecutive whole numbers larger than 1 into prime and composite numbers. The set of numbers most commonly used in classrooms is the set 1 through 100.

Boys and girls who are interested in further study of prime and composite numbers can complete these activities:

- Determine the prime numbers between 100 and 200, 100 and 300, or within any other limits, using the sieve to find the multiples of increasingly larger prime numbers—11, 13, 17, 19, 23, . . .

- Look for *twin primes*. Twin primes are two prime numbers that have exactly one composite number between them—3 and 5, 5 and 7, 11 and 13 are examples.

ACTIVITY 16-3 Sieve of Eratosthenes

- Begin with a blank hundreds chart.

```
 1  2  3  4  5  6  7  8  9  10
11 12 13 14 15 16 17 18 19 20
21 22 23 24 25 26 27 28 29 30
31 32 33 34 35 36 37 38 39 40
41 42 43 44 45 46 47 48 49 50
51 52 53 54 55 56 57 58 59 60
61 62 63 64 65 66 67 68 69 70
71 72 73 74 75 76 77 78 79 80
81 82 83 84 85 86 87 88 89 90
91 92 93 94 95 96 97 98 99 100
```

- Put a ring around 1.
- Two is the smallest prime number. Beginning with 4, mark out all of the multiples of 2 by putting a line through them.
- The next prime number is 3. Ask "Which of the multiples of 3 have already been marked out?" (Those that are multiples of 2.) Mark out the remaining multiples of 3.
- Ask, "Why are the 4 and its multiples already marked out?" (They are all multiples of 2.)
- Ask, "Is 5 a prime number?" (Yes.) Mark out the multiples of 5 that remain.
- Ask, "What is the smallest multiple of 7 that still remains?" (49.) Mark it out along with the remaining multiples of 7.
- Eleven is the next prime number. Ask, "What multiples of 11 are smaller than 100?" (22, 33, 44, 55, 66, 77, 88, 99.) "Are any of these left to be marked out?" (No.) "Why do you suppose no multiples of 11 are left?" (They are all multiples of smaller prime numbers.)

```
①  2  3  4  5  6  7  8  9  10
11 12 13 14 15 16 17 18 19 20
21 22 23 24 25 26 27 28 29 30
31 32 33 34 35 36 37 38 39 40
41 42 43 44 45 46 47 48 49 50
51 52 53 54 55 56 57 58 59 60
61 62 63 64 65 66 67 68 69 70
71 72 73 74 75 76 77 78 79 80
81 82 83 84 85 86 87 88 89 90
91 92 93 94 95 96 97 98 99 100
```

- Explain to the children that the numbers that have not been marked out are prime numbers. Make a list of these numbers.

- Test Goldbach's conjecture. Goldbach was a Russian mathematician who made a conjecture in 1742 that every even number greater than 2 can be written as the sum of a pair of prime numbers: $4 = 2 + 2$; $6 = 3 + 3$; $8 = 5 + 3$; $10 = 7 + 3$ or $5 + 5$. This conjecture has never been proven to be either true or false for all even numbers.

Give a statement that distinguishes between prime and composite numbers.

Demonstrate how markers, such as poker chips, can be used by children to discover the difference between prime and composite numbers.

Prepare a modern sieve of Eratosthenes for the numbers 1 through 100, and demonstrate how to use it to determine the prime numbers smaller than 100.

Self-check of Objectives 3, 4, and 5

3. Factoring Composite Numbers

The process of simplying common fractions (reducing to lowest terms) and determining common denominators for a pair of unlike fractions can be made systematic by using a factorization process. Children who learn to factor composite numbers can systematically determine the number by which to divide a fraction's numerator and denominator to simplify it. They can also use a factorization process to determine the least common multiple, or least common denominator, when they add or subtract unlike fractions.

A composite number is said to be factored completely when it is represented as a product expression that consists of two or more prime numbers. When the number 18 is factored completely, it is expressed as $2 \times 3 \times 3$; 36 is expressed as $2 \times 2 \times 3 \times 3$. Several procedures for factoring composite numbers will be discussed.

a. Use Basic Multiplication Facts Children can begin work with factoring by using small composite numbers, such as 4, 6, 9, 10, 15, and 21. These numbers have only a pair of prime number factors, so their prime factorization is complete as soon as the two factors are named. You can help children use basic facts to factor these numbers: "Which two prime numbers are multiplied to give a product of 21?" The basic multiplication fact $3 \times 7 = 21$ gives the answer.

b. Use Factor Trees Factor trees give a systematic way to factor numbers that are reasonably small but are the product of more than two prime numbers. Factor trees are created by expressing numbers in terms of successively smaller factors until all factors are prime numbers. Factor trees for 24 are shown in Figure 16-1. In (a) three different ways of beginning are shown; each begins with a different pair of factors. (The number pair 1 and 24 is not used.) In (b) the process is continued with each composite factor expressed by a pair of smaller factors. Note that 12 is factored in two ways in the two trees on the right and that the prime factors in any of the trees are represented by a repetition of their numerals. The tree on the left in (b) is completed because in its bottom line, 24 is expressed as the product of prime numbers. The completed trees for the other factorizations are shown in (c), where each bottom line expresses 24 as the product of prime numbers. The numerals at the bottom of each completed tree in (c) are 2, 2, 2, and 3.

Other numbers with two or more factor trees that can be used for practice are 16, 18, 28, 30, 36, and 40. After children have completed the factor trees for several small composite numbers, they should observe that the same prime numbers are in the bottom line of each number's factorization. For 24 there are three 2s and one 3; for 16 there are four 2s; and so on. Even though children do not have mathematical proof, they can observe that each composite number has only one prime factorization, if order of factors is disregarded. This property of numbers is called the *fundamental theorem of arithmetic*.

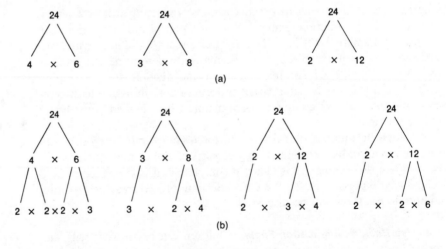

FIGURE 16-1
Different factor trees for the number 24

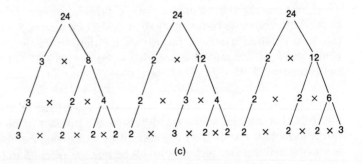

c. Use an Algorithm Factor trees are useful for numbers small enough for children to easily see at least one pair of factors. For larger numbers an algorithm for factoring numbers is useful. In the example in the margin an algorithm is used to factor 124. First, 124 is divided by 2 and the numeral for the quotient, "62," is written beneath the "124." Sixty-two is also divisible by 2. This division is completed, and the quotient's numeral is written beneath the "62." The number 31 is a prime number, so it is divided by itself. The three divisors show the prime factorization of 124 to be $2 \times 2 \times 31$. A second example is shown in the next algorithm in the margin. It shows that the prime factorization of 525 is $3 \times 5 \times 5 \times 7$.

$$
\begin{array}{r|r}
2 & 124 \\
2 & 62 \\
31 & 31 \\
\end{array}
$$

$$
\begin{array}{r|r}
3 & 525 \\
5 & 175 \\
5 & 35 \\
7 & 7 \\
\end{array}
$$

In these two examples the division by primes began with the smallest possible prime, which is 2 in the first example and 3 in the second. Each successive division was done with the smallest possible prime, and in both cases a prime number was repeated as a divisor. When the division is done this way, the prime numbers are written in order from smallest to largest. While it is not necessary to take the steps in this particular order, it is recommended for two reasons:

1. Children can recognize the divisibility by 2, 3, and 5 more easily than they can by the larger prime numbers.

2. When numbers have been completely factored, the factors are already ordered according to size, and the writing of prime product expressions is simplified. One of the advantages of writing product expressions in this manner becomes obvious when factoring of numerators and denominators is done to simplify common fractions.

Children can use basic multiplication facts, factor trees, and an algorithm to change composite numbers to their prime factor forms. Tell when each of these procedures should be used, using appropriate examples to illustrate.

Self-check
of Objective 6

4. Finding the Greatest Common Factor of Numbers

The process of finding the greatest common factor (GCF) of a pair of numbers is a useful skill when it is used to simplify (reduce to lowest terms) common fractions. Therefore children's work with GCF's should be coupled with simplifying common fractions. The meaning of the GCF and processes for finding greatest common factors are given in this chapter. The way GCFs are used to simplify common fractions is discussed in Chapter 12.

As the words *greatest common factor* suggest, for every pair of whole numbers there is only one largest whole number by which both may be divided. The greatest common factor of the pair 2 and 4 is 2; for the pair 8 and 12, it is 4; for 5 and 7, it is 1.

a. Using Venn Diagrams   A **Venn diagram** is a good way to show the GCF of a pair of numbers. Children who have used Venn diagrams earlier, perhaps as they sorted attribute materials or in problem-solving situations, will recognize the value of these diagrams in the new situation. If your children have not used Venn diagrams before, you must use care to see that the uses of these diagrams are clear to them now. Begin by using diagrams for pairs of small composite numbers.

ACTIVITY 16-4   Greatest Common Factors

- Have children name the prime factors for a pair of composite numbers, such as 4 and 6.
- Put the factors for 4 in circle *A* of a Venn diagram and the factors of 6 in circle *B*.

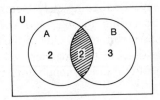

- Point out that the 2 in the overlapping (shaded) portion of the Venn diagram is the greatest common factor for the numbers 4 and 6.
- Repeat with other pairs of small numbers, such as 6 and 9, 5 and 10, and 6 and 14, which children can factor by inspection.
- Use other pairs of numbers, such as 36 and 42, for which factor trees or an algorithm might be needed.

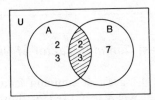

- Discuss the fact that the greatest common factor is the prime number or the product of the prime numbers in the intersection of the Venn diagram.
- Point out that when no numbers appear in the intersection, the GCF is 1.

---

b. Using an Algorithm Another systematic process is an algorithm that can be taught to mature fifth- and sixth-grade children. The procedure involves a series of divisions by common prime factors, beginning with the smallest prime factor for a pair of numbers. In the first example in the margin the GCF of 12 and 18 is determined. First 12 and 18 are divided by 2, the smallest prime number common to both. Next, the two quotients are divided by 3, which is the next smallest prime number common to both of them. The division by 3 results in two prime numbers, so the division is complete. The product of 2 and 3, the common divisors, gives 6 as the GCF for 12 and 18. The GCF of 120, 140, and 210 is determined in the second margin example. The product of 2 and 5 yields 10 as the GCF of these three numbers. In this example the factoring ends with division by 5, because 12, 14, and 21 have no common factor greater than 1.

2	12	18
3	6	9
	2	3

2	120	140	210
5	60	70	105
	12	14	21

Define the GCF for two or more numbers; then use the following two procedures to find the GCF of the numbers 24 and 56: Venn diagrams and the algorithm.

***Self-check
of Objective 7***

5. Finding the Least Common Multiple of Two or More Numbers

Children use the least common multiple (LCM) when a common denominator is needed before they can add or subtract two or more unlike fractions. There are rote processes that children can learn, but they are inefficient when denominators are large and are likely to be forgotten with time. It is better to use systematic procedures that children can understand and use confidently with numbers of any size. The three processes that follow can be developed over a period of time. Children first use the listing process and later, as they mature, they learn the factorization and algorithm processes.

a. Listing Multiples When children are finding the LCM for small numbers, they can inspect lists of multiples to identify the LCM. You can help them by presenting an activity like this:

ACTIVITY 16-5 Least Common Multiples

- Use the numbers 2 and 3. Ask, "What are the first several multiples of 2?" "What are the first several multiples of 3?" Ring the common multiples in the two lists. Point out that 6 is the smallest (least) number common to both sets of multiples.

2, 4, 6, 8, 10, 12, 14, 16, 18, 20, 22, 24, ...
3, 6, 9, 12, 15, 18, 21, 24, 27, 30, 33,...

- Repeat with other pairs of numbers.
- Show how the process can be used for three numbers.

4, 8, 12, 16, 20, 24, 28, 32, 36, 40, 44,...

5, 10, 15, 20, 25, 30, 35, 40, 45, 50, 55,...

8, 16, 24, 32, 40, 48, 56, 64, 72, 80, 88,...

b. Using a Factorization Process With larger numbers the process of finding the LCM for two or more numbers by inspection can be difficult, and a listing of multiples is tedious. A process that uses prime numbers is helpful for determining LCMs for larger numbers. To help children learn this process use activities like the following.

ACTIVITY 16-6 Factorization Process

- Begin with an addition-of-fractions situation:

$$1/6 + 1/8 = \square$$

- Determine the prime factorization of each denominator:

$$6 = 2 \times 3 \qquad 8 = 2 \times 2 \times 2$$

- Ask, "What will be the product if we multiply $2 \times 3 \times 2 \times 2 \times 2$?" (48.) Point out that 2 is common to the factorization of each number, so only three, rather than four, 2s are needed; the LCM is $2 \times 3 \times 2 \times 2$, or 24, not 48.
- A Venn diagram will help make the process clear to children who are familiar with its uses.

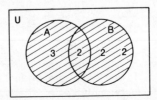

- Use a Venn diagram with a pair of larger numbers such as 15 and 12:

$$12 = 2 \times 2 \times 3 \qquad 15 = 3 \times 5$$
$$2 \times 2 \times 3 \times 5 = 60$$

- Children who are familiar with the concept of set union will recognize that the LCM for two or more numbers is determined by multiplying the factors that are in the union of factors in the prime factorization of the numbers.

c. Using an Algorithm   The algorithm for finding the GCF for numbers can also be used for finding the LCM of two or more numbers. In the algorithm in the margin the LCM for 12, 18, and 24 is determined. First, the three numbers are divided by 2, the smallest common prime divisor. The quotients of this division are divided by 3, which is a common divisor for all of them. There is no prime number divisor that is common to the three new quotients, so the algorithm continues with the division of 2 and 4 by 2. The 3 is brought down. All the quotients are now prime or are 1, so the division is complete. The LCM of 12, 18, and 24 is 72, which is the product of the expression $2 \times 3 \times 2 \times 3 \times 2$. The Venn diagram in Figure 16-2 is related to this algorithm. First, show that the prime numbers in the intersection of all three circles are the algorithm's first two divisors. Next, relate the prime number in the intersection of 12 and 24 to the third divisor. Finally, the numbers in the circles for 18 and 24 are the other two divisors.

2	12	18	24
3	6	9	12
2	2	3	4
	1	3	2

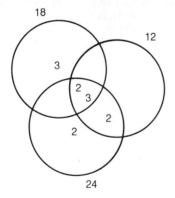

FIGURE 16-2
Venn diagram showing the factorizations of 12, 18, and 24. The lowest common multiple of the numbers is $2 \times 2 \times 2 \times 3 \times 3$, or 72.

Use at least two different procedures to find the LCMs of these sets of numbers: 4, 6, and 8; 3, 12, and 15.

Self-check of Objective 8

TESTS OF DIVISIBILITY

Tests of **divisibility** are used to determine if a number is divisible by a given number. "Divisible by" implies that division is completed with a remainder of zero. Children who know and apply divisibility tests save time as they factor composite numbers, because the tests enable them to determine quickly whether one number is a factor of another number. The tests for the prime numbers 2, 3, 5, 7, and 11 are particularly useful. The rules for divisibility that follow should be developed carefully so children will remember and use them at appropriate times. Most fifth- and sixth-grade children can learn the tests for 2, 5, and 10. The other tests are more difficult, and you may reserve instruction about them for your gifted and talented learners.

- *Divisibility by 2.* Every even number can be divided by 2.

- *Divisibility by 3.* To determine whether a number is divisible by 3, add the sum of its digits. If the sum is divisible by 3, the original number is divisible by 3. An example is 462: $4 + 6 + 2 = 12$; 12 is divisible by 3; so 462 is divisible by 3. The sum of the digits in 496 is 19; therefore 496 is not divisible by 3.

- *Divisibility by 4.* The test for 4 involves numbers in the one and tens places of the number to be tested. If the tens and ones are divisible by 4, the number is divisible by 4. Use 1344 as an example: $1344 = 1300 + 44$; 44 is divisible by 4, so 1344 is divisible by 4. In 1634, the number in the tens and ones places, 34, is not divisible by 4; neither is 1634.

- *Divisibility by 5.* Every whole number that ends in 0 or 5 is divisible by 5.

- *Divisibility by 6.* Any even number that is divisible by 3 is divisible by 6.

- *Divisibility by 7.* There are several tests for divisibility by 7. A useful one for reasonably small whole numbers is: Multiply the digit in the ones place by 2. Subtract the product from the number named by the remaining digits. If the difference is divisible by 7, the entire number is divisible by 7. This test shows that for the number 672, $2 \times 2 = 4$, $67 - 4 = 63$, and $63 \div 7 = 9$. Therefore 672 is divisible by 7. For 1001 the test gives $2 \times 1 = 2$, $100 - 2 = 98$, and $98 \div 7 = 14$. The number 1001 is divisible by 7.

- *Divisibility by 8.* A whole number is divisible by 8 if the part of the number that begins in the hundreds place is divisible by 8. The number 11,384 is divisible by 8 because 384 is divisible by 8. The number 16, 692 is not divisible by 8 because 692 is not divisible by 8.

- *Divisibility by 9.* A whole number is divisible by 9 if the sum of its digits is divisible by 9. The sum of the digits in the number 2331 is $2+3+3+1$, or 9; $9 \div 9 = 1$. The number 2331 is divisible by 9.

- *Divisibility by 10.* Any whole number that has a 0 in the ones place is divisible by 10.

- *Divisibility by 11.* There are several tests for divisibility by 11. A simple one to use with whole numbers involves subtracting the digit in the ones place of a number from the number named by the remaining digits. When the remainder is divisible by 11, the entire number is divisible by 11. If one subtraction does not make determination of divisibility by 11 obvious, repeat the process. For the number 121, apply the test as follows: $12 - 1 = 11$, $11 \div 11 = 1$. For the number 1452, $145 - 2 = 143$, $14 - 3 = 11$, $11 \div 11 = 1$. The number 1452 is divisible by 11.[3]

Explain how each test of divisibility shows which numbers are or are not divisible by 2, 3, 4, 5, 6, 7, 8, 9, 10, and 11.

***Self-check
of Objective 9***

PROBABILITY

As indicated in the first chapter most of the work with probability is confined to the upper grades of elementary school, in which it serves utilitarian and aesthetic purposes, and gives children background for future study of mathematics. You should not attempt to take children too far into the study of probability. Children's intuitive understanding will enable them to grasp the simpler concepts of the topic, but the thin dividing line between the simpler and more complex topics should not be crossed.[4] The activities presented here are examples of those that are appropriate for helping elementary-school children to learn some probability concepts and terms.

---

[3] The author is indebted to Leo Allison, mathematics instructor at Oakmont High School, Roseville, California, for information about this divisibility test. It is also described by H. Lawrence Ridge annd Joseph S. Renzulli in "Teaching Mathematics to Talented and Gifted Students," in *The Mathematics Education of Exceptional Children and Youth* (Reston, Virginia: National Council of Teachers of Mathematics, 1981), pp. 226–227.)

[4] John D. Wilkinson and Owen Nelson, "Probability and Statistics—Trial Teaching in Sixth Grade," *Arithmetic Teacher*, XIII, No. 2 (February 1966), p. 105.

1. Activities for Primary Grades

There are simple activities that can be begun in the primary grades. One such activity is the recording of sums that occur when two dice are rolled.

ACTIVITY 16-7   Rolling Dice

- Give each pair of children a pair of dice and a chart.

Tally Sheet										
2	3	4	5	6	7	8	9	10	11	12
I	I I	I I I	I I I	I I I I	I I I I I I	I I I	I I I I	I I	I I	I

- The children roll the dice and determine the total. Each time the dice are rolled, the total is recorded in the proper column of the chart.
- Depending upon the age and maturity of your children you may discuss why certain totals appear more frequently than others on the chart.

Jerry Shryock describes a **sampling** activity using colored popsicle sticks for third and fourth graders.[5]

ACTIVITY 16-8   Sampling Popsicle Sticks

- Mark 100 popsicle sticks with red dots, 100 with yellow dots, and 200 with blue dots; then place them in a paper bag.

---

[5] Jerry Shryock, "Statistical Sampling and Popsicle Sticks," in *Teaching Statistics and Probability* (Reston, Virginia: National Council of Teachers of Mathematics, 1981), pp. 45–49.

- Tell the children that there are sticks with red, blue, and yellow dots. Challenge them to think of a way to determine whether there are more sticks of one color than of the other colors without taking them all from the bag. Through discussion help them see that a random sample process can be used to meet the challenge.
- Mix the sticks thoroughly. Have a child draw one and note its color. Record the color and return the stick to the bag. Repeat the process until a certain number of draws, say 50, have been completed.

Tally Sheet		
Color of Dots	Count	Total
Red	~~HHT~~ ~~HHT~~ IIII	14
Yellow	~~HHT~~ ~~HHT~~ II	12
Blue	~~HHT~~ ~~HHT~~ ~~HHT~~ ~~HHT~~ IIII	24

- Use the tally of draws to help the children to conclude that there are more blue than red or yellow sticks.
- There are other aspects of this activity you may want to pursue with your children: Have the children make a graph of the count on the chart. Tell the children that there are 400 sticks; have them tell how many of each color they believe there are. Use the concept of ratio to determine the number of each color of stick if there had been 200 red sticks, 800 blue sticks, and so on.[6]

2. Activities for Intermediate Grades

As children mature, their probability activities can become more complex. Activities 16-9 and 16-10 are examples of ones for older children.

---

[6]This activity is adapted from the Shryock article.

These activities use beads in a bag. The beads should all be the same size and weight and should feel the same when touched.

ACTIVITY 16-9   Drawing Beads

- Begin with 2 beads, 1 red and 1 black. Draw a bead from the bag, note its color. Ask "What is the color of the bead that is still in the bag?" Help children to conclude that the chances of drawing a certain color of bead is 1 out of 2, or ½. The act of drawing a bead from the bag is called an event; the chances of the event being the drawing of a red bead is 1 out of 2.
- Have children work in pairs to verify this by drawing a red or a black bead from a bag. Have each pair of children draw and replace a bead 100 times and record their results in a simple table.

Red	Black
~~llll~~ ~~llll~~ ~~llll~~ ~~llll~~ ~~llll~~ ~~llll~~ ~~llll~~ ~~llll~~ ~~llll~~ l	~~llll~~ ~~llll~~ ~~llll~~ ~~llll~~ ~~llll~~ ~~llll~~ ~~llll~~ ~~llll~~ ~~llll~~ ~~llll~~ llll

- When each pair has completed 100 drawings, compile a master chart. The master chart should confirm the conclusion that the probability for each event is 1 in 2.
- Repeat with other bead combinations:
  - "What is the probability of drawing a red bead when you have two black and one red bead in the bag?"
  - "What is the probability of drawing a black bead when you have six red beads and six black beads in the bag?"
  - "What is the probability of drawing a black bead when there are three red beads and one black bead?"

Other readily available materials should be used along with or following work with beads so children can confirm that given events will occur when other types of materials are used. For example, when a red chip and a blue chip are used, children will see that the probability for each event is 1 in 2, just as it is with beads.

Later, children should use larger numbers of beads to discover how to predict probabilities when more than one bead at a time is removed from

FIGURE 16-3
(a) The two parts of a probability spoon. (b) The assembled spoon.

a container. Necessary equipment includes a container with an equal number of red and black beads—perhaps 50 of each—and a device for removing a given number of beads. An easily made device is a spoon fashioned from two pieces of masonite board. The top piece of masonite contains holes, or bowls, slightly larger than the beads. This piece is glued to the solid piece to complete the spoon (Figure 16-3). Make several spoons, each with a different number of bowls.

ACTIVITY 16-10 Probability Spoon

- Give each pair of children a bag containing 50 red and 50 black beads and a bead spoon. (A three-holed spoon is used here. One hole is lettered A, one is lettered B, and one is lettered C.)
- Be sure the children know what events can occur and how to record each one. When there are an equal number of the two beads and a three-holed spoon, four events are possible: three red, two red and one black, one red and two black, and three black. These events can be recorded as (3R, 0B), (2R, 1B), (1R, 2B), (0R, 3B) or simply as ordered pairs in which the first numeral refers to red beads and the second numeral refers to black beads: (3,0), (2,1), (1,2), (0,3). The children should readily see that there is only one way to draw three red beads or three black beads. They will probably need help to see that each of the other two events can occur three different ways. Use the lettered holes on the spoon to make this clear.
- Have children record results as beads are drawn until a chart listing all the possible outcomes is completed.

Events	Bowls		
	A	B	C
(3,0)	R	R	R
(2,1)	R	R	B
	B	R	R
	R	B	B
(1,2)	B	B	R
	R	B	B
	B	R	B
(0,3)	B	B	B

- The chart shows that there are eight possible outcomes when three beads are drawn. Help the children determine the probabilities for each event: (3,0) and (0,3) each have a probability of 1 in 8, whereas (2,1) and (1,2) each have a probability of 3 in 8.
- Have other pairs of children draw 2, 4, 5, or 6 beads at a time. (Remember that the greater the number of beads, the greater the amount of time needed to complete the task.)

Comparing tables of events in which different spoons are used will yield an interesting observation concerning the number of possible outcomes when two, three, four, and so on beads are drawn. There are four possible outcomes when two beads are drawn; the number increases to eight when three beads are drawn; there are sixteen possible outcomes when four beads are drawn. "Can you see a pattern that will enable us to predict the number of possible outcomes when we draw five beads?" (2^5, or 32.) "Six beads?" (2^6, or 64.) "Any number of beads?" (2^n.)

Other probability activities for children to follow are

1. Give each child a familiar object—thumb tack, small paper plate, or tetrahedron model with numbers or letters on the faces—and ask each one to determine the probabilities for each object to land a given way after it is tossed or spun. Some of the objects will lead to events for which probabilities can be easily established (for example, the tetrahedron model, assuming it is not weighted, but rather is *fair*) while others do not (paper plate).

2. Have children investigate the probabilities of multiple events. For example, "When we use our three-bowl spoon, what is the probability of drawing either three red or three black beads from the container?" "What is the probability that we will draw either all black beads or two black and one red bead from the container?"

3. Ask children to bring games that use dice or spinners for determining moves. Have them determine the probabilities for the occurrence of different events (moves).

3. Probability Terms

You can introduce the terms **event**, *impossible event*, *likely event*, *certain event*, and *equally likely event* to children in grades 5 and 6 by means of carefully sequenced activities and discussions. You can keep the work simple and still bring out the fact that every event, or happening, can be assigned a number that states the likelihood of its occurring. The more likely an event is to occur, the higher the number assigned to it. The numerical measure that refers to the likelihood of an event occurring is that event's probability. An impossible event, for example Christmas will come in the middle of summer in the northern hemisphere, is assigned a probability of 0. A certain event—for example, an airplane will cross the Atlantic Ocean when flying from New York to London in an easterly direction—is assigned a probability of 1. If an event can happen, but is unlikely to, the value of its probability is close to 9; and a likely event has a value that is close to 0. Two equally likely events are each assigned the value of ½.

One way to introduce children to the concept of the probability of an event is to discuss the likelihood of certain things occurring. The School Mathematics Study Group publication *Probability for Primary Grades, Teacher's Commentary* suggests these as good beginning topics.[7]

"Which is more likely on the fourth of July (here in our town), rain or snow?"

"Billy is a very good student. Which is he more likely to do in tomorrow's test, pass or fail?"

"A new boy has joined the class. Mary is to guess his birthday. Alice is to guess how many brothers and sisters he has. Who is more likely to guess right?"

"When Mary guesses the new boy's birthday, which (in her guess) is the more likely to be right, the entire birthday, or the month alone?"

In the first example the more likely event (in the United States) is rain, and this should be obvious to children. It is possible, of course, that neither event will occur. This gives you a chance to discuss the idea that even though *neither* event *may* happen, one is still *more likely* than the other. The second example is relatively simple, whereas the third and fourth will require careful consideration by children. In the final example an important principle is brought out. It is more likely that the birth month will be named than the birthday. However, it is impossible for the birthday (less likely event) to be given correctly if the birth month (more likely event) is given incorrectly. "In this case, the comparison in likelihood is derived not from past experience or numerical considerations, but from logical necessity."[8] You can adjust these topics to suit your children or use others of your own choosing.

---

[7] David W. Blakeslee and others, *Probability for Primary Grades, Teacher's Commentary*, rev. ed. (Stanford, Cal.: School Mathematics Study Group, Leland Stanford Junior University, 1966), pp. 7–9. The same topics appear in SMSG's companion book, *Probability for Intermediate Grades, Teacher's Commentary*, pp. 8–10.

[8] Blakeslee and others, p. 9.

**Self-check
of Objectives 10
and 11**

Demonstrate with appropriate materials probability investigations for children.

Define and give an example of each of these probability terms: *event, impossible event, certain event, unlikely event, likely event,* and *equally likely event.* Cite examples of situations that can serve as a means of introducing each term to children.

STATISTICS AND GRAPHS

One of the important problem-solving skills discussed in Chapter 5 is the compilation of data and construction of tables and graphs. The second National Assessment of Educational Progress shows that more attention needs to be given to this area of work. Children performed well when they answered questions that were based on a direct reading of graphs. They did less well when they were required to make predictions or solve problems based on information contained in graphs.[9] The results show that children need opportunities to examine graphs for trends and patterns and to solve problems using information from graphs.

A classroom should be equipped with both centimeter-squared paper and large sheets with inch or 2-centimeter squares, colored cubes and paper squares, and color crayons and pens.

1. Object Graphs

Object graphs are the easiest for young children to make and interpret. Each child can contribute to a graph by placing a model of one of the subjects represented by the data. Children's pets or their mode of transportation to school are suitable subjects for primary-grade children. Plastic animals or buses, cars, bicycles, and walking figures serve as models for these early graphing experiences.

ACTIVITY 16-11   Pet Statistics

- Poll the children about their pets. (You may choose to have children who have more than one pet limit their contribution to one pet only.)

---

[9] Barbara J. Bestgen, "Making and Interpreting Graphs: Results and Implications from National Assessment," *Arithmetic Teacher,* XXVIII, No. 4 (December 1980), p. 26.

Tally the results in a simple table. Be sure to include a "no pet" category.

Our Pets	
Horse	$\| \|$
Cat	̶H̶H̶t̶ $\| \|$
Fish	$\| \| \|$
Dog	̶H̶H̶t̶ $\| \| \| \|$
Mouse	$\| \|$
Guinea pig	$\|$
Turtle	$\|$
No pet	$\| \| \| \|$

- Give each child a plastic dog, cat, fish, or other pet. Children without pets can be given a small plastic basket to represent an empty pet bed.
- Write the names of the chosen pets on an already prepared graph form.
- Have the children place their plastic animals or baskets on the graph.

Our Pets	
Horse	🐴 🐴
Cat	🐈 🐈 🐈 🐈 🐈 🐈
Fish	🐟 🐟 🐟
Dog	🐕 🐕 🐕 🐕 🐕 🐕 🐕 🐕 🐕
Mouse	🐁 🐁
Guinea pig	🐹
Turtle	🐢
No pet	X X X X

- Use the graph for counting and comparing activities:
  - "How many children own cats? Dogs? Fish?"
  - "Do more children own cats than dogs? Dogs than horses?"
  - "How many fewer cat owners are there than dog owners?"
  - "Are there more children who have pets or more who do not have pets?"

2. Picture Graphs

The change from object graphs to **picture graphs** is easily made. Children can collect data about pets, transportation, eye color, favorite candy, and so on and then draw pictures and position them in the proper places on their graphs. The same sorts of questions asked about pets should be asked about each of the children's picture graphs.

3. Bar Graphs

Bar graphs should be introduced after children are familiar with object and picture graphs. The change to bar graphs is also easily made. After children have gathered their data, blocks or squares of colored paper can be used to represent subjects on the graph. Children who have blocks representing cats stack them on the edge of a table or in the chalkboard rail. Each of the other colors is stacked the same way. When squares of colored paper are used, they are carefully glued to a butcher-paper graph. Again use questions to guide the children's interpretation and evaluation of their data.

Older children's bar graphs can contain more information than ones made by younger children. For example, instead of containing data for one situation, such as the number of pets, a graph can contain data collected over a period of time. The graph in Figure 5-1 (Chapter 5) contains information about shoe colors that will be collected over a month's time. This graph presents a good opportunity for children to learn how to use a graph's key to obtain information on the meaning of the graph. Help them make predictions and compute answers to problems you pose. Ask questions such as these after several days of the project:

- Which color of shoe do you think will be worn most often during the month?

- Which color do you think will be worn least often?

- How many times were brown shoes worn on the first three days?

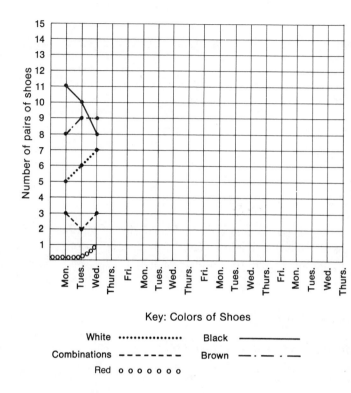

FIGURE 16-4
Line graph with data concerning color of children's shoes

Key: Colors of Shoes

White ···············   Black ———————

Combinations – – – – – – –   Brown —·—·—

Red o o o o o o o

4. Line Graphs

Line graphs made on coordinate grids are used to show data such as those collected during the shoe project. One way to record these data is shown in Figure 16-4. Another use of line graphs is to make geometric interpretations of situations containing two variables. The graph for the knitting-a-sweater problem in Chapter 5 (Problem 5-10) is an example of this use. You will recall that seven stitches are required for each inch of sleeve that is knitted. One variable is the inches of sleeve, and the other is the number of stitches per inch. The graph shows inches along the x axis and stitches along the y axis. It shows that if a sweater with a 15-inch sleeve is made, there will be 105 stitches in each sleeve when there are 7 stitches in each inch.

5. Circle Graphs

A **circle graph** showing the favorite colors of a group of children is shown in Figure 5-2. Other sources of data and a discussion of circle graphs are also contained in Chapter 5. Reread that section for information about these kinds of graphs.

Describe four types of graphs used by elementary-school children. Identify
one source of data for each graph you name.

THE CALCULATOR AND NUMBER THEORY, PROBABILITY, AND STATISTICS

These activities extend children's understanding of number theory, probability, and statistics. The calculator provides the means for simplifying the computation needed to complete each activity.

1. Number Theory

a. Finding Prime and Composite Numbers Which of these numbers are prime? Which are composite?

491   221   161   391   131   247   539   457

b. Testing Formulas Mathematicians have strived to develop a formula for determining prime numbers of any size. Test these two formulas for finding prime numbers: $n^2 - n + 41 = p$ and $n^2 - 79n + 1601 = p$. The first formula yields prime numbers for all whole-number replacements for n up to 41; the latter works for all whole-number replacements for n through 79.

c. Studying Prime and Composite Numbers[10] This investigation extends the activity with prime and composite numbers discussed previously. Have the children complete a chart similar to the one in Figure 16-5 for the numbers 1 through 50. When the chart is finished, direct the children's attention to these questions:

- Which numbers have two and only two factors? What kinds of numbers are these?

- Which numbers have three and only three factors? What will be the next number that has exactly three factors?

---

[10] This activity is adapted from William M. Fitzgerald and others, *Laboratory Manual for Elementary Mathematics* (Boston: Prindle, Weber & Schmidt, Inc., 1973), pp. 49–50. Adaptation made with permission of the publisher.

Number	Factors	Sum of Factors
1	1	1
2	1,2	3
3	1,3	4
4	1, 2, 4	7
5	1, 5	6
6	1, 2, 3, 6	12
7	1, 7	8
8	1, 2, 4, 8	15
9	1, 3, 9	13
10	1, 2, 5, 10	18
11	1,11	12
12	1, 2, 3, 4, 6, 12	28
13	1, 13	14
14	1, 2, 7, 14	24

FIGURE 16-5
The first fourteen counting numbers, their factors, and the sums of their factors

- Which numbers have four and only four factors? The numbers 8 and 27 have exactly four factors. How do they differ from the other numbers that have exactly four factors? Can you predict the next number of this kind? What number with exactly four factors follows 46?

- Which numbers have five and only five factors? Can you describe these numbers? What is the next number that has exactly five factors?

- Can you write a mathematical sentence that tells how to determine the sum of the factors when a number is prime? Can you write a sentence for finding the sum when a number has exactly three factors?

2. Probability and Pascal's Triangle

When a single coin is tossed, there are only two possible ways it can land; the coin can land either heads up or tails up. When two coins are tossed, there are four different outcomes: H-H, H-T, T-H, T-T. When three coins are tossed, these are the possible outcomes: H-H-H, H-H-T, H-T-H, T-H-H, H-T-T, T-H-T, T-T-H, and T-T-T. The number of ways one, two, and three coins can land are shown in this triangular arrangement of numbers:

$$1$$
1 coin	1—1
2 coins	1—2—1
3 coins	1—3—3—1

List all of the possible outcomes when four coins are tossed. What numbers indicate the ways four coins can land? Add these numbers to the triangle. Does the triangle give you enough information to predict the number of ways five coins can land? If not, list all of the possible outcomes for five coins. Extend the triangle to include complete rows for ten coins.

This arrangement of numbers is called **Pascal's triangle,** after the 17th century mathematician, Blaise Pascal, who studied and wrote about it. With it, many interesting questions can be considered:

- What is the sum of each row of the triangle? Can you describe the sequence of numbers that includes each sum?

- When six coins are tossed, what is the probability of getting three heads and three tails? What percent of the possible outcomes is this? What is the probability of getting four heads and four tails when eight coins are tossed? What percent of the possible outcomes is this? Will the percent of possible outcomes for five heads and five tails when ten coins are tossed be greater or less than the percent for four heads and four tails when eight coins are tossed? Why do you think this is so?

- When you toss seven coins, what is the probability of getting three heads and four tails? What is the probability of getting four heads and three tails? Is each of these probabilities the same percent of the total outcomes? How do you explain this?

- When you toss nine coins, what is the probability that you will get four heads? Can you give the probability of getting at least four heads?

3. Statistics—Target Average[11]

GAME　Finding the Average

Target Average　　　　　　　　　　　　　　**Partners** _____

1. Players take turns picking a number.
2. Each player picks as many numbers as indicated for the game.

---

[11] This activity is from George Immerzeel, *'77 Ideas for Using the Rockwell 18R in the Classroom* (Foxboro, Mass.: New Impressions, Inc., 1976), p. 93. (Used with permission.)

3. As you pick numbers, enter them in your calculator and add them.
4. After the last number is picked, divide by the number of numbers.
5. The player whose average is closest to the target is the winner.

12	9	3	19	26	44	49	25	65	16
15	96	20	51	78	18	15	19	30	0
47	13	45	29	14	45	21	41	14	39
16	76	33	12	48	30	45	6	40	19
2	10	21	20	17	22	35	28	10	34
17	49	37	17	33	60	39	13	40	35
0	87	14	55	65	31	93	24	18	47
18	11	87	32	15	50	15	36	2	13
31	62	23	75	18	89	57	10	35	91
27	43	18	31	11	27	61	28	37	43

Game 1	Game 2	Game 3
Pick 3 numbers	Pick 5 numbers	Pick 5 numbers
Target 15	Target 12	Target 20
Game 4	Game 5	Game 6
Pick 4 numbers	Pick 5 numbers	Pick 6 numbers
Target 30	Target 40	Target 50

Five activities for using the handheld calculator to extend children's under-standing of number theory, probability, and statistics are described. Explain each one, and demonstrate how the calculator is used for each.

Self-check
of Objective 13

SPECIAL STUDENTS AND NUMBER THEORY, PROBABILITY, AND STATISTICS

Topics discussed in this chapter provide students with basic skills for dealing with everyday situations and solving problems, as well as providing practice with number operations. Each of the topics is important and should be developed for all students to the extent that it is possible.

H. Lawrence Ridge and Joseph Renzulli[12] recommend that the topics of this chapter be especially emphasized with gifted and talented children. They indicate that many of these children are uneasy with the practical aspects of mathematics because they prefer to engage in abstract thought. Allowing gifted and talented children to concentrate solely on abstract thought deprives them of opportunities to develop the mathematical modeling and simulation skills they need to perform well in business and industry.

Many aspects of work with number theory, probability, statistics, and graphs provide opportunities for children to develop skills which have direct applications in many practical situations. For example, knowledge of systematic ways to determine greatest common factors and least common multiples is not only used when working with common fractions, as discussed in Chapter 12, but is also used in the derivation and solution of a variety of widely-applied formulas. Each of the chapter's topics give students opportunities to form bridges between the abstract and practical aspects of mathematics.

The following articles from yearbooks of the National Council of Teachers of Mathematics deal with this chapter's topics and contain useful information about ways to extend and enrich students' understandings and uses of mathematics:

From *Enrichment Mathematics for the Grades*, 27th Yearbook, 1963:

Sawyer, W. W. "Some Simple Laws of Physics," pp. 165–172.

Smith, Rolland R. "Probability in the Elementary School," pp. 127–133.

Tinnappel, Harold. "On Divisibility Rules," pp. 227–233.

———. "Using Sets to Study Odd, Even, and Prime Numbers," pp. 261–268.

From *Applications of School Mathematics*, 1979 Yearbook:

Pagni, David L. "Applications in School Mathematics: Human Variability," pp. 43–58.

Swift, James H. "Capture-Recapture Techniques as an Introduction to Statistical Inference," pp. 185–192.

Whitman, Nancy C. "Mauka-Makai and Other Directions," pp. 59–69.

---

[12] H. Lawrence Ridge and Joseph S. Renzulli, "Teaching Mathematics to the Talented and Gifted," in Vincent J. Glennon, ed. *The Mathematical Education of Exceptional Children and Youth; An Interdisciplinary Approach* (Reston, Virginia: National Council of Teachers of Mathematics, 1981), pp. 229–230.

From *Teaching Statistics and Probability*, 1981 Yerrbook:

Armstrong, Richard D. "An Area Model for Solving Probability Problems," pp. 135–142.

Bailey, Eris. "Triples—A Game to Introduce Facts of Chance," pp. 64–69.

Bohan, Harry, and Edith J. Moreland, "Developing Some Statistical Concepts in the Elementary School," pp. 60–63.

Bright, George W., John G. Harvey, and Margaret M. Wheeler. "Fair Games, Unfair Games," pp. 49–59.

Maher, Carolyn A. "Some Graphical Techniques for Examining Data Generated by Classroom Activities," pp. 109–117.

Matsumoto, Annette N. "Correlation, Junior Varsity Style," pp. 126–134.

From *Mathematics for the Middle Grades (5-9)*, 1982 Yearbook:

Casey, Rita J. "Beyond Four Walls: Mathematics in the Out-of-Doors," pp. 91–96.

Hatchett, Bunny C. "Math Mapping Begins at Home," pp. 97–101.

Ilani, Bat-Sheva, Naomi Taizi, and Maxim Bruckheimer. "Variations of a Game as a Strategy for Teaching Skills," pp. 200–225.

Kuhl, Opal. "Sports Card Math," pp. 162–165.

Sanok, Gloria. "Using Graphics to Represent Statistics," pp. 172–176.

Vance, James H. "An Opinion Poll: A Percent Activity for All Students," pp. 166–171.

Explain why topics discussed in this chapter can be especially beneficial to gifted and talented children.

Self-check of Objective 14

SUMMARY

Work with elementary number theory is largely investigative and exploratory, with children developing an intuitive understanding of number theory topics rather than a formalized set of definitions and rules. Topics

include odd and even numbers, prime and composite numbers, and tests
of divisibility. Primary-grade children use markers in arrays to distinguish between odd and even numbers. Older children learn about prime
and composite numbers in the same way. Children who understand prime
and composite numbers and who know how to find the prime factorizations of composite numbers have the background they need for understanding greatest common factors and least common multiples. Knowledge of GCFs and LCMs is used while working with fractional numbers
represented as common fractions.

Tests of divisibility, especially those for prime numbers such as 2, 3,
5, 7, and 11, are useful when finding the prime factorizations of composite numbers.

Children who have an understanding of probability and statistics and
graphs have a means of collecting, organizing, and interpreting information from the world around them. There are simple probability experiments for primary-grade children, and more sophisticated ones for older
children. Children themselves provide ample sources of statistical information to organize and then to prepare tables and graphs to report it.
Topics in this chapter provide many opportunities for gifted and talented
students to bridge the gap between abstract and practical mathematics.

STUDY QUESTIONS AND ACTIVITIES

1. Read "The Plight and Might of Number Seven," (see this chapter's reading list) and list some student activities suggested by
   Shmuel Avital. Identify students for whom you think each activity is appropriate.

2. Burton and Knifong discuss six approaches to prime numbers
   (see reading list). Read their article and identify each one. Discuss each approach's strengths and weaknesses. If one approach
   appeals to you, name it and tell why. Show that you understand
   the file card and toothpick activity discussed by these authors
   by picturing cards for these numbers: 2, 3, 4, 6, 7, 9.

3. "Hamann's Conjecture" is discussed by Maxine Frame (see
   reading list). This conjecture suggests that every even number
   from 2 through 250 can be expressed as the difference of two
   prime numbers. Give a definition of the word *conjecture;* then
   test Hamann's conjecture with at least 20 numbers between 2
   and 100, 100 and 200, and 200 and 250 to demonstrate that it is
   reasonable.

4. Twin primes are pairs of prime numbers separated by a single
   composite number. Identify the twin primes that follow 11 and

13 and come before 200. What are the first twin primes after 200?

5. The "Ideas for Teachers" and "From the File" sections of the *Arithmetic Teacher* appear each month. The first contains suggestions for lessons on one topic for several grades, and the second contains simulated file cards, each presenting a problem, puzzle, teaching tip, or other information. Review these sections for several back issues and add copies of useful ideas and files to your collection of teaching–learning aids.

KEY TERMS

number theory

odd and even numbers

prime and composite numbers

sieve of Eratosthenes

factor trees

Venn diagram

divisibility

sampling

event

object graphs

picture graphs

bar graphs

line graphs

circle graph

Pascal's triangle

FOR FURTHER READING

Adams, Verna M. "A Variation on the Algorithm for GCD and LCM," *Arithmetic Teacher*, XXX, No. 3 (November 1982), p. 46.

The algorithm for determining the prime factorization of two or more composite numbers discussed in this chapter is modified to yield the greatest common divisor as well as least common multiple for numbers.

Avital, Shmuel. "The Plight and Might of Number Seven," *Arithmetic Teacher*, XXV, No. 5 (February 1978), pp. 22–24. The number seven comes alive to visit the author and tell all about its special characteristics. Many interesting possibilities for student investigations of the number seven (and others) arise from this article.

Bestgen, Barbara J. "Making and Interpreting Graphs and Tables: Results and Implications from National Assessment," *Arithmetic Teacher*, XXVIII, No. 4 (December 1980), pp. 26–29.

The National Assessment of Educational Progress test indicates that children can read tables and graphs for single bits of information but have difficulty interpreting graphs and solving problems with information from them. The author offers five suggestions for improving children's ability to interpret and use information from graphs.

Burns, Marilyn. "Put Some Probability in Your Classroom," *Arithmetic Teacher*, XXX, No. 7 (March 1983), pp. 21–22.

A teacher's curiosity about a statement in the Sunday paper provided the basis for a probability activity for her sixth graders. Her procedures and children's responses are described.

Burton, Grace M., and J. Dan Knifong. "Definitions for Prime Numbers," *Arithmetic Teacher*, XXVII, No. 6 (February 1980), pp. 44–47.
Materials and procedures for teaching children about prime numbers are discussed. Other activities dealing with prime numbers are reviewed.

Christopher, Leonora. "Graphs Can Jazz Up the Mathematics Curriculum," *Arithmetic Teacher*, XXX, No. 1 (September 1982), pp. 28–30.
Reasons for using graphs are described. Materials that are needed and sources of data are included.

Dantzig, Tobias. *Number: The Language of Science*, 4th ed. (Garden City, N.Y.: Doubleday & Company, Inc., 1954). Chapter 3 is of particular interest because of its discussion of number theory.

Frame, Maxine R. "Hamann's Conjecture," *Arithmetic Teacher*, XXIII, No. 1 (January 1976), pp. 34–35. "Hamann's Conjecture" was made by a seventh-grade student when he discovered that every even number from 2 through 250 can be expressed as the difference of two prime numbers. (Hamann discovered later that his conjecture was not the first expression of this idea when he did some research about it.)

Horak, Virginia M. and Willis J. Horak. "Collecting and Displaying The Data Around Us," *Arithmetic Teacher*, XXX, No. 1 (September 1982), pp. 16–20.
Activities based on personal, home, and school grounds data are used with a variety of graphs. Easily made graphs are pictured and described.

Huff, Sara C. "Odds and Evens," *Arithmetic Teacher*, XXVII, No. 5 (January 1979), pp. 48–52. Colored pieces of cardboard, called "odds and evens" by the teacher and "magic counters" by second graders, served as a basis for investigations into the nature of odd and even numbers, addition of such numbers, and a game.

Johnson, Elizabeth M. "Bar Graphs for First Graders," *Arithmetic Teacher*, XXIX, No. 4 (December 1981), pp. 30–31.
A sequence of seven activities that ends with the construction of a bar graph is described. In addition to the graph itself, children deal with important concepts like "more than," "less than," "as many as," and so on.

Kerr, Donald R., Jr., and Donald Maki. "Mathematical Models to Provide Applications in the Classroom," *Applications in School Mathematics*, 1979 Yearbook of the National Council of Teachers of Mathematics (Reston, Va., The Council), pp. 1–7.
The process of forming mathematical models from real-world problems and special steps that must be taken to make the models appropriate for the classroom are described.

Lappan, Glenda, and Mary Jean Winter. "Prime Factorization," *Arithmetic Teacher*, XXVII, No. 7 (March 1980), pp. 24–27.
A variety of puzzles offers experiences in factoring numbers. Children are challenged by mazes, "strings," and other novel ways of investigating factorizations of numbers.

Nibbelink, William. "Graphing for Any Grade," *Arithmetic Teacher*, XXX, No. 3 (November 1982), pp. 28–31.
Nibbelink describes a way of introducing and making coordinate graphs that is suitable for children in all elementary grades. Step-by-step directions using a variety of data indicate how to use the graph in different grades.

O'Neil, David R., and Rosalie Jensen. "Looking at Facts," *Arithmetic Teacher*, XXIX, No. 8 (April 1982), pp. 12–15.
Eight exploratory activities dealing with probability and statistics for all grades are presented. A transition from three-dimensional graphs to bar graphs is demonstrated.

Parkerson, Elsa. "Patterns of Divisibility," *Arithmetic Teacher*, XXV, No. 4 (January 1978), p. 58. The patterns of divisibility by 3, 7, and 11 developed by a class of sixth graders are described and illustrated. The pattern for 11 is different from the one described in this chapter.

Robold, Alice I. "Patterns in Multiples," *Arithmetic Teacher*, XXIX, No. 9 (April 1982), pp. 21–23.
A square grid, bottle caps, and crayons are tools for investigating numbers and their multiples. The activities lead to understanding of prime and composite numbers and divisibility rules.

Roy, Sneh P. "LCM and GCF in the Hundred Chart," *Arithmetic Teacher*, XXVI, No. 4 (December 1978), p. 53. Counting on the hundred chart and marking certain numerals with circles and triangles serves as a means of determining the LCM and GCF for pairs of numbers.

Shulte, Albert P. "A Case for Statistics," *Arithmetic Teacher*, XXVI, No. 6 (February 1979), p. 24.
The author contends that children should not be made to wait until high school to begin their study of statistics. He presents five reasons for including statistics in the elementary curriculum.

———, ed. *Teaching Statistics and Probability*, 1981 Yearbook, National Council of Teachers of Mathematics (Reston, Virginia: The Council). Several chapters discuss programs and activities for elementary-school classrooms.

Souviney, Randall J. "Probability and Statistics," *Learning*, V, No. 4 (December 1976), pp. 51–52. Beginning with letters from children's names as a basis for analysis, a series of statistical and probability activities are possible. The activities could form a unit for grades 4 through 6.

———. "Quantifying Chance," *Arithmetic Teacher*, XXV, No. 3 (December 1977), pp. 24–26. Three activities using nonstandard dice, social studies book pages, and bags of colored marbles provide experiences for developing children's understanding of probability and their skill in making predictions about the occurrences of probability events.

Swafford, Jane, and Robert McGinty. "Story Numbers," *Arithmetic Teacher*, XXVI, No. 2 (October 1978), pp. 16–17. Another way of visualizing prime and composite numbers. Rectangular and triangular pieces of colored paper provide the models for constructing a city's skyline showing combinations of factors. All prime numbers form two-story buildings.

Tinnappel, Harold. "On Divisibility Rules," in *Enrichment Mathematics for the*

Grades, 27th Yearbook, National Council of Teachers of Mathematics (Washington, D.C.: The Council, 1963). Chapter 16 presents the rules for divisibility by 2, 3, 4, 5, 7, 9, and 11, and their proofs.

Woodward, Ernest. "A Second-Grade Probability and Graphing Lesson," *Arithmetic Teacher*, XXX, No. 7 (March 1983), pp. 23–24.
Dice and paper grids provide the means for introducing second grade children to the concept of probability through graphing the outcomes of multiple rolls of the dice.

Yates, Daniel S. "Using Mathematics to Predict," in *Practical Ways to Teach Basic Mathematical Skills*, Monograph (Richmond, Virginia: Virginia Teachers of Mathematics, 1978), pp. 148–175.
A variety of probability experiments and required materials are described. Most of the activities use easily constructed teacher-made materials.

17

Planning for Teaching

Upon completion of Chapter 17 you will be able to:

1. Describe seven elements that comprise an effective teacher-directed lesson.

2. Describe functions of classroom learning centers.

3. Explain how children's work at a learning center can be directed.

4. Describe a mathematics laboratory.

5. Describe five guidelines for planning activities for learning-handicapped children.

6. Describe three ways you can keep abreast of developments in elementary-school mathematics.

"The classroom teacher continues to be the gatekeeper in curriculum—the one who stages the learning opportunities." [1] The ways you stage learning opportunities should be based on theories of how children learn, the structure of mathematics, and your knowledge of the children you teach. In order to stage the best learning opportunities you must understand and use a repertoire of teaching strategies that maintains balance among different ways of guiding children's learning.

TEACHER-DIRECTED LESSONS

A textbook series commonly serves as the core of a school's mathematics program, providing the scope and sequence and the basis for many les-

[1] Ad Hoc Mathematics Framework Committee, *Mathematics Framework and the 1980 Addendum for California Public Schools Kindergarten Through Grade Twelve* (Sacramento: California State Department of Education, 1982), p. 100.

sons. A teacher's manual for each grade suggests procedures and materials for teaching lessons with the text. When you use a textbook series as the basis for your mathematics program, you must avoid the habit of having children open their books to a lesson's first page and follow along as you explain concepts and processes. This practice leads to a static program that becomes uninspiring. A lack of variety breeds negative attitudes and causes some children to discontinue their study of mathematics as quickly as possible.

A textbook can be an integral part of a lesson that presents a new concept or process. A lesson based on a text that combines manipulation of learning aids, discussion, modeling by the teacher or selected students, and written practice from the book is a practical way to guide children's learning of a new topic. Successful teachers know that well-developed plans are the foundation for effective lessons and activities. The seven steps discussed here are based on a scheme developed by Madeline Hunter and Douglas Russell, both of the Laboratory School at the University of California at Los Angeles.

It is assumed that certain preconditions exist before you prepare a particular lesson:

- You have a major goal clearly in mind. (Skill in subtraction with whole numbers serves as the major goal for the lesson that follows.)

- You are aware of the subtasks that lead to the major goal. (In this example subtasks for subtraction with whole numbers are used. Refer to the subtraction flow chart in Chapter 2.)

- The type(s) of mathematical behavior to be stressed—facts and skills, understanding and comprehension, application, and analysis—has been selected. (Refer to Figure 2-2 in Chapter 2.)

- Each child's status with regard to readiness for the lesson—cognitive, affective, pedagogical, maturational, and contextual—has been determined. (Refer to Chapter 3, "Assessment Procedures for Mathematics.")

Assume that you are ready to introduce subtraction of a two-place number from a two-place number with regrouping (subtask 7 in flow chart). Stated in performance terms your objective might be, "The student will use paper and pencil and the decomposition algorithm to compute the answer to examples like $63 - 45 = \square$." There are seven elements to consider as you plan your lesson:

- Setting the stage

- Statement of objective

- Instructional input

- Modeling

- Checking for understanding

- Guided practice

- Independent practice

1. Setting the Stage

You want to develop the children's mental readiness for what is to come. Hunter and Russell use the term **anticipatory set** to refer to an activity's purpose at this point in the lesson. You want to shift children's attention from activities that have preceded the mathematics period so that they focus on the lesson. One way to do this is to present a story problem that uses the new subtraction: "Yesterday evening I counted 42 peanuts in our peanut jar. I have given out 18 peanuts this morning. Can you tell me how many peanuts are in the jar now?" (Allow time for children to determine the answer in whatever ways they can. State the answer if it is determined.) Another way to start is to review a skill that is needed for the lesson, such as the use of beansticks to show tens and ones. A short oral review of basic subtraction facts is another way to begin.

2. Statement of Objective

This step in the lesson acquaints children with the specific objective. "Today you are going to learn a new kind of subtraction. You know how to do this: $\begin{array}{r} 36 \\ -15 \\ \hline \end{array}$. Now you are going to learn to do this kind of subtraction: $\begin{array}{r} 42 \\ -18 \\ \hline \end{array}$. How is it different from $\begin{array}{r} 36 \\ -15 \\ \hline \end{array}$?"

3. Instructional Input

You instruct children about the new work at this point in the lesson. Because this is a new subtask, you should begin at the concrete-manipulative level. A sequence of beanstick activities that you guide by posing situations and questions is one way to work. For the peanut problem used at the outset, have each child (or pair) work with a set of beansticks. Proceed this way:

- Pose a question: "Can you use the beansticks to tell how many peanuts were in the jar? (Each child represents 42 with beansticks.)

- Who remembers how many I have given out this morning?" Discuss the fact that we want to take away 18 beans.

- "How can you take away 18 beans when there are not enough loose beans to take away 8?"

- Guide the children to see that 1 ten stick can be exchanged for 10 loose beans. When this is done, there are 3 tens sticks and 12 loose beans.

- Ask, "Can you take away 18 beans now?"

- Children should recognize that they can take away 8 loose beans and 1 tens stick, or 18 beans.

- Repeat using other similar story situations.

A demonstration by you with an enlarged set of beansticks could be used instead of the guided learning activity. The same sequence of steps would be used.

4. Modeling

Modeling is the process of demonstrating how a process is completed. Now you make a transition from the manipulative materials to the decomposition algorithm. Put the algorithm $\begin{array}{r} 42 \\ -18 \\ \hline \end{array}$ on the chalkboard or overhead projector. Ask the children to identify the meaning of each numeral (The "42" stands for the number of peanuts in the jar yesterday afternoon; the "18" stands for the number you have given out since then.) Have them tell what the answer will stand for when it is determined. Model the steps in the algorithm by vocalizing each step as you work, as follows:

- "Watch carefully while I do this example. I will explain my thinking as I do it."

- Complete each step, thinking aloud:

  o "I can't subtract eight from two. I can exchange one ten for ten ones; I will have three tens left and enough ones to take away eight. Ten ones plus the two I began with make twelve ones. (You make a mark through the "4," put "3" by the "4," and put a small "1" next to the "2" to show 12 ones.)

  o "I can subtract eight from twelve. I put a "4" in the ones place of the answer."

  o "I subtract one from three in the tens column. The answer, "2," goes in the tens place of the answer."

  o "The answer tells me that there are 24 peanuts left in the peanut jar."

- Repeat with algorithms for the other previously used situations.

- Children can also model the steps for completing the algorithm. (Select children who are likely to model without prompting from you and who can articulate the steps clearly.)

5. Checking for Understanding

Now you want each child to demonstrate understanding of the algorithm. One way is for each child to work with an individual chalkboard. Show an example to be copied and completed. As each child displays an answer give other examples for those whose work is correct to copy and complete. Check each child's work for accuracy before a second example is begun. If there are children who obviously do not know how to do the subtraction, reteach the lesson for them. Whether you do it immediately or on another day, and whether with different learning aids or only the algorithm modeling, depends on your assessment of the extent of their misunderstanding.

6. Guided Practice

Guided practice follows checking for understanding. Assign the first five examples on the textbook page that formed the basis for this lesson. Move among the children as they work to commend those whose work is accurate and discuss any faulty work.

7. Independent Practice

Independent practice is assigned after children demonstrate understanding of the new subtraction during guided practice. Now they can be asked to complete the remaining examples on the text's page.

None of the seven steps is *always* a part of every lesson. A step may be omitted because it is inappropriate for a particular objective. For example, instruction in a new process is not done each day, so instructional input and modeling may not be necessary. In other instances children may not be ready for independent practice immediately following instruction in a new process. Concrete-manipulative activities and modeling may be spread over several days rather than completed in one lesson.

A form that contains an outline of the seven stages provides an easy means for preparing notes to guide your teaching. The form in Figure 17-1 is one you might use. It contains notes for the subtraction lesson.

Papers completed during an independent practice period should be carefully analyzed by you to determine which basic facts, if any, still

Name   J. Smith   Date – – – –

Subject *Mathematics*

Objective: The student will use paper and pencil and the decomposition algorithm to compute the answers to examples like 63-45 = ☐.

Setting the stage: Story situation — "I had 42 peanuts in my jar yesterday afternoon. Since then, I've given away 18 peanuts. How many peanuts are in the jar now?"

Materials: Peanut jar w/ 42 peanuts; beansticks, individual chalkboard, chalk, and eraser for each child; textbooks (P. 96)

FIGURE 17-1
Sample lesson plan

Instructional input: Child will use beansticks to represent 42 peanuts. Will show regrouping process to take 18 beans away. Will repeat, as necessary, with similar problem situations, e.g., distributing pieces of paper, sticks of gum, gold stars.

Model: Teacher will model process with algorithm. "Talk through" steps as children observe. Use peanut situation and other situations, as needed.

Checking for understanding: Children will repeat examples with chalkboard computation, plus two new examples.

$$
\begin{array}{r} 56 \\ -29 \\ \hline \end{array}
\qquad
\begin{array}{r} 31 \\ -17 \\ \hline \end{array}
$$

Guided practice: First 5 examples, practice page 96

Independent practice: Complete practice page 96.

need to be learned and whether there are patterned errors. Once you are convinced that a child understands a new process, provide further practice to make the learning permanent. These considerations will promote successful practice sessions:

- The kind and amount of practice are not likely to be the same for all children at all times.

- A variety of materials and procedures should be used.

- Practice sessions should be brief and occur regularly.

- Once a skill is learned, review practice sessions should be given periodically.

You have just read about seven elements of an effective teacher-directed lesson. Name each element and describe its function in a lesson.

Self-check of Objective 1

LEARNING CENTERS

Classroom **learning centers** serve several useful purposes. They provide a setting for

- Introducing a new concept or skill
- Practicing previously learned skills
- Working on individual or small-group enrichment activities

1. Introducing a New Concept or Skill

A sequence of activities at stations within a center can be used to introduce a new concept or skill. At a learning center children's work is guided by a set of serially numbered **problem cards,** or perhaps tape recorded instructions, that provide step-by-step instructions. Multiple sets of cards and sufficient manipulative materials should be provided to accommodate each individual or group.

A learning center can be used to introduce odd and even numbers. The teacher-directed activity described in Chapter 16 (Activity 16-1) can be replaced by one in which these problem cards are used:

ODD AND EVEN   (1)

1. Get a bag of poker chips.

2. Take 8 chips from the bag and put them on your
   table so they look like this:

   Count the chips in each row. <u>There are</u> ___ <u>chips</u>
   <u>in each row</u>.

3. Use a set of 10 chips this time. Put them in 2
   rows with an equal number of chips in each row.
   Draw a picture of your two rows of chips. <u>There</u>
   <u>are</u> ___ <u>chips in each row</u>.

FIGURE 17-2
Problem cards for work with
odd and even numbers

                                                        (2)

4. Put a set of 6 chips in 2 rows with an equal number
   of chips in each row. Draw a picture of your two
   rows of chips. <u>There are</u> ___ <u>chips in each row</u>.

5. Do the same things with each of these sets of chips.
   Draw a picture of each set of chips after you have
   put them in two rows. Tell how many chips are in
   each row by writing the answer on your paper.
   a. 4 chips   d. 20 chips
   b. 12 chips   e. 18 chips
   c. 16 chips   f. 30 chips

(3)

6. Make some other sets that have equal numbers of chips in each row when you make 2 rows. Draw a picture of each of your sets. Tell how many chips are in each of your sets.

7. Make a set of 7 chips and put them in 2 rows like this:

   Do the rows have the same numbers of chips in them? There are ___ chips in one row and ___ chips in the other row.

(4)

8. Make 2 rows with 5 chips. Draw a picture of your two rows. Did you put an equal number of chips in each row? There are ___ chips in one row and ___ chips in the other row.

9. Make 2 rows with the following sets of chips. Do it so there is always one more chip in one row than in the other row. Draw a picture of each of your sets after you have put them in 2 rows.
   a. 3 chips   d. 11 chips
   b. 9 chips   e. 19 chips
   c. 15 chips   f. 23 chips

(5)

10. You have counted chips and have put each set into 2 rows. Some sets were put into rows with equal numbers of chips in each row. Tell which sets these are. Some sets cannot be put into 2 rows with equal numbers of chips in each row. Tell which sets these are.

11. Sets that can be put into rows with equal numbers of chips in each row are sets with an EVEN number of chips in them. Write the numerals for some even numbers on your paper.

Sets that cannot be put into rows with equal numbers of chips in each row are sets with an ODD number of chips in them. Write the numerals for some odd numbers on your paper.

(6)

12. Make some different sets with an even number of chips in them. Tell how many chips are in each of your sets.

13. Make some sets with an odd number of chips in each one. Tell how many chips are in each of your sets.

A computer might be placed in a classroom learning center and new material presented by a computer tutorial program. Once a child's place in the computer program has been established, work time can be assigned at the machine. To justify a computer's cost it should be used throughout the day. Children's work can be scheduled for times other than the regular mathematics period. For example, a child can work at the computer while others read and then complete a reading assignment during part of the mathematics period.

2. Practicing Previously Learned Skills

Learning centers provide an ideal setting for practice. Practice materials include puzzles; games; cassette, computer, and filmloop programs; and preprogrammed devices. Materials associated with topics presented through teacher-directed lessons provide an alternative to practice pages from a textbook or teacher-prepared worksheets. Materials in a center should be changed frequently. It is better to remove an item before children's interest in it has peaked than to leave it until children become bored with it. The item will be received with enthusiasm when it is returned at a later time.

3. Working on Individual or Small-Group Enrichment Activities

Enrichment activities give variety to a program and extend children's learning to topics beyond those contained in textbooks. Chapter 14 contains a description of activities for enriching gifted and talented children's knowledge of measurement. All children can participate in exploratory activities at a center set up to initiate the activities. Even though this center is set up to encourage gifted and talented children to expand their study of measurement, any child who is interested should be encouraged to continue beyond the exploratory stage. You can encourage children to investigate a variety of topics through frequent use of centers focusing on different areas of mathematics.

4. Directing Work at a Center

A **contract** is one way to direct activities at a center. The work covered by a contract may be selected by a child or specified by you and may require a day, week, or longer period of time to complete. If problem cards, games, worksheets, computer programs, and other learning aids are keyed to a program's performance objectives, it is easy for you or a child to match center activities with objectives on a contract. A special form can be used or a contract can be written on a plain piece of paper.

A sample contract governing work at a center is illustrated in Figure 17-3. The contract contains information about five stations at a center called "Adding and Subtracting Rational Numbers." It includes a performance objective, instructions for each station, and a place for a child to check off activities as they are completed.

When a contract has been completed, it should be returned to you to be discussed and evaluated. You can meet with children in groups rather than individually to discuss their work. Discussion is important for at least two reasons: (1) Talking about the topic with you and their peers helps children to clear up misconceptions and internalize concepts. (2) You can better evaluate children's learning, noting and correcting mis-

FIGURE 17-3
Sample contract. Sources: Game in Station 3 is from Leonard M. Kennedy and Ruth L. Michon, *Games for Individualizing Mathematics Learning* (Columbus, Ohio: Charles E. Merrill, 1973), pp. 88–90. Film in Station 4 is from Jott Films, P.O. Box 745, Belmont, Cal. 94002. Cassette in Station 5 is from *Mathematics Teaching Tape Program, Primary Level* (Houghton Mifflin Company, 110 Tremont Street, Boston, Mass. 02107).

Adding and Subtracting Rational Numbers

Name _____
Date to be completed _____
Date returned to teacher _____

Performance Objective: When you have satisfactorily completed the activities at this center, you will be able to add and subtract fractional numbers represented by fractions having like denominators.

_____ *Station 1.* There are two envelopes containing materials for activities dealing with addition of fractional numbers. Read the directions on the envelopes, then complete the activities on each problem card. Write your answers on a response card. Return the materials to the right envelopes.

_____ *Station 2.* There are two envelopes containing materials for activities dealing with subtracting fractional numbers. Complete the activities and return the materials to the right envelopes. When you have finished all of the activities, staple your response card to your contract.

_____ *Station 3.* Choose a partner to play "Common Fraction Addition." The directions are on the cover of the box holding the game. Be sure to put the board and playing pieces back in the box when you are finished.

_____ *Station 4.* Watch the film loop *Fractions: Adding and Subtracting (Common Denominators).* You can watch the film more than once, if you wish.

_____ *Station 5.* The listening center has a cassette called *Adding Fractional Numbers.* Get one of the work sheets and put your name on it before you listen to the tape. When you have completed the work sheet, staple it to your contract.

understandings, and you can collect information for use in reporting pupil progress, whether by grades on a report card or by parent-teacher conferences. If center work is to continue, a new contract can be worked up for each child at the end of the discussion.

Center work must be planned with the same care as teacher-directed lessons. The assumptions listed earlier apply to selecting and organizing center activities. In addition to planning and organizing centers themselves care must be taken to orient children to center work. Children who will work together need to be selected. Children who have not worked at centers before need guidance when getting started. The first days need to be planned carefully, with more emphasis on procedures than mathematics activities. Once children learn to cope with procedures, their attention will shift to their own activities, and they will disregard what others are doing. Children differ in ability to adjust to new learning situations, so it is likely that some children will need specific instructions for a period of weeks, and others will become independent quite soon.

Describe three functions served by classroom learning centers.

    Explain how contracts are used to guide children's work at a learning center.

Self-checks
of Objectives 2 and 3

MATHEMATICS LABORATORIES

A **mathematics laboratory,** as defined in this book, is a special room in a school in which children learn mathematics. It is equipped with commercial aids, such as Cuisenaire rods, abacuses, geoboards, computers, calculators, and preprogrammed devices, and with other aids made by teachers and children. A mathematics teacher–specialist oversees all work, which may be directed by the specialist or an aide. Children may work individually or in groups of various sizes. Both teacher-directed and center activities are a part of the laboratory experience.

In some schools all mathematics instruction occurs in a laboratory. Children are assigned by class or by group. A child's place in a group is determined after a thorough diagnosis has been completed. Membership in a group is not permanent but remains flexible to accommodate each child's change in performance. In other schools only children with special needs work in a laboratory. Children with handicaps receive special help for problems that cannot be accommodated in a regular classroom. Gifted and talented children have opportunities to pursue topics of special interest. Teachers from the school and neighboring schools may come to the laboratory for workshops or to make things for their own classrooms.

The role of the mathematics textbook diminishes when well-conceived teacher-directed lessons and learning centers or laboratories assume greater prominence. Instead of being the primary source of activities a textbook then takes its place among other equally important materials. The text supplies the sequence for activities and serves as the basis for many directed lessons. It also provides pages of practice materials for children to complete on a selective basis. Not all children will complete the same exercises nor will all children complete the same number of pages.

***Self-check
of Objective 4***

Describe the main features of a school mathematics laboratory.

PLANNING FOR EXCEPTIONAL CHILDREN

Each of the chapters 7 through 16 ends with a discussion of activities and materials for working with exceptional children. A part of each discussion deals with ways to help learning-handicapped students improve their understanding of mathematics and their performance. The other part suggests ways to extend and enrich the program for gifted and talented students.

The discussion in each of these sections indicates that learning-handicapped children can develop skills in all areas of mathematics when they are presented with well sequenced lessons and appropriate learning materials. As a summary of the suggestions contained in the earlier chapters, the following guidelines are presented to help you organize and implement worthwhile lessons for these children:

- Plan and use a diagnostic teaching strategy that gives you immediate and continual feedback about each child's knowledge and understanding of mathematics, that is suitable for each child's level of maturity and understanding, and that takes handicaps into account. Have a variety of materials and procedures.

- Keep in mind a hierarchy of steps for each topic you teach. Make certain that there are no gaps in any topic's sequence.

- Do not isolate learning-handicapped children. Children learn better in a social context than when they work alone. Learning-handicapped children can contribute to group projects, and they benefit from working with other students.

- Do not focus on too narrow a range of topics. The broad interpretation of basics presented in this book should form the basis of the program for all children.

- Avoid concentrating on facts and skills alone. It is equally important to help learning-handicapped children to understand the mathematics they learn and see immediate uses for it. Applications through in- and extra-school situations should be stressed whenever possible.

You should also recognize that it is important for gifted and talented children to receive special attention. They should not be confined to a class's basic course of study or left to fend for themselves. You cannot assume that they will learn the basic understandings and skills without your help, so instruction in the basics is important. At the same time, however, they need to participate in more intensive investigations of many of the topics they study. The three-level enrichment model described in Chapter 3 is one way of meeting the needs of gifted and talented children. This plan exposes children to a wide variety of topics and allows them to choose special ones they want to study more intensively.

Describe orally or in writing four guidelines for working with learning handicapped children.

Self-check of Objective 5

CONCLUDING STATEMENT

One of the essential goals of any mathematics program is for children *to learn how to learn,* so they can continue to learn and understand mathematics after their formal education ends. In the same sense, every elementary school teacher must continue to learn about mathematics and how to teach it. After you have finished your studies, you can keep abreast of developments in the field of elementary school mathematics in several ways.

1. Reading

Professional books and journals provide up-to-date information concerning mathematics. No teacher should be content with the ideas from only one book about teaching mathematics. Even though the content of each book devoted to teaching mathematics in elementary school is similar, each author presents a different point of view. Also, each author usually discusses some topics not included in other books.

Arithmetic Teacher is a journal devoted entirely to elementary-school mathematics. Everyone who teaches mathematics to children should read it regularly. A one-year subscription to this journal is a benefit of membership in the National Council of Teachers of Mathematics. One can get information about the organization and all of its publications by writing the National Council of Teachers of Mathematics, 1906 Association Drive, Reston, VA 22091.

Other publications—*School Science and Mathematics*, *Learning Teacher*, and *Instructor*, for example—include articles dealing with elementary school mathematics.

2. Professional Meetings

The National Council of Teachers of Mathematics presents a number of mathematics conferences each year. In addition to an annual meeting each spring, nearly a dozen smaller meetings are held in various cities throughout the country. Each conference features speeches and workshops by authorities on teaching mathematics and displays of professional materials, as well as pupil-prepared exhibits. All teachers, whether or not they are NCTM members, are invited to these meetings. There is a fee for each one.

Throughout the country a number of state and local mathematics councils, clubs, or associations hold meetings in their areas. The names of these and their meeting dates are listed in *Arithmetic Teacher* from time to time.

3. College and University Courses and Workshops

Many colleges, universities, and school districts provide opportunities for continuing one's study of mathematics. Teachers can refine their teaching skills through courses and workshops of various types.

4. Miscellaneous Activities

Teachers may participate in other types of activities to improve their understanding of elementary-school mathematics. In many districts teachers select textbooks and other teaching materials. You can learn much about newer developments in the field by examining and evaluating new textbooks and learning aids. District and county offices frequently provide assistance through mathematics consultants or supervisors. Teachers who use these services usually find they learn much that helps them become better teachers. In every district a few teachers are especially effective in teaching mathematics to children. If you can, arrange for the opportunity to see these expert teachers working with children.

Each teacher must select from among the opportunities available those that will be most helpful to keep abreast of developments in elementary-school mathematics. Teachers who conscientiously strive to keep up with the subject may soon discover how little they actually know about it and will recognize more than ever the need for continual study.

Describe at least three ways you can keep abreast of developments in elementary-school mathematics.

Self-check
of Objective 6

SUMMARY

Teacher-directed lessons are frequently used to introduce new topics and concepts to children. An effective lesson will include seven elements: (1) setting the stage, (2) statement of objectives, (3) instructional input, (4) modeling, (5) checking for understanding, (6) guided practice, and (7) independent practice. A form that contains room for notes about each element serves as a guide for teaching a lesson.

A learning center provides another means for presenting information to children. It is also a practical way to provide practice activities and enrichment experiences for children. Problem cards, recorded instructions, and computer programs are ways of directing children's work in a center. Contracts are sometimes used to assign activities at centers. In some schools a mathematics laboratory provides the setting for children's mathematics work. A laboratory is a special room equipped with a variety of learning aids and is directed by a mathematics teacher–specialist. Sometimes only children with special needs are assigned work in a laboratory.

Teachers of learning-handicapped children should use a diagnostic-teaching strategy, adhere to a subject's hierarchy of steps, allow children to work in groups, provide opportunities for children to apply the mathematics they learn, and take a broad view of what is basic mathematics for children. Gifted and talented children should have a program that meets their special needs. The three-level model for enriching their learning advocated by Ridge and Renzulli is recommended as one way of providing for the mathematical needs of these children.

Teachers need to remain abreast of developments in elementary-school mathematics. Reading professional books and journals, and participation in professional meetings, college and university courses, and workshops are means of doing this.

STUDY QUESTIONS AND ACTIVITIES

1. Select a topic similar to the one used in this chapter, and prepare a plan for a lesson that introduces the topic to a group of
   children. Describe the background you believe children should
   possess before they participate in the lesson.

2. Visit a mathematics laboratory. Discuss its uses with the teacher
   in charge. In the teacher's view, what are the values of the laboratory? If possible, talk to several children to hear their reactions to the laboratory.

3. Select a topic for which you prepare a set of problem cards for
   a learning-center activity. Write performance objectives for your
   activity. What materials are required for your activity?

4. Arnold believes that a system of management by learning activities is superior to a system of management by objectives (see
   this chapter's reading list). What are the differences between
   the two systems? Why does he believe the system he prefers is
   superior?

KEY TERMS

anticipatory set   learning centers
modeling   problem cards
guided practice   contract
independent practice   mathematics laboratory

FOR FURTHER READING

Arnold, William R. "Management by Learning Activities: An Alternative to Ob-
      jectives, *Arithmetic Teacher*, XXV, No. 1 (October 1977), pp. 50–55. The
      author rejects the notion of management by objectives which, he says, ". . .
      features sequential learning of skills at the symbolic level of representation
      (and employs) pretests and posttests . . . to assess achievement." He con-
      tends that management by learning activities is the way to present material
      to children. Activities, organized as units, provide children with readiness,
      developmental, drill, and enrichment experiences that are much broader
      than the typical objective-based management scheme.

Chandler, Theodore A. "What's Wrong with Success and Praise?" *Arithmetic
      Teacher*, XXIX, No. 4 (December 1981), pp. 10–12.
      The article describes the dynamics of success and praise and suggests ways

to avoid pitfalls that make praise backfire. Six problems associated with praise are described, as are ways to use it successfully.

Cunningham, Betty. "Individualized Arithmetic Instruction for Fifth and Sixth Graders," *Arithmetic Teacher*, XXV, No. 8 (May 1978), pp. 44–46. Describes one teacher's plan for individualizing children's work. Includes a sample flow chart and samples of multiplication pre- and post-tests.

Danforth, Marion McC. "Aids for Learning Mathematics," *Arithmetic Teacher*, XXVI, No. 4 (December 1978), pp. 26–27. The aids Danforth describes are procedures for helping individuals overcome learning difficulties. Included are such things as giving specific objectives, having a child verbalize thought processes, using error-analysis cards, using analogies, giving directions several ways, using concrete materials, using cues to avoid errors, and removing frustration.

DeRidder, Charleen, and Donald J. Dessart. "Using a Directed Lesson," *Arithmetic Teacher*, XXX, No. 3 (November 1982), pp. 16–17.
A five-step sequence for presenting a specific mathematics skill is described. Teacher's activities at each step are explained.

Schussheim, Joan Y. "A Mathematics Laboratory, Alive and Well," *Arithmetic Teacher*, XXV, No. 8 (May 1978), pp. 15–21. Describes the room, its permanent centers, the operating procedures, and sample activities. Includes an extensive list of materials, with annotations and publishers' addresses.

Thornton, Carol A. "Math Centers for Young Learners," *Learning*, VI, No. 1 (August/September 1977), pp. 56–57. Describes the values of math centers and their uses to motivate and reinforce concepts, strategies, and skills. Includes eight pointers for effective use of centers and the distinction between centers and stations.

West, Tommie A. "Using a Textbook Effectively," *Arithmetic Teacher*, XXX, No. 2 (October 1982), pp. 8–9.
Steps in planning lessons around a text are explained. Ways to structure lessons, problems to assign, overcoming a text's weaknesses, and ways of correcting homework are discussed.

Appendix A

Prefixes and Suffixes of Mathematical Terms

PREFIXES

bi-, *L.*—twice, two
centi-, *L.*—hundred
deci-, *L.*—ten, tenth
deka-, *Gr.*—ten
dia-, *Gr.*—through
dodeca-, *Gr.*—twelve
geo-, *Gr.*—earth
hecto-, *Gr.*—hundred
hepta-, *Gr.*—seven
hexa-, *Gr.*—four
icosa-, *Gr.*—twenty
isos-, *Gr.*—equal
kilo-, *Gr.*—thousand
milli-, *L.*—thousand
octa-, *Gr.*—eight
para-, *Gr.*—side by side
penta-, *Gr.*—five
peri-, *Gr.*—around
poly-, *Gr.*—many
quadri-, *L.*—four
rect-, *L.*—right
tetra-, *Gr.*—four
tri-, *Gr.* and *L.*—three

SUFFIXES

-angle, *L.*—angle
-hedron, *Gr.*—side, face
-gon, *Gr.*—angle
-lateral, *L.*—side
-meter, *Gr.*—measure

Note: *L.* indicates Latin; *Gr.* indicates Greek.

Appendix B

Producers and Distributors of Mathematics Courseware for Microcomputers

Borg-Warner Educational Systems
600 West University Drive
Arlington Heights, IL 60004-1889

Creative Computing Press
39 East Hanover Avenue
Morris Plains, NJ 07950

CTB/McGraw-Hill
2500 Garden Road
Monterey, CA 93940

Developmental Learning Materials
One DLM Park
Allen, TX 75002

Edu-Ware Services, Inc.
P.O. Box 22222
Agoura, CA 91301

Follett Library Book Company
4506 Northwest Highway
Crystal Lake, IL 60014

Hartley Courseware, Inc.
Dimondale, MI 48821

Learning System, Ltd.
P.O. Box 9046
Fort Collins, CO 80525

The Micro Center
Department JM
P.O. Box 6
Pleasantville, NY 10570

Milliken Publishing Company
1100 Research Blvd.
St. Louis, MO 63132

Minn. Educational Computing Consortium
2520 Broadway Drive
St. Paul, MN 55113

Opportunities for Learning, Inc.
8950 Lurline Ave., Dept. JY
Chatsworth, CA 91311

Scholastic Inc.
905 Sylvan Avenue
Englewood Cliffs, NJ 07632

Scott, Foresman and Company
Electronic Publishing
Glenview, IL 60025

Sterling Swift Publishing Company
1600 Fortview Road
Austin, TX 78704

Sunburst Communications
Room TI
39 Washington Avenue
Pleasantville, NY 10570

Appendix C

Producers and Distributors of Mathematics Learning Aids

Activities Resources
P.O. Box 4875
Hayward, CA 94540

BJ's Educational Supply Store
1807 19th Street
Bakersfield, CA 93301

Burt Harrison & Company
P.O. Box 732
Weston, MA 02193-0732

Creative Publications
P.O. Box 10328
Palo Alto, CA 94303

Cuisenaire Company of America, Inc.
12 Church St.
Box D
New Rochelle, NY 10805

Dick Blick
P.O. Box 1267
Galesburg, IL 61401

Didax, Inc.
Educational Resources
6 Doulton Place
Peabody, MA 01960

Educat
P.O. Box 2891
Clinton, IA 52735

Educational Teaching Aids
159 West Kinzle St.
Chicago, IL 60610

Math House
Division of Mosaic Media, Inc.
Dept C183
P.O. Box 711
Glen Ellyn, IL 60137

Nasco
901 Janesville Ave.
Fort Atkinson, WI 53538

or

Nasco West
1524 Princeton Avenue
Modesto, CA 95352

Index

Abacus. *See* Materials, place value
Achievement test. *See* Assessment
Addend, 207
Addition, 5
  defined, 207
  fractional number
    common fraction, 336–341, 357–359
    decimal fraction, 374–375
  integer, 251–252
  whole number, 196–197, 206–231, 236–243, 254–261
    basic fact
      defined, 207
      learning, 220–223
      practicing, 223–225
    higher decade, 237–238
    introduction, 210–220
    low-stress algorithm, 257–258
    magic squares, 254–255
    palindromes, 254
    readiness activities, 209–210
    sequence of steps, 208
    vertical notation, 216–217
    with regrouping (carrying), 239–243
    without regrouping (carrying), 238–240
Adkins, Julia, 360
Algorithm
  common fraction
    addition, 337–341, 358–359
    division, 352–354, 358–359, 360
    multiplication, 345–350, 358–359
    subtraction, 342–344, 358–359
  defined, 5–6, 178
  factoring composite number, 495
  finding least common multiple, 499
  low-stress, 257–259, 310–311
    addition, 257–258, 310–311
    subtraction, 258–259
  whole number
    addition, 238–243
    division, 295–306
    multiplication, 237, 287–295
    Russian-peasant, 309
    subtraction
      decomposition, 5, 25–26, 190, 245–248, 524–528
      equal-addition, 248–250
      without decomposition, 243–245

An Agenda for Action: Recommendations for School Mathematics in the 1980s, 1, 81, 116
Anxiety. *See* Mathematics anxiety
Apple, the Personal Computer Magazine, 4
Application. *See* Problem solving
Approximation. *See* Estimation
Arithmetic Teacher, 182, 537–538
Array. *See* Multiplication
Assessment, 34–51, 256–257, 357–358, 527–528
  of daily work, 35, 36, 37, 48–49, 256–257, 357–358, 527, 529
  interview, 35, 36, 37, 50
  observation, 35, 36, 37, 49
  parent–teacher conference, 36, 38, 50–51
  procedures, 37–38
  test, 35, 36, 37–48, 410–411
    achievement, 40–41
    attitude, 36, 46–48
      attitude scale, 47–48
      semantic-differential, 46
      sentence completion, 48
    diagnostic, 35, 40–46
      commercial, 41
      teacher-made, 41–46
      subtraction, 45
    Piagetian-type, 36, 38–40, 410–411
  of uses of mathematics, 38, 50
Associative property. *See* Property
Attribute materials. *See* Materials
Authoritarian teaching, 70

Beansticks. *See* Materials, place value
Bitter, Gary, 134–135
Bley, Nancy, 52–53, 198, 357, 358, 395, 437
Bolduc, Elroy, 312
Books
  for children, 147
  for teachers, 156, 516–517
Brod, Rodney, 68
Brownell, William, 16, 23
Brush, Lorelei, 70–71, 72

Calculator, 2, 4, 116–120, 535
  activities, 99, 117, 195–197, 199, 224, 254–255, 308–309, 393–395, 512–515
  roll in program, 117–118, 224, 535
  selection of, 118–120

545